Following the News: The *Wall Street Journal*

Financial Markets and Institutions

The Addison-Wesley Series in Finance

Copeland/Weston/Shastri
Financial Theory and Corporate Policy

Dufey/Giddy
Cases in International Finance

Eakins
Finance: Investments, Institutions and Management

Eiteman/Stonehill/Moffett
Multinational Business Finance

Gitman
Principles of Managerial Finance

Gitman
Principles of Managerial Finance—Brief Edition

Gitman/Joehnk
Fundamentals of Investing

Gitman/Madura
Introduction to Finance

Hughes/MacDonald
International Banking: Text and Cases

Madura
Personal Finance

Marthinsen
Risk Takers: Uses and Abuses of Financial Derivatives

McDonald
Derivatives Markets

Megginson
Corporate Finance Theory

Melvin
International Money and Finance

Mishkin/Eakins
Financial Markets and Institutions

Moffett
Cases in International Finance

Moffett/Stonehill/Eiteman
Fundamentals of Multinational Finance

Rejda
Principles of Risk Management and Insurance

Solnik/McLeavey
International Investments

FIFTH EDITION

Financial Markets and Institutions

FREDERIC S. MISHKIN
Graduate School of Business,
Columbia University

STANLEY G. EAKINS
East Carolina University

PEARSON

Addison
Wesley

Boston San Francisco New York
London Toronto Sydney Tokyo Singapore Madrid
Mexico City Munich Paris Cape Town Hong Kong Montreal

Editor in Chief: Denise Clinton
Sponsoring Editor: Donna Battista
Director of Development: Sylvia Mallory
Assistant Development Editor: Amy Fleischer
Production Supervisor: Meredith Gertz
Supplements Editor: Kirsten Dickerson
Executive Marketing Manager: Stephen Frail
Design Manager: Regina Hagen Kolenda
Text Design: Dutton & Sherman Design
Cover Designer: Regina Hagen Kolenda
Media Producer: Bethany Tidd
Senior Manufacturing Buyer: Hugh Crawford
Project Coordination and Electronic Page Makeup: Argosy Publishing
Cover Image: © 2006 PictureQuest

Financial Markets and Institutions

Library of Congress Cataloging-in-Publication Data

Mishkin, Frederic S.
  Financial markets and institutions / Frederic S, Mishkin, Stanley G. Eakins.-- 5th ed.
    p. cm. -- (The Addison-Wesley series in finance)
  Includes index.
  ISBN 0-321-28029-6
1. Financial institutions--United States. 2. Money--United States. 3. Money market--United States. 4. Banks and banking--United States. I. Eakins, Stanley G. II. Title.
III. Series.

HG181.M558 2005
332.1'0973--dc22

2005041987

10 9 8 7 6 5 4 3 2 1—QWT—09 08 07 06 05

To My Dad

—F. S. M.

To My Wife, Laurie

—S. G. E.

CONTENTS IN BRIEF

CONTENTS IN DETAIL

Chapter 5   **How Do Risk and Term Structure Affect Interest Rates?**   101

Chapter 8 — Conduct of Monetary Policy: Tools, Goals, and Targets — 175

PART FOUR   FINANCIAL MARKETS   217

Chapter 9   The Money Markets   219

Chapter 13   The Foreign Exchange Market   317

Chapter 20

Banking Regulation   513

Chapter 23

Investment Banks, Security Brokers and Dealers, and Venture Capital Firms

CONTENTS ON THE WEB

The following updated chapter and appendices are available on our Companion Website at **www.aw-bc.com/mishkin_eakins**.

The fifth edition of *Financial Markets and Institutions* is a practical introduction to the workings of today's financial markets and institutions. Moving beyond the descriptions and definitions provided by other textbooks in the field, *Financial Markets and Institutions* encourages students to understand the connection between the theoretical concepts and their real-world applications. By enhancing students' analytical abilities and concrete problem-solving skills, this textbook prepares students for successful careers in the financial services industry or successful interactions with financial institutions, whatever their jobs.

To prepare students for their future careers, *Financial Markets and Institutions* provides the following features:

- A unifying analytic framework that uses a few basic principles to organize students' thinking. These principles include:

    Asymmetric information (agency) problems
    Conflicts of interest
    Transaction costs
    Supply and demand
    Asset market equilibrium
    Efficient markets
    Measurement and management of risk

- "The Practicing Manager," nearly twenty hands-on applications that emphasize the financial practitioner's approach to financial markets and institutions.
- A careful step-by-step development of models that enables students to master the material more easily
- A high degree of flexibility that allows professors to teach the course in the manner they prefer
- Complete integration of international perspectives throughout the text
- "The *Wall Street Journal:* Following the News" and "Case: The *Wall Street Journal,*" features to encourage the reading of a financial newspaper
- Numerous cases that increase students' interest by applying theory to real-world data and examples
- A focus on the impact of electronic (computer and telecommunications) technology on the financial system. The text makes extensive use of the Internet with Web exercises, Web sources for charts and tables, and Web references in the margins. It also features special E-Finance boxes that explain how changes in technology have affected financial markets and institutions.

What's New in the Fifth Edition

In addition to the expected updating of all data, there is major new material in every part of the text.

Conflicts of Interest

Recent corporate and accounting scandals have attracted tremendous public attention. Resulting bankruptcies have cost employees of these firms their jobs or pensions and may have played a role in the stock market crash that ensued in March 2000. Conflicts of interest—which occur when people who should act in the investing public's interests by providing reliable information have personal incentives to hide the truth—have contributed to these events. The growing concern in the financial community about the proliferation and effects of conflicts of interest has been echoed by the decision of many schools to add business ethics courses to their curriculums. To examine the impact of this issue on the financial industry, we have added a new chapter and a new set of boxes throughout the text that examine conflicts of interest.

New Chapter 16 An entirely new Chapter 16, "What Should Be Done About Conflicts of Interest in the Financial Industry?" defines conflicts of interest and explains why we should care about them. The chapter also surveys the different types of conflicts of interest in the financial services industry and discusses policies to remedy them. Placing this chapter before the chapters on the financial institutions industry in Part 6 allows us to introduce students to the basic concepts associated with this pervasive problem before we look at it in context. However, this chapter is self-contained and can be taught after Part 6 if professors prefer to cover the individual financial institutions before addressing conflicts of interest.

Conflicts of Interest Boxes To demonstrate the real-world implications of conflicts of interest, we have added a new type of box entitled "Conflicts of Interest" at key points in the discussion.

Mutual Funds

Scandals in the mutual fund industry have made headlines recently and increased students' overall interest in mutual funds. We now devote an entire chapter to this topic: Chapter 21, "The Mutual Fund Industry." This chapter discusses the history, growth, fee structure, and investment practices of the mutual fund industry. It also addresses many of the abuses that the industry has been charged with in recent years and explains the resulting regulatory action.

Expanded Coverage of the Money, Bond, and Stock Markets

We have increased our coverage of the money, bond, and stock markets by including separate chapters for each market. The expanded content includes more detail on valuation and marketing of securities, more examples of the valuation principles, and new discussions on the growth and influence of electronic communications networks (ECNs).

Other New Material on Financial Institutions

Continuing changes in financial markets and institutions have led us to make the following additions.

- Extensive discussion of recent accounting and corporate scandals and their impact on financial markets (Chapters 5, 11, and 16)

- New section on behavioral finance, which applies concepts from other social sciences such as anthropology, sociology and particularly psychology to analyze the behavior of securities prices (Chapter 6)
- New material on Federal Reserve transparency (Chapter 7)
- Discussions of the changes (implemented in 2003) in the way the Federal Reserve administers the discount window (Chapter 8)
- An updated discussion of the market for reserves and the Federal Reserve's setting of the federal funds rate (Chapter 8)
- Perspective on the growing concerns about the safety and soundness of Fannie Mae and Freddie Mac and their accounting scandals (Chapter 12)
- Detailed discussion of mutual fund abuses including the late trading and market timing scandals by Janus, Putnam, and other prominent mutual fund families (Chapter 21)

Increased International Perspective

Given the continuing, growing importance of the global economy, we have incorporated new material with an international focus. A special "global icon" designates these text sections and cases, and "Global" boxes report on specific international developments.

New to this edition:

- Analysis of how central banks set overnight rates in other countries (Chapter 7)
- A discussion of how the euro has fared over the last six years (Chapter 13)
- Examination of problems in the Chinese banking system (Chapter 20)
- An update on developments in Argentina (Chapter 15) and in the Japanese banking industry (Chapter 20)

Streamlined Coverage and Organization

Helpful comments from reviewers have encouraged us to improve the flow and streamline the organization of the fifth edition. Thus, despite the addition of substantial new material, our text has not increased in length. Please note that we have posted deleted material that may still be of interest to readers on the book's website (as described in the next subsection).

We have given new titles to all of the chapters in Part 2 to make them more meaningful to students. Chapter 3, "Understanding Interest Rates," has been changed to "What Do Interest Rates Mean and What Is Their Role in Valuation?" Chapter 4, "The Behavior of Interest Rates," has been changed to "Why Do Interest Rates Change?" Chapter 5, "The Risk and Term Structure of Interest Rates," has been changed to "How Do Risk and Term Structure Affect Interest Rates?" However, despite the title changes, the content has essentially remained the same.

Chapter 10 in the fourth edition, "The Stock Market and the Efficient Market Hypothesis," has been split into two chapters: Chapter 6, "Are Financial Markets Efficient?" and Chapter 11, "The Stock Market." Chapter 14 in the fourth edition, "Theory of Financial Structure," has been renamed and is now Chapter 15, "Why Do Financial Institutions Exist?" This is the first chapter in a new part of the book, Part 5, "Fundamentals of Financial Institutions," which also includes the new Chapter 16 on conflicts of interest. The material in Chapters 19 through 21 in the fourth edition has been reorganized into three new chapters: Chapter 21, "The Mutual Fund Industry," Chapter 22, "Insurance Companies and Pension Funds," and Chapter 23, "Investment Banks, Security Brokers and Dealers, and Venture Capital Firms," which includes the material on venture capital firms, investment banks, and brokerage firms.

New Pedagogy

In this edition, we have added a substantial number of *new* numerical problems that challenge students to use their quantitative skills to test their knowledge. In addition, a greatly enhanced set of lecture notes is available as PowerPoint presentation slides.

New Web Material

We have been able to both retain material and add new material for the book by posting content on the book's website at **www.aw-bc.com/mishkin_eakins**.

Animated Graphs Narrated animated graphs and figures help students master key concepts.

Web Chapter An entire chapter devoted to finance companies and financial conglomerates, Chapter 26, "Finance Companies," is posted on the website.

Web Appendices Appendices on the website include:

Chapter 4: Models of Asset Pricing

Chapter 4: Applying the Asset Market Approach to a Commodity Market: The Case of Gold

Chapter 4: Supply and Demand in the Market for Money: The Liquidity Preference Framework

Chapter 8: The Fed's Balance Sheet and the Monetary Base

Chapter 14: Balance of Payments

Chapter 20: Evaluating FDICIA and Other Proposed Reforms of the Banking Regulatory System

Chapter 25: More on Hedging with Financial Derivatives

Flexibility

There are as many ways to teach financial markets and institutions as there are instructors. Thus, there is a great need to make a textbook flexible in order to satisfy the diverse needs of instructors, and that has been a primary objective in writing this book. This textbook achieves this flexibility in the following ways:

- Core chapters provide the basic analysis used throughout the book, and other chapters or sections of chapters can be assigned or omitted according to instructor preferences. For example, Chapter 2 introduces the financial system and basic concepts such as transaction costs, adverse selection, and moral hazard. After covering Chapter 2, an instructor can decide to teach a more detailed treatment of financial structure or conflicts of interest in Chapters 15 and 16, or can skip these chapters and take any of a number of different paths.

- The approach to internationalizing the text using separate, marked international sections within chapters and separate chapters on the foreign exchange market and the international monetary system is comprehensive yet flexible. Although many instructors will teach all the international material, others will choose not to. Instructors who want less emphasis on international topics can easily skip Chapter 13 (on the foreign exchange market) and Chapter 14 (on the international financial system).

- "The Practicing Manager" applications, as well as Part 7 on the management of financial institutions, are self-contained and so can be skipped without loss of continuity. Thus, an instructor wishing to teach a less managerially oriented course, who might want to focus more on public policy issues, will have no trouble doing so. Alternatively, Part 7 can be taught earlier in the course, immediately after Chapter 17 on bank management.

The course outlines listed next for a semester teaching schedule illustrate how this book can be used for courses with a different emphasis. More detailed information about how the text can offer flexibility in your course is available in the *Instructor's Resource Manual.*

Financial markets and institutions emphasis: Chapters 1–5, 9–11, 15, 17, 18, 20, and six other chapters

Financial markets and institutions with international emphasis: Chapters 1–5, 9–11, 13–15, 17, 18, 20, and four other chapters

Managerial emphasis: Chapters 1–5, 17, 18, 20, 24, 25, and eight other chapters

Public policy emphasis: Chapters 1–5, 7, 8, 15, 16, 17, 20, and eight other chapters

Making It Easier to Teach Financial Markets and Institutions

The demands for good teaching at business schools have increased dramatically in recent years. To meet these demands, we have provided the instructor with supplementary materials, unavailable with any competing text, that should make teaching the course substantially easier.

Along with the usual items in the *Instructor's Resource Manual*—sample course outlines, chapter outlines, overviews, teaching tips, and answers to the end-of-chapter questions and quantitative problems—this manual includes over 850 pages of lecture notes. The lecture notes are comprehensive and outline all the major points covered in the text. They have been class-tested successfully by the authors and should make it much easier for other instructors to prepare their lecture notes as well. The lecture notes are perforated so that they can be easily detached for class use or to make transparency masters.

This edition of the book comes with a powerful teaching tool: an *Instructor's Resource CD-ROM.* Fully compatible with Windows and Macintosh computers, the

CD-ROM contains Word files for the entire contents of the *Instructor's Resource Manual* (including the lecture notes), PowerPoint presentations, Computerized Test Bank files, and animated graphs. Using this handy supplement, instructors can prepare student handouts such as solutions to problem sets made up of end-of-chapter problems or the outline of the lecture of the day. We have used handouts of this type in our classes and have found them to be very effective. To facilitate classroom presentation even further, the PowerPoint presentations include all the book's figures and tables in full color, as well as all the lecture notes; all are fully customizable. The Computerized Test Bank software (TestGen-EQ with QuizMaster-EQ for Windows and Macintosh) is a valuable test preparation tool that allows professors to view, edit, and add questions. Instructors have our permission and are encouraged to reproduce all of the materials on the CD-ROM and use them as they see fit in class.

Pedagogical Aids

A textbook must be a solid motivational tool. To this end, we have incorporated a wide variety of pedagogical features.

1. **Chapter Previews** at the beginning of each chapter tell students where the chapter is heading, why specific topics are important, and how they relate to other topics in the book.
2. **Cases** demonstrate how the analysis in the book can be used to explain many important real-world situations. A special set of cases called "Case: The *Wall Street Journal*" shows students how to read daily columns in this leading financial newspaper.
3. **"The Practicing Manager"** is a set of special cases that introduce students to real-world problems that managers of financial institutions have to solve.
4. **Numerical Examples** guide students through solutions to financial problems using formulas, time lines, and calculator key strokes.
5. **"The *Wall Street Journal:* Following the News" Boxes** introduce students to relevant news articles and data that are reported daily in the *Wall Street Journal* and explain how to read them.
6. **"Inside the Fed" Boxes** give students a feel for what is important in the operation and structure of the Federal Reserve System.
7. **"Global" Boxes** include interesting material with an international focus.
8. **"E-Finance" Boxes** relate how changes in technology have affected financial markets and institutions.
9. **"Conflicts of Interest" Boxes,** which outline conflicts of interest in different financial service industries.
10. **"Mini-Case" Boxes,** which highlight dramatic historical episodes or apply the theory to the data.
11. **Study Guides** are highlighted statements scattered throughout the text that provide hints on how to think about or approach a topic as students work their way through it.
12. **Summary Tables** are useful study aids for reviewing material.
13. **Key Statements** are important points that are set in boldface type so that students can easily find them for later reference.
14. **Graphs** with captions, numbering over 60, help students understand the interrelationship of the variables plotted and the principles of analysis.

15. **Summaries** at the end of each chapter list the chapter's main points.

16. **Key Terms** are important words or phrases that appear in boldface type when they are defined for the first time and are listed at the ends of the chapters.

17. **End-of-Chapter Questions,** help students learn the subject matter by applying economic concepts, and feature a special class of questions that students find particularly relevant, titled "Predicting the Future."

18. **End-of-Chapter Quantitative Problems,** numbering over 250, help students to develop their quantitative skills.

19. **Web Exercises** encourage students to collect information from on-line sources or use on-line resources to enhance their learning experience.

20. **Web Sources** report the URL source of the data used to create the many tables and charts.

21. **Marginal Web References** point the student to websites that provide information or data that supplement the text material.

22. **Glossary** at the back of the book defines all the key terms.

23. **Full Solutions to the Questions and Quantitative Problems** appear in the *Instructor's Resource Manual* and on the *Instructor's Resource CD-ROM.* Professors have the flexibility to share the solutions with their students as they see fit.

Supplementary Materials

The fifth edition of *Financial Markets and Institutions* includes the most comprehensive program of supplementary materials of any textbook in its field. These items are available to qualified domestic adopters but in some cases may not be available to international adopters. These include the following items:

For the Professor

1. **Instructor's Resource Manual,** prepared by the authors, which includes sample course outlines, chapter outlines, overviews, teaching tips, and complete solutions to questions and problems in the text. In addition it has **Power-Point slides,** numbering over 850 in transparency master format, that comprehensively outline the major points covered in the text.

2. **Enhanced PowerPoint** presentation prepared by Rick Swasey (Northeastern University). The presentation, which contains the lecture notes and the complete set of figures from the textbook, has been greatly expanded from the previous edition and now contains more than 850 slides.

3. **Instructor's Resource CD-ROM,** which contains Word files for the *Instructor's Resource Manual,* PowerPoint presentations, the Computerized Test Bank, and animated graphs.

4. **Test Bank,** updated and revised by James W. Eaton (Bridgewater College), available in both print and electronic form, which comprises over 2500 multiple-choice, true-false, and essay test items. The Test Bank is computerized so that the instructor can easily produce exams automatically.

5. **Mishkin-Eakins Companion Website** (located at **http://www.aw-bc.com/ mishkin_eakins**), which features a Web chapter on finance companies, Web appendices, animated graphs, and links to relevant data sources and Federal Reserve websites. The site also offers multiple-choice quizzes for each chapter. An on-line syllabus builder allows instructors to create a calendar of assignments for each class.

For the Student

1. **Study Guide and Workbook** (updated and revised by T. Shawn Strother, East Carolina University), which includes chapter synopses and completions, exercises, self-tests, and answers to the exercises and self-tests.
2. **Readings in Financial Markets and Institutions,** edited by James W. Eaton of Bridgewater College and Frederic S. Mishkin. Updated annually, with numerous new articles each year, this valuable resource is available on-line at the text's website (**www.aw-bc.com/mishkin_eakins**).
3. **Mishkin-Eakins Companion Website** (located at **www.aw-bc.com/ mishkin_eakins**) includes a Web chapter on finance companies, Web appendices, animated graphs, glossary flashcards, numerical and integrative mini-cases, self-assessment quizzes, Web exercises, and links from the textbook.

Acknowledgments

As always in so large a project, there are many people to thank. Our special gratitude goes to Bruce Kaplan, former economics editor at HarperCollins; Donna Battista, finance editor at Addison-Wesley; and Jane Tufts and Amy Fleischer, development editors. We also have been assisted by comments from my colleagues at Columbia and from my students.

In addition, we have been guided in this edition and its predecessors by the thoughtful comments of outside reviewers and correspondents. Their feedback has made this a better book. In particular, we thank:

Ibrahim J. Affanen, Indiana University of Pennsylvania

Senay Agca, George Washington University

Ronald Anderson, University of Nevada—Las Vegas

Bala G. Arshanapalli, Indiana University Northwest

James C. Baker, Kent State University

Joel Barber, Florida International University

Thomas M. Barnes, Alfred University

Marco Bassetto, Northwestern University

Dallas R. Blevins, University of Montevallo

Matej Blusko, University of Georgia

Paul J. Bolster, Northeastern University

Deanne Butchey, Florida International University

Mitch Charklewicz, Central Connecticut State University

Yea-Mow Chen, San Francisco State University

N.K. Chidambaran, Tulane University

Jeffrey A. Clark, Florida State University

Robert Bruce Cochran, San Jose State University

William Colclough, University of Wisconsin—La Crosse

Elizabeth Cooperman, University of Baltimore

Carl Davison, Mississippi State University

Erik Devos, Ohio University at SUNY Binghamton

Alan Durell, Dartmouth College

Franklin R. Edwards, Columbia University

Marty Eichenbaum, Northwestern University

Elyas Elyasiani, Temple University

Edward C. Erickson, California State University, Stanislaus

E. Bruce Fredrikson, Syracuse University

James Gatti, University of Vermont

Paul Girma, SUNY—New Paltz

Susan Glanz, St. John's University

Gary Gray, Pennsylvania State University

Charles Guez, University of Houston

Beverly L. Hadaway, University of Texas

John A. Halloran, University of Notre Dame

Billie J. Hamilton, East Carolina University

John H. Hand, Auburn University

Don P. Holdren, Marshall University

Adora Holstein, Robert Morris College

Sylvia C. Hudgins, Old Dominion University

Jerry G. Hunt, East Carolina University

Boulis Ibrahim, Heroit-Watt University

William E. Jackson, University of North
 Carolina—Chapel Hill
Joe James, Sam Houston State University
Melvin H. Jameson, University of Nevada—
 Las Vegas
Kurt Jessewein, Texas A&M International
 University
Jack Jordan, Seton Hall University
Taeho Kim, Thunderbird: The American Gradu-
 ate School of International Management
Taewon Kim, California State University, Los
 Angeles
Glen A. Larsen, Jr., University of Tulsa
James E. Larsen, Wright State University
Rick LeCompte, Wichita State University
Boyden E. Lee, New Mexico State University
Kartono Liano, Mississippi State University
John Litvan, Southwest Missouri State
Richard A. Lord, Georgia College
Robert L. Losey, American University
Anthony Loviscek, Seton Hall University
James Lynch, Robert Morris College
Judy E. Maese, New Mexico State University
William Marcum, Wake Forest University
David A. Martin, Albright College
Lanny Martindale, Texas A & M University
Joseph S. Mascia, Adelphi University
Khalid Metabdin, College of St. Rose
A. H. Moini, University of Wisconsin—
 Whitewater
Terry Nixon, Indiana University
William E. O'Connell, Jr., The College of
 William and Mary

Masao Ogaki, Ohio State University
Evren Ors, Southern Illinois University
Coleen C. Pantalone, Northeastern University
Scott Pardee, University of Chicago
James Peters, Fairleigh Dickinson University
Fred Puritz, SUNY—Oneonta
Mahmud Rahman, Eastern Michigan University
Anoop Rai, Hofstra University
Mitchell Ratner, Rider University
David Reps, Pace University—Westchester
Terry Richardson, Bowling Green University
Jack Rubens, Bryant College
Charles B. Ruscher, James Madison University
William Sackley, University of Southern
 Mississippi
Kevin Salyer, University of California—Davis
Siamack Shojai, Manhattan College
Donald Smith, Boston University
Sonya Williams Stanton, Ohio State University
Michael Sullivan, Florida International
 University
Rick Swasey, Northeastern University
Anjan Thackor, University of Michigan
Janet M. Todd, University of Delaware
James Tripp, Western Illinois University
Carlos Ulibarri, Washington State University
John Wagster, Wayne State University
David A. Whidbee, California State University—
 Sacramento
Arthur J. Wilson, George Washington University
Shee Q. Wong, University of Minnesota—Duluth
Criss G. Woodruff, Radford University
Tong Yu, University of Rhode Island

Finally, I want to thank my wife, Sally, my son, Matthew, and my daughter, Laura, who provide me with a warm and happy environment that enables me to do my work, and my father, Sydney, now deceased, who a long time ago put me on the path that led to this book.

Frederic S. Mishkin

I would like to thank Rick Mishkin for his excellent comments on my contributions. By working with Rick on this text, not only have I gained greater skill as a writer, but I have also gained a friend. I would also like to thank my wife, Laurie, for patiently reading each draft of this manuscript and for helping make this my best work. Through the years, her help and support have made this aspect of my career possible.

Stanley G. Eakins

© Peter Murphy

Frederic S. Mishkin is the Alfred Lerner Professor of Banking and Financial Institutions at the Graduate School of Business, Columbia University. He is also a research associate at the National Bureau of Economic Research, a Senior Fellow at the FDIC Center for Banking Research, and is the President of the Eastern Economic Association. Since receiving his Ph.D. from the Massachusetts Institute of Technology in 1976, he has taught at the University of Chicago, Northwestern University, Princeton University, and Columbia. He has also received an honorary professorship from the People's University of China (Renmin). From 1994 to 1997 he was executive vice president and director of research at the Federal Reserve Bank of New York and an associate economist of the Federal Open Market Committee of the Federal Reserve System.

Professor Mishkin's research focuses on monetary policy and its impact on financial markets and the aggregate economy. He is the author of more than ten books, including *A Rational Expectations Approach to Macroeconometrics: Testing Policy Ineffectiveness and Efficient Markets Models* (University of Chicago Press, 1983); *Money, Interest Rates, and Inflation* (Edward Elgar, 1993); *Inflation Targeting: Lessons from the International Experience* (Princeton University Press, 1999); *The Economics of Money, Banking, and Financial Markets,* 7th edition (Addison-Wesley, 2004); and has published over 100 articles in professional journals and books.

Professor Mishkin has served on the editorial board of the *American Economic Review,* has been an associate editor at the *Journal of Business and Economic Statistics, Journal of Applied Econometrics,* and the *Journal of Economic Perspectives,* and was the editor of the Federal Reserve Bank of New York's *Economic Policy Review.* He is currently an associate editor (member of the editorial board) at six academic journals: the *Journal of Money, Credit and Banking; Macroeconomics and Monetary Economics Abstracts; Journal of International Money and Finance; International Finance; Finance India; and Economic Policy Review.* He has been a consultant to the Board of Governors of the Federal Reserve System, the World Bank, and the International Monetary Fund, as well as to many central banks throughout the world. He was also a member of the International Advisory Board to the Financial Supervisory Service of South Korea. He is currently an academic consultant to and serves on the Economic Advisory Panel of the Federal Reserve Bank of New York.

Stanley G. Eakins has notable experience as a financial practitioner, serving as vice president and comptroller at the First National Bank of Fairbanks and as a commercial and real estate loan office. A founder of the Denali Title and Escrow Agency, a title insurance company in Fairbanks, Alaska, he also ran the operations side of a bank and was the chief finance officer for a multimillion-dollar construction and development company.

Professor Eakins received his Ph.D. from Arizona State University. He is the Associate Dean for the College of Business at East Carolina University. His research is focused primarily on the role of institutions in corporate control and how they influence investment practices. He is also interested in integrating multimedia tools into the learning environment and has received grants from East Carolina University in support of this work.

A contributor to journals such as the *Quarterly Journal of Business and Economics,* the *Journal of Financial Research,* and the *International Review of Financial Analysis,* Professor Eakins is also the author of *Finance: Institutions, Investments, and Management,* 2nd edition (Addison-Wesley, 2004).

PART 1

Introduction

CHAPTER 1

Why Study Financial Markets and Institutions?

Preview

On the evening news you have just heard that the bond market has been booming. Does this mean that interest rates will fall so that it is easier for you to finance the purchase of a new computer system for your small retail business? Will the economy improve in the future so that it is a good time to build a new building or add to the one you are in? Should you try to raise funds by issuing stocks or bonds or instead go to the bank for a loan? If you import goods from abroad, should you be concerned that they will become more expensive?

This book provides answers to these questions by examining how financial markets (such as those for bonds, stocks, and foreign exchange) and financial institutions (banks, insurance companies, mutual funds, and other institutions) work. Financial markets and institutions not only affect your everyday life but also involve huge flows of funds—trillions of dollars—throughout our economy, which in turn affect business profits, the production of goods and services, and even the economic well-being of countries other than the United States. What happens to financial markets and institutions is of great concern to our politicians and can even have a major impact on our elections. The study of financial markets and institutions will reward you with an understanding of many exciting issues. In this chapter we provide a road map of the book by outlining these exciting issues and exploring why they are worth studying.

Why Study Financial Markets?

Parts 2 and 3 of this book focus on **financial markets,** markets in which funds are transferred from people who have an excess of available funds to people who have a shortage. Financial markets such as the bond and stock markets are important in channeling funds from people who do not have a productive use for them to those who do. Indeed, well-functioning financial markets are a key factor in producing high economic growth, and poorly performing financial markets are one reason that many countries in the world remain desperately poor. Activities in financial markets also have direct effects on personal wealth, the behavior of businesses and consumers, and the cyclical performance of the economy.

Debt Markets and Interest Rates

A **security** (also called a *financial instrument*) is a claim on the issuer's future income or **assets** (any financial claim or piece of property that is subject to ownership). A **bond** is a debt security that promises to make payments periodically for a specified period of time.[1] Debt markets, also often referred to generically as the *bond market*, are especially important to economic activity because they enable corporations or governments to borrow to finance their activities and because the bond market is where interest rates are determined. The **interest rate** is the cost of borrowing or the price paid for the rental of funds (usually expressed as a percentage of the rental of $100 per year). There are many interest rates in the economy—mortgage interest rates, car loan rates, and interest rates on many different types of bonds.

Interest rates are important on a number of levels. On a personal level, high interest rates could deter you from buying a house or a car because the cost of financing it would be high. Conversely, high interest rates could encourage you to save because you can earn more interest income by putting aside some of your earnings as savings. On a more general level, interest rates have an impact on the overall health of the economy because they affect not only consumers' willingness to spend or save but also businesses' investment decisions. High interest rates, for example, may cause a corporation to postpone building a new plant that would ensure more jobs.

Daily, weekly, monthly, quarterly, and annual releases as well as historical data for selected interest rates, foreign exchange rates, etc., are available at **www.federalre serve.gov/ releases/**

The level of interest rates is especially important to financial institutions. A rise in interest rates raises the cost of acquiring funds for financial institutions such as banks and raises the income on assets such as loans. In addition, changes in interest rates affect the prices of securities such as stocks and bonds that are held by financial institutions. Changes in interest rates thus directly affect the profitability and value of financial institutions.

Because changes in interest rates have important effects on individuals, financial institutions, businesses, and the overall economy, it is important to explain fluctuations in interest rates, which have been substantial over the past 30 years. As a matter of fact, in no other 30-year period of U.S. history have interest-rate fluctuations been as great. For example, the interest rate on three-month Treasury bills peaked at over 16% in 1981. This interest rate then fell to 3% in late 1992 and 1993, rose to above 5% in the mid- to late 1990s, and then fell to a low of 1% in the mid-2000s, only to rise again thereafter.

Because different interest rates have a tendency to move in unison, economists frequently lump interest rates together and refer to "the" interest rate. As Figure 1 shows, however, interest rates on several types of bonds can differ substantially. The interest rate on three-month Treasury bills, for example, fluctuates more than the other interest rates and is lower, on average. The interest

---

[1]The definition of *bond* used throughout this book is the broad one in common use by academics, which covers short- as well as long-term debt instruments. However, some practitioners in financial markets use the word *bond* only to describe specific long-term debt instruments such as corporate bonds or U.S. Treasury bonds.

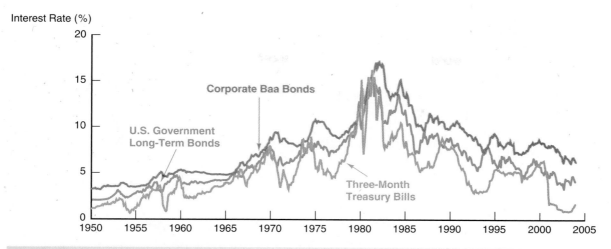

FIGURE 1 *Interest Rates on Selected Bonds, 1950–2004*

Source: http://www.federalreserve.gov/releases/H15/data.htm.

rate on Baa (medium-quality) corporate bonds is higher, on average, than the other interest rates, and the spread between it and the other rates became larger in the 1970s.

In Chapters 2, 9, 10, and 12 we study the role of debt markets in the economy, and in Chapters 3 through 5 we examine what an interest rate is, how the common movements in interest rates come about, and why interest rates on different securities vary.

The Stock Market

A **common stock** (typically just called a **stock**) is a security that represents a share of ownership in a corporation. It is a claim on the earnings and assets of the corporation. Issuing stock and selling it to the public is a way for corporations to raise funds to finance their activities. The stock market, in which claims on the earnings of corporations (shares of stock) are traded, is the most widely followed financial market in America (that's why it is often called simply "the market"). A big swing in the prices of shares in the stock market is always a big story on the evening news. People often express their opinion on where the market is heading and get very excited when they can brag about their latest "big killing," but get very depressed when they suffer a big loss. The attention the market receives can probably be best explained by one simple fact: It is a place where people get rich, and poor, quickly.

As Figure 2 indicates, stock prices have been extremely volatile. After the market rose in the 1980s, on "Black Monday" (October 19, 1987) it experienced the worst one-day drop in its entire history, with the Dow Jones Industrial Average (DJIA) falling by 22%. From then until 2000, the stock market experienced one of the great bull markets in its history, with the Dow climbing to a peak of over 11,000. With the collapse of the high-tech bubble in 2000, the stock market fell sharply, falling by over 30% by late 2002, and then recovered again to over the 10,000 level in 2004. These considerable fluctuations in stock prices affect the size of people's wealth and as a result may affect their willingness to spend.

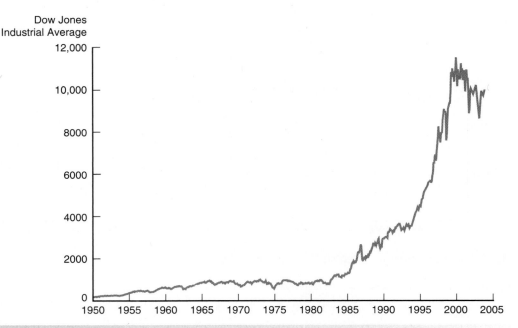

FIGURE 2 *Stock Prices as Measured by the Dow Jones Industrial Average, 1950–2004*

Source: http://finance.yahoo.com/?u.

The stock market is also an important factor in business investment decisions because the price of shares affects the amount of funds that can be raised by selling newly issued stock to finance investment spending. A higher price for a firm's shares means that it can raise a larger amount of funds, which can be used to buy production facilities and equipment.

In Chapter 2 we examine the role that the stock market plays in the financial system, and we return to the issue of how stock prices behave and respond to information in the marketplace in Chapters 6 and 11.

The Foreign Exchange Market

For funds to be transferred from one country to another, they have to be converted from the currency in the country of origin (say, dollars) into the currency of the country they are going to (say, euros). The **foreign exchange market** is where this conversion takes place, and so it is instrumental in moving funds between countries. It is also important because it is where the **foreign exchange rate,** the price of one country's currency in terms of another's, is determined.

Figure 3 shows the exchange rate for the U.S. dollar from 1970 to 2004 (measured as the value of the American dollar in terms of a basket of major foreign currencies). The fluctuations in prices in this market have also been substantial: The dollar weakened considerably from 1971 to 1973, rose slightly in value until 1976, and then reached a low point in the 1978–1980 period. From 1980 to early 1985, the dollar appreciated dramatically in value, but then fell sharply, appreciated again from 1995 to 2001, and then depreciated from 2001 to 2004.

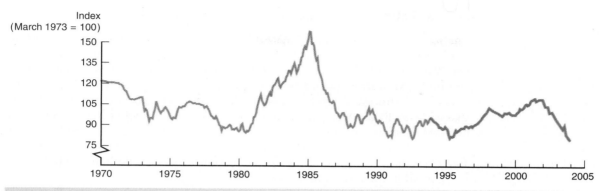

FIGURE 3 *Exchange Rate of the U.S. Dollar for a Basket of Foreign Currencies, 1970–2004*

Source: http://www.federalreserve.gov/releases/h10/Summary/indexn_m.txt.

What have these fluctuations in the exchange rate meant to the American public and businesses? A change in the exchange rate has a direct effect on American consumers because it affects the cost of foreign imports. In 2001, when the euro was worth around 85 cents, 100 euros of European goods (say, French wine) cost $85. When the dollar subsequently weakened, raising the cost of a euro to near $1.20, the same 100 euros of wine now cost $120. Thus a weaker dollar leads to more expensive foreign goods, makes vacationing abroad more expensive, and raises the cost of indulging your desire for imported delicacies. When the value of the dollar drops, Americans will decrease their purchases of foreign goods and increase their consumption of domestic goods (such as travel in the United States or American-made sweaters).

Conversely, a strong dollar means that U.S. goods exported abroad will cost more in foreign countries, and hence foreigners will buy fewer of them. Exports of steel, for example, declined sharply when the dollar strengthened in the 1980–1985 and 1995–2001 periods. A strong dollar benefited American consumers by making foreign goods cheaper but hurt American businesses and eliminated some jobs by cutting both domestic and foreign sales of their products. The decline in the value of the dollar from 1985–1995 and 2001–2004 has had the opposite effect: It has made foreign goods more expensive, but it has made American businesses more competitive. Fluctuations in the foreign exchange markets have major consequences for the American economy.

In Chapter 13 we study how exchange rates are determined in the foreign exchange market in which dollars are bought and sold for foreign currencies.

Why Study Financial Institutions?

The second major focus of this book is financial institutions. Financial institutions are what make financial markets work. Without them, financial markets would not be able to move funds from people who save to people who have productive investment opportunities. They thus also have important effects on the performance of the economy as a whole.

Central Banks and the Conduct of Monetary Policy

The most important financial institution in the financial system is the **central bank,** the government agency responsible for the conduct of monetary policy, which in the United States is the **Federal Reserve System** (also called simply **the Fed**). **Monetary policy** involves the management of interest rates and the quantity of **money,** also referred to as the **money supply** (defined as anything that is generally accepted in payment for goods and services or in the repayment of debt). Because monetary policy affects interest rates, inflation, and business cycles, all of which have a major impact on financial markets and institutions, we study how monetary policy is conducted by central banks in both the United States and abroad in Chapters 7 and 8.

Access general information, monetary policy, banking system, research and economic data from the Federal Reserve at www.federal reserve.gov

Structure of the Financial System

The financial system is complex, comprising many different types of private sector financial institutions, including banks, insurance companies, mutual funds, finance companies, and investment banks, all of which are heavily regulated by the government. If you wanted to make a loan to IBM or General Motors, for example, you would not go directly to the president of the company and offer a loan. Instead, you would lend to such companies indirectly through **financial intermediaries,** institutions such as commercial banks, savings and loan associations, mutual savings banks, credit unions, insurance companies, mutual funds, pension funds, and finance companies that borrow funds from people who have saved and in turn make loans to others.

Why are financial intermediaries so crucial to well-functioning financial markets? Why do they give credit to one party but not to another? Why do they usually write complicated legal documents when they extend loans? Why are they the most heavily regulated businesses in the economy?

We answer these questions by developing a coherent framework for analyzing financial structure both in the United States and in the rest of the world in Chapters 15 and 16.

Banks and Other Financial Institutions

Banks are financial institutions that accept deposits and make loans. Included under the term *banks* are firms such as commercial banks, savings and loan associations, mutual savings banks, and credit unions. Banks are the financial intermediaries that the average person interacts with most frequently. A person who needs a loan to buy a house or a car usually obtains it from a local bank. Most Americans keep a large proportion of their financial wealth in banks in the form of checking accounts, savings accounts, or other types of bank deposits. Because banks are the largest financial intermediaries in our economy, they deserve careful study. However, banks are not the only important financial institutions. Indeed, in recent years, other financial institutions such as insurance companies, finance companies, pension funds, mutual funds, and investment banks have been growing at the expense of banks, and so we need to study them as well. We study banks and all these other institutions in Parts 5 and 6.

Financial Innovation

In the good old days, when you took cash out of the bank or wanted to check your account balance, you got to say hello to the friendly teller. Nowadays you are more likely to interact with an automated teller machine when withdrawing cash, and can get your account balance from your home computer. To see why these options have been developed, we study why and how financial innovation takes place in Chapters 17, 18, and 20, with particular emphasis on how the dramatic improvements in information technology have led to new means of delivering financial services electronically, in what has become known as **e-finance.** We also study financial innovation because it shows us how creative thinking on the part of financial institutions can lead to higher profits. By seeing how and why financial institutions have been creative in the past, we obtain a better grasp of how they may be creative in the future. This knowledge provides us with useful clues about how the financial system may change over time and will help keep our knowledge about banks and other financial institutions from becoming obsolete.

Managing Risk in Financial Institutions

In recent years, the economic environment has become an increasingly risky place. Interest rates fluctuate wildly, stock markets have crashed both here and abroad, speculative crises have occurred in the foreign exchange markets, and failures of financial institutions have reached levels unprecedented since the Great Depression. To avoid wild swings in profitability (and even possibly failure) resulting from this environment, financial institutions must be concerned with how to cope with increased risk. We look at techniques that these institutions use when they engage in risk management in Chapter 24. Then in Chapter 25, we look at how these institutions make use of new financial instruments, such as financial futures, options, and swaps, to manage risk.

Applied Managerial Perspective

Another reason for studying financial institutions is that they are among the largest employers in the country and frequently pay very high salaries. Hence some of you have a very practical reason for studying financial institutions: It may help you get a good job in the financial sector. Even if your interests lie elsewhere, you should still care about how financial institutions are run because there will be many times in your life, as an individual, an employee, or the owner of a business, when you will interact with these institutions. Knowing how financial institutions are managed may help you get a better deal when you need to borrow from them or if you decide to supply them with funds.

This book emphasizes an applied managerial perspective in teaching you about financial markets and institutions by including special case applications headed "The Practicing Manager." These cases introduce you to the real-world problems that managers of financial institutions commonly face and need to solve in their day-to-day jobs. For example, how does the manager of a financial institution come up with a new financial product that will be profitable? How does a financial institution manager manage the risk that the institution faces from fluctuations in interest rates, stock prices, or foreign exchange rates? Should a manager hire an expert on Federal Reserve policymaking, referred to as a "Fed watcher," to help the institution discern where monetary policy might be going in the future?

Not only do the "Practicing Manager" cases, which answer these questions and others like them, provide you with some special analytic tools that you will need if you make your career at a financial institution, but they also give you a feel for what a job as the manager of a financial institution is all about.

How We Will Study Financial Markets and Institutions

Instead of focusing on a mass of dull facts that will soon become obsolete, this textbook stresses a unifying, analytic framework to study financial markets and institutions. This framework uses a few basic concepts to help organize your thinking about the determination of asset prices, the structure of financial markets, bank management, and the role of monetary policy in the economy. The basic concepts are equilibrium, basic supply and demand analysis to explain behavior in financial markets, the search for profits, and an approach to financial structure based on transaction costs and asymmetric information.

The unifying framework used in this book will not only keep your knowledge from becoming obsolete and make the material more interesting but also discourage you from memorizing a mass of facts that will be forgotten soon after the final exam. The framework also provides the tools you need to understand trends in the financial marketplace and in variables such as interest rates and exchange rates. To help you understand and apply the unifying analytic framework, simple models are constructed in which the variables held constant are carefully delineated, each step in the derivation of the model is clearly and carefully laid out, and the models are then used to explain various phenomena by focusing on changes in one variable at a time, holding all other variables constant. To reinforce the models' usefulness, this text also emphasizes the interaction of theoretical analysis and empirical data in order to expose you to real-life events and data. To make the study of financial markets and institutions even more relevant and to help you learn the material, the book contains, besides the "Practicing Manager" cases, numerous additional cases and mini-cases that demonstrate how the analysis in the book can be used to explain many real-world situations.

To function better in the real world outside the classroom, you must get into the lifelong habit of regularly following the financial news that appears in leading financial publications such as the *Wall Street Journal*. To help and encourage you to read the financial section of the newspaper, this book contains two special features. The first is a set of special boxed inserts titled "The *Wall Street Journal*: Following the News" that contain actual columns and data from the *Wall Street Journal* that typically appear daily or periodically. These boxes give you the detailed information and definitions you need to evaluate the data being presented. The second feature is a set of special case applications titled "Case: The *Wall Street Journal*" that expand on the "Following the News" boxes. These cases show you how the analytic framework in the book can be used directly to make sense of the daily columns in the United States' leading financial newspaper. In addition to these cases, this book also contains end-of-chapter questions and problems that ask you to apply the analytic concepts you have learned to other real-world issues. Particularly relevant is a special class of problems headed "Predicting the Future." These questions and problems give you an opportunity to review and apply many of the important financial concepts and tools presented throughout the book.

Exploring the Web

The World Wide Web has become an extremely valuable and convenient resource for financial research. We emphasize the importance of this tool in several ways. First, wherever we utilize the Web to find information to build the charts and tables that appear throughout the text, we include the source site's URL. These sites often contain additional information and are updated frequently. Second, in the margin of the text we have included the URLs of pertinent sites. Visit these sites to further explore a topic you find of particular interest. Finally, we have added Web exercises to the end of each chapter. These exercises prompt you to visit sites related to the chapter and to work with real-time data and information.

Website URLs are subject to frequent change. We have selected stable sites, but we realize that even government URLs change. The publisher's website (**www.aw-bc.com/mishkin_eakins**) will maintain an updated list of current URLs for your reference.

A sample Web exercise has been included in this chapter. This is an especially important example, since it demonstrates how to export data from a website into Excel for further analysis. We suggest you work through this problem on your own so that you will be able to perform this activity when prompted in subsequent Web exercises.

Web Exercise

You have been hired by Risky Ventures, Inc., as a consultant to help them analyze interest rate trends. They are initially interested in determining the historical relationship between long- and short-term interest rates. The biggest task you must immediately undertake is collecting market interest-rate data. You know the best source of this information is the Web.

1. You decide that your best indicator of long-term interest rates is the 10-year U.S. Treasury note. Your first task is to gather historical data. Go to **http://www.federalreserve.gov/releases/** and select "H.15 Selected Interest Rates Historical data." The site should look as follows:

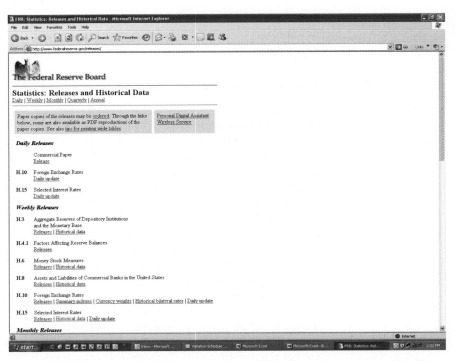

Click on "Historical data." Scroll down to "U.S. Government securities/Treasury constant maturities/10 year." Scroll over to the right and click on "annual."

2. While you have located an accurate source of historical interest-rate data, getting it onto a spreadsheet will be very tedious. You recall that Excel (Microsoft® Excel) will let you convert text data into columns. Begin by highlighting the two columns of data (the year and rate). Right click on the mouse and choose COPY. Now open Excel and put the cursor in a cell. Click paste. Now choose

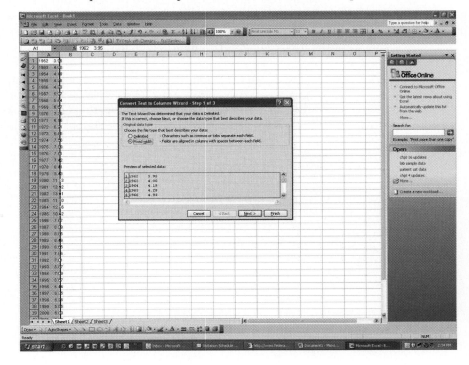

DATA from the tool bar and click on TEXT TO COLUMNS. Follow the wizard, checking the fixed-width option. The list of interest rates should now have the year in one column and the interest rate in the next column. Label your columns.

Repeat the above steps to collect the 1-year interest-rate series. Put it in the column next to the 10-year series. Be sure to line up the years correctly and delete any years that are not included in both series.

3. You now want to analyze the interest rates by graphing them. Again highlight the two columns of data you just created in Excel. Click on the charts icon on the tool bar (or INSERT/CHART). Select "scatter diagram" and choose any type of scatter diagram that connects the dots. Let the Excel wizard take you through the steps of completing the graph. (See the accompanying figure.)

4. Now go to **http://www.forecasts.org/data/index.htm**, click on "stock indices" at the top of the page, and choose "U.S. Stock indices—monthly option." Finally, choose the "Dow Jones Industrial Average" option and again repeat the instructions outlined in steps 2 and 3.

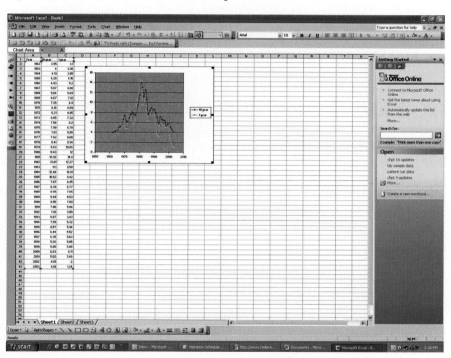

Concluding Remarks

The field of financial markets and institutions is an exciting one. Not only will you learn material that affects your life directly—for example, gaining skills that would be valuable in your career—but you will also gain a clearer understanding of events in financial markets and institutions you frequently hear about in the news media. Our study of financial markets and institutions will also introduce you to many of the controversies that are currently the subject of hot debate in the political arena.

Summary

1. Activities in financial markets have direct effects on individuals' wealth, the behavior of businesses, and the efficiency of our economy. Three financial markets deserve particular attention: the bond market (debt markets), where interest rates are determined; the stock market, which has a major effect on people's wealth and on firms' investment decisions; and the foreign exchange market, because fluctuations in the foreign exchange rate have major consequences for the American economy.

2. Because monetary policy affects interest rates, inflation, and business cycles, all of which have an important impact on financial markets and institutions, we need to understand how monetary policy is conducted by central banks in the United States and abroad.

3. Banks and other financial institutions channel funds from people who might not put them to productive use to people who can do so and thus play a crucial role in improving the efficiency of the economy.

4. Understanding how financial institutions are managed is important because there will be many times in your life, as an individual, an employee, or the owner of a business, when you will interact with them. The "Practicing Manager" cases provide special analytic tools that are useful if you make your career at a financial institution and also give you a feel for what a job as the manager of a financial institution is all about.

5. This textbook stresses an analytic way of thinking by developing a unifying framework for the study of financial markets and institutions using a few basic principles. This textbook also emphasizes the interaction of theoretical analysis and empirical data.

Key Terms

asset, *p. 4*
banks, *p. 8*
bond, *p. 4*
central bank, *p. 8*
common stock (stock), *p. 5*
e-finance, *p. 9*

Federal Reserve System (the Fed), *p. 8*
financial intermediaries, *p. 8*
financial markets, *p. 3*
foreign exchange market, *p. 6*

foreign exchange rate, *p. 6*
interest rate, *p. 4*
monetary policy, *p. 8*
money (money supply), *p. 8*
security, *p. 4*

Questions

1. Why are financial markets important to the health of the economy?

2. When interest rates rise, how might businesses and consumers change their economic behavior?

3. How can a change in interest rates affect the profitability of financial institutions?

4. Is everybody worse off when interest rates rise?

5. What effect might a fall in stock prices have on business investment?

6. What effect might a rise in stock prices have on consumers' decisions to spend?

7. How does a decline in the value of the pound sterling affect British consumers?

8. How does an increase in the value of the pound sterling affect American businesses?

9. How can changes in foreign exchange rates affect the profitability of financial institutions?

10. Looking at Figure 3, in what years would you have chosen to visit the Grand Canyon in Arizona rather than the Tower of London?

11. What is the basic activity of banks?

12. What are the other important financial intermediaries in the economy besides banks?

13. Can you think of any financial innovation in the past ten years that has affected you personally? Has it made you better or worse off? In what way?

14. What types of risks do financial institutions face?

15. Why do managers of financial institutions care so much about the activities of the Federal Reserve System?

Quantitative Problems

1. The following table lists foreign exchange rates between U.S. dollars and British pounds (GBP) during April.

Which day would have been the best day to convert $200 into British pounds? Which day would have been the worst day? What would be the difference in pounds?

Date	U.S. Dollars per GBP
4/1	1.9564
4/4	1.9293
4/5	1.914
4/6	1.9374
4/7	1.961
4/8	1.8925
4/11	1.8822
4/12	1.8558
4/13	1.796
4/14	1.7902
4/15	1.7785
4/18	1.7504
4/19	1.7255
4/20	1.6914
4/21	1.672
4/22	1.6684
4/25	1.6674
4/26	1.6857
4/27	1.6925
4/28	1.7201
4/29	1.7512

CHAPTER 2

Overview of the Financial System

Preview

Suppose that you want to start a business that manufactures a recently invented low-cost robot that cleans house (even does windows), mows the lawn, and washes the car, but you have no funds to put this wonderful invention into production. Walter has plenty of savings that he has inherited. If you and Walter could get together so that he could provide you with the funds, your company's robot would see the light of day, and you, Walter, and the economy would all be better off: Walter could earn a high return on his investment, you would get rich from producing the robot, and we would have cleaner houses, shinier cars, and more beautiful lawns.

Financial markets (bond and stock markets) and financial intermediaries (banks, insurance companies, pension funds) have the basic function of getting people such as you and Walter together by moving funds from those who have a surplus of funds (Walter) to those who have a shortage of funds (you). More realistically, when IBM invents a better computer, it may need funds to bring it to market, or a local government may need funds to build a road or a school. Well-functioning financial markets and financial intermediaries are crucial to our economic health. Indeed, when the financial system breaks down, as it has in Russia and in East Asia recently, severe economic hardship results.

To study the effects of financial markets and financial intermediaries on the economy, we need to acquire an understanding of their general structure and operation. In this chapter we learn about the major financial intermediaries and the instruments that are traded in financial markets.

This chapter offers a preliminary overview of the fascinating study of financial markets and institutions. We will return to a more detailed treatment of the regulation, structure, and evolution of financial markets and institutions in Parts 3 through 5.

Function of Financial Markets

Financial markets perform the essential economic function of channeling funds from households, firms, and governments that have saved surplus funds by spending less than their income to those who have a shortage of funds because they wish to spend more than their income. This function is shown schematically in Figure 1. Those who have saved and are lending funds, the lender-savers, are at the left, and those who must borrow funds to finance their spending, the borrower-spenders, are at the right. The principal lender-savers are households, but business enterprises and the government (particularly state and local government), as well as foreigners and their governments, sometimes also find themselves with excess funds and so lend them out. The most important borrower-spenders are businesses and the government (particularly the federal government), but households and foreigners also borrow to finance their purchases of cars, furniture, and houses. The arrows show that funds flow from lender-savers to borrower-spenders via two routes.

In *direct finance* (the route at the bottom of Figure 1), borrowers borrow funds directly from lenders in financial markets by selling them *securities* (also called *financial instruments*), which are claims on the borrower's future income or assets. Securities are assets for the person who buys them but **liabilities** (IOUs or debts) for the individual or firm that sells (issues) them. For example, if General Motors needs to borrow funds to pay for a new factory to manufacture computerized cars, it might borrow the funds from a saver by selling the saver a *bond*,

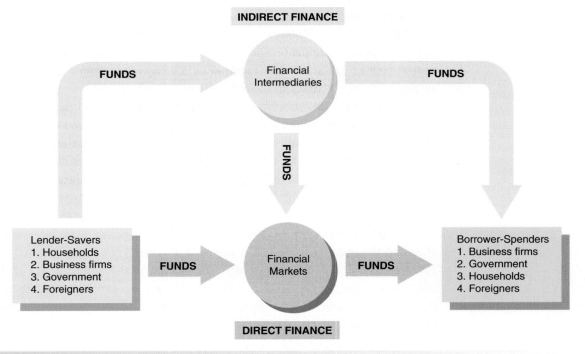

FIGURE 1 *Flows of Funds Through the Financial System*

a debt security that promises to make payments periodically for a specified period of time.

Why is this channeling of funds from savers to spenders so important to the economy? The answer is that the people who save are frequently not the same people who have profitable investment opportunities available to them, the entrepreneurs. Let's first think about this on a personal level. Suppose that you have saved $1000 this year, but no borrowing or lending is possible because there are no financial markets. If you do not have an investment opportunity that will permit you to earn income with your savings, you will just hold on to the $1000 and will earn no interest. However, Carl the Carpenter has a productive use for your $1000: He can use it to purchase a new tool that will shorten the time it takes him to build a house, thereby earning an extra $200 per year. If you could get in touch with Carl, you could lend him the $1000 at a rental fee (interest) of $100 per year, and both of you would be better off. You would earn $100 per year on your $1000, instead of the zero amount that you would earn otherwise, while Carl would earn $100 more income per year (the $200 extra earnings per year minus the $100 rental fee for the use of the funds).

In the absence of financial markets, you and Carl the Carpenter might never get together. Without financial markets, it is hard to transfer funds from a person who has no investment opportunities to one who has them; you would both be stuck with the status quo, and both of you would be worse off. Financial markets are thus essential to promoting economic efficiency.

The existence of financial markets is also beneficial even if someone borrows for a purpose other than increasing production in a business. Say that you are recently married, have a good job, and want to buy a house. You earn a good salary, but because you have just started to work, you have not yet saved much. Over time you would have no problem saving enough to buy the house of your dreams, but by then you would be too old to get full enjoyment from it. Without financial markets, you are stuck; you cannot buy the house and will continue to live in your tiny apartment.

If a financial market were set up so that people who had built up savings could lend you the funds to buy the house, you would be more than happy to pay them some interest in order to own a home while you are still young enough to enjoy it. Then, when you had saved up enough funds, you would pay back your loan. The overall outcome would be such that you would be better off, as would the persons who made you the loan. They would now earn some interest, whereas they would not if the financial market did not exist.

Now we can see why financial markets have such an important function in the economy. They allow funds to move from people who lack productive investment opportunities to people who have such opportunities. Thus financial markets are critical for producing an efficient allocation of capital, which contributes to higher production and efficiency for the overall economy. Indeed, as we will explore in Chapter 14, when financial markets break down during financial crises, as they have in Mexico, East Asia, and Argentina in recent years, severe economic hardship results, which can even lead to dangerous political instability.

Well-functioning financial markets also directly improve the well-being of consumers by allowing them to time their purchases better. They provide funds to young people to buy what they need and can eventually afford without forcing them to wait until they have saved up the entire purchase price. Financial markets that are operating efficiently improve the economic welfare of everyone in the society.

Structure of Financial Markets

Now that we understand the basic function of financial markets, let's look at their structure. The following descriptions of several categorizations of financial markets illustrate essential features of these markets.

Debt and Equity Markets

A firm or an individual can obtain funds in a financial market in two ways. The most common method is to issue a debt instrument, such as a bond or a mortgage, which is a contractual agreement by the borrower to pay the holder of the instrument fixed dollar amounts at regular intervals (interest and principal payments) until a specified date (the maturity date), when a final payment is made. The **maturity** of a debt instrument is the number of years (term) until that instrument's expiration date. A debt instrument is **short-term** if its maturity is less than a year and **long-term** if its maturity is ten years or longer. Debt instruments with a maturity between one and ten years are said to be **intermediate-term.**

The second method of raising funds is by issuing **equities,** such as common stock, which are claims to share in the net income (income after expenses and taxes) and the assets of a business. If you own one share of common stock in a company that has issued one million shares, you are entitled to 1 one-millionth of the firm's net income and 1 one-millionth of the firm's assets. Equities often make periodic payments (**dividends**) to their holders and are considered long-term securities because they have no maturity date. In addition, owning stock means that you own a portion of the firm and thus have the right to vote on issues important to the firm and to elect its directors.

The main disadvantage of owning a corporation's equities rather than its debt is that an equity holder is a *residual claimant;* that is, the corporation must pay all its debt holders before it pays its equity holders. The advantage of holding equities is that equity holders benefit directly from any increases in the corporation's profitability or asset value because equities confer ownership rights on the equity holders. Debt holders do not share in this benefit because their dollar payments are fixed. We examine the pros and cons of debt versus equity instruments in more detail in Chapter 15, which provides an analytical framework for understanding financial structure.

The total value of equities in the United States has typically fluctuated between $1 and $20 trillion since the early 1970s, depending on the prices of shares. Although the average person is more aware of the stock market than any other financial market, the size of the debt market greatly exceeds that of the equities market: The value of debt instruments ($35.1 trillion at the end of 2004) is more than 50% larger than the value of equities ($15.9 trillion at the end of 2004).

At www.nyse.com, find listed companies, quotes, company historical data, real-time market indices, and more.

Primary and Secondary Markets

A **primary market** is a financial market in which new issues of a security, such as a bond or a stock, are sold to initial buyers by the corporation or government agency borrowing the funds. A **secondary market** is a financial market in which securities that have been previously issued (and are thus secondhand) can be resold.

The primary markets for securities are not well known to the public because the selling of securities to initial buyers often takes place behind closed doors. An important financial institution that assists in the initial sale of securities in the primary market is the **investment bank.** It does this by **underwriting** securities: It guarantees a price for a corporation's securities and then sells them to the public.

The New York and American stock exchanges, in which previously issued stocks are traded, are the best-known examples of secondary markets, although the bond markets, in which previously issued bonds of major corporations and the U.S. government are bought and sold, actually have a larger trading volume. Other examples of secondary markets are foreign exchange markets, futures markets, and options markets. Securities brokers and dealers are crucial to a well-functioning secondary market. **Brokers** are agents of investors who match buyers with sellers of securities; **dealers** link buyers and sellers by buying and selling securities at stated prices.

When an individual buys a security in the secondary market, the person who has sold the security receives money in exchange for the security, but the corporation that issued the security acquires no new funds. A corporation acquires new funds only when its securities are first sold in the primary market. Nonetheless, secondary markets serve two important functions. First, they make it easier to sell these financial instruments to raise cash; that is, they make the financial instruments more **liquid.** The increased liquidity of these instruments then makes them more desirable and thus easier for the issuing firm to sell in the primary market. Second, they determine the price of the security that the issuing firm sells in the primary market. The firms that buy securities in the primary market will pay the issuing corporation no more than the price that they think the secondary market will set for this security. The higher the security's price in the secondary market, the higher will be the price that the issuing firm will receive for a new security in the primary market and hence the greater the amount of capital it can raise. Conditions in the secondary market are therefore the most relevant to corporations issuing securities. It is for this reason that books like this one, which deal with financial markets, focus on the behavior of secondary markets rather than that of primary markets.

Exchanges and Over-the-Counter Markets

Secondary markets can be organized in two ways. One is to organize **exchanges,** where buyers and sellers of securities (or their agents or brokers) meet in one central location to conduct trades. The New York and American stock exchanges for stocks and the Chicago Board of Trade for commodities (wheat, corn, silver, and other raw materials) are examples of organized exchanges.

The other method of organizing a secondary market is to have an **over-the-counter (OTC) market,** in which dealers at different locations have an inventory of securities and stand ready to buy and sell securities "over the counter" to anyone who comes to them and is willing to accept their prices. Because over-the-counter dealers are in computer contact and know the prices set by one another, the OTC market is very competitive and not very different from a market with an organized exchange.

Many common stocks are traded over the counter, although the majority of the largest corporations have their shares traded at organized stock exchanges such as the New York Stock Exchange. The U.S. government bond market, with

Detailed market and security information for the Nasdaq OTC stock exchange is available at www.nasdaq.com

a larger trading volume than the New York Stock Exchange, is set up as an over-the-counter market. Forty or so dealers establish a "market" in these securities by standing ready to buy and sell U.S. government bonds. Other over-the-counter markets include those that trade other types of financial instruments such as negotiable certificates of deposit, federal funds, banker's acceptances, and foreign exchange.

Money and Capital Markets

Another way of distinguishing between markets is on the basis of the maturity of the securities traded in each market. The **money market** is a financial market in which only short-term debt instruments (original maturity of less than one year) are traded; the **capital market** is the market in which longer-term debt (original maturity of one year or greater) and equity instruments are traded. Money market securities are usually more widely traded than longer-term securities and so tend to be more liquid. In addition, as we will see in Chapter 3, short-term securities have smaller fluctuations in prices than long-term securities, making them safer investments. As a result, corporations and banks actively use this market to earn interest on surplus funds that they expect to have only temporarily. Capital market securities, such as stocks and long-term bonds, are often held by financial intermediaries such as insurance companies and pension funds, which have little uncertainty about the amount of funds they will have available in the future.

Internationalization of Financial Markets

The growing internationalization of financial markets has become an important trend. Before the 1980s, U.S. financial markets were much larger than financial markets outside the United States, but in recent years the dominance of U.S. markets has been disappearing. The extraordinary growth of foreign financial markets has been the result of both large increases in the pool of savings in foreign countries such as Japan and the deregulation of foreign financial markets, which has enabled them to expand their activities. American corporations and banks are now more likely to tap international capital markets to raise needed funds, and American investors often seek investment opportunities abroad. Similarly, foreign corporations and banks raise funds from Americans, and foreigners are becoming important investors in the United States. A look at international bond markets and world stock markets will give us a picture of how this globalization of financial markets is taking place.

International Bond Market, Eurobonds, and Eurocurrencies

The traditional instruments in the international bond market are known as **foreign bonds.** Foreign bonds are sold in a foreign country and are denominated in that country's currency. For example, if the German automaker Porsche sells a bond in the United States denominated in U.S. dollars, it is classified as a foreign bond. Foreign bonds have been an important instrument in the international capital market for centuries. In fact, a large percentage of U.S. railroads built in the nineteenth century were financed by sales of foreign bonds in Britain.

A more recent innovation in the international bond market is the **Eurobond,** a bond denominated in a currency other than that of the country in which it is sold—for example, a bond denominated in U.S. dollars sold in London. Currently, over 80% of the new issues in the international bond market are Eurobonds, and the market for these securities has grown very rapidly. As a result, the Eurobond market has passed the U.S. corporate bond market as a source of new funds.

A variant of the Eurobond is **Eurocurrencies,** which are foreign currencies that are deposited in banks outside of the home country. The most important of the Eurocurrencies is **Eurodollars,** which are U.S. dollars deposited in foreign banks outside of the United States or in foreign branches of U.S. banks. These short-term deposits earn interest and so are similar to short-term Eurobonds. American banks borrow Eurodollar deposits from other banks or from their own foreign branches, and Eurodollars are now an important source of funds for American banks (over $100 billion outstanding).

Note that the new currency, the euro, can create some confusion about the terms *Eurobond, Eurocurrencies*, and *Eurodollars*. A bond denominated in euros is called a Eurobond only *if it is sold outside the countries that have adopted the euro*. In fact, most Eurobonds are not denominated in euros but are instead denominated in U.S. dollars. Similarly, Eurodollars have nothing to do with euros, but are instead U.S. dollars deposited in banks outside the United States.

World Stock Markets

Until recently, the U.S. stock market was by far the largest in the world, but foreign stock markets have been growing in importance. Now the United States is not always number one: In the 1980s, the value of stocks traded in Japan at times exceeded the value of stocks traded in the United States. The increased interest in foreign stocks has prompted the development in the United States of mutual funds specializing in trading in foreign stock markets. American investors now pay attention not only to the Dow Jones Industrial Average but also to stock price indexes for foreign stock markets such as the Nikkei 225 Average (Tokyo) and the Financial Times–Stock Exchange 100-Share Index (London).

The internationalization of financial markets is having profound effects on the United States. Foreigners, particularly the Japanese, are not only providing funds to corporations in the United States but are also helping finance a significant fraction of the federal government's huge budget deficit. Without these foreign funds, the U.S. economy would have grown far less rapidly in the last two decades. The internationalization of financial markets is also leading the way to a more integrated world economy in which flows of goods and technology between countries are more commonplace. In later chapters we will encounter many examples of the important roles that international factors play in our economy.

Function of Financial Intermediaries

As shown in Figure 1, funds can move from lenders to borrowers by a second route, called *indirect finance* because it involves a financial intermediary that stands between the lender-savers and the borrower-spenders and helps transfer funds from one to the other. A financial intermediary does this by borrowing funds from the lender-savers and then using these funds to make loans to borrower-spenders. For example, a bank might acquire funds by issuing a liability in the form of savings deposits (an asset for the public). It might then use the funds to acquire an asset by making a loan to General Motors or by buying a GM bond in the financial market. The ultimate result is that funds have been transferred from the public (the lender-savers) to GM (the borrower-spender) with the help of the financial intermediary (the bank).

The process of indirect finance using financial intermediaries, called **financial intermediation,** is the primary route for moving funds from lenders to borrowers. Indeed, although the media focus much of their attention on securities markets, particularly the stock market, financial intermediaries are a far more important source of financing for corporations than securities markets are. This is true not only for the United States but for other industrialized countries as well (see the "Global" box). Why are financial intermediaries and indirect finance so important in financial markets? To answer this question, we need to understand the role of transaction costs and information costs in financial markets.

THE *WALL STREET JOURNAL*: FOLLOWING THE NEWS

Foreign Stock Market Indexes

INTERNATIONAL STOCK MARKET INDEXES

COUNTRY	INDEX	12/8/04 CLOSE	NET CHG	% CHG	YTD NET CHG	YTD % CHG	P/E
World	DJ World Index	206.30	−0.95	−0.46	+19.35	+10.35	17
Argentina	Merval	1204.62	Closed	...	+132.67	+12.38	...
Australia	S&P/ASX 200	3897.70	−29.80	−0.76	+597.90	+18.12	16
Belgium	Bel-20	2906.39	−4.81	−0.17	+662.21	+29.51	12
Brazil	Sao Paulo Bovespa	24968.39	−20.23	−0.08	+2732.00	+12.29	13
Canada	S&P/TSX Composite	9003.74	+12.79	+0.14	+782.85	+9.52	17
Chile	Santiago IPSA	1786.90	Closed	...	+302.10	+20.35	17
China	Dow Jones CBN China 600	10740.49	+12.78	+0.12	−1476.12	−12.08	19
China	Dow Jones China 88	114.43	+0.03	+0.03	−21.30	−15.69	16
Europe	DJ STOXX 600	248.97	−0.47	−0.19	+19.66	+8.57	21
Europe	DJ STOXX 50	2768.29	−6.66	−0.24	+107.92	+4.06	20
Euro Zone	DJ Euro STOXX	263.36	−0.32	−0.12	+20.15	+8.29	21
Euro Zone	DJ Euro STOXX 50	2912.44	−5.99	−0.21	+151.78	+5.50	18
France	Paris CAC 40	3775.04	−12.41	−0.33	+217.14	+6.10	15
Germany	Frankfurt Xetra DAX	4201.35	−11.27	−0.27	+236.19	+5.96	14
Hong Kong	Hang Seng	14022.32	−213.46	−1.50	+1446.38	+11.50	16
India	Bombay Sensex	6261.52	−54.76	−0.87	+422.56	+7.24	17
Israel	Tel Aviv 25	593.84	−0.14	−0.02	+89.69	+17.79	...
Italy	S&P/MIB	30272	+99	+0.33	+3385	+12.59	18
Japan	Tokyo Nikkei Stock Average	10941.37	+67.74	+0.62	+264.73	+2.48	...
Japan	Tokyo Nikkei 300	212.74	+1.69	+0.80	+9.20	+4.52	...
Japan	Tokyo Topix Index	1099.69	+6.01	+0.55	+56.00	+5.37	115
Mexico	I.P.C. All-Share	12113.58	−4.73	−0.04	+3318.30	+37.73	17
Netherlands	Amsterdam AEX	343.31	−0.06	−0.02	+5.66	+1.68	10
Russia	DJ Russia Titans 10	1923.17	−118.97	−5.83	−251.96	−11.58	29
Singapore	Straits Times	2020.66	+4.40	+0.22	+265.14	+14.52	12
South Africa	Johannesburg All Share	12205.18	−107.83	−0.88	+1817.96	+17.50	14
South Korea	KOSPI	871.74	+10.67	+1.24	+61.03	+7.53	15
Spain	IBEX 35	8818.40	Closed	...	+1081.20	+13.97	17
Sweden	SX All Share	227.24	−1.40	−0.61	+33.07	+1.44	15
Switzerland	Zurich Swiss Market	5566.70	+5.60	+0.10	+78.90	+1.44	15
Taiwan	Weighted	5892.51	−32.77	−0.55	+1.82	+0.03	11
Turkey	Istanbul National 100	22625.44	−450.14	−1.95	+4000.42	+21.48	22
U.K.	London FTSE 100-share	4703.90	−24.80	−0.52	+227.00	+5.07	16
U.K.	London FTSE 250-share	6657.60	−3.90	−0.06	+855.30	+14.74	16

Foreign stock market indexes are published daily in the *Wall Street Journal*. The first two columns identify the foreign stock exchange and the market index; for example, the colored entry is for the Nikkei 300 for the Japanese Stock Exchange. The third column, "CLOSE," gives the closing value of the index, which was 212.74 for the Nikkei 300 on 12/18/2004. The "NET CHG" column indicates the change in the index from the previous trading day, +1.69, and the "% CHG" column indicates the percentage change in the index, +0.80. The next two columns indicate the year-to-date net change (+9.20) and percentage change of the index (+4.52%), respectively. The final column reports the price/earnings ratio where it is available.

Check out major world stock indexes, with charts, news, and components, at http://quote. yahoo.com/ m2?u

GLOBAL

The Importance of Financial Intermediaries to Securities Markets: An International Comparison

Patterns of financing corporations differ across countries, but one key fact emerges. Studies of the major developed countries, including the United States, Canada, Great Britain, Japan, Italy, Germany, and France, show that when businesses go looking for funds to finance their activities, they usually obtain them indirectly through financial intermediaries and not directly from securities markets. Even in the United States and Canada, which have the most developed securities markets in the world, loans from financial intermediaries are far more important for corporate finance than securities markets are. The countries that have made the least use of securities markets are Germany and Japan; in these two countries, financing from financial intermediaries has been almost ten times greater than that from securities markets. However, with the deregulation of Japanese securities markets in recent years, the share of corporate financing by financial intermediaries has been declining relative to the use of securities markets.

Although the dominance of financial intermediaries over securities markets is clear in all countries, the relative importance of bond versus stock markets differs widely across countries. In the United States, the bond market is far more important as a source of corporate finance: On average, the amount of new financing raised using bonds is ten times the amount using stocks. By contrast, countries such as France and Italy make use of equities markets more than the bond market to raise capital.

*See, for example, Colin Mayer, "Financial Systems, Corporate Finance, and Economic Development," in *Asymmetric Information, Corporate Finance, and Investment*, ed. R. Glenn Hubbard (Chicago: University of Chicago Press, 1990), pp. 307–332.

Transaction Costs

Transaction costs, the time and money spent in carrying out financial transactions, are a major problem for people who have excess funds to lend. As we have seen, Carl the Carpenter needs $1000 for his new tool, and you know that it is an excellent investment opportunity. You have the cash and would like to lend him the money, but to protect your investment, you have to hire a lawyer to write up the loan contract that specifies how much interest Carl will pay you, when he will make these interest payments, and when he will repay you the $1000. Obtaining the contract will cost you $500. When you figure in this transaction cost for making the loan, you realize that you can't earn enough from the deal (you spend $500 to make perhaps $100) and reluctantly tell Carl that he will have to look elsewhere.

This example illustrates that small savers like you or potential borrowers like Carl might be frozen out of financial markets and thus be unable to benefit from them. Can anyone come to the rescue? Financial intermediaries can.

Financial intermediaries can substantially reduce transaction costs because they have developed expertise in lowering them and because their large size allows them to take advantage of **economies of scale,** the reduction in transaction costs per dollar of transactions as the size (scale) of transactions increases. For example, a bank knows how to find a good lawyer to produce an airtight loan contract, and this contract can be used over and over again in its loan transactions, thus lowering the legal cost per transaction. Instead of a loan contract (which may not be all that well written) costing $500, a bank can hire a topflight lawyer for $5000 to draw up an airtight loan contract that can be used for 2000 loans at a cost of $2.50 per loan. At a cost of $2.50 per loan, it now becomes profitable for the financial intermediary to loan Carl the $1000.

Because financial intermediaries are able to reduce transaction costs substantially, they make it possible for you to provide funds indirectly to people with productive investment opportunities like Carl. In addition, a financial intermediary's low transaction costs mean that it can provide its customers with **liquidity services,** services that make it easier for customers to conduct transactions. For example, banks provide depositors with checking accounts that enable them to pay their bills easily. In addition, depositors can earn interest on checking and savings accounts and yet still convert them into goods and services whenever necessary.

Risk Sharing

Another benefit made possible by the low transaction costs of financial institutions is that they can help reduce the exposure of investors to **risk**—that is, uncertainty about the returns investors will earn on assets. Financial intermediaries do this through the process known as **risk sharing:** They create and sell assets with risk characteristics that people are comfortable with, and the intermediaries then use the funds they acquire by selling these assets to purchase other assets that may have far more risk. Low transaction costs for financial intermediaries allow them to do risk sharing at low cost, enabling them to earn a profit on the spread between the returns they earn on risky assets and the payments they make on the assets they have sold. This process of risk sharing is also sometimes referred to as the process of **asset transformation,** because in a sense risky assets are turned into safer assets for investors.

Financial intermediaries also promote risk sharing by helping individuals to diversify and thereby lower the amount of risk to which they are exposed. **Diversification** entails investing in a collection (**portfolio**) of assets whose returns do not always move together, with the result that overall risk is lower than for individual assets. (Diversification is just another name for the old adage that "you shouldn't put all your eggs in one basket.") Low transaction costs allow financial intermediaries to do this by pooling a collection of assets into a new asset and then selling it to individuals.

Asymmetric Information: Adverse Selection and Moral Hazard

The presence of transaction costs in financial markets explains, in part, why financial intermediaries and indirect finance play such an important role in financial markets. An additional reason is that in financial markets, one party often does not know enough about the other party to make accurate decisions. This inequality is called **asymmetric information.** For example, a borrower who takes out a loan usually has better information about the potential returns and risks associated with the investment projects for which the funds are earmarked than the lender does. Lack of information creates problems in the financial system on two fronts: before the transaction is entered into and after.

Adverse selection is the problem created by asymmetric information *before* the transaction occurs. Adverse selection in financial markets occurs when the potential borrowers who are the most likely to produce an undesirable *(adverse)* outcome—the bad credit risks—are the ones who most actively seek out a loan and are thus most likely to be selected. Because adverse selection makes it more likely that loans might be made to bad credit risks, lenders may decide not to make any loans even though there are good credit risks in the marketplace.

To understand why adverse selection occurs, suppose that you have two aunts to whom you might make a loan—Aunt Sheila and Aunt Louise. Aunt Louise is a conservative type who borrows only when she has an investment that she is quite sure will pay off. Aunt Sheila, by contrast, is an inveterate gambler who has just come across a get-rich-quick scheme that will make her a millionaire if she can just borrow $1000 to invest in it. Unfortunately, as with most get-rich-quick schemes, there is a high probability that the investment won't pay off and that Aunt Sheila will lose the $1000.

Which of your aunts is more likely to call you to ask for a loan? Aunt Sheila, of course, because she has so much to gain if the investment pays off. You, however, would not want to make a loan to her because there is a high probability that her investment will turn sour and she will be unable to pay you back.

If you knew both your aunts very well—that is, if information was not asymmetric—you wouldn't have a problem because you would know that Aunt Sheila is a bad risk and so you would not lend to her. Suppose, though, that you don't know your aunts well. You are more likely to lend to Aunt Sheila than to Aunt Louise because Aunt Sheila would be hounding you for the loan. Because of the possibility of adverse selection, you might decide not to lend to either of your aunts, even though there are times when Aunt Louise, who is an excellent credit risk, might need a loan for a worthwhile investment.

Moral hazard is the problem created by asymmetric information *after* the transaction occurs. Moral hazard in financial markets is the risk *(hazard)* that the borrower might engage in activities that are undesirable *(immoral)* from the lender's point of view because they make it less likely that the loan will be paid back. Because moral hazard lowers the probability that the loan will be repaid, lenders may decide that they would rather not make a loan.

As an example of moral hazard, suppose that you made a $1000 loan to another relative, Uncle Melvin, who needs the money to purchase a computer so that he can set up a business typing students' term papers. Once you have made the loan, however, Uncle Melvin is more likely to slip off to the track and play the horses. If he bets on a 20-to-1 long shot and wins with your money, he is able to pay you back your $1000 and live high off the hog with the remaining $19,000. But if he loses, as is likely, you don't get paid back, and all he has lost is his reputation as a reliable, upstanding uncle. Uncle Melvin therefore has an incentive to go to the track because his gains ($19,000) if he bets correctly may be much greater than the cost to him (his reputation) if he bets incorrectly. If you knew what Uncle Melvin was up to, you would prevent him from going to the track, and he would not be able to increase the moral hazard. However, because it is hard for you to keep informed about his whereabouts—that is, because information is asymmetric—there is a good chance that Uncle Melvin will go to the track and you will not get paid back. The risk of moral hazard might therefore discourage you from making the $1000 loan to Uncle Melvin, even if you were sure that you would be paid back if he used it to set up his business.

Another way of describing the moral hazard problem is that it leads to **conflicts of interest,** in which one party in a financial contract has incentives to act in its own interest rather than in the interests of the other party. Indeed, this is exactly what happens if your Uncle Melvin is tempted to go to the track and gamble at your expense.

The problems created by adverse selection and moral hazard are an important impediment to well-functioning financial markets. Again, financial intermediaries can alleviate these problems.

With financial intermediaries in the economy, small savers can provide their funds to the financial markets by lending these funds to a trustworthy intermediary, say, the Honest John Bank, which in turn lends the funds out either by making loans or by buying securities such as stocks or bonds. Successful financial intermediaries have higher earnings on their investments because they are better equipped than individuals to screen out good from bad credit risks, thereby reducing losses due to adverse selection. In addition, financial intermediaries have high earnings because they develop expertise in monitoring the parties they lend to, thus reducing losses due to moral hazard. The result is that financial intermediaries can afford to pay lender-savers interest or provide substantial services and still earn a profit.

As we have seen, financial intermediaries play an important role in the economy because they provide liquidity services, promote risk sharing, and solve information problems. The success of financial intermediaries in performing this role is evidenced by the fact that most Americans invest their savings with them and obtain loans from them. Financial intermediaries play a key role in improving economic efficiency because they help financial markets channel funds from lender-savers to people with productive investment opportunities. Without a well-functioning set of financial intermediaries, it is very hard for an economy to reach its full potential. We will explore further the role of financial intermediaries in the economy in Parts 5 and 6.

Financial Intermediaries

We have seen why financial intermediaries play such an important role in the economy. Now we look at the principal financial intermediaries and how they perform the intermediation function. They fall into three categories: depository institutions (banks), contractual savings institutions, and investment intermediaries. Table 1 provides a guide to the discussion of the financial intermediaries that fit into these three categories by describing their primary liabilities (sources of funds) and assets (uses of funds). The relative size of these intermediaries in the United States is indicated in Table 2, which lists the amount of their assets at the end of 1970, 1980, 1990, and 2004.

TABLE 1 *Primary Assets and Liabilities of Financial Intermediaries*

Type of Intermediary	Primary Liabilities (Sources of Funds)	Primary Assets (Uses of Funds)
Depository Institutions (Banks)		
Commercial banks	Deposits	Business and consumer loans, mortgages, U.S. government securities and municipal bonds
Savings and loan associations	Deposits	Mortgages
Mutual savings banks	Deposits	Mortgages
Credit unions	Deposits	Consumer loans
Contractual Savings Institutions		
Life insurance companies	Premiums from policies	Corporate bonds and mortgages
Fire and casualty insurance companies	Premiums from policies	Municipal bonds, corporate bonds and stock, U.S. government securities
Pension funds, government retirement funds	Employer and employee contributions	Corporate bonds and stock
Investment Intermediaries		
Finance companies	Commercial paper, stocks, bonds	Consumer and business loans
Mutual funds	Shares	Stocks, bonds
Money market mutual funds	Shares	Money market instruments

Source: Federal Reserve Flow of Funds Accounts.

Depository Institutions

Depository institutions (which for simplicity we refer to as *banks* throughout this text) are financial intermediaries that accept deposits from individuals and institutions and make loans. These institutions include commercial banks and the so-called **thrift institutions (thrifts):** savings and loan associations, mutual savings banks, and credit unions.

Commercial Banks These financial intermediaries raise funds primarily by issuing checkable deposits (deposits on which checks can be written), savings deposits (deposits that are payable on demand but do not allow their owner to write checks), and time deposits (deposits with fixed terms to maturity). They then use these funds to make commercial, consumer, and mortgage loans and to buy U.S. government securities and municipal bonds. There are approximately 8000 commercial banks in the United States, and as a group, they are the largest financial intermediary and have the most diversified portfolios (collections) of assets.

Savings and Loan Associations (S&Ls) and Mutual Savings Banks These depository institutions, of which there are approximately 1500, obtain funds primarily through savings deposits (often called *shares*) and time and checkable deposits. In the past, these institutions were constrained in their activities and mostly made mortgage loans for residential housing. Over time, these restrictions have been loosened so that the distinction between these depository institutions and commercial

TABLE 2   *Principal Financial Intermediaries*

Type of Intermediary	Value of Assets ($ billions, end of year)			
	1970	1980	1990	2004
Depository Institutions (Banks)				
Commercial banks	517	1481	3334	6141
Savings and loan associations and mutual savings banks	250	792	1365	1597
Credit unions	18	67	215	643
Contractual Savings Institutions				
Life insurance companies	201	464	1367	3969
Fire and casualty insurance companies	50	182	533	1116
Pension funds (private)	112	504	1629	4330
State and local government retirement funds	60	197	737	2046
Investment Intermediaries				
Finance companies	64	205	610	1385
Mutual funds	47	70	654	4969
Money market mutual funds	0	76	498	1912

Source: http://www.federalreserve.gov/releases/Z1/

banks has blurred. These intermediaries have become more alike and are now more competitive with each other.

Credit Unions These financial institutions, numbering about 10,000, are very small cooperative lending institutions organized around a particular group: union members, employees of a particular firm, and so forth. They acquire funds from deposits called *shares* and primarily make consumer loans. Thanks to the banking legislation in the 1980s, credit unions are also allowed to issue checkable deposits and can make mortgage loans in addition to consumer loans.

Contractual Savings Institutions

Contractual savings institutions, such as insurance companies and pension funds, are financial intermediaries that acquire funds at periodic intervals on a contractual basis. Because they can predict with reasonable accuracy how much they will have to pay out in benefits in the coming years, they do not have to worry as much as depository institutions about losing funds. As a result, the liquidity of assets is not as important a consideration for them as it is for depository institutions, and they tend to invest their funds primarily in long-term securities such as corporate bonds, stocks, and mortgages.

Life Insurance Companies Life insurance companies insure people against financial hazards following a death and sell annuities (annual income payments upon retirement). They acquire funds from the premiums that people pay to keep their policies in force and use them mainly to buy corporate bonds and mortgages. They also purchase stocks but are restricted in the amount that they can hold. Currently, with $3.1 trillion in assets, they are among the largest of the contractual savings institutions.

Fire and Casualty Insurance Companies These companies insure their policy-holders against loss from theft, fire, and accidents. They are very much like life insurance companies, receiving funds through premiums for their policies, but they have a greater possibility of loss of funds if major disasters occur. For this reason, they use their funds to buy more liquid assets than life insurance companies do. Their largest holding of assets is municipal bonds; they also hold corporate bonds and stocks and U.S. government securities.

Pension Funds and Government Retirement Funds Private pension funds and state and local government retirement funds provide retirement income in the form of annuities to employees who are covered by a pension plan. Funds are acquired by contributions from employers or from employees, who either have a contribution automatically deducted from their paychecks or contribute voluntarily. The largest asset holdings of pension funds are corporate bonds and stocks. The establishment of pension funds has been actively encouraged by the federal government both through legislation requiring pension plans and through tax incentives to encourage contributions.

Investment Intermediaries

This category of financial intermediaries includes finance companies, mutual funds, and money market mutual funds.

Finance Companies Finance companies raise funds by selling commercial paper (a short-term debt instrument) and by issuing stocks and bonds. They lend these funds to consumers, who make purchases of such items as furniture, automobiles, and home improvements, and to small businesses. Some finance companies are organized by a parent corporation to help sell its product. For example, Ford Motor Credit Company makes loans to consumers who purchase Ford automobiles.

Mutual Funds These financial intermediaries acquire funds by selling shares to many individuals and use the proceeds to purchase diversified portfolios of stocks and bonds. Mutual funds allow shareholders to pool their resources so that they can take advantage of lower transaction costs when buying large blocks of stocks or bonds. In addition, mutual funds allow shareholders to hold more diversified portfolios than they otherwise would. Shareholders can sell (redeem) shares at any time, but the value of these shares will be determined by the value of the mutual fund's holdings of securities. Because these fluctuate greatly, the value of mutual fund shares will too; therefore, investments in mutual funds can be risky.

Money Market Mutual Funds These relatively new financial institutions have the characteristics of a mutual fund but also function to some extent as a depository institution because they offer deposit-type accounts. Like most mutual funds, they sell shares to acquire funds that are then used to buy money market instruments that are both safe and very liquid. The interest on these assets is then paid out to the shareholders.

A key feature of these funds is that shareholders can write checks against the value of their shareholdings. There are generally restrictions on the use of the check-writing privilege, however; checks frequently cannot be written for amounts less than a set minimum, such as $500, and a substantial amount of money is required initially to open an account. In effect, shares in a money market mutual fund function like checking account deposits that pay interest, but with some restrictions on the check-writing privilege. Money market mutual funds have experienced extraordinary growth since 1971, when they first appeared. By 2004, their assets had climbed to $1.9 trillion.

Regulation of the Financial System

The United States Securities and Exchange Commission home page, www.sec.gov, contains vast SEC resources, laws and regulations, investor information, and litigation updates.

The financial system is among the most heavily regulated sectors of the American economy. The government regulates financial markets for three main reasons: to increase the information available to investors, to ensure the soundness of the financial system, and to improve control of monetary policy. We will examine how these three reasons have led to the present regulatory environment. As a study aid, the principal regulatory agencies of the U.S. financial system are listed in Table 3.

Increasing Information Available to Investors

Asymmetric information in financial markets means that investors may be subject to adverse selection and moral hazard problems that may hinder the efficient operation of financial markets. Risky firms or outright crooks may be the most eager to sell securities to unwary investors, and the resulting adverse selection problem may keep investors out of financial markets. Furthermore, once an investor has bought a security, thereby lending money to a firm, the borrower may have incentives to engage in risky activities or to commit outright fraud. The presence of this moral hazard problem may also keep investors away from financial markets. Government regulation can reduce adverse selection and moral hazard problems in financial markets and increase their efficiency by increasing the amount of information available to investors.

As a result of the stock market crash in 1929 and revelations of widespread fraud in the aftermath, political demands for regulation culminated in the Securities Act of 1933 and the establishment of the Securities and Exchange Commission (SEC). The SEC requires corporations issuing securities to disclose certain information about their sales, assets, and earnings to the public and restricts trading by the largest stockholders (known as insiders) in the corporation. By requiring disclosure of this information and by discouraging insider trading, which could be used to manipulate security prices, the SEC hopes that investors will be better informed and be protected from some of the abuses in financial markets that occurred before 1933. Indeed, in recent years, the SEC has been particularly active in prosecuting people involved in insider trading.

TABLE 3 *Principal Regulatory Agencies of the U.S. Financial System*

Regulatory Agency	Subject of Regulation	Nature of Regulations
Securities and Exchange Commission (SEC)	Organized exchanges and financial markets	Requires disclosure of information, restricts insider trading
Commodities Futures Trading Commission (CFTC)	Futures market exchanges	Regulates procedures for trading in futures markets
Office of the Comptroller of the Currency	Federally chartered commercial banks	Charters and examines the books of federally chartered commercial banks and imposes restrictions on assets they can hold
National Credit Union Administration (NCUA)	Federally chartered credit unions	Charters and examines the books of federally chartered credit unions and imposes restrictions on assets they can hold
State banking and insurance commissions	State-chartered depository institutions	Charter and examine the books of state-chartered banks and insurance companies, impose restrictions on assets they can hold, and impose restrictions on branching
Federal Deposit Insurance Corporation (FDIC)	Commercial banks, mutual savings banks, savings and loan associations	Provides insurance of up to $100,000 for each depositor at a bank, examines the books of insured banks, and imposes restrictions on assets they can hold
Federal Reserve System	All depository institutions	Examines the books of commercial banks that are members of the system, sets reserve requirements for all banks
Office of Thrift Supervision	Savings and loan associations	Examines the books of savings and loan associations, imposes restrictions on assets they can hold

Ensuring the Soundness of Financial Intermediaries

Asymmetric information can also lead to widespread collapse of financial intermediaries, referred to as a **financial panic.** Because providers of funds to financial intermediaries may not be able to assess whether the institutions holding their funds are sound or not, if they have doubts about the overall health of financial intermediaries, they may want to pull their funds out of both sound and unsound institutions. The possible outcome is a financial panic that produces large losses for the public and causes serious damage to the economy. To protect the public and the economy from financial panics, the government has implemented six types of regulations.

Restrictions on Entry State banking and insurance commissions, as well as the Office of the Comptroller of the Currency (an agency of the federal government), have created very tight regulations as to who is allowed to set up a financial intermediary. Individuals or groups that want to establish a financial intermediary, such as a bank or an insurance company, must obtain a charter from the state or the federal government. Only if they are upstanding citizens with impeccable credentials and a large amount of initial funds will they be given a charter.

Disclosure There are stringent reporting requirements for financial intermediaries. Their bookkeeping must follow certain strict principles, their books are subject to periodic inspection, and they must make certain information available to the public.

Restrictions on Assets and Activities There are restrictions on what financial intermediaries are allowed to do and what assets they can hold. Before you put your funds into a bank or some other such institution, you would want to know that your funds are safe and that the bank or other financial intermediary will be able to meet its obligations to you. One way of doing this is to restrict the financial intermediary from engaging in certain risky activities. Legislation passed in 1933 separates commercial banking from the securities industry so that banks do not engage in risky ventures associated with this industry. Another way is to restrict financial intermediaries from holding certain risky assets, or at least from holding a greater quantity of these risky assets than is prudent. For example, commercial banks and other depository institutions are not allowed to hold common stock because stock prices experience substantial fluctuations. Insurance companies are allowed to hold common stock, but their holdings cannot exceed a certain fraction of their total assets.

Deposit Insurance The government can insure people's deposits so that they do not suffer any financial loss if the financial intermediary that holds these deposits should fail. The most important government agency that provides this type of insurance is the Federal Deposit Insurance Corporation (FDIC), which insures each depositor at a commercial bank or mutual savings bank up to a loss of $100,000 per account. All commercial and mutual savings banks, with a few minor exceptions, make contributions into the FDIC's Bank Insurance Fund, which is used to pay off depositors in the case of a bank's failure. The FDIC was created in 1934 after the massive bank failures of 1930–1933 in which the savings of many depositors at commercial banks were wiped out. Similar government agencies exist for other depository institutions: The Savings Association Insurance Fund (part of the FDIC) provides deposit insurance for savings and loan associations, and the National Credit Union Share Insurance Fund (NCUSIF) does the same for credit unions.

Limits on Competition Politicians have often declared that unbridled competition among financial intermediaries promotes failures that will harm the public. Although the evidence that competition does this is extremely weak, it has not stopped the state and federal governments from imposing many restrictive regulations. These regulations have taken two forms. First are the restrictions on the opening of additional locations (branches). In the past, banks were not allowed to open up branches in other states, and in some states banks were restricted from opening additional locations.

Restrictions on Interest Rates Competition has also been inhibited by regulations that impose restrictions on interest rates that can be paid on deposits. For decades after 1933, banks were prohibited from paying interest on checking accounts. In addition, until 1986, the Federal Reserve System had the power under **Regulation Q** to set maximum interest rates that banks could pay on savings deposits. These regulations were instituted because of the widespread belief that unrestricted interest-rate competition helped encourage bank failures during the

Great Depression. Later evidence does not seem to support this view, and restrictions like Regulation Q have been abolished.

Improving Control of Monetary Policy

Because banks play a very important role in determining the supply of money (which in turn affects many aspects of the economy), much regulation of these financial intermediaries is intended to improve control over the money supply. One such regulation is **reserve requirements,** which make it obligatory for all depository institutions to keep a certain fraction of their deposits in accounts with the Federal Reserve System (the Fed), the central bank in the United States. Reserve requirements help the Fed exercise more precise control over the money supply. Deposit insurance regulation can also be rationalized along these lines: The FDIC gives depositors confidence in the banking system and eliminates widespread bank failures, which can in turn cause large, uncontrollable fluctuations in the quantity of money.

In later chapters, we will look more closely at government regulation of financial markets and will see whether it has improved the functioning of financial markets.

Financial Regulation Abroad

Not surprisingly, given the similarity of the economic system here and in Japan, Canada, and the nations of Western Europe, financial regulation in these countries is similar to financial regulation in the United States. The provision of information is improved by requiring corporations issuing securities to report details about assets and liabilities, earnings, and sales of stock and by prohibiting insider trading. The soundness of intermediaries is ensured by licensing, periodic inspection of financial intermediaries' books, and the provision of deposit insurance (although its coverage is smaller and its existence is often intentionally not advertised).

The major differences between financial regulation in the United States and abroad relate to bank regulation. In the past, the United States was the only industrialized country to subject banks to restrictions on branching, which limited banks' size and restricted them to certain geographic regions. U.S. banks are also the most restricted in the range of financial services they may provide and the assets they may hold. Banks abroad frequently hold shares in commercial firms; in Japan and Germany, those stakes can be sizable.

Summary

1. The basic function of financial markets is to channel funds from savers who have an excess of funds to spenders who have a shortage of funds. Financial markets can do this either through direct finance, in which borrowers borrow funds directly from lenders by selling them securities, or through indirect finance, which involves a financial intermediary who stands between the lender-savers and the borrower-spenders and helps transfer funds from one to the other. This channeling of funds improves the economic welfare of everyone in the society because it allows funds to move from people who have no productive investment opportunities to those who have such opportunities, thereby contributing to increased efficiency in the economy. In addition, it directly benefits consumers by allowing them to make purchases when they need them most.

2. Financial markets can be classified as debt and equity markets, primary and secondary markets, exchanges and over-the-counter markets, and money and capital markets.

3. An important trend in recent years is the growing internationalization of financial markets. Eurobonds, which are denominated in a currency other than that of the country in which they are sold, are now the dominant security in the international bond market and have surpassed U.S. corporate bonds as a source of new funds. Eurodollars, which are U.S. dollars deposited in foreign banks, are an important source of funds for American banks.

4. Financial intermediaries are financial institutions that acquire funds by issuing liabilities and in turn use those funds to acquire assets by purchasing securities or making loans. Financial intermediaries play such an important role in the financial system because they reduce transaction costs, allow risk sharing, and solve problems created by adverse selection and moral hazard. As a result, financial intermediaries allow small savers and borrowers to benefit from the existence of financial markets, thereby increasing the efficiency of the economy.

5. The principal financial intermediaries fall into three categories: (a) banks—commercial banks, savings and loan associations, mutual savings banks, and credit unions; (b) contractual savings institutions—life insurance companies, fire and casualty insurance companies, and pension funds; and (c) investment intermediaries—finance companies, mutual funds, and money market mutual funds.

6. The government regulates financial markets and financial intermediaries for three main reasons: to increase the information available to investors, to ensure the soundness of the financial system, and to improve control of monetary policy. Regulations include requiring disclosure of information to the public, restrictions on who can set up a financial intermediary, restrictions on what assets financial intermediaries can hold, the provision of deposit insurance, reserve requirements, and the setting of maximum interest rates that can be paid on checking accounts and savings deposits.

Key Terms

adverse selection, *p. 26*

asset transformation, *p. 26*

asymmetric information, *p. 26*

brokers, *p. 21*

capital market, *p. 22*

conflicts of interest, *p. 27*

dealers, *p. 21*

diversification, *p. 26*

dividends, *p. 20*

economies of scale, *p. 25*

equities, *p. 20*

Eurobonds, *p. 23*

Eurocurrencies, *p. 23*

Eurodollars, *p. 23*

exchanges, *p. 21*

financial intermediation, *p. 24*

financial panic, *p. 33*

foreign bonds, *p. 22*

intermediate-term, *p. 20*

investment banks, *p. 21*

liabilities, *p. 18*

liquid, *p. 21*

liquidity services, *p. 26*

long-term, *p. 20*

maturity, *p. 20*

money market, *p. 22*

moral hazard, *p. 27*

over-the-counter (OTC) market, *p. 21*

portfolio, *p. 26*

primary market, *p. 20*

Regulation Q, *p. 34*

reserve requirements, *p. 35*

risk, *p. 26*

risk sharing, *p. 26*

secondary market, *p. 20*

short-term, *p. 20*

thrift institutions (thrifts), *p. 29*

transaction costs, *p. 25*

underwriting, *p. 21*

Questions

1. Why is a share of IBM common stock an asset for its owner and a liability for IBM?

2. If I can buy a car today for $5000 and it is worth $10,000 next year in extra income to me because it enables me to get a job as a traveling anvil seller, should I take out a loan from Larry the Loan Shark at a 90% interest rate if no one else will give me a loan? Will I be better or worse off as a result of taking out this loan? Can you make a case for legalizing loan-sharking?

3. Some economists suspect that one of the reasons that economies in developing countries grow so slowly is that they do not have well-developed financial markets. Does this argument make sense?

4. In the nineteenth century the U.S. economy borrowed heavily from the British to build a railroad system. What was the principal debt instrument used? Why did this make both countries better off?

5. "Because corporations do not actually raise any funds in secondary markets, they are less important to the economy than primary markets." Comment.

6. If you suspect that a company will go bankrupt next year, which would you rather hold—bonds issued by the company or equities issued by the company? Why?

7. How can the adverse selection problem explain why you are more likely to make a loan to a family member than to a stranger?

8. Think of one example in which you have had to deal with the adverse selection problem.

9. Why do loan sharks worry less about moral hazard in connection with their borrowers than some other lenders do?

10. If you are an employer, what kinds of moral hazard problems might you worry about with your employees?

11. If there were no asymmetry in the information that a borrower and a lender had, could there still be a moral hazard problem?

12. "In a world without information and transaction costs, financial intermediaries would not exist." Is this statement true, false, or uncertain? Explain your answer.

13. Why might you be willing to make a loan to your neighbor by putting funds in a savings account earning a 5% interest rate at the bank and having the bank loan her the funds at a 10% interest rate, rather than loan her the funds yourself?

14. How does risk sharing benefit both financial intermediaries and private investors?

15. Discuss some of the manifestations of the globalization of world capital markets.

Web Exercises

Overview of the Financial System

1. One of the single best sources of information about financial institutions is the "U.S. Flow of Funds Report" produced by the Federal Reserve. This document contains data on most financial intermediaries. To access this report, go to **http://www.federalreserve.gov/releases/Z1/**. Click on the most current release. (You may have to load Acrobat Reader if your computer does not already have it. The site has a link for a free patch.) Go to the "Level Tables" and answer the following questions.

a. What is the date of the most current release?

b. What percent of assets do commercial banks hold in loans? What percent of assets are held in mortgage loans?

c. What percent of assets do savings and loans hold in mortgage loans?

d. What percent of assets do credit unions hold in mortgage loans and in consumer loans?

2. The most famous financial market in the world is the New York Stock Exchange. Check out their website at **http://www.nyse.com** and answer the following questions.

a. What is the mission of the NYSE?

b. Firms must pay a fee to list their shares for sale on the NYSE. What would be the fee for a firm with 5 million shares common outstanding?

PART 2

Fundamentals of Financial Markets

CHAPTER 3

What Do Interest Rates Mean and What Is Their Role in Valuation?

Preview

Interest rates are among the most closely watched variables in the economy. Their movements are reported almost daily by the news media because they directly affect our everyday lives and have important consequences for the health of the economy. They affect personal decisions such as whether to consume or save, whether to buy a house, and whether to purchase bonds or put funds into a savings account. Interest rates also affect the economic decisions of businesses and households, such as whether to use their funds to invest in new equipment for factories or to save their money in a bank.

At www.bloomberg. com/markets/ under the "Rates & Bonds" heading, you can access information on key interest rates, U.S. Treasury bonds, government bonds, and municipal bonds.

Before we can go on with the study of financial markets, we must understand exactly what the phrase *interest rates* means. In this chapter, we see that a concept known as the *yield to maturity* is the most accurate measure of interest rates; the yield to maturity is what financial economists mean when they use the term *interest rate*. We discuss how the yield to maturity is measured on credit market instruments and how it is used to value these instruments. We also see that a bond's interest rate does not necessarily indicate how good an investment the bond is because what it earns (its rate of return) does not necessarily equal its interest rate. Finally, we explore the distinction between real interest rates, which are adjusted for changes in the price level, and nominal interest rates, which are not.

Although learning definitions is not always the most exciting of pursuits, it is important to read carefully and understand the concepts presented in this chapter. Not only are they continually used throughout the remainder of this text, but a firm grasp of these terms will give you a clearer understanding of the role that interest rates play in your life as well as in the general economy.

Measuring Interest Rates

Different debt instruments have very different streams of cash payments to the holder (known as **cash flows**), with very different timing. Thus we first need to understand how we can compare the value of one kind of debt instrument with another before we see how interest rates are measured. To do this, we make use of the concept of *present value*.

Present Value

The concept of **present value** (or **present discounted value**) is based on the commonsense notion that a dollar of cash flow paid to you one year from now is less valuable to you than a dollar paid to you today: This notion is true because you can deposit a dollar in a savings account that earns interest and have more than a dollar in one year. Economists use a more formal definition, as explained in this section.

Let's look at the simplest kind of debt instrument, which we will call a **simple loan.** In this loan, the lender provides the borrower with an amount of funds (called the *principal*) that must be repaid to the lender at the *maturity date*, along with an additional payment for the interest. For example, if you made your friend Jane a simple loan of $100 for one year, you would require her to repay the principal of $100 in one year's time along with an additional payment for interest; say, $10. In the case of a simple loan like this one, the interest payment divided by the amount of the loan is a natural and sensible way to measure the interest rate. This measure of the so-called *simple interest rate*, i, is:

$$i = \frac{\$10}{\$100} = 0.10 = 10\%$$

If you make this $100 loan, at the end of the year you would have $110, which can be rewritten as:

$$\$100 \times (1 + 0.10) = \$110$$

If you then lent out the $110, at the end of the second year you would have:

$$\$110 \times (1 + 0.10) = \$121$$

or, equivalently,

$$\$100 \times (1 + 0.10) \times (1 + 0.10) = \$100 \times (1 + 0.10)^2 = \$121$$

Continuing with the loan again, you would have at the end of the third year:

$$\$121 \times (1 + 0.10) = \$100 \times (1 + 0.10)^3 = \$133$$

Generalizing, we can see that at the end of n years, your $100 would turn into:

$$\$100 \times (1 + i)^n$$

The amounts you would have at the end of each year by making the $100 loan today can be seen in the following timeline:

Today 0	Year 1	Year 2	Year 3	Year n
$100	$110	$121	$133	$100 \times (1 + 0.10)^n$

This timeline immediately tells you that you are just as happy having $100 today as having $110 a year from now (of course, as long as you are sure that Jane will pay you back). Or that you are just as happy having $100 today as having $121 two years from now, or $133 three years from now, or $100 × (1 + 0.10)^n in n years from now. The timeline tells us that we can also work backward from future amounts to the present. For example, $133 = $100 × (1 + 0.10)^3$ three years from now is worth $100 today, so that:

$$\$100 = \frac{\$133}{(1 + 0.10)^3}$$

The process of calculating today's value of dollars received in the future, as we have done above, is called *discounting the future*. We can generalize this process by writing today's (present) value of $100 as *PV*, the future cash flow of $133 as *CF*, and replacing 0.10 (the 10% interest rate) by i. This leads to the following formula:

$$PV = \frac{CF}{(1 + i)^n} \tag{1}$$

Intuitively, what Equation 1 tells us is that if you are promised $1 of cash flow for certain ten years from now, this dollar would not be as valuable to you as $1 is today because if you had the $1 today, you could invest it and end up with more than $1 in ten years.

EXAMPLE 1

Simple Present Value

What is the present value of $250 to be paid in two years if the interest rate is 15%?

Solution
The present value would be $189.04. Using Equation 1:

$$PV = \frac{CF}{(1 + i)^n}$$

where

CF = cash flow in two years = $250

i = annual interest rate = 0.15

n = number of years = 2

Thus

$$PV = \frac{\$250}{(1 + 0.15)^2} = \frac{\$250}{1.3225} = \$189.04$$

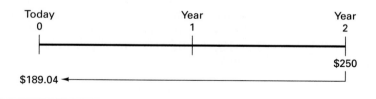

The concept of present value is extremely useful because it allows us to figure out today's value of a credit market instrument at a given simple interest rate *i* by just adding up the present value of all the future cash flows received. The present value concept allows us to compare the value of two instruments with very different timing of their cash flows.

Four Types of Credit Market Instruments

In terms of the timing of their cash flows, there are four basic types of credit market instruments.

1. A simple loan, which we have already discussed, in which the lender provides the borrower with an amount of funds, which must be repaid to the lender at the maturity date along with an additional payment for the interest. Many money market instruments are of this type: for example, commercial loans to businesses.

2. A **fixed-payment loan** (which is also called a **fully amortized loan**) in which the lender provides the borrower with an amount of funds, which must be repaid by making the same payment every period (such as a month), consisting of part of the principal and interest for a set number of years. For example, if you borrowed $1000, a fixed-payment loan might require you to pay $126 every year for 25 years. Installment loans (such as auto loans) and mortgages are frequently of the fixed-payment type.

3. A **coupon bond** pays the owner of the bond a fixed interest payment (coupon payment) every year until the maturity date, when a specified final amount (**face value** or **par value**) is repaid. The coupon payment is so named because the bondholder used to obtain payment by clipping a coupon off the bond and sending it to the bond issuer, who then sent the payment to the holder. Nowadays, it is no longer necessary to send in coupons to receive these payments. A coupon bond with $1000 face value, for example, might pay you a coupon payment of $100 per year for ten years, and at the maturity date repay you the face value amount of $1000. (The face value of a bond is usually in $1000 increments.)

    A coupon bond is identified by three pieces of information. First is the corporation or government agency that issues the bond. Second is the maturity date of the bond. Third is the bond's **coupon rate,** the dollar amount of the yearly coupon payment expressed as a percentage of the face value of the bond. In our example, the coupon bond has a yearly coupon payment of $100 and a face value of $1000. The coupon rate is then $100/$1000 = 0.10, or 10%. Capital market instruments such as U.S. Treasury bonds and notes and corporate bonds are examples of coupon bonds.

4. A **discount bond** (also called a **zero-coupon bond**) is bought at a price below its face value (at a discount), and the face value is repaid at the maturity date. Unlike a coupon bond, a discount bond does not make any interest payments; it just pays off the face value. For example, a discount bond with a face value of $1000 might be bought for $900; in a year's time the owner would be repaid the face value of $1000. U.S. Treasury bills, U.S. savings bonds, and long-term zero-coupon bonds are examples of discount bonds.

These four types of instruments require payments at different times: Simple loans and discount bonds make payment only at their maturity dates, whereas fixed-payment loans and coupon bonds have payments periodically until maturity. How would you decide which of these instruments provides you with more income? They all seem so different because they make payments at different times. To solve this problem, we use the concept of present value, explained earlier, to provide us with a procedure for measuring interest rates on these different types of instruments.

Yield to Maturity

Of the several common ways of calculating interest rates, the most important is the **yield to maturity,** the interest rate that equates the present value of cash flows received from a debt instrument with its value today. Because the concept behind the calculation of the yield to maturity makes good economic sense, financial economists consider it the most accurate measure of interest rates.

To understand the yield to maturity better, we now look at how it is calculated for the four types of credit market instruments.

Simple Loan   Using the concept of present value, the yield to maturity on a simple loan is easy to calculate. For the one-year loan we discussed, today's value is $100, and the cash flow in one year's time would be $110 (the repayment of $100 plus the interest payment of $10). We can use this information to solve for the yield to maturity i by recognizing that the present value of the future payments must equal today's value of a loan.

EXAMPLE 2   *Simple Loan*

If Pete borrows $100 from his sister and next year she wants $110 back from him, what is the yield to maturity on this loan?

Solution

The yield to maturity on the loan is 10%.

$$PV = \frac{CF}{(1 + i)^n}$$

where

$$PV = \text{amount borrowed} \quad = \$100$$
$$CF = \text{cash flow in one year} \quad = \$110$$
$$n \quad = \text{number of years} \quad = 1$$

Thus

$$\$100 = \frac{\$110}{(1 + i)}$$

$$(1 + i)\$100 = \$110$$

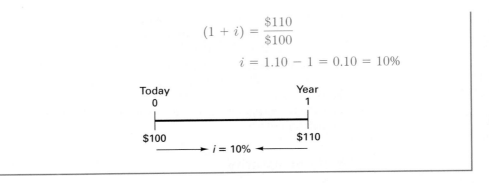

$$(1 + i) = \frac{\$110}{\$100}$$

$$i = 1.10 - 1 = 0.10 = 10\%$$

This calculation of the yield to maturity should look familiar because it equals the interest payment of $10 divided by the loan amount of $100; that is, it equals the simple interest rate on the loan. An important point to recognize is that **for simple loans, the simple interest rate equals the yield to maturity.** Hence the same term i is used to denote both the yield to maturity and the simple interest rate.

Study Guide

The key to understanding the calculation of the yield to maturity is equating today's value of the debt instrument with the present value of all of its future cash flows. The best way to learn this principle is to apply it to other specific examples of the four types of credit market instruments in addition to those we discuss here. See if you can develop the equations that would allow you to solve for the yield to maturity in each case.

Fixed-Payment Loan Recall that this type of loan has the same cash flow payment every year throughout the life of the loan. On a fixed-rate mortgage, for example, the borrower makes the same payment to the bank every month until the maturity date, when the loan will be completely paid off. To calculate the yield to maturity for a fixed-payment loan, we follow the same strategy we used for the simple loan—we equate today's value of the loan with its present value. Because the fixed-payment loan involves more than one cash flow payment, the present value of the fixed-payment loan is calculated as the sum of the present values of all cash flows (using Equation 1).

Suppose the loan is $1000, and the yearly cash flow payment is $85.81 for the next 25 years. The present value is calculated as follows: At the end of one year, there is a $85.81 cash flow payment with a PV of $\$85.81/(1 + i)$; at the end of two years, there is another $85.81 cash flow payment with a PV of $\$85.81/(1 + i)^2$; and so on until at the end of the twenty-fifth year, the last cash flow payment of $85.81 with a PV of $\$85.81/(1 + i)^{25}$ is made. Making today's value of the loan ($1000) equal to the sum of the present values of all the yearly cash flows gives us

$$\$1000 = \frac{\$85.81}{1 + i} + \frac{\$85.81}{(1 + i)^2} + \frac{\$85.81}{(1 + i)^3} + \cdots + \frac{\$85.81}{(1 + i)^{25}}$$

More generally, for any fixed-payment loan,

$$LV = \frac{FP}{1 + i} + \frac{FP}{(1 + i)^2} + \frac{FP}{(1 + i)^3} + \cdots + \frac{FP}{(1 + i)^n} \qquad (2)$$

where
$$LV = \text{loan value}$$
$$FP = \text{fixed yearly cash flow payment}$$
$$n = \text{number of years until maturity}$$

For a fixed-payment loan amount, the fixed yearly payment and the number of years until maturity are known quantities, and only the yield to maturity is not. So we can solve this equation for the yield to maturity i. Because this calculation is not easy, tables have been created that allow you to find i given the loan's numbers for LV, FP, and n. For example, in the case of the 25-year loan with yearly payments of $85.81, the yield to maturity from the table that solves Equation 2 is 7%. Real estate brokers always have such a table handy (or a pocket calculator that can solve such equations) so that they can immediately tell the prospective house buyer exactly what the yearly (or monthly) payments will be if the house purchase is financed by taking out a mortgage.

EXAMPLE 3   *Fixed-Payment Loan*

You decide to purchase a new home and need a $100,000 mortgage. You take out a loan from the bank that has an interest rate of 7%. What is the yearly payment to the bank to pay off the loan in 20 years?

Solution

The yearly payment to the bank is $9,439.29.

$$LV = \frac{FP}{1+i} + \frac{FP}{(1+i)^2} + \frac{FP}{(1+i)^3} + \cdots + \frac{FP}{(1+i)^n}$$

where

LV = loan value amount   = $100,000

i = annual interest rate = 0.07

n = number of years   = 20

Thus

$$\$100,000 = \frac{FP}{1+0.07} + \frac{FP}{(1+0.07)^2} + \frac{FP}{(1+0.07)^3} + \cdots + \frac{FP}{(1+0.07)^{20}}$$

To find the monthly payment for the loan using a financial calculator:

n = number of years   = 20

PV = amount of the loan (LV)   = $-100,000$

FV = amount of the loan after 20 years = 0

i = annual interest rate   = .07

Then push the *PMT* button = fixed yearly payment (*FP*) = $9,439.29.

Coupon Bond To calculate the yield to maturity for a coupon bond, follow the same strategy used for the fixed-payment loan: Equate today's value of the bond with its present value. Because coupon bonds also have more than one cash flow payment, the present value of the bond is calculated as the sum of the present values of all the coupon payments plus the present value of the final payment of the face value of the bond.

The present value of a $1000 face value bond with ten years to maturity and yearly coupon payments of $100 (a 10% coupon rate) can be calculated as follows: At the end of one year, there is a $100 coupon payment with a *PV* of $100/(1 + *i*); at the end of the second year, there is another $100 coupon payment with a *PV* of $100/(1 + *i*)^2; and so on until at maturity, there is a $100 coupon payment with a *PV* of $100/(1 + *i*)^{10} plus the repayment of the $1000 face value with a *PV* of $1000/(1 + *i*)^{10}. Setting today's value of the bond (its current price, denoted by *P*) equal to the sum of the present values of all the cash flows for this bond gives

$$P = \frac{\$100}{1 + i} + \frac{\$100}{(1 + i)^2} + \frac{\$100}{(1 + i)^3} + \cdots + \frac{\$100}{(1 + i)^{10}} + \frac{\$1000}{(1 + i)^{10}}$$

More generally, for any coupon bond,[1]

$$P = \frac{C}{1 + i} + \frac{C}{(1 + i)^2} + \frac{C}{(1 + i)^3} + \cdots + \frac{C}{(1 + i)^n} + \frac{F}{(1 + i)^n} \tag{3}$$

where
P = price of coupon bond
C = yearly coupon payment
F = face value of the bond
n = years to maturity date

In Equation 3, the coupon payment, the face value, the years to maturity, and the price of the bond are known quantities, and only the yield to maturity is not. Hence we can solve this equation for the yield to maturity i.[2] Just as in the case of the fixed-payment loan, this calculation is not easy, so bond tables have been created that allow you to read off the yield to maturity for a bond given its coupon rate, its years to maturity, and its price. Some business-oriented calculators have built-in programs that solve this equation for you.

EXAMPLE 4	*Coupon Bond*

EXAMPLE 4

Coupon Bond

Find the price of a 10% coupon bond with a face value of $1000, a 12.25% yield to maturity, and eight years to maturity.

Solution

The price of the bond is $889.20. To solve using a financial calculator:

n = years to maturity = 8

FV = face value of the bond = 1000

i = annual interest rate = 12.25%

PMT = yearly coupon payments = 100

Then push the *PV* button = price of the bond = $889.20.

---

[1]Most coupon bonds actually make coupon payments on a semiannual basis rather than once a year as assumed here. The effect on the calculations is only very slight and will be ignored here.

[2]In other contexts, it is also called the *internal rate of return*.

TABLE 1	Yields to Maturity on a 10% Coupon Rate Bond Maturing in Ten Years (Face Value = $1000)
Price of Bond ($)	Yield to Maturity (%)
1200	7.13
1100	8.48
1000	10.00
900	11.75
800	13.81

Table 1 shows the yields to maturity calculated for several bond prices. Three interesting facts emerge:

1. When the coupon bond is priced at its face value, the yield to maturity equals the coupon rate.
2. The price of a coupon bond and the yield to maturity are negatively related; that is, as the yield to maturity rises, the price of the bond falls. If the yield to maturity falls, the price of the bond rises.
3. The yield to maturity is greater than the coupon rate when the bond price is below its face value.

These three facts are true for any coupon bond and are really not surprising if you think about the reasoning behind the calculation of the yield to maturity. When you put $1000 in a bank account with an interest rate of 10%, you can take out $100 every year and you will be left with the $1000 at the end of ten years. This is similar to buying the $1000 bond with a 10% coupon rate analyzed in Table 1, which pays a $100 coupon payment every year and then repays $1000 at the end of ten years. If the bond is purchased at the par value of $1000, its yield to maturity must equal the interest rate of 10%, which is also equal to the coupon rate of 10%. The same reasoning applied to any coupon bond demonstrates that if the coupon bond is purchased at its par value, the yield to maturity and the coupon rate must be equal.

It is straightforward to show that the valuation of a bond and the yield to maturity are negatively related. As i, the yield to maturity, rises, all denominators in the bond price formula must necessarily rise. Hence a rise in the interest rate as measured by the yield to maturity means that the value and hence the price of the bond must fall. Another way to explain why the bond price falls when the interest rises is that a higher interest rate implies that the future coupon payments and final payment are worth less when discounted back to the present; hence, the price of the bond must be lower.

There is one special case of a coupon bond that is worth discussing because its yield to maturity is particularly easy to calculate. This bond is called a **perpetuity** or a **consol;** it is a perpetual bond with no maturity date and no

Check out a review of the key financial concepts of time value of money, annuities, and perpetuities at www.teachmefinance.com

repayment of principal that makes fixed coupon payments of $C forever. The formula in Equation 3 for the price of a perpetuity, P_c, simplifies to the following:[3]

$$P_c = \frac{C}{i_c} \tag{4}$$

where　　　　　　　　　P_c = price of the perpetuity (consol)
　　　　　　　　　　　　C = yearly payment
　　　　　　　　　　　　i_c = yield to maturity of the perpetuity (consol)

One nice feature of perpetuities is that you can immediately see that as i_c goes up, the price of the bond falls. For example, if a perpetuity pays $100 per year forever and the interest rate is 10%, its price will be $1000 = $100/0.10. If the interest rate rises to 20%, its price will fall to $500 = $100/0.20. We can also rewrite this formula as

$$i_c = \frac{C}{P_c} \tag{5}$$

EXAMPLE 5　　*Perpetuity*

What is the yield to maturity on a bond that has a price of $2000 and pays $100 annually forever?

Solution

The yield to maturity would be 5%.

$$i_c = \frac{C}{P_c}$$

where

C　= yearly payment　　　　　　　= $100

P_c　= price of perpetuity (consol)　= $2000

---

[3]The bond price formula for a perpetuity is

$$P_c = \frac{C}{1 + i_c} + \frac{C}{(1 + i_c)^2} + \frac{C}{(1 + i_c)^3} + \cdots$$

which can be written as

$$P_c = C(x + x^2 + x^3 + \ldots)$$

in which $x = 1/(1 + i)$. From your high school algebra you might remember the formula for an infinite sum:

$$1 + x + x^2 + x^3 + \cdots = \frac{1}{1 - x} \quad \text{for } x < 1$$

and so

$$P_c = C\left(\frac{1}{1 - x} - 1\right) = C\left[\frac{1}{1 - 1/(1 + i_c)} - 1\right]$$

which by suitable algebraic manipulation becomes

$$P_c = C\left(\frac{1 + i_c}{i_c} - \frac{i_c}{i_c}\right) = \frac{C}{i_c}$$

Thus

$$i_c = \frac{\$100}{\$2000}$$

$$i_c = 0.05 = 5\%$$

The formula in Equation 5, which describes the calculation of the yield to maturity for a perpetuity, also provides a useful approximation for the yield to maturity on coupon bonds. When a coupon bond has a long term to maturity (say, 20 years or more), it is very much like a perpetuity, which pays coupon payments forever. This is because the cash flows more than 20 years in the future have such small present discounted values that the value of a long-term coupon bond is very close to the value of a perpetuity with the same coupon rate. Thus i_c in Equation 5 will be very close to the yield to maturity for any long-term bond. For this reason, i_c, the yearly coupon payment divided by the price of the security, has been given the name **current yield** and is frequently used as an approximation to describe interest rates on long-term bonds.

Discount Bond The yield-to-maturity calculation for a discount bond is similar to that for the simple loan. Let us consider a discount bond such as a one-year U.S. Treasury bill, which pays a face value of $1000 in one year's time. If the current purchase price of this bill is $900, then equating this price to the present value of the $1000 received in one year, using Equation 1, gives

$$\$900 = \frac{\$1000}{1 + i}$$

and solving for i,

$$(1 + i) \times \$900 = \$1000$$

$$\$900 + \$900i = \$1000$$

$$\$900i = \$1000 - \$900$$

$$i = \frac{\$1000 - \$900}{\$900} = 0.111 = 11.1\%$$

More generally, for any one-year discount bond, the yield to maturity can be written as

$$i = \frac{F - P}{P} \tag{6}$$

where
$$F = \text{face value of the discount bond}$$
$$P = \text{current price of the discount bond}$$

In other words, the yield to maturity equals the increase in price over the year $F - P$ divided by the initial price P. In normal circumstances, investors earn positive returns from holding these securities and so they sell at a discount, meaning that the current price of the bond is below the face value. Therefore, $F - P$ should be positive, and the yield to maturity should be positive as well. However, this is not always the case, as extraordinary events in Japan indicated (see "Global" box).

GLOBAL

Negative T-Bill Rates? Japan Shows the Way

We normally assume that interest rates must always be positive. Negative interest rates would imply that you are willing to pay more for a bond today than you will receive for it in the future (as our formula for yield to maturity on a discount bond demonstrates). Negative interest rates therefore seem like an impossibility because you would do better by holding cash that has the same value in the future as it does today.

The Japanese have demonstrated that this reasoning is not quite correct. In November 1998, interest rates on Japanese six-month Treasury bills became negative, yielding an interest rate of −0.004%, with investors paying more for the bills than their face value. This was an extremely unusual event because no other country in the world has seen negative interest rates during the past 50 years. How could this happen?

As we will see in Chapter 4, the weakness of the Japanese economy and a negative inflation rate have driven Japanese interest rates to low levels, but they can't explain the negative rates. The answer is that large investors find it more convenient to hold these six-month bills as a store of value rather than holding cash because the bills are denominated in larger amounts and can be stored electronically. These advantages of the Japanese T-bills result in some investors being willing to hold them, given their negative rates, even though in monetary terms the investors would be better off holding cash. Clearly, the convenience of T-bills only goes so far, and thus their interest rates can go only a little bit below zero.

An important feature of this equation is that it indicates that for a discount bond, the yield to maturity is negatively related to the current bond price. This is the same conclusion that we reached for a coupon bond. For example, Equation 6 shows that a rise in the bond price from $900 to $950 means that the bond will have a smaller increase in its price over its lifetime, and the yield to maturity falls from 11.1% to 5.3%. Similarly, a fall in the yield to maturity means that the price of the discount bond has risen.

Summary The concept of present value tells you that a dollar in the future is not as valuable to you as a dollar today because you can earn interest on this dollar. Specifically, a dollar received n years from now is worth only $\$1/(1 + i)^n$ today. The present value of a set of future cash flows on a debt instrument equals the sum of the present values of each of the future cash flows. The yield to maturity for an instrument is the interest rate that equates the present value of the future cash flows on that instrument to its value today. Because the procedure for calculating the yield to maturity is based on sound economic principles, this is the measure that financial economists think most accurately describes the interest rate.

Our calculations of the yield to maturity for a variety of bonds reveal the important fact that **current bond prices and interest rates are negatively related: When the interest rate rises, the price of the bond falls, and vice versa.**

The Distinction Between Real and Nominal Interest Rates

So far in our discussion of interest rates, we have ignored the effects of inflation on the cost of borrowing. What we have up to now been calling the interest rate makes no allowance for inflation, and it is more precisely referred to as the **nominal interest rate,** which is to distinguish it from the **real interest rate,** the interest rate that is adjusted by subtracting expected changes in the price level (inflation) so that it more accurately reflects the true cost of borrowing.[4] The real interest rate is more accurately defined by the *Fisher equation*, named for Irving Fisher, one of the great monetary economists of the twentieth century. The Fisher equation states that the nominal interest rate i equals the real interest rate i_r plus the expected rate of inflation π^e.[5]

$$i = i_r + \pi^e \tag{7}$$

Rearranging terms, we find that the real interest rate equals the nominal interest rate minus the expected inflation rate:

$$i_r = i - \pi^e \tag{8}$$

To see why this definition makes sense, let us first consider a situation in which you have made a one-year simple loan with a 5% interest rate ($i = 5\%$) and you expect the price level to rise by 3% over the course of the year ($\pi^e = 3\%$). As a result of making the loan, at the end of the year you will have 2% more in **real terms,** that is, in terms of real goods and services you can buy.

In this case, the interest rate you have earned in terms of real goods and services is 2%; that is,

$$i_r = 5\% - 3\% = 2\%$$

as indicated by the Fisher definition.

At *www.martin capital.com/ charts.htm, click on "Interest Rates and Yields" and then "Nominal versus Real Market Rates" to view 30 years of nominal interest rates compared to real rates for the 30-year T-bond and 90-day T-bill.*

EXAMPLE 6   *Real and Nominal Interest Rates*

What is the real interest rate if the nominal interest rate is 8% and the expected inflation rate is 10% over the course of a year?

Solution

The real interest rate is −2%. Although you will be receiving 8% more dollars at the end of the year, you will be paying 10% more for goods. The result is that you will be able to buy 2% fewer goods at the end of the year, and you are 2% worse off in real terms.

$$i_r = i - \pi^e$$

---

[4]The real interest rate defined in the text is more precisely referred to as the *ex ante real interest rate* because it is adjusted for *expected* changes in the price level. This is the real interest rate that is most important to economic decisions, and typically it is what financial economists mean when they make reference to the "real" interest rate. The interest rate that is adjusted for *actual* changes in the price level is called the *ex post real interest rate*. It describes how well a lender has done in real terms *after the fact*.

[5]A more precise formulation of the Fisher equation is

$$i = i_r + \pi^e + (i_r \times \pi^e)$$

because

$$1 + i = (1 + i_r)(1 + \pi^e) = 1 + i_r + \pi^e + (i_r \times \pi^e)$$

and subtracting 1 from both sides gives us the first equation. For small values of i_r and π^e, the term $i_r \times \pi^e$ is so small that we ignore it, as in the text.

where

i = nominal interest rate = 0.08

π^{e} = expected inflation rate = 0.10

Thus

$$i_r = 0.08 - 0.10 = -0.02 = -2\%$$

As a lender, you are clearly less eager to make a loan in Example 6 because in terms of real goods and services you have actually earned a negative interest rate of 2%. By contrast, as the borrower, you fare quite well because at the end of the year, the amounts you will have to pay back will be worth 2% less in terms of goods and services—you as the borrower will be ahead by 2% in real terms. ***When the real interest rate is low, there are greater incentives to borrow and fewer incentives to lend.***

The distinction between real and nominal interest rates is important because the real interest rate, which reflects the real cost of borrowing, is likely to be a better indicator of the incentives to borrow and lend. It appears to be a better guide to how people will be affected by what is happening in credit markets. Figure 1, which presents estimates from 1953 to 2004 of the real and nominal interest rates on three-month U.S. Treasury bills, shows us that nominal and real rates often do not move together. (This is also true for nominal and real interest rates in the

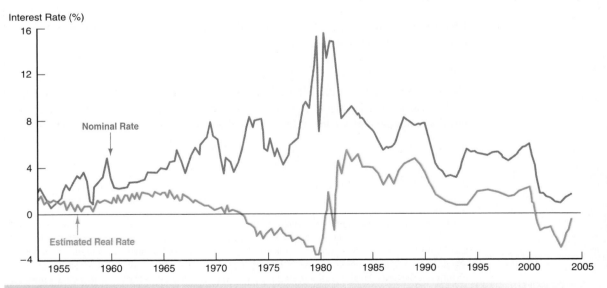

FIGURE 1 *Real and Nominal Interest Rates (Three-Month Treasury Bill), 1953–2004*

Sources: Nominal rates from the Citibase databank. The real rate is constructed using the procedure outlined in Frederic S. Mishkin, "The Real Interest Rate: An Empirical Investigation," *Carnegie–Rochester Conference Series on Public Policy* 15 (1981): 151–200. This involves estimating expected inflation as a function of past interest rates, inflation, and time trends and then subtracting the expected inflation measure from the nominal interest rate.

rest of the world.) In particular, when nominal rates in the United States were high in the 1970s, real rates were actually extremely low, often negative. By the standard of nominal interest rates, you would have thought that credit market conditions were tight in this period because it was expensive to borrow. However, the estimates of the real rates indicate that you would have been mistaken. In real terms, the cost of borrowing was actually quite low.[6]

Until recently, real interest rates in the United States were not observable, because only nominal rates were reported. This all changed in January 1997, when the U.S. Treasury began to issue **indexed bonds**, bonds whose interest and principal payments are adjusted for changes in the price level (see "Mini-Case" box on p. 56).

The Distinction Between Interest Rates and Returns

Many people think that the interest rate on a bond tells them all they need to know about how well off they are as a result of owning it. If Irving the Investor thinks he is better off when he owns a long-term bond yielding a 10% interest rate and the interest rate rises to 20%, he will have a rude awakening: As we will shortly see, Irving has lost his shirt! How well a person does by holding a bond or any other security over a particular time period is accurately measured by the **return,** or, in more precise terminology, the **rate of return.** For any security, the rate of return is defined as the payments to the owner plus the change in its value, expressed as a fraction of its purchase price. To make this definition clearer, let us see what the return would look like for a $1000-face-value coupon bond with a coupon rate of 10% that is bought for $1000, held for one year, and then sold for $1200. The payments to the owner are the yearly coupon payments of $100, and the change in its value is $1200 − $1000 = $200. Adding these together and

---

[6]Because most interest income in the United States is subject to federal income taxes, the true earnings in real terms from holding a debt instrument are not reflected by the real interest rate defined by the Fisher equation but rather by the *after-tax real interest rate*, which equals the nominal interest rate *after income tax payments have been subtracted*, minus the expected inflation rate. For a person facing a 30% tax rate, the after-tax interest rate earned on a bond yielding 10% is only 7% because 30% of the interest income must be paid to the Internal Revenue Service. Thus the after-tax real interest rate on this bond when expected inflation is 20% equals −13% (= 7% − 20%). More generally, the after-tax real interest rate can be expressed as

$$i(1 - \tau) - \pi^e$$

where τ = the income tax rate.

   This formula for the after-tax real interest rate also provides a better measure of the effective cost of borrowing for many corporations and individuals in the United States because in calculating income taxes, they can deduct interest payments on loans from their income. Thus if you face a 30% tax rate and take out a mortgage loan with a 10% interest rate, you are able to deduct the 10% interest payment and thus lower your taxes by 30% of this amount. Your after-tax nominal cost of borrowing is then 7% (10% minus 30% of the 10% interest payment), and when the expected inflation rate is 20%, the effective cost of borrowing in real terms is again −13% (= 7% − 20%).

   As the example (and the formula) indicates, after-tax real interest rates are always below the real interest rate defined by the Fisher equation. For a further discussion of measures of after-tax real interest rates, see Frederic S. Mishkin, "The Real Interest Rate: An Empirical Investigation," *Carnegie-Rochester Conference Series on Public Policy* 15 (1981): 151–200.

MINI-CASE

With TIPS, Real Interest Rates Have Become Observable in the United States

When the U.S. Treasury decided to issue TIPS (Treasury Inflation Protection Securities), a version of indexed coupon bonds, it was somewhat late in the game. Other countries such as the United Kingdom, Canada, Australia, and Sweden had already beaten the United States to the punch. (In September 1998, the U.S. Treasury also began issuing the Series I savings bond, which provides inflation protection for small investors.)

These indexed securities have successfully acquired a niche in the bond market, enabling governments to raise more funds. In addition, because their interest and principal payments are adjusted for changes in the price level, the interest rate on these bonds provides a direct measure of a real interest rate. These indexed bonds are very useful to policymakers, especially monetary policymakers, because by subtracting their interest rate from a nominal interest rate, they generate more insight into expected inflation, a valuable piece of information. For example, on December 15, 2004, the interest rate on the ten-year Treasury bond was 4.16%, while that on the ten-year TIPS was 1.65%. Thus the implied expected inflation rate for the next ten years, derived from the difference between these two rates, was 2.51%. The private sector finds the information provided by TIPS very useful: Many commercial and investment banks routinely publish the expected U.S. inflation rates derived from these bonds.

expressing them as a fraction of the purchase price of $1000 gives us the one-year holding-period return for this bond:

$$\frac{\$100 + \$200}{\$1000} = \frac{\$300}{\$1000} = 0.30 = 30\%$$

You may have noticed something quite surprising about the return that we have just calculated: It equals 30%, yet as Table 1 indicates, initially the yield to maturity was only 10%. This demonstrates that ***the return on a bond will not necessarily equal the interest rate on that bond.*** We now see that the distinction between interest rate and return can be important, although for many securities the two may be closely related.

Study Guide

The concept of return discussed here is extremely important because it is used continually throughout the book. Make sure that you understand how a return is calculated and why it can differ from the interest rate. This understanding will make the material presented later in the book easier to follow.

More generally, the return on a bond held from time t to time $t + 1$ can be written as

$$R = \frac{C + P_{t+1} - P_t}{P_t} \qquad (9)$$

where

R = return from holding the bond from time t to time $t + 1$

P_t = price of the bond at time t

P_{t+1} = price of the bond at time $t + 1$

C = coupon payment

| EXAMPLE 7 | *Rate of Return* |

What would the rate of return be on a bond bought for $1000 and sold one year later for $800? The bond has a face value of $1000 and a coupon rate of 8%.

Solution

The rate of return on the bond for holding it one year is -12%.

$$R = \frac{C + P_{t+1} - P_t}{P_t}$$

where

C	= coupon payment = 1000×0.08	= $80
P_{t+1}	= price of the bond one year later	= $800
P_t	= price of the bond today	= $1000

Thus

$$R = \frac{\$80 + (\$800 - \$1000)}{\$1000} = \frac{-120}{1000} = -0.12 = -12\%$$

A convenient way to rewrite the return formula in Equation 9 is to recognize that it can be split into two separate terms:

$$R = \frac{C}{P_t} + \frac{P_{t+1} - P_t}{P_t}$$

The first term is the current yield i_c (the coupon payment over the purchase price):

$$\frac{C}{P_t} = i_c$$

The second term is the **rate of capital gain,** or the change in the bond's price relative to the initial purchase price:

$$\frac{P_{t+1} - P_t}{P_t} = g$$

where g = rate of capital gain. Equation 9 can then be rewritten as

$$R = i_c + g \tag{10}$$

which shows that the return on a bond is the current yield i_c plus the rate of capital gain g. This rewritten formula illustrates the point we just discovered. Even for a bond for which the current yield i_c is an accurate measure of the yield to maturity, the return can differ substantially from the interest rate. Returns will differ from the interest rate especially if there are sizable fluctuations in the price of the bond that produce substantial capital gains or losses.

TABLE 2 *One-Year Returns on Different-Maturity 10% Coupon Rate Bonds When Interest Rates Rise from 10% to 20%*

(1)	(2)	(3)	(4)	(5)	(6)
Years to Maturity When Bond Is Purchased	Initial Current Yield (%)	Initial Price ($)	Price Next Year ($)	Rate of Capital Gain (%)	Rate of Return (2 + 5) (%)
30	10	1000	503	−49.7	−39.7
20	10	1000	516	−48.4	−38.4
10	10	1000	597	−40.3	−30.3
5	10	1000	741	−25.9	−15.9
2	10	1000	917	− 8.3	+ 1.7
1	10	1000	1000	0.0	+10.0

To explore this point even further, let's look at what happens to the returns on bonds of different maturities when interest rates rise. Table 2 calculates the one-year return on several 10% coupon rate bonds all purchased at par when interest rates on all these bonds rise from 10% to 20%. Several key findings in this table are generally true of all bonds:

- The only bond whose return equals the initial yield to maturity is one whose time to maturity is the same as the holding period (see the last bond in Table 2).
- A rise in interest rates is associated with a fall in bond prices, resulting in capital losses on bonds whose terms to maturity are longer than the holding period.
- The more distant a bond's maturity, the greater the size of the price change associated with an interest-rate change.
- The more distant a bond's maturity, the lower the rate of return that occurs as a result of the increase in the interest rate.
- Even though a bond has a substantial initial interest rate, its return can turn out to be negative if interest rates rise.

At first it frequently puzzles students that a rise in interest rates can mean that a bond has been a poor investment (as it puzzles poor Irving the Investor). The trick to understanding this is to recognize that a rise in the interest rate means that the price of a bond has fallen. A rise in interest rates therefore means that a capital loss has occurred, and if this loss is large enough, the bond can be a poor investment indeed. For example, we see in Table 2 that the bond that has 30 years to maturity when purchased has a capital loss of 49.7% when the interest rate rises from 10% to 20%. This loss is so large that it exceeds the current yield of 10%, resulting in a negative return (loss) of −39.7%. If Irving does not sell the bond, the capital loss is often referred to as a "paper loss." This is a loss nonetheless because if he had not bought this bond and had instead put his money in the bank, he would now be able to buy more bonds at their lower price than he presently owns.

Maturity and the Volatility of Bond Returns: Interest-Rate Risk

The finding that the prices of longer-maturity bonds respond more dramatically to changes in interest rates helps explain an important fact about the behavior of bond markets: ***Prices and returns for long-term bonds are more volatile than those for shorter-term bonds.*** Price changes of +20% and −20% within a year, with corresponding variations in returns, are common for bonds more than 20 years away from maturity.

We now see that changes in interest rates make investments in long-term bonds quite risky. Indeed, the riskiness of an asset's return that results from interest-rate changes is so important that it has been given a special name, **interest-rate risk.** Dealing with interest-rate risk is a major concern of managers of financial institutions and investors, as we will see in later chapters (see also the "Mini-Case" box below).

Although long-term debt instruments have substantial interest-rate risk, short-term debt instruments do not. Indeed, bonds with a maturity that is as short as the holding period have no interest-rate risk.[7] We see this for the coupon bond at the bottom of Table 2, which has no uncertainty about the rate of return because it equals the yield to maturity, which is known at the time the bond is purchased. The key to understanding why there is no interest-rate risk for *any* bond whose time to maturity matches the holding period is to recognize that (in this case) the price at the end of the holding period is already fixed at the face value. The change in interest rates can then have no effect on the price at the end of the holding period for these bonds, and the return will therefore be equal to the yield to maturity known at the time the bond is purchased.

MINI-CASE

Helping Investors Select Desired Interest-Rate Risk

Because many investors want to know how much interest-rate risk they are exposed to, some mutual fund companies try to educate investors about the perils of interest-rate risk, as well as to offer investment alternatives that match their investors' preferences.

Vanguard Group, for example, offers eight separate high-grade bond mutual funds. In its prospectus, Vanguard separates the funds by the average maturity of the bonds they hold and demonstrates the effect of interest-rate changes by computing the percentage change in bond value resulting from a 1% increase and decrease in interest rates. Three of the funds invest in bonds with average maturities of one to three years, which Vanguard rates as having the lowest interest-rate risk. Three other funds hold bonds with average maturities of five to ten years, which Vanguard rates as having medium interest-rate risk. Two funds hold long-term bonds with maturities of 15 to 30 years, which Vanguard rates as having high interest-rate risk.

By providing this information, Vanguard hopes to increase its market share in the sales of bond funds. Not surprisingly, Vanguard is one of the most successful mutual fund companies in the business.

---

[7]The statement that there is no interest-rate risk for any bond whose time to maturity matches the holding period is literally true only for discount bonds and zero-coupon bonds that make no intermediate cash payments before the holding period is over. A coupon bond that makes an intermediate cash payment before the holding period is over requires that this payment be reinvested at some future date. Because the interest rate at which this payment can be reinvested is uncertain, there is some uncertainty about the return on this coupon bond even when the time to maturity equals the holding period. However, the riskiness of the return on a coupon bond from reinvesting the coupon payments is typically quite small, and so the basic point that a coupon bond with a time to maturity equaling the holding period has very little risk still holds true.

Reinvestment Risk

Up to now, we have been assuming that all holding periods are short and equal to the maturity on short-term bonds and are thus not subject to interest-rate risk. However, if an investor's holding period is longer than the term to maturity of the bond, the investor is exposed to a type of interest-rate risk called **reinvestment risk.** Reinvestment risk occurs because the proceeds from the short-term bond need to be reinvested at a future interest rate that is uncertain.

To understand reinvestment risk, suppose that Irving the Investor has a holding period of two years and decides to purchase a $1000 one-year bond at face value and will then purchase another one at the end of the first year. If the initial interest rate is 10%, Irving will have $1100 at the end of the year. If the interest rate on one-year bonds rises to 20% at the end of the year, as in Table 2, Irving will find that buying $1100 worth of another one-year bond will leave him at the end of the second year with $1100 × (1 + 0.20) = $1320. Thus Irving's two-year return will be ($1320 − $1000)/$1000 = 0.32 = 32%, which equals 14.9% at an annual rate. In this case, Irving has earned more by buying the one-year bonds than if he had initially purchased the two-year bond with an interest rate of 10%. Thus when Irving has a holding period that is longer than the term to maturity of the bonds he purchases, he benefits from a rise in interest rates. Conversely, if interest rates on one-year bonds fall to 5% at the end of the year, Irving will have only $1155 at the end of two years: $1100 × (1 + 0.05). Thus his two-year return will be ($1155 − $1000)/$1000 = 0.155 = 15.5%, which is 7.2% at an annual rate. With a holding period greater than the term to maturity of the bond, Irving now loses from a fall in interest rates.

We have thus seen that when the holding period is longer than the term to maturity of a bond, the return is uncertain because the future interest rate when reinvestment occurs is also uncertain—in short, there is reinvestment risk. We also see that if the holding period is longer than the term to maturity of the bond, the investor benefits from a rise in interest rates and is hurt by a fall in interest rates.

Summary

The return on a bond, which tells you how good an investment it has been over the holding period, is equal to the yield to maturity in only one special case: when the holding period and the maturity of the bond are identical. Bonds whose term to maturity is longer than the holding period are subject to interest-rate risk: Changes in interest rates lead to capital gains and losses that produce substantial differences between the return and the yield to maturity known at the time the bond is purchased. Interest-rate risk is especially important for long-term bonds, where the capital gains and losses can be substantial. This is why long-term bonds are not considered to be safe assets with a sure return over short holding periods. Bonds whose term to maturity is shorter than the holding period are also subject to reinvestment risk. Reinvestment risk occurs because the proceeds from the short-term bond need to be reinvested at a future interest rate that is uncertain.

The Practicing Manager

CALCULATING DURATION TO MEASURE INTEREST-RATE RISK

Earlier in our discussion of interest-rate risk, we saw that when interest rates change, a bond with a longer term to maturity has a larger change in its price and hence more interest-rate risk than a bond with a shorter term to maturity. Although this is a useful general fact, in order to measure interest-rate risk, the manager of a financial institution needs more precise information on the actual capital gain or loss that occurs when the interest rate changes by a certain amount. To do this, the manager needs to make use of the concept of **duration,** the average lifetime of a debt security's stream of payments.

The fact that two bonds have the same term to maturity does not mean that they have the same interest-rate risk. A long-term discount bond with ten years to maturity, a so-called zero-coupon bond, makes all of its payments at the end of the ten years, whereas a 10% coupon bond with ten years to maturity makes substantial cash payments before the maturity date. Since the coupon bond makes payments earlier than the zero-coupon bond, we might intuitively guess that the coupon bond's *effective maturity,* the term to maturity that accurately measures interest-rate risk, is shorter than it is for the zero-coupon discount bond.

Indeed, this is exactly what we find in Example 8.

EXAMPLE 8   *Rate of Capital Gain*

Calculate the rate of capital gain or loss on a ten-year zero-coupon bond for which the interest rate has increased from 10% to 20%. The bond has a face value of $1000.

Solution

The rate of capital gain or loss is −49.7%.

$$g = \frac{P_{t+1} - P_t}{P_t}$$

where

P_{t+1} = price of the bond one year from now $= \dfrac{\$1000}{(1 + 0.20)^9} = \$193.81$

P_t = price of the bond today $= \dfrac{\$1000}{(1 + 0.10)^{10}} = \$385.54$

Thus

$$g = \frac{\$193.81 - \$385.54}{\$385.54}$$

$$g = -0.497 = -49.7\%$$

But as we have already calculated in Table 2, the capital gain on the 10% ten-year coupon bond is −40.3%. We see that interest-rate risk for the ten-year coupon bond is less than for the ten-year zero-coupon bond, so the effective maturity on the coupon bond (which measures interest-rate risk) is, as expected, shorter than the effective maturity on the zero-coupon bond.

Calculating Duration

To calculate the duration or effective maturity on any debt security, Frederick Macaulay, a researcher at the National Bureau of Economic Research, invented the concept of duration more than half a century ago. Because a zero-coupon bond makes no cash payments before the bond matures, it makes sense to define its effective maturity as equal to its actual term to maturity. Macaulay then realized that he could measure the effective maturity of a coupon bond by recognizing that a coupon bond is equivalent to a set of zero-coupon discount bonds. A ten-year 10% coupon bond with $1000 face value has cash payments identical to the following set of zero-coupon bonds: a $100 one-year zero-coupon bond (which pays the equivalent of the $100 coupon payment made by the $1000 ten-year 10% coupon bond at the end of one year), a $100 two-year zero-coupon bond (which pays the equivalent of the $100 coupon payment at the end of two years), . . . , a $100 ten-year zero-coupon bond (which pays the equivalent of the $100 coupon payment at the end of ten years), and a $1000 ten-year zero-coupon bond (which pays back the equivalent of the coupon bond's $1000 face value). This set of coupon bonds is shown in the following timeline:

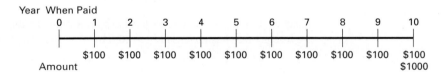

This same set of coupon bonds is listed in column (2) of Table 3, which calculates the duration on the ten-year coupon bond when its interest rate is 10%.

To get the effective maturity of this set of zero-coupon bonds, we would want to sum up the effective maturity of each zero-coupon bond, weighting it by the percentage of the total value of all the bonds that it represents. In other words, the duration of this set of zero-coupon bonds is the weighted average of the effective maturities of the individual zero-coupon bonds, with the weights equaling the proportion of the total value represented by each zero-coupon bond. We do this in several steps in Table 3. First we calculate the present value of each of the zero-coupon bonds when the interest rate is 10% in column (3). Then in column (4) we divide each of these present values by $1000, the total present value of the set of zero-coupon bonds, to get the percentage of the total value of all the bonds that each bond represents. Note that the sum of the weights in column (4) must total 100%, as shown at the bottom of the column.

To get the effective maturity of the set of zero-coupon bonds, we add up the weighted maturities in column (5) and obtain the figure of 6.76 years. This figure for the effective maturity of the set of zero-coupon bonds is the duration of the 10% ten-year coupon bond because the bond is equivalent to

TABLE 3 *Calculating Duration on a $1000 Ten-Year 10% Coupon Bond When Its Interest Rate Is 10%*

(1)	(2)	(3)	(4)	(5)
Year	Cash Payments (Zero-Coupon Bonds) ($)	Present Value (PV) of Cash Payments (i = 10%) ($)	Weights (% of total PV = PV/$1000) (%)	Weighted Maturity (1 × 4)/100 (years)
1	100	90.91	9.091	0.09091
2	100	82.64	8.264	0.16528
3	100	75.13	7.513	0.22539
4	100	68.30	6.830	0.27320
5	100	62.09	6.209	0.31045
6	100	56.44	5.644	0.33864
7	100	51.32	5.132	0.35924
8	100	46.65	4.665	0.37320
9	100	42.41	4.241	0.38169
10	100	38.55	3.855	0.38550
10	1000	385.54	38.554	3.85500
Total		1000.00	100.000	6.75850

this set of zero-coupon bonds. In short, we see that **duration is a weighted average of the maturities of the cash payments.**

The duration calculation done in Table 3 can be written as follows:

$$DUR = \sum_{t=1}^{n} t \frac{CP_t}{(1 + i)^t} \bigg/ \sum_{t=1}^{n} \frac{CP_t}{(1 + i)^t} \tag{11}$$

where DUR = duration

   t = years until cash payment is made

   CP_t = cash payment (interest plus principal) at time t

   i = interest rate

   n = years to maturity of the security

This formula is not as intuitive as the calculation done in Table 3, but it does have the advantage that it can easily be programmed into a calculator or computer, making duration calculations very easy.

If we calculate the duration for an 11-year 10% coupon bond when the interest rate is again 10%, we find that it equals 7.14 years, which is greater than the 6.76 years for the ten-year bond. Thus we have reached the expected conclusion: **All else being equal, the longer the term to maturity of a bond, the longer its duration.**

You might think that knowing the maturity of a coupon bond is enough to tell you what its duration is. However, that is not the case. To see this and to give you more practice in calculating duration, in Table 4 we again calculate the duration for the ten-year 10% coupon bond, but when the current interest rate is 20% rather than 10% as in Table 3. The calculation in Table 4 reveals that the duration of the coupon bond at this higher interest rate has fallen from 6.76 years to 5.72 years. The explanation is fairly straightforward. When the interest rate is higher, the cash payments in the future are discounted more heavily and become less important in present-value terms relative to the total present value of all the payments. The relative weight for these cash payments drops as we see in Table 4, and so the effective maturity of the bond falls. We have come to an important conclusion: ***All else being equal, when interest rates rise, the duration of a coupon bond falls.***

The duration of a coupon bond is also affected by its coupon rate. For example, consider a ten-year 20% coupon bond when the interest rate is 10%. Using the same procedure, we find that its duration at the higher 20% coupon rate is 5.98 years versus 6.76 years when the coupon rate is 10%. The explanation is that a higher coupon rate means that a relatively greater amount of the cash payments are made earlier in the life of the bond, and so the effective maturity of the bond must fall. We have thus established a third fact about duration: ***All else being equal, the higher the coupon rate on the bond, the shorter the bond's duration.***

Study Guide

To make certain that you understand how to calculate duration, practice doing the calculations in Tables 3 and 4. Try to produce the tables for calculating duration in the case of an 11-year 10% coupon bond and also for the ten-year 20% coupon bond mentioned in the text when the current interest rate is 10%. Make sure your calculations produce the same results found in the text. You can get more practice by doing some of the problems involving duration calculations at the end of the chapter.

One additional fact about duration makes this concept useful when applied to a portfolio of securities. Our examples have shown that duration is equal to the weighted average of the durations of the cash payments (the effective maturities of the corresponding zero-coupon bonds). So if we calculate the duration for two different securities, it should be easy to see that the duration of a portfolio of the two securities is just the weighted average of the durations of the two securities, with the weights reflecting the proportion of the portfolio invested in each.

EXAMPLE 9   *Duration*

A manager of a financial institution is holding 25% of a portfolio in a bond with a five-year duration and 75% in a bond with a ten-year duration. What is the duration of the portfolio?

Solution

The duration of the portfolio is 8.75 years.

$$(0.25 \times 5) + (0.75 \times 10) = 1.25 + 7.5 = 8.75 \text{ years}$$

TABLE 4 *Calculating Duration on a $1000 Ten-Year 10% Coupon Bond When Its Interest Rate Is 20%*

(1) Year	(2) Cash Payments (Zero-Coupon Bonds) ($)	(3) Present Value (PV) of Cash Payments (i = 20%) ($)	(4) Weights (% of total PV = PV/$580.76) (%)	(5) Weighted Maturity (1 × 4)/100 (years)
1	100	83.33	14.348	0.14348
2	100	69.44	11.957	0.23914
3	100	57.87	9.965	0.29895
4	100	48.23	8.305	0.33220
5	100	40.19	6.920	0.34600
6	100	33.49	5.767	0.34602
7	100	27.91	4.806	0.33642
8	100	23.26	4.005	0.32040
9	100	19.38	3.337	0.30033
10	100	16.15	2.781	0.27810
10	$1000	161.51	27.808	2.78100
Total		580.76	100.000	5.72204

We now see that ***the duration of a portfolio of securities is the weighted average of the durations of the individual securities, with the weights reflecting the proportion of the portfolio invested in each.*** This fact about duration is often referred to as the *additive property of duration*, and it is extremely useful because it means that the duration of a portfolio of securities is easy to calculate from the durations of the individual securities.

To summarize, our calculations of duration for coupon bonds have revealed four facts:

1. The longer the term to maturity of a bond, everything else being equal, the greater its duration.

2. When interest rates rise, everything else being equal, the duration of a coupon bond falls.

3. The higher the coupon rate on the bond, everything else being equal, the shorter the bond's duration.

4. Duration is additive: The duration of a portfolio of securities is the weighted average of the durations of the individual securities, with the weights reflecting the proportion of the portfolio invested in each.

Duration and Interest-Rate Risk

Now that we understand how duration is calculated, we want to see how it can be used by the practicing financial institution manager to measure interest-rate risk. Duration is a particularly useful concept because it provides a good approximation, particularly when interest-rate changes are small, for how much the security price changes for a given change in interest rates, as the following formula indicates:

$$\%\Delta P \approx -DUR \times \frac{\Delta i}{1 + i} \tag{12}$$

where $\%\Delta P = (P_{t+1} - P_t)/P_t$ = percentage change in the price of the security from t to $t + 1$ = rate of capital gain

DUR = duration

i = interest rate

EXAMPLE 10   *Duration and Interest-Rate Risk*

A pension fund manager is holding a ten-year 10% coupon bond in the fund's portfolio and the interest rate is currently 10%. What loss would the fund be exposed to if the interest rate rises to 11% tomorrow?

Solution

The approximate percentage change in the price of the bond is −6.15%.

As the calulation in Table 3 shows, the duration of a ten-year 10% coupon bond is 6.76 years.

$$\%\Delta P \approx -DUR \times \frac{\Delta i}{1 + i}$$

where

DUR = duration   = 6.76

Δi = change in interest rate = 0.11 − 0.10 = 0.01

i = current interest rate   = 0.10

Thus

$$\%\Delta P \approx -6.76 \times \frac{0.01}{1 + 0.10}$$

$$\%\Delta P \approx -0.0615 = -6.15\%$$

EXAMPLE 11   *Duration and Interest-Rate Risk*

Now the pension manager has the option to hold a ten-year coupon bond with a coupon rate of 20% instead of 10%. As mentioned earlier, the duration for this 20% coupon bond is 5.98 years when the interest rate is 10%. Find the approximate change in the bond price when the interest rate increases from 10% to 11%.

Solution

This time the approximate change in bond price is −5.4%. This change in bond price is much smaller than for the higher-duration coupon bond.

$$\%\Delta P \approx -DUR \times \frac{\Delta i}{1 + i}$$

where

DUR = duration $\qquad\qquad$ = 5.98
Δi $\quad$ = change in interest rate = 0.11 − 0.10 = 0.01
i $\quad$ = current interest rate $\qquad$ = 0.10

Thus

$$\%\Delta P \approx -5.98 \times \frac{0.01}{1 + 0.10}$$

$$\%\Delta P \approx -0.054 = -5.4\%$$

The pension fund manager realizes that the interest-rate risk on the 20% coupon bond is less than on the 10% coupon, so he switches the fund out of the 10% coupon bond and into the 20% coupon bond.

Examples 10 and 11 have led the pension fund manager to an important conclusion about the relationship of duration and interest-rate risk: ***The greater the duration of a security, the greater the percentage change in the market value of the security for a given change in interest rates. Therefore, the greater the duration of a security, the greater its interest-rate risk.***

This reasoning applies equally to a portfolio of securities. So by calculating the duration of the fund's portfolio of securities using the methods outlined here, a pension fund manager can easily ascertain the amount of interest-rate risk the entire fund is exposed to. As we will see in Chapter 24, duration is a highly useful concept for the management of interest-rate risk that is widely used by managers of banks and other financial institutions.

Summary

1. The yield to maturity, which is the measure that most accurately reflects the interest rate, is the interest rate that equates the present value of future cash flows of a debt instrument with its value today. Application of this principle reveals that bond prices and interest rates are negatively related: When the interest rate rises, the price of the bond must fall, and vice versa.

2. The real interest rate is defined as the nominal interest rate minus the expected rate of inflation. It is a better measure of the incentives to borrow and lend than the nominal interest rate, and it is a more accurate indicator of the tightness of credit market conditions than the nominal interest rate.

3. The return on a security, which tells you how well you have done by holding this security over a stated period of time, can differ substantially from the interest rate as measured by the yield to maturity. Long-term bond prices have substantial fluctuations when interest rates change and thus bear interest-rate risk. The resulting capital gains and losses can be large, which is why long-term bonds are not considered to be safe assets with a sure return. Bonds whose maturity is shorter than the holding period are also subject to reinvestment risk, which occurs because the proceeds from the short-term bond need to be reinvested at a future interest rate that is uncertain.

4. Duration, the average lifetime of a debt security's stream of payments, is a measure of effective maturity, the term to maturity that accurately measures interest-rate risk. Everything else being equal, the duration of a bond is greater the longer the maturity of a bond, when interest rates fall, or when the coupon rate of a coupon bond falls. Duration is additive: The duration of a portfolio of securities is the weighted average of the durations of the individual securities, with the weights reflecting the proportion of the portfolio invested in each. The greater the duration of a security, the greater the percentage change in the market value of the security for a given change in interest rates. Therefore, the greater the duration of a security, the greater its interest-rate risk.

Key Terms

cash flows, *p. 42*

coupon bond, *p. 44*

coupon rate, *p. 44*

current yield, *p. 51*

discount bond (zero-coupon bond), *p. 44*

duration, *p. 61*

face value (par value), *p. 44*

fixed-payment loan (fully amortized loan), *p. 44*

indexed bond, *p. 55*

interest-rate risk, *p. 59*

nominal interest rate, *p. 52*

perpetuity (consol), *p. 49*

present value (present discounted value), *p. 42*

rate of capital gain, *p. 57*

real interest rate, *p. 52*

real terms, *p. 53*

reinvestment risk, *p. 60*

return (rate of return), *p. 55*

simple loan, *p. 42*

yield to maturity, *p. 45*

Questions

1. Write down the formula that is used to calculate the yield to maturity on a 20-year 10% coupon bond with $1000 face value that sells for $2000.

2. If there is a decline in interest rates, which would you rather be holding, long-term bonds or short-term bonds? Why? Which type of bond has the greater interest-rate risk?

3. A financial adviser has just given you the following advice: "Long-term bonds are a great investment because their interest rate is over 20%." Is the financial adviser necessarily right?

4. If mortgage rates rise from 5% to 10% but the expected rate of increase in housing prices rises from 2% to 9%, are people more or less likely to buy houses?

Quantitative Problems

1. Calculate the present value of a $1000 zero-coupon bond with 5 years to maturity if the yield to maturity is 6%.

2. A lottery claims its grand prize is $10 million, payable over 20 years at $500,000 per year. If the first payment is made immediately, what is this grand prize really worth? Use a discount rate of 6%.

3. Consider a bond with a 7% annual coupon and a face value of $1000. Complete the following table.

Years to Maturity	Yield to Maturity	Current Price
3	5	
3	7	
6	7	
9	7	
9	9	

What relationships do you observe between maturity and discount rate and the current price?

4. Consider a coupon bond that has a $1000 par value and a coupon rate of 10%. The bond is currently selling for $1150 and has eight years to maturity. What is the bond's yield to maturity?

5. You are willing to pay $15,625 now to purchase a perpetuity that will pay you and your heirs $1250 each year, forever, starting at the end of this year. If your required rate of return does not change, how much would you be willing to pay if this were a 20-year, annual payment, ordinary annuity instead of a perpetuity?

6. What is the price of a perpetuity that has a coupon of $50 per year and a yield to maturity of 2.5%? If the yield to maturity doubles, what will happen to its price?

7. Property taxes in DeKalb County are roughly 2.66% of the purchase price every year. If you just bought a $100,000 home, what is the PV of all the future property tax payments? Assume that the house remains worth $100,000 forever, property tax rates never change, and that a 9% discount rate is used for discounting.

8. Assume you just deposited $1000 into a bank account. The current real interest rate is 2%, and inflation is expected to be 6% over the next year. What nominal rate would you require from the bank over the next year? How much money will you have at the end of one year? If you are saving to buy a stereo that currently sells for $1050, will you have enough to buy it?

9. A ten-year, 7% coupon bond with a face value of $1000 is currently selling for $871.65. Compute your rate of return if you sell the bond next year for $880.10.

10. You have paid $980.30 for an 8% coupon bond with a face value of $1000 that matures in five years. You plan on holding the bond for one year. If you want to earn a 9% rate of return on this investment, what price must you sell the bond for? Is this realistic?

11. Calculate the duration of a $1000, 6% coupon bond with three years to maturity. Assume that all market interest rates are 7%.

12. Consider the bond in the previous question. Calculate the expected price change if interest rates drop to 6.75% using the duration approximation. Calculate the actual price change using discounted cash flow.

13. The duration of a $100 million portfolio is 10 years. $40 million in new securities are added to the portfolio, increasing the duration of the portfolio to 12.5 years. What is the duration of the $40 million in new securities?

14. A bank has two 3-year commercial loans with a present value of $70 million. The first is a $30 million loan that requires a single payment of $37.8 million in three years, with no other payments till then. The second loan is for $40 million. It requires an annual interest payment of $3.6 million. The principal of $40 million is due in 3 years.

   a. What is the duration of the bank's commercial loan portfolio?

   b. What will happen to the value of its portfolio if the general level of interest rates increases from 8% to 8.5%?

15. Consider a bond that promises the following cash flows. The required discount rate is 12%.

Year	0	1	2	3	4
Promised Payments		160	170	180	230

You plan to buy this bond, hold it for 2.5 years, and then sell the bond.

   a. What total cash will you receive from the bond after the 2.5 years? Assume that periodic cash flows are reinvested at 12%.

   b. If immediately after buying this bond, all market interest rates drop to 11% (including your reinvestment rate), what will be the impact on your total cash flow after 2.5 years? How does this compare to part (a)?

   c. Assuming all market interest rates are 12%, what is the duration of this bond?

Web Exercises

Understanding Interest Rates

1. Investigate the data available from the Federal Reserve at **http://www.federalreserve.gov/releases/**. Then answer the following questions.

   a. What is the difference in the interest rates on commercial paper for financial firms versus non-financial firms?

   b. What was the interest rate on the one-month Eurodollar at the end of 1971?

   c. What is the most recent interest rate reported for the 10-year Treasury note?

2. Figure 1 in the chapter shows the estimated real and nominal rates for three-month Treasury bills. Go to **http://www.martincapital.com/charts. htm**. Click on "interest rates and yields" then on "Nominal versus Real Market Rates."

   a. Compare the three-month real rate to the long-term real rate. Which is greater?

   b. Compare the short-term nominal rate to the long-term nominal rate. Which appears most volatile?

CHAPTER 4

Why Do Interest Rates Change?

Preview

In the early 1950s, nominal interest rates on three-month Treasury bills were about 1% at an annual rate; by 1981, they had reached over 15%, then fell to 3% in 1993, rose above 5% by the mid-1990s, dropped to near 1% in 2003, then began rising again in mid-2004. What explains these substantial fluctuations in interest rates? One reason we study financial markets and institutions is to provide some answers to this question.

In this chapter we examine why the overall level of *nominal* interest rates (which we refer to simply as "interest rates") changes and the factors that influence their behavior. We learned in Chapter 3 that interest rates are negatively related to the price of bonds, so if we can explain why bond prices change, we can also explain why interest rates fluctuate. Here we will apply supply and demand analysis to examine how bond prices and interest rates change.

Determinants of Asset Demand

An **asset** is a piece of property that is a store of value. Items such as money, bonds, stocks, art, land, houses, farm equipment, and manufacturing machinery are all assets. Facing the question of whether to buy and hold an asset or whether to buy one asset rather than another, an individual must consider the following factors:

1. **Wealth,** the total resources owned by the individual, including all assets
2. **Expected return** (the return expected over the next period) on one asset relative to alternative assets
3. **Risk** (the degree of uncertainty associated with the return) on one asset relative to alternative assets
4. **Liquidity** (the ease and speed with which an asset can be turned into cash) relative to alternative assets

Wealth

When we find that our wealth has increased, we have more resources available with which to purchase assets and so, not surprisingly, the quantity of assets we demand increases.[1] Therefore, the effect of changes in wealth on the quantity demanded of an asset can be summarized as follows: ***Holding everything else constant, an increase in wealth raises the quantity demanded of an asset.***

Expected Returns

In Chapter 3 we saw that the return on an asset (such as a bond) measures how much we gain from holding that asset. When we make a decision to buy an asset, we are influenced by what we expect the return on that asset to be. If an Exxon-Mobil Corporation bond, for example, has a return of 15% half of the time and 5% the other half of the time, its expected return (which you can think of as the average return) is 10%. More formally, the expected return on an asset is the weighted average of all possible returns, where the weights are the probabilities of occurrence of that return:

$$R^e = p_1 R_1 + p_2 R_2 + \ldots + p_n R_n \tag{1}$$

where
R^e = expected return
n = number of possible outcomes (states of nature)
R_i = return in the ith state of nature
p_i = probability of occurrence of the return R_i

EXAMPLE 1   *Expected Return*

What is the expected return on the Exxon-Mobil bond if the return is 12% two-thirds of the time and 8% one-third of the time?

Solution

The expected return is 10.68%.

$$R^e = p_1 R_1 + p_2 R_2$$

---

[1]Although it is possible that some assets (called *inferior assets*) might have the property that the quantity demanded does not increase as wealth increases, such assets are rare. Hence we will always assume that demand for an asset increases as wealth increases.

where

p_1 = probability of occurrence of return 1 $= \frac{2}{3}$ $= 0.67$

R_1 = return in state 1 $= 12\%$ $= 0.12$

p_2 = probability of occurrence return 2 $= \frac{1}{3}$ $= 0.33$

R_2 = return in state 2 $= 8\%$ $= 0.08$

Thus

$$R^e = (.67)(0.12) + (.33)(0.08) = 0.1068 = 10.68\%$$

If the expected return on the Exxon-Mobil bond rises relative to expected returns on alternative assets, holding everything else constant, then it becomes more desirable to purchase it, and the quantity demanded increases. This can occur in either of two ways: (1) when the expected return on the Mobil Oil bond rises while the return on an alternative asset—say, stock in IBM—remains unchanged or (2) when the return on the alternative asset, the IBM stock, falls while the return on the Mobil Oil bond remains unchanged. To summarize, ***an increase in an asset's expected return relative to that of an alternative asset, holding everything else unchanged, raises the quantity demanded of the asset.***

Risk

The degree of risk or uncertainty of an asset's returns also affects the demand for the asset. Consider two assets, stock in Fly-by-Night Airlines and stock in Feet-on-the-Ground Bus Company. Suppose that Fly-by-Night stock has a return of 15% half of the time and 5% the other half of the time, making its expected return 10%, while stock in Feet-on-the-Ground has a fixed return of 10%. Fly-by-Night stock has uncertainty associated with its returns and so has greater risk than stock in Feet-on-the-Ground, whose return is a sure thing.

To see this more formally, we can use a measure of risk called the **standard deviation.** The standard deviation of returns on an asset is calculated as follows. First you need to calculate the expected return, R^e; then you subtract the expected return from each return to get a deviation; then you square each deviation and multiply it by the probability of occurrence of that outcome; finally, you add up all these weighted squared deviations and take the square root. The formula for the standard deviation, σ, is thus:

$$\sigma = \sqrt{p_1(R_1 - R^e)^2 + p_2(R_2 - R^e)^2 + \cdots + p_n(R_n - R^e)^2} \qquad (2)$$

The higher the standard deviation, σ, the greater the risk of an asset.

EXAMPLE 2   *Standard Deviation*

What is the standard deviation of the returns on the Fly-by-Night Airlines stock and Feet-on-the Ground Bus Company, with the same return outcomes and probabilities described above? Of these two stocks, which is riskier?

Solution

Fly-by-Night Airlines has a standard deviation of returns of 5%.

$$\sigma = \sqrt{p_1(R_1 - R^e)^2 + p_2(R_2 - R^e)^2}$$

$$R^e = p_1R_1 + p_2R_2$$

where

p_1 = probability of occurrence of return 1 $= \dfrac{1}{2}$		$= 0.50$
R_1 = return in state 1	$= 15\%$	$= 0.15$
p_2 = probability of occurrence of return 2 $= \dfrac{1}{2}$		$= 0.50$
R_2 = return in state 2	$= 5\%$	$= 0.05$
R^e = expected return	$= (.50)(0.15) + (.50)(0.05)$	$= 0.10$

Thus

$$\sigma = \sqrt{(.50)(0.15 - 0.10)^2 + (.50)(0.05 - 0.10)^2}$$

$$\sigma = \sqrt{(.50)(0.0025) + (.50)(0.0025)} = \sqrt{0.0025} = 0.05 = 5\%$$

Feet-on-the-Ground Bus Company has a standard deviation of returns of 0%.

$$\sigma = \sqrt{p_1(R_1 - R^e)^2}$$

$$R^e = p_1R_1$$

where

p_1 = probability of occurrence of return 1 $= 1.0$

R_1 = return in state 1 $= 10\%$ $= 0.10$

R^e = expected return $= (1.0)(0.10)$ $= 0.10$

Thus

$$\sigma = \sqrt{(1.0)(0.10 - 0.10)^2}$$

$$= \sqrt{0} = 0 = 0\%$$

Clearly, Fly-by-Night Airlines is a riskier stock because its standard deviation of returns of 5% is higher than the zero standard deviation of returns for Feet-on-the-Ground Bus Company, which has a certain return.

A *risk-averse* person prefers stock in the Feet-on-the-Ground (the sure thing) to Fly-by-Night stock (the riskier asset), even though the stocks have the same expected return, 10%. By contrast, a person who prefers risk is a *risk preferrer* or *risk lover*. Most people are risk-averse, especially in their financial decisions: Everything else being equal, they prefer to hold the less risky asset. Hence, *holding everything else constant, if an asset's risk rises relative to that of alternative assets, its quantity demanded will fall.*[2]

Liquidity

Another factor that affects the demand for an asset is how quickly it can be converted into cash at low cost—its liquidity. An asset is liquid if the market in which it is traded has depth and breadth, that is, if the market has many buyers and sellers. A house is not a very liquid asset because it may be hard to find a buyer quickly; if a house must be sold to pay off bills, it might have to be sold for a much lower price. And the transaction costs in selling a house (broker's commissions, lawyer's fees, and so on) are substantial. A U.S. Treasury bill, by contrast, is a highly liquid asset. It can be sold in a well-organized market where there are many buyers, so it can be sold quickly at low cost. *The more liquid an asset is relative to alternative assets, holding everything else unchanged, the more desirable it is, and the greater will be the quantity demanded.*

Summary

All the determining factors we have just discussed can be summarized by stating that, holding all of the other factors constant:

1. The quantity demanded of an asset is usually positively related to wealth, with the response being greater if the asset is a luxury than if it is a necessity.
2. The quantity demanded of an asset is positively related to its expected return relative to alternative assets.
3. The quantity demanded of an asset is negatively related to the risk of its returns relative to alternative assets.
4. The quantity demanded of an asset is positively related to its liquidity relative to alternative assets.

These results are summarized in Table 1.

Supply and Demand in the Bond Market

We approach the analysis of interest-rate determination by studying the supply of and demand for bonds. Because interest rates on different securities tend to move together, in this chapter we will act as if there is only one type of security and a single interest rate in the entire economy. In Chapter 5, we will expand our analysis to look at why interest rates on different securities differ.

The first step is to use the analysis of the determinants of asset demand to obtain a **demand curve,** which shows the relationship between the quantity

---

[2]Diversification, the holding of many risky assets in a portfolio, reduces the overall risk an investor faces. If you are interested in how diversification lowers risk and what impact this has on the price of an asset, you can look at an appendix to this chapter describing models of asset pricing that is on the book's website at **www.aw-bc.com/mishkin_eakins**.

TABLE 1 SUMMARY   *Response of the Quantity of an Asset Demanded to Changes in Income or Wealth, Expected Returns, Risk, and Liquidity*

Variable	Change in Variable	Change in Quantity Demanded
Income or wealth	↑	↑
Expected return relative to other assets	↑	↑
Risk relative to other assets	↑	↓
Liquidity relative to other assets	↑	↑

Note: Only increases (↑) in the variables are shown. The effect of decreases in the variables on the change in demand would be the opposite of those indicated in the rightmost column.

demanded and the price when all other economic variables are held constant (that is, values of other variables are taken as given). You may recall from previous finance and economics courses that the assumption that all other economic variables are held constant is called *ceteris paribus*, which means "other things being equal" in Latin.

Demand Curve

To clarify our analysis, let us consider the demand for one-year discount bonds, which make no coupon payments but pay the owner the $1000 face value in a year. If the holding period is one year, then as we have seen in Chapter 3, the return on the bonds is known absolutely and is equal to the interest rate as measured by the yield to maturity. This means that the expected return on this bond is equal to the interest rate i, which, using Equation 6 in Chapter 3, is

$$i = R^e = \frac{F - P}{P}$$

where
i = interest rate = yield to maturity
R^e = expected return
F = face value of the discount bond
P = initial purchase price of the discount bond

This formula shows that a particular value of the interest rate corresponds to each bond price. If the bond sells for $950, the interest rate and expected return is

$$\frac{(\$1000 - \$950)}{\$950} = 0.053 = 5.3\%$$

At this 5.3% interest rate and expected return corresponding to a bond price of $950, let us assume that the quantity of bonds demanded is $100 billion, which is plotted as point A in Figure 1. To display both the bond price and the corresponding interest rate, Figure 1 has two vertical axes. The left vertical axis shows the bond price, with the price of bonds increasing from $750 near the bottom of the axis toward $1000 at the top. The right vertical axis shows the interest rate, which increases in the *opposite* direction from 0% at the top of the axis to 33% near the bottom. The right and left vertical axes run in opposite directions because,

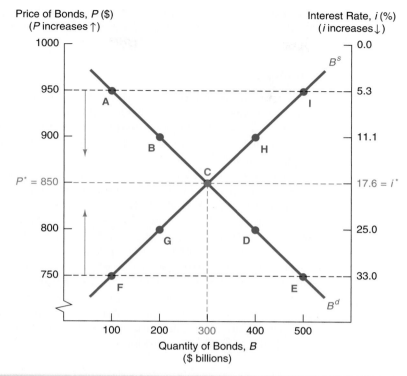

Price of Bonds, P ($)
(P increases ↑)

Interest Rate, i (%)
(i increases ↓)

FIGURE 1 *Supply and Demand for Bonds*

Equilibrium in the bond market occurs at point C, the intersection of the bond demand curve B^d and the bond supply curve B^s. The equilibrium price is P^* = $850, and the equilibrium interest rate is i^* = 17.6%. (*Note*: P and i increase in opposite directions. P on the left vertical axis increases as we go up the axis from $750 near the bottom to $1000 at the top, while i on the right vertical axis increases as we go down the axis from 0% at the top to 33% near the bottom.)

as we learned in Chapter 3, bond price and interest rate are always negatively related: As the price of the bond rises, the interest rate on the bond necessarily falls.

At a price of $900, the interest rate and expected return equals

$$\frac{(\$1000 - \$900)}{\$900} = 0.111 = 11.1\%$$

Because the expected return on these bonds is higher, with all other economic variables (such as income, expected returns on other assets, risk, and liquidity) held constant, the quantity demanded of bonds will be higher as predicted by our analysis of the determinants of asset demand. Point B in Figure 1 shows that the quantity of bonds demanded at the price of $900 has risen to $200 billion. Continuing with this reasoning, if the bond price is $850 (interest rate and expected return = 17.6%), the quantity of bonds demanded (point C) will be greater than at point B. Similarly, at the lower prices of $800 (interest rate = 25%) and $750 (interest rate = 33.3%), the quantity of bonds demanded will be even higher (points D and E). The curve B^d, which connects these points, is the demand curve for bonds. It has the usual downward slope, indicating that at lower prices of the bond (everything else being equal), the quantity demanded is higher.[3]

Supply Curve

An important assumption behind the demand curve for bonds in Figure 1 is that all other economic variables besides the bond's price and interest rate are held constant. We use the same assumption in deriving a **supply curve,** which shows the relationship between the quantity supplied and the price when all other economic variables are held constant.

When the price of the bonds is $750 (interest rate = 33.3%), point F shows that the quantity of bonds supplied is $100 billion for the example we are considering. If the price is $800, the interest rate is the lower rate of 25%. Because at this interest rate it is now less costly to borrow by issuing bonds, firms will be willing to borrow more through bond issues, and the quantity of bonds supplied is at the higher level of $200 billion (point G). An even higher price of $850, corresponding to a lower interest rate of 17.6%, results in a larger quantity of bonds supplied of $300 billion (point C). Higher prices of $900 and $950 result in even greater quantities of bonds supplied (points H and I). The B^s curve, which connects these points, is the supply curve for bonds. It has the usual upward slope found in supply curves, indicating that as the price increases (everything else being equal), the quantity supplied increases.

Market Equilibrium

In finance and economics, **market equilibrium** occurs when the amount that people are willing to buy (*demand*) equals the amount that people are willing to sell (*supply*) at a given price. In the bond market, this is achieved when the quantity of bonds demanded equals the quantity of bonds supplied:

$$B^d = B^s \tag{3}$$

In Figure 1, equilibrium occurs at point C, where the demand and supply curves intersect at a bond price of $850 (interest rate of 17.6%) and a quantity of bonds of $300 billion. The price of $P^* = 850$, where the quantity demanded equals the quantity supplied, is called the *equilibrium* or *market-clearing* price. Similarly, the interest rate of $i^* = 17.6\%$ that corresponds to this price is called the equilibrium or market-clearing interest rate.

The concepts of market equilibrium and equilibrium price or interest rate are useful because there is a tendency for the market to head toward them. We can see that it does in Figure 1 by first looking at what happens when we have a bond price that is above the equilibrium price. When the price of bonds is set too high, at, say, $950, the quantity of bonds supplied at point I is greater than the quantity of bonds demanded at point A. A situation like this, in which the quantity of bonds supplied exceeds the quantity of bonds demanded, is called a condition of **excess supply.** Because people want to sell more bonds than others want to buy, the price of the bonds will fall, and this is why the downward arrow is drawn

---

[3]Note that although our analysis indicates that the demand curve is downward-sloping, it does not imply that the curve is a straight line. For ease of exposition, however, we will draw demand curves and supply curves as straight lines.

in the figure at the bond price of $950. As long as the bond price remains above the equilibrium price, there will continue to be an excess supply of bonds, and the price will continue to fall. This will stop only when the price has reached the equilibrium price of $850, where the excess supply of bonds has been eliminated.

Now let's look at what happens when the price of bonds is below the equilibrium price. If the price of the bonds is set too low, at, say, $750, the quantity demanded at point E is greater than the quantity supplied at point F. This is called a condition of **excess demand.** People now want to buy more bonds than others are willing to sell, and so the price of bonds will be driven up. This is illustrated by the upward arrow drawn in the figure at the bond price of $750. Only when the excess demand for bonds is eliminated by the price rising to the equilibrium level of $850 is there no further tendency for the price to rise.

We can see that the concept of equilibrium price is a useful one because it indicates where the market will settle. Because each price on the left vertical axis of Figure 1 corresponds to a value of the interest rate on the right vertical axis, the same diagram also shows that the interest rate will head toward the equilibrium interest rate of 17.6%. When the interest rate is below the equilibrium interest rate, as it is when it is at 5.3%, the price of the bond is above the equilibrium price, and there will be an excess supply of bonds. The price of the bond then falls, leading to a rise in the interest rate toward the equilibrium level. Similarly, when the interest rate is above the equilibrium level, as it is when it is at 33.3%, there is excess demand for bonds, and the bond price will rise, driving the interest rate back down to the equilibrium level of 17.6%.

Supply and Demand Analysis

Our Figure 1 is a conventional supply and demand diagram with price on the left vertical axis and quantity on the horizontal axis. Because the interest rate that corresponds to each bond price is also marked on the right vertical axis, this diagram allows us to read the equilibrium interest rate, giving us a model that describes the determination of interest rates. It is important to recognize that a supply and demand diagram like Figure 1 can be drawn for *any* type of bond because the interest rate and price of a bond are *always* negatively related for any type of bond, be it a discount bond or a coupon bond.

Loanable Funds Framework

Throughout this book we will use diagrams like Figure 1 and analyze interest rate behavior in terms of the supply and demand for bonds. However, the analysis of the bond market that we have developed here has another interpretation with a different terminology. Here we discuss this other terminology, which is couched in terms of the supply and demand for loanable funds used by some economists. We include this discussion in case you come across this other terminology, but you will not need to make use of it to understand how interest rates are determined.

One disadvantage of the diagram in Figure 1 is that interest rates run in an unusual direction on the right vertical axis: As we go up the right axis, interest rates fall. Because financial economists are typically more concerned with the value of interest rates than with the price of bonds, we could plot the supply of and demand for bonds on a diagram that has only a left vertical axis that provides the values of the interest rates running in the usual direction, rising as we

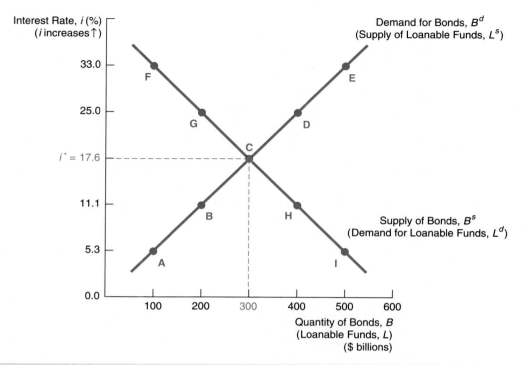

FIGURE 2 *A Comparison of Terminology: Loanable Funds and Supply and Demand for Bonds*

The demand for bonds is equivalent to the supply of loanable funds, and the supply of bonds is equivalent to the demand for loanable funds. (*Note*: *i* increases as we go up the vertical axis, in contrast to Figure 1, in which the opposite occurs.)

go up the axis. Figure 2 is such a diagram, in which points A through I match the corresponding points in Figure 1.

However, making interest rates run the "usual" direction on the vertical axis presents us with a problem. Our demand curve for bonds, points A through E, now looks peculiar because it has an upward slope. This upward slope is, however, completely consistent with our usual demand analysis, which produces a negative relationship between price and quantity. The inverse relationship between bond prices and interest rates means that in moving from point A to point B to point C, bond prices are falling and, consistent with usual demand analysis, the quantity demanded is rising. Similarly, our supply curve for bonds, points F through I, has an unusual-looking downward slope but is completely consistent with the usual view that price and the quantity supplied are positively related.

One way to give the demand curve the usual downward slope and the supply curve the usual upward slope is to rename the horizontal axis and the demand and supply curves. Because a firm supplying bonds is in fact taking out a loan from a person buying a bond, "supplying a bond" is equivalent to "demanding a loan." Thus the supply curve for bonds can be reinterpreted as indicating the *quantity of loans demanded* for each value of the interest rate. If we rename the horizontal axis **loanable funds,** defined as the quantity of loans, the supply of bonds can be reinterpreted as the *demand for loanable funds*. Similarly, the demand curve for bonds can be reidentified as the *supply of loanable funds* because buying (demanding) a bond is equivalent to supplying a loan. Figure 2 relabels the curves and the horizontal axis using the loanable funds terminology in parentheses, and now the renamed loanable funds demand curve has the usual downward slope and the renamed loanable funds supply curve the usual upward slope.

Because supply and demand diagrams that explain how interest rates are determined in the bond market most commonly use the loanable funds terminology, this analysis is frequently referred to as the **loanable funds framework.** However, because in later chapters describing the conduct of monetary policy we focus on how the demand for and supply of bonds is affected, we will continue to conduct supply and demand analysis in terms of bonds, as in Figure 1, rather than loanable funds. Whether the analysis is done in terms of loanable funds or in terms of the demand for and supply of bonds, the results are the same; the two ways of analyzing the determination of interest rates are equivalent.

An important feature of the analysis here is that supply and demand are always in terms of *stocks* (amounts at a given point in time) of assets, not in terms of *flows*. This approach is somewhat different from certain loanable funds analyses, which are conducted in terms of flows (loans per year). The **asset market approach** for understanding behavior in financial markets—which emphasizes stocks of assets rather than flows in determining asset prices—is now the dominant methodology used by financial economists because correctly conducting analyses in terms of flows is very tricky, especially when we encounter inflation.[4]

Changes in Equilibrium Interest Rates

We will now use the supply and demand framework for bonds to analyze why interest rates change. To avoid confusion, it is important to make the distinction between *movements along* a demand (or supply) curve and *shifts in* a demand (or supply) curve. When quantity demanded (or supplied) changes as a result of a change in the price of the bond (or, equivalently, a change in the interest rate), we have a *movement along* the demand (or supply) curve. The change in the quantity demanded when we move from point A to B to C in Figure 1 or Figure 2, for example, is a movement along a demand curve. A *shift in* the demand (or supply) curve, by contrast, occurs when the quantity demanded (or supplied) changes *at each given price (or interest rate)* of the bond in response to a change in some other factor besides the bond's price or interest rate. When one of these factors changes, causing a shift in the demand or supply curve, there will be a new equilibrium value for the interest rate.

In the following pages we will look at how the supply and demand curves shift in response to changes in variables, such as expected inflation and wealth, and what effects these changes have on the equilibrium value of interest rates.

Shifts in the Demand for Bonds

Our analysis of the determinants of asset demand at the beginning of the chapter provides a framework for deciding what factors cause the demand curve for bonds to shift. These factors include changes in four parameters:

---

[4]The asset market approach developed in the text is useful in understanding not only how interest rates behave but also how any asset price is determined. A second appendix to this chapter, which is on this book's website at **www.aw-bc.com/mishkin_eakins**, shows how the asset market approach can be applied to understanding the behavior of commodity markets; in particular, the gold market.

1. Wealth
2. Expected returns on bonds relative to alternative assets
3. Risk of bonds relative to alternative assets
4. Liquidity of bonds relative to alternative assets

To see how a change in each of these factors (holding all other factors constant) can shift the demand curve, let us look at some examples. (As a study aid, Table 2 summarizes the effects of changes in these factors on the bond demand curve.)

Wealth When the economy is growing rapidly in a business cycle expansion and wealth is increasing, the quantity of bonds demanded at each bond price (or interest rate) increases as shown in Figure 3. To see how this works, consider point B on the initial demand curve for bonds B_1^d. It tells us that at a bond price of $900 and an interest rate of 11.1%, the quantity of bonds demanded is $200 billion. With higher wealth, the quantity of bonds demanded at the same interest rate must rise, say, to $400 billion (point B′). Similarly, the higher wealth causes the quantity demanded at a bond price of $800 and an interest rate of 25% to rise from $400 billion to $600 billion (point D to D′). Continuing with this reasoning for every point on the initial demand curve B_1^d, we can see that the demand curve shifts to the right from B_1^d to B_2^d as is indicated by the arrows.

The conclusion we have reached is that *in a business cycle expansion with growing wealth, the demand for bonds rises and the demand curve for bonds shifts to the right.* Using the same reasoning, *in a recession, when income and wealth are falling, the demand for bonds falls, and the demand curve shifts to the left.*

Another factor that affects wealth is the public's propensity to save. If households save more, wealth increases and, as we have seen, the demand for bonds rises and the demand curve for bonds shifts to the right. Conversely, if people save less, wealth and the demand for bonds will fall and the demand curve shifts to the left.

Expected Returns For a one-year discount bond and a one-year holding period, the expected return and the interest rate are identical. No component of the expected return is unrelated to the bond price or the interest rate.

For bonds with maturities of greater than one year, the expected return may differ from the interest rate. For example, we saw in Chapter 3, Table 2, that a rise in the interest rate on a long-term bond from 10% to 20% would lead to a sharp decline in price and a very negative return. Hence if people begin to think that interest rates will be higher next year than they had originally anticipated, the expected return today on long-term bonds would fall, and the quantity demanded would fall at each interest rate. *Higher expected interest rates in the future decrease the demand for long-term bonds and shift the demand curve to the left.*

By contrast, a revision downward of expectations of future interest rates would mean that long-term bond prices would be expected to rise more than originally anticipated, and the resulting higher expected return today would raise the quantity demanded at each bond price and interest rate. *Lower expected interest rates in the future increase the demand for long-term bonds and shift the demand curve to the right* (as in Figure 3).

Changes in expected returns on other assets can also shift the demand curve for bonds. If people suddenly became more optimistic about the stock market

TABLE 2 SUMMARY *Factors That Shift the Demand Curve for Bonds*

Variable	Change in Variable	Change in Quantity Demanded	Shift in Demand Curve
Wealth	↑	↑	
Expected interest rate	↑	↓	
Expected inflation	↑	↓	
Riskiness of bonds relative to other assets	↑	↓	
Liquidity of bonds relative to other assets	↑	↑	

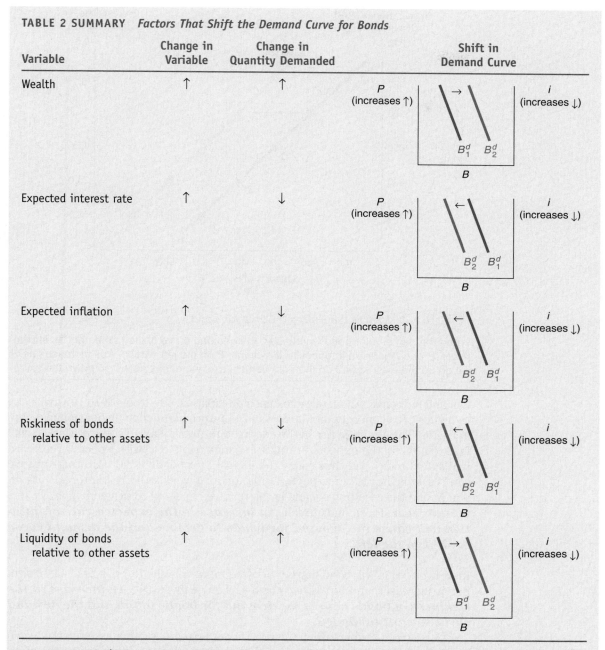

Note: Only increases (↑) in the variables are shown. The effect of decreases in the variables on the change in demand would be the opposite of those indicated in the remaining columns.

and began to expect higher stock prices in the future, both expected capital gains and expected returns on stocks would rise. With the expected return on bonds held constant, the expected return on bonds today relative to stocks would fall, lowering the demand for bonds and shifting the demand curve to the left.

A change in expected inflation is likely to alter expected returns on physical assets (also called *real assets*) such as automobiles and houses, which affect the

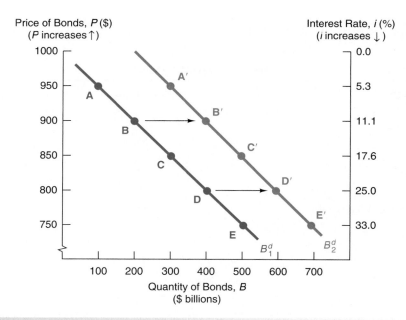

FIGURE 3 *Shift in the Demand Curve for Bonds*

When the demand for bonds increases, the demand curve shifts to the right as shown. (*Note: P* and *i* increase in opposite directions. *P* on the left vertical axis increases as we go up the axis, while *i* on the right vertical axis increases as we go down the axis.)

demand for bonds. An increase in expected inflation, say, from 5% to 10%, will lead to higher prices on cars and houses in the future and hence higher nominal capital gains. The resulting rise in the expected returns today on these real assets will lead to a fall in the expected return on bonds relative to the expected return on real assets today and thus cause the demand for bonds to fall. Alternatively, we can think of the rise in expected inflation as lowering the real interest rate on bonds, and the resulting decline in the relative expected return on bonds as causing the demand for bonds to fall. *An increase in the expected rate of inflation will cause the demand for bonds to decline and the demand curve to shift to the left.*

Risk If prices in the bond market become more volatile, the risk associated with bonds increases, and bonds become a less attractive asset. *An increase in the riskiness of bonds causes the demand for bonds to fall and the demand curve to shift to the left.*

Conversely, an increase in the volatility of prices in another asset market, such as the stock market, would make bonds more attractive. *An increase in the riskiness of alternative assets causes the demand for bonds to rise and the demand curve to shift to the right* (as in Figure 3).

Liquidity If more people started trading in the bond market and as a result it became easier to sell bonds quickly, the increase in their liquidity would cause the quantity of bonds demanded at each interest rate to rise. *Increased liquidity of bonds results in an increased demand for bonds, and the demand curve shifts to the right* (see Figure 3). *Similarly, increased liquidity of alternative assets lowers the demand for bonds and shifts the demand*

curve to the left. The reduction of brokerage commissions for trading common stocks that occurred when the fixed-rate commission structure was abolished in 1975, for example, increased the liquidity of stocks relative to bonds, and the resulting lower demand for bonds shifted the demand curve to the left.

Shifts in the Supply of Bonds

Certain factors can cause the supply curve for bonds to shift, among them these:

1. Expected profitability of investment opportunities
2. Expected inflation
3. Government activities

We will look at how the supply curve shifts when each of these factors changes (when all others remain constant). (As a study aid, Table 3 summarizes the effects of changes in these factors on the bond supply curve.)

Expected Profitability of Investment Opportunities The more profitable investments that a firm expects it can make, the more willing it will be to borrow in order

TABLE 3 SUMMARY *Factors That Shift the Supply of Bonds*

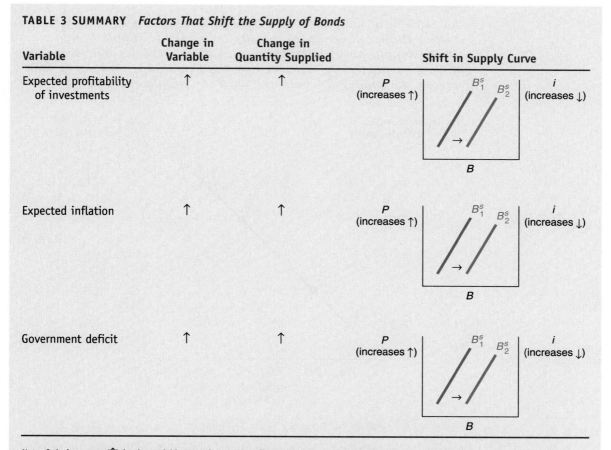

Variable	Change in Variable	Change in Quantity Supplied	Shift in Supply Curve		
Expected profitability of investments	↑	↑	P (increases ↑)		i (increases ↓)
Expected inflation	↑	↑	P (increases ↑)		i (increases ↓)
Government deficit	↑	↑	P (increases ↑)		i (increases ↓)

Note: Only increases (↑) in the variables are shown. The effect of decreases in the variables on the change in supply would be the opposite of those indicated in the remaining columns.

to finance these investments. When the economy is growing rapidly, as in a business cycle expansion, investment opportunities that are expected to be profitable abound, and the quantity of bonds supplied at any given bond price and interest rate will increase (see Figure 4). Therefore, ***in a business cycle expansion, the supply of bonds increases, and the supply curve shifts to the right. Likewise, in a recession, when there are far fewer expected profitable investment opportunities, the supply of bonds falls, and the supply curve shifts to the left.***

Expected Inflation As we saw in Chapter 3, the real cost of borrowing is more accurately measured by the real interest rate, which equals the (nominal) interest rate minus the expected inflation rate. For a given interest rate, when expected inflation increases, the real cost of borrowing falls; hence the quantity of bonds supplied increases at any given bond price and interest rate. ***An increase in expected inflation causes the supply of bonds to increase and the supply curve to shift to the right*** (see Figure 4).

Government Activities The activities of the government can influence the supply of bonds in several ways. The U.S. Treasury issues bonds to finance government deficits, the gap between the government's expenditures and its revenues. When these deficits are large, as they have been recently, the Treasury sells more bonds, and the quantity of bonds supplied at each bond price and interest rate increases. ***Higher government deficits increase the supply of bonds and shift the supply curve to the right*** (see Figure 4). ***On the other hand, government surpluses, as occurred in the late 1990s and early 2000s, decrease the supply of bonds and shift the supply curve to the left.***

Weekly updates on domestic and global economic, monetary, and policy trends influencing inflation are available at www.forecasts. org/inflation watch/index. htm.

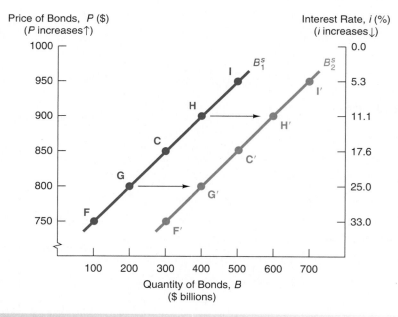

FIGURE 4 *Shift in the Supply Curve for Bonds*

When the supply of bonds increases, the supply curve shifts to the right. (*Note: P* and *i* increase in opposite directions. *P* on the left vertical axis increases as we go up the axis, while *i* on the right vertical axis increases as we go down the axis.)

State and local governments and other government agencies also issue bonds to finance their expenditures, and this can also affect the supply of bonds. We will see in later chapters that the conduct of monetary policy involves the purchase and sale of bonds, which in turn influences the supply of bonds.

Case

CHANGES IN THE EQUILIBRIUM INTEREST RATE DUE TO EXPECTED INFLATION OR BUSINESS CYCLE EXPANSIONS

We can now use our knowledge of how supply and demand curves shift to analyze how the equilibrium interest rate can change. The best way to do this is to pursue several cases that are particularly relevant to our understanding of how monetary policy affects interest rates.

Study Guide

Supply and demand analysis for the bond market is best learned by practicing case applications. When there is a case in the text and we look at how the interest rate changes because some economic variable increases, see if you can draw the appropriate shifts in the supply and demand curves when this same economic variable decreases. While you are practicing applications, keep two things in mind:

1. When you examine the effect of a variable change, remember that we are assuming that all other variables are unchanged; that is, we are making use of the *ceteris paribus* assumption.
2. Remember that the interest rate is negatively related to the bond price, so when the equilibrium bond price rises, the equilibrium interest rate falls. Conversely, if the equilibrium bond price moves downward, the equilibrium interest rate rises.

Changes in Expected Inflation: The Fisher Effect

We have already done most of the work to evaluate how a change in expected inflation affects the nominal interest rate in that we have already analyzed how a change in expected inflation shifts the supply and demand curves. Figure 5 shows the effect on the equilibrium interest rate of an increase in expected inflation.

Suppose that expected inflation is initially 5% and the initial supply and demand curves B_1^s and B_1^d intersect at point 1, where the equilibrium bond price is P_1 and the equilibrium interest rate is i_1. If expected inflation rises to 10%, the expected return on bonds relative to real assets falls for any given bond price and interest rate. As a result, the demand for bonds falls, and the demand curve shifts to the left from B_1^d to B_2^d. The rise in expected inflation also shifts the supply curve. At any given bond price and interest rate, the real cost of borrowing has declined, causing the quantity of bonds supplied to increase, and the supply curve shifts to the right from B_1^s to B_2^s.

When the demand and supply curves shift in response to the change in expected inflation, the equilibrium moves from point 1 to point 2, which is the intersection of B_2^d and B_2^s. The equilibrium bond price has fallen from P_1 to P_2, and because the bond price is negatively related to the interest rate (as is indicated by the interest rate rising as we go down the right vertical axis), this means that the interest rate has risen from i_1 to i_2. Note that Figure 5 has been drawn so that the equilibrium quantity of bonds remains the same for both point 1 and point 2. However, depending on the size of

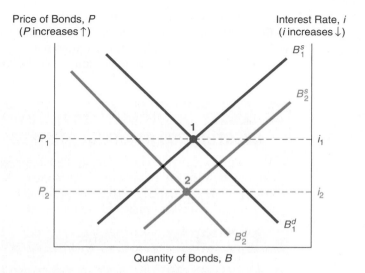

Price of Bonds, P
(P increases ↑)

Interest Rate, i
(i increases ↓)

Quantity of Bonds, B

FIGURE 5 *Response to a Change in Expected Inflation*

When expected inflation rises, the supply curve shifts from B_1^s to B_2^s, and the demand curve shifts from B_1^d to B_2^d. The equilibrium moves from point 1 to point 2, with the result that the equilibrium bond price (left axis) falls from P_1 to P_2 and the equilibrium interest rate (right axis) rises from i_1 to i_2. (*Note: P* and *i* increase in opposite directions. *P* on the left vertical axis increases as we go up the axis, while *i* on the right vertical axis increases as we go down the axis.)

the shifts in the supply and demand curves, the equilibrium quantity of bonds could either rise or fall when expected inflation rises.

Our supply and demand analysis has led us to an important observation: ***When expected inflation rises, interest rates will rise.*** This result has been named the **Fisher effect,** after Irving Fisher, the economist who first pointed out the relationship of expected inflation to interest rates. The accuracy of this prediction is shown in Figure 6. The interest rate on three-month Treasury bills has usually moved along with the expected inflation rate. Consequently, it is understandable that many economists recommend that the fight against inflation must be won if we want to lower interest rates.

Business Cycle Expansion

Figure 7 analyzes the effects of a business cycle expansion on interest rates. In a business cycle expansion, the amount of goods and services being produced in the economy rises, so national income increases. When this occurs, businesses will be more willing to borrow because they are likely to have many profitable investment opportunities for which they need financing. Hence at a given bond price and interest rate, the quantity of bonds that firms want to sell (that is, the supply of bonds) will increase. This means that in a business cycle expansion, the supply curve for bonds shifts to the right (see Figure 7) from B_1^s to B_2^s.

The expanding economy will also affect the demand for bonds. Our discussion of the determinants of asset demand tells us that as the economy

Annual Rate (%)

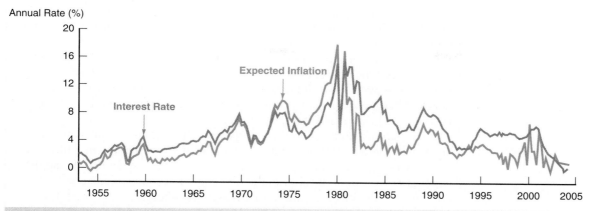

FIGURE 6   *Expected Inflation and Interest Rates (Three-Month Treasury Bills), 1953–2004*

Source: Expected inflation calculated using procedures outlined in Frederic S. Mishkin, "The Real Interest Rate: An Empirical Investigation," *Carnegie-Rochester Conference Series on Public Policy* 15 (1981): 151–200. This involves estimating expected inflation as a function of past interest rates, inflation, and time trends.

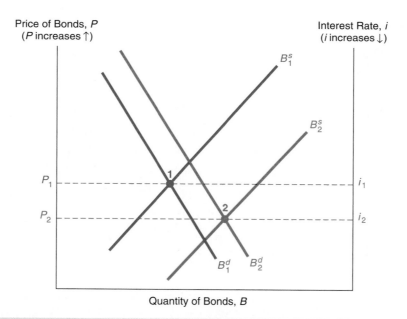

FIGURE 7   *Response to a Business Cycle Expansion*

In a business cycle expansion, when income and wealth are rising, the demand curve shifts rightward from B_1^d to B_2^d, and the supply curve shifts rightward from B_1^s to B_2^s. If the supply curve shifts to the right more than the demand curve, as in this figure, the equilibrium bond price (left axis) moves down from P_1 to P_2, and the equilibrium interest rate (right axis) rises from i_1 to i_2. (*Note*: P and i increase in opposite directions. P on the left vertical axis increases as we go up the axis, while i on the right vertical axis increases as we go down the axis.)

expands, wealth is likely to increase and the demand for bonds will rise as well. We see this in Figure 7, where the demand curve has shifted to the right from B_1^d to B_2^d.

Given that both the supply and demand curves have shifted to the right, we know that the new equilibrium reached at the intersection of B_2^d and B_2^s must also move to the right. However, depending on whether the supply curve shifts more than the demand curve or vice versa, the new equilibrium interest rate can either rise or fall.

The supply and demand analysis used here gives us an ambiguous answer to the question of what will happen to interest rates in a business cycle expansion. The figure has been drawn so that the shift in the supply curve is greater than the shift in the demand curve, causing the equilibrium bond price to fall to P_2, leading to a rise in the equilibrium interest rate to i_2. The reason the figure has been drawn so that a business cycle expansion and a rise in income lead to a higher interest rate is that this is the outcome we actually see in the data. Figure 8 plots the movement of the interest rate on three-month U.S. Treasury bills from 1951 to 2004 and indicates when the business cycle is undergoing recessions (shaded areas). As you can see, the interest rate rises during business cycle expansions and falls during recessions, which is what the supply and demand diagram indicates.

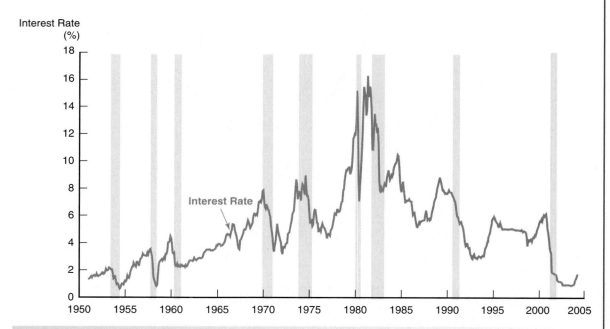

FIGURE 8 *Business Cycle and Interest Rates (Three-Month Treasury Bills), 1951–2004*

Shaded areas indicate periods of recession. The figure shows that interest rates rise during business cycle expansions and fall during contractions, which is what Figure 7 suggests would happen.

Source: Federal Reserve Board at www.federalreserve.gov/releases.

Case

EXPLAINING LOW JAPANESE INTEREST RATES

In the 1990s and early 2000s, Japanese interest rates became the lowest in the world. Indeed, in November 1998, an extraordinary event occurred: Interest rates on Japanese six-month Treasury bills turned slightly negative (see Chapter 3). Why did Japanese rates drop to such low levels?

In the late 1990s, Japan had been experiencing a prolonged recession, accompanied by a negative inflation rate. Using these facts, analysis similar to that used in the preceding case explains the low Japanese interest rates.

Negative inflation causes the demand for bonds to rise because the expected return on real assets falls, thereby raising the relative expected return on bonds and in turn causing the demand curve to shift to the right. The negative inflation also raises the real interest rate and therefore the real cost of borrowing for any given nominal rate, thereby causing the supply of bonds to contract and the supply curve to shift to the left. The outcome is then exactly the opposite of that graphed in Figure 5: The rightward shift of the demand curve and leftward shift of the supply curve lead to a rise in the bond price and a fall in interest rates.

The business cycle contraction in Japan also leads to lower interest rates because the resulting lack of investment opportunities decreases the supply of bonds, shifting the supply curve to the left. Although the demand curve also shifts to the left because wealth decreases during the business cycle contraction, we have seen in the preceding case that the demand curve shifts less than the supply curve, so that we get exactly the opposite outcome as that in Figure 7: The bond price rises, and the interest rates fall.

Usually we think that low interest rates are a good thing because they make it cheap to borrow. But the Japanese example shows that just as there is a fallacy in the adage "You can never be too rich or too thin"—maybe you can't be too rich, but you certainly can be too thin and do damage to your health—there is a fallacy in always thinking that lower interest rates are better. In Japan, the low and even negative interest rates are a sign that the Japanese economy is in real trouble, with falling prices and a contracting economy. Only when the Japanese economy returns to health will interest rates rise back to more normal levels.

Case

The *Wall Street Journal*

THE "CREDIT MARKETS" COLUMN

Now that we have an understanding of how supply and demand determine prices and interest rates in the bond market, we can use our analysis to understand discussions about bond prices and interest rates appearing in the financial press. Every day, the *Wall Street Journal* reports on developments in the bond market on the previous business day in its "Credit Markets" column, an example of which is found in the "Following the News" box on page 93. Let's see how statements in the "Credit Markets" column can be explained using our supply and demand framework.

The column featured in the "Following the News" box begins by stating that August's better job growth ends the notion that Treasury bonds will revisit the recent rally that had been lifting prices. This is exactly what our supply and demand analysis says should happen.

A stronger economy raises the supply of bonds because of increased investment opportunities and thus shifts the supply curve to the right, while it also increases the demand for bonds and shifts the demand curve to the right because a stronger economy raises wealth and income. However, as illustrated in Figure 7, because the supply curve generally shifts by more than the demand curve when the economy gets stronger, the price of bonds is likely to fall rather than rise.

The column also points out that the prospect of a stronger economy confirms that the Fed will maintain a measured pace of rate increases. Higher future interest rates imply that the price of bonds will be lower in the future, thus decreasing their expected return. The lower expected return causes the demand for bonds to be lower, so that the demand curve would shift to the left and the price of bonds would be lower. This provides another reason why the price of bonds is more likely to fall rather than rise.

However, the column also says that there is unlikely to be an aggressive rise in long-term bond yields because the Fed is expected to remain vigilant on inflation. The fact that inflation is not expected to get out of control means that the scenario depicted in Figure 6 is unlikely to happen, in which the demand curve shifts to the left because the relative expected return on bonds falls relative to real assets and the supply curve shifts to the right because the real cost of borrowing would fall for any given bond price and interest rate. Thus the likelihood of a sharp rise in interest rates is not high.

THE *WALL STREET JOURNAL*: FOLLOWING THE NEWS

The "Credit Markets" Column

The "Credit Markets" column appears daily in the *Wall Street Journal*; an example is presented here. It is found in the third section, "Money and Investing."

CREDIT MARKETS

Jobs Report Yields No Surprises

Stronger Data Likely Mean Interest Rates Will Keep Rising at a Deliberate Pace

By MICHAEL MACKENZIE
Dow Jones Newswires

NEW YORK — So much for the monthly jobs shocker.

The August employment report, which nearly matched consensus forecasts, was a reality check Friday for a government bond market that had grown accustomed to monthly payrolls data well out of line with market expectations. Investors and analysts believe August's better, though unspectacular, rate of job growth, confirms that the Federal Reserve will maintain a measured pace of rate increases for 2004, including a quarter-point move at the Sept. 21 Fed policy meeting.

"If there were any doubts about a Fed-rate hike on Sept. 21, this should dispel them," said Stephen Stanley, chief economist at RBS Greenwich Capital, in Greenwich, Conn., which sees quarter-percentage-point rate increases at each of the three remaining Fed meetings in 2004.

Coming on the heels of weaker payrolls data in June and July, the faster pace of payrolls growth in August ends the notion of Treasurys revisiting the technically driven rally that had been lifting prices. But yields may not rise sharply, given the expectations of a moderate pace of Fed-rate increases and possibly uneven news on economic growth.

Analysts expect most of the movement in the yield of the two-year note—the most sensitive of the actively traded Treasury benchmarks to monetary-policy expectations. "The front end is the most vulnerable part of the curve in the wake of the payroll data," noted Anton Pil, global head of fixed income at JP Morgan Private Bank in New York.

Yield Comparisons

Based on Merill Lynch Bond indexes, priced as of midafternoon Eastern time.

	9/3	9/2	52-WEEK HIGH	52-WEEK LOW
Corp. Govt. Master Treasury	3.96%	3.85%	4.47%	3.18%
1-10 yr	3.03	2.90	3.45	2.07
10+ yr	4.90	4.81	5.43	4.36
Agencies				
1-10 yr	3.36	3.22	3.86	2.25
10+ yr	5.27	5.16	5.93	4.66
Corporate				
1-10 yr High Quality	3.76	3.64	4.26	2.84
Medium Quality	4.33	4.22	4.86	3.48
10+ yr High Quality	5.73	5.65	6.26	5.23
Medium Quality	6.13	6.05	6.77	5.60
Yankee bonds (1)	4.33	4.22	4.81	3.53
Current-coupon mortgages (2)				
GNMA 4.99% (3)	5.21	5.12	5.82	4.53
FNMA 5.48%	5.23	5.12	5.92	4.58
FHLMC 5.48%	5.26	5.16	5.97	4.61
High-yield corporates	7.50	7.49	8.78	6.88
Tax-Exempt Bonds				
7-12 yr G.O. (AA)	3.67	3.61	4.33	3.08
12-22 yr G.O. (AA)	4.18	4.13	4.93	3.85
22+ yr revenue (A)	4.87	4.82	5.42	4.31

Note: High quality rated AAA-AA; medium quality A-BBB/Baa; high yield, BB/Ba-C.
(1) Dollar-denominated, SEC-registered bonds of foreign issuers sold in the U.S. (2) Reflects the 52-week high and low of mortgage-backed securities indexes rather than the individual securities shown. (3) Government guaranteed.

Helping to cap any aggressive rise in longer yields is the fact that the outlook for measured rate increases "sends a clear message to holders of long-dated Treasurys that the Fed will remain vigilant on inflation," added Mr. Pil.

The two-year yield, which moves inversely to its price, jumped 0.12 percentage point Friday, after the labor report.

Bond trading halted early that day, and the market was closed yesterday in the U.S. in observance of Labor Day.

At the 2 p.m. EDT early close on Friday, the benchmark 10-year note was down 19/32 point, or $5.94 per $1,000 face value, at 99 23/32. Its yield rose to 4.287% from 4.215% Thursday. The 30-year bond was down 27/32 point at 104

21/32 to yield 5.055%, up from 5.000% Thursday.

The August gain in payrolls is "a good number for the Fed and the president, and a bad number for traders," said Mike Franzese, head of U.S. trading at Zions First National Bank in Jersey City, N.J.

Following the jobs report, all respondents in a Dow Jones Newswires/CNBC survey of primary dealers in government securities predicted that the Sept. 21 Fed policy meeting will result in a quarter-percentage-point rise, to 1.75%, in the federal-funds-rate target. Primary dealers underwrite Treasury debt auctions and deal directly with the Fed.

The Practicing Manager

PROFITING FROM INTEREST-RATE FORECASTS

Given the importance of interest rates, the media frequently report interest-rate forecasts, as the "Following the News" box pn pages 94–95 indicates. Because changes in interest rates have a major impact on the profitability of financial institutions, financial managers care a great deal about the path of future interest rates. Managers of financial institutions obtain interest-rate forecasts either by hiring their own staff economists to generate forecasts or by purchasing forecasts from other financial institutions or economic forecasting firms.

Several methods are used to produce interest-rate forecasts. One of the most popular is based on the supply and demand for bonds framework described in this chapter, and it is used by financial institutions such as Salomon Smith Barney, Morgan Guaranty Trust Company, and the Prudential Insurance Company.[5] Using this framework, analysts predict what will happen to the factors that affect the supply of and demand for bonds—factors such as the strength of the economy, the profitability of investment opportunities, the expected inflation rate, and the size of government deficits and borrowing. They then use the supply and demand analysis outlined in the chapter to come up with their interest-rate forecasts. A variation of this approach makes use of the *Flow of Funds Accounts* produced by the Federal Reserve. These data show the sources and uses of funds by different sectors of the American economy. By looking at how well the supply of credit and the demand for credit by different sectors match up, forecasters attempt to predict future changes in interest rates.

Forecasting done with the supply and demand for bonds framework often does not make use of formal economic models but rather depends on the judgment or "feel" of the forecaster. An alternative method of forecasting interest rates makes use of **econometric models,** models whose equations are estimated with statistical procedures using past data. These models involve interlocking equations that, once input variables such as the behavior of government spending and monetary policy are plugged in, produce simultaneous forecasts of many variables including interest rates. The basic assumption of these forecasting models is that the estimated relationships between variables will continue to hold up in the future. Given this assumption, the forecaster makes predictions of the expected path of the input variables and then lets the model generate forecasts of variables such as interest rates.

Many of these econometric models are quite large, involving hundreds and sometimes over a thousand equations, and consequently require computers to produce their forecasts. Prominent examples of these large-scale econometric models used by the private sector include those developed by Wharton Econometric Forecasting Associates, Chase Econometric Associates, and Data Resources, Inc. To generate its interest-rate forecasts, the Board of Governors of the Federal Reserve System makes use of its own large-scale econometric model, although it makes use of judgmental forecasts as well.

---

[5]Another framework used to produce forecasts of interest rates, developed by John Maynard Keynes, analyzes the supply and demand for money and is called the *liquidity preference framework.* This framework is discussed in a third appendix to this chapter which can be found on the book's website at **www.aw-bc.com/mishkin_eakins.**

Managers of financial institutions rely on these forecasts to make decisions about which assets they should hold. A manager who believes that the forecast that long-term interest rates will fall in the future is reliable would seek to purchase long-term bonds for the asset account because, as we have seen in Chapter 3, the drop in interest rates will produce large capital gains. Conversely, if forecasts say that interest rates are likely to rise in the future, the manager will prefer to hold short-term bonds or loans in the portfolio in order to avoid potential capital losses on long-term securities.

Forecasts of interest rates also help managers decide whether to borrow long-term or short-term. If interest rates are forecast to rise in the future, the financial institution manager will want to lock in the low interest rates by borrowing long-term; if the forecasts say that interest rates will fall, the manager will seek to borrow short-term in order to take advantage of low interest-rate costs in the future.

Clearly, good forecasts of future interest rates are extremely valuable to the financial institution manager, who, not surprisingly, would be willing to pay a lot for accurate forecasts. Unfortunately, interest-rate forecasting is a perilous business, and even the top forecasters, to their embarrassment, are frequently far off in their forecasts.

THE *WALL STREET JOURNAL*: FOLLOWING THE NEWS

Forecasting Interest Rates

Forecasting interest rates is a time-honored profession. Financial economists are hired (sometimes at very high salaries) to forecast interest rates because businesses need to know what the rates will be in order to plan their future spending, and banks and investors require interest-rate forecasts in order to decide which assets to buy. Interest-rate forecasters predict what will happen to the factors that affect the supply and demand for bonds and for money—factors such as the strength of the economy, the profitability of investment opportunities, the expected inflation rate, and the size of government budget deficits and borrowing. They then use the supply and demand analysis we have outlined in this chapter to come up with their interest-rate forecasts.

The *Wall Street Journal* reports interest-rate forecasts by leading prognosticators twice a year (early January and July) in its "Economy" column or in its "Credit Markets" column, which surveys developments in the bond market daily. Forecasting interest rates is a perilous business. To their embarrassment, even the top experts are frequently far off in their forecasts.

THE WALL STREET JOURNAL
FORECASTING SURVEY FOR 2004 AND 2005

In percent except for dollar vs. yen and dollar vs. euro, ranked by first-quarter GDP forecasts

	JULY 2004 SURVEY						NEWS FORECASTS FOR 2005									
	3-MO. TREASURY BILL[1] DEC.	10-YR NOTE DEC.	GDP[2] Q1 2004	CPI[3] NOV.	$U.S. VS. EURO DEC.	UNEM-PLOY-MENT NOV.	3-MO. TREASURY BILL[1] JUNE	10-YR NOTE JUNE	GDP[2] Q1 2005	Q2 2005	Q3 2005	Q4 2005	CPI[3] MAY	$U.S. VS. YEN JUNE	$U.S. VS. EURO JUNE	UNEM-PLOY-MENT MAY
Gail Fesler, Conference Board	1.75	4.75	5.9	2.6	1.08	5.0	3.25	4.50	5.5	5.3	4.1	3.3	3.3	110	1.26	5.0
Jim Mell/Arun Raha, Eaton Corp.	2.10	4.70	4.1	3.5	1.18	5.4	3.10	4.40	4.5	4.6	3.6	4.7	2.5	105	1.32	5.2
John Ryding/David Malpass, Bear Sterns	2.20	5.00	4.9	2.7	1.20	5.3	3.40	5.40	4.4	4.1	3.5	3.6	2.4	98	1.25	5.1
David Lereah, National Assoc. of Realtors	2.05	5.10	4.3	2.5	1.20	5.3	2.80	4.70	4.3	4.4	4.2	3.9	2.5	100	1.40	5.2
Joe Carson, Alliance Bernstein	New Participant						3.00	5.00	4.2	4.6	4.1	4.3	3.0	100	1.35	5.2
Brian S. Wesbury, Griffin, Kubik	2.30	5.50	5.6	3.3	1.15	5.4	3.20	5.40	4.2	4.2	4.1	4.3	3.0	108	1.27	5.0
William T. Wilson, Keystone India	2.30	4.80	4.8	2.5	1.20	5.5	3.70	4.80	4.1	3.5	3.5	3.5	3.1	112	1.28	5.4
William B. Hummer, Wayne Hummer Invest.	2.02	5.10	4.2	2.4	1.16	5.3	3.30	4.90	4.1	3.8	3.6	3.5	2.5	101	1.22	5.4
Stephen Gallagher, SG CIB	2.00	5.15	4.6	2.7	1.15	5.3	3.25	4.75	4.1	3.8	3.5	3.5	2.2	100	1.32	5.2
David L. Littmann, Comerica Bank	1.88	5.60	4.6	2.8	1.10	5.3	2.85	4.65	4.1	3.6	3.5	3.5	2.9	115	1.20	5.1
Richard J. DeKaser, National City Corp.	2.00	4.80	4.5	2.9	1.26	5.3	2.80	4.80	4.0	4.2	3.8	3.6	2.2	100	1.35	5.2
Peter Hooper, Deutsche Bank	2.00	5.40	5.1	3.0	1.30	5.0	3.35	5.00	4.0	4.1	4.0	4.1	2.4	97	1.38	5.3

Lawrence Kudlow, Kudlow & Co.	2.50	5.25	6.0	3.0	1.15	5.4	3.10	4.80	**4.0**	4.2	4.2	4.3	2.5	110	1.27	5.2
Ian Sheperdson, High Frequency	2.50	5.25	5.0	3.2	1.15	5.1	3.25	5.50	**4.0**	4.5	4.5	3.5	2.1	110	1.20	5.0
Sung Won Sohn, Hanmi Bank[5]	1.85	5.14	4.5	2.0	1.20	5.4	2.85	4.60	**3.9**	3.9	3.9	4.1	2.0	102	1.35	5.3
Saul Hymans, University of Michigan	1.96	4.95	5.0	2.9	1.28	5.5	2.90	4.85	**3.9**	3.5	3.3	3.4	2.4	100	1.34	5.2
Robert DiClemente, Citigroup	2.00	5.00	5.1	2.8	1.27	5.4	3.15	4.55	**3.9**	4.0	4.5	4.0	2.3	102	1.30	5.2
James F. Smith, SIOR and UNC	1.94	4.53	5.3	1.4	0.99	4.7	2.81	4.52	**3.9**	3.1	4.6	4.8	-0.9	117	1.12	4.7
David W. Berson, Fannie Mae	2.05	5.11	4.3	2.7	1.25	5.3	2.95	4.45	**3.9**	3.9	4.0	3.7	2.8	101	1.33	5.3
Mickey Levy, Bank of America	2.20	5.10	3.6	2.9	1.14	5.4	3.10	4.60	**3.8**	3.8	3.9	3.9	2.5	103	1.32	5.3
J. Prakken/C. Varvares, Macroeconomic Advis.	1.88	5.25	4.6	2.6	1.20	5.3	2.80	4.90	**3.8**	3.8	3.9	4.0	2.4	102	1.32	5.3
Neal Soss, CSFB	N.A.	5.10	4.2	3.3	1.20	5.4	N.A.	4.65	**3.7**	3.7	3.7	3.7	2.2	100	1.30	5.2
Gene Huang, FedEx Corp.	1.40	5.00	3.2	2.8	1.22	5.5	2.90	5.10	**3.6**	3.3	3.1	3.4	2.8	102	1.34	5.3
Daniel E. Laufenberg, American Express	2.10	5.20	4.2	2.6	1.22	5.4	3.50	5.10	**3.6**	3.1	3.8	3.7	2.4	105	1.28	5.2
Allen Sinal, Decision Economics	2.41	5.47	4.2	3.6	1.25	5.1	3.31	4.58	**3.6**	3.4	3.1	2.8	3.0	97	1.46	5.2
Tim McGee, US Trust	2.25	5.05	4.0	2.9	1.20	5.3	3.40	4.60	**3.5**	3.6	3.8	3.6	2.2	95	1.40	5.2
Susan M. Sterne, Economic Analysis Assoc.	3.00	5.50	4.9	3.1	1.18	5.0	3.30	5.20	**3.5**	3.1	4.2	3.8	2.5	106	1.28	5.0
Scott Anderson, Wells Fargo		New Participant					2.85	4.70	**3.5**	3.6	3.4	3.6	2.8	100	1.36	5.2
Ram Bhagavatula, The Royal Bank of Scotland	2.15	5.15	4.3	3.2	1.17	5.3	3.35	5.25	**3.5**	4.2	4.0	3.5	2.4	100	1.28	5.0
Henry Witinfore, Barclays Capital	2.20	5.35	4.8	3.0	1.10	5.0	2.95	4.80	**3.5**	4.0	3.5	3.5	2.4	98	1.28	4.9
David Wyss, Standard & Poors	2.00	5.10	4.4	3.1	1.28	5.4	3.00	4.60	**3.5**	3.4	3.1	2.9	2.2	98	1.40	5.2
David Resler, Nomura Securities International	2.25	5.30	3.9	3.3	1.17	5.5	3.00	4.80	**3.5**	3.7	3.9	3.8	2.5	101	1.38	5.4
Mark Zandi, Economy.com	1.90	5.25	4.1	2.5	1.2	5.6	3.10	5.00	**3.4**	29	3.0	3.2	2.6	105	1.30	5.5
Narlman Behravesh, Global Insight	2.15	5.15	4.6	3.2	1.28	5.4	3.00	4.75	**3.3**	3.3	3.0	2.9	2.3	99	1.41	5.3
Maria Florini Ramirez, MFR	2.30	5.25	4.1	3.0	1.20	5.4	2.95	5.25	**3.3**	3.3	3.2	3.1	2.8	97	1.35	5.2
Gary Thayer, A.G. Edwards	1.80	4.90	4.7	2.2	1.24	5.2	3.10	4.80	**3.3**	2.9	4.0	3.0	2.4	111	1.50	5.4
J. Dewey Deane, Vanderbilt University	2.10	5.25	4.3	2.2	1.24	5.2	3.00	5.00	**3.3**	3.0	3.0	3.0	4.0	105	1.50	5.4
Donald H. Straszhelm, Straszhelm Global Advis.	2.25	5.50	4.3	2.3	1.20	5.4	3.00	4.75	**3.3**	3.3	3.0	3.0	2.5	100	1.40	5.5
Richard Berner/David Greenlaw, Morgan Stanley	2.22	5.10	4.5	3.0	1.20	5.4	3.15	4.90	**3.2**	3.6	4.3	4.5	2.2	95	1.37	5.5
Maury Harris, UBS	2.15	5.00	4.0	2.7	1.32	5.5	3.40	4.80	**3.2**	2.7	3.0	3.0	1.9	103	1.36	5.3
Nicholas S. Perna, Perna Associates	2.35	5.29	3.9	3.2	1.17	5.3	3.14	5.21	**3.1**	3.5	3.4	3.7	2.9	100	1.43	5.2
Edward Leamer, UCLA Anderson Forecast	1.74	5.25	3.0	4.0	N.A.	5.8	2.50	5.20	**3.1**	3.1	2.8	2.7	2.7	N.A.	N.A.	5.5
Douglas Duncan, Mortgage Bankers Association	1.80	5.20	4.2	3.4	N.A.	5.4	2.30	4.40	**3.1**	3.2	3.2	3.2	1.4	N.A.	N.A.	5.5
Tracy Herrick, Private Bank of the Peninsula	2.05	5.60	4.3	3.2	1.27	5.2	3.35	4.25	**3.0**	2.6	2.2	1.8	3.3	106	1.28	5.3
Stuart G. Hoffman, PNC Financial	1.95	5.20	3.8	2.9	1.18	5.4	2.95	4.70	**3.0**	3.2	3.4	3.4	2.7	99	1.36	5.2
Paul L. Kasriel, Northern Trust Co.	1.90	5.05	3.9	3.1	1.25	5.2	2.40	4.65	**3.0**	3.5	3.7	3.5	2.7	100	1.35	5.5
Mike Cosgrove, Econoclast	1.85	5.00	3.7	2.0	1.15	5.3	2.90	4.50	**3.0**	3.5	3.5	3.1	2.3	110	1.25	5.3
John Lonski, Moody's	2.30	5.20	4.2	3.2	1.17	5.4	3.05	4.70	**3.0**	3.6	4.3	4.5	2.5	105	1.30	5.3
Ethan S. Harris, Lehman Brothers	2.50	5.30	4.1	3.5	1.25	5.2	3.00	4.40	**3.0**	3.5	3.7	3.7	2.6	100	1.45	5.2
Kurt Karl, Swiss Re	2.30	5.20	3.7	2.6	1.25	5.3	3.30	4.70	**3.0**	3.0	3.4	3.3	2.3	100	1.37	5.2
John Silvia, Wachovia	2.15	5.10	4.5	2.2	1.16	5.4	3.15	4.60	**2.8**	3.1	3.2	3.2	2.8	100	1.38	5.4
Richard D. Rippe, Prudential Equity Group	1.80	5.00	4.4	2.6	1.25	5.4	2.95	4.80	**2.7**	4.1	4.2	4.4	2.5	98	1.36	5.2
William Dudley, Goldman, Sachs & Co.	2.10	4.70	4.0	2.9	1.30	5.4	3.00	5.00	**2.5**	3.5	3.5	3.0	2.6	98	1.35	5.2
David Rosenberg, Merrill Lynch	N.A.	5.25	N.A.	3.0	1.33	5.5	2.40	3.80	**2.5**	3.0	3.3	3.8	2.2	89	1.32	5.6
Ellen Hughes-Cromwick, Ford Motor	1.60	4.75	3.8	2.1	1.22	5.5	2.75	5.25	**2.2**	2.7	3.2	3.4	2.4	103	1.33	5.4
Robert Shrouds/Robert Fry, Dupont	2.00	5.20	4.2	3.1	1.22	5.3	2.75	4.50	**1.5**	2.5	3.0	3.0	2.3	105	1.35	5.4
AVERAGES[4]	2.08	5.14	4.4	2.9	1.20	5.3	3.04	4.79	**3.5**	3.6	3.6	3.6	2.5	102	1.33	5.3
ACTUAL Numbers as of Dec. 31	2.21	4.22	3.9	3.5	1.36	5.4										

N.A.=Not Available; [1]Treasury bill rates are on a bond-equivalent basis; [2]Real gross domestic product; annualized growth rate; [3]Year-to-year change in the consumer price index ; [4]Averages are for economists called at time of survey; [5]Did not participate in January survey.

Summary

1. The quantity demanded of an asset is (a) positively related to wealth, (b) positively related to the expected return on the asset relative to alternative assets, (c) negatively related to the riskiness of the asset relative to alternative assets, and (d) positively related to the liquidity of the asset relative to alternative assets.

2. Diversification (the holding of more than one asset) benefits investors because it reduces the risk they face, and the benefits are greater the less returns on securities move together.

3. The supply and demand analysis for bonds, known as the loanable funds framework, provides one theory of how interest rates are determined. It predicts that interest rates will change when there is a change in demand because of changes in income (or wealth), expected returns, risk, or liquidity, or when there is a change in supply because of changes in the attractiveness of investment opportunities, the real cost of borrowing, or government activities.

Key Terms

asset, *p. 71*
asset market approach, *p. 81*
demand curve, *p. 75*
econometric model, *p. 94*
excess demand, *p. 79*
excess supply, *p. 78*

expected return, *p. 71*
Fisher effect, *p. 88*
liquidity, *p. 71*
loanable funds, *p. 80*
loanable funds framework,
   p. 81

market equilibrium, *p. 78*
risk, *p. 71*
standard deviation, *p. 73*
supply curve, *p. 78*
wealth, *p. 71*

Questions

1. Explain why you would be more or less willing to buy a share of Polaroid stock in the following situations:

   a. Your wealth falls.

   b. You expect it to appreciate in value.

   c. The bond market becomes more liquid.

   d. You expect gold to appreciate in value.

   e. Prices in the bond market become more volatile.

2. Explain why you would be more or less willing to buy a house under the following circumstances:

   a. You just inherited $100,000.

   b. Real estate commissions fall from 6% of the sales price to 4% of the sales price.

   c. You expect Polaroid stock to double in value next year.

   d. Prices in the stock market become more volatile.

   e. You expect housing prices to fall.

3. "The more risk-averse people are, the more likely they are to diversify." Is this statement true, false, or uncertain? Explain your answer.

4. I own a professional football team, and I plan to diversify by purchasing shares in either a company that owns a pro basketball team or a pharmaceutical company. Which of these two investments is more likely to reduce the overall risk I face? Why?

5. "No one who is risk-averse will ever buy a security that has a lower expected return, more risk, and less liquidity than another security." Is this statement true, false, or uncertain? Explain your answer.

For items 6–14, answer each question by drawing the appropriate supply and demand diagrams.

6. An important way in which the Federal Reserve decreases the money supply is by selling bonds to the public. Using a supply and demand analysis for bonds, show what effect this action has on interest rates.

7. Using the supply and demand for bonds framework, show why interest rates are procyclical (rising when the economy is expanding and falling during recessions).

8. Why should a rise in the price level (but not in expected inflation) cause interest rates to rise when the nominal money supply is fixed?

9. Find the "Credit Markets" column in the *Wall Street Journal*. Underline the statements in the column that explain bond price movements, and draw the appropriate supply and demand diagrams that support these statements.

10. What effect will a sudden increase in the volatility of gold prices have on interest rates?

11. How might a sudden increase in people's expectations of future real estate prices affect interest rates?

12. Explain what effect a large federal deficit might have on interest rates.

13. Using a supply and demand analysis for bonds, show what the effect is on interest rates when the riskiness of bonds rises.

14. Will there be an effect on interest rates if brokerage commissions on stocks fall? Explain your answer.

Predicting the Future

15. The president of the United States announces in a press conference that he will fight the higher inflation rate with a new anti-inflation program. Predict what will happen to interest rates if the public believes him.

16. The chairman of the Fed announces that interest rates will rise sharply next year, and the market believes him. What will happen to today's interest rate on AT&T bonds, such as the $8\frac{1}{8}$ s of 2022?

17. Predict what will happen to interest rates if the public suddenly expects a large increase in stock prices.

18. Predict what will happen to interest rates if prices in the bond market become more volatile.

19. If the next chair of the Federal Reserve Board has a reputation for advocating an even slower rate of money growth than the current chair, what will happen to interest rates? Discuss the possible resulting situations.

Quantitative Problems

1. You own a $1000-par zero-coupon bond that has five years of remaining maturity. You plan on selling the bond in one year, and believe that the required yield next year will have the following probability distribution:

Probability	Required Yield %
0.1	6.60%
0.2	6.75%
0.4	7.00%
0.2	7.20%
0.1	7.45%

  a. What is your expected price when you sell the bond?

  b. What is the standard deviation of the bond price?

2. Consider a $1000-par junk bond paying a 12% annual coupon with two years, to maturity. The issuing company has a 20% chance of defaulting this year; in which case, the bond would not pay anything. If the company survives the first year, paying the annual coupon payment, it then has a 25% chance of defaulting in the second year. If the company defaults in the second year, neither the final coupon payment nor par value of the bond will be paid.

  a. What price must investors pay for this bond to expect a 10% yield to maturity?

  b. At that price, what is the expected holding period return and standard deviation of returns? Assume that periodic cash flows are reinvested at 10%.

3. Last month, corporations supplied $250 billion in one-year discount bonds to investors at an average market rate of 11.8%. This month, an additional $25 billion in one-year discount bonds became available, and market rates increased to 12.2%. Assuming a loanable funds framework for interest rates, and that the demand curve remains constant, derive a linear equation for the demand for bonds, using prices instead of interest rates.

4. An economist has concluded that, near the point of equilibrium, the demand curve and supply curve for one-year discount bonds can be estimated using the following equations:

$$B^d: \text{Price} = \frac{-2}{5}\text{Quantity} + 940$$
$$B^s: \text{Price} = \text{Quantity} + 500$$

  a. What is the expected equilibrium price and quantity of bonds in this market?

  b. Given your answer to part (a), which is the expected interest rate in this market?

5. The demand curve and supply curve for one-year discount bonds were estimated using the following equations:

$$B^d: \text{Price} = \frac{-2}{5}\text{Quantity} + 940$$
$$B^s: \text{Price} = \text{Quantity} + 500$$

Following a dramatic increase in the value of the stock market, many retirees started moving money out of the stock market and into bonds. This resulted in a parallel shift in the demand for bonds, such that the price of bonds at all quantities increased $50. Assuming no change in the supply equation for bonds, what is the new equilibrium price and quantity? What is the new market interest rate?

6. The demand curve and supply curve for one-year discount bonds were estimated using the following equations:

$$B^d: \text{Price} = \frac{-2}{5}\text{Quantity} + 990$$
$$B^s: \text{Price} = \text{Quantity} + 500$$

As the stock market continued to rise, the Federal Reserve felt the need to increase the interest rates. As a result, the new market interest rate increased to 19.65%, but the equilibrium quantity remained unchanged. What are the new demand and supply equations? Assume parallel shifts in the equations.

Web Exercises

The Behavior of Interest Rates

1. One of the largest single influences on the level of interest rates is inflation. There are a number of sites that report inflation over time. Go to **ftp://ftp.bls.gov/pub/special.requests/cpi/cpiai.txt** and review the data available. Note that the last columns report various averages. Move these data into an Excel spreadsheet using the method in Chapter 1. What has the average rate of inflation been since 1950, 1960, 1970, 1980, and 1990? What year had the lowest level of inflation? What year had the highest level of inflation?

2. Increasing prices erode the purchasing power of the dollar. It is interesting to compute what goods would have cost at some point in the past after adjusting for inflation. Go to **www.jsc.nasa.gov/bu2/inflate.html**. What would a car that cost $22,000 today have cost during the year that you were born?

Web Appendices

Please visit our website at **www.aw-bc.com/mishkin_eakins** to read the Web appendices to Chapter 4:

- Appendix 1: *Models of Asset Pricing*
- Appendix 2: *Supply and Demand in the Market for Money: The Liquidity Preference Framework*
- Appendix 3: *Applying the Asset Market Approach to a Commodity Market: The Case of Gold*

How Do Risk and Term Structure Affect Interest Rates?

Preview

In our supply and demand analysis of interest-rate behavior in Chapter 4, we examined the determination of just one interest rate. Yet we saw earlier that there are enormous numbers of bonds on which the interest rates can and do differ. In this chapter we complete the interest-rate picture by examining the relationship of the various interest rates to one another. Understanding why they differ from bond to bond can help businesses, banks, insurance companies, and private investors decide which bonds to purchase as investments or which ones to sell.

We first look at why bonds with the same term to maturity have different interest rates. The relationship among these interest rates is called the **risk structure of interest rates**, although risk, liquidity, and income tax rules all play a role in determining the risk structure. A bond's term to maturity also affects its interest rate, and the relationship among interest rates on bonds with different terms to maturity is called the **term structure of interest rates**. In this chapter we examine how risk and term structure cause fluctuations in interest rates relative to one another and look at a number of theories that explain these fluctuations.

Risk Structure of Interest Rates

Figure 1 shows the yields to maturity for several categories of long-term bonds from 1919 to 2004. It shows us two important features of interest-rate behavior for bonds of the same maturity: Interest rates on different categories of bonds differ from one another in any given year, and the spread (or difference) between the interest rates varies over time. The interest rates on municipal bonds, for example, are above those on U.S. government (Treasury) bonds in the late 1930s but lower thereafter. In addition, the spread between the interest rates on Baa corporate bonds (riskier than Aaa corporate bonds) and U.S. government bonds is

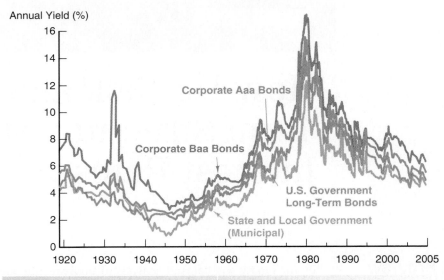

Annual Yield (%)

FIGURE 1   *Long-Term Bond Yields, 1919–2004*

Source: http://www.federalreserve.gov/releases/H15/data.htm.

very large during the Great Depression years 1930–1933, is smaller during the 1940s–1960s, and then widens again afterwards. What factors are responsible for these phenomena?

Default Risk

One attribute of a bond that influences its interest rate is its risk of **default,** which occurs when the issuer of the bond is unable or unwilling to make interest payments when promised or pay off the face value when the bond matures. A corporation suffering big losses, such as Chrysler Corporation did in the 1970s, might be more likely to suspend interest payments on its bonds.[1] The default risk on its bonds would therefore be quite high. By contrast, U.S. Treasury bonds have usually been considered to have no default risk because the federal government can always increase taxes to pay off its obligations. Bonds like these with no default risk are called **default-free bonds.** (However, during the budget negotiations in Congress in 1995 and 1996, the Republicans threatened to let Treasury bonds default, and this had an impact on the bond market, as the case following this section indicates.) The spread between the interest rates on bonds with default risk and default-free bonds, called the **risk premium,** indicates how much additional interest people must earn in order to be willing to hold that risky bond. Our supply and demand analysis of the bond market in Chapter 4 can be used to explain why a bond with default risk always has a positive risk premium and why the higher the default risk is, the larger the risk premium will be.

---

[1]Chrysler did not default on its loans in this period, but it would have were it not for a government bailout plan intended to preserve jobs that in effect provided Chrysler with funds that were used to pay off creditors.

To examine the effect of default risk on interest rates, let us look at the supply and demand diagrams for the default-free (U.S. Treasury) and corporate long-term bond markets in Figure 2. To make the diagrams somewhat easier to read, let's assume that initially there is no possibility of default on the corporate bonds, so they are default-free like U.S. Treasury bonds. In this case, these two bonds have the same attributes (identical risk and maturity); their equilibrium prices and interest rates will initially be equal $(P_1^c = P_1^T$ and $i_1^c = i_1^T)$, and the risk premium on corporate bonds $(i_1^c - i_1^T)$ will be zero.

If the possibility of a default increases because a corporation begins to suffer large losses, the default risk on corporate bonds will increase, and the expected

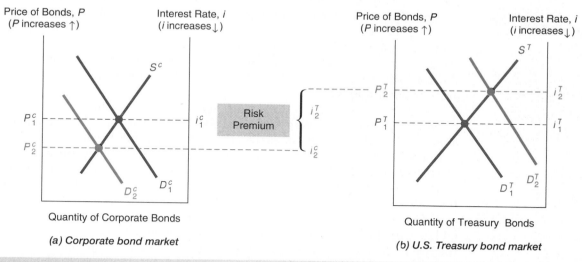

FIGURE 2 *Response to an Increase in Default Risk on Corporate Bonds*

An increase in default risk on corporate bonds shifts the demand curve from D_1^c to D_2^c. Simultaneously, it shifts the demand curve for Treasury bonds from D_1^T to D_2^T. The equilibrium price for corporate bonds (left axis) falls from P_1^c to P_2^c, and the equilibrium interest rate on corporate bonds (right axis) rises from i_1^c to i_2^c. In the Treasury market, the equilibrium bond price rises from P_1^T to P_2^T, and the equilibrium interest rate falls from i_1^T to i_2^T. The brace indicates the difference between i_2^c and i_2^T, the risk premium on corporate bonds. (*Note:* P and i increase in opposite directions. P on the left vertical axis increases as we go up the axis, while i on the right vertical axis increases as we go down the axis.)

return on these bonds will decrease. In addition, the corporate bond's return will be more uncertain as well. Our analysis of the determinants of asset demand predicts that because the expected return on the corporate bond falls relative to the expected return on the default-free Treasury bond while its relative riskiness rises, the corporate bond is less desirable (holding everything else equal), and demand for it will fall. The demand curve for corporate bonds in panel (a) of Figure 2 then shifts to the left from D_1^c to D_2^c.

At the same time, the expected return on default-free Treasury bonds increases relative to the expected return on corporate bonds while their relative riskiness declines. The Treasury bonds thus become more desirable, and demand rises, as shown in panel (b) by the rightward shift in the demand curve for these bonds from D_1^T to D_2^T.

As we can see in Figure 2, the equilibrium price for corporate bonds (left axis) falls from P_1^c to P_2^c, and since the bond price is negatively related to the interest rate, the equilibrium interest rate on corporate bonds (right axis) rises from i_1^c to i_2^c. At the same time, however, the equilibrium price for the Treasury bonds rises from P_1^T to P_2^T, and the equilibrium interest rate falls from i_1^T to i_2^T. The spread between the interest rates on corporate and default-free bonds—that is, the risk premium on corporate bonds—has risen from zero to $i_2^c - i_2^T$. We can now conclude that *a bond with default risk will always have a positive risk premium, and an increase in its default risk will raise the risk premium.*

Because default risk is so important to the size of the risk premium, purchasers of bonds need to know whether a corporation is likely to default on its bonds. This information is provided by **credit-rating agencies,** investment advisory firms that rate the quality of corporate and municipal bonds in terms of the probability of default. Table 1 provides the ratings and their descriptions for the two largest credit-rating agencies, Moody's Investor Service and Standard and Poor's Corporation. Bonds with relatively low risk of default are called *investment-grade* securities and have a rating of Baa (or BBB) and above. Bonds with ratings below Baa (or BBB) have higher default risk and have been aptly dubbed speculative-grade or **junk bonds.**

Next let's look back at Figure 1 and see if we can explain the relationship between interest rates on corporate and U.S. Treasury bonds. Corporate bonds always have higher interest rates than U.S. Treasury bonds because they always have some risk of default, whereas U.S. Treasury bonds do not. Because Baa-rated corporate bonds have a greater default risk than the higher-rated Aaa bonds, their risk premium is greater, and the Baa rate therefore always exceeds the Aaa rate.

We can use the same analysis to explain the huge jump in the risk premium on Baa corporate bond rates during the Great Depression years 1930–1933 and the rise in the risk premium in the last 30 years (see Figure 1). The depression period saw a very high rate of business failures and defaults. As we would expect, these factors led to a substantial increase in default risk for bonds issued by vulnerable corporations, and the risk premium for Baa bonds reached unprecedentedly high levels. The 1970s and following decades again saw higher levels of business failures and defaults, although they were still well below Great Depression levels. Again, as expected, default risks and risk premiums for corporate bonds rose, widening the spread between interest rates on corporate bonds and Treasury bonds.

TABLE 1 *Bond Ratings by Moody's and Standard & Poor's*

Moody's	Standard & Poor's	Description	Examples of Corporations with Bonds Outstanding in 2004
Aaa	AAA	Highest quality (lowest default risk)	General Electric, United Parcel Service, Nestle
Aa	AA	High quality	3M, Koch Ind., Illinois Tool Works
A	A	Upper medium grade	Honeywell, Rockwell Intl., General Dynamics, Boeing
Baa	BBB	Medium grade	Itt Ind., Northrop, Goodrich, FedEx
Ba	BB	Lower medium grade	Westinghouse, Allied Waste Products, IKON Office Solutions
B	B	Speculative	Jacuzzi, Sabreliner Corp., American Airlines
Caa, Ca	CCC, CC, C	Poor (high default risk)	Delta Airlines, McDermott, Schutt Int.
C	D	Lowest grade	US Airways, United Airlines, Citation Corp.

Access ratings of various bonds and institutions at www.standardandpoors.com/. Click on "Credit rating."

Case

THE ENRON BANKRUPTCY AND THE Baa–Aaa SPREAD

In December 2001, the Enron Corporation, a firm specializing in trading in the energy market, and once the seventh-largest corporation in the United States, was forced to declare bankruptcy after it became clear that it had used shady accounting to hide its financial problems. Because of the scale of the bankruptcy and the questions it raised about the quality of the information in accounting statements, the Enron collapse had a major impact on the corporate bond market. Let's see how our supply and demand analysis explains the behavior of the spread between interest rates on lower quality (Baa-rated) and highest quality (Aaa-rated) corporate bonds in the aftermath of the Enron failure.

As a consequence of the Enron bankruptcy, many investors began to doubt the financial health of corporations with lower credit ratings such as Baa. The increase in default risk for Baa bonds made them less desirable at any given interest rate, decreased the quantity demanded, and shifted the demand curve for Baa bonds to the left. As shown in panel (a) of Figure 2, the interest rate on Baa bonds should have risen, which is indeed what happened. Interest rates on Baa bonds rose by 24 basis points (0.24 percentage points) from 7.81% in November 2001 to 8.05% in December 2001. But the increase in the perceived default risk for Baa bonds after the Enron bankruptcy made the highest-quality (Aaa) bonds relatively more attractive and shifted the demand curve for these securities to the right—an outcome described by some analysts as a "flight to quality." Just as our analysis predicts in Figure 2, interest rates on Aaa bonds fell by 20 basis points, from 6.97% in November to 6.77% in December. The overall outcome was that the spread between interest rates on Baa and Aaa bonds rose by 44 basis points from 0.84% before the bankruptcy to 1.28% afterward.

Case

WHAT IF TREASURY SECURITIES WERE NO LONGER DEFAULT-FREE?

Throughout our history, the U.S. Treasury has never defaulted on its securities. However, in late 1995 and early 1996, a budget battle between congressional Republicans and President Clinton almost led to an unprecedented default. In an attempt to get their way in the budget negotiations, the Republicans threatened to refuse to raise the federal government debt ceiling. If the threat had been carried out, the Treasury would have missed interest payments on its debt because it would not have been able to issue new debt to cover its interest outlays and other expenditures when the debt ceiling was reached. Default was averted when a budget compromise was finally reached and the debt ceiling was raised after several shutdowns of the federal government in which "nonessential" government workers were sent home. What would have been the impact of a Treasury default?

Our analysis in Figure 2 provides the answer. Default on Treasury bonds would mean that they would no longer be considered default-free and would now have the attributes of corporate bonds in panel (a) of Figure 2. The increase in default risk would decrease the quantity of Treasury bonds demanded at any given interest rate and would thus cause their demand curve to shift to the left. As we see in panel (a), this would result in a fall in their bond price and a rise in their interest rate. Indeed, just as our analysis predicts, when budget talks stalled on December 18, 1995, and fear of a possible government default rose, the Treasury bond market slumped: Bond prices fell, and the interest rate on 30-year Treasury bonds rose by 11/100s of a percentage point, the largest one-day rise in more than six months.

Liquidity

Another attribute of a bond that influences its interest rate is its liquidity. As we learned in Chapter 4, a liquid asset is one that can be quickly and cheaply converted into cash if the need arises. The more liquid an asset is, the more desirable it is (holding everything else constant). U.S. Treasury bonds are the most liquid of all long-term bonds because they are so widely traded that they are the easiest to sell quickly and the cost of selling them is low. Corporate bonds are not as liquid because fewer bonds for any one corporation are traded; thus it can be costly to sell these bonds in an emergency because it may be hard to find buyers quickly.

How does the reduced liquidity of the corporate bonds affect their interest rates relative to the interest rate on Treasury bonds? We can use supply and demand analysis to show that the lower liquidity of corporate bonds relative to Treasury bonds increases the spread between the interest rates on these two bonds. Let us start the analysis by assuming that initially corporate and Treasury bonds are equally liquid and all their other attributes are the same. As shown in Figure 3, their equilibrium prices and interest rates will initially be equal: $P_1^c = P_1^T$ and $i_1^c = i_1^T$, If the corporate bond becomes less liquid than the Treasury bond because it is less widely traded, then as our analysis of the determinants of asset demand indicates, its demand will fall, shifting its demand curve from D_1^c to D_2^c

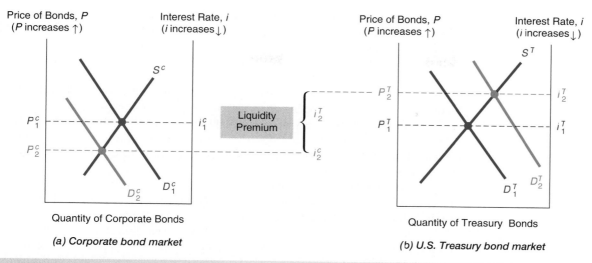

FIGURE 3 *Response to a Decrease in the Liquidity of Corporate Bonds*

A decrease in the liquidity of corporate bonds shifts the demand curve from D_1^c to D_2^c. Simultaneously, it shifts the demand curve for Treasury bonds from D_1^T to D_2^T. The equilibrium price for corporate bonds (left axis) falls from P_1^c to P_2^c, and the equilibrium interest rate on corporate bonds (right axis) rises from i_1^c to i_2^c. In the Treasury market, the equilibrium bond price rises from P_1^T to P_2^T, and the equilibrium interest rate falls from i_1^T to i_2^T. The brace indicates the difference between i_2^c and i_2^T, the liquidity premium on corporate bonds. (*Note:* P and i increase in opposite directions. P on the left vertical axis increases as we go up the axis, while i on the right vertical axis increases as we go down the axis.)

as in panel (a). The Treasury bond now becomes relatively more liquid in comparison with the corporate bond, so its demand curve shifts rightward from D_1^T to D_2^T as in panel (b). The shifts in the curves in Figure 3 show that the price of the less liquid corporate bond falls and its interest rate rises, while the price of the more liquid Treasury bond rises and its interest rate falls.

The result is that the spread between the interest rates on the two bond types has risen. Therefore, the differences between interest rates on corporate bonds and Treasury bonds (that is, the risk premiums) reflect not only the corporate bond's default risk but its liquidity too. This is why a risk premium is sometimes called a *liquidity premium*. More accurately, it should be called a "risk and liquidity premium," but convention dictates that it be called a *risk premium*.

Income Tax Considerations

Returning to Figure 1, we are still left with one puzzle—the behavior of municipal bond rates. Municipal bonds are certainly not default-free: State and local governments have defaulted on the municipal bonds they have issued in the past, particularly during the Great Depression and even more recently in the case of Orange County, California, in 1994 (more on this in Chapter 25). Also, municipal bonds are not as liquid as U.S. Treasury bonds.

Why is it, then, that these bonds have had lower interest rates than U.S. Treasury bonds for at least 40 years, as indicated in Figure 1? The explanation lies in the fact that interest payments on municipal bonds are exempt from federal income taxes, a factor that has the same effect on the demand for municipal bonds as an increase in their expected return.

Let us imagine that you have a high enough income to put you in the 40% income tax bracket, where for every extra dollar of income you have to pay 40 cents to the government. If you own a $1000 face value U.S. Treasury bond that sells for $1000 and has a coupon payment of $100, you get to keep only $60 of the payment after taxes. Although the bond has a 10% interest rate, you actually earn only 6% after taxes.

Suppose, however, that you put your savings into a $1000 face value municipal bond that sells for $1000 and pays only $80 in coupon payments. Its interest rate is only 8%, but because it is a tax-exempt security, you pay no taxes on the $80 coupon payment, so you earn 8% after taxes. Clearly, you earn more on the municipal bond after taxes, so you are willing to hold the riskier and less liquid municipal bond even though it has a lower interest rate than the U.S. Treasury bond. (This was not true before World War II, when the tax-exempt status of municipal bonds did not convey much of an advantage because income tax rates were extremely low.)

EXAMPLE 1   *Income Tax Considerations*

Suppose you had the opportunity to buy either a municipal bond or a corporate bond, both of which have a face value and purchase price of $1000. The municipal bond has coupon payments of $60 and a coupon rate of 6%. The corporate bond has coupon payments of $80 and an interest rate of 8%. Which bond would you choose to purchase, assuming a 40% tax rate?

Solution

You would choose to purchase the municipal bond because it will earn you $60 in coupon payments and an interest rate after taxes of 6%. Since municipal bonds are tax-exempt, you pay no taxes on the $60 coupon payments and earn 6% after taxes. However, you have to pay taxes on corporate bonds. You will keep only 60% of the $80 coupon payment because the other 40% goes to taxes. Therefore, you receive $48 of the coupon payment and have an interest rate of 4.8% after taxes. Buying the municipal bond would yield you higher earnings.

Another way of understanding why municipal bonds have lower interest rates than Treasury bonds is to use the supply and demand analysis displayed in Figure 4. To begin with, we assume that municipal and Treasury bonds have identical attributes and so have the same bond prices and interest rates as drawn in the figure: $P_1^m = P_1^T$ and $i_1^m = i_1^T$. Once the municipal bonds are given a tax advantage that raises their after-tax expected return relative to Treasury bonds and makes them more desirable, demand for them rises, and their demand curve shifts to the right from D_1^m to D_2^m. The result is that their equilibrium bond price rises from P_1^m to P_2^m, and their equilibrium interest rate falls from i_1^m to i_2^m. By contrast, Treasury bonds have now become less desirable relative to municipal bonds,

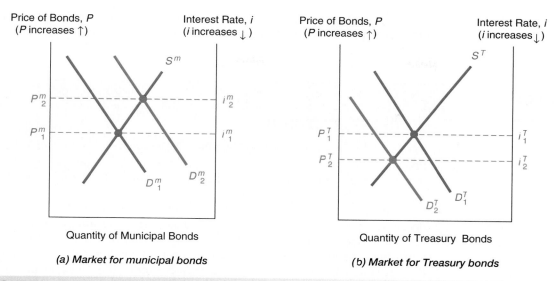

(a) Market for municipal bonds   **(b) Market for Treasury bonds**

FIGURE 4   *Interest Rates on Municipal and Treasury Bonds*

When the municipal bond is given tax-free status, demand for the municipal bond shifts rightward from D_1^m to D_2^m and demand for the Treasury bond shifts leftward from D_1^T to D_2^T. The equilibrium price of the municipal bond (left axis) rises from P_1^m to P_2^m, so its interest rate (right axis) falls from i_1^m to i_2^m while the equilibrium price of the Treasury bond falls from P_1^T to P_2^T and its interest rate rises from i_1^T to i_2^T. The result is that municipal bonds end up with lower interest rates than those on Treasury bonds. (*Note: P* and *i* increase in opposite directions. *P* on the left vertical axis increases as we go up the axis, while *i* on the right vertical axis increases as we go down the axis.)

demand for Treasury bonds decreases, and D_1^T shifts to D_2^T. The Treasury bond price falls from P_1^T to P_2^T, and the interest rate rises from i_1^T to i_2^T. The resulting lower interest rates for municipal bonds and higher interest rates for Treasury bonds explains why municipal bonds can have interest rates below those of Treasury bonds.[2]

Summary

The risk structure of interest rates (the relationship among interest rates on bonds with the same maturity) is explained by three factors: default risk, liquidity, and the income tax treatment of the bond's interest payments. As a bond's default risk increases, the risk premium on that bond (the spread between its interest rate and the interest rate on a default-free Treasury bond) rises. The greater liquidity of Treasury bonds also explains why their interest rates are lower than interest

---

[2]In contrast to corporate bonds, Treasury bonds are exempt from state and local income taxes. Using the analysis in the text, you should be able to show that this feature of Treasury bonds provides an additional reason why interest rates on corporate bonds are higher than those on Treasury bonds.

rates on less liquid bonds. If a bond has a favorable tax treatment, as do municipal bonds, whose interest payments are exempt from federal income taxes, its interest rate will be lower.

Case

EFFECTS OF THE BUSH TAX CUT ON BOND INTEREST RATES

The Bush tax cut passed in 2001 schedules a reduction of the top income tax bracket from 39% to 35% over a ten-year period. What is the effect of this income tax decrease on interest rates in the municipal bond market relative to those in the Treasury bond market?

The supply and demand analysis in Figure 4 provides the answer. A decreased income tax rate for rich people means that the after-tax expected return on tax-free municipal bonds relative to that on Treasury bonds is lower because the interest on Treasury bonds is now taxed at a lower rate. Because municipal bonds now become less desirable, this change shifts the demand curve to the left, which lowers their price and raises their interest rate. Conversely, the lower income tax rate makes Treasury bonds more desirable; that shifts their demand curve to the right, raises their price, and lowers their interest rates.

Our analysis thus shows that the Bush tax cut raises the interest rates on municipal bonds relative to interest rates on Treasury bonds.

Term Structure of Interest Rates

We have seen how risk, liquidity, and tax considerations (collectively embedded in the risk structure) can influence interest rates. Another factor that influences the interest rate on a bond is its term to maturity: Bonds with identical risk, liquidity, and tax characteristics may have different interest rates because the time remaining to maturity is different. A plot of the yields on bonds with differing terms to maturity but the same risk, liquidity, and tax considerations is called a **yield curve,** and it describes the term structure of interest rates for particular types of bonds, such as government bonds. The "Following the News" box shows several yield curves for Treasury securities that were published in the *Wall Street Journal.* Yield curves can be classified as upward-sloping, flat, and downward-sloping (the last sort is often referred to as an **inverted yield curve**). When yield curves slope upward, as in the "Following the News" box, the long-term interest rates are above the short-term interest rates; when yield curves are flat, short- and long-term interest rates are the same; and when yield curves are inverted, long-term interest rates are below short-term interest rates. Yield curves can also have more complicated shapes in which they first slope up and then down, or vice versa. Why do we usually see upward slopes of the yield curve as in the "Following the News" box but sometimes other shapes?

Besides explaining why yield curves take on different shapes at different times, a good theory of the term structure of interest rates must explain the following three important empirical facts:

1. As we see in Figure 5, interest rates on bonds of different maturities move together over time.

THE *WALL STREET JOURNAL:* FOLLOWING THE NEWS

Yield Curves

The *Wall Street Journal* publishes a daily plot of the yield curves for Treasury securities, an example of which is presented here. It is typically found next to the "Credit Markets" column.

The numbers on the vertical axis indicate the interest rate for the Treasury security, with the maturity given by the numbers on the horizontal axis. For example, the yield curve marked "Monday" indicates that the interest rate on the three-month Treasury bill was 2.2%, while the two-year bill had an interest rate of 3.0% and the ten-year bond had an interest rate of 4.2%. As you can see, the yield curves in the plot has a steep upward slope.

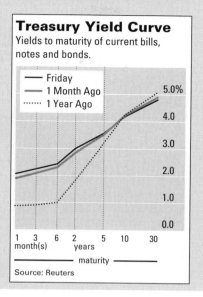

Treasury Yield Curve
Yields to maturity of current bills, notes and bonds.

Source: Reuters

Check out today's Treasury yield curve at www.stockcharts. com/charts/ YieldCurve.html

2. When short-term interest rates are low, yield curves are more likely to have an upward slope; when short-term interest rates are high, yield curves are more likely to slope downward and be inverted.
3. Yield curves almost always slope upward, as in the "Following the News" box.

Three theories have been put forward to explain the term structure of interest rates, that is, the relationship among interest rates on bonds of different maturities reflected in yield curve patterns: (1) pure expectations theory, (2) market segmentation theory, and (3) liquidity premium theory. The pure expectations theory does a good job of explaining the first two facts on our list but not the third. The market segmentation theory can explain fact 3 but not the other two facts, which are well explained by the pure expectations theory. Because each theory explains facts that the other cannot, a natural way to seek a better understanding of the term structure is to combine features of both theories, which leads us to the liquidity premium theory, which can explain all three facts.

If the liquidity premium theory does a better job of explaining the facts and is consequently widely accepted, why do we spend time discussing the other two theories? There are two reasons. First, the ideas in these two theories provide the groundwork for the liquidity premium theory. Second, it is important to see how financial economists modify theories to improve them when they find that the predicted results are inconsistent with the empirical evidence.

Pure Expectations Theory

The **pure expectations theory** of the term structure states the following commonsense proposition: The interest rate on a long-term bond will equal an average of short-term interest rates that people expect to occur over the life of the

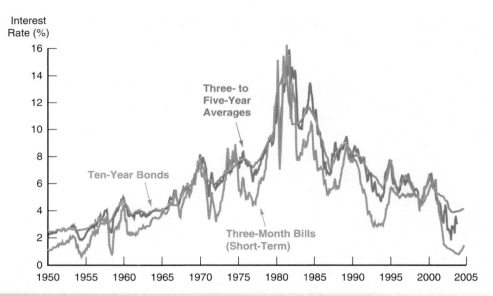

FIGURE 5 *Movements over Time of Interest Rates on U.S. Government Bonds with Different Maturities*

Sources: http://www.federalreserve.gov/releases/H15/data/m/tcm3y.txt, http://www.federalreserve.gov/releases/H15/data/m/tcm5y.txt, http://www.federalreserve.gov/releases/H15/data.htm.

long-term bond. For example, if people expect that short-term interest rates will be 10% on average over the coming five years, the expectations hypothesis predicts that the interest rate on bonds with five years to maturity will be 10% too. If short-term interest rates were expected to rise even higher after this five-year period so that the average short-term interest rate over the coming 20 years is 11%, then the interest rate on 20-year bonds would equal 11% and would be higher than the interest rate on five-year bonds. We can see that the explanation provided by the pure expectations theory for why interest rates on bonds of different maturities differ is that short-term interest rates are expected to have different values at future dates.

The key assumption behind this theory is that buyers of bonds do not prefer bonds of one maturity over another, so they will not hold any quantity of a bond if its expected return is less than that of another bond with a different maturity. Bonds that have this characteristic are said to be *perfect substitutes*. What this means in practice is that if bonds with different maturities are perfect substitutes, the expected return on these bonds must be equal.

To see how the assumption that bonds with different maturities are perfect substitutes leads to the pure expectations theory, let us consider the following two investment strategies:

1. Purchase a one-year bond, and when it matures in one year, purchase another one-year bond.
2. Purchase a two-year bond and hold it until maturity.

CHAPTER 5 HOW DO RISK AND TERM STRUCTURE AFFECT INTEREST RATES?

113

Because both strategies must have the same expected return if people are holding both one- and two-year bonds, the interest rate on the two-year bond must equal the average of the two one-year interest rates.

EXAMPLE 2   *Pure Expectations Theory*

The current interest rate on a one-year bond is 9%, and you expect the interest rate on the one-year bond next year to be 11%. What is the expected return over the two years? What interest rate must a two-year bond have to equal the two one-year bonds?

Solution

The expected return over the two years will average 10% per year ([9% + 11%]/2 = 10%). The bondholder will be willing to hold both the one- and two-year bonds only if the expected return per year of the two-year bond equals 10%. Therefore, the interest rate on the two-year bond must equal 10%, the average interest rate on the two one-year bonds. Graphically, we have:

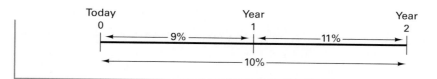

We can make this argument more general. For an investment of $1, consider the choice of holding, for two periods, a two-period bond or two one-period bonds. Using the definitions

i_t = today's (time t) interest rate on a one-period bond

i_{t+1}^e = interest rate on a one-period bond expected for next period (time $t + 1$)

i_{2t} = today's (time t) interest rate on the two-period bond

the expected return over the two periods from investing $1 in the two-period bond and holding it for the two periods can be calculated as

$$(1 + i_{2t})(1 + i_{2t}) - 1 = 1 + 2i_{2t} + (i_{2t})^2 - 1$$

This calculation is derived by recognizing that after the second period, the $1 investment is worth $(1 + i_{2t}) (1 + i_{2t})$. Then subtracting the $1 initial investment from this amount and dividing by the initial $1 investment gives the rate of return calculated in the previous equation. Because $(i_{2t})^2$ is extremely small—if $i_{2t} = 10\% = 0.10$, then $(i_{2t})^2 = 0.01$—we can simplify the expected return for holding the two-period bond for the two periods to

$$2i_{2t}$$

With the other strategy, in which one-period bonds are bought, the expected return on the $1 investment over the two periods is

$$(1 + i_t)(1 + i_{t+1}^e) - 1$$
$$= 1 + i_t + i_{t+1}^e + i_t(i_{t+1}^e) - 1$$

After the first period, the \$1 investment becomes $1 + i_t$, and this is reinvested in the one-period bond for the next period, yielding an amount $(1 + i_t)(1 + i^e_{t+1})$. Subtracting the \$1 initial investment from this amount and dividing by the initial investment of \$1 gives the expected return for the strategy of holding one-period bonds for the two periods. Because $i_t(i^e_{t+1})$ is also extremely small— if $i_t = i^e_{t+1} = 0.10$, then $i_t(i^e_{t+1}) = 0.01$—we can simplify this to

$$i_t + i^e_{t+1}$$

Both bonds will be held only if these expected returns are equal, that is, when

$$2i_{2t} = i_t + i^e_{t+1}$$

Solving for i_{2t} in terms of the one-period rates, we have

$$i_{2t} = \frac{i_t + i^e_{t+1}}{2} \qquad (1)$$

which tells us that the two-period rate must equal the average of the two one-period rates. Graphically, we have

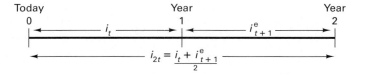

We can conduct the same steps for bonds with a longer maturity so that we can examine the whole term structure of interest rates. Doing so, we will find that the interest rate of i_{nt} on an n-period bond must equal

$$i_{nt} = \frac{i_t + i^e_{t+1} + i^e_{t+2} + \cdots + i^e_{t+(n-1)}}{n} \qquad (2)$$

Equation 2 states that the n-period interest rate equals the average of the one-period interest rates expected to occur over the n-period life of the bond. This is a restatement of the pure expectations theory in more precise terms.[3]

EXAMPLE 3   *Pure Expectations Theory*

The one-year interest rates over the next five years are expected to be 5%, 6%, 7%, 8%, and 9%. Given this information, what are the interest rates on a two-year bond and a five-year bond? Explain what is happening to the yield curve.

Solution

The interest rate on the two-year bond would be 5.5%.

$$i_{nt} = \frac{i_t + i^e_{t+1} + i^e_{t+2} + \cdots + i^e_{t+(n-1)}}{n}$$

---

[3]The analysis here has been conducted for discount bonds. Formulas for interest rates on coupon bonds would differ slightly from those used here but would convey the same principle.

where

$$i_t = \text{year 1 interest rate} = 5\%$$
$$i^e_{t+1} = \text{year 2 interest rate} = 6\%$$
$$n = \text{number of years} = 2$$

Thus

$$i_{2t} = \frac{5\% + 6\%}{2} = 5.5\%$$

The interest rate on the five-year bond would be 7%.

$$i_{nt} = \frac{i_t + i^e_{t+1} + i^e_{t+2} + \cdots + i^e_{t+(n-1)}}{n}$$

where

$$i_t = \text{year 1 interest rate} = 5\%$$
$$i^e_{t+1} = \text{year 2 interest rate} = 6\%$$
$$i^e_{t+2} = \text{year 3 interest rate} = 7\%$$
$$i^e_{t+3} = \text{year 4 interest rate} = 8\%$$
$$i^e_{t+4} = \text{year 5 interest rate} = 9\%$$
$$n = \text{number of years} = 5$$

Thus

$$i_{5t} = \frac{5\% + 6\% + 7\% + 8\% + 9\%}{5} = 7.0\%$$

Using the same equation for the one-, three-, and four-year interest rates, you will be able to verify the one-year to five-year rates as 5.0%, 5.5%, 6.0%, 6.5%, and 7.0% respectively. The rising trend in short-term interest rates produces an upward-sloping yield curve along which interest rates rise as maturity lengthens.

The pure expectations theory provides an elegant explanation of why the term structure of interest rates (as represented by yield curves) changes at different times. When the yield curve is upward-sloping, the pure expectations theory suggests that short-term interest rates are expected to rise in the future, as we have seen in our numerical example. In this situation, in which the long-term rate is currently above the short-term rate, the average of future short-term rates is expected to be higher than the current short-term rate, which can occur only if short-term interest rates are expected to rise. This is what we see in our numerical example. When the yield curve slopes downward and is inverted, the average of future short-term interest rates is expected to be below the current short-term rate, implying that short-term interest rates are expected to fall, on average, in the future. Only when the yield curve is flat does the pure expectations theory suggest that short-term interest rates are not expected to change, on average, in the future.

The pure expectations theory also explains fact 1—that interest rates on bonds with different maturities move together over time. Historically, short-term interest rates have had the characteristic that if they increase today, they will tend to be higher in the future. Hence a rise in short-term rates will raise people's expectations of future short-term rates. Because long-term rates are related to the average of expected future short-term rates, a rise in short-term rates will also raise long-term rates, causing short- and long-term rates to move together.

The pure expectations theory also explains fact 2—that yield curves tend to have an upward slope when short-term interest rates are low and are inverted when short-term rates are high. When short-term rates are low, people generally expect them to rise to some normal level in the future, and the average of future expected short-term rates is high relative to the current short-term rate. Therefore, long-term interest rates will be substantially above current short-term rates, and the yield curve would then have an upward slope. Conversely, if short-term rates are high, people usually expect them to come back down. Long-term rates would then drop below short-term rates because the average of expected future short-term rates would be below current short-term rates and the yield curve would slope downward and become inverted.[4]

The pure expectations theory is an attractive theory because it provides a simple explanation of the behavior of the term structure, but unfortunately it has a major shortcoming: It cannot explain fact 3—that yield curves usually slope upward. The typical upward slope of yield curves implies that short-term interest rates are usually expected to rise in the future. In practice, short-term interest rates are just as likely to fall as they are to rise, and so the pure expectations theory suggests that the typical yield curve should be flat rather than upward-sloping.

Market Segmentation Theory

As the name suggests, the **market segmentation theory** of the term structure sees markets for different-maturity bonds as completely separate and segmented. The interest rate for each bond with a different maturity is then determined by the supply of and demand for that bond with no effects from expected returns on other bonds with other maturities.

The key assumption in market segmentation theory is that bonds of different maturities are not substitutes at all, so the expected return from holding a bond of one maturity has no effect on the demand for a bond of another maturity. This theory of the term structure is at the opposite extreme to the pure expectations theory, which assumes that bonds of different maturities are perfect substitutes.

The argument for why bonds of different maturities are not substitutes is that investors have strong preferences for bonds of one maturity but not for another, so they will be concerned with the expected returns only for bonds of the maturity they prefer. This might occur because they have a particular holding period in mind, and if they match the maturity of the bond to the desired holding

---

[4]The pure expectations theory explains another important fact about the relationship between short-term and long-term interest rates. As you can see looking back at Figure 5, short-term interest rates are more volatile than long-term rates. If interest rates are mean-reverting—that is, if they tend to head back down after they are at unusually high levels or go back up when they are at unusually low levels—then an average of these short-term rates must necessarily have lower volatility than the short-term rates themselves. Because the pure expectations theory suggests that the long-term rate will be an average of future short-term rates, it implies that the long-term rate will have lower volatility than short-term rates.

period, they can obtain a certain return with no risk at all.[5] (We have seen in Chapter 3 that if the term to maturity equals the holding period, the return is known for certain because it equals the yield exactly, and there is no interest-rate risk.) For example, people who have a short holding period would prefer to hold short-term bonds. Conversely, if you were putting funds away for your young child to go to college, your desired holding period might be much longer, and you would want to hold longer-term bonds.

In market segmentation theory, differing yield curve patterns are accounted for by supply and demand differences associated with bonds of different maturities. If, as seems sensible, investors generally prefer bonds with shorter maturities that have less interest-rate risk, market segmentation theory can explain fact 3, that yield curves typically slope upward. Because the demand for long-term bonds is relatively lower than that for short-term bonds in the typical situation, long-term bonds will have lower prices and higher interest rates, and hence the yield curve will typically slope upward.

Although market segmentation theory can explain why yield curves usually tend to slope upward, it has a major flaw in that it cannot explain facts 1 and 2. Because it views the market for bonds of different maturities as completely segmented, there is no reason for a rise in interest rates on a bond of one maturity to affect the interest rate on a bond of another maturity. Therefore, it cannot explain why interest rates on bonds of different maturities tend to move together (fact 1). Second, because it is not clear how demand and supply for short- versus long-term bonds changes with the level of short-term interest rates, the theory cannot explain why yield curves tend to slope upward when short-term interest rates are low and to be inverted when short-term interest rates are high (fact 2).

Because each of our two theories explains empirical facts that the other cannot, a logical step is to combine the theories, which leads us to the liquidity premium theory.

Liquidity Premium Theory

The **liquidity premium theory** of term structure states that the interest rate on a long-term bond will equal an average of short-term interest rates expected to occur over the life of the long-term bond plus a liquidity premium that responds to supply and demand conditions for that bond.

The liquidity premium theory's key assumption is that bonds of different maturities are substitutes, which means that the expected return on one bond *does* influence the expected return on a bond of a different maturity, but it allows investors to prefer one bond maturity over another. In other words, bonds of different maturities are assumed to be substitutes but not perfect substitutes. Investors tend to prefer shorter-term bonds because these bonds bear less interest-rate risk. For this reason, investors must be offered a positive liquidity premium to induce them to hold longer-term bonds. Such an outcome would modify the pure

---

[5]The statement that there is no uncertainty about the return if the term to maturity equals the holding period is literally true only for a discount bond. For a coupon bond with a long holding period, there is some risk because coupon payments must be reinvested before the bond matures. Our analysis here is thus being conducted for discount bonds. However, the gist of the analysis remains the same for coupon bonds because the amount of this risk from reinvestment is small when coupon bonds have the same term to maturity as the holding period.

expectations theory by adding a positive liquidity premium to the equation that describes the relationship between long- and short-term interest rates. The liquidity premium theory is thus written

$$i_{nt} = \frac{i_t + i_{t+1}^e + i_{t+2}^e + \cdots + i_{t+(n-1)}^e}{n} + l_{nt} \tag{3}$$

where l_{nt} = the liquidity premium for the n-period bond at time t, which is always positive and rises with the term to maturity of the bond, n.

The relationship between the pure expectations theory and the liquidity premium theory is shown in Figure 6. There we see that because the liquidity premium is always positive and typically grows as the term to maturity increases, the yield curve implied by the liquidity premium theory is always above the yield curve implied by the pure expectations theory and generally has a steeper slope. (Note that for simplicity we are assuming that the pure expectations yield curve is flat.)

EXAMPLE 4

Liquidity Premium Theory

As in Example 3, let's suppose that the one-year interest rates over the next five years are expected to be 5%, 6%, 7%, 8%, and 9%. Investors' preferences for holding short-term bonds have the liquidity premiums for one-year to five-year bonds as 0%, 0.25%, 0.5%, 0.75%, and 1.0%, respectively. What is the interest rate on a two-year bond and a five-year bond? Compare these findings with the answer from Example 3 dealing with the pure expectations theory.

Solution

The interest rate on the two-year bond would be 5.75%.

$$i_{nt} = \frac{i_t + i_{t+1}^e + i_{t+2}^e + \cdots + i_{t+(n-1)}^e}{n} + l_{nt}$$

where

$\quad i_t \quad$ = year 1 interest rate = 5%

$\quad i_{t+1}^e$ = year 2 interest rate = 6%

$\quad l_{nt} \quad$ = liquidity premium = 0.25%

$\quad n \quad$ = number of years   = 2

Thus

$$i_{2t} = \frac{5\% + 6\%}{2} + 0.25\% = 5.75\%$$

The interest rate on the five-year bond would be 8%.

$$i_{nt} = \frac{i_t + i_{t+1}^e + i_{t+2}^e + \cdots + i_{t+(n-1)}^e}{n} + l_{nt}$$

where

$\quad i_t \quad$ = year 1 interest rate = 5%

$\quad i_{t+1}^e$ = year 2 interest rate = 6%

$$i_{t+2}^e = \text{year 3 interest rate} = 7\%$$

$$i_{t+3}^e = \text{year 4 interest rate} = 8\%$$

$$i_{t+4}^e = \text{year 5 interest rate} = 9\%$$

$$l_{2t} = \text{liquidity premium} = 1\%$$

$$n = \text{number of years} = 5$$

Thus

$$i_{5t} = \frac{5\% + 6\% + 7\% + 8\% + 9\%}{5} + 1\% = 8.0\%$$

If you did similar calculations for the one-, three-, and four-year interest rates, the one-year to five-year interest rates would be as follows: 5.0%, 5.75%, 6.5%, 7.25%, and 8.0%, respectively. Comparing these findings with those for the pure expectations theory, we can see that the liquidity preference theory produces yield curves that slope more steeply upward because of investors' preferences for short-term bonds.

Let's see if the liquidity premium theory is consistent with all three empirical facts we have discussed. It explains fact 1 that interest rates on different-maturity bonds move together over time: A rise in short-term interest rates indicates that short-term interest rates will, on average, be higher in the future, and the first term in Equation 3 then implies that long-term interest rates will rise along with them.

It also explains why yield curves tend to have an especially steep upward slope when short-term interest rates are low and to be inverted when short-term rates are high (fact 2). Because investors generally expect short-term interest rates

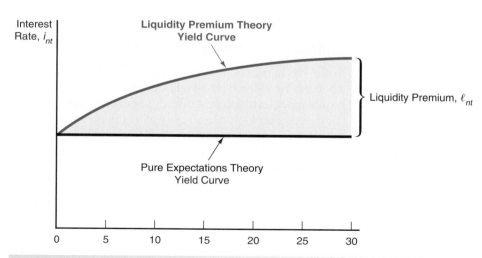

FIGURE 6 *The Relationship Between the Liquidity Premium and Pure Expectations Theories*

Because the liquidity premium is always positive and grows as the term to maturity increases, the yield curve implied by the liquidity premium theory is always above the yield curve implied by the pure expectations theory and has a steeper slope.

to rise to some normal level when they are low, the average of future expected short-term rates will be high relative to the current short-term rate. With the additional boost of a positive liquidity premium, long-term interest rates will be substantially above current short-term rates, and the yield curve would then have a steep upward slope. Conversely, if short-term rates are high, people usually expect them to come back down. Long-term rates would then drop below short-term rates because the average of expected future short-term rates would be so far below current short-term rates that despite positive liquidity premiums, the yield curve would slope downward.

The liquidity premium theory explains fact 3 that yield curves typically slope upward by recognizing that the liquidity premium rises with a bond's maturity because of investors' preferences for short-term bonds. Even if short-term interest rates are expected to stay the same on average in the future, long-term interest rates will be above short-term interest rates, and yield curves will typically slope upward.

How can the liquidity premium theory explain the occasional appearance of inverted yield curves if the liquidity premium is positive? It must be that at times short-term interest rates are expected to fall so much in the future that the average of the expected short-term rates is well below the current short-term rate. Even when the positive liquidity premium is added to this average, the resulting long-term rate will still be below the current short-term interest rate.

As our discussion indicates, a particularly attractive feature of the liquidity premium theory is that it tells you what the market is predicting about future short-term interest rates just by looking at the slope of the yield curve. A steeply rising yield curve, as in panel (a) of Figure 7, indicates that short-term interest rates are expected to rise in the future. A moderately steep yield curve, as in panel (b), indicates that short-term interest rates are not expected to rise or fall much in the future. A flat yield curve, as in panel (c), indicates that short-term rates are expected to fall moderately in the future. Finally, an inverted yield curve, as in panel (d), indicates that short-term interest rates are expected to fall sharply in the future.

Evidence on the Term Structure

In the 1980s, researchers examining the term structure of interest rates questioned whether the slope of the yield curve provides information about movements of future short-term interest rates.[6] They found that the spread between long- and short-term interest rates does not always help predict future short-term interest rates, a finding that may stem from substantial fluctuations in the liquidity premium for long-term bonds. More recent research using more discriminating tests now favors a different view. It shows that the term structure contains quite a bit of information for the very short run, over the next several months, and the long run, over several years, but is unreliable at predicting movements in interest rates over the intermediate term, the time in between.[7]

---

[6]Robert J. Shiller, John Y. Campbell, and Kermit L. Schoenholtz, "Forward Rates and Future Policy: Interpreting the Term Structure of Interest Rates," *Brookings Papers on Economic Activity* 1 (1983): 173–217; N. Gregory Mankiw and Lawrence H. Summers, "Do Long-Term Interest Rates Overreact to Short-Term Interest Rates?" *Brookings Papers on Economic Activity* 1 (1984): 243–247.

[7]Eugene Fama, "The Information in the Term Structure," *Journal of Financial Economics* 13 (1984): 509–528; Eugene Fama and Robert Bliss, "The Information in Long-Maturity Forward

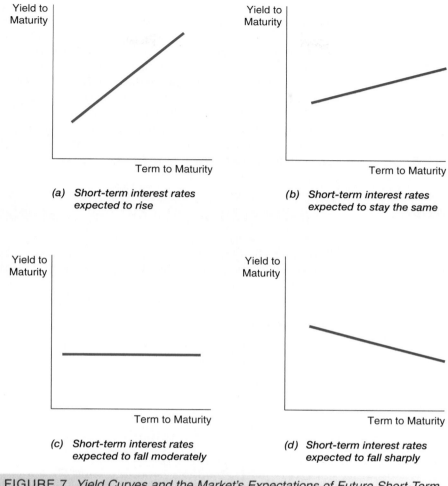

(a) **Short-term interest rates expected to rise**

(b) **Short-term interest rates expected to stay the same**

(c) **Short-term interest rates expected to fall moderately**

(d) **Short-term interest rates expected to fall sharply**

FIGURE 7 *Yield Curves and the Market's Expectations of Future Short-Term Interest Rates*

Summary

The liquidity premium theory is the most widely accepted theory of the term structure of interest rates because it explains the major empirical facts about the term structure so well. It combines the features of both the pure expectations theory and market segmentation theory by asserting that a long-term interest rate will be the sum of a liquidity premium and the average of the short-term interest rates that are expected to occur over the life of the bond.

Rates," *American Economic Review* 77 (1987): 680–692; John Y. Campbell and Robert J. Shiller, "Cointegration and Tests of the Present Value Models," *Journal of Political Economy* 95 (1987): 1062–1088; John Y. Campbell and Robert J. Shiller, "Yield Spreads and Interest Rate Movements: A Bird's Eye View," *Review of Economic Studies* 58 (1991): 495–514.

The liquidity premium theory explains the following facts: (1) Interest rates on bonds of different maturities tend to move together over time, (2) yield curves usually slope upward, and (3) when short-term interest rates are low, yield curves are more likely to have a steep upward slope, whereas when short-term interest rates are high, yield curves are more likely to be inverted.

The theory also helps us predict the movement of short-term interest rates in the future. A steep upward slope of the yield curve means that short-term rates are expected to rise, a mild upward slope means that short-term rates are expected to remain the same, a flat slope means that short-term rates are expected to fall moderately, and an inverted yield curve means that short-term rates are expected to fall sharply.

Case

INTERPRETING YIELD CURVES, 1980–2004

Figure 8 illustrates several yield curves that have appeared for U.S. government bonds in recent years. What do these yield curves tell us about the public's expectations of future movements of short-term interest rates?

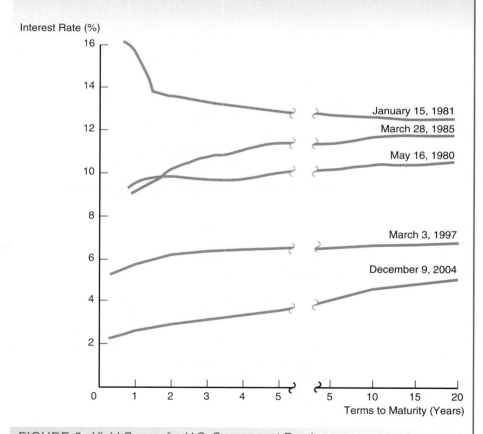

FIGURE 8   *Yield Curves for U.S. Government Bonds*

Sources: Federal Reserve Bank of St. Louis; *U.S. Financial Data,* various issues; *Wall Street Journal,* various dates.

Study Guide

Try to answer the question before reading further in the text. If you have trouble answering it with the liquidity premium theory, first try answering it with the pure expectations theory (which is simpler because you don't have to worry about the liquidity premium). When you understand what the expectations of future interest rates are in this case, modify your analysis by taking the liquidity premium into account.

The steep inverted yield curve that occurred on January 15, 1981, indicated that short-term interest rates were expected to decline sharply in the future. In order for longer-term interest rates with their positive liquidity premium to be well below the short-term interest rate, short-term interest rates must be expected to decline so sharply that their average is far below the current short-term rate. Indeed, the public's expectations of sharply lower short-term interest rates evident in the yield curve were realized soon after January 15; by March, three-month Treasury bill rates had declined from the 16% level to 13%.

The steep upward-sloping yield curves on March 28, 1985, and December 9, 2004, indicated that short-term interest rates would climb in the future. The long-term interest rate is above the short-term interest rate when short-term interest rates are expected to rise because their average plus the liquidity premium will be above the current short-term rate. The moderately upward-sloping yield curves on May 16, 1980, and March 3, 1997, indicated that short-term interest rates were expected neither to rise nor to fall in the near future. In this case, their average remains the same as the current short-term rate, and the positive liquidity premium for longer-term bonds explains the moderate upward slope of the yield curve.

The Practicing Manager

USING THE TERM STRUCTURE TO FORECAST INTEREST RATES

As was discussed in Chapter 4, interest-rate forecasts are extremely important to managers of financial institutions because future changes in interest rates have a significant impact on the profitability of their institutions. Furthermore, interest-rate forecasts are needed when managers of financial institutions have to set interest rates on loans that are promised to customers in the future. Our discussion of the term structure of interest rates has indicated that the slope of the yield curve provides general information about the market's prediction of the future path of interest rates. For example, a steeply upward-sloping yield curve indicates that short-term interest rates are predicted to rise in the future, and a downward-sloping yield curve indicates that short-term interest rates are predicted to fall. However, a financial institution manager needs much more specific information on interest-rate forecasts than this. Here we show how the manager of a financial institution can generate specific forecasts of interest rates using the term structure.

To see how this is done, let's start the analysis using the approach we took in developing the pure expectations theory. Recall that because bonds of different maturities are perfect substitutes, we assumed that the expected return over two periods from investing \$1 in a two-period bond, which is $(1 + i_{2t})(1 + i_{2t}) - 1$, must equal the expected return from investing \$1 in one-period bonds, which is $(1 + i_t)(1 + i_{t+1}^e) - 1$. This is shown graphically as follows:

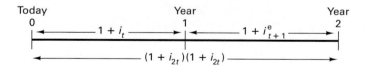

In other words,

$$(1 + i_t)(1 + i_{t+1}^e) - 1 = (1 + i_{2t})(1 + i_{2t}) - 1$$

Through some tedious algebra we can solve for i_{t+1}^e:

$$i_{t+1}^e = \frac{(1 + i_{2t})^2}{1 + i_t} - 1 \tag{4}$$

This measure of i_{t+1}^e is called the **forward rate** because it is the one-period interest rate that the pure expectations theory of the term structure indicates is expected to prevail one period in the future. To differentiate forward rates derived from the term structure from actual interest rates that are observed at time t, we call these observed interest rates **spot rates.**

Going back to Example 3, which we used to discuss the pure expectations theory earlier in this chapter, at time t the one-year interest rate is 5% and the two-year rate is 5.5%. Plugging these numbers into Equation 4 yields the following estimate of the forward rate one period in the future:

$$i_{t+1}^e = \frac{(1 + 0.055)^2}{1 + 0.05} - 1 = 0.06 = 6\%$$

Not surprisingly, this 6% forward rate is identical to the expected one-year interest rate one year in the future that we used in Example 3. This is exactly what we should find, as our calculation here is just another way of looking at the pure expectations theory.

We can also compare holding the three-year bond against holding a sequence of one-year bonds, which reveals the following relationship:

$$(1 + i_t)(1 + i_{t+1}^e)(1 + i_{t+2}^e) - 1 = (1 + i_{3t})(1 + i_{3t})(1 + i_{3t}) - 1$$

and plugging in the estimate for i_{t+1}^e derived in Equation 4, we can solve for i_{t+2}^e:

$$i_{t+2}^e = \frac{(1 + i_{3t})^3}{(1 + i_{2t})^2} - 1$$

Continuing with these calculations, we obtain the general solution for the forward rate n periods into the future:

$$i_{t+n}^e = \frac{(1 + i_{n+1t})^{n+1}}{(1 + i_{nt})^n} - 1 \tag{5}$$

Our discussion indicated that the pure expectations theory is not entirely satisfactory because investors must be compensated with liquidity premiums to induce them to hold longer-term bonds. Hence we need to modify our analysis, as we did when discussing the liquidity premium theory, by allowing for these liquidity premiums in estimating predictions of future interest rates.

Recall from the discussion of those theories that because investors prefer to hold short-term rather than long-term bonds, the n-period interest rate differs from that indicated by the pure expectations theory by a liquidity premium of l_{nt}. So to allow for liquidity premiums, we need merely subtract l_{nt} from i_{nt} in our formula to derive i_{t+n}^e:

$$i_{t+n}^e = \frac{(1 + i_{n+1t} - l_{n+1t})^{n+1}}{(1 + i_{nt} - l_{nt})^n} - 1 \tag{6}$$

This measure of i_{t+n}^e is referred to, naturally enough, as the *adjusted forward-rate forecast*.

In the case of i_{t+1}^e, Equation 6 produces the following estimate

$$i_{t+1}^e = \frac{(1 + i_{2t} - l_{2t})^2}{1 + i_t} - 1$$

Using Example 4 in our discussion of the liquidity premium theory, at time t the l_{2t} liquidity premium is 0.25%, $l_{1t} = 0$, the one-year interest rate is 5%, and the two-year interest rate is 5.75%. Plugging these numbers into our equation yields the following adjusted forward-rate forecast for one period in the future:

$$i_{t+1}^e = \frac{(1 + 0.0575 - 0.0025)^2}{1 + 0.05} - 1 = 0.06 = 6\%$$

which is the same as the expected interest rate used in Example 3, as it should be.

Our analysis of the term structure thus provides managers of financial institutions with a fairly straightforward procedure for producing interest-rate forecasts. First they need to estimate l_{nt}, the values of the liquidity premiums for various n. Then they need merely apply the formula in Equation 6 to derive the market's forecasts of future interest rates.

EXAMPLE 5   *Forward Rate*

A customer asks a bank if it would be willing to commit to making the customer a one-year loan at an interest rate of 8% one year from now. To compensate for the costs of making the loan, the bank needs to charge one percentage point more than the expected interest rate on a Treasury bond with the same maturity if it is to make a profit. If the bank manager estimates the liquidity premium to be 0.4%, and the one-year Treasury bond rate is 6% and the two-year bond rate is 7%, should the manager be willing to make the commitment?

Solution

The bank manager is unwilling to make the loan because at an interest rate of 8%, the loan is likely to be unprofitable to the bank.

$$i_{t+n}^e = \frac{(1 + i_{n+1t} - l_{n+1t})^{n+1}}{(1 + i_{nt} - l_{nt})^n} - 1$$

where

i_{n+1t} = two-year bond rate = 0.07

l_{n+1t} = liquidity premium = 0.004

i_{nt} = one-year bond rate = 0.06

l_{1t} = liquidity premium = 0

n = number of years = 1

Thus

$$i_{t+1}^e = \frac{(1 + 0.07 - 0.004)^2}{1 + 0.06} - 1 = 0.072 = 7.2\%$$

The market's forecast of the one-year Treasury bond rate one year in the future is therefore 7.2%. Adding the 1% necessary to make a profit on the one-year loan means that the loan is expected to be profitable only if it has an interest rate of 8.2% or higher.

As we will see in Chapter 6, the bond market's forecasts of interest rates may be the most accurate ones possible. If this is the case, the estimates of the market's forecasts of future interest rates using the simple procedure outlined here may be the best interest-rate forecasts that a financial institution manager can obtain.

Study Guide

To make sure you understand how to generate interest-rate forecasts from the term structure, calculate the forecasts of the one-year interest rates using Equation 6 for two, three, and four years in the future using the liquidity premiums and one-year through five-year interest rates in Example 4. The resulting forecasts should equal the expected future interest rates found in the example. Problems at the end of the chapter will give you more practice in generating interest-rate forecasts from the term structure.

Summary

1. Bonds with the same maturity will have different interest rates because of three factors: default risk, liquidity, and tax considerations. The greater a bond's default risk, the higher its interest rate relative to other bonds; the greater a bond's liquidity, the lower its interest rate; and bonds with tax-exempt status will have lower interest rates than they otherwise would. The relationship among interest rates on bonds with the same maturity that arise because of these three factors is known as the risk structure of interest rates.

2. Several theories of the term structure provide explanations of how interest rates on bonds with different terms to maturity are related. The pure expectations theory views long-term interest rates as equaling the average of future short-term interest rates expected to occur over the life of the bond; by contrast, market segmentation theory treats the determination of interest rates for each bond's maturity as the outcome of supply and demand in that market only. Neither of these theories by itself can explain both the fact that interest

rates on bonds of different maturities move together over time and the fact that yield curves usually slope upward.

3. The liquidity premium theory combines the features of the other two theories and by so doing is able to explain the facts just mentioned. It views long-term interest rates as equaling the average of future short-term interest rates expected to occur over the life of the bond plus a liquidity premium that reflects the supply of and demand for bonds of different maturities.

4. These theories allow us to infer the market's expectations about the movement of future short-term interest rates from the yield curve. A steeply upward-sloping curve indicates that future short-term rates are expected to rise, a mildly upward-sloping curve indicates that short-term rates are expected to stay the same, a flat curve indicates that short-term rates are expected to decline slightly, and an inverted yield curve indicates that a substantial decline in short-term rates is expected in the future.

Key Terms

credit-rating agencies, *p. 104*
default, *p. 102*
default-free bonds, *p. 102*
forward rate, *p. 124*
inverted yield curve, *p. 110*
junk bonds, *p. 104*
liquidity premium theory,
   p. 117

market segmentation theory,
   p. 116
pure expectations theory,
   p. 111
risk premium, *p. 102*
risk structure of interest rates,
   p. 101

spot rate, *p. 124*
term structure of interest rates,
   p. 101
yield curve, *p. 110*

Questions

1. Which should have the higher risk premium on its interest rates, a corporate bond with a Moody's Baa rating or a corporate bond with a C rating? Why?

2. Why do U.S. Treasury bills have lower interest rates than large-denomination negotiable bank CDs?

3. Risk premiums on corporate bonds are usually anticyclical; that is, they decrease during business cycle expansions and increase during recessions. Why is this so?

4. "If bonds of different maturities are close substitutes, their interest rates are more likely to move together." Is this statement true, false, or uncertain? Explain your answer.

5. If yield curves, on average, were flat, what would this say about the liquidity premiums in the term structure? Would you be more or less willing to accept the pure expectations theory?

6. If a yield curve looks like the following one, what is the market predicting about the movement of future short-term interest rates? What might the yield curve indicate about the market's predictions about the inflation rate in the future?

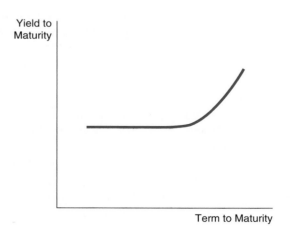

7. If a yield curve looks like the one shown on the next page, what is the market predicting about the movement of future short-term interest rates? What might the yield curve indicate about the market's predictions about the inflation rate in the future?

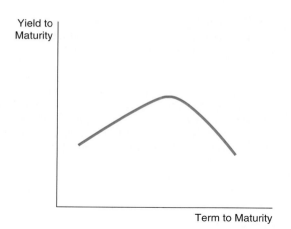

Yield to Maturity / Term to Maturity

8. What effect would reducing income tax rates have on the interest rates of municipal bonds? Would interest rates of Treasury securities be affected and, if so, how?

Predicting the Future

9. Predict what will happen to interest rates on a corporation's bonds if the federal government guarantees today that it will pay creditors if the corporation goes bankrupt in the future. What will happen to the interest rates on Treasury securities?

10. Predict what would happen to the risk premiums on corporate bonds if brokerage commissions were lowered in the corporate bond market.

11. If the income tax exemption on municipal bonds were abolished, what would happen to the interest rates on these bonds? What effect would it have on interest rates on U.S. Treasury securities?

Quantitative Problems

1. Assuming that the pure expectations theory is the correct theory of the term structure, calculate the interest rates in the term structure for maturities of one to five years, and plot the resulting yield curves for the following series of one-year interest rates over the next five years:

  a. 5%, 7%, 7%, 7%, 7%

  b. 5%, 4%, 4%, 4%, 4%

How would your yield curves change if people preferred shorter-term bonds over longer-term bonds?

2. Government economists have forecasted one-year T-bill rates for the following five years, as follows:

Year	1-year rate (%)
1	4.25
2	5.15
3	5.50
4	6.25
5	7.10

You have a liquidity premium of 0.25% for the next two years and 0.50% thereafter. Would you be willing to purchase a four-year T-bond at a 5.75% interest rate?

3. How does the after-tax yield on a $1,000,000 municipal bond with a coupon rate of 8% paying interest annually, compare with that of a $1,000,000 corporate bond with a coupon rate of 10% paying interest annually? Assume that you are in the 25% tax bracket.

4. Consider the decision to purchase either a five-year corporate bond or a five-year municipal bond. The corporate bond is a 12% annual coupon bond with a par value of $1000. It is currently yielding 11.5%. The municipal bond has an 8.5% annual coupon and a par value of $1000. It is currently yielding 7%. Which of the two bonds would be more beneficial to you? Assume that your marginal tax rate is 35%.

5. Debt issued by Southeastern Corporation currently yields 12%. A municipal bond of equal risk currently yields 8%. At what marginal tax rate would an investor be indifferent between these two bonds?

6. One-year T-bill rates are expected to steadily increase by 150 basis points per year over the next six years. Determine the required interest rate on a three-year T-bond and a six-year T-bond if the current one-year interest rate is 7.5%. Assume that the pure expectations hypothesis for interest rates holds.

7. The one-year interest rate over the next ten years will be 3%, 4.5%, 6%, 7.5%, 9%, 10.5%, 13%, 14.5%, 16%, and 17.5%. Using the pure expectations theory, what will be the interest rates on a three-year bond, six-year bond, and nine-year bond?

8. Using the information from the previous question, now assume that investors prefer holding short-term bonds. A liquidity premium of 10 basis points is required for each year of a bond's maturity. What will be the interest rates on a three-year bond, six-year bond, and nine-year bond?

9. Which bond would produce a greater return if the pure expectations theory were to hold true, a two-year bond with an interest rate of 15% or two one-year bonds with sequential interest payments of 13% and 17%?

10. Little Monsters, Inc., borrowed $1,000,000 for two years from NorthernBank, Inc., at an 11.5% interest rate. The current risk-free rate is 2%, and Little Monsters' financial condition warrants a default risk premium of 3% and a liquidity risk premium of 2%. The maturity risk premium for a two-year loan is 1%, and inflation is expected to be 3% next year. What does this information imply about the rate of inflation in the second year?

11. One-year T-bill rates are 2% currently. If interest rates are expected to go up after three years by 2% every year, what should be the required interest rate on a 10-year bond issued today? Assume that the pure expectations theory holds.

12. One-year T-bill rates over the next four years are expected to be 3%, 4%, 5%, and 5.5%. If four-year T-bonds are yielding 4.5%, what is the liquidity premium on this bond?

13. At your favorite bond store, Bonds-R-Us, you see the following prices:

One-year $100 zero selling for $90.19

Three-year 10% coupon $1000 par bond selling for $1000

Two-year 10% coupon $1000 par bond selling for $1000

Assume that the pure expectations theory for the term structure of interest rates holds, no liquidity premium exists, and the bonds are equally risky. What is the implied one-year rate two years from now?

14. You observe the following market interest rates, for both borrowing and lending:

One-year rate = 5%

Two-year rate = 6%

One-year rate one year from now = 7.25%

How can you take advantage of these rates to earn a riskless profit? Assume that the pure expectations theory for interest rates holds.

15. If the interest rates on one- to five-year bonds are currently 4%, 5%, 6%, 7%, and 8% and the term premiums for one- to five-year bonds are 0%, 0.25%, 0.35%, 0.40%, and 0.50%, predict what the one-year interest rate will be two years from now.

Web Exercises

The Risk and Term Structure of Interest Rates

1. The amount of additional interest investors receive due to the various premiums changes over time. Sometimes the risk premiums are much larger than at other times. For example, the default risk premium was very small in the late 1990s, when the economy was healthy and business failures were rare. It follows that this risk premium increases during recessions.

   Go to **http://www.federalreserve.gov/releases/release/H.15** (historical data) and find the interest rate listings for AAA and Baa-rated bonds at three points in time: the most recent, June 1, 1995, and June 1, 1992. Prepare a graph that shows these three time periods (see Figure 1 in this chapter for an example). Are the risk premiums stable, or do they change over time?

2. Figure 8 in this chapter shows a number of yield curves at various points in time. Go to **http://www.bloomberg.com** and click on "Markets" at the top of the page. Find the Treasury yield curve. Does the current yield curve fall above or below the most recent one listed in Figure 8? Is the current yield curve flatter or steeper than the most recent one reported in Figure 8?

3. Investment companies attempt to explain to investors the nature of the risk the investor incurs when buying shares in their mutual funds. For example, Vanguard carefully explains interest-rate risk and offers alternative funds with different interest-rate risks. Go to **http://majestic.van guard.com/FP/DA**.

   a. Select the bond fund you would recommend to an investor who has very low tolerance for risk and a short investment horizon. Justify your answer.

   b. Select the bond fund you would recommend to an investor who has very high tolerance for risk and a long investment horizon. Justify your answer.

CHAPTER 6

Are Financial Markets Efficient?

Preview

Throughout our discussion so far of how financial markets work, you may have noticed that the subject of expectations keeps cropping up again and again. Expectations of returns, risk, and liquidity are central elements in the demand for assets; expectations of inflation have a major impact on bond prices and interest rates; expectations about the likelihood of default are the most important factor that determines the risk structure of interest rates; and expectations of future short-term interest rates play a central role in determining the term structure of interest rates. Not only are expectations critical in understanding behavior in financial markets, but as we will see later in this book, they are also central to our understanding of how financial institutions operate.

To understand how expectations are formed so that we can understand how securities prices move over time, we look at the *efficient market hypothesis*. In this chapter we examine the basic reasoning behind the efficient market hypothesis in order to explain some puzzling features of the operation and behavior of financial markets. You will see, for example, why changes in stock prices are unpredictable and why listening to a stock broker's hot tips may not be a good idea.

Theoretically, the efficient market hypothesis should be a powerful tool for analyzing behavior in financial markets. But to establish that it is *in reality* a useful tool, we must compare the theory with the data. Does the emperical evidence support the theory? Though mixed, the available evidence indicates that for many purposes, this theory is a good starting point for analyzing expectations.

The Efficient Market Hypothesis

To learn more about the efficient market hypothesis, go to www.investor home.com/emh.htm

To more fully understand how expectations affect securities prices, we need to look at how information in the market affects these prices. To do this we examine the **efficient market hypothesis** (also referred to as the **theory of efficient capital markets**), which states that prices of securities in financial markets fully reflect all available information. But what does this mean?

You may recall from Chapter 3 that the rate of return from holding a security equals the sum of the capital gain on the security (the change in the price) plus any cash payments, divided by the initial purchase price of the security:

$$R = \frac{P_{t+1} - P_t + C}{P_t} \tag{1}$$

where R = rate of return on the security held from time t to time $t + 1$ (say, the end of 2002 to the end of 2003)

P_{t+1} = price of the security at time $t + 1$, the end of the holding period

P_t = the price of the security at time t, the beginning of the holding period

C = cash payment (coupon or dividend payments) made in the period t to $t + 1$

Let's look at the expectation of this return at time t, the beginning of the holding period. Because the current price and the cash payment C are known at the beginning, the only variable in the definition of the return that is uncertain is the price next period, P_{t+1}.[1] Denoting the expectation of the security's price at the end of the holding period as P^e_{t+1}, the expected return R^e is

$$R^e = \frac{P^e_{t+1} - P_t + C}{P_t}$$

The efficient market hypothesis views expectations as equal to optimal forecasts using all available information. What exactly does this mean? An optimal forecast is the best guess of the future using all available information. This does not mean that the forecast is perfectly accurate, but only that it is the *best possible* given the available information. This can be written more formally as

$$P^e_{t+1} = P^{of}_{t+1}$$

which in turn implies that the expected return on the security will equal the optimal forecast of the return:

$$R^e = R^{of} \tag{2}$$

Unfortunately, we cannot observe either R^e or P^e_{t+1}, so the equations above by themselves do not tell us much about how the financial market behaves. However, if we can devise some way to measure the value of R^e, these equations will have important implications for how prices of securities change in financial markets.

---

[1]There are cases where C might not be known at the beginning of the period, but that does not make a substantial difference to the analysis. We would in that case assume that not only price expectations but also the expectations of C are optimal forecasts using all available information.

The supply and demand analysis of the bond market developed in Chapter 4 shows us that the expected return on a security (the interest rate in the case of the bond examined) will have a tendency to head toward the equilibrium return that equates the quantity demanded to the quantity supplied. Supply and demand analysis enables us to determine the expected return on a security with the following equilibrium condition: The expected return on a security R^e equals the equilibrium return R^*, which equates the quantity of the security demanded to the quantity supplied; that is,

$$R^e = R^* \tag{3}$$

The academic field of finance explores the factors (risk and liquidity, for example) that influence the equilibrium returns on securities. For our purposes, it is sufficient to know that we can determine the equilibrium return and thus determine the expected return with the equilibrium condition.

We can derive an equation to describe pricing behavior in an efficient market by using the equilibrium condition to replace R^e with R^* in Equation 2. In this way we obtain

$$R^{of} = R^* \tag{4}$$

This equation tells us that **current prices in a financial market will be set so that the optimal forecast of a security's return using all available information equals the security's equilibrium return.** Financial economists state it more simply: A security's price fully reflects all available information in an efficient market.

EXAMPLE 1   *The Efficient Market Hypothesis*

Suppose that a share of Microsoft had a closing price yesterday of $90, but new information was announced after the market closed that caused a revision in the forecast of the price for next year to go to $120. If the annual equilibrium return on Microsoft is 15%, what does the efficient market hypothesis indicate the price will go to today when the market opens? (Assume that Microsoft pays no dividends.)

Solution

The price would rise to $104.35 after the opening.

$$R^{of} = \frac{P^{of}_{t+1} - P_t + C}{P_t} = R^*$$

where

R^{of}	= optimal forecast of the return = 15%	= 0.15	
R^*	= equilibrium return = 15%	= 0.15	
P^{of}_{t+1}	= optimal forecast of price next year	= \$120	
P_t	= price today after opening		
C	= cash (dividend) payment	= 0	

Thus

$$0.15 = \frac{\$120 - P_t}{P_t}$$

$$P_t \times 0.15 = \$120 - P_t$$

$$P_t(1.15) = \$120$$

$$P_t = \$104.35$$

Rationale Behind the Hypothesis

Let's see what the efficient market condition means in practice and why it is a sensible characterization of pricing behavior. Suppose that the equilibrium return on a security, say, Exxon-Mobil common stock, is 10% at an annual rate, and its current price P_t is lower than the optimal forecast of tomorrow's price P_{t+1}^{of} so that the optimal forecast of the return at an annual rate is 50%, which is greater than the equilibrium return of 10%. We are now able to predict that, on average, Exxon's return would be abnormally high. This situation is called an **unexploited profit opportunity** because, on average, people would be earning more than they should, given the characteristics of that security. Knowing that, on average, you can earn such an abnormally high rate of return on Exxon because $R^{of} > R^*$, you would buy more, which would in turn drive up its current price relative to the expected future price P_{t+1}^{of}, thereby lowering R^{of}. When the current price had risen sufficiently so that R^{of} equals R^* and the efficient market condition (Equation 4) is satisfied, the buying of Exxon will stop, and the unexploited profit opportunity will have disappeared.

Similarly, a security for which the optimal forecast of the return is −5% while the equilibrium return is 10% ($R^{of} < R^*$) would be a poor investment because, on average, it earns less than the equilibrium return. In such a case, you would sell the security and drive down its current price relative to the expected future price until R^{of} rose to the level of R^* and the efficient market condition is again satisfied. What we have shown can be summarized as follows:

$$\left. \begin{array}{l} R^{of} > R^* \rightarrow P_t\uparrow \rightarrow R^{of}\downarrow \\ R^{of} < R^* \rightarrow P_t\downarrow \rightarrow R^{of}\uparrow \end{array} \right\} \quad \text{until } R^{of} = R^*$$

Another way to state the efficient market condition is this: ***In an efficient market, all unexploited profit opportunities will be eliminated.***

An extremely important factor in this reasoning is that ***not everyone in a financial market must be well informed about a security or have rational expectations for its price to be driven to the point at which the efficient market condition holds.*** Financial markets are structured so that many participants can play. As long as a few (who are often referred to as "smart money") keep their eyes open for unexploited profit opportunities, they will eliminate the profit opportunities that appear because in so doing, they make a profit. The efficient market hypothesis makes sense because it does not require everyone in a market to be cognizant of what is happening to every security.

Stronger Version of the Efficient Market Hypothesis

Many financial economists take the efficient market hypothesis one step further in their analysis of financial markets. Not only do they define an efficient market as one in which expectations are optimal forecasts using all available information, but they also add the condition that an efficient market is one in which prices reflect the true fundamental (intrinsic) value of the securities. Thus in an efficient market, all prices are always correct and reflect **market fundamentals** (items that have a direct impact on future income streams of the securities). This stronger view of market efficiency has several important implications in the academic field of finance. First, it implies that in an efficient capital market, one investment is as good as any other because the securities' prices are correct. Second, it implies that a security's price reflects all available information about the intrinsic value of the security. Third, it implies that security prices can be used by managers of both financial and nonfinancial firms to assess their cost of capital (cost of financing their investments) accurately and hence that security prices can be used to help them make the correct decisions about whether a specific investment is worth making or not. The stronger version of market efficiency is a basic tenet of much analysis in the finance field.

Evidence on the Efficient Market Hypothesis

Early evidence on the efficient market hypothesis was quite favorable to it, but in recent years, deeper analysis of the evidence suggests that the hypothesis may not always be entirely correct. Let's first look at the earlier evidence in favor of the hypothesis and then examine some of the more recent evidence that casts some doubt on it.

Evidence in Favor of Market Efficiency

Evidence in favor of market efficiency has examined the performance of investment analysts and mutual funds, whether stock prices reflect publicly available information, the random-walk behavior of stock prices, and the success of so-called technical analysis.

Performance of Investment Analysts and Mutual Funds We have seen that one implication of the efficient market hypothesis is that when purchasing a security, you cannot expect to earn an abnormally high return, a return greater than the equilibrium return. This implies that it is impossible to beat the market. Many studies shed light on whether investment advisers and mutual funds (some of which charge steep sales commissions to people who purchase them) beat the market. One common test that has been performed is to take buy and sell recommendations from a group of advisers or mutual funds and compare the performance of the resulting selection of stocks with the market as a whole. Sometimes the advisers' choices have even been compared to a group of stocks chosen by putting a copy of the financial page of the newspaper on a dartboard and throwing darts. The *Wall Street Journal,* for example, has a regular feature called "Investment Dartboard" that compares how well stocks picked by investment advisers do relative to stocks picked by throwing darts. Do the advisers win?

To their embarrassment, the dartboard beats them as often as they beat the dart-board. Furthermore, even when the comparison includes only advisers who have been successful in the past in predicting the stock market, the advisers still don't regularly beat the dartboard.

Consistent with the efficient market hypothesis, mutual funds are also not found to beat the market. Mutual funds not only do not outperform the market on average, but when they are separated into groups according to whether they had the highest or lowest profits in a chosen period, the mutual funds that did well in the first period did not beat the market in the second period.[2]

The conclusion from the study of investment advisers and mutual fund performance is this: ***Having performed well in the past does not indicate that an investment adviser or a mutual fund will perform well in the future.*** This is not pleasing news to investment advisers, but it is exactly what the efficient market hypothesis predicts. It says that some advisers will be lucky and some will be unlucky. Being lucky does not mean that a forecaster actually has the ability to beat the market. (An exception that proves the rule is discussed in the Mini-Case box on p.137.)

Do Stock Prices Reflect Publicly Available Information? The efficient market hypothesis predicts that stock prices will reflect all publicly available information. Thus if information is already publicly available, a positive announcement about a company will not, on average, raise the price of its stock because this information is already reflected in the stock price. Early empirical evidence also confirmed this conjecture from the efficient market hypothesis: Favorable earnings announcements or announcements of stock splits (a division of a share of stock into multiple shares, which is usually followed by higher earnings) do not, on average, cause stock prices to rise.[3]

Random-Walk Behavior of Stock Prices The term **random walk** describes the movements of a variable whose future changes cannot be predicted (are random) because, given today's value, the variable is just as likely to fall as to rise. An important implication of the efficient market hypothesis is that stock prices should approximately follow a random walk; that is, ***future changes in stock prices should, for all practical purposes, be unpredictable.*** The random-walk implication of the efficient market hypothesis is the one most commonly mentioned in the press because it is the most readily comprehensible to the public.

---

[2]An early study that found that mutual funds do not outperform the market is Michael C. Jensen, "The Performance of Mutual Funds in the Period 1945–64," *Journal of Finance* 23 (1968): 389–416. More recent studies on mutual fund performance are Mark Grimblatt and Sheridan Titman, "Mutual Fund Performance: An Analysis of Quarterly Portfolio Holdings," *Journal of Business* 62 (1989): 393–416; R. A. Ippolito, "Efficiency with Costly Information: A Study of Mutual Fund Performance, 1965–84," *Quarterly Journal of Economics* 104 (1989): 1–23; J. Lakonishok, A. Shleifer, and R. Vishny, "The Structure and Performance of the Money Management Industry," *Brookings Papers on Economic Activity, Microeconomics* (1992); and B. Malkiel, "Returns from Investing in Equity Mutual Funds, 1971–1991," *Journal of Finance* 50 (1995): 549–72.

[3]Ray Ball and Philip Brown, "An Empirical Evaluation of Accounting Income Numbers," *Journal of Accounting Research* 6 (1968): 159–178; Eugene F. Fama, Lawrence Fisher, Michael C. Jensen, and Richard Roll, "The Adjustment of Stock Prices to New Information," *International Economic Review* 10 (1969): 1–21.

MINI-CASE

An Exception That Proves the Rule: Ivan Boesky

The efficient market hypothesis indicates that investment advisers should not have the ability to beat the market. Yet that is exactly what Ivan Boesky was able to do until 1986, when he was charged by the Securities and Exchange Commission with making unfair profits (rumored to be in the hundreds of millions of dollars) by trading on inside information. In an out-of-court settlement, Boesky was banned from the securities business, fined $100 million, and sentenced to three years in jail. (After serving his sentence, Boesky was released from jail in 1990.) If the stock market is efficient, can the SEC legitimately claim that Boesky was able to beat the market? The answer is yes.

Ivan Boesky was the most successful of the so-called *arbs* (short for *arbitrageurs*) who made hundreds of millions in profits for himself and his clients by investing in the stocks of firms that were about to be taken over by other firms at an above-market price. Boesky's continuing success was assured by an arrangement whereby he paid cash (sometimes in a suitcase) to Dennis Levine, an investment banker who had inside information about when a takeover was to take place because his firm was arranging the financing of the deal. When Levine found out that a firm was planning a takeover, he would inform Boesky, who would then buy the stock of the company being taken over and sell it after the stock had risen.

Boesky's ability to make millions year after year in the 1980s is an exception that proves the rule that financial analysts cannot continually outperform the market; yet it supports the efficient markets claim that only information *unavailable to the market* enables an investor to do so. Boesky profited from knowing about takeovers before the rest of the market; this information was known to him but unavailable to the market.

In fact, when people mention the "random-walk theory of stock prices," they are in reality referring to the efficient market hypothesis.

The case for random-walk stock prices can be demonstrated. Suppose that people could predict that the price of Happy Feet Corporation (HFC) stock would rise 1% in the coming week. The predicted rate of capital gains and rate of return on HFC stock would then be over 50% at an annual rate. Since this is very likely to be far higher than the equilibrium rate of return on HFC stock ($R^{of} > R^*$), the efficient market hypothesis indicates that people would immediately buy this stock and bid up its current price. The action would stop only when the predictable change in the price dropped to near zero so that $R^{of} = R^*$.

Similarly, if people could predict that the price of HFC stock would fall by 1%, the predicted rate of return would be negative ($R^{of} < R^*$), and people would immediately sell. The current price would fall until the predictable change in the price rose back to near zero, where the efficient market condition again holds. The efficient market hypothesis suggests that the predictable change in stock prices will be near zero, leading to the conclusion that stock prices will generally follow a random walk.[4]

Financial economists have used two types of tests to explore the hypothesis that stock prices follow a random walk. In the first, they examine stock market

---

[4]Note that the random-walk behavior of stock prices is only an *approximation* derived from the efficient market hypothesis. It would hold exactly only for a stock for which an unchanged price leads to its having the equilibrium return. Then, when the predictable change in the stock price is exactly zero, $R^{of} = R^*$.

records to see if changes in stock prices are systematically related to past changes and hence could have been predicted on that basis. The second type of test examines the data to see if publicly available information other than past stock prices could have been used to predict changes. These tests are somewhat more stringent because additional information (money supply growth, government spending, interest rates, corporate profits) might be used to help forecast stock returns. Early results from both types of tests generally confirmed the efficient market view that stock prices are not predictable and follow a random walk.[5]

Technical Analysis A popular technique used to predict stock prices, called *technical analysis,* is to study past stock price data and search for patterns such as trends and regular cycles. Rules for when to buy and sell stocks are then established on the basis of the patterns that emerge. The efficient market hypothesis suggests that technical analysis is a waste of time. The simplest way to understand why is to use the random-walk result derived from the efficient market hypothesis that holds that past stock price data cannot help predict changes. Therefore, technical analysis, which relies on such data to produce its forecasts, cannot successfully predict changes in stock prices.

Two types of tests bear directly on the value of technical analysis. The first performs the empirical analysis described earlier to evaluate the performance of any financial analyst, technical or otherwise. The results are exactly what the efficient market hypothesis predicts: Technical analysts fare no better than other financial analysts; on average, they do not outperform the market, and successful past forecasting does not imply that their forecasts will outperform the market in the future. The second type of test (first performed by Sidney Alexander) takes the rules developed in technical analysis for when to buy and sell stocks and applies them to new data.[6] The performance of these rules is then evaluated by the profits that would have been made using them. These tests also discredit technical analysis: It does not outperform the overall market.

---

[5]The first type of test, using only stock market data, is referred to as a test of *weak-form efficiency* because the information that can be used to predict stock prices is restricted solely to past price data. The second type of test is referred to as a test of *semistrong-form efficiency* because the information set is expanded to include all publicly available information, not just past stock prices. A third type of test is called a test of *strong-form efficiency* because the information set includes insider information, known only to the owners of the corporation, as when they plan to declare a high dividend. Strong-form tests do sometimes indicate that insider information can be used to predict changes in stock prices. This finding does not contradict efficient markets theory because the information is not available to the market and hence cannot be reflected in market prices. In fact, there are strict laws against using insider information to trade in financial markets. For an early survey on the three forms of tests, see Eugene F. Fama, "Efficient Capital Markets: A Review of Theory and Empirical Work," *Journal of Finance* 25 (1970): 383–416.

[6]Sidney Alexander, "Price Movements in Speculative Markets: Trends or Random Walks?" *Industrial Management Review,* May 1961, pp. 7–26; and Sidney Alexander, "Price Movements in Speculative Markets: Trends or Random Walks? No. 2" in The *Random Character of Stock Prices,* ed. Paul Cootner (Cambridge, Mass.: MIT Press, 1964), pp. 338–372. More recent evidence also seems to discredit technical analysis, for example, F. Allen and R. Karjalainen, "Using Genetic Algorithms to Find Technical Trading Rules," *Journal of Financial Economics* (1999) 51: 245–71. However, some other research is more favorable to technical analysis, e.g., P. Sullivan, A. Timmerman, and H. White, "Data-Snooping, Technical Trading Rule Performance and the Bootstrap," Centre for Economic Policy Research Discussion Paper No. 1976, 1998.

Case

SHOULD FOREIGN EXCHANGE RATES FOLLOW A RANDOM WALK?

Although the efficient market hypothesis is usually applied to the stock market, it can also be used to show that foreign exchange rates, like stock prices, should generally follow a random walk. To see why this is the case, consider what would happen if people could predict that a currency would appreciate by 1% in the coming week. By buying this currency, they could earn a greater than 50% return at an annual rate, which is likely to be far above the equilibrium return for holding a currency. As a result, people would immediately buy the currency and bid up its current price, thereby reducing the expected return. The process would stop only when the predictable change in the exchange rate dropped to near zero so that the optimal forecast of the return no longer differed from the equilibrium return. Likewise, if people could predict that the currency would depreciate by 1% in the coming week, they would sell it until the predictable change in the exchange rate was again near zero. The efficient market hypothesis therefore implies that future changes in exchange rates should, for all practical purposes, be unpredictable; in other words, exchange rates should follow random walks. This is exactly what empirical evidence finds.[7]

Evidence Against Market Efficiency

All the early evidence supporting the efficient market hypothesis appeared to be overwhelming, causing Eugene Fama, a prominent financial economist, to state in his famous 1970 survey of the empirical evidence on the efficient market hypothesis, "The evidence in support of the efficient markets model is extensive, and (somewhat uniquely in economics) contradictory evidence is sparse."[8] However, in recent years, the theory has begun to show a few cracks, referred to as *anomalies*, and empirical evidence indicates that the efficient market hypothesis may not always be generally applicable.

Small-Firm Effect   One of the earliest reported anomalies in which the stock market did not appear to be efficient is called the *small-firm effect.* Many empirical studies have shown that small firms have earned abnormally high returns over long periods of time, even when the greater risk for these firms has been taken into account.[9] The small-firm effect seems to have diminished in recent years but is still a challenge to the theory of efficient markets. Various theories have been

---

[7]See Richard A. Meese and Kenneth Rogoff, "Empirical Exchange Rate Models of the Seventies: Do They Fit out of Sample?" *Journal of International Economics* 14 (1983): 3–24.

[8]Eugene F. Fama, "Efficient Capital Markets: A Review of Theory and Empirical Work," *Journal of Finance* 25 (1970): 383–416.

[9]For example, see Marc R. Reinganum, "The Anomalous Stock Market Behavior of Small Firms in January: Empirical Tests of Tax Loss Selling Effects," *Journal of Financial Economics* 12 (1983): 89–104; Jay R. Ritter, "The Buying and Selling Behavior of Individual Investors at the Turn of the Year," *Journal of Finance* 43 (1988): 701–717; and Richard Roll, "Vas Ist Das? The Turn-of-the-Year Effect: Anomaly or Risk Mismeasurement?" *Journal of Portfolio Management* 9 (1988): 18–28.

developed to explain the small-firm effect, suggesting that it may be due to rebalancing of portfolios by institutional investors, tax issues, low liquidity of small-firm stocks, large information costs in evaluating small firms, or an inappropriate measurement of risk for small-firm stocks.

January Effect Over long periods of time, stock prices have tended to experience an abnormal price rise from December to January that is predictable and hence inconsistent with random-walk behavior. This so-called **January effect** seems to have diminished in recent years for shares of large companies but still occurs for shares of small companies.[10] Some financial economists argue that the January effect is due to tax issues. Investors have an incentive to sell stocks before the end of the year in December because they can then take capital losses on their tax return and reduce their tax liability. Then when the new year starts in January, they can repurchase the stocks, driving up their prices and producing abnormally high returns. Although this explanation seems sensible, it does not explain why institutional investors such as private pension funds, which are not subject to income taxes, do not take advantage of the abnormal returns in January and buy stocks in December, thus bidding up their price and eliminating the abnormal returns.[11]

Market Overreaction Recent research suggests that stock prices may overreact to news announcements and that the pricing errors are corrected only slowly.[12] When corporations announce a major change in earnings, say, a large decline, the stock price may overshoot, and after an initial large decline, it may rise back to more normal levels over a period of several weeks. This violates the efficient market hypothesis because an investor could earn abnormally high returns, on average, by buying a stock immediately after a poor earnings announcement and then selling it after a couple of weeks when it has risen back to normal levels.

Excessive Volatility A closely related phenomenon to market overreaction is that the stock market appears to display excessive volatility; that is, fluctuations in stock prices may be much greater than is warranted by fluctuations in their fundamental value. In an important paper, Robert Shiller of Yale University found that fluctuations in the S&P 500 stock index could not be justified by the subsequent fluctuations in the dividends of the stocks making up this index. There has been much subsequent technical work criticizing these results, but Shiller's work, along with research that finds that there are smaller fluctuations in stock prices when

---

[10]For example, see Donald B. Keim, "The CAPM and Equity Return Regularities," *Financial Analysts Journal* 42 (May–June 1986): 19–34.

[11]Another anomaly that makes the stock market seem less than efficient is the fact that the *Value Line Survey,* one of the most prominent investment advice newsletters, has produced stock recommendations that have yielded abnormally high returns on average. See Fischer Black, "Yes, Virginia, There Is Hope: Tests of the Value Line Ranking System," *Financial Analysts Journal* 29 (September–October 1973): 10–14, and Gur Huberman and Shmuel Kandel, "Market Efficiency and Value Line's Record," *Journal of Business* 63 (1990): 187–216. Whether the excellent performance of the *Value Line Survey* will continue in the future is, of course, a question mark.

[12]Werner F. M. De Bondt and Richard Thaler, "Further Evidence on Investor Overreaction and Stock Market Seasonality," *Journal of Finance* 62 (1987): 557–580.

stock markets are closed, has produced a consensus that stock market prices appear to be driven by factors other than fundamentals.[13]

Mean Reversion Some researchers have also found that stock returns display **mean reversion:** Stocks with low returns today tend to have high returns in the future, and vice versa. Hence stocks that have done poorly in the past are more likely to do well in the future because mean reversion indicates that there will be a predictable positive change in the future price, suggesting that stock prices are not a random walk. Other researchers have found that mean reversion is not nearly as strong in data after World War II and so have raised doubts about whether it is currently an important phenomenon. The evidence on mean reversion remains controversial.[14]

New Information Is Not Always Immediately Incorporated into Stock Prices Although it is generally found that stock prices adjust rapidly to new information, as is suggested by the efficient market hypothesis, recent evidence suggests that, inconsistent with the efficient market hypothesis, stock prices do not instantaneously adjust to profit announcements. Instead, on average stock prices continue to rise for some time after the announcement of unexpectedly high profits, and they continue to fall after surprisingly low profit announcements.[15]

Overview of the Evidence on the Efficient Market Hypothesis

As you can see, the debate on the efficient market hypothesis is far from over. The evidence seems to suggest that the efficient market hypothesis may be a reasonable starting point for evaluating behavior in financial markets. However, there

---

[13]Robert Shiller, "Do Stock Prices Move Too Much to Be Justified by Subsequent Changes in Dividends?" *American Economic Review* 71 (1981): 421–436, and Kenneth R. French and Richard Roll, "Stock Return Variances: The Arrival of Information and the Reaction of Traders," *Journal of Financial Economics* 17 (1986): 5–26.

[14]Evidence for mean reversion has been reported by James M. Poterba and Lawrence H. Summers, "Mean Reversion in Stock Prices: Evidence and Implications," *Journal of Financial Economics* 22 (1988): 27–59; Eugene F. Fama and Kenneth R. French, "Permanent and Temporary Components of Stock Prices," *Journal of Political Economy* 96 (1988): 246–273; and Andrew W. Lo and A. Craig MacKinlay, "Stock Market Prices Do Not Follow Random Walks: Evidence from a Simple Specification Test," *Review of Financial Studies* 1 (1988): 41–66. However, Myung Jig Kim, Charles R. Nelson, and Richard Startz, "Mean Reversion in Stock Prices? A Reappraisal of the Evidence," *Review of Economic Studies* 58 (1991): 515–528, question whether some of these findings are valid. For an excellent summary of this evidence, see Charles Engel and Charles S. Morris, "Challenges to Stock Market Efficiency: Evidence from Mean Reversion Studies," Federal Reserve Bank of Kansas City *Economic Review,* September-October 1991, pp. 21–35. See also N. Jegadeesh and Sheridan Titman, "Returns to Buying Winners and Selling Losers: Implications for Stock Market Efficiency," *Journal of Finance* 48 (1993): 65–92, which shows that mean reversion also occurs for individual stocks.

[15]For example, see R. Ball and P. Brown, "An Empirical Evaluation of Accounting Income Numbers," *Journal of Accounting Research* (1968) 6: 159–78; L. Chan, N. Jegadeesh, and J. Lakonishok, "Momentum Strategies," *Journal of Finance* (1996) 51: 1681–171; and Eugene Fama, "Market Efficiency, Long-Term Returns and Behavioral Finance," *Journal of Financial Economics* (1998) 49: 283–306.

do seem to be important violations of market efficiency that suggest that the efficient market hypothesis may not be the whole story and so may not be generalizable to all behavior in financial markets.

The Practicing Manager

PRACTICAL GUIDE TO INVESTING IN THE STOCK MARKET

The efficient market hypothesis has numerous applications to the real world. It is especially valuable because it can be applied directly to an issue that concerns managers of financial institutions (and the general public as well): how to make profits in the stock market. A practical guide to investing in the stock market, which we develop here, provides a better understanding of the use and implications of the efficient market hypothesis.

How Valuable Are Published Reports by Investment Advisers?

Suppose that you have just read in the "Heard on the Street" column of the *Wall Street Journal* that investment advisers are predicting a boom in oil stocks because an oil shortage is developing. Should you proceed to withdraw all your hard-earned savings from the bank and invest it in oil stocks?

The efficient market hypothesis tells us that when purchasing a security, we cannot expect to earn an abnormally high return, a return greater than the equilibrium return. Information in newspapers and in the published reports of investment advisers is readily available to many market participants and is already reflected in market prices. So acting on this information will not yield abnormally high returns, on average. As we have seen, the empirical evidence for the most part confirms that recommendations from investment advisers cannot help us outperform the general market. Indeed, as the Mini-Case box below suggests, human investment advisers in San Francisco do not on average even outperform an orangutan!

Probably no other conclusion is met with more skepticism by students than this one when they first hear it. We all know or have heard of somebody who has been successful in the stock market for a period of many years. We wonder, how could someone be so consistently successful if he or she did not really know how to predict when returns would be abnormally high? The following story, reported in the press, illustrates why such anecdotal evidence is not reliable.

MINI-CASE

Should You Hire an Ape as Your Investment Adviser?

The *San Francisco Chronicle* came up with an amusing way of evaluating how successful investment advisers are at picking stocks. They asked eight analysts to pick five stocks at the beginning of the year and then compared the performance of their stock picks to those chosen by Jolyn, an orangutan living at Marine World/Africa USA in Vallejo, California. Consistent with the results found in the "Investment Dartboard" feature of the *Wall Street Journal,* Jolyn beat the investment advisers as often as they beat her. Given this result, you might be just as well off hiring an orangutan as your investment adviser as you would hiring a human being!

A get-rich-quick artist invented a clever scam. Every week, he wrote two letters. In letter A, he would pick team A to win a particular football game, and in letter B, he would pick the opponent, team B. A mailing list would then be separated into two groups, and he would send letter A to the people in one group and letter B to the people in the other. The following week he would do the same thing but would send these letters only to the group who had received the first letter with the correct prediction. After doing this for ten games, he had a small cluster of people who had received letters predicting the correct winning team for every game. He then mailed a final letter to them, declaring that since he was obviously an expert predictor of the outcome of football games (he had picked winners ten weeks in a row) and since his predictions were profitable for the recipients who bet on the games, he would continue to send his predictions only if he were paid a substantial amount of money. When one of his clients figured out what he was up to, the con man was prosecuted and thrown in jail!

What is the lesson of the story? Even if no forecaster is an accurate predictor of the market, there will always be a group of consistent winners. A person who has done well regularly in the past cannot guarantee that he or she will do well in the future. Note that there will also be a group of persistent losers, but you rarely hear about them because no one brags about a poor forecasting record.

Should You Be Skeptical of Hot Tips?

Suppose that your broker phones you with a hot tip to buy stock in the Happy Feet Corporation (HFC) because it has just developed a product that is completely effective in curing athlete's foot. The stock price is sure to go up. Should you follow this advice and buy HFC stock?

The efficient market hypothesis indicates that you should be skeptical of such news. If the stock market is efficient, it has already priced HFC stock so that its expected return will equal the equilibrium return. The hot tip is not particularly valuable and will not enable you to earn an abnormally high return.

You might wonder, though, if the hot tip is based on new information and would give you an edge on the rest of the market. If other market participants have gotten this information before you, the answer is no. As soon as the information hits the street, the unexploited profit opportunity it creates will be quickly eliminated. The stock's price will already reflect the information, and you should expect to realize only the equilibrium return. But if you are one of the first to know the new information (as Ivan Boesky was—see the Mini-Case box), it can do you some good. Only then can you be one of the lucky ones who, on average, will earn an abnormally high return by helping eliminate the profit opportunity by buying HFC stock.

Do Stock Prices Always Rise When There Is Good News?

If you follow the stock market, you might have noticed a puzzling phenomenon: When good news about a stock, such as a particularly favorable earnings report, is announced, the price of the stock frequently does not rise. The efficient market hypothesis and the random-walk behavior of stock prices explain this phenomenon.

Because changes in stock prices are unpredictable, when information is announced that has already been expected by the market, the stock price will remain unchanged. The announcement does not contain any new information that should lead to a change in stock prices. If this were not the case and the announcement led to a change in stock prices, it would mean that the change was predictable. Because that is ruled out in an efficient market, **stock prices will respond to announcements only when the information being announced is new and unexpected.** If the news is expected, there will be no stock price response. This is exactly what the evidence that we described earlier suggests will occur—that stock prices reflect publicly available information.

Sometimes a stock price declines when good news is announced. Although this seems somewhat peculiar, it is completely consistent with the workings of an efficient market. Suppose that although the announced news is good, it is not as good as expected. HFC's earnings may have risen 15%, but if the market expected earnings to rise by 20%, the new information is actually unfavorable, and the stock price declines.

Efficient Markets Prescription for the Investor

What does the efficient market hypothesis recommend for investing in the stock market? It tells us that hot tips, investment advisers' published recommendations, and technical analysis—all of which make use of publicly available information—cannot help an investor outperform the market. Indeed, it indicates that anyone without better information than other market participants cannot expect to beat the market. So what is an investor to do?

The efficient market hypothesis leads to the conclusion that such an investor (and almost all of us fit into this category) should not try to outguess the market by constantly buying and selling securities. This process does nothing but boost the income of brokers, who earn commissions on each trade.[16] Instead, the investor should pursue a "buy and hold" strategy—purchase stocks and hold them for long periods of time. This will lead to the same returns, on average, but the investor's net profits will be higher because fewer brokerage commissions will have to be paid.[17]

It is frequently a sensible strategy for a small investor, whose costs of managing a portfolio may be high relative to its size, to buy into a mutual fund rather than individual stocks. Because the efficient market hypothesis indicates that no mutual fund can consistently outperform the market, an investor should not buy into one that has high management fees or that pays sales commissions to brokers but rather should purchase a no-load (commission-free) mutual fund that has low management fees.

As we have seen, the evidence indicates that it will not be easy to beat the prescription suggested here, although some of the anomalies to the efficient market hypothesis suggest that an extremely clever investor (which rules out most of us) may be able to outperform a buy-and-hold strategy.

---

[16]The investor may also have to pay Uncle Sam capital gains taxes on any profits that are realized when a security is sold—an additional reason why continual buying and selling does not make sense.

[17]The investor can also minimize risk by holding a diversified portfolio. The investor will be better off by pursuing a buy-and-hold strategy with a diversified portfolio or with a mutual fund that has a diversified portfolio.

Case

WHAT DO THE BLACK MONDAY CRASH OF 1987 AND THE TECH CRASH OF 2000 TELL US ABOUT THE EFFICIENT MARKET HYPOTHESIS?

On October 19, 1987, dubbed "Black Monday," the Dow Jones Industrial Average declined more than 20%, the largest one-day decline in U.S. history. The collapse of the high-tech companies' share prices from their peaks in March 2000 caused the heavily tech-laden NASDAQ index to fall from around 5000 in March 2000 to around 1500 in 2001 and 2002, for a decline of well over 60%. These two crashes have caused many economists to question the validity of the efficient market hypothesis. They do not believe that an efficient market could have produced such massive swings in share prices. To what degree should these stock market crashes make us doubt the validity of the efficient market hypothesis?

Nothing in the efficient market hypothesis rules out large changes in stock prices. A large change in stock prices can result from new information that produces a dramatic decline in optimal forecasts of the future valuation of firms. However, economists are hard pressed to come up with fundamental changes in the economy that can explain the Black Monday and tech crashes. One lesson from these crashes is that factors other than market fundamentals probably have an effect on stock prices. Hence these crashes have convinced many economists that the stronger version of the efficient market hypothesis, which states that asset prices reflect the true fundamental (intrinsic) value of securities, is incorrect. They attribute a large role in determination of stock prices to market psychology and to the institutional structure of the marketplace. However, nothing in this view contradicts the basic reasoning behind the weaker version of the efficient market hypothesis—that market participants eliminate unexploited profit opportunities. Even though stock market prices may not always solely reflect market fundamentals, this does not mean that rational expectations do not hold. As long as stock market crashes are unpredictable, the basic lessons of the theory of rational expectations hold.

Some economists have come up with theories of what they call *rational bubbles* to explain stock market crashes. A **bubble** is a situation in which the price of an asset differs from its fundamental market value. In a rational bubble, investors can have rational expectations that a bubble is occurring because the asset price is above its fundamental value but continue to hold the asset anyway. They might do this because they believe that someone else will buy the asset for a higher price in the future. In a rational bubble, asset prices can therefore deviate from their fundamental value for a long time because the bursting of the bubble cannot be predicted and so there are no unexploited profit opportunities.

However, other economists believe that the Black Monday crash of 1987 and the tech crash of 2000 suggest that there may be unexploited profit opportunities and that the theory of rational expectations and the efficient market hypothesis might be fundamentally flawed. The controversy over whether capital markets are efficient continues.

Behavioral Finance

Doubts about the efficient market hypothesis, particularly after the stock market crash of 1987, have led to a new field of study, **behavioral finance,** which applies concepts from other social sciences such as anthropology, sociology, and particularly psychology to understand the behavior of securities prices.[18]

As we have seen, the efficient market hypothesis assumes that unexploited profit opportunities are eliminated by "smart money." But can smart money dominate ordinary investors so that financial markets are efficient? Specifically, the efficient market hypothesis suggests that smart money sells when a stock price goes up irrationally, with the result that the stock falls back down to what is justified by fundamentals. However, for this to occur, smart money must be able to engage in **short sales,** in which they borrow stock from brokers and then sell it in the market, with the hope that they earn a profit by buying the stock back again ("covering the short") after it has fallen in price. However, work by psychologists suggests that people are subject to loss aversion: That is, they are more unhappy when they suffer losses than they are happy from making gains. Short sales can result in losses way in excess of an investor's initial investment if the stock price climbs sharply above the price at which the short sale is made (and these losses have the possibility of being unlimited if the stock price climbs to astronomical heights). Loss aversion can thus explain an important phenomenon: Very little short selling actually takes place. Short selling may also be constrained by rules restricting it because it seems unsavory that someone would make money from another person's misfortune. The fact that there is so little short selling can explain why stock prices sometimes get overvalued. Not enough short selling can take place by smart money to drive stock prices back down to their fundamental value.

Psychologists have also found that people tend to be overconfident in their own judgments (just as in "Lake Woebegon," everyone believes they are above average). As a result, it is no surprise that investors tend to believe that they are smarter than other investors and so are willing to assume that the market typically doesn't get it right and therefore to trade on their beliefs. This can explain why securities markets have so much trading volume, something that the efficient market hypothesis does not predict.

Overconfidence and social contagion provide an explanation for stock market bubbles. When stock prices go up, investors attribute their profits to their intelligence and talk up the stock market. This word-of-mouth enthusiasm and the media then can produce an environment in which even more investors think stock prices will rise in the future. The result is then a so-called positive feedback loop in which prices continue to rise, producing a speculative bubble, which finally crashes when prices get too far out of line with fundamentals.[19]

The field of behavioral finance is a young one, but it holds out hope that we might be able to explain some features of securities markets' behavior that are not well explained by the efficient market hypothesis.

---

[18]Surveys of this field can be found in Hersh Shefrin, *Beyond Greed and Fear: Understanding of Behavioral Finance and the Psychology of Investing* (Boston: Harvard Business School Press, 2000); Andrei Shleifer, *Inefficient Markets* (Oxford: Oxford University Press, 2000); and Robert J. Shiller, "From Efficient Market Theory to Behavioral Finance," Cowles Foundation Discussion Paper No. 1385 (October 2002).

[19]See Robert J. Shiller, *Irrational Exuberance* (New York: Broadway Books, 2001).

Summary

1. The efficient market hypothesis states that current security prices will fully reflect all available information because in an efficient market, all unexploited profit opportunities are eliminated. The elimination of unexploited profit opportunities necessary for a financial market to be efficient does not require that all market participants be well informed.

2. The evidence on the efficient market hypothesis is quite mixed. Early evidence on the performance of investment analysts and mutual funds, whether stock prices reflect publicly available information, the random-walk behavior of stock prices, and the success of so-called technical analysis was quite favorable to the efficient market hypothesis. However, in recent years, evidence on the small-firm effect, the January effect, market overreaction, excessive volatility, mean reversion, and that new information is not always incorporated into stock prices suggests that the hypothesis may not always be entirely correct. The evidence seems to suggest that the efficient market hypothesis may be a reasonable starting point for evaluating behavior in financial markets but may not be generalizable to all behavior in financial markets.

3. The efficient market hypothesis indicates that hot tips, investment advisers' published recommenda-

tions, and technical analysis cannot help an investor outperform the market. The prescription for investors is to pursue a buy-and-hold strategy—purchase stocks and hold them for long periods of time. Empirical evidence generally supports these implications of the efficient market hypothesis in the stock market.

4. The stock market crashes of 1987 and 2000 have convinced many financial economists that the stronger version of the efficient market hypothesis, which states that asset prices reflect the true fundamental (intrinsic) value of securities, is not correct. It is less clear that the stock market crashes show that the weaker version of the efficient market hypothesis is wrong. Even if the stock market was driven by factors other than fundamentals, the crashes do not clearly demonstrate that many of the basic lessons of the efficient market hypothesis are no longer valid as long as the crashes could not have been predicted.

5. The new field of behavioral finance applies concepts from other social sciences such as anthropology, sociology, and particularly psychology to understand the behavior of securities prices. Loss aversion, overconfidence, and social contagion can explain why trading volume is so high, stock prices get overvalued, and speculative bubbles occur.

Key Terms

behavioral finance, *p. 146*
bubble, *p. 145*
efficient market hypothesis, *p. 132*
January effect, *p. 140*

market fundamentals, *p. 135*
mean reversion, *p. 141*
random walk, *p. 136*
short sale, *p. 146*

theory of efficient capital markets, *p. 132*
unexploited profit opportunity, *p. 134*

Questions

1. "Forecasters' predictions of inflation are notoriously inaccurate, so their expectations of inflation cannot be optimal." Is this statement true, false, or uncertain? Explain your answer.

2. "Whenever it is snowing when Joe Commuter gets up in the morning, he misjudges how long it will take him to drive to work. Otherwise, his expectations of the driving time are perfectly accurate. Considering that it snows only once every ten years where Joe lives, Joe's expectations are almost always perfectly accurate." Are Joe's expectations optimal? Why or why not?

3. If a forecaster spends hours every day studying data to forecast interest rates but his expectations are not as accurate as predicting that tomorrow's interest rates will be identical to today's interest rate, are his expectations optimal?

4. "If stock prices did not follow a random walk, there would be unexploited profit opportunities in the market." Is this statement true, false, or uncertain? Explain your answer.

5. Suppose that increases in the money supply lead to a rise in stock prices. Does this mean that when you see that the money supply has had a sharp rise in

the past week, you should go out and buy stocks? Why or why not?

6. If I read in the *Wall Street Journal* that the "smart money" on Wall Street expects stock prices to fall, should I follow that lead and sell all my stocks?

7. If my broker has been right in her five previous buy and sell recommendations, should I continue listening to her advice?

8. Can a person with optimal expectations expect the price of IBM to rise by 10% in the next month?

9. "If most participants in the stock market do not follow what is happening to the monetary aggregates, prices of common stocks will not fully reflect information about them." Is this statement true, false, or uncertain? Explain your answer.

10. "An efficient market is one in which no one ever profits from having better information than the rest." Is this statement true, false, or uncertain? Explain your answer.

11. If higher money growth is associated with higher future inflation and if announced money growth turns out to be extremely high but is still less than the market expected, what do you think would happen to long-term bond prices?

12. "Foreign exchange rates, like stock prices, should follow a random walk." Is this statement true, false, or uncertain? Explain your answer.

13. Can we expect the value of the dollar to rise by 2% next week if our expectations are optimal?

14. "Human fear is the source of stock market crashes, so these crashes indicate that expectations in the stock market cannot be optimal." Is this statement true, false, or uncertain? Explain your answer.

Quantitative Problems

1. A company has just announced a 3-for-1 stock split, effective immediately. Prior to the split, the company had a market value of $5 billion with 100 million shares outstanding. Assuming that the split conveys no new information about the company, what is the value of the company, the number of shares outstanding, and price per share after the split? If the actual market price immediately following the split is $17.00 per share, what does this tell us about market efficiency?

2. If the public expects a corporation to lose $5 a share this quarter and it actually loses $4, which is still the largest loss in the history of the company, what does the efficient market hypothesis say will happen to the price of the stock when the $4 loss is announced?

Web Exercises

The Efficient Market Hypothesis

1. Visit **http://www.forecasts.org/data/index.htm**. Click on "Stock Index" at the very top of the page. Now choose "U.S. Stock Indices-monthly." Review the indices for the DJIA, the S&P 500, and the NASDAQ composite. Which index appears most volatile? In which index would you have rather invested in 1985 if the investment had been allowed to compound until now?

2. The Internet is a great source of information on stock prices and stock price movements. There are many sites that provide up-to-the minute data on stock market indices. One of the best is found at **http://finance.lycos.com/home/livecharts**. This site provides free real-time streaming of stock market data. Type $indu in the submit box to have the chart display the Dow Jones Industrial Average. Look at the stock trend over various intervals by adjusting the update frequency (click on INT at the top of the chart). Have stock prices been going up or down over the last day, week, month, and year?

PART 3

Central Banking and the Conduct of Monetary Policy

CHAPTER 7

Structure of Central Banks and the Federal Reserve System

Preview

The most important players in financial markets throughout the world are central banks, the government authorities in charge of monetary policy. Central banks' actions affect interest rates, the amount of credit, and the money supply, all of which have direct impacts not only on financial markets but also on aggregate output and inflation. To understand the role that central banks play in financial markets and the overall economy, we need to understand how these organizations work. Who controls central banks and determines their actions? What motivates their behavior? Who holds the reins of power?

In this chapter we look at the institutional structure of major central banks and particularly focus on the Federal Reserve System, the most important central bank in the world. We start by focusing on the formal institutional structure of the Fed and then examine the more relevant informal structure that determines where the true power within the Federal Reserve System lies. By understanding who makes the decisions, we will have a better idea of how they are made. We then look at several other major central banks and see how they are organized. With this information, we will be more able to comprehend the actual conduct of monetary policy described in the following chapters.

Origins of the Federal Reserve System

Of all the central banks in the world, the Federal Reserve System probably has the most unusual structure. To understand why this structure arose, we must go back before 1913, when the Federal Reserve System was created.

Before the twentieth century, a major characteristic of American politics was the fear of centralized power, as seen in the checks and balances of the Constitution and the preservation of states' rights. This fear of centralized power was one source of the American resistance to the establishment of a central bank (see Chapter 18). Another source was the traditional American distrust of moneyed interests, the most prominent symbol of which was a central bank. The open hostility of the American public to the existence of a central bank resulted in the demise of the first two experiments in central banking, whose function was to police the banking system: The First Bank of the United States was disbanded in 1811, and the national charter of the Second Bank of the United States expired in 1836 after its renewal was vetoed in 1832 by President Andrew Jackson.

The termination of the Second Bank's national charter in 1836 created a severe problem for American financial markets because there was no lender of last resort who could provide reserves to the banking system to avert a bank panic. Hence in the nineteenth and early twentieth centuries, nationwide bank panics became a regular event, occurring every 20 years or so, culminating in the panic of 1907. The 1907 panic resulted in such widespread bank failures and such substantial losses to depositors that the public was finally convinced that a central bank was needed to prevent future panics.

The hostility of the American public to banks and centralized authority created great opposition to the establishment of a single central bank like the Bank of England. Fear was rampant that the moneyed interests on Wall Street (including the largest corporations and banks) would be able to manipulate such an institution to gain control over the economy and that federal operation of the central bank might result in too much government intervention in the affairs of private banks. Serious disagreements existed over whether the central bank should be a private bank or a government institution. Because of the heated debates on these issues, a compromise was struck. In the great American tradition, Congress wrote an elaborate system of checks and balances into the Federal Reserve Act of 1913, which created the Federal Reserve System with its 12 regional Federal Reserve banks (see the "Inside the Fed" box below).

INSIDE THE FED

The Political Genius of the Founders of the Federal Reserve System

The history of the United States has been one of public hostility to banks and especially to a central bank. How were the politicians who founded the Federal Reserve able to design a system that has become one of the most prestigious institutions in the United States?

The answer is that the founders recognized that if power was too concentrated in either Washington or New York, cities that Americans love to hate, an American central bank might not have enough public support to operate effectively. They thus decided to set up a decentralized system with 12 Federal Reserve banks spread throughout the country to make sure that all regions of the country were represented in monetary policy deliberations. In addition, they made the Federal Reserve banks quasi-private institutions overseen by directors from the private sector living in that district who represent views from that region and are in close contact with the president of the Federal Reserve bank. The unusual structure of the Federal Reserve System has promoted a concern in the Fed with regional issues as is evident in Federal Reserve bank publications. Without this unusual structure, the Federal Reserve System might have been far less popular with the public, making the institution far less effective.

Formal Structure of the Federal Reserve System

The formal structure of the Federal Reserve System was intended by writers of the Federal Reserve Act to diffuse power along regional lines, between the private sector and the government, and among bankers, businesspeople, and the public. This initial diffusion of power has resulted in the evolution of the Federal Reserve System to include the following entities: the **Federal Reserve banks,** the **Board of Governors of the Federal Reserve System,** the **Federal Open Market Committee (FOMC),** the Federal Advisory Council, and around 3600 member commercial banks. Figure 1 outlines the relationships of these entities to one another and to the three policy tools of the Fed (open market operations, the discount rate, and reserve requirements) discussed in Chapter 8.

Check out information on the structure of the Federal Reserve System at www.federalreserve.gov/pubs/frseries/frseri.htm

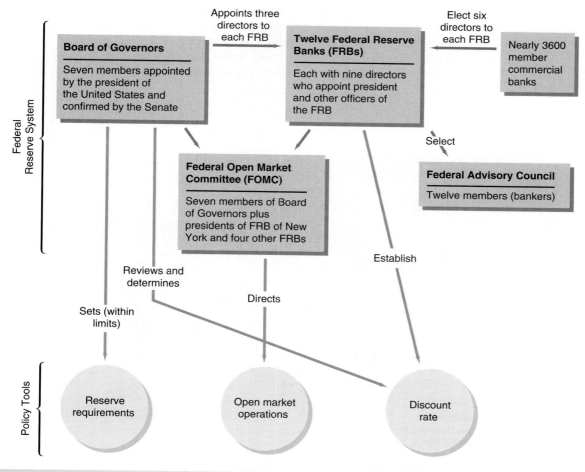

FIGURE 1 *Formal Structure and Allocation of Policy Tools in the Federal Reserve*

Federal Reserve Banks

Each of the 12 Federal Reserve districts has one main Federal Reserve bank, which may have branches in other cities in the district. The locations of these districts, the Federal Reserve banks, and their branches are shown in Figure 2. The three largest Federal Reserve banks in terms of assets are those of New York, Chicago, and San Francisco—combined they hold over 50% of the assets (discount loans, securities, and other holdings) of the Federal Reserve System. The New York bank, with around one-quarter of the assets, is the most important of the Federal Reserve banks (see the "Inside the Fed" box on page 155).

Each of the Federal Reserve banks is a quasi-public (part private, part government) institution owned by the private commercial banks in the district who are members of the Federal Reserve System. These member banks have purchased stock in their district Federal Reserve bank (a requirement of membership), and the dividends paid by that stock are limited by law to 6% annually. The member banks elect six directors for each district bank; three more are appointed by the Board of Governors. Together, these nine directors appoint the president of the bank (subject to the approval of the Board of Governors).

The directors of a district bank are classified into three categories, A, B, and C: The three A directors (elected by the member banks) are professional bankers, and the three B directors (also elected by the member banks) are prominent leaders from industry, labor, agriculture, or the consumer sector. The three C directors, who are appointed by the Board of Governors to represent the public interest,

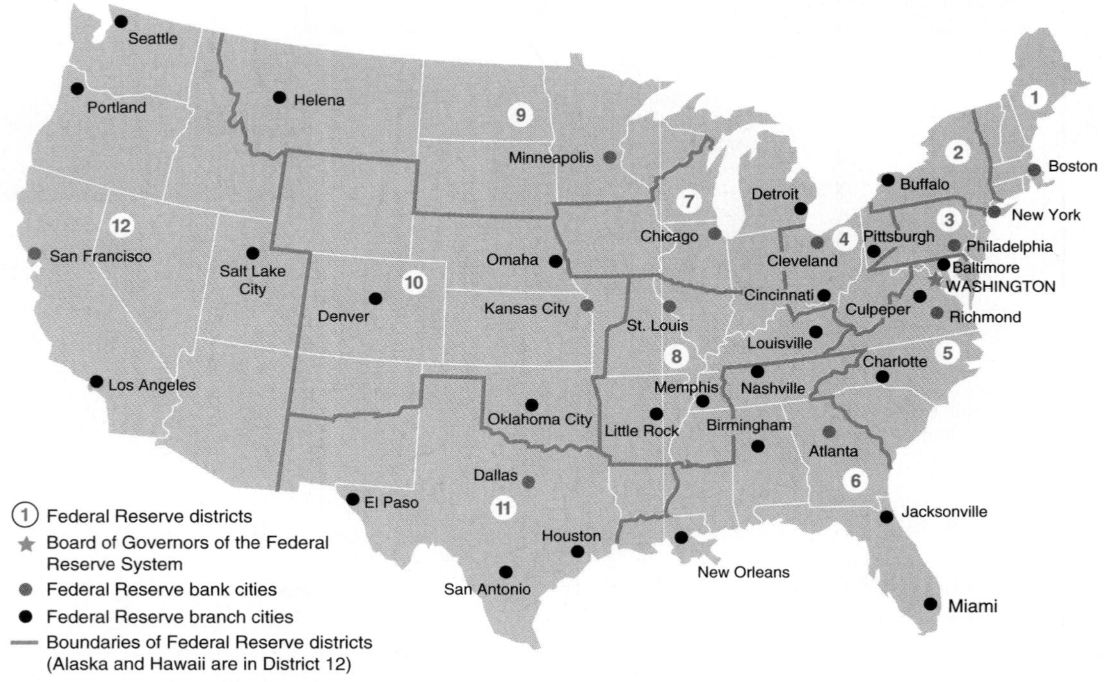

Find addresses and phone numbers of Federal Reserve banks, branches, and RCPCs as well as links to the main pages of the 12 reserve banks and Board of Governors at www.federalreserve.gov/otherfrb.htm

(1) Federal Reserve districts
★ Board of Governors of the Federal Reserve System
● Federal Reserve bank cities
● Federal Reserve branch cities
— Boundaries of Federal Reserve districts (Alaska and Hawaii are in District 12)

FIGURE 2 *Federal Reserve System*

Source: Federal Reserve Bulletin.

INSIDE THE FED

Special Role of the Federal Reserve Bank of New York

The Federal Reserve Bank of New York plays a special role in the Federal Reserve System for several reasons. First, its district contains many of the largest commercial banks in the United States, the safety and soundness of which are paramount to the health of the U.S. financial system. The Federal Reserve Bank of New York conducts examinations of bank holding companies and state-chartered banks in its district, making it the supervisor of some of the most important financial institutions in our financial system. Not surprisingly, given this responsibility, the Bank Supervision group is one of the largest units of the New York Fed and is by far the largest bank supervision group in the Federal Reserve System.

The second reason for the New York Fed's special role is its active involvement in the bond and foreign exchange markets. The New York Fed houses the open market desk, which conducts open market operations—the purchase and sale of bonds—that determine the amount of reserves in the banking system. Because of this involvement in the Treasury securities market, as well as its walking-distance location near the New York and American Stock Exchanges, the officials at the Federal Reserve Bank of New York are in constant contact with the major domestic financial markets in the United States. In addition, the Federal Reserve Bank of New York also houses the foreign exchange desk, which conducts foreign exchange interventions on behalf of the Federal Reserve System and the U.S. Treasury. Its involvement in these financial markets means that the New York Fed is an important source of information on what is happening in domestic and foreign financial markets, particularly during crisis periods, as well as a liaison between officials in the Federal Reserve System and private participants in the markets.

The third reason for the Federal Reserve Bank of New York's prominence is that it is the only Federal Reserve bank to be a member of the Bank for International Settlements (BIS). Thus the president of the New York Fed, along with the chairman of the Board of Governors, represent the Federal Reserve System in its regular monthly meetings with other major central bankers at the BIS. This close contact with foreign central bankers and interaction with foreign exchange markets means that the New York Fed has a special role in international relations, both with other central bankers and with private market participants. Adding to its prominence in international circles is that the New York Fed is the repository for over $100 billion of the world's gold, an amount greater than the gold at Fort Knox.

Finally, the president of the Federal Reserve Bank of New York, currently Timothy F. Geithner, is the only permanent member of the FOMC among the Federal Reserve bank presidents, serving as the vice chairman of the committee. Thus he, the chairman, and the vice chairman of the Board of Governors are the three most important officials in the Federal Reserve System.

---

are not allowed to be officers, employees, or stockholders of banks. This design for choosing directors was intended by the framers of the Federal Reserve Act to ensure that the directors of each Federal Reserve bank would reflect all constituencies of the American public.

The 12 Federal Reserve banks perform the following functions:

- Clear checks.
- Issue new currency.
- Withdraw damaged currency from circulation.
- Evaluate proposed mergers and applications for banks to expand their activities.
- Administer and make discount loans to banks in their districts.
- Act as liaisons between the business community and the Federal Reserve System.
- Examine bank holding companies and state-chartered member banks.

- Collect data on local business conditions.
- Use their staffs of professional economists to research topics related to the conduct of monetary policy.

The 12 Federal Reserve banks are involved in monetary policy in several ways:

- Their directors "establish" the discount rate (although the discount rate in each district is reviewed and determined by the Board of Governors).
- They decide which banks, member and nonmember alike, can obtain discount loans from the Federal Reserve bank.
- Their directors select one commercial banker from each bank's district to serve on the Federal Advisory Council, which consults with the Board of Governors and provides information that helps in the conduct of monetary policy.
- Five of the 12 bank presidents each have a vote in the Federal Open Market Committee, which directs **open market operations** (the purchase and sale of government securities that affect both interest rates and the amount of reserves in the banking system). As explained in the "Inside the Fed" box, the president of the New York Fed always has a vote in the FOMC, making it the most important of the banks; the other four votes allocated to the district banks rotate annually among the remaining 11 presidents.

Member Banks

All *national banks* (commercial banks chartered by the Office of the Comptroller of the Currency) are required to be members of the Federal Reserve System. Commercial banks chartered by the states are not required to be members, but they can choose to join. Currently, around one-third of the commercial banks in the United States are members of the Federal Reserve System, having declined from a peak figure of 49% in 1947.

Before 1980, only member banks were required to keep reserves as deposits at the Federal Reserve banks. Nonmember banks were subject to reserve requirements determined by their states, which typically allowed them to hold much of their reserves in interest-bearing securities. Because no interest is paid on reserves deposited at the Federal Reserve banks, it was costly to be a member of the system, and as interest rates rose, the relative cost of membership rose, and more and more banks left the system.

This decline in Fed membership was a major concern of the Board of Governors (one reason was that it lessened the Fed's control over the money supply, making it more difficult for the Fed to conduct monetary policy). The chairman of the Board of Governors repeatedly called for new legislation that required all commercial banks to be members of the Federal Reserve System. One result of the Fed's pressure on Congress was a provision in the Depository Institutions Deregulation and Monetary Control Act of 1980: All depository institutions became subject (by 1987) to the same requirements to keep deposits at the Fed, so member and nonmember banks would be on an equal footing in terms of reserve requirements. In addition, all depository institutions were given access to the Federal Reserve facilities, such as the discount window (discussed in Chapter 8) and

Fed check clearing, on an equal basis. These provisions ended the decline in Fed membership and reduced the distinction between member and nonmember banks.

Board of Governors of the Federal Reserve System

At the head of the Federal Reserve System is the seven-member Board of Governors, headquartered in Washington, D.C. Each governor is appointed by the president of the United States and confirmed by the Senate. To limit the president's control over the Fed and insulate the Fed from other political pressures, the governors serve one nonrenewable 14-year term, with one governor's term expiring every other January.[1] The governors (many are professional economists) are required to come from different Federal Reserve districts to prevent the interests of one region of the country from being overrepresented. The chairman of the Board of Governors is chosen from among the seven governors and serves a four-year term. It is expected that once a new chairman is chosen, the old chairman resigns from the Board of Governors, even if there are many years left to his or her term as a governor.

The Board of Governors is actively involved in decisions concerning the conduct of monetary policy. All seven governors are members of the FOMC and vote on the conduct of open market operations. Because there are only 12 voting members on this committee (seven governors and five presidents of the district banks), the board has the majority of the votes. The board also sets reserve requirements (within limits imposed by legislation) and effectively controls the discount rate by the "review and determination" process, whereby it approves or disapproves the discount rate "established" by the Federal Reserve banks. The chairman of the board advises the president of the United States on economic policy, testifies in Congress, and speaks for the Federal Reserve System to the media. The chairman and other governors may also represent the United States in negotiations with foreign governments on economic matters. The board has a staff of professional economists (larger than those of individual Federal Reserve banks), which provides economic analysis that the board uses in making its decisions. (The "Inside the Fed" box on page 158 discusses the role of the research staff.)

Through legislation, the Board of Governors has often been given duties not directly related to the conduct of monetary policy. In the past, for example, the board set the maximum interest rates payable on certain types of time deposits under Regulation Q. (After 1986, ceilings on time deposits were eliminated, but there is still a restriction on paying any interest on business demand deposits.) Under the Credit Control Act of 1969 (which expired in 1982), the board had the ability to regulate and control credit once the president of the United States approved. The Board of Governors also sets margin requirements, the fraction of the purchase price of the securities that has to be paid for with cash rather than

---

[1]Although technically the governor's term is nonrenewable, a governor can resign just before the term expires and then be reappointed by the president. This explains how one governor, William McChesney Martin Jr., served for 28 years. Since Martin, the chairman from 1951 to 1970, retired from the board in 1970.

INSIDE THE FED

Role of the Research Staff

The Federal Reserve System is the largest employer of economists not just in the United States but in the world. The system's research staff has around 1000 people, half of whom are economists. Of these 500 economists, 250 are at the Board of Governors, 100 are at the Federal Reserve Bank of New York, and the remainder are at the other Federal Reserve banks. What do all these economists do?

The most important task of the Fed's economists is to follow the incoming data from government agencies and private sector organizations on the economy and provide guidance to the policymakers on where the economy may be heading and what the impact of monetary policy actions on the economy might be. Before each FOMC meeting, the research staff at each Federal Reserve bank briefs its president and the senior management of the bank on its forecast for the U.S. economy and the issues that are likely to be discussed at the meeting. The research staff also provides briefing materials or a formal briefing on the economic outlook for the bank's region, something that each president discusses at the FOMC meeting. Meanwhile, at the Board of Governors, economists maintain a large econometric model (a model whose equations are estimated with statistical procedures) that helps them produce their forecasts of the national economy, and they too brief the governors on the national economic outlook.

The research staffers at the banks and the board also provide support for the bank supervisory staff, tracking developments in the banking sector and other financial markets and institutions and providing bank examiners with technical advice that they might need in the course of their examinations. Because the Board of Governors has to decide on whether to approve bank mergers, the research staff at both the board and the bank in whose district the merger is to take place prepare information on what effect the proposed merger might have on the competitive environment. To assure compliance with the Community Reinvestment Act, economists also analyze a bank's performance in its lending activities in different communities.

Because of the increased influence of developments in foreign countries on the U.S. economy, the research staff, particularly at the New York Fed and the board, produce reports on the major foreign economies. They also conduct research on developments in the foreign exchange market because of its growing importance in the monetary policy process and to support the activities of the foreign exchange desk. Economists also help support the operation of the open market desk by projecting reserve growth and the growth of the monetary aggregates.

Staff economists also engage in basic research on the effects of monetary policy on output and inflation, developments in the labor markets, international trade, international capital markets, banking and other financial institutions, financial markets, and the regional economy, among other topics. This research is published widely in academic journals and in Reserve bank publications. (Federal Reserve bank reviews are a good source of supplemental material for finance students.)

Another important activity of the research staff primarily at the Reserve banks is in the public education area. Staff economists are called on frequently to make presentations to the board of directors at their banks or to make public speeches in their district.

borrowed funds. It also sets the salary of the president and all officers of each Federal Reserve bank and reviews each bank's budget. Finally, the board has substantial bank regulatory functions: It approves bank mergers and applications for new activities, specifies the permissible activities of bank holding companies, and supervises the activities of foreign banks in the United States.

Federal Open Market Committee (FOMC)

The FOMC usually meets eight times a year (about every six weeks) and makes decisions regarding the conduct of open market operations, which influence the monetary base. The FOMC is often referred to as the "Fed" in the press: For example, when the media say that the Fed is meeting, they actually mean that the FOMC is meeting. The committee consists of the seven members of the Board of Governors, the president of the Federal Reserve Bank of New York, and presidents of four other Federal Reserve banks. The chairman of the Board of Governors also presides as the chairman of the FOMC. Even though only presidents of five of the Federal Reserve banks are voting members of the FOMC, the other seven presidents of the district banks attend FOMC meetings and participate in discussions. Hence they have some input into the committee's decisions.

Because open market operations are the most important policy tool that the Fed has for controlling the money supply, the FOMC is necessarily the focal point for policymaking in the Federal Reserve System. Although reserve requirements and the discount rate are not actually set by the FOMC, decisions in regard to these policy tools are effectively made there. The FOMC does not actually carry out securities purchases or sales. Rather it issues directives to the trading desk at the Federal Reserve Bank of New York, where the manager for domestic open market operations supervises a roomful of people who execute the purchases and sales of the government or agency securities. The manager communicates daily with the FOMC members and their staffs concerning the activities of the trading desk.

Find general information on the FOMC, including its schedule of meetings, statements, minutes, and transcripts, information on its members, and the beige book at www.federalreserve.gov/fomc

The FOMC Meeting

The FOMC meeting takes place in the boardroom on the second floor of the main building of the Board of Governors in Washington. The seven governors and the 12 Reserve Bank presidents, along with the secretary of the FOMC, the board's director of the Research and Statistics Division and his deputy, and the directors of the Monetary Affairs and International Finance Divisions, sit around a massive conference table. Although only five of the Reserve Bank presidents have voting rights on the FOMC at any given time, all actively participate in the deliberations. Seated around the sides of the room are the directors of research at each of the Reserve banks and other senior board and Reserve Bank officials, who, by tradition, do not speak at the meeting.

Except for the meetings before the February and July testimony by the chairman of the Board of Governors before Congress, the meetings start on Tuesdays at 9:00 A.M. sharp with a quick approval of the minutes of the previous meeting of the FOMC. The first substantive agenda item is the reports by the manager of system open market operations on foreign currency and domestic open market operations and other issues related to these topics. After the governors and Reserve Bank presidents finish asking questions and discussing these reports, a vote is taken to ratify them.

The next stage in the meeting is a presentation of the board staff's national economic forecast, which is referred to as the "green book" forecast (see the "Inside the Fed" box), by the director of the Research and Statistics Division at the board. After the governors and Reserve Bank presidents have queried the division director about the forecast, the so-called *go-round* occurs: Each bank president presents an overview of economic conditions in his or her district and the bank's assessment of the national outlook, and each governor, except for the chairman, gives a view of the national outlook. By tradition, remarks avoid the topic of monetary policy at this time.

After a coffee break, everyone returns to the boardroom and the agenda turns to current monetary policy and the domestic policy directive. The board's director of the Monetary Affairs Division then leads off the discussion by outlining the

INSIDE THE FED

Green, Blue, and Beige: What Do These Colors Mean at the Fed?

Three research documents play an important role in the monetary policy process and at Federal Open Market Committee meetings. The national forecast for the next two years, generated by the Federal Reserve Board of Governors' Research and Statistics Division, is placed between green covers and is thus known as the "green book." It is provided to all who attend the FOMC meeting. The "blue book," in blue covers, is also provided to all participants at the FOMC meeting. It contains the projections for the monetary aggregates prepared by the Monetary Affairs Division at the Board of Governors and contains typically three alternative scenarios for monetary policy (labeled A, B, and C). The "beige book," with beige covers, is produced by the Reserve banks and details evidence gleaned either from surveys or from talks with key businesses and financial institutions on the state of the economy in each of the Federal Reserve districts. This is the only one of the three books that is distributed publicly, and it often receives a lot of attention in the press.

different scenarios for monetary policy actions outlined in the blue book (see the "Inside the Fed" box above) and may describe an issue relating to how monetary policy should be conducted. After a question-and-answer period, the chairman (currently Alan Greenspan) sets the stage for the following discussion by presenting his views on the state of the economy and then typically makes a recommendation for what monetary policy action should be taken. Then each of the FOMC members as well as the nonvoting bank presidents expresses his or her views on monetary policy, and the chairman summarizes the discussion and proposes specific wording for the statement to the open market desk. The secretary of the FOMC formally reads the proposed statement, and the members of the FOMC vote.[2]

Then there is an informal buffet lunch, and while eating, the participants hear a presentation on the latest developments in Congress on banking legislation and other legislation relevant to the Federal Reserve. Around 2:15 P.M. the meeting breaks up and the public announcement is made about the outcome of the meeting: whether the federal funds rate target has been raised, lowered, or left unchanged, and an assessment of the "balance of risks" in the future, whether toward higher inflation or toward a weaker economy.[3] The postmeeting announcement is an innovation initiated in 1994. Before then, no such announcement was made, and the markets had to guess what policy action was taken. The decision to announce this information was a step in the direction of greater openness by the Fed.

---

[2]The decisions expressed in the directive may not be unanimous, and the dissenting views are made public. However, except in rare cases, the chairman's vote is always on the winning side.

[3]The meetings before the February and July chairman's testimony before Congress, in which the *Monetary Report to Congress* is presented, have a somewhat different format. Rather than start Tuesday morning at 9 A.M. like the other meetings, they start in the afternoon on Tuesday and go over to Wednesday, with the usual announcement around 2:15 P.M. These longer meetings consider the longer-term economic outlook as well as the current conduct of open market operations.

Informal Structure of the Federal Reserve System

The Federal Reserve Act and other legislation give us some idea of the formal structure of the Federal Reserve System and who makes decisions at the Fed. What is written in black and white, however, does not necessarily reflect the reality of the power and decision-making structure.

As envisioned in 1913, the Federal Reserve System was to be a highly decentralized system designed to function as 12 separate, cooperating central banks. In the original plan, the Fed was not responsible for the health of the economy through its control of the money supply and its ability to affect interest rates. Over time, it has acquired the responsibility for promoting a stable economy, and this responsibility has caused the Federal Reserve System to evolve slowly into a more unified central bank.

The framers of the Federal Reserve Act of 1913 intended the Fed to have only one basic tool of monetary policy, the control of discount loans to member banks. The use of open market operations as a tool for monetary control was not yet well understood, and reserve requirements were fixed by the Federal Reserve Act. The discount tool was to be controlled by the joint decision of the Federal Reserve banks and the Federal Reserve Board (which later became the Board of Governors), so that both would share equally in the determination of monetary policy. However, the board's ability to "review and determine" the discount rate effectively allowed it to dominate the district banks in setting this policy.

Banking legislation during the Great Depression years centralized power within the newly created Board of Governors by giving it effective control over the remaining two tools of monetary policy, open market operations and changes in reserve requirements. The Banking Act of 1933 granted the FOMC authority to determine open market operations, and the Banking Act of 1935 gave the board the majority of votes in the FOMC. The Banking Act of 1935 also gave the board authority to change reserve requirements.

Since the 1930s, then, the Board of Governors has acquired the reins of control over the tools for conducting monetary policy. In recent years, the power of the board has become even greater. Although the directors of a Federal Reserve bank choose its president with the approval of the board, the board sometimes suggests a choice (often a professional economist) for president of a Federal Reserve bank to the directors of the bank, who then often follow the board's suggestions. Since the board sets the salary of the bank's president and reviews the budget of each Federal Reserve bank, it has further influence over the district banks' activities.

If the Board of Governors has so much power, what power do the Federal Advisory Council and the "owners" of the Federal Reserve banks—the member banks—actually have within the Federal Reserve System? The answer is almost none. Although member banks own stock in the Federal Reserve banks, they have none of the usual benefits of ownership. First, they have no claim on the earnings of the Fed and get paid only a 6% annual dividend, regardless of how much the Fed earns. Second, they have no say over how their property is used by the Federal Reserve System, in contrast to stockholders of private corporations. Third, there is usually only a single candidate for each of the six A and B directorships "elected" by the member banks, and this candidate is frequently suggested by the president of the Federal Reserve bank (who, in turn, is approved by the Board of Governors). The net result is that member banks are essentially frozen out of the political process at the Fed and have little effective power. Fourth, as its name implies, the Federal Advisory Council has only an advisory capacity and has no authority over Federal Reserve policymaking. Although the member bank "owners" do not have the usual power associated with being a stockholder, they do play an important but subtle role in the Federal Reserve System (see the "Inside the Fed" box below).

A fair characterization of the Federal Reserve System as it has evolved is that it functions as a central bank, headquartered in Washington, D.C., with branches in 12 cities. Because all aspects of the Federal Reserve System are essentially controlled by the Board of Governors, who controls the board? Although the chairman of the Board of Governors does not have legal authority to exercise control over this body, he effectively does so through his ability to act as spokesperson for the Fed and negotiate with Congress and the president of the United States. He also exercises control by setting the agenda of board and FOMC meetings. For example, the fact that the agenda at the FOMC has the chairman speak first about monetary policy enables him to have greater influence over what the policy action will be. The chairman also influences the board through the force of stature and personality. Chairmen of the Board of Governors (including Marriner S. Eccles, William McChesney Martin Jr., Arthur Burns, Paul A. Volcker, and Alan Greenspan) have typically had strong personalities and have wielded great power.

The chairman also exercises power by supervising the board's staff of professional economists and advisers. Because the staff gathers information for the board and conducts the analyses that the board uses in its decisions, it also has some influence over monetary policy. In addition, in the past, several appointments to the board itself have come from within the ranks of its professional staff, making the chairman's influence even farther-reaching and longer-lasting than a four-year term.

INSIDE THE FED

Role of Member Banks in the Federal Reserve System

Although the member bank stockholders in each Federal Reserve bank have little direct power in the Federal Reserve System, they do play an important role. Their six representatives on the board of directors of each bank have a major oversight function. Along with the three public interest directors, they oversee the audit process for the Federal Reserve bank, making sure it is being run properly, and also share their management expertise with the senior management of the bank. Because they vote on recommendations by each bank to raise, lower, or maintain the discount rate at its current level, they engage in discussions about monetary policy and transmit their private sector views to the president and senior management of the

bank. They also get to understand the inner workings of the Federal Reserve banks and the system so that they can help explain the position of the Federal Reserve to their contacts in the private and political sectors. Advisory councils like the Federal Advisory Council and others that are often set up by the district banks—for example, the Small Business and Agriculture Advisory Council and the Thrift Advisory Council at the New York Fed—are a conduit for the private sector to express views on both the economy and the state of the banking system.

So even though the owners of the Reserve banks do not have the usual voting rights, they are important to the Federal Reserve System because they make sure it does not get out of touch with the needs and opinions of the private sector.

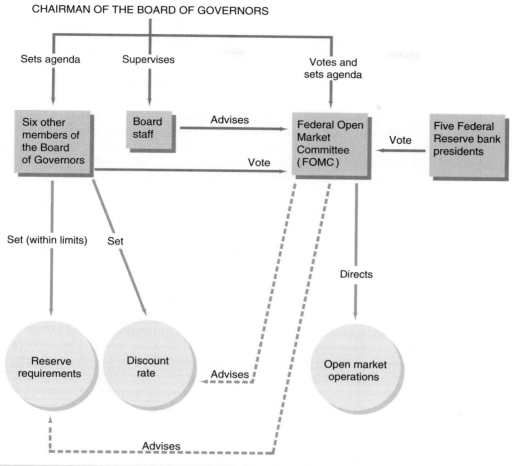

FIGURE 3 *Informal Power Structure of the Federal Reserve System*

The informal power structure of the Fed, in which power is centralized in the chairman of the Board of Governors, is summarized in Figure 3.

How Independent Is the Fed?

When we look, in the next chapter, at how the Federal Reserve conducts monetary policy, we will want to know why it decides to take certain policy actions but not others. To understand its actions, we must understand the incentives that motivate the Fed's behavior. How free is the Fed from presidential and congressional pressures? Do economic, bureaucratic, or political considerations guide it? Is the Fed truly independent of outside pressures?

Stanley Fischer, who was a professor at MIT and then the Deputy Managing Director of the International Monetary Fund, has defined two different types of independence of central banks: **instrument independence,** the ability of the central bank to set monetary policy instruments, and **goal independence,** the ability of the central bank to set the goals of monetary policy. The Federal Reserve has both types of independence and is remarkably free of the political pressures that influence other government agencies. Not only are the members of the Board of Governors appointed for a 14-year term (and so cannot be ousted from office), but also the term is technically not renewable, eliminating some of the incentive for the governors to curry favor with the president and Congress.

Probably even more important to its independence from the whims of Congress is the Fed's independent and substantial source of revenue from its holdings of securities and, to a lesser extent, from its loans to banks. In recent years, for example, the Fed has had net earnings after expenses of around $20 billion per year—not a bad living if you can find it! Because it returns the bulk of these earnings to the Treasury, it does not get rich from its activities, but this income gives the Fed an important advantage over other government agencies: It is not subject to the appropriations process usually controlled by Congress. Indeed, the General Accounting Office, the auditing agency of the federal government, cannot audit the monetary policy or foreign exchange market functions of the Federal Reserve. Because the power to control the purse strings is usually synonymous with the power of overall control, this feature of the Federal Reserve System contributes to its independence more than any other factor.

Yet the Federal Reserve is still subject to the influence of Congress because the legislation that structures it is written by Congress and is subject to change at any time. When legislators are upset with the Fed's conduct of monetary policy, they frequently threaten to take control of the Fed's finances and force it to submit a budget request like other government agencies. An example is the call by Senators Dorgan and Reid in 1996 for Congress to have budgetary authority over the nonmonetary activities of the Federal Reserve. This is a powerful club to wave, and it certainly has some effect in keeping the Fed from straying too far from congressional wishes.

Congress has also passed legislation to make the Federal Reserve more accountable for its actions. In 1975, Congress passed House Concurrent Resolution 133, which requires the Fed to announce its objectives for the growth rates of the monetary aggregates. In the Full Employment and Balanced Growth Act of 1978 (the Humphrey-Hawkins Act), the Fed is required to explain how these objectives are consistent with the economic plans of the president of the United States. More recently, Representative Henry Gonzalez, the former chairman of the House Banking Committee, pressured the Fed to be less secretive in its deliberations about monetary policy—with some success, as the Fed's move to a post-FOMC announcement testifies.

The president can also influence the Federal Reserve. Because congressional legislation can affect the Fed directly or affect its ability to conduct monetary policy, the president can be a powerful ally through his influence on Congress. Second, although ostensibly a president might be able to appoint only one or two members to the Board of Governors during each presidential term, in actual practice the president appoints members far more often. One reason is that most governors do not serve out a full 14-year term. (Governors' salaries are substantially below what they can earn in the private sector, thus providing an incentive for them to take private sector jobs before their term expires.) In addition, the president is able to appoint a new chairman of the Board of Governors every four years, and a chairman who is not reappointed is expected to resign from the board so that a new member can be appointed.

The power that the president enjoys through his appointments to the Board of Governors is limited, however. Because the term of the chairman is not necessarily concurrent with that of the president, a president may have to deal with a chairman of the Board of Governors appointed by a previous administration. Alan Greenspan, for example, was appointed chairman in 1987 by President Ronald Reagan and was reappointed to another term by another Republican president, George Bush. When Bill Clinton, a Democrat, became president in 1993, Greenspan had several years left to his term. Clinton was put under tremendous pressure to reappoint Greenspan when his term expired and did so in 1996, even though Greenspan is a Republican.[4]

You can see that the Federal Reserve has extraordinary independence for a government agency and is one of the most independent central banks in the world. Nonetheless, the Fed is not free from political pressures. Indeed, to understand the Fed's behavior, we must recognize that public support for the actions of the Federal Reserve plays a very important role.[5]

Structure and Independence of Foreign Central Banks

In contrast to the Federal Reserve System, which is decentralized into 12 district banks, which are privately owned, central banks in other industrialized countries consist of one centralized unit that is owned by the government. Here we examine the structure and degree of independence of four of the most important foreign central banks: the Bank of Canada, the Bank of England, the Bank of Japan, and the European Central Bank.

Bank of Canada

Canada was late in establishing a central bank: The Bank of Canada was founded in 1934. Its directors are appointed by the government to three-year terms, and they appoint the governor, who has a seven-year term. A governing council, consisting of the four deputy governors and the governor, is the policymaking body comparable to the FOMC that makes decisions about monetary policy.

The Bank Act was amended in 1967 to give the ultimate responsibility for monetary policy to the government. So on paper, the Bank of Canada is not as instrument independent as the Federal Reserve. In practice, however, the Bank of Canada does essentially control monetary policy. In the event of a disagreement

---

[4]Similarly, William McChesney Martin Jr., the chairman from 1951 to 1970, was appointed by President Truman (Dem.) but was reappointed by Presidents Eisenhower (Rep.), Kennedy (Dem.), and Nixon (Rep.). Also Paul Volcker, the chairman from 1979 to 1987, was appointed by President Carter (Dem.) but was reappointed by President Reagan (Rep.).

[5]An inside view of how the Fed interacts with the public and the politicians can be found in Bob Woodward, *Maestro: Greenspan's Fed and the American Boom* (New York: Simon and Schuster, 2000).

between the bank and the government, the minister of finance can issue a directive that the bank must follow. However, because the directive must be in writing and specific and applicable for a specified period, it is unlikely that such a directive would be issued, and none has been to date. The goal for monetary policy, a target for inflation, is set jointly by the Bank of Canada and the government, so the Bank of Canada has less goal independence than the Fed.

Bank of England

Founded in 1694, the Bank of England is one of the oldest central banks. The Bank Act of 1946 gave the government statutory authority over the Bank of England. The Court (equivalent to a board of directors) of the Bank of England is made up of the governor and two deputy governors, who are appointed for five-year terms, and 16 nonexecutive directors, who are appointed for three-year terms.

Until 1997, the Bank of England was the least independent of the central banks examined in this chapter because the decision to raise or lower interest rates resided not within the Bank of England but with the chancellor of the Exchequer (the equivalent of the U.S. secretary of the Treasury). All of this changed when the new Labour government came to power in May 1997. At this time, the new chancellor of the Exchequer, Gordon Brown, made a surprise announcement that the Bank of England would henceforth have the power to set interest rates. However, the Bank was not granted total instrument independence: The government can overrule the Bank and set rates "in extreme economic circumstances" and "for a limited period." Nonetheless, as in Canada, because overruling the Bank would be so public and is supposed to occur only in highly unusual circumstances and for a limited time, it is unlikely that the government will ever overrule the Bank.

The decision to set interest rates resides in the Monetary Policy Committee, made up of the governor, four other central bank officials (two deputy governors and two other central bank officials chosen by the governor), plus four outside economic experts appointed by the chancellor. (Surprisingly, two of the four outside experts initially appointed to this committee were not British citizens—one was Dutch and the other American, although both were residents of the United Kingdom.) The inflation target for the Bank of England is set by the chancellor of the Exchequer, so the Bank of England is also less goal independent than the Fed.

Bank of Japan

The Bank of Japan (Nippon Ginko) was founded in 1882 during the Meiji Restoration. Monetary policy is determined by the Policy Board, which is composed of the governor, two vice governors, and six outside members appointed by the cabinet and approved by the parliament, all of whom serve for five-year terms.

Until recently, the Bank of Japan was not formally independent of the government, with ultimate power residing with the Ministry of Finance. However, the new Bank of Japan Law, which took effect in April 1998—the first major change in the powers of the Bank of Japan in 55 years—has changed this. In addition to stipulating that the objective of monetary policy is to attain price stability, the law granted greater instrument and goal independence to the Bank of Japan. Before this, the government had two voting members on the Policy Board, one from the Ministry of Finance and the other from the Economic Planning Agency. Now the government may send two representatives from these agencies to board meetings, but they no longer have voting rights, although they do have the ability to request delays in monetary policy decisions. In addition, the Ministry of Finance lost its authority to oversee many of the operations of the Bank of Japan, particularly the right to dismiss senior officials. However, the Ministry of Finance continues to have control over the part of the Bank's budget that is unrelated to monetary policy. Some critics of the new law argue that giving the ministry veto power over most of the Bank's budget might limit its independence to some extent.

European Central Bank

The Maastricht Treaty established the European Central Bank (ECB) and the European System of Central Banks (ESCB), which began operation in January 1999. The structure of the central bank is patterned after the U.S. Federal Reserve System in that central banks for each country have a role similar to that of the Federal Reserve banks. The executive board of the ECB is made up of the president, a vice president, and four other members, who are appointed for eight-year terms. The monetary policymaking body of the bank includes the five members of the executive board and the central-bank governors from the 11 euro countries, all of whom must have five-year terms at a minimum.

Gather general information about the organizational structure of ECB, its history and goals, its monetary policy strategy and operational framework by clicking on "About the ECB" at www.ecb.int

The European Central Bank will be the most independent in the world, even more independent than the German central bank, the Bundesbank, which, before the establishment of the ECB, was considered the world's most independent central bank, along with the Swiss National Bank. The ECB is instrument and goal independent of both the European Union and the national governments and has complete control over monetary policy. In addition, the ECB's mandated mission is the pursuit of price stability. The ECB is far more independent than any other central bank in the world because its charter cannot be changed by legislation: It can be changed only by revision of the Maastricht Treaty, a difficult process because all signatories to the treaty would have to agree.

The Trend Toward Greater Independence

As our survey of the structure and independence of the major central banks indicates, in recent years we have been seeing a remarkable trend toward increasing independence. It used to be that the Federal Reserve was substantially more independent than almost all other central banks, with the exception of those in Germany and Switzerland. Now the newly established European Central Bank is far more independent than the Fed, and greater independence has been granted to central banks like the Bank of England and the Bank of Japan, putting them more on a par with the Fed, as well as to central banks in such diverse countries as New Zealand, Sweden, and the euro nations. Both theory and experience suggest that more independent central banks produce better monetary policy, thus providing an impetus for this trend.

Explaining Central Bank Behavior

One view of government bureaucratic behavior is that bureaucracies serve the public interest (this is the *public interest view*). Yet some economists have developed a theory of bureaucratic behavior that suggests other factors that influence how bureaucracies operate. The *theory of bureaucratic behavior* suggests that the objective of a bureaucracy is to maximize its own welfare, just as a consumer's behavior is motivated by the maximization of personal welfare and a firm's behavior is motivated by the maximization of profits. The welfare of a bureaucracy is related to its power and prestige. Thus this theory suggests that an important factor affecting a central bank's behavior is its attempt to increase its power and prestige.

What predictions does this view of a central bank like the Fed suggest? One is that the Federal Reserve will fight vigorously to preserve its autonomy, a prediction verified time and time again as the Fed has continually counterattacked congressional attempts to control its budget. In fact, it is extraordinary how effectively the Fed has been able to mobilize a lobby of bankers and businesspeople to preserve its independence when threatened.

Another prediction is that the Federal Reserve will try to avoid conflict with powerful groups that may threaten to curtail its power and reduce its autonomy. The Fed's behavior may take several forms. One possible factor explaining why the Fed is sometimes slow to increase interest rates and so smooths out their fluctuations is that it wishes to avoid a conflict with the president and Congress over increases in interest rates. The desire to avoid conflict with Congress and the president may also explain why in the past the Fed was not at all transparent about its actions and is still not fully transparent (see the "Inside the Fed" box below).

The desire of the Fed to hold as much power as possible also explains why it vigorously pursued a campaign to gain control over more banks. The campaign

INSIDE THE FED

Federal Reserve Transparency

As the theory of bureaucratic behavior predicts, the Fed has incentives to hide its actions from the public and from politicians to avoid conflicts with them. In the past, this motivation led to a penchant for secrecy in the Fed, about which one former Fed official remarked that "a lot of staffers would concede that [secrecy] is designed to shield the Fed from political oversight."* For example, the Fed pursued an active defense of delaying its release of FOMC directives to Congress and the public. However, as we have seen, in 1994, it began to reveal the FOMC directive immediately after each FOMC meeting. In 1999, it also began to immediately announce the "bias" toward which

direction monetary policy was likely to go, later expressed as the balance of risks in the economy. In 2002, the Fed started to report the roll call vote on the federal funds rate target taken at the FOMC meeting. In December 2004, it moved up the release date of the minutes of FOMC meetings from six weeks to three weeks after the meeting. Thus the Fed has increased its transparency in recent years. Yet, even today, the Fed is not fully transparent: It does not publish its forecasts of the economy, nor its target for the inflation rate, as some other central banks do.

---

*Quoted in "Monetary Zeal: How the Federal Reserve Under Volcker Finally Slowed Down Inflation," *Wall Street Journal,* December 7, 1984, p. 23.

culminated in legislation that expanded jurisdiction of the Fed's reserve requirements to *all* banks (not just the member commercial banks) by 1987.

The theory of bureaucratic behavior seems applicable to the Federal Reserve's
actions, but we must recognize that this view of the Fed as being solely concerned
with its own self-interest is too extreme. Maximizing one's welfare does not rule
out altruism. (You might give generously to a charity because it makes you feel
good about yourself, but in the process you are helping a worthy cause.) The
Fed is surely concerned that it conduct monetary policy in the public interest.
However, much uncertainty and disagreement exist over what monetary policy
should be. When it is unclear what is in the public interest, other motives may influence the Fed's behavior. In these situations, the theory of bureaucratic behavior
may be a useful guide to predicting what motivates the Fed.

Should the Fed Be Independent?

As we have seen, the Federal Reserve is probably the most independent government agency in the United States. Every few years, the question arises in Congress
as to whether the independence of the Fed should be curtailed. Politicians who
strongly oppose a Fed policy often want to bring it under their supervision in order
to impose a policy more to their liking. Should the Fed be independent, or would
we be better off with a central bank under the control of the president or Congress?

The Case for Independence

The strongest argument for an independent Federal Reserve rests on the view that
subjecting the Fed to more political pressures would impart an inflationary bias to
monetary policy. In the view of many observers, politicians in a democratic society are shortsighted because they are driven by the need to win their next election. With this as the primary goal, they are unlikely to focus on long-run objectives,
such as promoting a stable price level. Instead, they will seek short-run solutions
to problems, like high unemployment and high interest rates, even if the short-run
solutions have undesirable long-run consequences. For example, we saw in
Chapter 4 that high money growth might lead initially to a drop in interest rates
but might cause an increase later as inflation heats up. Would a Federal Reserve
under the control of Congress or the president be more likely to pursue a policy
of excessive money growth when interest rates are high, even though it would
eventually lead to inflation and even higher interest rates in the future? The advocates of an independent Federal Reserve say yes. They believe that a politically
insulated Fed is more likely to be concerned with long-run objectives and thus
be a defender of a sound dollar and a stable price level.

A variation on the preceding argument is that the political process in America leads to the so-called **political business cycle,** in which just before an election, expansionary policies are pursued to lower unemployment and interest rates.
After the election, the bad effects of these policies—high inflation and high interest rates—come home to roost, requiring contractionary policies that politicians
hope the public will forget before the next election. There is some evidence that
such a political business cycle exists in the United States, and a Federal Reserve

under the control of Congress or the president might make the cycle even more pronounced.

Putting the Fed under the control of the president (making it more subject to influence by the Treasury) is also considered dangerous because the Fed can be used to facilitate Treasury financing of large budget deficits by its purchases of Treasury bonds.[6] Treasury pressure on the Fed to "help out" might lead to a more inflationary bias in the economy. An independent Fed is better able to resist this pressure from the Treasury.

Another argument for Fed independence is that control of monetary policy is too important to leave to politicians, a group that has repeatedly demonstrated a lack of expertise at making hard decisions on issues of great economic importance, such as reducing the budget deficit or reforming the banking system. Another way to state this argument is in terms of the principal-agent problem discussed in Chapters 15 and 19. Both the Federal Reserve and politicians are agents of the public (the principals), and as we have seen, both politicians and the Fed have incentives to act in their own interest rather than in the interest of the public. The argument supporting Federal Reserve independence is that the principal-agent problem is worse for politicians than for the Fed because politicians have fewer incentives to act in the public interest.

Indeed, some politicians may prefer to have an independent Fed, which can be used as a public "whipping boy" to take some of the heat off their shoulders. It is possible that a politician who in private opposes an inflationary monetary policy will be forced to support such a policy in public for fear of not being reelected. An independent Fed can pursue policies that are politically unpopular yet in the public interest.

The Case Against Independence

Proponents of a Fed under the control of the president or Congress argue that it is undemocratic to have monetary policy (which affects almost everyone in the economy) controlled by an elite group responsible to no one. The current lack of accountability of the Federal Reserve has serious consequences: If the Fed performs badly, there is no provision for replacing members (as there is with politicians). True, the Fed needs to pursue long-run objectives, but elected officials of Congress vote on long-run issues also (foreign policy, for example). If we push the argument further that policy is always performed better by elite groups like the Fed, we end up with such conclusions as the Joint Chiefs of Staff should determine military budgets or the IRS should set tax policies with no oversight from the president or Congress. Would you advocate this degree of independence for the Joint Chiefs or the IRS?

The public holds the president and Congress responsible for the economic well-being of the country, yet they lack control over the government agency that

---

[6]The Federal Reserve Act prohibited the Fed from buying Treasury bonds directly from the Treasury (except to roll over maturing securities); instead the Fed buys Treasury bonds on the open market. One possible reason for this prohibition is consistent with the foregoing argument: The Fed would find it harder to facilitate Treasury financing of large budget deficits.

may well be the most important factor in determining the health of the economy. In addition, to achieve a cohesive program that will promote economic stability, monetary policy must be coordinated with fiscal policy (management of government spending and taxation). Only by placing monetary policy under the control of the politicians who also control fiscal policy can these two policies be prevented from working at cross-purposes.

Another argument against Federal Reserve independence is that an independent Fed has not always used its freedom successfully. The Fed failed miserably in its stated role as lender of last resort during the Great Depression, and its independence certainly didn't prevent it from pursuing an overly expansionary monetary policy in the 1960s and 1970s that contributed to rapid inflation in this period.

Our earlier discussion also suggests that the Federal Reserve is not immune from political pressures.[7] Its independence may encourage it to pursue a course of narrow self-interest rather than the public interest.

There is yet no consensus on whether Federal Reserve independence is a good thing, although public support for independence of the central bank seems to have been growing in both the United States and abroad. As you might expect, people who like the Fed's policies are more likely to support its independence, while those who dislike its policies advocate a less independent Fed.

Central Bank Independence and Macroeconomic Performance Throughout the World

We have seen that advocates of an independent central bank believe that macroeconomic performance will be improved by making the central bank more independent. Recent research seems to support this conjecture: When central banks are ranked from least independent to most independent, inflation performance is found to be the best for countries with the most independent central banks.[8] Although a more independent central bank appears to lead to a lower inflation rate, this is not achieved at the expense of poorer real economic performance. Countries with independent central banks are no more likely to have high unemployment or greater output fluctuations than countries with less independent central banks.

---

[7]For evidence on this issue, see Robert E. Weintraub, "Congressional Supervision of Monetary Policy," *Journal of Monetary Economics* 4 (1978): 341–362. Some economists suggest that lessening the independence of the Fed might even reduce the incentive for politically motivated monetary policy; see Milton Friedman, "Monetary Policy: Theory and Practice," *Journal of Money, Credit and Banking* 14 (1982): 98–118.

[8]Alberto Alesina and Lawrence H. Summers, "Central Bank Independence and Macroeconomic Performance: Some Comparative Evidence," *Journal of Money, Credit and Banking* 25 (1993): 151–162. However, Adam Posen, "Central Bank Independence and Disinflationary Credibility: A Missing Link," Federal Reserve Bank of New York Staff Report No. 1, May 1995, has cast some doubt on whether the causality runs from central bank independence to improved inflation performance.

Summary

1. The Federal Reserve System was created in 1913 to lessen the frequency of bank panics. Because of public hostility to central banks and the centralization of power, the Federal Reserve System was created with many checks and balances to diffuse power.

2. The formal structure of the Federal Reserve System consists of 12 regional Federal Reserve banks, around 4000 member commercial banks, the Board of Governors of the Federal Reserve System, the Federal Open Market Committee, and the Federal Advisory Council.

3. Although on paper the Federal Reserve System appears to be decentralized, in practice it has come to function as a unified central bank controlled by the Board of Governors, especially the board's chairman.

4. The Federal Reserve is more independent than most agencies of the U.S. government, but it is still subject to political pressures because the legisla-tion that structures the Fed is written by Congress and can be changed at any time. The theory of bureaucratic behavior indicates that one factor driving the Fed's behavior is its attempt to increase its power and prestige. This view explains many of the Fed's actions, although the agency may also try to act in the public interest.

5. The case for an independent Federal Reserve rests on the view that curtailing the Fed's independence and subjecting it to more political pressures would impart an inflationary bias to monetary policy. An independent Fed can afford to take the long view and not respond to short-run problems that will result in expansionary monetary policy and a political business cycle. The case against an independent Fed holds that it is undemocratic to have monetary policy (so important to the public) controlled by an elite that is not accountable to the public. An independent Fed also makes the coordination of monetary and fiscal policy difficult.

Key Terms

Board of Governors of the Federal Reserve System, p. 153

Federal Open Market Committee (FOMC), p. 153

Federal Reserve banks, p. 153
goal independence, p. 164
instrument independence, p. 164

open market operations, p. 156
political business cycle, p. 169

Questions

1. Why was the Federal Reserve System set up with 12 regional Federal Reserve banks rather than one central bank, as in other countries?

2. What political realities might explain why the Federal Reserve Act of 1913 placed two Federal Reserve banks in Missouri?

3. "The Federal Reserve System resembles the U.S. Constitution in that it was designed with many checks and balances." Discuss.

4. In what ways can the regional Federal Reserve banks influence the conduct of monetary policy?

5. Which entities in the Federal Reserve System control the discount rate? Reserve requirements? Open market operations?

6. Do you think that the 14-year nonrenewable terms for governors effectively insulate the Board of Governors from political pressure?

7. Over time, which entities have gained power in the Federal Reserve System and which have lost power? Why do you think this has happened?

8. The Fed is the most independent of all U.S. government agencies. What is the main difference between it and other government agencies that explains its greater independence?

9. What is the primary tool that Congress uses to exercise some control over the Fed?

10. In the 1960s and 1970s, the Federal Reserve System lost member banks at a rapid rate. How can the theory of bureaucratic behavior explain the Fed's campaign for legislation to require all commercial banks to become members? Was the Fed successful in this campaign?

11. "The theory of bureaucratic behavior indicates that the Fed never operates in the public interest." Is

this statement true, false, or uncertain? Explain your answer.

12. Why might eliminating the Fed's independence lead to a more pronounced political business cycle?

13. "The independence of the Fed leaves it completely unaccountable for its actions." Is this statement true, false, or uncertain? Explain your answer.

14. "The independence of the Fed has meant that it takes the long view and not the short view." Is this statement true, false, or uncertain? Explain your answer.

15. The Fed promotes secrecy by not releasing FOMC minutes to Congress or the public immediately. Discuss the pros and cons of this policy.

Web Exercises

Structure of Central Banks and the Federal Reserve System

1. Go to **http://www.federalreserve.gov/general. htm**. Choose "Structure of the Federal Reserve." According to the Federal Reserve, what is the most important responsibility of the Board of Governors?

2. Go to the previously mentioned site and click on "Monetary Policy" to find the beige book. According to the summary of the most recently published book, is the economy weakening or recovering?

CHAPTER 8

Conduct of Monetary Policy: Tools, Goals, and Targets

Preview

Understanding the conduct of monetary policy is important because it affects not only the money supply and interest rates but also the level of economic activity and hence our well-being. To explore this subject, we look first at the Federal Reserve's balance sheet and how the tools of monetary policy affect the money supply and interest rates. Then we examine in more detail how the Fed uses these tools and what goals the Fed and other countries' central banks establish for monetary policy. After examining strategies for conducting monetary policy, we can evaluate central banks' conduct of monetary policy in the past, with the hope that it will give us some clues to where monetary policy may head in the future.

The Federal Reserve's Balance Sheet

The conduct of monetary policy by the Federal Reserve involves actions that affect its balance sheet (holdings of assets and liabilities). Here we discuss the following simplified balance sheet:[1]

Federal Reserve System	
Assets	Liabilities
Government securities	Currency in circulation
Discount loans	Reserves

Liabilities

The two liabilities on the balance sheet, currency in circulation and reserves, are often referred to as the *monetary liabilities* of the Fed. They are an important part of the money supply story because increases in either or both will lead to an increase in the money supply (everything else being constant). The sum of

---

[1]A detailed discussion of the Fed's balance sheet and the factors that affect reserves and the monetary base can be found in the appendix to this chapter, which you can find on this book's website at **www.aw-bc.com/mishkin_eakins.**

175

Historic and cur-
rent data on the
aggregate
reserves of depos-
itory institutions
and the mone-
tary base is
available at
http://www.
federalreserve.
gov/releases/H3

the Fed's monetary liabilities (currency in circulation and reserves) and the U.S. Treasury's monetary liabilities (Treasury currency in circulation, primarily coins) is called the **monetary base.** When discussing the monetary base, we will focus only on the monetary liabilities of the Fed because the monetary liabilities of the Treasury account for less than 10% of the base.[2]

1. *Currency in circulation.* The Fed issues currency (those green-and-gray pieces of paper in your wallet that say "Federal Reserve Note" at the top). Currency in circulation is the amount of currency in the hands of the public (outside of banks)—an important component of the money supply. (Currency held by depository institutions is also a liability of the Fed but is counted as part of reserves.)

   Federal Reserve notes are IOUs from the Fed to the bearer and are also liabilities, but unlike most, they promise to pay back the bearer solely with Federal Reserve notes; that is, they pay off IOUs with other IOUs. Accordingly, if you bring a $100 bill to the Federal Reserve and demand payment, you will receive two $50s, five $20s, ten $10s, or one hundred $1 bills.

   People are more willing to accept IOUs from the Fed than from you or me because Federal Reserve notes are a recognized medium of exchange; that is, they are accepted as a means of payment and so function as money. Unfortunately, neither you nor I can convince people that our own IOUs are worth anything more than the paper they are written on.[3]

2. *Reserves.* All banks have an account at the Fed in which they hold deposits. **Reserves** consist of deposits at the Fed plus currency that is physically held by banks (called vault cash because it is stored in bank vaults). Reserves are assets for the banks but liabilities for the Fed because the banks can demand payment on them at any time and the Fed is obliged to satisfy its obligation by paying Federal Reserve notes. As you will see, an increase in reserves leads to an increase in the level of deposits and hence in the money supply.

   Total reserves can be divided into two categories: reserves that the Fed requires banks to hold (**required reserves**) and any additional reserves the banks choose to hold (**excess reserves**). For example, the Fed might require that for every dollar of deposits at a depository institution, a certain fraction (say, 10 cents) must be held as reserves. This fraction (10%)

---

[2]It is also safe to ignore the Treasury's monetary liabilities when discussing the monetary base because the Treasury cannot actively supply its monetary liabilities to the economy due to legal restrictions.

[3]The currency item on the Fed's balance sheet refers only to currency in circulation, that is, the amount in the hands of the public. Currency that has been printed by the U.S. Bureau of Engraving and Printing is not automatically a liability of the Fed. For example, consider the importance of having $1 million of your own IOUs printed up. You give out $100 worth to other people and keep the other $999,900 in your pocket. The $999,900 of IOUs does not make you richer or poorer and does not affect your indebtedness. You care only about the $100 of liabilities from the $100 of circulated IOUs. The same reasoning applies for the Fed in regard to its Federal Reserve notes.

For similar reasons, the currency component of the money supply, no matter how it is defined, includes only currency in circulation. It does not include any additional currency that is not yet in the hands of the public. The fact that currency has been printed but is not circulating means that it is not anyone's asset or liability and thus cannot affect anyone's behavior. Therefore; it makes sense not to include it in the money supply.

is called the **required reserve ratio.** Currently, the Fed pays no interest on reserves.

Assets

The two assets on the Fed's balance sheet are important for two reasons. First, changes in the asset items lead to changes in reserves and consequently to changes in the money supply. Second, because these assets (government securities and discount loans) earn interest while the liabilities (currency in circulation and reserves) do not, the Fed makes billions of dollars every year—its assets earn income, and its liabilities cost nothing. Although it returns most of its earnings to the federal government, the Fed does spend some of it on "worthy causes," such as supporting economic research.

1. *Government securities.* This category of assets covers the Fed's holdings of securities issued by the U.S. Treasury. As you will see, the Fed provides reserves to the banking system by purchasing securities, thereby increasing its holdings of these assets. An increase in government securities held by the Fed leads to an increase in the money supply.
2. *Discount loans.* The Fed can provide reserves to the banking system by making discount loans to banks. An increase in discount loans can also be the source of an increase in the money supply. The interest rate charged banks for these loans is called the **discount rate.**

Open Market Operations

Open market operations, the central bank's purchase or sale of bonds in the open market, are the most important monetary policy tool because they are the primary determinant of changes in reserves in the banking system and interest rates. To see how they work, let's use T-accounts to examine what happens when the Fed conducts an open market purchase in which $100 of bonds are bought from the public.

When the person or corporation that sells the $100 of bonds to the Fed deposits the Fed's check in the local bank, the nonbank public's T-account after this transaction is

Nonbank Public		
Assets		Liabilities
Securities	−$100	
Checkable deposits	+$100	

When the bank receives the check, it credits the depositor's account with the $100 and then deposits the check in its account with the Fed, thereby adding to its reserves. The banking system's T-account becomes

Banking System		
Assets		Liabilities
Reserves	+$100	Checkable deposits	+$100

The effect on the Fed's balance sheet is that it has gained $100 of securities in its assets column, while reserves have increased by $100, as shown in its liabilities column:

Federal Reserve System			
Assets		Liabilities	
Securities	+$100	Reserves	+$100

As you can see, the result of the Fed's open market purchase is an expansion of reserves and deposits in the banking system. Another way of seeing this is to recognize that open market purchases of bonds expand reserves because the central bank pays for the bonds with reserves. Because the monetary base equals currency plus reserves, we have shown that an open market purchase increases the monetary base by an equal amount. Also because deposits are an important component of the money supply, another result of the open market purchase is an increase in the money supply. This leads to the following important conclusion: ***An open market purchase leads to an expansion of reserves and deposits in the banking system and hence to an expansion of the monetary base and the money supply.***

Similar reasoning indicates that when a central bank conducts an open market sale, the public pays for the bonds by writing a check that causes deposits and reserves in the banking system to fall. Thus ***an open market sale leads to a contraction of reserves and deposits in the banking system and hence to a decline in the monetary base and the money supply.***

Discount Lending

Open market operations are not the only way the Federal Reserve can affect the amount of reserves. Reserves are also changed when the Fed makes a discount loan to a bank. For example, suppose that the Fed makes a $100 discount loan to the First National Bank. The Fed then credits $100 to the bank's reserve account. The effects on the balance sheets of the banking system and the Fed are illustrated by the following T-accounts:

Banking System				Federal Reserve System			
Assets		Liabilities		Assets		Liabilities	
Reserves	+$100	Discount loans	+$100	Discount loans	+$100	Reserves	+$100

We thus see that ***a discount loan leads to an expansion of reserves, which can be lent out as deposits, thereby leading to an expansion of the monetary base and the money supply.*** Similar reasoning indicates that ***when a bank repays its discount loan and so reduces the total amount of discount lending, the amount of reserves decreases along with the monetary base and the money supply.***

The Market for Reserves and the Federal Funds Rate

We have just seen how open market operations and discount lending affect the balance sheet of the Fed and the amount of reserves. Now we will analyze the market for reserves to see how the resulting changes in reserves affect the **federal funds rate,** the interest rate on overnight loans of reserves from one bank to another. The federal funds rate is particularly important in the conduct of monetary policy because it is the interest rate that the Fed tries to influence directly. Thus it is indicative of the Fed's stance on monetary policy.

Open market operations and discount policy are the principal tools that the Fed uses to influence the federal funds rate. In addition, there is a third tool, **reserve requirements,** the regulations making it obligatory for depository institutions to keep a certain fraction of their deposits as reserves with the Fed. We will also analyze how reserve requirements affect the market for reserves and thereby affect the federal funds rate.

Supply and Demand in the Market for Reserves

The analysis of the market for reserves proceeds in a fashion similar to the analysis of the bond market we conducted in Chapter 4. We derive demand and supply curves for reserves, and the market equilibrium in which the quantity of reserves demanded equals the quantity supplied then determines the federal funds rate, the interest rate charged on the loans of these reserves.

Demand Curve   To derive the demand curve for reserves, we need to ask what happens to the quantity of reserves demanded, holding everything else constant, as the federal funds rate changes. Recall that the amount of reserves can be split up into two components: (1) required reserves, which equal the required reserve ratio times the amount of deposits on which reserves are required, and (2) excess reserves, the additional reserves banks choose to hold. Therefore, the quantity of reserves demanded equals required reserves plus the quantity of excess reserves demanded. Excess reserves are insurance against deposit outflows, and the cost of holding these excess reserves is their opportunity cost, the interest rate that could have been earned on lending these reserves out, which is equivalent to the federal funds rate. Thus as the federal funds rate decreases, the opportunity cost of holding excess reserves falls and, holding everything else constant, including the quantity of required reserves, the quantity of reserves demanded rises. Consequently, the demand curve for reserves, R^d, slopes downward in Figure 1.

Supply Curve   The supply of reserves, R^s, can be broken up into two components: the amount of reserves that are supplied by the Fed's open market operations, called nonborrowed reserves (R_n), and the amount of reserves borrowed from the Fed, that is, the amount of discount loans, which are often referred to as borrowed reserves. The primary cost of borrowing discount loans from the Fed is the interest rate the Fed charges on these loans, the discount rate (i_d). Because borrowing federal funds is a substitute for taking out discount loans from the Fed, if the federal funds rate i_{ff} is below the discount rate i_d, then banks will not borrow from the Fed and discount loans will be zero because borrowing in the federal funds market is cheaper. Thus, as long as i_{ff} remains below i_d, the supply of reserves will just equal the amount of nonborrowed reserves supplied by the Fed, R_n, and so the supply curve will be vertical as shown in Figure 1. However,

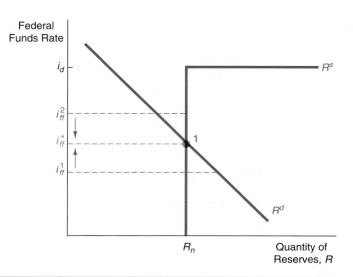

FIGURE 1 *Equilibrium in the Market for Reserves*

Equilibrium occurs at the intersection of the supply curve R^s and the demand curve R^d at point 1 and an interest rate of i_{ff}^*.

as the federal funds rate begins to rise above the discount rate, banks would want to keep borrowing more and more at i_d and then lending out the proceeds in the federal funds market at the higher rate, i_{ff}. The result is that the supply curve becomes flat (infinitely elastic) at i_d, as shown in Figure 1.

Market Equilibrium   Market equilibrium occurs where the quantity of reserves demanded equals the quantity supplied, $R^s = R^d$. Equilibrium therefore occurs at the intersection of the demand curve R^d and the supply curve R^s at point 1, with an equilibrium federal funds rate of i_{ff}^*. When the federal funds rate is above the equilibrium rate at i_{ff}^2, there are more reserves supplied than demanded (excess supply) and so the federal funds rate falls to i_{ff}^* as shown by the downward arrow. On the other hand, when the federal funds rate is below the equilibrium rate at i_{ff}^1, there are more reserves demanded than supplied (excess demand) and so the federal funds rate rises as shown by the upward arrow. (Note that Figure 1 is drawn so that i_d is above i_{ff}^* because the Federal Reserve now keeps the discount rate substantially above the target for the federal funds rate.)

How Changes in the Tools of Monetary Policy Affect the Federal Funds Rate

Now that we understand how the federal funds rate is determined, we can examine how changes in the three tools of monetary policy—open market operations, discount lending, and reserve requirements—affect the market for reserves and the equilibrium federal funds rate.

Open Market Operations   We have already seen that an open market purchase leads to a greater quantity of reserves supplied; this is true at any given federal funds rate because of the higher amount of nonborrowed reserves, which rises

www.federalre serve.gov/fomc/ fundsrate.htm lists historical federal funds rates and also discusses Federal Reserve targets.

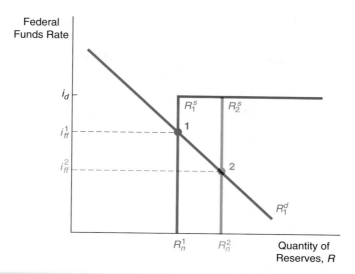

FIGURE 2 *Response to an Open Market Operation*

An open market purchase increases nonborrowed reserves and hence the reserves supplied, and shifts the supply curve from R_1^s to R_2^s. The equilibrium moves from point 1 to point 2, lowering the federal funds rate from i_{ff}^1 to i_{ff}^2.

---

from R_n^1 to R_n^2. An open market purchase therefore shifts the supply curve to the right from R_1^s to R_2^s and moves the equilibrium from point 1 to point 2, lowering the federal funds rate from i_{ff}^1 to i_{ff}^2 (see Figure 2).[4] The same reasoning implies that an open market sale decreases the quantity of reserves supplied, shifts the supply curve to the left, and causes the federal funds rate to rise.

The result is that **an open market purchase causes the federal funds rate to fall, whereas an open market sale causes the federal funds rate to rise.**

Discount Lending The effect of a discount rate change depends on whether the demand curve intersects the supply curve in its vertical section versus its flat section. Panel (a) of Figure 3 shows what happens if the intersection occurs at the vertical section of the supply curve so there is no discount lending. In this case, when the discount rate is lowered by the Fed from i_d^1 to i_d^2, the vertical section of the supply curve where there is no discount lending just shortens, as in R_2^s, while the intersection of the supply and demand curve remains at the same point. Thus, in this case there is no change in the equilibrium federal funds rate, which remains at i_{ff}^1. Because this is the typical situation—since the Fed now usually keeps the discount rate above its target for the federal funds rate—the conclusion is that **most changes in the discount rate have no effect on the federal funds rate.**

Information on the operation of the discount window and data on current and historical interest rates can be found at www.frbdiscount window.org/

---

[4]We come to the same conclusion using the money supply framework along with the liquidity preference framework in Web appendix 3 of Chapter 4. An open market purchase raises reserves and the money supply, and then the liquidity preference framework shows that interest rates fall.

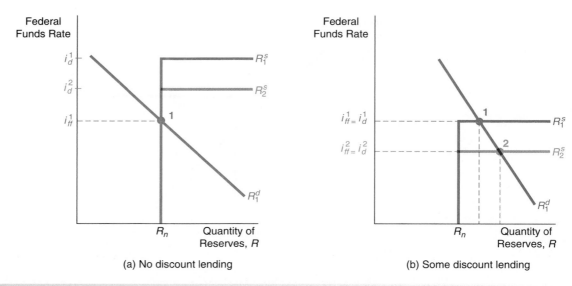

(a) No discount lending   (b) Some discount lending

FIGURE 3 *Response to a Change in the Discount Rate*

In panel (a) when the discount rate is lowered by the Fed from i_d^1 to i_d^2, the vertical section of the supply curve just shortens, as in R_2^s, so that the equilibrium federal funds rate remains unchanged at i_{ff}^1. In panel (b) when the discount rate is lowered by the Fed from i_d^1 to i_d^2, the horizontal section of the supply curve R_2^s falls, and the equilibrium federal funds rate falls from i_{ff}^1 to i_{ff}^2.

However, if the demand curve intersects the supply curve on its flat section, so there is some discount lending, as in panel (b) of Figure 3, changes in the discount rate do affect the federal funds rate. In this case, initially discount lending is positive and the equilibrium federal funds rate equals the discount rate, $i_{ff}^1 = i_d^1$. When the discount rate is lowered by the Fed from i_d^1 to i_d^2, the horizontal section of the supply curve R_2^s falls, moving the equilibrium from point 1 to point 2, and the equilibrium federal funds rate falls from i_{ff}^1 to i_{ff}^2 ($= i_d^2$) in panel (b).

Reserve Requirements   When the required reserve ratio increases, required reserves increase, and hence the quantity of reserves demanded increases for any given interest rate. Thus a rise in the required reserve ratio shifts the demand curve to the right from R_1^d to R_2^d in Figure 4, moves the equilibrium from point 1 to point 2, and in turn raises the federal funds rate from i_{ff}^1 to i_{ff}^2.

The result is that ***when the Fed raises reserve requirements, the federal funds rate rises.***[5]

Similarly, a decline in the required reserve ratio lowers the quantity of reserves demanded, shifts the demand curve to the left, and causes the federal funds rate to fall. ***When the Fed decreases reserve requirements, it leads to a fall in the federal funds rate.***

www.federalre serve.gov/ monetarypolicy/ reservereq.htm contains historical data and discussion about reserve requirements.

---

[5]Because an increase in the required reserve ratio means that the same amount of reserves is able to support a smaller amount of deposits, a rise in the required reserve ratio leads to a decline in the money supply. Using the liquidity preference framework, the fall in the money supply results in a rise in interest rates, yielding the same conclusion in the text that raising reserve requirements leads to higher interest rates.

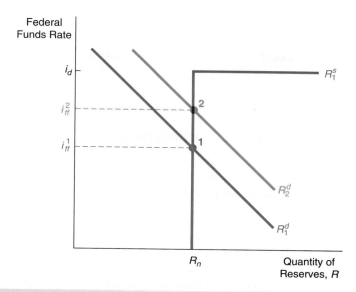

FIGURE 4 *Response to a Change in Required Reserves*

When the Fed raises reserve requirements, required reserves increase, which increases the demand for reserves. The demand curve shifts from R_1^d to R_2^d, the equilibrium moves from point 1 to point 2, and the federal funds rate rises from i_{ff}^1 to i_{ff}^2.

Tools of Monetary Policy

Now that we understand how the three tools of monetary policy—open market operations, discount lending, and reserve requirements—can be used by the Fed to manipulate the money supply and interest rates, we will examine each of them in turn to see how the Fed wields them in practice and how relatively useful each tool is.

Open Market Operations

There are two types of open market operations: **Dynamic open market operations** are intended to change the level of reserves, and **defensive open market operations** are intended to offset movements in other factors that affect reserves, such as changes in Treasury deposits with the Fed. The Fed conducts open market operations in U.S. Treasury and government agency securities, especially U.S. Treasury bills.[6] The Fed conducts most of its open market operations in Treasury securities because the market for these securities is the most liquid and has the largest trading volume. It has the capacity to absorb the Fed's substantial volume of transactions without experiencing excessive price fluctuations that would disrupt the market.

As we saw in Chapter 7, the decision-making authority for open market operations is the Federal Open Market Committee (FOMC), which sets a target for the

---

[6]To avoid conflicts of interest, the Fed does not conduct open market operations in privately issued securities. (For example, think of the conflict if the Federal Reserve purchased bonds issued by a company owned by the chairman's brother-in-law.)

federal funds rate. The actual execution of these operations, however, is conducted by the trading desk at the Federal Reserve Bank of New York. The best way to see how these transactions are executed is to look at a typical day at the trading desk, located in a newly built trading room on the ninth floor of the Federal Reserve Bank of New York.

A Day at the Trading Desk

The head of domestic open market operations, currently Sandy Krieger, supervises the analysts and traders who execute the purchases and sales of securities. To get a grip on what might happen in the federal funds market that day, her work-day and her staff's begins with a review of developments in the federal funds market the previous day and with an update on the actual amount of reserves in the banking system the day before. Later in the morning, Sandy's staff issues updated reports that contain detailed forecasts of what will be happening to some of the short-term factors affecting the supply and demand of reserves.

This information will help Sandy and her staff decide how large a change in reserves is needed to obtain a desired level of the federal funds rate. If the amount of reserves in the banking system is too large, many banks will have excess reserves to lend that other banks may have little desire to borrow, and the federal funds rate will probably fall. If the level of reserves is too low, banks seeking to borrow reserves from the few banks that have excess reserves to lend may push the funds rate higher than the desired level. Also during the morning, the staff will monitor the behavior of the federal funds rate and contact some of the major participants in the funds market, which may provide independent information about whether a change in reserves is needed to achieve the desired level of the federal funds rate.

Early in the morning, members of Sandy's staff contact several representatives of the so-called **primary dealers,** government securities dealers (who operate out of private firms or commercial banks) that the open market desk trades with. Her staff finds out how the dealers view market conditions to get a feel for what may happen to the prices of the securities they trade in over the course of the day. They also call the Treasury to get updated information on the expected level of Treasury balances at the Fed in order to refine their estimates of the supply of reserves.

Afterward, members of the Monetary Affairs Division at the Board of Governors are contacted, and the New York Fed's forecasts of reserve supply and demand are compared with the Board's. On the basis of these projections and the observed behavior of the federal funds market, the desk will formulate and propose a course of action to be taken that day, which may involve plans to add reserves to or drain reserves from the banking system through open market operations. If an operation is contemplated, the type, size, and maturity will be discussed.

The whole process is currently completed by midmorning, at which time a daily conference call is arranged linking the desk with the Office of the Director of Monetary Affairs at the Board and with one of the four voting Reserve Bank presidents outside of New York. During the call, a member of Sandy's unit will outline the desk's proposed reserve management strategy for the day. After the plan is approved, the desk is instructed to execute immediately any temporary open market operations that were planned for that day. (Outright operations, to be described shortly, may be conducted at other times of the day.)

The desk is linked electronically with its domestic open market trading counterparties by a computer system called TRAPS (Trading Room Automated Processing System), and all open market operations are now performed over this system. A message will be electronically transmitted simultaneously to all the primary dealers over TRAPS indicating the type and maturity of the operation being arranged. The dealers are given several minutes to respond via TRAPS with their propositions. The propositions are then assembled and displayed on a computer screen for evaluation. The desk will select all propositions, beginning with the most attractively priced, up to the point where the desired amount is purchased or sold, and it will then notify each dealer via TRAPS which of its propositions have been chosen. The entire selection process is typically completed in a matter of minutes.

These temporary transactions are of two basic types. In a **repurchase agreement** (often called a **repo**), the Fed purchases securities with an agreement that the seller will repurchase them in a short period of time, anywhere from 1 to 15 days from the original date of purchase. Because the effects on reserves of a repo are reversed on the day the agreement matures, a repo is actually a temporary open market purchase and is an especially desirable way of conducting a defensive open market purchase that will be reversed shortly. When the Fed wants to conduct a temporary open market sale, it engages in a **matched sale-purchase transaction** (sometimes called a **reverse repo**) in which the Fed sells securities and the buyer agrees to sell them back to the Fed in the near future.

At times, the desk may see the need to address a persistent reserve shortage or surplus and wish to arrange an operation that will have a permanent impact on the supply of reserves. Outright transactions, which involve a purchase or sale of securities that is not self-reversing, are also conducted over TRAPS. These operations are traditionally executed at times of day when temporary operations are not being conducted.

Discount Policy

The Federal Reserve facility at which discount loans are made to banks is called the **discount window.** The easiest way to understand how the Fed affects the volume of discount loans is by looking at how the discount window operates.

Operation of the Discount Window

The Fed's discount loans to banks are of three types: primary credit, secondary credit, and seasonal credit.[7] *Primary credit* is the discount lending that plays the most important role in monetary policy. Healthy banks are allowed to borrow all they want from the primary credit facility, and it is therefore referred to as a *standing lending facility.* The interest rate on these loans is the discount rate, and as we mentioned before, it is set higher than the federal funds

---

[7]The procedures for administering the discount window were changed in January 2003. The primary credit facility replaced an adjustment credit facility whose discount rate was typically set below market interest rates, so banks were restricted in their access to this credit. In contrast, now healthy banks can borrow all they want from the primary credit facility. The secondary credit facility replaced the extended credit facility which focused somewhat more on longer-term credit extensions. The seasonal credit facility remains basically unchanged.

rate target, usually by 100 basis points (one percentage point), and thus in most circumstances the amount of discount lending under the primary credit facility is very small. Then why does the Fed have this facility?

The answer is that the facility is intended to be a backup source of liquidity for sound banks so that the federal funds rate never rises too far above the federal funds target. To see how the primary credit facility works, let's see what happens if there is a large increase in the demand for reserves, say because deposits have surged unexpectedly and have led to an increase in required reserves. This situation is analyzed in Figure 5. Suppose that initially, the demand and supply curve for reserves intersect at point 1 so that the federal funds rate is at its target level, i_{ff}^T. Now the increase in required reserves shifts the demand curve to R_2^d and the equilibrium moves to point 2. The result is that discount lending increases from zero to DL_2 and the federal funds rate rises to i_d and can rise no further. The primary credit facility has thus put a ceiling on the federal funds rate of i_d.

Secondary credit is given to banks that are in financial trouble and are experiencing severe liquidity problems. The interest rate on secondary credit is set at 50 basis points (0.5 percentage points) above the discount rate. This interest rate on these loans is set at a higher, penalty rate to reflect the less-sound condition of these borrowers. *Seasonal credit* is given to meet the needs of a limited number of small banks in vacation and agricultural areas that have a seasonal pattern of deposits. The interest rate charged on seasonal credit is tied to the average of the federal funds rate and certificate of deposit rates. The Federal Reserve has questioned the need for the seasonal credit facility because of improvements in credit markets and is thus contemplating eliminating it in the future.

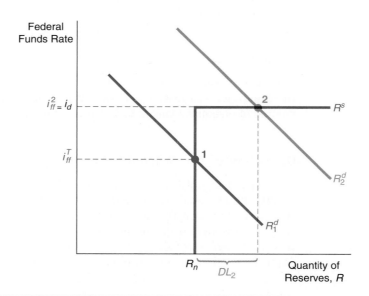

FIGURE 5   *How the Primary Credit Facility Puts a Ceiling on the Federal Funds Rate*

The rightward shift of the demand curve to reserves from R_1^d to R_2^d moves the equilibrium from point 1 to point 2 where $i_{ff}^2 = i_d$ and discount lending rises from zero to DL_2.

Lender of Last Resort

In addition to its use as a tool to influence reserves in the banking system and the money supply, discounting is important in preventing financial panics. When the Federal Reserve System was created, its most important role was intended to be as the **lender of last resort;** it was to provide reserves to banks when no one else would in order to prevent bank failures from spinning out of control, thereby preventing bank and financial panics. Discounting is a particularly effective way to provide reserves to the banking system during a banking crisis because reserves are immediately channeled to the banks that need them most.

Using the discount tool to avoid financial panics by performing the role of lender of last resort is an extremely important requirement of successful monetary policymaking. Financial panics can also severely damage the economy because they interfere with the ability of these markets to move funds to people with productive investment opportunities (see Chapter 15).

Unfortunately, the discount tool has not always been used by the Fed to prevent financial panics, as the massive failures during the Great Depression attest. The Fed learned from its mistakes of that period and has performed admirably in its role of lender of last resort in the post–World War II period. The Fed has used its discount weapon several times to avoid bank panics by extending loans to troubled banking institutions, thereby preventing further bank failures. The largest of these occurred in 1984, when the Fed lent Continental Illinois, at that time one of the ten largest banks in the United States, over $5 billion.

At first glance, it might appear as though the presence of the FDIC, which insures depositors from losses due to a bank's failure up to a limit of $100,000 per account, would make the lender-of-last-resort function of the Fed superfluous. (The FDIC is described in detail in Chapter 20.) There are two reasons why this is not the case. First, it is important to recognize that the FDIC's insurance fund amounts to around 1% of the amount of these deposits outstanding. If a large number of bank failures occurred, the FDIC would not be able to cover all the depositors' losses. Indeed, the large number of bank failures in the 1980s and early 1990s, described in Chapter 20, led to large losses and a shrinkage in the FDIC's insurance fund, which reduced the FDIC's ability to cover depositors' losses. This fact has not weakened the confidence of small depositors in the banking system because the Fed has been ready to stand behind the banks to provide whatever reserves are needed to prevent bank panics. Second, the nearly $500 billion of large-denomination deposits in the banking system are not guaranteed by the FDIC because they exceed the $100,000 limit. A loss of confidence in the banking system could still lead to runs on banks from the large-denomination depositors, and bank panics could still occur despite the existence of the FDIC. The importance of the Federal Reserve's role as lender of last resort is, if anything, more important today because of the high number of bank failures experienced in the 1980s and early 1990s.

Not only can the Fed be a lender of last resort to banks, but it can also play the same role for the financial system as a whole. The existence of the Fed's discount window can help prevent financial panics that are not triggered by bank failures, as was the case during the Black Monday stock market crash of October 1987 and the terrorist destruction of the World Trade Center in September 2001 (see the "Inside the Fed" box on p. 189).

Although the Fed's role as the lender of last resort has the benefit of preventing bank and financial panics, it does have a cost. If a bank expects that the

Fed will provide it with discount loans when it gets into trouble, as occurred with Continental Illinois, it will be willing to take on more risk knowing that the Fed will come to the rescue. The Fed's lender-of-last-resort role has thus created a moral hazard problem similar to the one created by deposit insurance (discussed in Chapter 20): Banks take on more risk, thus exposing the deposit insurance agency, and hence taxpayers, to greater losses. The moral hazard problem is most severe for large banks, which may believe that the Fed and the FDIC view them as "too big to fail"; that is, they will always receive Fed loans when they are in trouble because their failure would be likely to precipitate a bank panic.

Similarly, Federal Reserve actions to prevent financial panic, as occurred after the October 1987 stock market crash and the September 11, 2001, terrorist attack, may encourage financial institutions other than banks to take on greater risk. They, too, expect the Fed to ensure that they could get loans if a financial panic seemed imminent. When the Fed considers using the discount weapon to prevent panics, it therefore needs to consider the trade-off between the moral hazard cost of its role as lender of last resort and the benefit of preventing financial panics. This trade-off explains why the Fed must be careful not to perform its role as lender of last resort too frequently.

Reserve Requirements

Changes in reserve requirements affect the demand for reserves: A rise in reserve requirements means that banks must hold more reserves, and a reduction means that they are required to hold less. The Depository Institutions Deregulation and Monetary Control Act of 1980 provided a simple scheme for setting reserve requirements. All depository institutions, including commercial banks, savings and loan associations, mutual savings banks, and credit unions, are now subject to the same reserve requirements, as follows: Required reserves on all checkable deposits—including non-interest-bearing checking accounts, NOW accounts, super-NOW accounts, and ATS (automatic transfer savings) accounts—are equal to 3% of the bank's first $47.6 million of checkable deposits[8] and 10% of the checkable deposits over $47.6 million, and the percentage set initially at 10% can be varied between 8% and 14% at the Fed's discretion. In extraordinary circumstances, the percentage can be raised as high as 18%.

Reserve requirements have been rarely used as a monetary policy tool because raising them can cause immediate liquidity problems for banks with low excess reserves. When the Fed has raised these requirements in the past, it has usually softened the blow by conducting open market purchases or by making the discount window more available, thus providing reserves to banks that needed them. Continually fluctuating reserve requirements would also create more uncertainty for banks and make their liquidity management more difficult.

Advantages of Open Market Operations Over the Other Tools

Of the three tools of monetary policy available to the Fed, the primary tool used is open market operations. This is because open market operations have several advantages over the other tools of monetary policy.

---

[8]The $47.6 million figure is as of the beginning of 2005. Each year, the figure is adjusted upward by 80% of the percentage increase in checkable deposits in the United States.

INSIDE THE FED

Discounting to Prevent a Financial Panic: The Black Monday Stock Market Crash of October 1987 and the Terrorist Destruction of the World Trade Center in September 2001

Although October 19, 1987, dubbed "Black Monday," will go down in the history books as the largest one-day percentage decline in stock prices to date (the Dow Jones Industrial Average declined by more than 20%), it was on Tuesday, October 20, 1987, that financial markets almost stopped functioning. Felix Rohatyn, one of the most prominent men on Wall Street, stated flatly: "Tuesday was the most dangerous day we had in 50 years."* Much of the credit for prevention of a market meltdown after Black Monday must be given to the Federal Reserve System and the chairman of the Board of Governors, Alan Greenspan.

The stress of keeping markets functioning during the sharp decline in stock prices on Monday, October 19, meant that many brokerage houses and specialists (dealer-brokers who maintain orderly trading on the stock exchanges) were severely in need of additional funds to finance their activities. However, understandably enough, New York banks, as well as foreign and regional U.S. banks, growing very nervous about the financial health of securities firms, began to cut back credit to the securities industry at the very time when it was most needed. Panic was in the air. One chairman of a large specialist firm commented that on Monday, "from 2 P.M. on, there was total despair. The entire investment community fled the market. We were left alone on the field." It was time for the Fed, like the cavalry, to come to the rescue.

Upon learning of the plight of the securities industry, Alan Greenspan and E. Gerald Corrigan, then president of the Federal Reserve Bank of New York and the Fed official most closely in touch with Wall Street, became fearful of a spreading collapse of securities firms. To prevent this from occurring, Greenspan announced before the market opened on Tuesday, October 20, the Federal Reserve System's "readiness to serve as a source of liquidity to support the economic and financial system." In addition to this extraordinary announcement, the Fed made it clear that it would provide discount loans to any bank that would make loans to the securities industry, although this did not prove to be necessary. As one New York banker said, the Fed's message was, "We're here. Whatever you need, we'll give you."

The outcome of the Fed's timely action was that a financial panic was averted. The markets kept functioning on Tuesday, and a market rally ensued that day, with the Dow Jones Industrial Average climbing over 100 points.

A similar lender-of-last resort operation was carried out in the aftermath of the destruction of the World Trade Center on Tuesday, September 11, 2001, in the worst terrorist incident in U.S. history. Because of the disruption of the most important financial center in the world, the liquidity needs of the financial system skyrocketed. To satisfy this need and so keep the financial system from seizing up, within a few hours of the incident, the Fed made a similar announcement to that made after the crash of 1987, stating, "The Federal Reserve System is open and operating. The discount window is available to meet liquidity needs."** The Fed then proceeded to provide $45 billion to banks through the discount window, a 200-fold increase over the previous week. As a result of this action, along with as much as $80 billion of reserves injected into the banking system through open market operations, the financial system kept functioning. When the stock market reopened on Monday, September 17, trading was orderly, although the Dow Jones average did decline 7%.

The terrorists were able to bring down the twin towers of the World Trade Center with over 3000 dead. However, they were unable to bring down the U.S. financial system because of the timely actions of the Federal Reserve.

---

*"Terrible Tuesday: How the Stock Market Almost Disintegrated a Day After the Crash," *Wall Street Journal,* November 20, 1987, p. 1. This article provides a fascinating and more detailed view of the events described here and is the source of all the quotations cited.
**"Economic Front: How Policy Makers Regrouped to Defend the Financial System," *Wall Street Journal,* Tuesday, September 18, 2001, p. A1, provides more detail on this episode.

First, open market operations occur at the initiative of the Fed, which has complete control over their volume. This control is not found, for example, in discount operations, in which the Fed can encourage or discourage banks to take out discount loans by altering the discount rate but cannot directly control the volume of discount loans.

Second, open market operations are flexible and precise; they can be used to any extent. No matter how small a change in reserves is desired, open market operations can achieve it with a small purchase or sale of securities. Conversely, if the desired change in reserves or the monetary base is very large, the open market operations tool is strong enough to do the job through a very large purchase or sale of securities.

Third, open market operations are easily reversed. If a mistake is made in conducting an open market operation, the Fed can immediately reverse it. If the Fed decides that the federal funds rate is too low because it has made too many open market purchases, it can immediately make a correction by conducting open market sales.

Fourth, open market operations can be implemented quickly; they involve no administrative delays. When the Fed decides that it wants to change reserves, it just places orders with securities dealers, and the trades are executed immediately.

Goals of Monetary Policy

The site http://stats.bls.gov/ contains statistics on employment level, summary of the employment situation, and other useful information related to employment issues.

Six basic goals are continually mentioned by personnel at the Federal Reserve and other central banks when they discuss the objectives of monetary policy: (1) high employment, (2) economic growth, (3) price stability, (4) interest-rate stability, (5) stability of financial markets, and (6) stability in foreign exchange markets.

High Employment

The Employment Act of 1946 and the Full Employment and Balanced Growth Act of 1978 (more commonly called the Humphrey-Hawkins Act) commit the U.S. government to promoting high employment consistent with a stable price level. High employment is a worthy goal for two main reasons: (1) the alternative situation, high unemployment, causes much human misery, with families suffering financial distress, loss of personal self-respect, and increase in crime (though this last conclusion is highly controversial), and (2) when unemployment is high, the economy has not only idle workers but also idle resources (closed factories and unused equipment), resulting in a loss of output (lower GDP).

Although it is clear that high employment is desirable, how high should it be? At what point can we say that the economy is at full employment? At first, it might seem that full employment is the point at which no worker is out of a job, that is, when unemployment is zero. But this definition ignores the fact that some unemployment, called *frictional unemployment*, which involves searches by workers and firms to find suitable matchups, is beneficial to the economy. For example, a worker who decides to look for a better job might be unemployed for a while during the job search. Workers often decide to leave work temporarily to pursue other activities (raising a family, travel, returning to school), and when they decide to reenter the job market, it may take some time for them to find the right job. The benefit of having some unemployment is similar to the benefit of having a nonzero vacancy rate in the market for rental apartments. As many of you who have looked for an apartment have discovered, when the vacancy rate in the rental market is too low, you will have a difficult time finding the right apartment.

Another reason that unemployment is not zero when the economy is at full employment is due to what is called *structural unemployment*, a mismatch between job requirements and the skills or availability of local workers. Clearly, this kind of unemployment is undesirable. Nonetheless, it is something that monetary policy can do little about.

The goal for high employment should therefore not seek an unemployment level of zero but rather a level above zero consistent with full employment at which the demand for labor equals the supply of labor. This level is called the **natural rate of unemployment.**

Although this definition sounds neat and authoritative, it isn't, because it leaves a troublesome question unanswered: What unemployment rate is consistent with full employment? On the one hand, in some cases, it is obvious that the unemployment rate is too high: The unemployment rate in excess of 20% during the Great Depression, for example, was clearly far too high. In the early 1960s, on the other hand, policymakers thought that a reasonable goal was 4%, a level that was probably too low because it led to accelerating inflation. Current estimates of the natural rate of unemployment place it between 5% and 6%, but even this estimate is subject to a great deal of uncertainty and disagreement. In addition, it is possible that appropriate government policy, such as the provision of better information about job vacancies or job training programs, might decrease the natural rate of unemployment.

Economic Growth

The goal of steady economic growth is closely related to the high-employment goal because businesses are more likely to invest in capital equipment to increase productivity and economic growth when unemployment is low. Conversely, if unemployment is high and factories are idle, it does not pay for a firm to invest in additional plants and equipment. Although the two goals are closely related, policies can be specifically aimed at promoting economic growth by directly encouraging firms to invest or by encouraging people to save, which provides more funds for firms to invest. In fact, this is the stated purpose of so-called supply-side economics policies, which are intended to spur economic growth by providing tax incentives for businesses to invest in factories and equipment and for taxpayers to save more. There is also an active debate over what growth role monetary policy can play in boosting growth.

Price Stability

Over the past few decades, policymakers in the United States have become more aware of the social and economic costs of inflation and more concerned with a stable price level as a goal of economic policy. (The growing commitment to price stability is also evident in Europe—see the "Global" box on p. 192.) Price stability is desirable because a rising price level (inflation) creates uncertainty in the economy, and that may hamper economic growth. For example, the information conveyed by the prices of goods and services is harder to interpret when the overall level of prices is changing, which complicates decision making for consumers, businesses, and government. Not only do public opinion surveys indicate that the public is very hostile to inflation, but also a growing body of evidence suggests that inflation leads to lower economic growth.[9] The most extreme example

---

[9]For example, see Stanley Fischer, "The Role of Macroeconomic Factors in Growth," *Journal of Monetary Economics* 32 (1993): 485–512.

GLOBAL

The Growing European Commitment to Price Stability

Not surprisingly, given Germany's experience with hyperinflation in the 1920s, its central bank has the strongest commitment to price stability. In contrast to statutes for the German central bank, the statutes of other central banks in Europe set various objectives for policy, including all the goals outlined here in the text. However, European policymakers have been coming around to the view that the primary objective for a central bank should be price stability. The increased importance of this goal is reflected in the December 1991 Treaty of European Union, known as the Maastricht Treaty, which proposed the creation of the European System of Central Banks, which would function very much like the Federal Reserve System. The statute of the European System of Central Banks sets price stability as the primary objective of this system and indicates that the general economic policies of the European Union are to be supported only if they are not in conflict with price stability.

of unstable prices is *hyperinflation*, such as Argentina, Brazil, and Russia have experienced in the recent past. Many economists attribute the slower growth that these countries have experienced to their problems with hyperinflation.

Inflation also makes it hard to plan for the future. For example, it is more difficult to decide how much funds should be put aside to provide for a child's college education in an inflationary environment. Further, inflation may strain a country's social fabric: Conflict may result because each group in the society may compete with other groups to make sure that its income keeps up with the rising level of prices.

Interest-Rate Stability

Interest-rate stability is desirable because fluctuations in interest rates can create uncertainty in the economy and make it harder to plan for the future. Fluctuations in interest rates that affect consumers' willingness to buy houses, for example, make it more difficult for consumers to decide when to purchase a house and for construction firms to plan how many houses to build. A central bank may also want to reduce upward movements in interest rates for the reasons we discussed in Chapter 7: Upward movements in interest rates generate hostility toward central banks like the Fed and lead to demands that their power be curtailed.

Stability of Financial Markets

As our analysis in Chapter 15 will show, financial crises can interfere with the ability of financial markets to channel funds to people with productive investment opportunities, thereby leading to a sharp contraction in economic activity. The promotion of a more stable financial system in which financial crises are avoided is thus an important goal for a central bank. Indeed, as discussed in Chapter 7, the Federal Reserve System was created in response to the bank panic of 1907 to promote financial stability.

The stability of financial markets is also fostered by interest-rate stability because fluctuations in interest rates create great uncertainty for financial institutions. An increase in interest rates produces large capital losses on long-term bonds and mortgages, losses that can cause the failure of the financial institutions holding them. In recent years, more pronounced interest-rate fluctuations have been a particularly severe problem for savings and loan associations and mutual savings banks, many of which got into serious financial trouble in the 1980s and early 1990s.

Stability in Foreign Exchange Markets

With the increasing importance of international trade to the U.S. economy, the value of the dollar relative to other currencies has become a major consideration for the Fed. As we will see in Chapter 13, a rise in the value of the dollar makes American industries less competitive with those abroad, and declines in the value of the dollar stimulate inflation in the United States. In addition, preventing large changes in the value of the dollar makes it easier for firms and individuals purchasing or selling goods abroad to plan ahead. Stabilizing extreme movements in the value of the dollar in foreign exchange markets is thus viewed as a worthy goal of monetary policy. In other countries, which are even more dependent on foreign trade, stability in foreign exchange markets takes on even greater importance.

Conflict Among Goals

Although many of the goals mentioned are consistent with each other—high employment with economic growth, interest-rate stability with financial market stability—this is not always the case. The goal of price stability often conflicts with the goals of interest-rate stability and high employment in the short run (but probably not in the long run). For example, when the economy is expanding and unemployment is falling, both inflation and interest rates may start to rise. If the central bank tries to prevent a rise in interest rates, this may cause the economy to overheat and stimulate inflation. But if a central bank raises interest rates to prevent inflation, in the short run unemployment may rise. The conflict among goals may thus present central banks like the Federal Reserve with some hard choices.

Central Bank Strategy: Use of Targets

The central bank's problem is that it wishes to achieve certain goals, such as price stability with high employment, but it does not directly influence the goals. It has a set of tools to employ (open market operations, changes in the discount rate, and changes in reserve requirements) that can affect the goals indirectly after a period of time (typically more than a year). If the central bank waits to see what the price level and employment will be one year later, it will be too late to make any corrections to its policy—mistakes will be irreversible.

All central banks consequently pursue a different strategy for conducting monetary policy by aiming at variables that lie between their tools and the achievement of their goals. The strategy is as follows: After deciding on its goals for employment and the price level, the central bank chooses a set of variables to aim for, called **intermediate targets,** such as the monetary aggregates (various measures of the money supply denoted by M1, M2, or M3) or interest rates (short- or long-term), which have a direct effect on employment and the price level. However, even these intermediate targets are not directly affected by the central bank's policy tools. Therefore, it chooses another set of variables to aim for, called **operating targets,** or alternatively called *instruments*, such as reserve aggregates (reserves, non-borrowed reserves, monetary base, or nonborrowed base) or interest rates (fed-eral funds rate or Treasury bill rate), which are more responsive to its policy tools. (Nonborrowed reserves are total reserves minus borrowed reserves, which are the amount of discount loans; the monetary base is the sum of currency plus reserves in the banking system; the nonborrowed base is the monetary base minus bor-rowed reserves; and the federal funds rate is the interest rate on funds loaned overnight between banks.)[10]

The central bank pursues this strategy because it is easier to hit a goal by aim-ing at targets than by aiming at the goal directly. Specifically, by using interme-diate and operating targets, it can more quickly judge whether its policies are on the right track, rather than waiting until it sees the final outcome of its policies on employment and the price level.[11] By analogy, NASA employs the strategy of using targets when it is trying to send a spaceship to the moon. It will check to see whether the spaceship is positioned correctly as it leaves the atmosphere (we can think of this as NASA's "operating target"). If the spaceship is off course at this stage, NASA engineers will adjust its thrust (a policy tool) to get it back on target. NASA may check the position of the spaceship again when it is halfway to the moon (NASA's "intermediate target") and can make further midcourse cor-rections if necessary.

The central bank's strategy works in a similar way. Suppose that the central bank's employment and price-level goals are consistent with a nominal GDP growth rate of 5%. If the central bank feels that the 5% nominal GDP growth rate will be achieved by a 4% growth rate for M2 (its intermediate target), which will in turn be achieved by a growth rate of 3% for nonborrowed reserves (its operat-ing target), it will carry out open market operations (its tool) to achieve the 3% growth in nonborrowed reserves. After implementing this policy, the central bank may find that nonborrowed reserves is growing too slowly, say, at a 2% rate; then it can correct this too slow growth by increasing the amount of its open market purchases. Somewhat later, the central bank will begin to see how its policy is affecting the growth rate of the money supply. If M2 is growing too fast, say, at a 7% rate, the central bank may decide to reduce its open market purchases or make open market sales to reduce the M2 growth rate.

One way of thinking about this strategy (illustrated in Figure 6) is that the central bank is using its operating and intermediate targets to direct monetary pol-icy (the spaceship) toward the achievement of its goals. After the initial setting of the policy tools (the liftoff), an operating target such as nonborrowed reserves, which the central bank can control fairly directly, is used to reset the tools so

---

[10]There is some ambiguity as to whether to call a particular variable an operating target or an intermediate target. The monetary base and the Treasury bill rate are often viewed as possible intermediate targets, even though they may function as operating targets as well. In addition, if the Fed wants to pursue a goal of interest-rate stability, an interest rate can be both a goal and a target.

[11]This reasoning for the use of monetary targets has come under attack because information on employment and the price level can be useful in evaluating policy. See Benjamin M. Friedman, "The Inefficiency of Short-Run Monetary Targets for Monetary Policy," *Brookings Papers on Economic Activity* 2 (1977): 292–346.

Tools of the Central Bank

Open market operations
Discount policy
Reserve requirements

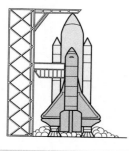
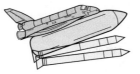

Operating Targets

Reserve aggregates
(reserves, nonborrowed
reserves, monetary base,
nonborrowed base)
Interest rates (short-term
such as federal funds rate)

Intermediate Targets

Monetary aggregates
(M1, M2, M3)
Interest rates (short-
and long-term)

Goals

High employment,
price stability,
financial market
stability, and so on

FIGURE 6 *Central Bank Strategy*

that monetary policy is channeled toward achieving the intermediate target of a certain rate of money supply growth. Midcourse corrections in the policy tools can be made again when the central bank sees what is happening to its intermediate target, thus directing monetary policy so that it will achieve its goals of high employment and price stability (the spaceship reaches the moon).

Choosing the Targets

As we see in Figure 6, there are two different types of target variables: interest rates and aggregates (monetary aggregates and reserve aggregates). In our example, the central bank chose a 3% growth rate of nonborrowed reserves to achieve a 5% rate of growth for nominal GDP. Alternatively, it could have to set the federal funds rate at, say, 2% to achieve the same goal. Can the central bank choose to pursue both of these targets at the same time? The answer is no. The application of the supply and demand analysis of the market for reserves we developed earlier in the chapter explains why a central bank must choose one or the other.

Let's first see why an aggregate target involves losing control of the interest rate. Figure 7 contains a supply and demand diagram for the market for reserves. Although the central bank expects the demand curve for reserves to be at R^{d*}, it fluctuates between $R^{d'}$ and $R^{d''}$ because of unexpected fluctuations in deposits (and hence required reserves) or changes in banks' desire to hold excess reserves. If the central bank has a nonborrowed reserves target of R_n^* (say, because it has a target growth rate of the money supply of 4%), it expects that the federal funds rate will be i_{ff}^*. However, as the figure indicates, the fluctuations in the reserves demand curve between $R^{d'}$ and $R^{d''}$ will result in a fluctuation in the federal funds rate between $i_{ff}^{'}$ and $i_{ff}^{''}$. Pursuing an aggregate target implies that interest rates will fluctuate.

The supply and demand diagram in Figure 8 shows the consequences of an interest-rate target set at i_{ff}^*. Again the central bank expects the reserves demand curve to be at R^{d*}, but it fluctuates between $R^{d'}$ and $R^{d''}$ due to unexpected changes

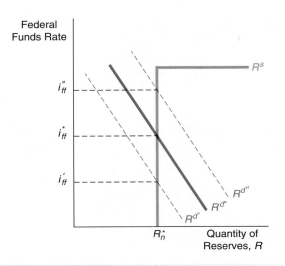

FIGURE 7 *Result of Targeting on Nonborrowed Reserves*

Targeting on nonborrowed reserves of R_n^* will lead to fluctuations in the federal funds rate between i_{ff}' and i_{ff}'' because of fluctuations in the demand for reserves between $R^{d'}$ and $R^{d''}$.

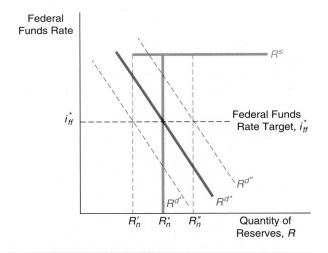

FIGURE 8 *Result of Targeting on the Federal Funds Rate*

Targeting on the interest rate i_{ff}^* will lead to fluctuation of nonborrowed reserves because of fluctuations in the demand for reserves between $R^{d'}$ and $R^{d''}$.

in deposits or banks' desire to hold excess reserves. If the demand curve rises to $R^{d''}$, the federal funds rate will begin to rise above i_{ff}^* and the central bank will engage in open market purchases of bonds until it raises the supply of nonborrowed reserves to R_n'', at which point the equilibrium federal funds rate is again at i_{ff}^*. Conversely, if the demand curve falls to $R^{d'}$ and lowers the federal funds rate, the central bank would keep making open market sales until nonborrowed reserves fall to R_n' and the federal funds rate is i_{ff}^*. The central bank's adherence to the interest-rate target thus leads to a fluctuating quantity of nonborrowed reserves and the money supply.

The conclusion from the supply and demand analysis is that interest-rate and reserve (monetary) aggregate targets are incompatible. A central bank can hit one or the other, but not both. Because a choice between them has to be made, we need to examine what criteria should be used to decide on the target variable.

Criteria for Choosing Intermediate Targets

The rationale behind a central bank's strategy of using targets suggests three criteria for choosing an intermediate target: It must be measurable, it must be controllable by the central bank, and it must have a predictable effect on the goal.

Measurability Quick and accurate measurement of an intermediate-target variable is necessary because the intermediate target will be useful only if it signals when policy is off track more rapidly than the goal. What good does it do for the central bank to plan to hit a 4% growth rate for M2 if it has no way of quickly and accurately measuring M2? Data on the monetary aggregates are obtained after a two-week delay, and interest-rate data are available almost immediately. Data on a variable like GDP that serves as a goal, by contrast, are compiled quarterly and are made available with a month's delay. In addition, the GDP data are less accurate than data on the monetary aggregates or interest rates. On these grounds alone, focusing on interest rates and monetary aggregates as intermediate targets rather than on a goal like GDP can provide clearer signals about the status of the central bank's policy.

At first glance, interest rates seem to be more measurable than monetary aggregates and hence more useful as intermediate targets. Not only are the data on interest rates available more quickly than on monetary aggregates, but they are also measured more precisely and are rarely revised, in contrast to the monetary aggregates, which are subject to a fair amount of revision. However, as we learned in Chapter 3, the interest rate that is quickly and accurately measured, the nominal interest rate, is typically a poor measure of the real cost of borrowing, which indicates with more certainty what will happen to GDP. This real cost of borrowing is more accurately measured by the real interest rate—the interest rate adjusted for expected inflation ($i_r = i - \pi^e$). Unfortunately, the real interest rate is extremely hard to measure because we have no direct way to measure expected inflation. Since both interest rate and monetary aggregates have measurability problems, it is not clear whether one should be preferred to the other as an intermediate target.

Controllability A central bank must be able to exercise effective control over a variable if it is to function as a useful target. If the central bank cannot control an intermediate target, knowing that it is off track does little good because the bank has no way of getting back on track. Some economists have suggested that nominal GDP should be used as an intermediate target, but since the central bank has little direct control over nominal GDP, it will not provide much guidance on how the Fed should set its policy tools. A central bank does, however, have a good deal of control over the monetary aggregates and interest rates.

Our discussion of the money supply process and the central bank's policy tools indicates that a central bank does have the ability to exercise a powerful effect on the money supply, although its control is not perfect. We have also seen that open market operations can be used to set interest rates by directly affecting the price of bonds. Because a central bank can set interest rates directly whereas it cannot completely control the money supply, it might appear that interest rates dominate the monetary aggregates on the controllability criterion. However, a central bank cannot set real interest rates because it does not have control over expectations of inflation. So again, a clear-cut case cannot be made that interest rates are preferable to monetary aggregates as an intermediate target or vice versa.

Predictable Effect on Goals   The most important characteristic a variable must have to be useful as an intermediate target is that it must have a predictable impact on a goal. If a central bank can accurately and quickly measure the price of tea in China and can completely control its price, what good will it do? The central bank cannot use the price of tea in China to affect unemployment or the price level in its country. Because the ability to affect goals is so critical to the usefulness of an intermediate-target variable, the linkage of the money supply and interest rates with the goals—output, employment, and the price level—is a matter of much debate.

Criteria for Choosing Operating Targets

The choice of an operating target can be based on the same criteria used to evaluate intermediate targets. Both the federal funds rate and reserve aggregates are measured accurately and are available daily with almost no delay; both are easily controllable using the policy tools that we discussed earlier in the chapter. When we look at the third criterion, however, we can think of the intermediate target as the goal for the operating target. An operating target that has a more predictable impact on the most desirable intermediate target is preferred. If the desired intermediate target is an interest rate, the preferred operating target will be an interest-rate variable like the federal funds rate because interest rates are closely tied to each other (as we saw in Chapter 5). However, if the desired intermediate target is a monetary aggregate, a reserve aggregate operating target such as the monetary base will be preferred. Because there does not seem to be much reason to choose an interest rate over a reserve aggregate on the basis of measurability or controllability, the choice of which operating target is better rests on the choice of the intermediate target (the goal of the operating target).

Fed Policy Procedures: Historical Perspective

The well-known adage "The road to hell is paved with good intentions" applies as much to the Federal Reserve as it does to human beings. Understanding a central bank's goals and the strategies it can use to pursue them cannot tell us how monetary policy is actually conducted. To understand the practical results of the theoretical underpinnings, we have to look at how central banks have actually conducted policy in the past. First we will look at the Federal Reserve's past policy procedures: its choice of goals, policy tools, operating targets, and intermediate targets. This historical perspective will not only show us how our central bank carries out its duties but will also help us interpret the Fed's activities and see where U.S. monetary policy may be heading in the future. Once we are done studying the Fed, we will then examine central banks' experiences in other countries.

The Early Years: Discount Policy as the Primary Tool

When the Fed was created, changing the discount rate was the primary tool of monetary policy—the Fed had not yet discovered that open market operations were a more powerful tool for influencing the money supply, and the Federal Reserve Act made no provisions for changes in reserve requirements. The guiding principle for the conduct of monetary policy was that as long as loans were being made for "productive" purposes—that is, to support the production of goods and services—providing reserves to the banking system to make these loans would not be inflationary.[12] This theory, now thoroughly discredited, became known as the **real bills doctrine.** In practice, it meant that the Fed would make loans to member commercial banks when they showed up at the discount window with *eligible paper*, loans to facilitate the production and sale of goods and services. (Note that since the 1920s, the Fed has not conducted discount operations in this way.) The Fed's act of making loans to member banks was initially called *rediscounting* because the original bank loans to businesses were made by discounting (loaning less than) the face value of the loan, and the Fed would be discounting them again. (Over time, when the Fed's emphasis on eligible paper diminished, the Fed's loans to banks became known as *discounts*, and the interest rate on these loans the *discount rate*, which is the terminology we use today.)

By the end of World War I, the Fed's policy of rediscounting eligible paper and keeping interest rates low to help the Treasury finance the war had led to a raging inflation; in 1919 and 1920, the inflation rate averaged 14%. The Fed decided that it could no longer follow the passive policy prescribed by the real bills doctrine because it was inconsistent with the goal of price stability, and for the first time the Fed accepted the responsibility of playing an active role in influencing the economy. In January 1920, the Fed raised the discount rate from $4\frac{3}{4}\%$ to 6%, the largest jump in its history, and eventually raised it further to 7% in June 1920, where it remained for nearly a year. The result of this policy was a sharp decline in the money supply and an especially sharp recession in 1920–1921. Although the blame for this severe recession can clearly be laid at the Fed's doorstep, in one sense the Fed's policy was very successful: After an initial decline in the price level, the inflation rate went to zero, paving the way for the prosperous Roaring Twenties.

Discovery of Open Market Operations

In the early 1920s, a particularly important event occurred: The Fed accidentally discovered open market operations. When the Fed was created, its revenue came exclusively from the interest it received on the discount loans that it made to mem-

---

[12]Another guiding principle was the maintenance of the gold standard, which we will discuss in Chapter 14.

ber banks. After the 1920–1921 recession, the volume of discount loans shrank dramatically, and the Fed was pressed for income. It solved this problem by purchasing income-earning securities. In doing so, the Fed noticed that reserves in the banking system grew and interest rates fell. A new monetary policy tool was born, and by the end of the 1920s, it was the most important weapon in the Fed's arsenal.

The Great Depression

The stock market boom in 1928 and 1929 created a dilemma for the Fed. It wanted to temper the boom by raising the discount rate, but it was reluctant to do so because that would mean raising interest rates to businesses and individuals who had legitimate needs for credit. Finally, in August 1929, the Fed raised the discount rate, but by then it was too late; the speculative excesses of the market boom had already occurred, and the Fed's action only hastened the stock market crash and pushed the economy into recession.

The weakness of the economy, particularly in the agricultural sector, led to a "contagion of fear" that triggered substantial withdrawals from banks, building to a full-fledged bank panic in November and December 1930. For the next two years, the Fed sat idly by while one bank panic after another occurred, culminating in the final panic in March 1933, at which point the new president, Franklin Delano Roosevelt, declared a bank holiday. (Why the Fed failed to engage in its lender-of-last-resort role during this period is discussed in the "Inside the Fed" box on p. 201.) The spate of bank panics from 1930 to 1933 were the most severe in U.S. history, and Roosevelt aptly summed up the problem in his statement, "The only thing we have to fear is fear itself." By the time the panics were over in March 1933, more than one-third of the commercial banks in the United States had failed.

War Finance and the Pegging of Interest Rates: 1942–1951

With the entrance of the United States into World War II in late 1941, government spending skyrocketed, and to finance it, the Treasury issued huge amounts of bonds. The Fed agreed to help the Treasury finance the war cheaply by pegging interest rates at the low levels that had prevailed before the war: $\frac{3}{8}$% on Treasury bills and $2\frac{1}{2}$% on long-term Treasury bonds. Whenever interest rates would rise above these levels and the price of bonds would begin to fall, the Fed would make open market purchases, thereby bidding up bond prices and driving interest rates down again. The result was a rapid growth in the monetary base and the money supply. The Fed had thus in effect relinquished its control of monetary policy to meet the financing needs of the government.

When the war ended, the Fed continued to peg interest rates, and because there was little pressure on them to rise, this policy did not result in an explosive growth in the money supply. When the Korean War broke out in 1950, however, interest rates began to climb, and the Fed found that it was again forced to expand the money supply at a rapid rate. Because inflation began to heat up (the consumer price index rose 8% between 1950 and 1951), the Fed decided that it was time to reassert its control over monetary policy by abandoning the interest-rate peg. An often bitter debate ensued between the Fed and the Treasury, which wanted to keep its interest costs down and so favored a continued peg-

INSIDE THE FED

Bank Panics of 1930–1933: Why Did the Fed Let Them Happen?

The Federal Reserve System was totally passive during the bank panics of the Great Depression period and did not perform its intended role of lender of last resort to prevent them. In retrospect, the Fed's behavior seems quite extraordinary, but hindsight is always clearer than foresight.

The primary reason for the Fed's inaction was that Federal Reserve officials did not understand the negative impact bank failures could have on the money supply and economic activity. Friedman and Schwartz report that the Federal Reserve officials "tended to regard bank failures as regrettable consequences of bank management or bad banking practices, or as inevitable reactions to prior speculative excesses, or as a consequence but hardly a cause of the financial and economic collapse in process." In addition, bank failures in the early stages of the bank panics "were concentrated among smaller banks and, since the most influential figures in the system were big-city bankers who deplored the existence of smaller banks, their disappearance may have been viewed with complacency."*

Friedman and Schwartz also point out that political infighting may have played an important role in the passivity of the Fed during this period. The Federal Reserve Bank of New York, which until 1928 was the dominant force in the Federal Reserve System, strongly advocated an active program of open market purchases to provide reserves to the banking system during the bank panics. However, other powerful figures in the Federal Reserve System opposed the New York bank's position, and the bank was outvoted. (Friedman and Schwartz's discussion of the politics of the Federal Reserve System during this period makes for fascinating reading, and you might enjoy their highly readable book.)

*Milton Friedman and Anna Jacobson Schwartz, *A Monetary History of the United States, 1867–1960* (Princeton, N.J.: Princeton University Press, 1963), p. 358.

ging of interest rates at low levels. In March 1951, the Fed and the Treasury came to an agreement known as the Accord, in which pegging was abandoned but the Fed promised that it would not allow interest rates to rise precipitously. After Eisenhower's election as president in 1952, the Fed was given complete freedom to pursue its monetary policy objectives.

Targeting Money Market Conditions: The 1950s and 1960s

With its freedom restored, the Federal Reserve, then under the chairmanship of William McChesney Martin Jr., took the view that monetary policy should be grounded in intuitive judgment based on a feel for the money market. The policy procedure that resulted can be described as one in which the Fed targeted money market conditions, and particularly interest rates.

By the late 1960s, the rising chorus of criticism from monetarists who advocated an increased focus on monetary aggregates in the conduct of monetary policy and concerns about inflation finally led the Fed to abandon its focus on money market conditions.

Targeting Monetary Aggregates: The 1970s

In 1970, Arthur Burns was appointed chairman of the Board of Governors, and soon thereafter the Fed stated that it was committing itself to the use of monetary aggregates as intermediate targets.

Every six weeks, the Federal Open Market Committee would set target ranges for the growth rate of various monetary aggregates and would determine what federal funds rate (the interest rate on funds loaned overnight between banks) it thought consistent with these aims. The target ranges for the growth in monetary aggregates were fairly broad—a typical range for the growth of M1 (a monetary aggregate that consists primarily of currency and checkable deposits) might be 3% to 6%; for M2 (a monetary aggregate that adds to M1 money market mutual funds and deposit accounts, small-denomination time deposits, saving deposits, and overnight repurchase agreements and Eurodollars), 4% to 7%—while the range for the federal funds rate was a narrow band, say, from $7\frac{1}{2}\%$ to $8\frac{1}{4}\%$. The trading desk at the Federal Reserve Bank of New York was then instructed to meet both sets of targets, but as we saw earlier, interest-rate targets and monetary aggregate targets might not be compatible. If the two targets were incompatible—say, the federal funds rate began to climb higher than the top of its target band when M1 was growing too rapidly—the trading desk was instructed to give precedence to the federal funds rate target. In the situation just described, this would mean that although M1 growth was too high, the trading desk would make open market purchases to keep the federal funds rate within its target range.

The Fed was actually using the federal funds rate as its operating target. During the six-week period between FOMC meetings, an unexpected rise in income (which would cause the federal funds rate to hit the top of its target band) would then induce open market purchases and a too rapid growth of the money supply. When the FOMC met again, it would try to bring money supply growth back on track by raising the target range on the federal funds rate. However, if income continued to rise unexpectedly, money growth would overshoot again. This is exactly what occurred from June 1972 to June 1973, when the economy boomed unexpectedly: M1 growth greatly exceeded its target, increasing at approximately an 8% rate, while the federal funds rate climbed from $4\frac{1}{2}\%$ to $8\frac{1}{2}\%$. The economy soon became overheated, and inflationary pressures began to mount.

The opposite chain of events occurred at the end of 1974, when the economic contraction was far more severe than anyone had predicted. The federal funds rate fell dramatically from over 12% to 5% and persistently bumped against the bottom of its target range. The trading desk conducted open market sales to keep the federal funds rate from falling, and money growth dropped precipitously, actually turning negative by the beginning of 1975. Clearly, this sharp drop in money growth when the United States was experiencing one of the worst economic contractions of the postwar era was a serious mistake.

Using the federal funds rate as an operating target promoted a procyclical monetary policy despite the Fed's lip service to monetary aggregate targets. If the Federal Reserve really intended to pursue monetary aggregate targets, it seems peculiar that it would have chosen an interest rate for an operating target rather than a reserve aggregate. (However, as the discussion of the conduct of Japanese monetary policy later in this chapter makes clear, more effective monetary control can be achieved even when an interest rate is used as an operating target.) The explanation for why the Fed chose an interest rate as an operating target is that it was still very concerned with achieving interest-rate stability and was reluctant to relinquish control over interest-rate movements. The incompatibility of the Fed's policy procedure with its stated intent of targeting on the monetary aggregates had become very clear by October 1979, when the Fed's policy procedures underwent drastic revision.

New Fed Operating Procedures: October 1979–October 1982

In October 1979, two months after Paul Volcker became chairman of the Board of Governors, the Fed finally deemphasized the federal funds rate as an operating target by widening its target range more than fivefold: A typical range might be from 10% to 15%. The primary operating target became nonborrowed reserves that the Fed would set after estimating the volume of discount loans the banks would borrow. Not surprisingly, the federal funds rate underwent much greater fluctuations after it was deemphasized as an operating target. What is surprising, however, is that the deemphasis of the federal funds target did not result in improved monetary control: After October 1979, the fluctuations in the rate of money supply growth *increased* rather than decreased as would have been expected. In addition, the Fed missed its M1 growth target ranges in all three years of the 1979–1982 period.[13] What went wrong?

There are several possible answers to this question. The first is that the economy was exposed to several shocks during this period that made monetary control more difficult: the acceleration of financial innovation and deregulation, which added new categories of deposits such as NOW accounts to the measures of monetary aggregates; the imposition by the Fed of credit controls from March to July 1980, which restricted the growth of consumer and business loans; and the back-to-back recessions of 1980 and 1981–1982.[14]

A more persuasive explanation for poor monetary control, however, is that controlling the money supply was never really the intent of Volcker's policy shift. Despite Volcker's statements about the need to target monetary aggregates, he was not committed to these targets. Rather, he was far more concerned with using interest-rate movements to wring inflation out of the economy. Volcker's primary reason for changing the Fed's operating procedure was to free his hand to manipulate interest rates in order to fight inflation. It was necessary to abandon interest-rate targets if Volcker were to be able to raise interest rates sharply when a slowdown in the economy was required to dampen inflation. This view of Volcker's strategy suggests that the Fed's announced attachment to monetary aggregate targets may have been a smokescreen to keep the Fed from being blamed for the high interest rates that would result from the new policy.

Interest-rate movements support this interpretation of Fed strategy. After the October 1979 announcement, short-term interest rates were driven up by nearly 5%, until in March 1980 they exceeded 15%. With the imposition of credit controls in March 1980 and the rapid decline in real GDP in the second quarter of 1980, the

---

[13]The M1 target ranges and actual growth rates for 1980–1982 were as follows:

Year	Target Range (%)	Actual Growth (%)
1980	4.5–7.0	7.5
1981	6.0–8.5	5.1
1982	2.5–5.5	8.8

Source: Board of Governors of the Federal Reserve System, *Monetary Policy Objectives, 1981–1983.*

[14]Another explanation focuses on the technical difficulties of monetary control when using a nonborrowed reserves operating target under a system of lagged reserve requirements, in which required reserves for a given week are calculated on the basis of the level of deposits two weeks earlier. See David Lindsey, "Nonborrowed Reserve Targeting and Monetary Control," in *Improving Money Stock Control*, ed. Laurence Meyer (Boston: Kluwer-Nijhoff, 1983), pp. 3–41.

Fed eased up on its policy and allowed interest rates to decline sharply. When recovery began in July 1980, inflation remained persistent, still exceeding 10%. Because the inflation fight was not yet won, the Fed tightened the screws again, sending short-term rates above the 15% level for a second time. The 1981–1982 recession and its large decline in output and high unemployment began to bring inflation down. The inflationary psychology apparently broken, interest rates were allowed to fall.

The Fed's anti-inflation strategy during the October 1979–October 1982 period was neither intended nor likely to produce smooth growth in the monetary aggregates. Indeed, the large fluctuations in interest rates and the business cycle, along with financial innovation, helped generate volatile money growth.

Deemphasis of Monetary Aggregates: October 1982–Early 1990s

In October 1982, with inflation in check, the Fed returned, in effect, to a policy of smoothing interest rates. It did this by placing less emphasis on monetary aggregate targets and shifting to borrowed reserves (discount loan borrowings) as an operating target. To see how a borrowed reserves target produces interest-rate smoothing, let's consider what happens when the economy expands so that interest rates are driven up. The rise in interest rates increases the incentives for banks to borrow more from the Fed, so borrowed reserves rise. To prevent the resulting rise in borrowed reserves from exceeding the target level, the Fed must lower interest rates by bidding up the price of bonds through open market purchases. The outcome of targeting on borrowed reserves, then, is that the Fed prevents a rise in interest rates.

The deemphasis of monetary aggregates and the change to a borrowed reserves target led to much smaller fluctuations in the federal funds rate after October 1982, but large fluctuations in money supply growth continued. Finally, in February 1987, the Fed announced that it would no longer even set M1 targets. The abandonment of M1 targets was defended on two grounds. The first was that the rapid pace of financial innovation and deregulation had made the definition and measurement of money very difficult. The second is that there had been a breakdown in the stable relationship between M1 and economic activity. These two arguments suggested that a monetary aggregate such as M1 might no longer be a reliable guide for monetary policy. As a result, the Fed switched its focus to the broader monetary aggregate M2, which it felt had a more stable relationship with economic activity. However, in the early 1990s, this relationship also broke down, and in July 1993, Board of Governors Chairman Alan Greenspan testified before Congress that the Fed would no longer use any monetary targets, including M2, as a guide for conducting monetary policy. Finally, legislation in 2000 amending the Federal Reserve Act dropped the requirement that the Fed report target ranges for monetary aggregates to Congress.

Federal Funds Targeting Again: Early 1990s and Beyond

Having abandoned monetary aggregates as a guide for monetary policy, the Federal Reserve returned to using a federal funds target in the early 1990s. Indeed, from late 1992 until February 1994, a period of a year and a half, the Fed kept the federal funds rate targeted at the constant rate of 3%, a low level last seen in the 1960s. The explanation for this unusual period of keeping the federal funds rate pegged so low for such a long period of time was fear on the part of the Federal Reserve that the credit crunch (described in Chapter 17) was putting a drag on the economy (the "headwinds" referred to by Greenspan) that was producing a sluggish recovery from the 1990–1991 recession. Starting in February 1994, after the economy returned to rapid growth, the Fed began a preemptive strike to head off any future inflationary pressures by raising the federal funds rate in steps to 6% by early 1995. The Fed not only has engaged in preemptive strikes against a rise in inflation but has acted preemptively against negative shocks to demand. It lowered the federal funds rate in early 1996 to deal with a possible slowing in the economy, and took the dramatic step of reducing the federal funds rate by three-quarters of a percentage point when the collapse of Long Term Capital Management in the fall of 1998 (discussed in Chapter 23) led to concerns about the health of the financial system. With the strong growth of the economy in 1999 and heightened concerns about inflation, the Fed reversed course and began to raise the federal funds rate again. The Fed's timely actions kept the economy on track, helping to produce the longest business cycle expansion in U.S. history. With a weakening economy, in January 2001, the Fed reversed course again, and began to sharply reduce the federal funds rate from its height of 6.5% to below the 2% level.

In February 1994, with the first change in the federal funds rate in a year and half, the Fed adopted a new policy procedure. Instead of keeping the federal funds target secret, as it had done previously, the Fed now announced any federal funds rate target change. As mentioned in Chapter 7, at around 2:15 P.M., after every FOMC meeting, the Fed now announces whether the federal funds rate target has been raised, lowered, or kept the same. This move to greater transparency of Fed policy was followed by another such move when, in February 1999, the Fed indicated that in the future it would announce the direction of bias to where the federal funds rate will head in the future. However, dissatisfaction with the confusion that the bias announcement created for market participants led the Fed to revise its policy, and starting in February 2000, the Fed switched to an announcement of a statement outlining the "balance of risks" in the future, whether toward higher inflation or toward a weaker economy. As a result of these announcements, the outcome of the FOMC meeting is now big news, and the media devotes much more attention to FOMC meetings because announced changes in the federal funds rate feed into changes in other interest rates that affect consumers and businesses.

International Considerations

The increasing importance of international trade to the American economy has brought international considerations to the forefront of Federal Reserve policy-making in recent years. By 1985, the strength of the dollar had contributed to a deterioration in American competitiveness with foreign businesses. In public pronouncements, Chairman Volcker and other Fed officials made it clear that the dollar was at too high a value and needed to come down. Because, as we will see in Chapter 13, expansionary monetary policy is one way to lower the value of the dollar, it is no surprise that the Fed engineered an acceleration in the growth rates of the monetary aggregates in 1985 and 1986 and that the value of the dollar declined. By 1987, policymakers at the Fed agreed that the dollar had fallen sufficiently, and sure enough, monetary growth in the United States slowed. These monetary policy actions by the Fed were encouraged by the process of **international**

GLOBAL

International Policy Coordination: The Plaza Agreement and the Louvre Accord

By 1985, the decrease in the competitiveness of American corporations as a result of the strong dollar was raising strong sentiment in Congress for restricting imports. This protectionist threat to the international trading system stimulated finance ministers and the heads of central banks from the Group of Five (G-5) industrial countries—the United States, the United Kingdom, France, West Germany, and Japan—to reach an agreement at New York's Plaza Hotel in September 1985 to bring down the value of the dollar. From September 1985 until the beginning of 1987, the value of the dollar did indeed undergo a substantial decline, falling by 35% on average relative to foreign currencies. At this point, there was growing controversy over the decline in the dollar, and another meeting of policymakers from the G-5 countries plus Canada took

place in February 1987 at the Louvre Museum in Paris. There the policymakers agreed that exchange rates should be stabilized around the levels currently prevailing. Although the value of the dollar did continue to fluctuate relative to foreign currencies after the Louvre Accord, its downward trend had been checked as intended.

Because subsequent exchange rate movements were pretty much in line with the Plaza Agreement and the Louvre Accord, these attempts at international policy coordination have been considered successful. However, other aspects of the agreements were not adhered to by all signatories. For example, West German and Japanese policymakers agreed that their countries should pursue more expansionary policies by increasing government spending and cutting taxes, and the United States agreed to try to bring down its budget deficit. At that time, the United States was not particularly successful in lowering its deficit, and the Germans were reluctant to pursue expansionary policies because of their concerns about inflation.

policy coordination (agreements among countries to enact policies cooperatively) that led to the Plaza Agreement in 1985 and the Louvre Accord in 1987 (see the "Global" box above). International considerations, although not the primary focus of the Federal Reserve, are likely to be a major factor in the conduct of American monetary policy in the future.

Monetary Targeting in Other Countries

To understand more about how monetary policy is conducted, we must compare our experiences with those of other nations. Here we examine how central banks in other countries have conducted monetary policy. Note that many of their experiences parallel those in the United States.

As we noted in our study of the conduct of U.S. monetary policy, the Federal Reserve has flirted with monetary targeting as its basic monetary policy strategy. And the Fed was not alone in adopting a monetary targeting framework in the 1970s; many other central banks did as well. Why did monetary targeting become so popular in the 1970s?[15]

The primary reason was the rise in inflation throughout the industrialized world. Central banks realized that using nominal interest rates as a target variable

---

[15]The discussion here is based on Ben Bernanke and Frederic S. Mishkin, "Central Bank Behavior and the Strategy of Monetary Policy: Observations from Six Industrialized Countries," in *NBER Macroeconomics Annual, 1992*, ed. Oliver Blanchard and Stanley Fischer (Cambridge, Mass.: MIT Press, 1992), pp. 183–228.

could lead to rising inflationary pressures. They believed that monetary aggregates could serve as a guidepost, or *nominal anchor,* that could promote a less inflationary monetary policy. Of probably even more importance, central banks believed that monetary targets could help send almost immediate signals to both the public and markets about the stance of monetary policy and the intentions of the policymakers to keep inflation in check. These signals might then help fix inflation expectations and help produce lower wage and price increases and thus less actual inflation.

We examine the experiences of four foreign countries—the United Kingdom, Canada, Germany, and Japan—to evaluate the extent to which monetary targeting has been a successful strategy for monetary policy.

United Kingdom

As in the United States, the British introduced monetary targeting in late 1973 in response to mounting concerns about inflation. The Bank of England targeted M3, a broader monetary target than the Fed used, but did not pursue it seriously: Announced targets were consistently overshot, and the Bank of England frequently revised its targets midstream or abandoned them entirely. The outcome was greater volatility of British monetary aggregates compared to American ones. After inflation accelerated in the late 1970s, Prime Minister Margaret Thatcher in 1980 introduced the Medium-Term Financial Strategy, which proposed a gradual deceleration of M3 growth. Unfortunately, the M3 targets ran into problems similar to those of the M1 targets in the United States: They were not reliable indicators of the tightness of monetary policy. After 1983, arguing that financial innovation was wreaking havoc with the relationship between M3 and national income, the Bank of England began to deemphasize M3 in favor of a narrower monetary aggregate, M0 (the monetary base). The target for M3 was temporarily suspended in October 1985 and was completely dropped in 1987, and monetary targets were abandoned altogether when the nation tied its exchange rate to the deutsche mark and became part of the European Monetary System (EMS) in October 1990.

Canada

The Canadian experience with monetary policy closely parallels that of the United States. This is not surprising given the strong ties between the two economies and the fact that the value of the Canadian dollar has been closely linked to the U.S dollar.

In response to rising inflation in the early 1970s, the Bank of Canada introduced a program of "monetary gradualism" under which M1 growth would be controlled within a gradually falling target range. Monetary gradualism was no more successful in Canada than the initial attempts at monetary targeting in the United States and the United Kingdom. By 1978, only three years after monetary targeting had begun, the Bank of Canada began to distance itself from this strategy out of concern for the exchange rate. Because of the conflict with exchange rate goals, as well as the uncertainty about M1 as a reliable guide to monetary policy, the M1 targets were abandoned in November 1982. From November 1982 to January 1988, the Bank of Canada pursued a monetary policy strategy without an explicit nominal anchor, but in January 1988, John Crow, the governor (head) of the Bank of Canada, announced that the bank would subsequently pursue an objective of price stability.

Germany

Germany's central bank, the Bundesbank, also responded to rising inflation in the early 1970s by adopting monetary targets in 1975. The monetary aggregate chosen was a narrow one known as *central bank money*, the sum of currency in circulation and bank deposits weighted by the 1974 required reserve ratios. The Bundesbank has allowed growth outside of its target ranges for periods of two to three years, and overshoots of its targets have subsequently been reversed. The primary reason for allowing deviations from its targets has been exchange rate considerations, which have been important to international agreements such as the European Monetary System, the Plaza Agreement, and the Louvre Accord. In 1988, the Bundesbank switched targets from central bank money to M3. German monetary policy using monetary targeting has been quite successful in maintaining a low and stable inflation rate.

The reunification of Germany in 1990 created some difficult problems for monetary policy. The Bundesbank was torn between trying to restrain the inflationary pressures created by reunification and keeping its exchange rate in line with those in other European countries. These strains contributed to an exchange rate crisis in Europe in September 1992, which will be discussed further in Chapter 14. The Bundesbank continued to subscribe to monetary targeting until it became part of the European System of Central Banks in January 1999, but recent research suggests that its commitment may have been weaker than its rhetoric suggested.[16]

Japan

The increase in oil prices in late 1973 was a major shock for Japan, which experienced a huge jump in the inflation rate to greater than 20% in 1974—a surge facilitated by money growth in 1973 in excess of 20%. The Bank of Japan, like the other central banks discussed here, began to pay more attention to money growth rates. In 1978, the Bank of Japan began to announce "forecasts" at the beginning of each quarter for M2 + CDs. Although the Bank of Japan was not officially committed to monetary targeting, monetary policy appeared to be more money-focused after 1978. For example, after the second oil price shock in 1979, the Bank of Japan quickly reduced M2 + CDs growth, rather than allowing it to shoot up as occurred after the first oil shock. The Bank of Japan conducted monetary policy with operating procedures that are similar in many ways to those that the Federal Reserve has used in the United States. The Bank of Japan uses the interest rate in the Japanese interbank market (which has a function similar to that of the federal funds market in the United States) as its daily operating target, just as the Fed has done.

The Bank of Japan's monetary policy performance during the 1978–1987 period was much better than the Fed's. Money growth in Japan slowed gradually, beginning in the mid-1970s, and was much less variable than in the United States. The outcome was a more rapid braking of inflation and an average inflation rate that was lower in Japan. In addition, these excellent results on inflation were achieved with lower variability in real output in Japan than in the United States. The success of Japanese monetary policy in the 1978–1987 period using an interest rate as an operating target, in contrast to the lack of success in the 1970–1979

---

[16]See Richard Clarida and Mark Gertler, "How the Bundesbank Conducts Monetary Policy," National Bureau of Economic Research Working Paper No. 5581, May 1996.

period in the United States when the Fed used a similar operating procedure, suggests that using an interest rate as an operating target is not necessarily a barrier to successful monetary policy. More important might be a commitment to a low inflation rate, something that was true for the Bank of Japan in this period.

In parallel with the United States, financial innovation and deregulation in Japan began to reduce the usefulness of the M2 + CDs monetary aggregate as an indicator of monetary policy. Because of concerns about the appreciation of the yen, the Bank of Japan significantly increased the rate of money growth from 1987 to 1989. Many observers blame speculation in Japanese land and stock prices (the so-called bubble economy) on the increase in money growth, and to reduce this speculation, in 1989 the Bank of Japan switched to a tighter monetary policy aimed at slower money growth. The aftermath has been a substantial decline in land and stock prices and the collapse of the bubble economy.

Lessons from Monetary Targeting Experiences

There are several lessons to be drawn from the experience with monetary targeting in the four countries and the United States. First, successful use of monetary targeting seems to require that the central bank pursue its targeting strategy seriously. Countries like the United States, Canada, and especially the United Kingdom were unable to use monetary targeting to bring inflation under control because the procedures they used to implement the targets did not imply a strong commitment to the strategy and they consistently overshot their monetary targets. Germany and Japan, by contrast, were more successful in using monetary aggregates to keep inflation in check. This did not mean that the Bundesbank and the Bank of Japan always met their targets; more critical to their success was that they subsequently reversed overshoots of the targets. A further lesson from the Japanese experience is that the success of monetary targeting can be achieved with operating procedures that focus on interest rates as the operating target. The final lesson is that the breakdown in the relationship between monetary aggregates and the goal variables, nominal GDP and inflation, in many countries made the monetary targeting strategy untenable. As the former governor of the Bank of Canada, John Crow, is said to have stated, "We didn't abandon monetary aggregates; they abandoned us."

The New International Trend in Monetary Policy Strategy: Inflation Targeting

Although central banks have abandoned monetary targeting, the reasons they adopted it in the first place remain. Central banks still see the need to have a nominal anchor that will promote price stability. Another nominal anchor for monetary policy can be the foreign exchange rate. As we will see in Chapter 14, some countries have achieved low inflation by tying the value of their currency to the currency of a country with a good inflation record. However, the problem with this strategy is that, as shown in Chapter 14, with a fixed exchange rate, a country no longer exercises control over its own monetary policy and so cannot use monetary policy to respond to domestic shocks.

The search for a nominal anchor has led many countries to pursue inflation targeting as their basic monetary strategy. To understand what inflation targeting is all about, we look at the experience in three countries: New Zealand, which was the first to adopt this strategy; Canada; and the United Kingdom.[17]

New Zealand

As part of a general reform of the government's role in the economy, the New Zealand parliament in 1989 passed the Reserve Bank of New Zealand Act, which became effective on February 1, 1990. Besides increasing the independence of the central bank, the Reserve Bank of New Zealand, transforming it from one of the least independent to one of the most independent among the developed countries, the act also committed the Reserve Bank to the sole objective of price stability. The act stipulated that the minister of finance and the governor of the Reserve Bank should negotiate and make public a "policy targets agreement" that sets out the targets against which monetary policy performance will be evaluated. These agreements have specified numerical target ranges for inflation and the dates by which they were to be reached. An unusual feature of the New Zealand legislation is that the governor of the Reserve Bank is held personally accountable for the success of monetary policy. If the goals set forth in the policy targets agreement are not met, the governor is subject to dismissal.

The first policy targets agreement, signed by the minister of finance and the governor of the Reserve Bank on March 2, 1990, directed the Reserve Bank to achieve an annual inflation rate within the 0% to 2% range, and subsequent agreements stuck with this range until the end of 1996, when the range was changed to 0% to 3%, and later in 2002, when it was changed to 1% to 3%. As a result of tight monetary policy, the inflation rate was brought down from above 5% to below 2% by the end of 1992, but at the cost of a deep recession and a sharp rise in unemployment. Since then, inflation typically has remained within the target range, with the exception of a brief period in 1995, when it exceeded the upper limit by a few tenths of a percentage point. (Under the Reserve Bank Act, the governor, Don Brash, could have been dismissed, but after parliamentary debate, he was retained in his job.) Since 1992, New Zealand's growth rate has on average been strong, with some years exceeding 5%, and unemployment has come down significantly.

Canada

On February 26, 1991, a joint announcement by the minister of finance and the governor of the Bank of Canada established formal inflation targets. The target ranges were 2% to 4% by the end of 1992, 1.5% to 3.5% by June 1994, and 1% to 3% by December 1996. After the new government took office in late 1993, the target range was set at 1% to 3% starting December 1995 and has been kept there by subsequent governments. Canadian inflation has also fallen dramatically since the adoption of inflation targets, from above the 5% level in 1991 to within the target range of 1% to 3% since 1995. However, as in New Zealand, this decline was not without cost: Unemployment soared beyond the 10% level from 1991 until 1994 but then declined substantially.

---

[17]The discussion here is based on Frederic S. Mishkin and Adam S. Posen, "Inflation Targeting: Lessons from Four Countries," Federal Reserve Bank of New York, *Economic Policy Review* 3 (1997): 9–110, and Ben S. Bernanke, Thomas Laubach, Frederic S. Mishkin, and Adam S. Posen, *Inflation Targeting: Lessons from the International Experience* (Princeton, N.J.: Princeton University Press, 1999).

United Kingdom

When the United Kingdom left the European Monetary System after the speculative attack on the pound in September 1992 (more on this in Chapter 14), the British decided to turn to inflation targets to replace the exchange rate as the nominal anchor. As you may recall from Chapter 7, the central bank in the United Kingdom, the Bank of England, at that time did not have statutory authority over monetary policy; it could only make recommendations. Thus it was the chancellor of the Exchequer (the equivalent of the U.S. Treasury secretary) who announced an inflation target for the nation on October 8, 1992. Three weeks later, he "invited" the governor of the Bank of England to issue on a quarterly basis a report on the progress being made in achieving the target—an invitation that the governor accepted. The inflation target range was set at 1% to 4% until the next election (May 1997), with the intent that the inflation rate should settle down to the lower half of the range (below 2.5%). In 1997, the range was changed to a point target of 2.5% and eventually to 2%. Along with this inflation target, the government implemented the institutional changes mentioned in Chapter 7, which, along with the governor's report, gave the Bank of England a more independent voice on monetary policy, culminating in the granting of the power to set interest rates to the Bank in May 1997.

Before the adoption of inflation targets, inflation had already been falling in the United Kingdom, from a peak of 9% at the beginning of 1991 to 4% at the time of adoption. After a small upward movement in early 1993, inflation continued to fall until by the third quarter of 1994 it was at 2.2%, within the intended range articulated by the chancellor. Subsequently inflation rose, climbing above the 2.5% level by 1996, but has remained close to the target since then. Meanwhile, growth of the U.K. economy has been strong, causing a reduction in the unemployment rate.

Lessons from Inflation Targeting Experiences

Several lessons can be drawn from the inflation targeting experiences in these three countries. First, as the New Zealand and Canadian experience indicates, inflation targets have not been able to produce a decline in inflation without a substantial decline in output and a rise in unemployment. Hopes that inflation targets would lead to disinflation at a lower cost have not been realized. Second, inflation targets have so far worked well in keeping inflation at moderate levels. One important advantage of inflation targets is that they keep the goal of price stability in the public's eye, thus making the central bank more accountable for keeping inflation low, which can also help reduce political pressures on the central bank to pursue inflationary monetary policy.

How successful will inflation targeting be at keeping inflation low in the countries examined here? It is still too early to tell. Nonetheless, many other countries have followed New Zealand, Canada, and the United Kingdom in adopting inflation targets, including Australia, Israel, Sweden, Switzerland, Brazil, Chile, South Africa, Poland, and Thailand. The growing popularity of inflation targeting indicates that it might become the wave of the future for central bank strategy.

The Practicing Manager

USING A FED WATCHER

As we have seen, the most important player in the determination of the U.S. money supply and interest rates is the Federal Reserve. When the Fed wants to inject reserves into the system, it conducts open market purchases of bonds, which cause their prices to increase and their interest rates to fall, at least in the short term. If the Fed withdraws reserves from the system, it sells bonds, thereby depressing their price and raising their interest rates. From a longer-run perspective, if the Fed pursues an expansionary monetary policy with high money growth, inflation will rise and interest rates will rise as well. Contractionary monetary policy is likely to lower inflation in the long run and lead to lower interest rates.

Knowing what actions the Fed might be taking can thus help financial institution managers predict the future course of interest rates with greater accuracy. Because, as we have seen, changes in interest rates have a major impact on a financial institution's profitability, the managers of these institutions are particularly interested in scrutinizing the Fed's behavior. To help in this task, managers hire so-called Fed watchers, experts on Federal Reserve behavior who may have worked in the Federal Reserve System and so have an insider's view of Federal Reserve operations.

Divining what the Fed is up to is by no means easy. Chapter 7 suggested that the Fed has a penchant for secrecy. The Fed does not disclose the content of the minutes of FOMC meetings at which it decides the course of monetary policy until six weeks after each meeting. In addition, the Fed does not provide information on the amount of certain transactions and frequently tries to obscure from the market whether it is injecting reserves into the banking system by making open market purchases and sales simultaneously.

Fed watchers, with their specialized knowledge of the ins and outs of the Fed, scrutinize the public pronouncements of Federal Reserve officials to get a feel for where monetary policy is heading. They also carefully study the data on past Federal Reserve actions and current events in the bond markets to determine what the Fed is up to.

If a Fed watcher tells a financial institution manager that Federal Reserve concerns about inflation are high and the Fed will pursue a tight monetary policy and raise short-term interest rates in the near future, the manager may decide immediately to acquire funds at the currently low interest rates in order to keep the cost of funds from rising. If the financial institution trades foreign exchange, the rise in interest rates and the attempt by the Fed to keep inflation down might lead the manager to instruct traders to purchase dollars in the foreign exchange market. As we will see in Chapter 13, these actions by the Fed would be likely to cause the value of the dollar to appreciate, so the purchase of dollars by the financial institution should lead to substantial profits.

If, conversely, the Fed watcher thinks that the Fed is worried about a weak economy and will thus pursue an expansionary policy and lower interest rates, the financial institution manager will take very different actions. Now the manager might instruct loan officers to make as many loans as possible so as to lock in the higher interest rates that the financial institution can earn currently. Or the manager might buy bonds, anticipating that interest rates will fall and their prices will rise, giving the institution a nice profit. The more expansionary policy is also likely to lower the value of the dollar in the foreign exchange market, so the financial institution manager might tell foreign exchange traders to buy foreign currencies and sell dollars in order to make a profit when the dollar falls in the future.

A Fed watcher who is right is a very valuable commodity to a financial institution. Successful Fed watchers are actively sought out by financial institutions and often earn high salaries, well into the six-figure range.

Summary

1. The conduct of monetary policy involves actions that affect the Federal Reserve's balance sheet. Open market purchases lead to an expansion of reserves and deposits in the banking system and hence to an expansion of the monetary base and the money supply. An increase in discount loans leads to an expansion of reserves, thereby causing an expansion of the monetary base and the money supply.

2. A supply and demand analysis of the market for reserves yields the following results: (a) When the Fed makes an open market purchase, lowers the discount rate, or lowers reserve requirements, the federal funds rate declines; (b) when the Fed makes an open market sale, raises the discount rate, or raises reserve requirements, the federal funds rate rises.

3. The three basic tools of monetary policy are open market operations, discount policy, and reserve requirements. Open market operations are the primary tool used by the Fed to control the money supply because they occur at the initiative of the Fed, are flexible, are easily reversed, and can be implemented quickly.

4. The six basic goals of monetary policy are high employment, economic growth, price stability, interest-rate stability, stability of financial markets, and stability in foreign exchange markets.

5. By using intermediate and operating targets, a central bank like the Fed can more quickly judge whether its policies are on the right track and make midcourse corrections, rather than waiting to see the final outcome of its policies on such goals as employment and the price level. The Fed's policy tools directly affect its operating targets, which in turn affect the intermediate targets, which in turn affect the goals.

6. Because interest-rate and monetary aggregate targets are incompatible, a central bank must choose between them on the basis of three criteria: measurability, controllability, and the ability to affect goal variables predictably. Unfortunately, these criteria do not establish an overwhelming case for one set of targets over another.

7. The historical record of the Fed's conduct of monetary policy reveals that the Fed has switched its operating targets many times, returning to a federal funds rate target in recent years.

8. In response to the rise in inflation in the early 1970s, central banks around the world also began to target monetary aggregates. Monetary targeting seems to have been most effective when it has been pursued seriously, which does not mean that targets were always met; more critical to success was a reversal of overshoots of the targets. Unfortunately, the breakdown in many countries of the relationship between monetary aggregates and the goal variables, nominal GDP and inflation, made the monetary targeting strategy untenable.

9. After disappointments with monetary targeting, the search for a nominal anchor has led several countries to pursue inflation targeting as their basic monetary strategy. Although inflation targeting so far has been successful in keeping inflation rates low in countries that have adopted it, hopes that inflation targets would lead to disinflation at a lower cost have not been realized.

10. Because predicting the Federal Reserve's actions can help managers of financial institutions predict the course of future interest rates, which has a major impact on the financial institutions' profitability, such managers value the services of Fed watchers, experts on Federal Reserve behavior.

Key Terms

defensive open market
  operations, *p. 183*
discount rate, *p. 177*
discount window, *p. 185*
dynamic open market
  operations, *p. 183*
excess reserves, *p. 176*
federal funds rate, *p. 179*
intermediate target, *p. 194*
international policy
  coordination, *p. 205*

lender of last resort, *p. 187*
matched sale-purchase transaction (reverse repo), *p. 185*
monetary base, *p. 176*
natural rate of unemployment,
  p. 191
open market operations, *p. 177*
operating target, *p. 194*
primary dealer, *p. 184*

real bills doctrine, *p. 199*
repurchase agreement (repo),
  p. 185
required reserve ratio, *p. 177*
required reserves, *p. 176*
reserve requirements, *p. 179*
reserves, *p. 176*

Questions

1. "Unemployment is a bad thing, and the government should make every effort to eliminate it." Do you agree or disagree? Explain your answer.

2. Which goals of the Fed frequently conflict?

3. "If the demand for reserves did not fluctuate, the Fed could pursue both a nonborrowed reserves target and an interest-rate target at the same time." Is this statement true, false, or uncertain? Explain your answer.

4. Classify each of the following as either an operating target or an intermediate target, and explain why.
   a. The three-month Treasury bill rate
   b. The monetary base
   c. M2

5. What procedures can the Fed use to control the three-month Treasury bill rate? Why does control of this interest rate imply that the Fed will lose control of the money supply?

6. If the Fed has an interest-rate target, why will an increase in the demand for reserves lead to a rise in the money supply?

7. "Interest rates can be measured more accurately and more quickly than the money supply. Hence an interest rate is preferred over the money supply as an intermediate target." Do you agree or disagree? Explain your answer.

8. Compare the monetary base to M2 on the grounds of controllability and measurability. Which do you prefer as an intermediate target? Why?

9. "Discounting is no longer needed because the presence of the FDIC eliminates the possibility of bank panics." Is this statement true, false, or uncertain? Explain your answer.

10. The benefits of using Fed discount operations to prevent bank panics are straightforward. What are the costs?

11. Explain why the rise in the discount rate in 1920 led to a sharp decline in the money supply.

12. Excess reserves are frequently called idle reserves, suggesting that they are not useful. Does the episode of the rise in reserve requirements in 1936–1937 bear out this view?

13. How did the Fed's failure to perform its role as the lender of last resort contribute to the decline of the money supply in the 1930–1933 period?

14. Why is pegging the nominal interest rate problematic for a central bank?

15. How have the Federal Reserve's concerns about the value of the U.S. exchange rate affected monetary policy?

16. "The failure of the Fed to control the money supply in the 1970s and 1980s suggests that the Fed is not able to control the money supply." Do you agree or disagree? Explain your answer.

17. "When the economy enters a recession, either a free reserve target or an interest-rate target will lead to a slower rate of growth for the money supply." Explain why this statement is true. What does it say about the use of free reserves or interest rates as targets?

18. How can bank behavior and the Fed's behavior cause money supply growth to be procyclical (rising in booms and falling in recessions)?

19. Which is more likely to produce smaller fluctuations in the federal funds rate, a nonborrowed reserves target or a borrowed reserves target? Why?

20. Why might the Fed say that it wants to control the money supply but in reality not be serious about doing so?

Quantitative Problems

1. Consider a bank policy to maintain 12% of deposits as reserves. The bank currently has $10 million in deposits and holds $400,000 in excess reserves. What is the required reserve on a new deposit of $50,000?

2. Estimates of unemployment for the upcoming year have been developed as follows:

Economy	Probability	Unemployment Rate (%)
Bust	0.15	20
Average	0.5	10
Good	0.2	5
Boom	0.15	1

What is the expected unemployment rate? The standard deviation?

3. The Federal Reserve wants to increase the supply of reserves, so it purchases $1 million dollars worth of bonds from the public. Show the effect of this open market operation using T-accounts.

4. Use T-accounts to show the effect of the Federal Reserve being paid back a $500,000 discount loan from a bank.

5. The short-term nominal interest rate is 5%, with an expected inflation of 2%. Economists forecast that next year's nominal rate will increase by 100 basis points, but inflation will fall to 1.5%. What is the expected change in real interest rates?

6. If the required reserve ratio is 10%, how much of a new $10,000 deposit can a bank lend? What is the potential impact on the money supply? Recall from introductory macroeconomics that the money multiplier = 1/(required reserve ratio).

7. A bank currently holds $150,000 in excess reserves. If the current reserve requirement is 12.5%, how much could the money supply change? How could this happen?

8. The trading desk at the Federal Reserve sold $100,000,000 in T-bills to the public. If the current reserve requirement is 8.0%, how much could the money supply change?

Web Exercises

Conduct of Monetary Policy: Tools, Goals, and Targets

1. The Federal Open Market Committee (FOMC) meets about every six weeks to assess the state of the economy and to determine what actions the central bank should take. The minutes of these meetings are released after the next scheduled meeting. However, a brief press release is made available immediately. Find the schedule of minutes and press releases at **http://www.federalreserve. gov/fomc/**.

   a. When was the last scheduled meeting of the FOMC? When is the next meeting?

   b. Review the press release from the last meeting. What did the committee decide to do about short-term interest rates?

   c. Review the most recently published meeting minutes. What areas of the economy seemed to be of most concern to the committee members?

2. It is possible to access other central bank websites to learn about their structure. One example is the European Central Bank (ECB). Go to **http://www. ecb.int/**. On the ECB home page, locate the link to the current exchange rate between the euro and the dollar. When the euro debuted in January 1999 it was valued at $1.18. What is it at now?

Web Appendices

Please visit our Web site at **www.aw-bc.com/mishkin_ eakins** to read the Web appendix to Chapter 8, *The Fed's Balance Sheet and the Monetary Base.*

PART 4

Financial Markets

CHAPTER 9

The Money Markets

Preview

If you were to review Microsoft's annual report for 2003, you would find that the company had over $6 billion in cash and equivalents. The firm also listed $42 billion in short-term securities. The firm chose to hold nearly $50 billion in highly liquid short-term assets in order to be ready to take advantage of investment opportunities and to avoid the risks associated with other types of investments. Microsoft will have much of these funds invested in the money markets. Recall that money market securities are short-term, low-risk, and very liquid. Because of the high degree of safety and liquidity these securities exhibit, they are close to being money, hence their name.

The money markets have been active since the early 1800s but have become much more important since 1970, when interest rates rose above historic levels. In fact, the rise in short-term rates, coupled with a regulated ceiling on the rate that banks could pay for deposits, resulted in a rapid outflow of funds from financial institutions in the late 1970s and early 1980s. This outflow in turn caused many banks and savings and loans to fail. The industry regained its health only after massive changes were made to bank regulations with regard to money market interest rates.

This chapter carefully reviews the money markets and the securities that are traded there. In addition, we discuss why the money markets are important to our financial system.

The Money Markets Defined

The term *money market* is actually a misnomer. Money—currency—is not traded in the money markets. Because the securities that do trade there are short-term and highly liquid, however, they are close to being money. Money market securities, which are discussed in detail later in this chapter, have three basic characteristics in common:

- They are usually sold in large denominations.
- They have low default risk.
- They mature in one year or less *from their original issue date.* Most money market instruments mature in less than 120 days.

Money market transactions do not take place in any one particular location or building. Instead, traders usually arrange purchases and sales between participants over the phone and complete them electronically. Because of this characteristic, money market securities usually have an active *secondary market.* This means that after the security has been sold initially, it is relatively easy to find buyers who will purchase it in the future. An active secondary market makes money market securities very flexible instruments to use to fill short-term financial needs. For example, Microsoft's annual report states that "we consider all highly liquid interest-earning investments with a maturity of 3 months or less at date of purchase to be cash equivalents."

Another characteristic of the money markets is that they are **wholesale markets.** This means that most transactions are very large, usually in excess of $1 million. The size of these transactions prevents most individual investors from participating directly in the money markets. Instead, dealers and brokers, operating in the trading rooms of large banks and brokerage houses, bring customers together. These traders will buy or sell $50 or $100 million in mere seconds—certainly not a job for the faint of heart!

As you may recall from Chapter 2, flexibility and innovation are two important characteristics of any financial market, and the money markets are no exception. Despite the wholesale nature of the money market, innovative securities and trading methods have been developed to give small investors access to money market securities. We will discuss these securities and their characteristics later in the chapter, and in greater detail in Chapter 21.

Why Do We Need the Money Markets?

In theory, the money markets should not be needed. The banking industry exists primarily to provide short-term loans and to accept short-term deposits. Banks should have an efficiency advantage in gathering information, an advantage that should eliminate the need for the money markets. Thanks to continuing relationships with customers, banks should be able to offer loans more cheaply than diversified markets, which must evaluate each borrower every time a new security is offered. Furthermore, short-term securities offered for sale in the money markets are neither as liquid nor as safe as deposits placed in banks and thrifts. Given the advantages that banks have, why do the money markets exist at all?

The banking industry exists primarily to mediate the asymmetric information problem between saver-lenders and borrower-spenders, and banks can earn profits by capturing economies of scale while providing this service. However, the banking industry is subject to more regulations and governmental costs than are the money markets. In situations where the asymmetric information problem is not severe, the money markets have a distinct cost advantage over banks in providing short-term funds.

Money Market Cost Advantages

Banks must put aside a portion of their deposits in the form of reserves that are held without interest at the Federal Reserve. Thus, for every dollar deposited, the bank can invest only between 90 to 97 cents.[1] This means that it must pay a lower interest rate to the depositor than if the full deposit could be invested.

Interest-rate regulations were a second competitive obstacle for banks. One of the principal purposes of the banking regulations of the 1930s was to reduce competition among banks. Without competition, regulators felt, banks were less likely to fail. The cost to consumers of the greater profits banks earned because of the lack of free market competition was justified by the greater economic stability that a healthy banking system would provide.

One way that banking profits were assured was by regulations that set a ceiling on the rate of interest that banks could pay for funds. The Glass-Steagall Act of 1933 prohibited payment of interest on checking accounts and limited the interest that could be paid on time deposits. The limits on interest rates were not particularly relevant until the late 1950s. The limits became especially troublesome to banks in the late 1970s and early 1980s when inflation pushed short-term interest rates above the level that banks could pay. Investors pulled their money out of banks and put it into money market security accounts offered by many brokerage firms. These new investors caused the money markets to grow rapidly.

Banks continue to provide valuable intermediation, as we will see in several later chapters. In some situations, however, the cost structure of the banking industry makes it unable to compete effectively in the market for short-term funds against the less restricted money markets.

The Purpose of the Money Markets

The well-developed secondary market for money market instruments makes the money market an ideal place for a firm or financial institution to "warehouse" surplus funds until they are needed. Similarly, the money markets provide a low-cost source of funds to firms, the government, and intermediaries that need a short-term infusion of funds.

Most investors in the money market who are temporarily warehousing funds are ordinarily not trying to earn unusually high returns on their money market funds. Rather, they use the money market as an interim investment that provides a higher return than holding cash or money in banks. They may feel that market conditions are not right to warrant the purchase of additional stock, or they may expect interest rates to rise and hence not want to purchase bonds. It is important to keep in mind that holding idle surplus cash is expensive for an investor because cash balances earn no income for the owner. Idle cash represents an *opportunity cost* in terms of lost interest income. Recall from Chapter 4 that an asset's opportunity cost is the amount of interest sacrificed by not holding an alternative asset. The money markets provide a means to invest idle funds and to reduce this opportunity cost.

---

[1]The reserve requirement on nonpersonal time deposits with an original maturity of less than $1\frac{1}{2}$ years was reduced from 3% to 0% in December 1990.

Investment advisers often hold some funds in the money market so that they will be able to act quickly to take advantage of investment opportunities they identify. Most investment funds and financial intermediaries also hold money market securities to meet investment or deposit outflows.

The sellers of money market securities find that the money market provides a low-cost source of temporary funds. Table 1 shows the interest rates available on a variety of money market instruments sold by a variety of firms and institutions. For example, banks may issue federal funds (we will define the money market securities later in this chapter) to obtain funds in the money market to meet short-term reserve requirement shortages. The government funds a large portion of the U.S. debt with Treasury bills. Finance companies like GMAC (General Motors Acceptance Company, the financing division of General Motors) may enter the money market to raise the funds that it uses to make car loans.

Why do corporations and the U.S. government sometimes need to get their hands on funds quickly? The primary reason is that cash inflows and outflows are rarely synchronized. Government tax revenues, for example, usually come only at certain times of the year, but expenses are incurred all year long. The government can borrow short-term funds that it will pay back when it receives tax revenues. Businesses also face problems caused by revenues and expenses occurring at different times. The money markets provide an efficient, low-cost way of solving these problems.

Who Participates in the Money Markets?

An obvious way to discuss the players in the money market would be to list those who borrow and those who lend. The problem with this approach is that most money market participants operate on both sides of the market. For example, any large bank will borrow aggressively in the money market by selling large commercial CDs. At the same time, it will lend short-term funds to businesses through

TABLE 1   *Sample Money Market Rates, Decemnber 15, 2004*

Instrument	Interest Rate (%)
Prime rate	5.25
Federal funds	2.25
Commercial paper	2.30
Certificate of deposit	2.36
Banker's acceptance	2.35
London interbank offer rate	2.41
Foreign prime rates	
Canada	4.25
European Central Bank	2.00
Japan	1.375
Treasury bills	2.20
Merrill Lynch Ready Assets Trust	1.38

Source: Wall Street Journal, December 15, 2004, p. C15.

its commercial lending departments. Nevertheless, we can identify the primary money market players—the U.S. Treasury, the Federal Reserve System, commercial banks, businesses, investments and securities firms, and individuals—and discuss their roles (summarized in Table 2).

U.S. Treasury Department

The U.S. Treasury Department is unique because it is always a demander of money market funds and never a supplier. The U.S. Treasury is the largest of all money market borrowers worldwide. It issues Treasury bills (often called T-bills) and other securities that are popular with other money market participants. Short-term issues enable the government to raise funds until tax revenues are received. The Treasury also issues T-bills to replace maturing issues.

Federal Reserve System

The Federal Reserve is the Treasury's agent for the distribution of all government securities. The Fed holds vast quantities of Treasury securities that it sells if it believes that the money supply should be reduced. Similarly, the Fed will purchase Treasury securities if it believes that the money supply should be expanded. The Fed's responsibility for the money supply makes it the single most

TABLE 2 *Money Market Participants*	
Participant	**Role**
U.S. Treasury Department	Sells U.S. Treasury securities to fund the national debt
Federal Reserve System	Buys and sells U.S. Treasury securities as its primary method of controlling the money supply
Commercial banks	Buy U.S. Treasury securities; sell certificates of deposit and make short-term loans; offer individual investors accounts that invest in money market securities
Businesses	Buy and sell various short-term securities as a regular part of their cash management
Investment companies (brokerage firms)	Trade on behalf of commercial accounts
Finance companies (commercial leasing companies)	Lend funds to individuals
Insurance companies (property and casualty insurance companies)	Maintain liquidity needed to meet unexpected demands
Pension funds	Maintain funds in money market instruments in readiness for investment in stocks and bonds
Individuals	Buy money market mutual funds
Money market mutual funds	Allow small investors to participate in the money market by aggregating their funds to invest in large-denomination money market securities

influential participant in the U.S. money market. The Federal Reserve's role in controlling the economy through open market operations was discussed further in Chapters 7 and 8.

Commercial Banks

Commercial banks hold a larger percentage of U.S. government securities than any other group of financial institutions, approximately 12%. This is partly because of regulations that limit the investment opportunities available to banks. Specifically, banks are prohibited from owning risky securities, such as stocks or corporate bonds. There are no restrictions against holding Treasury securities because of their low risk and liquidity.

Banks are also the major issuer of negotiable certificates of deposit (CDs), banker's acceptances, federal funds, and repurchase agreements (we will discuss these securities in the next section). In addition to using money market securities to help manage their own liquidity, many banks trade on behalf of their customers.

Not all commercial banks deal for their customers in the secondary money market. The ones that do are among the largest in the country and are often referred to as *money center banks*. The biggest money center banks include Citigroup, Bank of America, J.P. Morgan, and Wachovia.

Businesses

Many businesses buy and sell securities in the money markets. Such activity is usually limited to major corporations because of the large dollar amounts involved. As discussed earlier, the money markets are used extensively by businesses both to warehouse surplus funds and to raise short-term funds. We will discuss the specific money market securities that businesses issue later in this chapter.

Investment and Securities Firms

The other financial institutions that participate in the money markets are listed in Table 2.

Investment Companies Large diversified brokerage firms are active in the money markets. The largest of these include Bear Stearns, Salomon Smith Barney, Merrill Lynch, PaineWebber, and Morgan Stanley Dean Witter. The primary function of these dealers is to "make a market" for money market securities by maintaining an inventory from which to buy or sell. These firms are very important to the liquidity of the money market because they ensure that both buyers and sellers can readily market their securities. We discuss investment companies in Chapter 23.

Finance Companies Finance companies raise funds in the money markets primarily by selling commercial paper. They then lend the funds to consumers for the purchase of durable goods such as cars, boats, or home improvements. Finance companies and related firms are discussed in Chapter 26 (on the Web).

Insurance Companies Property and casualty insurance companies must maintain liquidity because of their unpredictable need for funds. When four hurricanes hit

Florida in 2004, for example, insurance companies paid out billions of dollars in benefits to policyholders. To meet this demand for funds, the insurance companies sold some of their money market securities to raise cash. Insurance companies are discussed in Chapter 22.

Pension Funds Pension funds invest a portion of their cash in the money markets so that they can take advantage of investment opportunities that they may identify in the stock or bond markets. Like insurance companies, pension funds must have sufficient liquidity to meet their obligations. However, because their obligations are reasonably predictable, large money market security holdings are unnecessary. Pension funds are discussed in Chapter 22.

Individuals

When inflation rose in the late 1970s, the interest rates that banks were offering on deposits became unattractive to individual investors. At this same time, brokerage houses began promoting money market mutual funds, which paid much higher rates.

Banks could not stop large amounts of cash from moving out to mutual funds because regulations capped the rate they could pay on deposits. To combat this flight of money from banks, the authorities revised the regulations. Banks quickly raised rates in an attempt to recapture individual investors' dollars. This halted the rapid movement of funds, but money market mutual funds remain a popular individual investment option. The advantage of mutual funds is that they give investors with relatively small amounts of cash to invest access to large-denomination securities. We will discuss money market mutual funds in more depth in Chapter 21.

Money Market Instruments

A variety of money market instruments are available to meet the diverse needs of market participants. One security will be perfect for one investor; a different security may be best for another. In this section we gain a greater understanding of money market security characteristics and how money market participants use them to manage their cash.

Treasury Bills

To finance the national debt, the U.S. Treasury Department issues a variety of debt securities. The most widely held liquid security is the Treasury bill. Treasury bills have 91-day, 182-day, or 12-month maturities. The Treasury bill had a minimum denomination of $10,000 until 1998, at which time new $1000 T-bills became available. The Fed has set up a direct purchase option that individuals may use to purchase Treasury bills over the Internet. First available in September 1998, this method of buying securities represented an effort to make Treasury securities more widely available.

The government does not actually pay interest on Treasury bills. Instead they are issued at a discount from par (their value at maturity). The investor's yield comes from the increase in the value of the security between the time it was purchased and the time it matures.

Case

DISCOUNTING THE PRICE OF TREASURY SECURITIES TO PAY THE INTEREST

Most money market securities do not pay interest. Instead, the investor pays less for the security than it will be worth when it matures, and the increase in price provides a return. This is called **discounting** and is common to short-term securities because they often mature before the issuer can mail out interest checks. (We discussed discounting in Chapter 3.)

The yield on an investment is found by computing the increase in value in the security during its holding period and dividing by the amount paid for the security. This yield is converted into an annual yield by multiplying by 365 divided by the number of days until maturity. This gives the following equation:

$$i_{yt} = \frac{F - P}{P} \times \frac{365}{n} \tag{1}$$

where

i_{yt} = annualized yield on the investment
F = face value (amount paid to the investor at maturity)
P = purchase price
n = number of days until maturity

EXAMPLE 1 *Discounting*

You decide to purchase a 91-day Treasury bill for $9850. When it matures, the bill will be worth $10,000. What is the bill's annualized yield?

Solution

You would earn 6.11% on the 91-day investment in the Treasury bill.

$$i_{yt} = \frac{F - P}{P} \times \frac{365}{n}$$

where

F = face value (amount paid to investor at maturity) = $10,000
P = purchase price = $9850
n = number of days until maturity = 91

Thus

$$i_{yt} = \frac{\$10{,}000 - \$9850}{\$9850} \times \frac{365}{91} = 0.0611 = 6.11\%$$

EXAMPLE 2 *Discounting*

Now suppose that you decide to sell the Treasury bill 31 days before it matures. By selling before it matures, you will receive $9948. What is the bill's annualized yield?

Solution

On this 60-day investment in the Treasury bill, you would earn 6.05%.

$$i_{yt} = \frac{F - P}{P} \times \frac{365}{n}$$

where

F = face value (in this case amount paid to investor before maturity) = $9948

P = purchase price $\qquad$ = $9850

n = number of days security held = $91 - 31$ $\qquad$ = 60

Thus

$$i_{yt} = \frac{\$9948 - \$9850}{\$9850} \times \frac{365}{60} = 0.0605 = 6.05\%$$

Risk Treasury bills have virtually zero default risk because even if the government ran out of money, it could simply print more to redeem them when they mature. The risk of unexpected changes in inflation is also low because of the short term to maturity. The market for Treasury bills is extremely deep and liquid. A **deep market** is one with many different buyers and sellers. A **liquid market** is one in which securities can be bought and sold quickly and with low transaction costs. Investors in markets that are deep and liquid have little risk that they will not be able to sell their securities when they want to.

The budget debates in early 1996 almost caused the government to default on its debt, despite the long-held belief that such a thing could not happen. Congress attempted to force President Clinton to sign a budget bill by refusing to approve a temporary spending package. If the stalemate had lasted much longer, we would have witnessed the first-ever U.S. government security default. We can only speculate what the long-term effect on interest rates might have been if the market decided to add a default risk premium to all government securities.

Treasury Bill Auctions Every Thursday, the Treasury announces how many 91-day (13-week) and 182-day (26-week) Treasury bills it will offer for sale. Buyers must submit bids by the following Monday, and awards are made the following morning. The 52-week Treasury bills are offered similarly, but only once a month. The Treasury accepts the bids offering the highest price. The highest bidder is satisfied first. Subsequent bidders are satisfied in the order of their bid amount until the total amount of securities is distributed. Note that this implies that not everyone at the auction pays the same price for the securities.

Find information about upcoming auctions, results, debt buyback operations, and historical information at www.publicdebt.treas.gov/of/ofaucrt.htm

As an alternative to the **competitive bidding** procedure just outlined, the Treasury also permits **noncompetitive bidding.** When competitive bids are offered, investors state both the amount of securities desired and the price they are willing to pay. By contrast, noncompetitive bids include only the amount of securities the investor wants. The price is set as the weighted average of the competitive bids accepted. For example, if 30% of the issue was sold for $98 per $100 of par value, 50% for $97, and the remaining 20% for $96, the weighted average would be

Weighted average price = 0.30($98) + 0.50($97) + 0.20($96) = $97.10

TABLE 3   *Treasury Bill Auction Results, November 2, 2004*

	13-Week
Applications	$37,788,182,000
Accepted bids	$21,000,082,000
Accepted at market yield	15.56%
Accepted noncompetitively	$1,511,154,000
Auction price (Rate)	99.507 (1.95%)

Source: Wall Street Journal, November 2, 2004; p. C2.

Bidders submitting noncompetitive bids would pay $97.10 per $100 of Treasury bills purchased.

Table 3 presents the results of a typical Treasury auction as reported in the *Wall Street Journal.* About 15% of the bids submitted to the Fed for 13-week securities were accepted at the market yield. A relatively small number of bids were submitted noncompetitively.

In 1976, the Treasury switched the entire marketable portion of the federal debt over to **book entry** securities, replacing engraved pieces of paper. In a book entry system, ownership of Treasury securities is documented only in the Fed's computer: Essentially, a ledger entry replaces the actual security. This procedure reduces the cost of issuing Treasury securities as well as the cost of transferring them as they are bought and sold in the secondary market.

The Treasury auction of securities is supposed to be highly competitive and fair. To ensure proper levels of competition, no one dealer is allowed to purchase more than 35% of any one issue. About 40 primary dealers regularly participate in the auction. Salomon Smith Barney was caught violating the limits on the percentage of one issue a dealer may purchase, with serious consequences. (See the "Mini-Case" box on the Salomon Smith Barney scandal.)

MINI-CASE

Treasury Bill Auctions Go Haywire

Every Thursday, the Treasury announces how many 91-day and 182-day Treasury bills it will offer for sale. Buyers must submit bids by the following Monday, and awards are made the next morning. Fifty-two-week Treasury bills are offered similarly once a month. The Treasury accepts the bids offering the highest price.

The Treasury auction of securities is supposed to be highly competitive and fair. To ensure proper levels of competition, no one dealer is allowed to purchase more than 35% of any one issue. About 40 primary dealers regularly participate in the auction.

In 1991, the disclosure that Salomon Smith Barney had broken the rules to corner the market cast the fairness of the auction in doubt. Salomon Smith

Barney purchased 35% of the Treasury securities in its own name by submitting a relatively high bid. It then bought additional securities in the names of its customers, often without their knowledge or consent. Salomon then bought the securities from the customers. As a result of these transactions, Salomon cornered the market and was able to charge a monopoly-like premium. The investigation of Salomon Smith Barney revealed that during one auction in May 1991, the brokerage managed to gain control of 94% of an $11 billion issue. During the scandal that followed this disclosure, John Gutfreund, the firm's chairman, and several other top executives with Salomon retired. The Treasury has instituted new rules since then to ensure that the market remains competitive.

Treasury Bill Interest Rates Treasury bills are very close to being risk-free. As expected for a risk-free security, the interest rate earned on Treasury bill securities is among the lowest in the economy. Investors in Treasury bills have found that in some years, their earnings did not even compensate them for changes in purchasing power due to inflation. Figure 1 shows the interest rate on Treasury bills and the inflation rate over the period 1973–2004. As discussed in Chapter 3, the *real rate* of interest has occasionally been less than zero. For example, in 1973–1977, 1990–1991, and again in the most recent few years, the inflation rate matched or exceeded the earnings on T-bills. Clearly, the T-bill is not an investment to be used for anything but temporary storage of excess funds, because it barely keeps up with inflation.

Federal Funds

Federal funds are short-term funds transferred (loaned or borrowed) between financial institutions, usually for a period of one day. The term *federal funds* (or *fed funds*) is misleading. Fed funds really have nothing to do with the federal government. The term is a holdover from when the fed funds market began in the 1920s and banks with excess reserves loaned them to banks that needed them. The interest rate for borrowing these funds was close to the rate that the Federal Reserve charged on discount loans.

Purpose of Fed Funds The Federal Reserve has set minimum reserve requirements that all banks must maintain to ensure that they have adequate liquidity. To meet these reserve requirements, banks must maintain a certain percentage of their total deposits with the Federal Reserve. The main purpose for fed funds is to

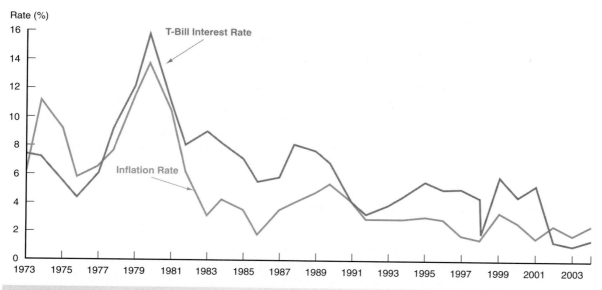

FIGURE 1 *Treasury Bill Interest Rate and the Inflation Rate, January 1973–January 2004*

Source: ftp://ftp.bls.gov/special.requests/cpi/cpiai.txt.

provide banks with an immediate infusion of reserves should they be short. Banks can borrow directly from the Federal Reserve, but many prefer to borrow from other banks so that they do not alert the Fed to any liquidity problems. The reason that banks like to lend in the fed funds market is that money held at the Federal Reserve in excess of what is required does not earn any interest. So even though the interest rate on fed funds is low, it beats the alternative. One indication of the popularity of fed funds is that on a typical day a quarter of a trillion dollars in fed funds will change hands.

Terms for Fed Funds Fed funds are usually overnight investments. Banks analyze their reserve position on a daily basis and either borrow or invest in fed funds, depending on whether they have excess or deficit reserves. Suppose that a bank finds that it has $50 million in excess reserves. It will call its correspondent banks (banks that have reciprocal accounts) to see if they need reserves that day. The bank will sell its excess funds to the bank that offers the highest rate. Once an agreement has been reached, the bank with excess funds will wire the funds to the borrowing bank. This involves telecommunicating to the Federal Reserve bank instructions to take funds out of the seller's account at the Fed and deposit the funds in the borrower's account. The next day, the funds are transferred back, and the process begins again.

Most fed funds borrowings are unsecured. Typically, the entire agreement is supported only by oral communication between buyer and seller.

Federal Funds Interest Rates The forces of supply and demand set the fed funds interest rate. This is a competitive market that analysts watch closely for indications of what is happening to short-term rates. The fed funds rate reported by the press is known as the *effective rate,* which is defined in the *Federal Reserve Bulletin* as the weighted average of rates on trades through New York brokers.

The Federal Reserve cannot directly control fed funds rates. It can and does indirectly influence them by adjusting the level of reserves available to banks in the system. The Fed can increase the amount of money in the financial system by buying securities, as was demonstrated in Chapter 8. When investors sell securities to the Fed, the proceeds are deposited in their banks' accounts at the Federal Reserve. These deposits increase the supply of reserves in the financial system and lower interest rates. If the Fed removes reserves by selling securities, fed funds rates will increase. The Fed will often announce its intention to raise or lower the fed funds rate in advance. Though these rates directly affect few businesses or consumers, analysts consider them an important indicator of the direction in which the Federal Reserve wants the economy to move. Figure 2 compares the fed funds rate with the T-bill rate. Clearly, the two track together.

Repurchase Agreements

Repurchase agreements (repos) work much the same as fed funds except that nonbanks can participate. A firm can sell Treasury securities in a repurchase agreement whereby the firm agrees to buy back the securities at a specified future date. Most repos have a very short term, the most common being for 3 to 14 days. There is a market, however, for one- to three-month repos.

The Use of Repurchase Agreements Government securities dealers frequently engage in repos. The dealer may sell the securities to a bank with the promise

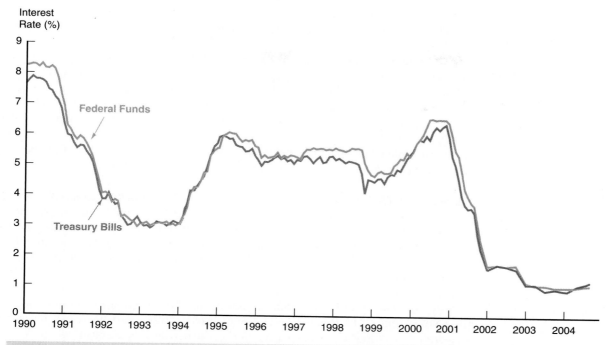

FIGURE 2 *Federal Funds and Treasury Bill Interest Rates, January 1990–January 2004*

Source: http://www.federalreserve.gov/releases/H15/data.htm/.

to buy the securities back the next day. This makes the repo essentially a short-term collateralized loan. Securities dealers use the repo to manage their liquidity and to take advantage of anticipated changes in interest rates.

The Federal Reserve also uses repos in conducting monetary policy. We presented the details of monetary policy in Chapter 8. Recall that the conduct of monetary policy typically requires that the Fed adjust bank reserves on a temporary basis. To accomplish this adjustment, the Fed will buy or sell Treasury securities in the repo market. The maturities of Federal Reserve repos never exceed 15 days.

Interest Rate on Repos Because repos are collateralized with Treasury securities, they are usually low-risk investments and therefore have low interest rates. Though rare, losses have occurred in these markets. For example, in 1985, ESM Government Securities and Bevill, Bresler & Schulman declared bankruptcy. These firms had used the same securities as collateral for more than one loan. The resulting losses to municipalities that had purchased the repos exceeded $500 million. Such losses also caused the failure of the state-insured thrift insurance system in Ohio.

Negotiable Certificates of Deposit

A negotiable certificate of deposit is a bank-issued security that documents a deposit and specifies the interest rate and the maturity date. Because a maturity date is specified, a CD is a **term security** as opposed to a **demand deposit:** Term securities have a specified maturity date; demand deposits can be withdrawn at any time. A negotiable CD is also called a **bearer instrument.** This means that whoever holds the instrument at maturity receives the principal and interest. The CD can be bought and sold until maturity.

Terms of Negotiable Certificates of Deposit The denominations of negotiable certificates of deposit range from $100,000 to $10 million. Few negotiable CDs are denominated less than $1 million. The reason that these instruments are so large is that dealers have established the round lot size to be $1 million. A round lot is the minimum quantity that can be traded without incurring higher than normal brokerage fees.

Negotiable CDs typically have a maturity of one to four months. Some have six-month maturities, but there is little demand for ones with longer maturities.

History of the CD Citibank issued the first large certificates of deposit in 1961. The bank offered the CD to counter the long-term trend of declining demand deposits at large banks. Corporate treasurers were minimizing their cash balances and investing their excess funds in safe, income-generating money market instruments such as T-bills. The attraction of the CD was that it paid a market interest rate. There was a problem, however. The rate of interest that banks could pay on CDs was restricted by Regulation Q. As long as interest rates on most securities were low, this regulation did not affect demand. But when interest rates rose above the level permitted by Regulation Q, the market for these certificates of deposit evaporated. In response, banks began offering the certificates overseas, where they were exempt from Regulation Q limits. In 1970, Congress amended Regulation Q to exempt certificates of deposit over $100,000. By 1972, the CD represented approximately 40% of all bank deposits. The certificate of deposit is now the second most popular money market instrument, behind only the T-bill.

Interest Rate on CDs Figure 3 plots the interest rate on negotiable CDs along with that on T-bills. The rates paid on negotiable CDs are negotiated between the bank and the customer. They are similar to the rate paid on other money market instruments because the level of risk is relatively low. Large money center banks can offer rates a little lower than other banks because many investors in the market believe that the government would never allow one of the nation's largest banks to fail. This belief makes these banks' obligations less risky. CD rates tend to be slightly above the T-bill rate because of the slightly greater chance of default.

Commercial Paper

Commercial paper securities are unsecured promissory notes, issued by corporations, that mature in no more than 270 days. Because these securities are unsecured, only the largest and most creditworthy corporations issue commercial paper. The interest rate the corporation is charged reflects the firm's level of risk.

Terms and Issuance Commercial paper always has an original maturity of less than 270 days. This is to avoid the need to register the security issue with the Securities and Exchange Commission. (To be exempt from SEC registration, the issue must have an original maturity of less than 270 days and be intended for current transactions.) Most commercial paper actually matures in 20 to 45 days. Like T-bills, most commercial paper is issued on a discounted basis.

Find detailed information on commercial paper, including criteria used for calculating commercial paper interest rates and historical discount rates, at www.federalreserve.gov/releases/CP/

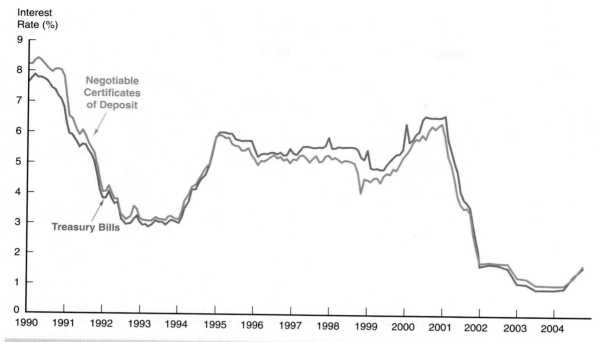

FIGURE 3 *Interest Rates on Negotiable Certificates of Deposit and on Treasury Bills, 1990–2004*

Source: http://www.federalreserve.gov/releases.

About 60% of commercial paper is sold directly by the issuer to the buyer. The balance is sold by dealers in the commercial paper market. A strong secondary market for commercial paper does not exist. A dealer will redeem commercial paper if a purchaser has a dire need for cash, though this is generally not necessary.

History of Commercial Paper Commercial paper has been used in various forms since the 1920s. In 1969, a tight-money environment caused bank holding companies to issue commercial paper to finance new loans. In response, to keep control over the money supply, the Federal Reserve imposed reserve requirements on bank-issued commercial paper in 1970. These reserve requirements removed the major advantage to banks of using commercial paper. Bank holding companies still use commercial paper to fund leasing and consumer finance.

The use of commercial paper increased substantially in the early 1980s because of the rising cost of bank loans. Figure 4 graphs the interest rate on commercial paper against the bank prime rate for the period January 1990–January 2002. Commercial paper has become an important alternative to bank loans primarily because of its lower cost.

Market for Commercial Paper Nonbank corporations use commercial paper extensively to finance the loans that they extend to their customers. For example, General Motors Acceptance Corporation (GMAC) borrows money by issuing commercial paper and uses the money to make loans to consumers buying General Motors cars. Similarly, Household Finance and Chrysler Credit use commercial

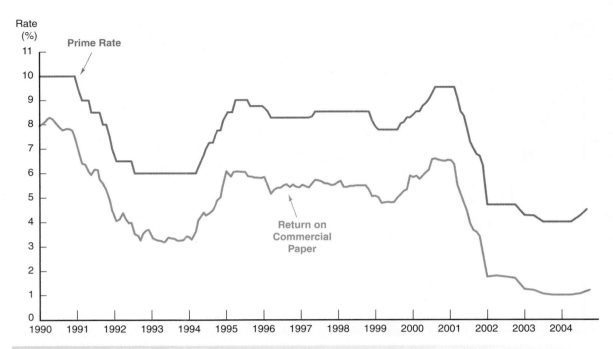

FIGURE 4 *Return on Commercial Paper and the Prime Rate, 1990–2004*

Source: http://www.federalreserve.gov/releases.

paper to fund loans made to consumers. The total number of firms issuing commercial paper varies between 600 to 800, depending on the level of interest rates. Most of these firms use one of about 30 commercial paper dealers who match up buyers and sellers. The large New York City money center banks are very active in this market. Some of the larger issuers of commercial paper choose to distribute their securities with **direct placements.** In a direct placement, the issuer bypasses the dealer and sells directly to the end investor. The advantage of this method is that the issuer saves the 0.125% commission that the dealer charges.

Most issuers of commercial paper back up their paper with a line of credit at a bank. This means that in the event the issuer cannot pay off or roll over the maturing paper, the bank will lend the firm funds for this purpose. The line of credit reduces the risk to the purchasers of the paper and so lowers the interest rate. The bank that provides the backup line of credit agrees in advance to make a loan to the issuer if needed to pay off the outstanding paper. The bank charges a fee of 0.5% to 1% for this commitment. Issuers pay this fee because they are able to save more than this in lowered interest costs by having the line.

Commercial banks were the original purchasers of commercial paper. Today the market has greatly expanded to include large insurance companies, nonfinancial businesses, bank trust departments, and government pension funds. These firms are attracted by the relatively low default risk, short maturity, and high yields these securities offer. Currently, about $1.5 trillion in commercial paper is outstanding (see Figure 5).

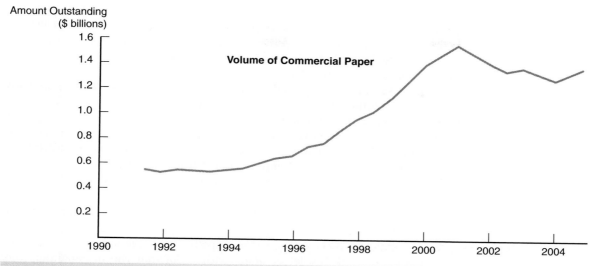

Amount Outstanding
($ billions)

FIGURE 5 *Volume of Commercial Paper Outstanding*

Source: http:www.federalreserve.gov/releases/cp/histouts.txt.

Banker's Acceptances

A banker's acceptance is an order to pay a specified amount of money to the bearer on a given date. Banker's acceptances have been in use since the twelfth century. However, they were not major money market securities until the volume of international trade ballooned in the 1960s. They are used to finance goods that have not yet been transferred from the seller to the buyer. For example, suppose that Builtwell Construction Company wants to buy a bulldozer from Komatsu in Japan. Komatsu does not want to ship the bulldozer without being paid because Komatsu has never heard of Builtwell and realizes that it would be difficult to collect if payment were not forthcoming. Similarly, Builtwell is reluctant to send money to Japan before receiving the equipment. A bank can intervene in this standoff by issuing a banker's acceptance.

Using a Banker's Acceptance The transaction would begin with Builtwell obtaining a letter of credit from its bank. A letter of credit simply says that if Builtwell has not paid its obligation by a certain time, the bank will make payment. This particular letter of credit will also authorize the exporter (Komatsu or its bank) to draw a time draft for the amount of the sale. A time draft is like a postdated check: It can be cashed only after a certain date. Builtwell sends the order for the bulldozer, along with the letter of credit, to Komatsu.

When Komatsu receives these documents, it is willing to ship the equipment because the bank's credit standing has been substituted for that of the actual buyer. Once the equipment has been shipped, Komatsu will present the letter of credit and the shipping documents to its own bank in Japan. This bank will create the time draft authorized by the letter of credit and send it to Builtwell's bank. When Builtwell's bank receives the time draft and the shipping documents, it will stamp the time draft "accepted" and return it to Komatsu's bank.

This accepted time draft is now a banker's acceptance. Because it is backed by the credit of a bank, it can be traded on the secondary market. Typically, the exporter's bank will sell it so that the exporter can receive funds before the maturity date. It will be sold at a discount so that the buyer can earn a fair return for holding it until its maturity date.

The transaction is completed when Builtwell deposits the funds in its bank to cover the amount of the time draft (now a banker's acceptance). When the banker's acceptance finally matures and is presented for payment, the issuing bank withdraws funds from Builtwell's account to make payment. Of course, if for some reason Builtwell was unable to make the required deposit, its bank would pay the acceptance anyway and attempt to collect from Builtwell later.

Let us summarize the steps for using banker's acceptances.

1. The importer requests its bank to send an irrevocable letter of credit to the exporter.
2. The exporter receives the letter, ships the goods, and is paid by presenting to its bank the letter along with proof that the merchandise was shipped.
3. The exporter's bank creates a time draft based on the letter of credit and sends it along with proof of shipment to the importer's bank.
4. The importer's bank stamps the time draft "accepted" and sends the banker's acceptance back to the exporter's bank so that the exporter's bank can sell it on the secondary market to collect payment.
5. The importer deposits funds at its bank sufficient to cover the banker's acceptance when it matures.

Advantages of Banker's Acceptances As the bulldozer example demonstrates, banker's acceptances are crucial to international trade. Without them, many transactions simply would not occur because the parties would not feel properly protected from losses. There are other advantages as well:

- The exporter is paid immediately. This is important when delivery times are long after shipment.
- The exporter is shielded from foreign exchange risk because the local bank pays in domestic funds.
- The exporter does not have to assess the creditworthiness of the importer because the importer's bank guarantees payment.

Secondary Market for Banker's Acceptances Because banker's acceptances are payable to the bearer, they can be bought and sold until they mature. They are sold on a discounted basis like commercial paper and T-bills. Dealers in this market match up firms that want to discount a banker's acceptance (sell it for immediate payment) with companies wishing to invest in banker's acceptances.

Interest rates on banker's acceptances are low because the risk of default is very low. For example, no investor in banker's acceptances in the United States has suffered a loss of principal in more than 60 years. The reason is that only large money center banks are involved in this market.

Eurodollars

Many contracts around the world call for payment in U.S. dollars due to the dollar's stability. For this reason, many companies and governments choose to hold dollars. Prior to World War II, most of these deposits were held in New York money center banks. However, as a result of the Cold War that followed, there was fear that deposits held on U.S. soil could be expropriated. Some large London banks responded to this opportunity by offering to hold dollar-denominated deposits in British banks. These deposits were dubbed Eurodollars (see the "Global" box).

The Eurodollar market has continued to grow rapidly. The primary reason is that depositors receive a higher rate of return on a dollar deposit in the Eurodollar market than in the domestic market. At the same time, the borrower is able to receive a more favorable rate in the Eurodollar market than in the domestic market. This is because multinational banks are not subject to the same regulations restricting U.S. banks and because they are willing and able to accept narrower spreads between the interest paid on deposits and the interest earned on loans.

London Interbank Market Some large London banks act as brokers in the interbank Eurodollar market. Recall that fed funds are used by banks to make up temporary shortfalls in their reserves. Eurodollars are an alternative to fed funds. Banks from around the world buy and sell overnight funds in this market. The rate paid by banks buying funds is the **London interbank bid rate (LIBID).** Funds are offered for sale in this market at the **London interbank offer rate (LIBOR).** Because many banks participate in this market, it is extremely competitive. The spread between the bid and the offer rate seldom exceeds 0.125%. Eurodollar deposits are time deposits, which means that they cannot be withdrawn for a specified period of time. Although the most common time period is overnight, different maturities are available. Each maturity has a different rate.

The overnight LIBOR and the fed funds rate tend to be very close to each other. This is because they are near-perfect substitutes. Suppose that the fed funds rate exceeded the overnight LIBOR. Banks that need to borrow funds will borrow overnight Eurodollars, thus tending to raise rates, and banks with funds to

GLOBAL

Ironic Birth of the Eurodollar Market

One of capitalism's great ironies is that the Eurodollar market, one of the most important financial markets used by capitalists, was fathered by the Soviet Union. In the early 1950s, during the height of the Cold War, the Soviets had accumulated a substantial amount of dollar balances held by banks in the United States. Because the Russians feared that the U.S. government might freeze these assets in the United States, they wanted to move the deposits to Europe, where they would be safe from expropriation. (This fear was not unjustified—consider the U.S. freeze on Iranian assets in 1979 and Iraqi assets in 1990.) However, they also wanted to keep the deposits in dollars so that they could be used in their international transactions. The solution was to transfer the deposits to European banks but to keep the deposits denominated in dollars. When the Soviets did this, the Eurodollar was born.

lend will lend fed funds, thus tending to lower rates. The demand and supply pressure will cause a rapid adjustment that will drive the two rates together.

At one time, most short-term loans with adjustable interest rates were tied to the Treasury bill rate. However, the market for Eurodollars is so broad and deep that it has recently become the standard rate against which others are compared. For example, the U.S. commercial paper market now quotes rates as a spread over LIBOR, rather than over the T-bill rate.

The Eurodollar market is not limited to London banks anymore. The primary brokers in this market maintain offices in all of the major financial centers worldwide.

Eurodollar Certificates of Deposit   Because Eurodollars are time deposits with fixed maturities, they are to a certain extent illiquid. As usual, the financial markets created new types of securities to combat this problem. These new securities were transferable negotiable certificates of deposit (negotiable CDs). Because most Eurodollar deposits have a relatively short term to begin with, the market for Eurodollar negotiable CDs is relatively limited, comprising less than 10% of the amount of regular Eurodollar deposits. The market for the negotiable CDs is still thin.

Other Eurocurrencies   The Eurodollar market is by far the largest short-term security market in the world. This is due to the international popularity of the U.S. dollar for trade. However, the market is not limited to dollars. It is possible to have an account denominated in Japanese yen held in a London or New York bank. Such an account would be termed a Euroyen account. Similarly, you may also have Euromark or Europeso accounts denominated in marks and pesos, respectively, and held in various banks around the world. Keep in mind that if market participants have a need for a particular security and are willing to pay for it, the financial markets stand ready and willing to create it.

Comparing Money Market Securities

Although money market securities share many characteristics, such as liquidity, safety, and short maturities, they all differ in some aspects.

Interest Rates

Figure 6 compares the interest rates on many of the money market instruments we have discussed. The most notable feature of this graph is that all of the money market instruments appear to move very closely together over time. This is because all have very low risk and a short term. They all have deep markets and so are priced competitively. In addition, because these instruments have so many of the same risk and term characteristics, they are close substitutes. Consequently, if one rate should temporarily depart from the others, market supply and demand forces would soon cause a correction.

The *Wall Street Journal* reports money market rates in a table called "Money Rates," which appears daily in the third section. This table contains a brief description of each security and the most recent available interest rate. The "Following the News" box shows a "Money Rates" table from the *Wall Street Journal*.

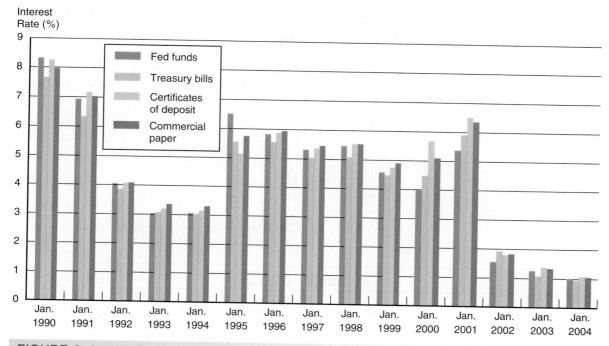

FIGURE 6 *Interest Rates on Money Market Securities, 1990–2004*

Source: http://www.federalreserve.gov/releases.

Liquidity

As we discussed in Chapter 3, the *liquidity* of a security refers to how quickly, easily, and cheaply it can be converted into cash. Typically, the depth of the secondary market where the security can be resold determines its liquidity. For example, the secondary market for Treasury bills is extensive and well developed. As a result, Treasury bills can be converted into cash quickly and with little cost. By contrast, there is no well-developed secondary market for commercial paper. Most holders of commercial paper hold the securities until maturity. In the event that a commercial paper investor needed to sell the securities to raise cash, it is likely that brokers would charge relatively high fees.

In some ways, the depth of the secondary market is not as critical for money market securities as it is for long-term securities such as stocks and bonds. This is because money market securities are short-term to start with. Nevertheless, many investors desire *liquidity intervention:* They seek an intermediary to provide liquidity where it did not previously exist. This is one function of money market mutual funds (discussed in Chapter 21).

Table 4 summarizes the money market securities and the depth of the secondary market.

How Money Market Securities Are Valued

Suppose you work for Merrill Lynch and that it is your job to submit the bid for Treasury bills this week. How would you know what price to submit? Your first step

THE *WALL STREET JOURNAL*: FOLLOWING THE NEWS

Money Market Rates

The *Wall Street Journal* publishes daily a listing of interest rates on many different financial instruments in its "Money Rates" column. (See "Today's Contents" on page 1 of the *Journal* for the location.)

The four interest rates in the "Money Rates" column that are discussed most frequently in the media are these:

Prime rate: The base interest rate on corporate bank loans, an indicator of the cost of business borrowing from banks

Federal funds rate: The interest rate charged on overnight loans in the federal funds market, a sensitive indicator of the cost to banks of borrowing funds from other banks and the stance of monetary policy

Treasury bill rate: The interest rate on U.S. Treasury bills, an indicator of general interest-rate movements

Federal Home Loan Mortgage Corporation rates: Interest rates on "Freddie Mac"—guaranteed mortgages, an indicator of the cost of financing residential housing purchases

MONEY RATES

Wednesday, November 3, 2004

PRIME RATE: 4.75% (effective 09/22/04). The base rate on corporate loans posted by at least 75% of the nation's 30 largest banks.

DISCOUNT RATE (PRIMARY): 2.75% (effective 09/21/04).

FEDERAL FUNDS: 1.750% high, 1.688% low, 1.719% near closing bid, 1.750% offered. Effective rate: 1.73%. Source: Prebon Yamane (USA) Inc. Federal-funds target rate: 1.750% (effective 09/21/04).

CALL MONEY: 3.50% (effective 09/22/04).

COMMERCIAL PAPER: Placed directly by General Electric Capital Corp.: 1.90% 30 days; 1.98% 31 to 43 days; 2.00% 44 to 60 days; 2.07% 61 to 90 days; 2.12% 91 to 119 days; 2.16% 120 to 149 days; 2.21% 150 to 179 days; 2.26% 180 to 209 days; 2.29% 210 to 239 days; 2.32% 240 to 270 days.

EURO COMMERCIAL PAPER: Placed directly by General Electric Capital Corp.: 2.05% 30 days; 2.10% two months; 2.11% three months; 2.12% four months; 2.14% five months; 2.16% six months.

DEALER COMMERCIAL PAPER: High-grade unsecured notes sold through dealers by major corporations: 1.97% 30 days; 2.09% 60 days; 2.14% 90 days.

CERTIFICATES OF DEPOSIT: 1.98% one month; 2.15% three months; 2.30% six months.

BANKERS ACCEPTANCES: 1.97% 30 days; 2.08% 60 days; 2.12% 90 days; 2.18% 120 days; 2.24% 150 days; 2.28% 180 days. Source: Prebon Yamane (USA) Inc.

EURODOLLARS: 2.00% – 1.98% one month; 2.11% – 2.09% two months; 2.15% – 2.13% three months; 2.22% – 2.18% four months; 2.28% – 2.23% five months; 2.31% – 2.28% six months. Source: Prebon Yamane (USA) Inc.

LONDON INTERBANK OFFERED RATES (LIBOR): 2.0500% one month; 2.2000% three months; 2.3575% six months; 2.6100% one year. Effective rate for contracts entered into two days from date appearing at top of this column.

EURO LIBOR: 2.09425% one month; 2.15600% three months; 2.20663% six months; 2.33600% one year. Effective rate for contracts entered into two days from date appearing at top of this column.

EURO INTERBANK OFFERED RATES (EURIBOR): 2.094% one month; 2.158% three months; 2.208% six months; 2.338% one year. Source: Reuters.

FOREIGN PRIME RATES: Canada 4.25%; European Central Bank 2.00%; Japan 1.375%; Switzerland 2.52%; Britain 4.75%.

TREASURY BILLS: Results of the Monday, November 1, 2004, auction of short-term U.S. government bills, sold at a discount from face value in units of $1,000 to $1 million: 1.950% 13 weeks; 2.140% 26 weeks. Tuesday, November 2, 2004 auction: 1.835% 4 weeks.

OVERNIGHT REPURCHASE RATE: 1.74%. Source: Garban Intercapital.

FREDDIE MAC: Posted yields on 30-year mortgage commitments. Delivery within 30 days 5.37%, 60 days 5.43%, standard conventional fixed-rate mortgages: 2.875%, 2% rate capped one-year adjustable rate mortgages.

FANNIE MAE: Posted yields on 30 year mortgage commitments (priced at par) for delivery within 30 days 5.48%, 60 days 5.54%, standard conventional fixed-rate mortgages; 3.35%, 6/2 rate capped one-year adjustable rate mortgages. Constant Maturity Debt Index: 2.141% three months; 2.329% six months; 2.555% one year.

MERRILL LYNCH READY ASSETS TRUST: 1.18%.

CONSUMER PRICE INDEX: September 189.9, up 2.5% from a year ago. Bureau of Labor Statistics.

---

would be to determine the yield that you require. Let us assume that, based on your understanding of interest rates learned in Chapters 3 and 4, you decide you need a 2% return. To simplify our calculations, let us also assume we are bidding on securities with a one-year maturity. We know that our Treasury bill will pay $1000 when it matures, so to compute how much we will pay today we find the present value of $1000. The process of computing a present value was discussed in Example 1 in Chapter 3. The formula is

$$PV = \frac{FV}{(1 + i)^n}$$

TABLE 4 *Money Market Securities and Their Markets*

Money Market Security	Issuer	Buyer	Usual Maturity	Secondary Market
Treasury bills	U.S. government	Consumers and companies	13 weeks, 26 weeks, 1 year	Excellent
Federal funds	Banks	Banks	1 to 7 days	None
Repurchase agreements	Businesses and banks	Businesses and banks	1 to 15 days	Good
Negotiable certificates of deposit	Large money center banks	Businesses	14 to 120 days	Good
Commercial paper	Finance companies and businesses	Businesses	1 to 270 days	Poor
Banker's acceptance	Banks	Businesses	30 to 180 days	Good
Eurodollar deposits	Non-U.S. banks	Businesses, governments, and banks	1 day to 1 year	Poor

In this example FV = $1000, the interest rate = 0.02, and the period until maturity is 1, so

$$\text{Price} = \frac{\$1000}{(1 + 0.02)} = \$980.39$$

Note what happens to the price of the security as interest rates rise. Since we are dividing by a larger number, the current price will decrease. For example, if interest rates rise to 3%, the value of the security would fall to $970.87 [$1000/(1.03) = $970.87].

This method of discounting the future maturity value back to the present is the method used to price most money market securities.

Summary

1. Money market securities are short-term instruments with an original maturity of less than one year. These securities trade in the money markets. They include Treasury bills, commercial paper, federal funds, repurchase agreements, negotiable certificates of deposit, banker's acceptances, and Eurodollars.

2. Money market securities are used to "warehouse" funds until needed. The returns earned on these investments are low due to their low risk and high liquidity.

3. Many participants in the money markets both buy and sell money market securities. The U.S. Treasury, commercial banks, businesses, and individuals all benefit by having access to low-risk short-term investments.

4. Interest rates on all money market securities tend to follow one another closely over time. Treasury bill returns are the lowest because they are virtually devoid of default risk. Banker's acceptances and negotiable certificates of deposit are next lowest because they are backed by the creditworthiness of large money center banks.

Key Terms

bearer instrument, *p. 231*
book entry, *p. 228*
competitive bidding, *p. 227*
deep market, *p. 227*
demand deposit, *p. 231*
direct placement, *p. 234*

discounting, *p. 226*
liquid market, *p. 227*
London interbank bid rate,
  (LIBID), *p. 237*
London interbank offer rate,
  (LIBOR), *p. 237*

noncompetitive bidding, *p. 227*
term security, *p. 231*
wholesale market, *p. 220*

Questions

1. What characteristics define the money markets?

2. Is a Treasury bond issued 29 years ago with six months remaining before it matures a money market instrument?

3. Why do banks not eliminate the need for money markets?

4. Distinguish between a term security and a demand security.

5. What was the purpose motivating regulators to impose interest ceilings on bank savings accounts? What impact did this eventually have on the money markets?

6. Why does the U.S. government use the money markets?

7. Why do businesses use the money markets?

8. What purpose initially motivated Merrill Lynch to offer money market mutual funds to its customers?

9. Why are more funds from property and casualty insurance companies than funds from life insurance companies invested in the money markets?

10. Which of the money market securities is the most liquid and considered the most risk-free? Why?

11. Distinguish between competitive bidding and non-competitive bidding for Treasury securities.

12. Who issues federal funds, and what is the usual purpose of these funds?

13. Does the Federal Reserve *directly* set the federal funds interest rate?

14. Who issues commercial paper and for what purpose?

15. Why are banker's acceptances so popular for international transactions?

Quantitative Problems

1. What would be your annualized yield on the purchase of a 182-day Treasury bill for $4925 that pays $5000 at maturity?

2. What is the annualized yield on a Treasury bill that you purchase for $9940 that will mature in 91 days for $10,000?

3. If you want to earn an annualized yield of 3.5%, what is the most you can pay for a 91-day Treasury bill that pays $5000 at maturity?

4. What is the annualized yield on a Treasury bill that you purchase for $9900 that will mature in 91 days for $10,000?

5. The price of 182-day commercial paper is $7840. If the annualized yield is 4.04%, what will the paper pay at maturity?

6. How much would you pay for a Treasury bill that matures in one year and pays $10,000 if you require a 1.8% return?

7. The price of $8000 face value commercial paper is $7930. If the annualized yield is 4%, when will the paper mature?

8. How much would you pay for a Treasury bill that matures in one year and pays $10,000 if you require a 3% return?

9. The annualized yield on a particular money market instrument, is 3.75%. The face value is $200,000 and it matures in 51 days. What is its price? What would be the price if it had 71 days to maturity?

10. The annualized yield is 3% for 91-day commercial paper, and 3.5% for 182-day commercial paper. What is the expected 91-day commercial paper rate 91 days from now?

11. Assume that 45% of a Treasury bill auction was sold for $998 per $1000 par value, 35% was sold for $997, and the last 20% was sold for $996. What would be the weighted average price paid by a noncompetitive bid?

12. In a Treasury auction of $2.5 billion par value 91-day T-bills, the following bids were submitted:

Bidder	Bid Amount	Price
1	$500 million	$0.9940
2	$750 million	$0.9901
3	$1.5 billion	$0.9925
4	$1 billion	$0.9936
5	$600 million	$0.9939

If only these competitive bids are received, who will receive T-bills, in what quantity, and at what price?

13. If the Treasury also received $750 million in non-competitive bids, who will receive T-bills, in what quantity, and at what price?

Web Exercises

The Money Markets

1. Up-to-date interest rates are available from the Federal Reserve at **http://www.federalreserve.gov/releases**. Locate the current rate on the following securities:

a. Prime rate

b. Federal funds

c. Commercial paper (financial)

d. Certificates of deposit

e. Discount rate

f. One-month Eurodollar deposits

Compare these rates on a–d to those reported in Table 1. Have short-term rates generally increased or decreased?

2. The Treasury conducts auctions of money market treasury securities at regular intervals. Go to **http://www.publicdebt.treas/gov/of/ofaucrt.htm** and locate the schedule of auctions. When is the next auction of 4-week bills? When is the next auction of 13- and 26-week bills? How often are these securities auctioned?

CHAPTER 10

The Bond Market

Preview

The last chapter discussed short-term securities that trade in a market we call the money market. This chapter talks about the first of several securities that trade in a market we call the capital market. Capital markets are for securities with an original maturity that is greater than one year. These securities include bonds, stocks, and mortgages. We will devote an entire chapter to each major type of capital market security due to their importance to investors, businesses, and the economy. This chapter begins with a brief introduction on how the capital markets operate before launching into the study of bonds. In the next chapter we will study stocks and the stock market. We will conclude our look at the capital markets in Chapter 12 with mortgages.

Purpose of the Capital Market

Firms that issue capital market securities and the investors who buy them have very different motivations than those who operate in the money markets. Firms and individuals use the money markets primarily to warehouse funds for short periods of time until a more important need or a more productive use for the funds arises. By contrast, firms and individuals use the capital markets for long-term investments.

Suppose that after a careful financial analysis, your firm determines that it needs a new plant to meet the increased demand for its products. This analysis will be made using interest rates that reflect the *current* long-term cost of funds to the firm. Now suppose that your firm chooses to finance this plant by issuing money market securities, such as commercial paper. As long as interest rates do not rise, all is well: When these short-term securities mature, they can be reissued at the same interest rate. However, if interest rates rise, as they did in 1980, the firm may find that it does not have the cash flows or income to support the plant because when the short-term securities mature, the firm will have to reissue them at a higher interest rate. If long-term securities, such as bonds or stock, had been used, the increased interest rates would not have been as critical. The primary reason that individuals and firms choose to borrow long-term is to reduce the risk that interest rates will rise before they pay off their debt. This reduction in risk comes at a cost, however. As you may recall from Chapter 5, most long-term interest rates are higher than short-term rates due to risk premiums. Despite the need to pay higher interest rates to borrow in the capital markets, these markets remain very active.

Capital Market Participants

The primary issuers of capital market securities are federal and local governments and corporations. The federal government issues long-term notes and bonds to fund the national debt. State and municipal governments also issue long-term notes and bonds to finance capital projects, such as school and prison construction. Governments never issue stock because they cannot sell ownership claims.

Corporations issue both bonds and stock. One of the most difficult decisions a firm faces can be whether it should finance its growth with debt or equity. The distribution of a firm's capital between debt and equity is its capital structure. (The factors that influence the capital structure decision are discussed in Chapter 15.) Corporations may enter the capital markets because they do not have sufficient capital to fund their investment opportunities. Alternatively, firms may choose to enter the capital markets because they want to preserve their capital to protect against unexpected needs. In either case, the availability of efficiently functioning capital markets is crucial to the continued health of the business sector.

The largest purchasers of capital market securities are households. Frequently, individuals and households deposit funds in financial institutions that use the funds to purchase capital market instruments such as bonds or stock.

Capital Market Trading

Initial public offering news and information, including advanced search tools for IPO offerings, venture capital research reports, etc., is available at www.ipomonitor. com

Find listed companies, member information, real-time market indices, and current stock quotes at www.nyse.com

Capital market trading occurs in either the *primary market* or the *secondary market*. The primary market is where new issues of stocks and bonds are introduced. Investment funds, corporations, and individual investors can all purchase securities offered in the primary market. You can think of a primary market transaction as one where the issuer of the security actually receives the proceeds of the sale. When firms sell securities for the very first time, the issue is an **initial public offering (IPO).** Subsequent sales of a firm's new stocks or bonds to the public are simply primary market transactions (as opposed to an initial one).

The capital markets have well-developed secondary markets. A secondary market is where the sale of previously issued securities takes place, and it is important because most investors plan to sell long-term bonds before they reach maturity and eventually to sell their holdings of stock as well. There are two types of exchanges in the secondary market for capital securities: *organized exchanges* and *over-the-counter exchanges*. Whereas most money market transactions originate over the phone, most capital market transactions, measured by volume, occur in organized exchanges. An organized exchange has a building where securities (including stocks, bonds, options, and futures) trade. Exchange rules govern trading to ensure the efficient and legal operation of the exchange, and the exchange's board constantly reviews these rules to ensure that they result in competitive trading.

Types of Bonds

Bonds are securities that represent a debt owed by the issuer to the investor. Bonds obligate the issuer to pay a specified amount at a given date, generally with periodic interest payments. The par, face, or maturity value of the bond is the amount that the issuer must pay at maturity. The coupon rate is the rate of interest that the issuer must pay. This rate is usually fixed for the duration of the bond and does not fluctuate with market interest rates. If the repayment terms of a bond are not met, the holder of a bond has a claim on the assets of the issuer. Look at Figure 1. The face value of the bond is given in the top right corner. The interest rate of $8\frac{5}{8}\%$, along with the maturity date, is reported several times on the face of the bond.

Long-term bonds traded in the capital market include long-term government notes and bonds, municipal bonds, and corporate bonds.

Treasury Bonds

The U.S. Treasury issues notes and bonds to finance the national debt. The difference between a note and a bond is that notes have an original maturity of 1 to 10 years while bonds have an original maturity of 10 to 20 years. (Recall from Chapter 9 that Treasury *bills* mature in less than one year.) Table 1 summarizes the maturity differences among Treasury securities. The prices of Treasury notes, bonds, and bills are quoted as a percentage of $100 face value. (Later in this chapter we explain how newspaper bond quotes can be converted into market prices.)

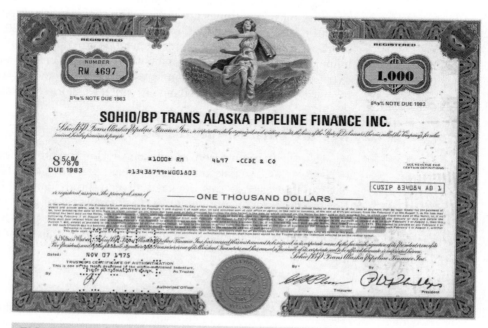

FIGURE 1 *Sohio/BP Corporate Bond*

Source: Eakins, *Finance: Investments, Institutions, & Management,* p. 39.

TABLE 1	*Treasury Securities*
Type	**Maturity**
Treasury bill	Less than 1 year
Treasury note	1 to 10 years
Treasury bond	10 to 20 years

On November 1, 2001, the Treasury announced that it would no longer issue 30-year Treasury securities. The motivation for this change was to reduce the interest cost on the government debt by using shorter-term securities that usually carry a lower interest rate. The announcement caused an immediate increase in 30-year bond prices as investors snapped up those that were available.

Federal government notes and bonds are free of default risk because the government can always print money to pay off the debt if necessary.[1] This does *not* mean that these securities are risk-free. We will discuss interest-rate risk applied to bonds later in this chapter.

Treasury Bond Interest Rates

Treasury bonds have very low interest rates because they have no default risk. Although investors in Treasury bonds have found themselves earning less than the rate of inflation in some years (see Figure 2), most of the time the interest rate on Treasury notes and bonds is above that on money market securities because of interest-rate risk.

Figure 3 plots the yield on 20-year Treasury bonds against the yield on 90-day Treasury bills. Two things are noteworthy in this graph. First, in most years, the rate of return on the short-term bill is below that on the 20-year bond. Second, short-term rates are more volatile than long-term rates. Short-term rates are more influenced by the current rate of inflation. Investors in long-term securities expect extremely high or low inflation rates to return to more normal levels, so long-term rates do not typically change as much as short-term rates.

Treasury Inflation-Indexed Securities

In 1997, the Treasury Department began offering an innovative bond designed to remove inflation risk from holding treasuries. The new inflation-indexed bonds have an interest rate that does not change throughout the term of the security. However, the principal amount used to compute the interest payment does change based on the consumer price index. At maturity, the securities are redeemed at the greater of their inflation-adjusted principal or par amount at original issue.

---

[1]We noted in Chapter 9 that Treasury bills were also considered default-risk-free except that a budget stalemate in 1996 almost caused default. The same small chance of default applies to Treasury bonds.

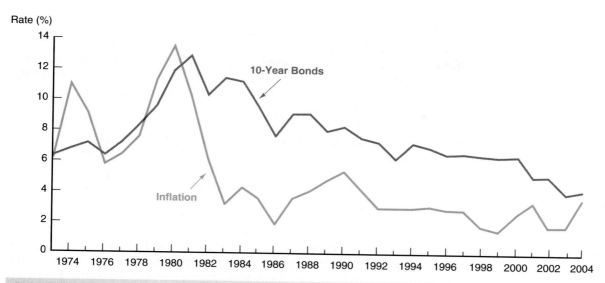

FIGURE 2 *Interest Rate on Treasury Bonds and the Inflation Rate, 1973–2004*

Sources: http://www.federalreserve.gov/releases and ftp://ftp.bls.gov/pub/special.requests/cpi/cpiai.txt.

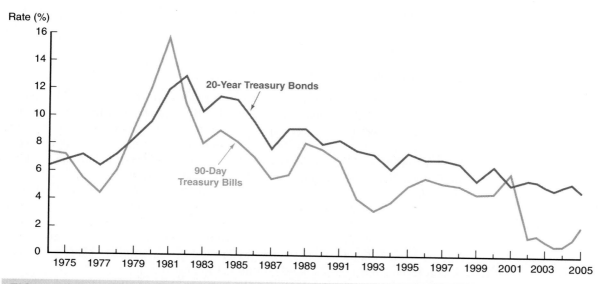

FIGURE 3 *Interest Rate on Treasury Bills and Treasury Bonds, 1973–2004 (January of each year)*

Source: http://www.federalreserve.gov/releases.

The advantage of inflation-indexed securities is that they give both individual and institutional investors a chance to buy a security whose value won't be eroded by inflation. These securities can be used by retirees who want to hold a very low-risk portfolio.

Treasury STRIPS

In addition to bonds, notes, and bills, in 1985 the Treasury began issuing to depository institutions bonds in book entry form called **Separate Trading of Registered Interest and Principal Securities,** more commonly called **STRIPS.** Recall from Chapter 9 that to be sold in book entry form means that no physical document exists; instead, the security is issued and accounted for electronically. A STRIP separates the periodic interest payments from the final principal repayment. When a Treasury fixed-principal or inflation-indexed note or bond is stripped, each interest payment and the principal payment becomes a separate zero-coupon security. Each component has its own identifying number and can be held or traded separately. For example, a Treasury note with five years remaining to maturity consists of a single principal payment at maturity and ten interest payments, one every six months for five years. When this note is stripped, each of the ten interest payments and the principal payment becomes a separate security. Thus, the single Treasury note becomes 11 separate securities that can be traded individually. STRIPS are also called **zero-coupon securities** because the only time an investor receives a payment during the life of a STRIP is when it matures.

Before the government introduced these securities, the private sector had created them indirectly. In the early 1980s, Merrill Lynch created the Treasury Investment Growth Fund (TIGRs, pronounced "tigers"), in which it purchased Treasury securities and then stripped them to create principal-only securities and interest-only securities. Currently, more than $50 billion in stripped Treasury securities are outstanding.

Agency Bonds

Congress has authorized a number of U.S. agencies to issue bonds. The government does not explicitly guarantee agency bonds, though most investors feel that the government would not allow the agencies to default. Issuers of agency bonds include the Government National Mortgage Association, the Farmers Home Administration, the Federal Housing Administration, the Veterans Administrations, the Federal National Mortgage Association (Fannie Mae), the Federal Land Banks, the Federal Home Loan Mortgage Corporation, and the Student Loan Marketing Association. These agencies issue bonds to raise funds that are used for purposes that Congress has deemed to be in the national interest. For example, the Government National Mortgage Association (Ginnie Mae) issues bonds to raise funds that are used to finance home loans. Similarly, the Student Loan Marketing Association (Sallie Mae) issues bonds to fund student loans.

The risk on agency bonds is actually very low. They are usually secured by the loans that are made with the funds raised by the bond sales. In addition, the federal agencies may use their lines of credit with the Treasury Department should they have trouble meeting their obligations. Finally, it is unlikely that the federal government would permit its agencies to default on their obligations.

Despite this low level of risk, these securities offer interest rates that are significantly higher than those available on Treasury securities. For example, on June 8, 2004, 30-year Fannie Mae bonds yielded 6.11%, while 30-year Treasury bonds yielded 5.46%. A portion of the higher yield available on agencies may be due to their lower liquidity: Though a secondary market in agency securities exists, it is not as well developed or as deep as the market for government securities. (Chapter

5 discusses the effect liquidity has on interest rates.) Many investors feel that agency bonds represent an attractive alternative to low-interest-rate Treasuries.

Municipal Bonds

Municipal bonds are securities issued by local, county, and state governments. The proceeds from these bonds are used to finance public interest projects such as schools, utilities, and transportation systems. Municipal bonds that are issued to pay for essential public projects are exempt from federal taxation. As we saw in Chapter 5, this allows the municipality to borrow at a lower cost because investors will be satisfied with lower interest rates on tax-exempt bonds. You can use the following equation to determine what tax-free rate of interest is equivalent to a taxable rate:

www.bloomberg. com/markets/ rates/index.html supplies the latest municipal bond events, experts' insights and analyses, and a municipal bond yields table.

$$\text{Equivalent tax-free rate} = \text{taxable interest rate} \times (1 - \text{marginal tax rate})$$

EXAMPLE 1   *Municipal Bonds*

Suppose that the interest rate on a taxable corporate bond is 9% and that the marginal tax is 28%. Suppose a tax-free municipal bond with a rate of 6.75% were available. Which security would you choose?

Solution

The tax-free municipal interest rate is 6.48%.

$$\text{Equivalent tax-free rate} = \text{taxable interest rate} \times (1 - \text{marginal tax rate})$$

where

Taxable interest rate = 0.09

Marginal tax rate = 0.28

Thus

$$\text{Equivalent tax-free rate} = 0.09 \times (1 - 0.28) = 0.0648 = 6.48\%$$

Since the tax-free municipal bond rate (6.75%) is higher than the equivalent tax-free rate (6.48%), choose the municipal bond.

There are two types of municipal bonds: general obligation bonds and revenue bonds. **General obligation bonds** do not have specific assets pledged as security or a specific source of revenue allocated for their repayment. Instead, they are backed by the "full faith and credit" of the issuer. This phrase means that the issuer promises to use every resource available to repay the bond as promised. Most general obligation bond issues must be approved by the taxpayers because the taxing authority of the government is pledged for their repayment.

Revenue bonds, by contrast, are backed by the cash flow of a particular revenue-generating project. For example, revenue bonds may be issued to build a toll bridge, with the tolls being pledged as repayment. If the revenues are not sufficient to repay the bonds, they may go into default, and investors may suffer losses. This occurred on a large scale in 1983 when the Washington Public Power

Supply System (since called "WHOOPS") used revenue bonds to finance the construction of two nuclear power plants. As a result of falling energy costs and tremendous cost overruns, the plants never became operational, and buyers of these bonds lost their investments. Revenue bonds tend to be issued more frequently than general obligation bonds (see Figure 4). Note that the low interest rates seen in recent years have prompted municipalities to issue record amounts of bonds.

Risk in the Municipal Bond Market

Municipal bonds are not default-free. For example, defaults on municipal bonds amounted to $1.4 billion in 1990. This was primarily attributed to the weaker economy in 1990; however, it points out that governments are not exempt from financial distress. Unlike the federal government, local governments cannot print money, and there are real limits on how high they can raise taxes without driving the population away.

Corporate Bonds

When large corporations need to borrow funds for long periods of time, they may issue bonds. Most corporate bonds have a face value of $1000 and pay interest semiannually (twice per year). Most are also callable, meaning that the issuer may redeem the bonds after a specified date.

The **bond indenture** is a contract that states the lender's rights and privileges and the borrower's obligations. Any collateral offered as security to the bondholders will also be described in the indenture.

The degree of risk varies widely among issues because the risk of default depends on the company's health, which can be affected by a number of variables. The interest rate on corporate bonds varies with the level of risk, as we discussed

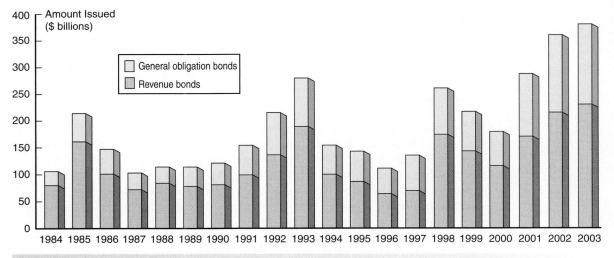

FIGURE 4 *Issuance of Revenue and General Obligation Bonds, 1984–2003 (End of year)*

Source: Federal Reserve Bulletin, various issues, Table 1.45.

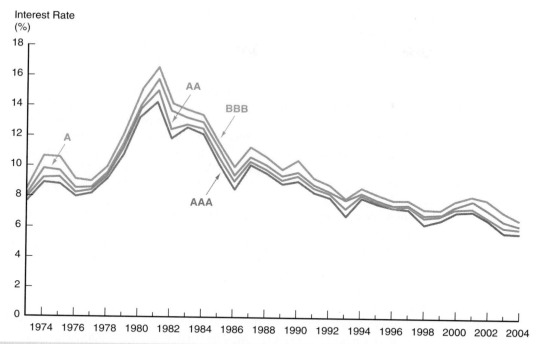

FIGURE 5 *Corporate Bond Interest Rates, 1973–2004 (End of year)*

Source: *Federal Reserve Bulletin,* Table 1.35, various issues.

in Chapter 5. As Figure 5 shows, bonds with lower risk and a higher rating (AAA being the highest) have lower interest rates than more risky bonds (BBB). A bond's interest rate will depend on its features and characteristics, which are described in the following sections.

Characteristics of Corporate Bonds

At one time bonds were sold with attached coupons that the owner of the bond clipped and mailed to the firm to receive interest payments. These were called *bearer bonds* because payments were made to whoever had physical possession of the bonds. The Internal Revenue Service did not care for this method of payment, however, because it made tracking interest income difficult. Bearer bonds have now been largely replaced by **registered bonds,** which do not have coupons. Instead, the owner must register with the firm to receive interest payments. The firms are required to report to the IRS the name of the person who receives interest income. Despite the fact that bearer bonds with attached coupons have been phased out, the interest paid on bonds is still called the "coupon interest payment," and the interest rate on bonds is the coupon interest rate.

Restrictive Covenants   A corporation's financial managers are hired, fired, and compensated at the direction of the board of directors, which represents the corporation's *stockholders.* This arrangement implies that the managers will be more interested in protecting stockholders than they are in protecting bondholders. You

At **http://bonds. yahoo.com,** *access information on 10-year Treasury yield, composite bond rates for U.S. Treasury bonds, municipal bonds, and corporate bonds.*

should recognize this as an example of the moral hazard problem introduced in Chapter 2 and discussed further in Chapter 15. Managers may not use the funds provided by the bonds as the bondholders might prefer. Since bondholders cannot look to managers for protection when the firm gets into trouble, they must include rules and restrictions on managers designed to protect the bondholders' interests. These are known as **restrictive covenants.** They usually limit the amount of dividends the firm can pay and the ability of the firm to issue additional debt. Other financial policies, such as the firm's involvement in mergers, may also be restricted. Restrictive covenants are included in the bond indenture. Typically, the interest rate will be lower the more restrictions are placed on management through restrictive covenants because the bonds will be considered safer by investors.

Call Provisions   Most corporate indentures include a **call provision,** which states that the issuer has the right to force the holder to sell the bond back. The call provision usually requires a waiting period between the time the bond is initially issued and the time when it can be called. The price bondholders are paid for the bond is usually set at the bond's par price or slightly higher (usually by one year's interest cost). For example, a 10% coupon rate $1000 bond may have a call price of $1100.

If interest rates fall, the price of the bond will rise. If rates fall enough, the price will rise above the call price, and the firm will call the bond. Because call provisions put a limit on the amount that bondholders can earn from the appreciation of a bond's price, investors do not like call provisions.

A second reason that issuers of bonds include call provisions is to make it possible for them to buy back their bonds according to the terms of the **sinking fund.** A sinking fund is a requirement in the bond indenture that the firm pay off a portion of the bond issue each year. This provision is attractive to bondholders because it reduces the probability of default when the issue matures. Because a sinking fund provision makes the issue more attractive, the firm can reduce the bond's interest rate.

A third reason firms usually issue only callable bonds is that firms may have to retire a bond issue if the covenants of the issue restrict the firm from some activity that it feels is in the best interest of stockholders. Suppose that a firm needed to borrow additional funds to expand its storage facilities. If the firm's bonds carried a restriction against adding debt, the firm would have to retire its existing bonds before issuing new bonds or taking out a loan to build the new warehouse.

Finally, a firm may choose to call bonds if it wishes to alter its capital structure. A maturing firm with excess cash flow may wish to reduce its debt load if few attractive investment opportunities are available.

Because bondholders do not generally like call provisions, callable bonds must have a higher yield than comparable noncallable bonds. Despite the higher cost, firms still typically issue callable bonds because of the flexibility this feature provides the firm.

Conversion   Some bonds can be converted into shares of common stock. This feature permits bondholders to share in the firm's good fortunes if the stock price rises. Most convertible bonds will state that the bond can be converted into a certain number of common shares at the discretion of the bondholder. The conversion ratio will be such that the price of the stock must rise substantially before conversion is likely to occur.

Issuing convertible bonds is one way firms avoid sending a negative signal to the market. If a firm chooses to issue stock, the market usually interprets this action as indicating that the stock price is relatively high or that it is going to fall in the future. The market makes this interpretation because it believes that managers are most concerned with looking out for the interests of existing stockholders and will not issue stock when it is undervalued. If managers believe that the firm will perform well in the future, they can, instead, issue convertible bonds. If the managers are correct and the stock price rises, the bondholders will convert to stock at a relatively high price that managers believe is fair. Alternatively, bondholders have the option not to convert if managers turn out to be wrong about the company's future.

Bondholders like a conversion feature. It is very similar to buying just a bond but receiving both a bond and a stock option (stock options are discussed fully in Chapter 25). The price of the bond will reflect the value of this option and so will be higher than the price of comparable nonconvertible bonds. The higher price received for the bond by the firm implies a lower interest rate.

Types of Corporate Bonds

A variety of corporate bonds are available. They are usually distinguished by the type of collateral that secures the bond and by the order in which the bond is paid off if the firm defaults.

Secured Bonds Secured bonds are ones with collateral attached. *Mortgage bonds* are used to finance a specific project. For example, a building may be the collateral for bonds issued for its construction. In the event that the firm fails to make payments as promised, mortgage bondholders have the right to liquidate the property in order to be paid. Because these bonds have specific property pledged as collateral, they are less risky than comparable unsecured bonds. As a result, they will have a lower interest rate.

Equipment trust certificates are bonds secured by tangible non-real-estate property, such as heavy equipment or airplanes. Typically, the collateral backing these bonds is more easily marketed than the real property backing mortgage bonds. As with mortgage bonds, the presence of collateral reduces the risk of the bonds and so lowers their interest rates.

Unsecured Bonds *Debentures* are long-term unsecured bonds that are backed only by the general creditworthiness of the issuer. No specific collateral is pledged to repay the debt. In the event of default, the bondholders must go to court to seize assets. Collateral that has been pledged to other debtors is not available to the holders of debentures. *Debentures* usually have attached to them a contract that spells out the terms of the bond and the responsibilities of management. The contract attached to the debenture is called an *indenture*. (Be careful not to confuse the terms *debenture* and *indenture*.) Debentures have lower priority than secured bonds if the firm defaults. As a result, they will have a higher interest rate than otherwise comparable secured bonds.

Subordinated debentures are similar to debentures except that they have a lower priority claim. This means that in the event of a default, subordinated debenture holders are paid only after nonsubordinated bondholders have been paid in full. As a result, subordinated debenture holders are at greater risk of loss.

Variable-rate bonds (which may be secured or unsecured) are a financial innovation spurred by increased interest-rate variability in the 1980s and 1990s. The interest rate on these securities is tied to another market interest rate, such as the rate on Treasury bonds, and is adjusted periodically. The interest rate on the bonds will change over time as market rates change.

Junk Bonds Recall from Chapter 5 that all bonds are rated by various companies according to their default risk. These companies study the issuer's financial characteristics and make a judgment about the issuer's possibility of default. A bond with a rating of AAA has the highest grade possible. Bonds *at or above* Moody's Baa or Standard and Poor's BBB rating are considered of investment grade. Those rated *below* this level are usually considered speculative (see Table 2). Speculative-grade bonds are often called **junk bonds.** Before the late 1970s, primary issues of speculative-grade securities were very rare; almost all new bond issues consisted of investment-grade bonds. However, when companies ran into financial difficulties, their bond ratings would fall. Holders of these downgraded bonds found that they were difficult to sell because no well-developed secondary market existed. It is easy to understand why investors would be leery of these securities, as they were usually unsecured.

In 1977, Michael Milken, at the investment banking firm of Drexel Burnham Lambert, recognized that there were many investors who would be willing to take on greater risk if they were compensated with greater returns. First, however, Milken had to address two problems that hindered the market for low-grade bonds. The first was that they suffered from poor liquidity. Whereas underwriters of investment-grade bonds continued to make a market after the bonds were issued, no such market maker existed for junk bonds. Drexel agreed to assume this role as market maker for junk bonds. That assured that a secondary market existed, an important consideration for investors, who seldom want to hold the bonds to maturity.

The second problem with the junk bond market was that there was a very real chance that the issuing firms would default on their bond payments. By comparison, the default risk on investment-grade securities was negligible. To reduce the probability of losses, Milken acted much as a commercial bank for junk bond issuers. He would renegotiate the firm's debt or advance additional funds if needed to prevent the firm from defaulting. Milken's efforts substantially reduced the default risk, and the demand for junk bonds soared.

During the early and mid-1980s, many firms took advantage of junk bonds to finance the takeover of other firms. When a firm greatly increases its debt level (by issuing junk bonds) to finance the purchase of another firm's stock, the increase in leverage makes the bonds high-risk. Frequently, part of the acquired firm is eventually sold to pay down the debt incurred by issuing the junk bonds. Some 1800 firms accessed the junk bond market during the 1980s.

Milken and his brokerage firm were very well compensated for their efforts. Milken earned a fee of 2% to 3% of each junk bond issue, which made Drexel the most profitable firm on Wall Street in 1987. Milken's personal income between 1983 and 1987 was in excess of $1 billion.

Unfortunately for holders of junk bonds, both Milken and Drexel were caught and convicted of insider trading. With Drexel unable to support the junk bond market, 250 companies defaulted between 1989 and 1991. Drexel itself filed bankruptcy in 1990 due to losses on its own holdings of junk bonds. Milken was

TABLE 2 *Debt Ratings*

Standard and Poor's	Moody's	Average Interest Rate* (%)	Definition
AAA	Aaa	6.00	Best quality and highest rating. Capacity to pay interest and repay principal is extremely strong. Smallest degree of investment risk.
AA	Aa	6.35	High quality. Very strong capacity to pay interest and repay principal and differs from AAA/Aaa in a small degree.
A	A	6.49	Strong capacity to pay interest and repay principal. Possess many favorable investment attributes and are considered upper-medium-grade obligations. Somewhat more susceptible to the adverse effects of changes in circumstances and economic conditions.
BBB	Baa	6.72	Medium-grade obligations. Neither highly protected nor poorly secured. Adequate capacity to pay interest and repay principal. May lack long-term reliability and protective elements to secure interest and principal payments.
BB	Ba		Moderate ability to pay interest and repay principal. Have speculative elements and future cannot be considered well assured. Adverse business, economic, and financial conditions could lead to inability to meet financial obligations.
B	B		Lack characteristics of desirable investment. Assurance of interest and principal payments over long period of time may be small. Adverse conditions likely to impair ability to meet financial obligations.
CCC	Caa		Poor standing. Identifiable vulnerability to default and dependent on favorable business, economic, and financial conditions to meet timely payment of interest and repayment of principal.
CC	Ca		Represent obligations that are speculative to a high degree. Issues often default and have other marked shortcomings.
C	C		Lowest-rated class of bonds. Have extremely poor prospects of attaining any real investment standard. May be used to cover a situation where bankruptcy petition has been filed, but debt service payments are continued.
CI			Reserved for income bonds on which no interest is being paid.
D			Payment default.
NR			No public rating has been requested.
(+) or (−)			Ratings from AA to CCC may be modified by the addition of a plus or minus sign to show relative standing within the major rating categories.

*Average interest rates are reported in the *Bulletin* only for the top four risk categories.

Source: Federal Reserve Bulletin, Table 1.35, Lines 27–30. August 2004.

sentenced to three years in prison for his part in the scandal. *Fortune* magazine reported that Milken's personal fortune still exceeded $400 million.[2]

The junk bond market has recovered since its low in 1990 and now continues to permit medium-size firms to obtain financing that might otherwise be unavailable to them because of the relatively high risk.

Financial Guarantees for Bonds

Financially weaker security issuers frequently purchase **financial guarantees** to lower the risk of their bonds. A financial guarantee ensures that the lender (bond purchaser) will be paid both principal and interest in the event the issuer defaults. Large, well-known insurance companies write what are actually insurance policies to back bond issues. With such a financial guarantee, bond buyers no longer have to be concerned with the financial health of the bond issuer. Instead, they are interested only in the strength of the insurer. Essentially, the credit rating of the insurer is substituted for the credit rating of the issuer. The resulting reduction in risk lowers the interest rate demanded by bond buyers. Of course, issuers must pay a fee to the insurance company for the guarantee. Financial guarantees make sense only when the cost of the insurance is less than the interest savings that result.

Financial guarantees were developed in the early 1970s to insure municipal bonds. More recently, their use has been expanded to cover a variety of corporate bonds as well.

Bond Yield Calculations

Chapter 3 introduced interest rates and described the concept of yield to maturity. If you buy a bond and hold it until it matures, you will earn the yield to maturity. This represents the most accurate measure of the yield from holding a bond.

Current Yield

The **current yield** is an approximation of the yield to maturity on coupon bonds that is often reported because it is easily calculated. It is defined as the yearly coupon payment divided by the price of the security,

$$i_c = \frac{C}{P} \tag{1}$$

where
i_c = current yield
P = price of the coupon bond
C = yearly coupon payment

This formula is identical to the formula in Equation 5 of Chapter 3, which describes the calculation of the yield to maturity for a perpetuity. Hence for a perpetuity, the current yield is an exact measure of the yield to maturity. When a coupon bond has a long term to maturity (say, 20 years or more), it is very

---

[2]A complete history of Milken was reported in *Fortune*, September 30, 1996, pp. 80–105.

much like a perpetuity, which pays coupon payments forever. Thus you would expect the current yield to be a rather close approximation of the yield to maturity for a long-term coupon bond, and you can safely use the current yield calculation instead of looking up the yield to maturity in a bond table. However, as the time to maturity of the coupon bond shortens (say, it becomes less than five years), it behaves less and less like a perpetuity and so the approximation afforded by the current yield becomes worse and worse.

We have also seen that when the bond price equals the par value of the bond, the yield to maturity is equal to the coupon rate (the coupon payment divided by the par value of the bond). Because the current yield equals the coupon payment divided by the bond price, the current yield is also equal to the coupon rate when the bond price is at par. This logic leads us to the conclusion that when the bond price is at par, the current yield equals the yield to maturity. This means that the nearer the bond price is to the bond's par value, the better the current yield will approximate the yield to maturity.

The current yield is negatively related to the price of the bond. In the case of our 10% coupon rate bond, when the price rises from $1000 to $1100, the current yield falls from 10% (= $100/$1000) to 9.09% (= $100/$1100). As Table 1 in Chapter 3 indicates, the yield to maturity is also negatively related to the price of the bond; when the price rises from $1000 to $1100, the yield to maturity falls from 10% to 8.48%. In this we see an important fact: The current yield and the yield to maturity always move together; a rise in the current yield always signals that the yield to maturity has also risen.

EXAMPLE 2

Current Yield

What is the current yield for a bond that has a par value of $1000 and a coupon interest rate of 10.95%? The current market price for the bond is $921.01.

Solution

The current yield is 11.89%.

$$i_c = \frac{C}{P}$$

where

C = yearly payment $= 0.1095 \times \$1000 = \$109.50$

P = price of the bond $= \$921.01$

Thus

$$i_c = \frac{\$109.50}{\$921.01} = 0.1189 = 11.89\%$$

The general characteristics of the current yield (the yearly coupon payment divided by the bond price) can be summarized as follows: The current yield better approximates the yield to maturity when the bond's price is nearer to the bond's par value and the maturity of the bond is longer. It becomes a worse approximation when the bond's price is further from the bond's par value and the bond's maturity is shorter. Regardless of whether the current yield is a good approximation of the yield to maturity, a change in the current yield *always* signals a change in the same direction of the yield to maturity.

Yield on a Discount Basis

Before the advent of calculators and computers, dealers in U.S. Treasury bills found it difficult to calculate interest rates as a yield to maturity. Instead, they quoted the interest rate on bills as a **yield on a discount basis** (or **discount yield**), and they still do so today. Formally, the yield on a discount basis is defined by the following formula:

$$i_{db} = \frac{F - P}{F} \times \frac{360}{\text{days to maturity}} \qquad (2)$$

where i_{db} = yield on a discount basis
F = face value of the discount bond
P = purchase price of the discount bond

This method for calculating interest rates has two peculiarities. First, it uses the percentage gain on the face value of the bill, $(F - P)/F$, rather than the percentage gain on the purchase price of the bill, $(F - P)/P$, used in calculating the yield to maturity. Second, it puts the yield on an annual basis by taking the year to be 360 days long rather than 365 days.

Because of these peculiarities, the discount yield understates the interest rate on bills as measured by the yield to maturity. On our one-year bill, which is selling for $900 and has a face value of $1000, the yield on a discount basis would be as follows:

$$i_{db} = \frac{\$1000 - \$900}{\$1000} \times \frac{360}{365} = 0.099 = 9.9\%$$

whereas the yield to maturity for this bill, which we calculated before, is 11.1%. The discount yield understates the yield to maturity by a factor of over 10%. A little more than 1% can be attributed to the understatement of the length of the year: When the bill has one year to maturity, the second term on the right-hand side of the formula is 360/365 = 0.986 rather than 1.0, as it should be.

The more serious source of the understatement, however, is the use of the percentage gain on the face value rather than on the purchase price. Because, by definition, the purchase price of a discount bond is always less than the face value, the percentage gain on the face value is necessarily smaller than the percentage gain on the purchase price. The greater the difference between the purchase price and the face value of the discount bond, the more the discount yield understates the yield to maturity. Because the difference between the purchase price and the face value gets larger as maturity gets longer, we can draw the following conclusion about the relationship of the yield on a discount basis to the yield to maturity: The yield on a discount basis always understates the yield to maturity, and this understatement becomes more severe the longer the maturity of the discount bond.

Another important feature of the discount yield is that, like the yield to maturity, it is negatively related to the price of the bond. For example, when the price of the bond rises from $900 to $950, the formula indicates that the yield on a discount basis declines from 9.9% to 4.9%. At the same time, the yield to maturity declines from 11.1% to 5.3%. Here we see another important factor about the relationship of yield on a discount basis to yield to maturity: They always move together; that is, a rise in the discount yield always means that the yield to maturity has risen, and a decline in the discount yield means that the yield to maturity has declined as well.

EXAMPLE 3

Yield on a Discount Basis

What is the discount yield (or yield on a discount basis) for a one-year bond that was purchased for $875 and has a face value of $1000?

Solution

The discount yield (or yield on a discount basis) is 12.33%.

$$i_{db} = \frac{F - P}{F} \times \frac{360}{\text{days to maturity}}$$

where

F = face value of the bond   = $1000

P = purchase price of the bond   = $875

days to maturity = one year   = 365 days

Thus

$$i_{db} = \frac{\$1000 - \$875}{\$1000} \times \frac{360}{365}$$

$$i_{db} = 0.1250 \times 0.9863 = 0.1233 = 12.33\%$$

The characteristics of the yield on a discount basis can be summarized as follows: Yield on a discount basis understates the more accurate measure of the interest rate, the yield to maturity; and the longer the maturity of the discount bond, the greater this understatement becomes. Even though the discount yield is a somewhat misleading measure of the interest rates, however, a change in the discount yield always indicates a change in the same direction for the yield to maturity.

Case

The *Wall Street Journal*

THE BOND PAGE

Now that we understand the different interest-rate definitions, let's apply our knowledge and take a look at what kind of information appears on the bond page of a typical newspaper, in this case the *Wall Street Journal*. The "Following the News" boxes on pp. 262–264 contain the *Journal*'s listings for three different types of bonds on Wednesday, November 4, 2004. The first box contains the information on U.S. Treasury bonds and notes. Both are coupon bonds, the only difference being their time to maturity from when they were originally issued: Notes have a time to maturity of less than ten years; bonds have a time to maturity of more than ten years.

The information found in the "Rate" and "Maturity" columns identifies the bond by coupon rate and maturity date. For example, T-bond 1 has a coupon rate of 6.50%, indicating that it pays out $65.00 per year on a $1000 face value bond and matures in May 2005. In bond market parlance, it is referred to as the Treasury's 6.5s of 2005. The next three columns tell us about the bond's price. By convention, all prices in the bond market are quoted per $100 of face value. Furthermore, the numbers after the colon represent thirty-seconds. In the case of T-bond 1, the first price of 102:07 represents $102\frac{7}{32} = 102.219$, or an actual price of $1022.19 for a $1000 face value bond. The bid price tells you what price you will receive if you sell the bond, and the asked price tells you what you must pay for the bond. (You might want to think of the bid price as the "wholesale" price and the asked price as the "retail" price.) The "Chg." column indicates how much the bid price has changed in 32nds (in this case, $-\frac{1}{32}$) from the previous trading day.

Notice that for all the bonds and notes, the asked price is more than the bid price. Can you guess why this is so? The difference between the two (the *spread*) provides the bond dealer who trades these securities with a profit. For T-bond 1, the dealer who buys it at 102:07 and sells it for 102:08 makes a profit of $\frac{1}{32}$. This profit is what enables the dealer to make a living and provide the service of allowing you to buy and sell bonds at will.

THE *WALL STREET JOURNAL*: FOLLOWING THE NEWS

Treasury Bonds and Notes

Bond prices and interest rates are published daily. In the *Wall Street Journal*, the prices and yields on Trea-

sury bonds and notes can be found in the "Treas./Govt. Issues" section of the paper, under the general heading of "Treasury Bonds, Notes & Bills."

GOVT. BOND & NOTES

	Rate	Maturity Mo/Yr	Bid	Asked	Chg.	Ask Yld.
T-bond 1	6.500	May 05n	102:07	102:08	−1	2.15
	6.750	May 05n	102:11	102:12	−1	2.19
	12.000	May 05	105:03	105:04	−2	2.14
	1.250	May 05n	99:15	99:16	—	2.14
	3.875	Apr 29i	133:19	133:20	−18	2.11
	6.125	Aug 29	117:23	117:24	6	4.88
	6.250	May 30	119:29	119:30	6	4.88
	5.375	Feb 31	108:09	108:10	5	4.81

Representative Over-the-Counter quotation based on transactions of $1 million or more. Treasury bond, note and bill quotes are as of mid-afternoon. Colons in bid-and-asked quotes represent 32nds; 101:01 means 101 1/32. Net changes in 32nds. n-Treasury note. i-inflation-indexed issue. Treasury bill quotes in hundredths, quoted on terms of a rate of discount. Days to maturity calculated from settlement date. All yields are to maturity and based on the asked quote. Latest 13-week and 26-week bills are boldfaced. For bonds callable prior to maturity, yields are computed to the earliest call date for issues quoted above par and to the maturity date for issues quoted below par. *When issued.
　　Source: eSpeed/Cantor Fitzgerald
　　U.S. Treasury strips as of 3 p.m. Eastern time, also based on transactions of $1 million or more. Colons in bid and asked quotes represent 32nds; 99:01 means 99 1/32. Net changes in 32nds. Yields calculated on the asked quotation. ci-stripped coupon interest. bp-Treasury bond, stripped principal. np-Treasury note, stripped principal. For bonds callable prior to maturity, yields are computed to the earliest call date for issues quoted above par and to the maturity date for issues below par.
　　Source: Bear, Stearns & Co. via Street Software Technology Inc.

The "Ask Yld." column provides the yield to maturity, which is 2.15% for T-bond 1. It is calculated with the method described in Chapter 3 using the asked price as the price of the bond. The asked price is used in the calculation because the yield to maturity is most relevant to a person who is going to buy and hold the security and thus earn the yield. The person selling the security is not going to be holding it and hence is less concerned with the yield.

Two other categories of bonds are reported much like the Treasury bonds and notes in the newspaper. Government agency and miscellaneous securities include securities issued by U.S. government agencies such as Ginnie Mae, which makes loans to savings and loan institutions, and international agencies such as the World Bank. Tax-exempt bonds are the other category reported in a manner similar to Treasury bonds and notes. Tax-exempt bonds include bonds issued by local government and public authorities whose interest payments are exempt from federal income taxes.

The second "Following the News" box quotes yields on U.S. Treasury bills, which, as we have seen, are discount bonds. Since there is no coupon, these securities are identified solely by their maturity dates, which you can see in the first column. The next column, "Days to Mat.," provides the

THE *WALL STREET JOURNAL*: FOLLOWING THE NEWS

Treasury Bills

In the *Wall Street Journal*, the yields on Treasury bills can also be found in the "Treas./Govt. Issues" section

of the paper, under the general heading of "Treasury Bonds, Notes & Bills."

TREASURY BILLS

Maturity	Days to Mat.	Bid	Asked	Chg.	Ask Yld.
Nov 12 04	7	1.54	1.53	−0.08	1.55
Nov 18 04	13	1.65	1.64	0.03	1.66
Nov 26 04	21	1.80	1.79	0.06	1.82
Dec 02 04	27	1.82	1.81	0.01	1.84
Dec 09 04	34	1.75	1.74	0.03	1.77
Dec 16 04	41	1.75	1.74	0.08	1.77
Dec 23 04	48	1.82	1.81	0.04	1.84
Dec 30 04	55	1.84	1.83	0.02	1.86
Jan 06 05	62	1.84	1.83	0.02	1.86
Jan 13 05	69	1.87	1.86	0.03	1.89
Jan 20 05	76	1.87	1.86	0.02	1.89
Jan 27 05	83	1.88	1.87	0.02	1.90
Feb 03 05	90	1.94	1.93	0.02	1.97
Feb 10 05	97	1.96	1.95	0.01	1.99
Feb 17 05	104	1.97	1.96	0.01	2.00
Feb 24 05	111	1.98	1.97	0.02	2.01
Mar 03 05	118	2.02	2.01	0.03	2.05
Mar 10 05	125	2.04	2.03	0.03	2.07
Mar 17 05	132	2.06	2.05	0.02	2.09
Mar 24 05	139	2.06	2.05	0.01	2.10
Mar 31 05	146	2.07	2.06	0.01	2.11
Apr 07 05	153	2.09	2.08	—	2.13
Apr 14 05	160	2.10	2.09	0.01	2.14
Apr 21 05	167	2.12	2.11	0.02	2.16
Apr 28 05	174	2.13	2.12	0.02	2.17
May 05 05	181	2.14	2.13	0.02	2.18

number of days to maturity of the bill. Dealers in these markets always refer to prices by quoting the yield on a discount basis. The "Bid" column gives the discount yield for people selling the bills to dealers, and the "Asked" column gives the discount yield for people buying the bills from dealers. As with bonds and notes, the dealers' profits are made by the asked price being higher than the bid price, leading to the asked discount yield being lower than the bid discount yield.

The "Chg." column indicates how much the asked discount yield changed from the previous day. When financial analysts talk about changes in the yield, they frequently describe the changes in terms of **basis points,** which are hundredths of a percentage point. For example, a financial analyst would describe the −.08 change in the asked discount yield for the November 12, 2004, T-bill by saying that it had fallen by 8 basis points.

As we learned earlier, the yield on a discount basis understates the yield to maturity, which is reported in the column headed "Ask Yld." This is evident from a comparison of the "Ask Yld." and "Asked" columns. As we would also expect from our discussion of the calculation of yields on a discount basis, the understatement grows as the maturity of the bill lengthens.

The third "Following the News" box has quotations for the five most active fixed-coupon corporate bonds. The first column identifies the issuing company. In our example, we see that General Motors was the most actively traded bond that day. The second column reports the coupon rate (8.375 for GM). The maturity date of the bond is reported in the next column. The GM bond matures on July 15, 2033. The last price the bond sold for that day and the last yield are reported in the next two columns. Note that the GM bond is selling for a premium so the yield is below the coupon rate. The EST SPREAD reports the number of basis points between the

---

THE *WALL STREET JOURNAL*: FOLLOWING THE NEWS

Corporate Bonds

In the *Wall Street Journal,* data on the most active corporate bonds is reported below the NASDAQ stock listing.

CORPORATE BONDS

Friday, November 5, 2004

Forty most active fixed-coupon corporate bonds

Company (TICKER)	Coupon	Maturity	Last Price	Last Yield	*Est Spread	Ust†	Est $ Vol (000's)
General Motors (GM)	8.375	Jul 15, 2033	106.460	7.806	290	30	581,679
Ford Motor Credit (F)	7.000	Oct 01, 2013	106.002	6.114	194	10	267,867
Ford Motor (F)	7.450	Jul 16, 2031	99.103	7.527	263	30	175,967
General Motors (GM)	7.125	Jul 15, 2013	104.164	6.488	231	10	152,847
Comcast Holdings (CMCSA)	7.050	Mar 15, 2033	112.400	6.122	122	30	145,800

Volume represents total volume for each issue; price/yield data are for trades of $1 million and greater. *Estimated spreads, in basis points (100 basis points is one percentage point), over the 2,3, 4, 10, or 30-year hot run Treasury note/bond. 2-year: 2.500 10/06; 3-year: 2.750 08/07; 5-year: 3.375 10/09; 10-year: 4.250 08/14; 30-year: 5.375 02/31. †Comparable U.S. Treasury issue.

Source: MarketAxess Corporate BondTicker

corporate bond and the comparable maturity Treasury bond. The UST is the term of the Treasury security used for computing the EST SPREAD. For example, GM bonds are selling for 290 basis points above the 30-year Treasury. The last column reports the volume in thousands.

Finding the Value of Coupon Bonds

Before we look specifically at how to price bonds, let us first look at the general theory behind computing the price of any business asset. Luckily, the value of all financial assets is found the same way. The current price is the present value of all future cash flows. Recall the discussion of present value from Chapter 3. If you have the present value of a future cash flow, you can exactly reproduce that future cash flow by investing the present value amount at the discount rate. For example, the present value of $100 that will be received in one year is $90.90 if the discount rate is 10%. An investor is completely indifferent between having the $90.90 today or having the $100 in one year. This is because the $90.90 can be invested at 10% to provide $100.00 in the future ($90.90 × 1.10 = $100). This represents the essence of value. The current price must be such that the seller is indifferent between continuing to receive the cash flow stream provided by the asset or receiving the offer price.

One question we might ask is why prices fluctuate if everyone knows how value is established. It is because not everyone agrees about what the future cash flows are going to be. Let us summarize how to find the value of a security

1. Identify the cash flows that result from owning the security.
2. Determine the discount rate required to compensate the investor for holding the security.
3. Find the present value of the cash flows estimated in step 1 using the discount rate determined in step 2.

The rest of this chapter focuses on how one important asset is valued: bonds. The next chapter discusses stock valuation.

Finding the Price of Semiannual Bonds

Recall that a bond usually pays interest semiannually in an amount equal to the coupon interest rate times the face amount (or par value) of the bond. When the bond matures, the holder will also receive a lump sum payment equal to the face amount. Most corporate bonds have a face amount of $1000. Basic bond terminology is reviewed in Table 3.

The issuing corporation will usually set the coupon rate close to the rate available on other similar outstanding bonds at the time the bond is offered for sale. Unless the bond has an adjustable rate, the coupon interest payment remains unchanged throughout the life of the bond.

The first step in finding the value of the bond is to identify the cash flows the holder of the bond will receive. The value of the bond is the present value of these cash flows. The cash flows consist of the interest payments and the final lump sum repayment.

TABLE 3   *Bond Terminology*

Coupon interest rate	The stated annual interest rate on the bond. It is usually fixed for the life of the bond.
Current yield	The coupon interest payment divided by the current market price of the bond.
Face amount	The maturity value of the bond. The holder of the bond will receive the face amount from the issuer when the bond matures. *Face amount* is synonymous with *par value*.
Indenture	The contract that accompanies a bond and specifies the terms of the loan agreement. It includes management restrictions, called covenants.
Market rate	The interest rate currently in effect in the market for securities of like risk and maturity. The market rate is used to value bonds.
Maturity	The number of years or periods until the bond matures and the holder is paid the face amount.
Par value	The same as *face amount*.
Yield to maturity	The yield an investor will earn if the bond is purchased at the current market price and held until maturity.

In the second step these cash flows are discounted back to the present using an interest rate that represents the yield available on other bonds of like risk and maturity.

The technique for computing the price of a simple bond with annual cash flows was discussed in detail in Chapter 3. Let us now look at a more realistic example. Most bonds pay interest semiannually. To adjust the cash flows for semiannual payments, divide the coupon payment by 2 since only half of the annual payment is paid each six months. Similarly, to find the interest rate effective during one-half of the year, the market interest rate must be divided by 2. The final adjustment is to double the number of periods because there will be two periods per year. Equation 3 shows how to compute the price of a semiannual bond:[3]

$$P_{semi} = \frac{C/2}{1+i} + \frac{C/2}{(1+i)^2} + \frac{C/2}{(1+i)^3} + \cdots + \frac{C/2}{(1+i)^{2n}} + \frac{F}{(1+i)^{2n}} \qquad (3)$$

where

P_{semi} = price of semiannual coupon bond
C = yearly coupon payment
F = face value of the bond
n = years to maturity date
$i = \frac{1}{2}$ annual market interest rate

---

[3]There is a theoretical argument for discounting the final cash flow using the full-year interest rate with the original number of periods. Derivative securities are sold, in which the principal and interest cash flows are separated and sold to different investors. The fact that one investor is receiving semiannual interest payments should not affect the value of the principal-only cash flow. However, virtually every text, calculator, and spreadsheet computes bond values by discounting the final cash flow using the same interest rate and number of periods as is used to compute the present value of the interest payments. To be consistent, we will use that method in this text.

| EXAMPLE 4 | *Bond Valuation, Semiannual Payment Bond* |

Let us compute the price of a Chrysler bond recently listed in the *Wall Street Journal*. The bonds have a 10% coupon rate, a $1000 par value (maturity value), and mature in two years. Assume semiannual compounding and that market rates of interest are 12%.

Solution

1. Begin by identifying the cash flows. Compute the coupon interest payment by multiplying 0.10 times $1000 to get $100. Since the coupon payment is made each six months, it will be one-half of $100, or $50. The final cash flow consists of repayment of the $1000 face amount of the bond. This does not change because of semiannual payments.
2. We need to know what market rate of interest is appropriate to use for computing the present value of the bond. We are told that bonds being issued today with similar risk have coupon rates of 12%. Divide this amount by 2 to get the interest rate over six months. This provides an interest rate of 6%.
3. Find the present value of the cash flows. Note that with semiannual compounding the number of periods must be doubled. This means that we discount the bond payments for four periods.

Solution: Equation

$$P = \frac{\$100/2}{(1+.06)} + \frac{\$100/2}{(1+.06)^2} + \frac{\$100/2}{(1+.06)^3} + \frac{\$100/2}{(1+.06)^4} + \frac{\$1000}{(1+.06)^4}$$

$$P = \$47.17 + \$44.50 + \$41.98 + \$39.60 + \$792.10 = \$965.35$$

Solution: Financial Calculator

$N = 4$

$FV = \$1000$

$I = 6\%$

$PMT = \$50$

Compute PV = price of bond = $965.35.

Notice that the market price for the bond in Example 4 is below the $1000 par value of the bond. When the bond sells for less than the par value, it is selling at a **discount.** When the market price exceeds the par value, the bond is selling at a **premium.**

What determines whether a bond will sell for a premium or a discount? Suppose that you are asked to invest in an old bond that has a coupon rate of 10% and $1000 par. You would not be willing to pay $1000 for this bond if new bonds with similar risk were available yielding 12%. The seller of the old bond would have to lower the price on the 10% bond to make it an attractive investment. In fact, the seller would have to lower the price until the yield earned by a buyer of the old bond exactly equaled the yield on similar new bonds. This means that as interest rates in the market rise, the value of bonds with fixed interest rates falls.

Similarly, as interest rates available in the market on new bonds fall, the value of old fixed-interest-rate bonds rises.

Investing in Bonds

Bonds represent one of the most popular long-term alternatives to investing in stocks (see Figure 6). Bonds are lower risk than stocks because they have a higher priority of payment. This means that when the firm is having difficulty meeting its obligations, bondholders get paid before stockholders. Additionally, should the firm have to liquidate, bondholders must be paid before stockholders.

Even healthy firms with sufficient cash flow to pay both bondholders and stockholders frequently have very volatile stock prices. This volatility scares many investors out of the stock market. Bonds are the most popular alternative. They offer relative security and dependable cash payments, making them ideal for retired investors and those who want to live off their investments.

Many investors think that bonds represent a very low risk investment since the cash flows are relatively certain. It is true that high-grade bonds seldom default; however, bond investors face fluctuations in price due to market interest-rate movements in the economy. As interest rates rise and fall, the value of bonds changes in the opposite direction. As discussed in Chapter 3, the possibility of suffering a loss because of interest-rate changes is called **interest-rate risk.** The longer the time until the bond matures, the greater will be the change in price. This does not cause a loss to those investors who do not sell their bonds; however, many investors do not hold their bonds until maturity. If they attempt to sell their bonds after interest rates have risen, they will receive less than they paid. Interest-rate risk is an important consideration when deciding whether to invest in bonds.

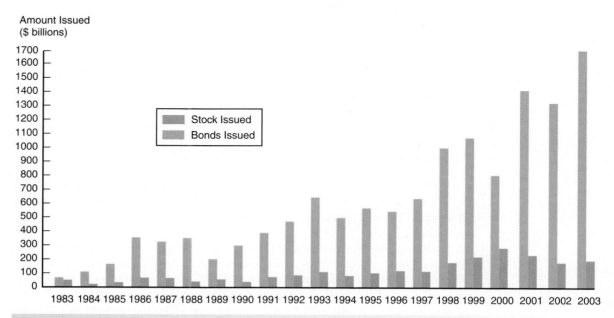

FIGURE 6   *Bonds and Stocks Issued, 1983–2003*

Source: Federal Reserve Bulletin, various issues. Table 1.46.

Summary

1. The capital markets exist to provide financing for long-term capital assets. Households, often through investments in pension and mutual funds, are net investors in the capital markets. Corporations and the federal and state governments are net users of these funds.

2. The three main capital market instruments are bonds, stocks, and mortgages. Bonds represent borrowing by the issuing firm. Stock represents ownership in the issuing firm. Mortgages are long-term loans secured by real property. Only corporations can issue stock. Corporations and governments can issue bonds. In any given year, far more funds are raised with bonds than with stock.

3. Firm managers are hired by stockholders to protect and increase their wealth. Bondholders must rely on a contract called an indenture to protect their interests. Bond indentures contain covenants that restrict the firm from activities that increase risk and hence the chance of default on the bonds. Bond indentures also contain many provisions that make

them more or less attractive to investors, such as a call option, convertibility, or a sinking fund.

4. The value of any business asset is computed the same way, by computing the present value of the cash flows that will go to the holder of the asset. For example, a commercial building is valued by computing the present value of the net cash flows the owner will receive. We compute the value of bonds by finding the present value of the cash flows, which consist of periodic interest payments and a final principal payment.

5. The value of bonds fluctuates with current market prices. If a bond has an interest payment based on a 5% coupon rate, no investor will buy it at face value if new bonds are available for the same price with interest payments based on 8% coupon interest. To sell the bond, the holder will have to discount the price until the yield to the holder equals 8%. The amount of the discount is greater the longer the term to maturity.

Key Terms

basis points, *p. 264*
bond indenture, *p. 252*
call provision, *p. 254*
current yield, *p. 258*
discount, *p. 267*
financial guarantee, *p. 258*
general obligation bond, *p. 251*

initial public offering, *p. 246*
interest-rate risk, *p. 268*
junk bond, *p. 256*
premium, *p. 267*
registered bond, *p. 253*
restrictive covenant, *p. 254*
revenue bond, *p. 251*

Separate Trading of Registered Interest and Principal Securities (STRIPS), *p. 250*
sinking fund, *p. 254*
yield on a discount basis (discount yield), *p. 260*
zero-coupon securities, *p. 250*

Questions

1. Contrast investors' use of capital markets with their use of money markets.

2. What are the primary capital market securities, and who are the primary purchasers of these securities?

3. Distinguish between the primary market and the secondary market for securities.

4. A bond provides information about its par value, coupon interest rate, and maturity date. Define each of these.

5. The U.S. Treasury issues bills, notes, and bonds. How do these three securities differ?

6. As interest rates in the market change over time, the market price of bonds rises and falls. The

change in the value of bonds due to changes in interest rates is a risk incurred by bond investors. What is this risk called?

7. In addition to Treasury securities, some agencies of the government issue bonds. List three such agencies, and state what the funds raised by the bond issues are used for.

8. A call provision on a bond allows the issuer to redeem the bond at will. Investors do not like call provisions and so require higher interest on callable bonds. Why do issuers continue to issue callable bonds anyway?

9. What is a sinking fund? Do investors like bonds that contain this feature?

10. What is the document called that lists the terms of a bond?

11. Describe the two ways whereby capital market securities pass from the issuer to the public.

Quantitative Problems

1. A bond makes an annual $80 interest payment (8% coupon). The bond has five years before it matures, at which time it will pay $1000. Assuming a discount rate of 10%, what should be the price of the bond? (Review Chapter 3.)

2. A zero-coupon bond has a par value of $1000 and matures in 20 years. Investors require a 10% annual return on these bonds. For what price should the bond sell? (Note: Zero-coupon bonds do not pay any interest. Review Chapter 3.)

3. Consider the two bonds described below:

	Bond A	Bond B
Maturity (yr)	15	20
Coupon rate (%)		
(paid semiannually)	10	6
Par value	$1000	$1000

    a. If both bonds had a required return of 8%, what would the bonds' prices be?

    b. Describe what it means if a bond sells at a discount, a premium, and at its face amount (par value). Are these two bonds selling at a discount, premium, or par?

    c. If the required return on the two bonds rose to 10%, what would the bonds' prices be?

4. A two-year $1000 par zero-coupon bond is currently priced at $819.00. A two-year $1000 annuity is currently priced at $1712.52. If you want to invest $50,000 in one of the two securities, which is a better buy? Hint: Compute the yield of each security.

5. Consider the following cash flows. All market interest rates are 12%.

Year	0	1	2	3	4
Cash Flow		160	170	180	230

    a. What price would you pay for these cash flows? What total wealth do you expect after $2\frac{1}{2}$ years if you sell the rights to the remaining cash flows? Assume interest rates remain constant.

    b. What is the duration of these cash flows?

    c. Immediately after buying these cash flows, all market interest rates drop to 11%. What is the impact on your total wealth after $2\frac{1}{2}$ years?

6. The yield on a corporate bond is 10%, and it is currently selling at par. The marginal tax rate is 20%. A par value municipal bond with a coupon rate of 8.50% is available. Which security is a better buy?

7. If the municipal bond rate is 4.25% and the corporate bond rate is 6.25%, what is the marginal tax rate, assuming investors are indifferent between the two bonds?

8. M&E, Inc., has an outstanding convertible bond. The bond can be converted into 20 shares of common equity (currently trading at $52/share). The bond has five years of remaining maturity, a $1000 par value, and a 6% annual coupon. M&E's straight debt is currently trading to yield 5%. What is the minimum price of the bond?

9. Assume the debt in the previous question is trading at $1035. How can you earn a riskless profit from this situation (arbitrage)?

10. A ten-year, $1000 par value bond with a 5% annual coupon is trading to yield 6%. What is the current yield?

11. A $1000 par bond with an annual coupon has only one year until maturity. Its current yield is 6.713%, and its yield to maturity is 10%. What is the price of the bond?

12. A one-year discount bond with a face value of $1000 was purchased for $900. What is the yield to maturity? What is the yield on a discount basis?

13. A seven-year, $1000 par bond has an 8% annual coupon and is currently yielding 7.5%. The bond can be called in two years at a call price of $1010. What is the bond yielding, assuming it will be called (known as the yield to call)?

14. A 20-year $1000 par value bond has a 7% annual coupon. The bond is callable after the tenth year for a call premium of $1025. If the bond is trading with a yield to call of 6.25%, what is the bond's yield to maturity?

15. A ten-year $1000 par value bond has a 9% semi-annual coupon and a nominal yield to maturity of 8.8%. What is the price of the bond?

16. Your company owns the following bonds:

Bond	Market Value	Duration
A	$13 million	2
B	$18 million	4
C	$20 million	3

If general interest rates rise from 8% to 8.5%, what is the approximate change in the value of the port-folio?

Web Exercises

The Bond Market

1. Stocks tend to get more publicity than bonds, but many investors, especially those nearing or in retirement, find that bonds are more consistent with their risk preferences. One site that will help an investor choose among bonds can be found at **http://bonds.yahoo.com**. Click on the calculators tab and choose the calculator titled, "Which bond is better." Look at the example provided. Do the results change if you assume a 28% tax bracket and that you will sell the bond in two years?

CHAPTER 11

The Stock Market

Preview

In the last chapter we identified the capital markets as where long-term securities trade. We then examined the bond market and discussed how bond prices are established. In this chapter we continue our investigation of the capital markets by taking a close look at the stock market. The market for stocks is undoubtedly the financial market that receives the most attention and scrutiny. Great fortunes are made and lost as investors attempt to anticipate the market's ups and downs. We have witnessed an unprecedented period of volatility over the last decade. Stock indexes hit record highs in the late 1990s, largely led by technology companies, and then fell precipitously in 2000. In this chapter we begin looking at how this important market works.

We begin by discussing the markets where stocks trade. We will then examine the fundamental theories that underlie the valuation of stocks. These theories are critical to an understanding of the forces that cause the value of stocks to rise and fall minute by minute and day by day. We will learn that determining a value for a common stock is very difficult and that it is this difficulty that leads to so much volatility in the stock markets.

Investing in Stocks

A share of stock in a firm represents ownership. A stockholder owns a percentage interest in a firm, consistent with the percentage of outstanding stock held.

Investors can earn a return from stock in one of two ways. Either the price of the stock rises over time, or the firm pays the stockholder dividends. Frequently, investors earn a return from both sources. Stock is riskier than bonds because stockholders have a lower priority than bondholders when the firm is in trouble, the returns to investors are less assured because dividends can be easily changed, and stock price increases are not guaranteed. Despite these risks, it is possible to make a great deal of money by investing in stock, whereas that is very unlikely by investing in bonds. Another distinction between stock and bonds is that stock does not mature.

Ownership of stock gives the stockholder certain rights regarding the firm. One is the right of a *residual claimant:* Stockholders have a claim on all assets and income left over after all other claimants have been satisfied. If nothing is left over, they get nothing. As noted, however, it is possible to get rich as a stockholder if the firm does well.

Most stockholders have the *right to vote* for directors and on certain issues, such as amendments to the corporate charter and whether new shares should be issued.

Notice that the stock certificate shown in Figure 1 does not list a maturity date, face value, or an interest rate, which were indicated on the bond shown in Chapter 10.

Common Stock Versus Preferred Stock

There are two types of stock, common and preferred. A share of **common stock** in a firm represents an ownership interest in that firm. Common stockholders vote, receive dividends, and hope that the price of their stock will rise. There are various classes of common stock, usually denoted as type A, type B, and so on. Unfortunately, the type does not have any meaning that is standard across all companies. The differences among the types usually involve either the distribution of dividends or voting rights. It is important for an investor in stocks to know exactly what rights go along with the shares of stock being contemplated.

Preferred stock is a form of equity from a legal and tax standpoint. However, it differs from common stock in several important ways. First, because preferred

FIGURE 1 *Wien Consolidated Airlines Stock*

Source: Eakins, *Finance Investments, Institutions, & Management,* p. 43.

stockholders receive a fixed dividend that never changes, a share of preferred stock is as much like a bond as it is like common stock. Second, because the dividend does not change, the price of preferred stock is relatively stable. Third, preferred stock-holders do not usually vote unless the firm has failed to pay the promised dividend. Finally, preferred stockholders hold a claim on assets that has priority over the claims of common shareholders but after that of creditors such as bondholders.

Less than 25% of new equity issues are preferred stock, and only about 5% of all capital is raised using preferred stock. This may be because preferred dividends are not tax-deductible to the firm but bond interest payments are. Consequently, issuing preferred stock usually costs the firm more than issuing debt, even though it shares many of the characteristics of a bond.

How Stocks Are Sold

Literally billions of shares of stock are sold each business day in the United States. The orderly flow of information, stock ownership, and funds through the stock markets is a critical feature of well-developed and efficient markets. This efficiency encourages investors to buy stocks and to provide equity capital to businesses with valuable growth opportunities. We traditionally discuss stocks as trading on either an organized exchange or over the counter. Recently, this distinction is blurring as electronic trading grows in both volume and influence.

Organized Securities Exchanges   Organized exchanges account for over 72% of the total dollar volume of domestic stock shares traded. Organized exchanges also support trading in bonds. The largest of the organized stock exchanges in the United States is the New York Stock Exchange (NYSE). The NYSE occupies a building in downtown New York City, and only traders who are members of the exchange may engage in trading. To become a member, an individual or firm must buy a "seat." There are 1366 seats on the NYSE, most of them owned by brokerage houses. Today seats on the New York Stock Exchange can sell for as much as $1.2 million (see the "Mini-Case" box below), depending on the market's perception of the profit potential in being a trader. Average daily volume on the NYSE in 2003 was 1.41 billion shares of stocks, with a total of about 350 billion shares traded during the year.

There are also major organized stock exchanges around the world. The most active exchange in the world is the Nikkei in Tokyo. Other major exchanges include the London Stock Exchange in England, the DAX in Germany, and the Toronto Stock Exchange in Canada.

Find listed companies, member information, real-time market indices, and current stock quotes at www.nyse.com

---

MINI-CASE

The Most Expensive Seat in Town

In October 2004 a seat on the NYSE sold for $1.035 million, a $300,000 decrease from the price a year earlier. Owning one of the 1366 NYSE seats is the admission ticket to trading on the world's largest stock exchange. Membership gives the holders the right to trade stocks and vote at exchange meetings. The highest price ever paid for a Big Board seat was $2.65 million on August 23, 1999. As expensive as a seat on the exchange is, consider this: It doesn't even include a chair. If you want to sit down, you have to bring your own stool.

Source: www.NYSE.com/glossary

To have a stock listed for trading on one of the organized exchanges, a firm must file an application and meet certain criteria set by the exchange designed to enhance trading. For example, the NYSE encourages only the largest firms to list so that transaction volume will be high. To list on the NYSE, a firm must meet the following minimum requirements:

- Earnings of at least $10 million for the last three years
- $500 million market value with $100 million in revenues

About 3000 companies around the world list their shares on the New York Stock Exchange. More than 70% of NYSE-listed companies have joined the exchange since 1986. The average firm on the exchange has a market value of $3.5 billion. On October 28, 1998, the NYSE volume topped 1 billion shares for the first time.[1] By 2004, daily volume was regularly in excess of 1 billion shares.

The NYSE switched to a decimal system of reporting stock prices on January 29, 2001. Prior to this change, prices were quoted in eighths. This change was prompted by the Securities and Exchange Commission (SEC) in the hope that it would reduce bid-ask spreads.

The second-largest organized stock exchange in the United States is the American Stock Exchange. About 700 firms trade on it. The American Stock Exchange has less restrictive listing requirements. Regional exchanges, such as the Philadelphia and Pacific Stock Exchange, are even easier to list on. Some firms choose to list on more than one exchange, believing that more exposure will increase the demand for their stock and hence its price. Many firms also believe that there is a certain amount of prestige in being listed on one of the major exchanges. They may even include this fact in their advertising. There is little conclusive research to support this belief, however. Microsoft, for example, is not listed on any organized exchange, yet its stock had a total market value of over $287 billion in late 2004.

Over-the-Counter Markets   If Microsoft's stock is not traded on any of the organized stock exchanges, where does it sell its stock? Securities not listed on one of the exchanges trade in the over-the-counter (OTC) market. This market is not organized in the sense of having a building where trading takes place. Instead, trading occurs over sophisticated telecommunications networks. One such network is called the **National Association of Securities Dealers Automated Quotation System (NASDAQ).** This system, introduced in 1971, provides current bid and ask prices on about 3300 actively traded securities. Dealers "make a market" in these stocks by buying for inventory when investors want to sell and selling from inventory when investors want to buy. These dealers provide small stocks with the liquidity that is essential to their acceptance in the market. Total volume on the NASDAQ is usually slightly lower than on the NYSE; however, NASDAQ volume has been growing and occasionally exceeds NYSE volume.

Not all publicly traded stocks list on one of the organized exchanges or on NASDAQ. Securities that trade very infrequently or trade primarily in one region of the country are usually handled by the regional offices of various brokerage houses. These offices often maintain small inventories of regionally popular securities. Dealers that make a market for stocks that trade in low volume are very important to the success of the over-the-counter market. Without these dealers

---

[1]*NYSE Fact Book,* 2004 data, May 2004.

standing ready to buy or sell shares, investors would be reluctant to buy shares of stock in regional or unknown firms, and it would be very difficult for start-up firms to raise needed capital. Recall from Chapter 4 that the more liquid an asset is, the greater the quantity demanded. By providing liquidity intervention, dealers increase demand for thinly traded securities.

Organized Versus Over-the-Counter Trading   There is a significant difference between how organized and OTC exchanges operate. Organized exchanges are characterized as auction markets that use floor traders who specialize in particular stocks. These specialists oversee and facilitate trading in a group of stocks. Floor traders, representing various brokerage firms with buy and sell orders, meet at the trading post on the exchange and learn about current bid and ask prices. These quotes are called out loud. In about 90% of trades, the specialist matches buyers with sellers. In the other 10% the specialists may intervene by taking ownership of the stock themselves or by selling stock from inventory. It is the specialist's duty to maintain an orderly market in the stock even if that means buying stock in a declining market.

About one of four orders on the New York Stock Exchange is filled by floor traders personally approaching the specialist on the exchange. The other three-quarters of trades are executed by the SuperDOT system (Super Designated Order Turnaround system). The SuperDOT is an electronic order routing system that transmits orders directly to the specialist who trades in a stock. This allows for much faster communication of trades than is possible using floor traders. Super-DOT is for trades under 100,000 shares and gives priority to trades of under 2100 shares.

Whereas organized exchanges have specialists who facilitate trading, over-the-counter markets have market makers. Rather than trading stocks in an auction format, they trade on an electronic network where bid and ask prices are set by the market makers. There are usually multiple market makers for any particular stock. They each enter their bid and ask quotes. Once this is done, they are obligated to buy or sell at least 1000 securities at that price. Once a trade has been executed, they may enter a new bid and ask quote. Market makers are important to the economy in that they assure there is continuous liquidity for every stock, even those with little transaction volume. Market makers are compensated by the spread between the bid price (the price they pay for stocks) and ask price (the price they sell the stocks for). They also receive commissions on trades.

Although NASDAQ, the NYSE, and the other exchanges are heavily regulated, they are still public for-profit businesses. They have shareholders, directors, and officers who are interested in market share and generating profits. This means that the NYSE is vigorously competing with NASDAQ for the high-volume stocks that generate the big fees. For example, the NYSE has been trying to entice Microsoft to leave the NASDAQ and list with them for many years.

Electronic Communications Networks (ECNs)   ECNs have been challenging both NASDAQ and the organized exchanges for business in recent years. An ECN is an electronic network that brings together major brokerages and traders so that they can trade between themselves and bypass the middleman. ECNs have a number of advantages that have led to their rapid growth.

- *Transparency:* All unfilled orders are available for review by ECN traders. This provides valuable information about supply and demand that traders can use to set their strategy. Although some exchanges make this information available, it is not always as current or complete as what the ECN provides.

- *Cost reduction:* Because the middleman and that commission is cut out of the deal, transaction costs can be lower for trades executed over an ECN. The spread is usually reduced and sometimes eliminated.
- *Faster execution:* Since ECNs are fully automated, trades are matched and confirmed faster than can be done when there is human involvement. For many traders this is not of great significance, but for those trying to trade on small price fluctuations, this is critical.
- *After-hours trading:* Prior to the advent of ECNs only institutional traders had access to trading securities after the exchanges had closed for the day. Many news reports and information become available after the major exchanges have closed, and small investors were locked out of trading on this data. Since ECNs never close, trading can continue around the clock.

Along with the advantages of ECNs there are disadvantages. The primary one is that they work well only for stocks with substantial volume. Since ECNs require there to be a seller to match against each buyer and vice versa, thinly traded stocks may go long intervals without trading.

The largest ECN is Instinet. It is mainly for institutional traders. Instinet also owns Island, which is for active individual trades. One of the fastest-growing ECNs is Archipelago, which calls itself an exchange. It is partnered with the Pacific Stock Exchange and has grown from virtually no activity in 2001 to frequently handling trades of over a trillion shares per day by 2004. The exchange features a trading system that searches for the best way to execute each order. Archipelago (known as ArcaEx) trades in all firms listed on the NYSE, NASDAQ, and American Stock Exchange.

The major exchanges are fighting the ECNs by expanding their own automatic trading systems. For example, the NYSE recently announced changes to its own Direct+ order routing system to make it more competitive. Although the NYSE still dominates the American stock market in terms of share and dollar volume, its live auction format may not survive technological challenges for many more years (see the "Mini-Case" box on p. 279).

Computing the Price of Common Stock

One basic principle of finance is that the value of any investment is found by computing the value today of all cash flows the investment will generate over its life. For example, a commercial building will sell for a price that reflects the net cash flows (rents – expenses) it is projected to have over its useful life. Similarly, we value common stock as the value in today's dollars of all future cash flows. The cash flows a stockholder may earn from stock are dividends, the sales price, or both. The "Following the News" box shows how stock market prices are reported each day.

To develop the theory of stock valuation, we begin with the simplest possible scenario. This assumes that you buy the stock, hold it for one period to get a dividend, then sell the stock. We call this the *one-period valuation model*.

At http://stock charts.com/ charts/historical. access detailed stock quotes, charts, and historical stock data.

MINI-CASE

NASDAQ: Fighting for Its Life Against ECNs

In the 1970s, NASDAQ introduced a unique and updated computer-trading system that captured business and volume from the traditional auction-style exchanges. Now it is being one-upped at its own game. Archipelago is an electronic communications network that has taken the leap to becoming a full-fledged exchange and in this position is threatening the leadership and profitability of the existing exchanges. It has developed a trading system that automatically searches for the best prices for stocks and bypasses the aging NASDAQ system. It is often quicker and cheaper than alternative systems.

NASDAQ reports that the trading volume in its own listed stocks dropped from 86.6% at the beginning of 2003 to 47.8% by early 2004. A large part of the trading was picked up by Archipelago and rival Instinet.

To fight the growing competition, NASDAQ made a dramatic cut in its fees. For example, the levy on trades from its biggest customers was slashed from a tenth of a cent per share to a hundredth of a cent. Unfortunately, the fee cuts and loss of volume are cutting NASDAQ's bottom line. In the first quarter of 2004 its net revenue dropped by 21% to $4.6 million. In contrast, Archipelago's profits surged 67% to $21.6 million, and Instinet's profits rose to $19 million.

As the stock market titans battle it out for market share, traders will undoubtedly benefit from lower trading cost and improved service. Who will emerge as the leader in the second half of the decade is yet to be decided.

Source: BusinessWeek, May 31, 2004, p. 82.

The One-Period Valuation Model

Suppose that you have some extra money to invest for one year. After a year you will need to sell your investment to pay tuition. After watching *Wall Street Week* on TV you decide that you want to buy Intel Corp. stock. You call your broker and find that Intel is currently selling for $50 per share and pays $0.16 per year in dividends. The analyst on *Wall Street Week* predicts that the stock will be selling for $60 in one year. Should you buy this stock?

To answer this question you need to determine whether the current price accurately reflects the analyst's forecast. To value the stock today, you need to find the present discounted value of the expected cash flows (future payments) using the formula in Equation 1 of Chapter 3 in which the discount factor used to discount the cash flows is the required return on investments in equity rather than the interest rate. The cash flows consist of one dividend payment plus a final sales price, which, when discounted back to the present, leads to the following equation that computes the current price of the stock.

$$P_0 = \frac{Div_1}{(1 + k_e)} + \frac{P_1}{(1 + k_e)} \tag{1}$$

where P_0 = the current price of the stock. The zero subscript refers to time period zero, or the present.

Div_1 = the dividend paid at the end of year 1.

k_e = the required return on investments in equity.

P_1 = the price at the end of the first period. This is the assumed sales price of the stock.

THE *WALL STREET JOURNAL*: FOLLOWING THE NEWS

Stock Prices

Stock prices are published daily, and in the *Wall Street Journal* they are reported in the sections "NYSE—

Composite Transactions," "Amex—Composite Transactions," and "Over-the-Counter Markets." The New York Stock Exchange (NYSE) and American Stock Exchange (Amex) stocks' prices are quoted in the following format:

YTD %CHG	52 WEEKS HI	52 WEEKS LO	STOCK (SYM)	DIV	YLD %	PE	VOL 100S	LAST	NET CHG
6.3	35.19	24.65	IntAlum IAL	1.20	4.1	27	31	29.09	0.13
−1.6	100.43	81.90	IBM IBM	.72	.8	19	65203	91.20	0.73
10.0	39.97	31.01	IntFlavor IFF	.70	1.8	19	2715	38.41	0.01
−3.4	47.12	28.22	IntGameTch IGT	.48f	1.4	26	35847	34.50	−0.39
−10.1	45.01	36.57	IntPaper IP	1.00	2.6	dd	20850	38.75	0.43

Source: Wall Street Journal. November 4, 2004, p. C8.

The following information is included in each column. International Business Machines (IBM) common stock is used as an example.

Ytd % Chg: Year-to-date percentage change in price. Since this listing is for close of business November 3, 2004, the −1.6 reflects the decrease in price since Janurary 1, 2004.

52 Weeks Hi: Highest price of a share in the past 52 weeks: $100.43 for IBM stock

52 Weeks Lo: Lowest price of a share in the past 52 weeks: 81.90 for IBM stock

Stock: Company name: IBM for International Business Machines

Sym: Symbol that identifies company: IBM

Div: Annual dividends per share: $0.72 for IBM

Yld %: Yield for stock expressed as annual dividends divided by today's closing price: 0.8% (= 0.72 ÷ 91.20) for IBM stock

PE: Price earnings ratio; the stock price divided by the annual earnings per share: 19.

Vol 100s: Number of shares (in hundreds) traded that day: 6,520,300 shares for IBM

Last: Closing price (last price) that day: $91.20.

Net Chg: Change in the closing price from the previous day: +$0.73

Prices quoted for shares traded over the counter (through dealers rather than on an organized exchange) are sometimes quoted with the same information, but in many cases only the bid price (the price the dealer is willing to pay for the stock) and the asked price (the price the dealer is willing to sell the stock for) are quoted.

EXAMPLE 1   *Stock Valuation*

Find the price of the Intel stock given the figures reported above. You will need to know the required return on equity to find the present value of the cash flows. Since a stock is more risky than a bond, you will require a higher return than that offered in the bond market. Assume that after careful consideration you decide that you would be satisfied to earn 12% on the investment.

Solution

Putting the numbers into Equation 1 yields the following:

$$P_0 = \frac{.16}{1 + 0.12} + \frac{\$60}{1 + 0.12} = \$.14 + \$53.57 = \$53.71$$

Based on your analysis you find that the stock is worth $53.71. Since the stock is currently available for $50 per share, you would choose to buy it. Why is the stock selling for less than $53.71? It may be because other investors place a different risk on the cash flows or estimate the cash flows to be less than you do.

The Generalized Dividend Valuation Model

The one-period dividend valuation model can be extended to any number of periods. The concept remains the same. The value of stock is the present value of all future cash flows. The only cash flows that an investor will receive are dividends and a final sales price when the stock is ultimately sold. The generalized formula for stock can be written as in Equation 2.

$$P_0 = \frac{D_1}{(1 + k_e)^1} + \frac{D_2}{(1 + k_e)^2} + \cdots + \frac{D_n}{(1 + k_e)^n} + \frac{P_n}{(1 + k_e)^n} \qquad (2)$$

If you were to attempt to use Equation 2 to find the value of a share of stock, you would soon realize that you must first estimate the value the stock will have at some point in the future before you can estimate its value today. In other words, you must find P_n in order to find P_0. However, if P_n is far in the future, it will not affect P_0. For example, the present value of a share of stock that sells for $50 seventy-five years from now using a 12% discount rate is just one cent [$50/(1.12^{75})$ = $0.01]. This means that the current value of a share of stock can be found as simply the present value of the future dividend stream. The **generalized dividend model** is rewritten in Equation 3 without the final sales price.

$$P_0 = \sum_{t=1}^{\infty} \frac{D_t}{(1 + k_e)^t} \qquad (3)$$

Consider the implications of Equation 3 for a moment. The generalized dividend model says that the price of stock is determined only by the present value of the dividends and that nothing else matters. Many stocks do not pay dividends, so how is it that these stocks have value? *Buyers of the stock expect that the firm will pay dividends someday.* Most of the time a firm institutes dividends as soon as it has completed the rapid growth phase of its life cycle. The stock price increases as the time approaches for the dividend stream to begin.

The generalized dividend valuation model requires that we compute the present value of an infinite stream of dividends, a process that could be difficult, to say the least. Therefore, simplified models have been developed to make the calculations easier. One such model is the **Gordon growth model** that assumes constant dividend growth.

The Gordon Growth Model

Many firms strive to increase their dividends at a constant rate each year. Equation 4 rewrites Equation 3 to reflect this constant growth in dividends.

$$P_0 = \frac{D_0 \times (1 + g)^1}{(1 + k_e)^1} + \frac{D_0 \times (1 + g)^2}{(1 + k_e)^2} + \cdots + \frac{D_0 \times (1 + g)^\infty}{(1 + k_e)^\infty} \qquad (4)$$

where

$$D_0 = \text{the most recent dividend paid}$$
$$g = \text{the expected constant growth rate in dividends}$$
$$k_e = \text{the required return on an investment in equity}$$

Equation 4 has been simplified using algebra to obtain Equation 5.[2]

$$P_0 = \frac{D_0 \times (1 + g)}{(k_e - g)} = \frac{D_1}{(k_e - g)} \tag{5}$$

This model is useful for finding the value of stock, given a few assumptions:

1. *Dividends are assumed to continue growing at a constant rate forever.* Actually, as long as they are expected to grow at a constant rate for an extended period of time, the model should yield reasonable results. This is because errors about distant cash flows become small when discounted to the present.
2. *The growth rate is assumed to be less than the required return on equity, k_e.* Myron Gordon, in his development of the model, demonstrated that this is a reasonable assumption. In theory, if the growth rate were faster than the rate demanded by holders of the firm's equity, in the long run the firm would grow impossibly large.

EXAMPLE 2   *Stock Valuation, Constant Growth*

Find the current market price of Coca-Cola stock assuming dividends grow at a constant rate of 10.95%, D_0 = $1.00, and the required return is 13%.

Solution

$$P_0 = \frac{D_0 \times (1 + g)}{k_e - g}$$

---

[2]To generate Equation 5 from Equation 4, first multiply both sides of Equation 4 by $(1 + k_e)/(1 + g)$ and subtract Equation 4 from the result. This yields

$$\frac{P_0 \times (1 + k_e)}{(1 + g)} - P_0 = D_0 - \frac{D_0 \times (1 + g)^\infty}{(1 + k_e)^\infty}$$

Assuming that k_e is greater than g, the term on the far right will approach zero and can be dropped. Thus, after factoring P_0 out of the left-hand side,

$$P_0 \times \left[\frac{1 + k_e}{1 + g} - 1\right] = D_0$$

Next simplify by combining terms to

$$P_0 \times \frac{(1 + k_e) - (1 + g)}{1 + g} = D_0$$

$$P_0 = \frac{D_0 \times (1 + g)}{k_e - g} = \frac{D_1}{k_e - g}$$

$$P_0 = \frac{\$1.00 \times (1.1095)}{.13 - .1095}$$

$$P_0 = \frac{\$1.1095}{0.0205} = \$54.12$$

Coca Cola stock should sell for $54.12 if the assumptions regarding the constant growth rate and required return are correct.

Price Earnings Valuation Method

Theoretically, the best method of stock valuation is the dividend valuation approach. Sometimes, however, it is difficult to apply. If a firm is not paying dividends or has a very erratic growth rate, the results may not be satisfactory. Other approaches to stock valuation are sometimes applied. Among the more popular is the price/earnings multiple.

The **price earnings ratio (PE)** is a widely watched measure of how much the market is willing to pay for $1 of earnings from a firm. A high PE has two interpretations.

1. A higher than average PE may mean that the market expects earnings to rise in the future. This would return the PE to a more normal level.
2. A high PE may alternatively indicate that the market feels the firm's earnings are very low risk and is therefore willing to pay a premium for them.

The PE ratio can be used to estimate the value of a firm's stock. Note that algebraically the product of the PE ratio times expected earnings is the firm's stock price.

$$\frac{P}{E} \times E = P \qquad\qquad (6)$$

Firms in the same industry are expected to have similar PE ratios in the long run. The value of a firm's stock can be found by multiplying the average industry PE times the expected earnings per share.

EXAMPLE 3

Stock Valuation, PE Ratio Approach

The average industry PE ratio for restaurants similar to Applebee's, a pub restaurant chain, is 23. What is the current price of Applebee's if earnings per share are projected to be $1.13?

Solution

Using Equation 6 and the data given we find:

$$P_0 = P/E \times E$$

$$P_0 = 23 \times \$1.13 = \$26$$

The PE ratio approach is especially useful for valuing privately held firms and firms that do not pay dividends. The weakness of the PE approach to valuation is that by using an industry average PE ratio, firm-specific factors that might contribute to a

> long-term PE ratio above or below the average are ignored in the analysis. A skilled analyst will adjust the PE ratio up or down to reflect unique characteristics of a firm when estimating its stock price.

How the Market Sets Security Prices

Suppose you went to an auto auction. The cars are available for inspection before the auction begins, and you find a little Mazda Miata that you like. You test-drive it in the parking lot and notice that it makes a few strange noises, but you decide that you would still like the car. You decide $5000 would be a fair price that would allow you to pay some repair bills should the noises turn out to be serious. You see that the auction is ready to begin, so you go in and wait for the Miata to enter.

Suppose there is another buyer who also spots the Miata. He test-drives the car and recognizes that the noises are simply the result of worn brake pads that he can fix himself at a nominal cost. He decides that the car is worth $7000. He also goes in and waits for the Miata to enter.

Who will buy the car and for how much? Suppose only the two of you are interested in the Miata. You begin the bidding at $4000. He ups your bid to $4500. You bid your top price of $5000. He counters with $5100. The price is now higher than you are willing to pay, so you stop bidding. The car is sold to the more informed buyer for $5100.

This simple example raises a number of points. First, the price is set by the buyer willing to pay the highest price. The price is not necessarily the highest price the asset could fetch, but it is incrementally greater than what any other buyer is willing to pay.

Second, the market price will be set by the buyer who can take best advantage of the asset. The buyer who purchased the car knew that he could fix the noise easily and cheaply. Because of this he was willing to pay more for the car than you were. The same concept holds for other assets. For example, a piece of property or a building will sell to the buyer who can put the asset to the most productive use. Consider why one company often pays a substantial premium over current market prices to acquire ownership of another (target) company. The acquiring firm may believe that it can put the target firm's assets to work better than they are currently and that this justifies the premium price.

Finally, the example shows the role played by information in asset pricing. Superior information about an asset can increase its value by reducing its risk. When you consider buying a stock, there are many unknowns about the future cash flows. The buyer who has the best information about these cash flows will discount them at a lower interest rate than will a buyer who is very uncertain.

Now let us apply these ideas to stock valuation. Suppose that you are considering the purchase of stock expected to pay dividends of $2 next year. The firm is expected to grow at 3% indefinitely. You are quite *uncertain* about both the constancy of the dividend stream and the accuracy of the estimated growth rate. To compensate yourself for this risk, you require a return of 15%.

Now suppose Jennifer, another investor, has spoken with industry insiders and feels more confident about the projected cash flows. Jennifer only requires a 12% return because her perceived risk is lower than yours. Bud, on the other hand, is dating the CEO of the company. He knows with near certainty what the future of the firm actually is. He thinks that both the estimated growth rate and the estimated cash flows are lower than what they will *actually* be in the future. Because he sees almost no risk in this investment, he only requires a 7% return.

What are the values each investor will give to the stock? Applying the Gordon growth model yields the following stock prices.

Investor	Discount Rate	Stock Price
You	15%	$16.67
Jennifer	12%	$22.22
Bud	7%	$50.00

You are willing to pay $16.67 for the stock. Jennifer would pay up to $22.22, and Bud would pay $50. The investor with the lowest perceived risk is willing to pay the most for the stock. If there were no other traders, the market price would be just above $22.22. If you already held the stock, you would sell it to Bud.

The point of this section is that the players in the market, bidding against each other, establish the market price. When new information is released about a firm, expectations change, and with them, prices change. New information can cause changes in expectations about the level of future dividends or the risk of those dividends. Since market participants are constantly receiving new information and constantly revising their expectations, it is reasonable that stock prices are constantly changing as well.

Errors in Valuation

In this chapter, we learned about several asset valuation models. An interesting exercise is to apply these models to real firms. Students who do this find that computed stock prices do not match market prices much of the time. Students often question whether the models are wrong or incomplete or whether they are simply being used incorrectly. There are many opportunities for errors in applying the models. These include problems estimating growth, estimating risk, and forecasting dividends.

Problems with Estimating Growth

The constant growth model requires the analyst to estimate the constant rate of growth the firm will experience. You may estimate future growth by computing the historical growth rate in dividends, sales, or net profits. This approach fails to consider any changes in the firm or economy that may affect the growth rate. Robert Haugen, a professor of finance at the University of California, writes in his book, *The New Finance,* that competition will prevent high-growth firms from being able to maintain their historical growth rate. He demonstrates that, despite this, the stock prices of historically high-growth firms tend to reflect a continuation of the high growth rate. The result is that investors in these firms receive lower returns than they would by investing in mature firms. This just points out that even the experts have trouble estimating future growth rates. Table 1 shows the stock price for a firm with a 15% required return, a $2 dividend, and a range of different growth rates. The stock price varies from $14.43 at 1% growth to $228 at 14% growth rate. Estimating growth at 13% instead of 12% results in a $38.33 price difference.

TABLE 1 *Stock Prices for a Security with D_0 = $2.00, k_e = 15%, and Constant Growth Rates as Listed*

Growth (%)	Price
1	$ 14.43
3	17.17
5	21.00
10	44.00
11	55.50
12	74.67
13	113.00
14	228.00

TABLE 2 *Stock Prices for a Security with D_0 = $2.00, g = 5%, and Required Returns as Listed*

Required Return (%)	Price
10	$42.00
11	35.00
12	30.00
13	26.25
14	23.33
15	21.00

Problems with Estimating Risk

The dividend valuation model requires the analyst to estimate the required return for the firm's equity. Table 2 shows how the price of a share of stock offering a $2 dividend and a 5% growth rate changes with different estimates of the required return. Clearly, stock price is highly dependent on the required return, despite our uncertainty regarding how it is found.

Problems with Forecasting Dividends

Even if we are able to accurately estimate a firm's growth rate and its required return, we are still faced with the problem of determining how much of the firm's earnings will be paid as dividends. Clearly, many factors can influence the dividend payout ratio. These will include the firm's future growth opportunities and management's concern over future cash flows.

Putting all of these concerns together, we see that stock analysts are seldom very certain that their stock price projections are accurate. This is why stock prices fluctuate so widely on news reports. For example, information that the economy is slowing can cause analysts to revise their growth expectations. When this happens across a broad spectrum of stocks, major market indexes can change.

Does all this mean that you should not invest in the market? No, it only means that short-term fluctuations in stock prices are expected and natural. Over the long term, the stock price will adjust to reflect the true earnings of the firm. If high-quality firms are chosen for your portfolio, they should provide fair returns over time.

Case

THE SEPTEMBER 11 TERRORIST ATTACK, THE ENRON SCANDAL, AND THE STOCK MARKET

In 2001, two big shocks hit the stock market: the September 11 terrorist attack and the Enron scandal. Our analysis of stock price evaluation, again using the Gordon growth model, can help us understand how these events affected stock prices.

The September 11 terrorist attack raised the possibility that terrorism against the United States would paralyze the country. These fears led to a downward revision of the growth prospects for U.S. companies, thus lowering the dividend growth rate g in the Gordon model. The resulting rise in the denominator in Equation 5 should lead to a decline in P_0 and hence a decline in stock prices.

Increased uncertainty for the U.S. economy would also raise the required return on investment in equity. A higher k_e also leads to a rise in the denominator in Equation 5, a decline in P_0, and a general fall in stock prices. As the Gordon model predicts, the stock market fell by over 10% immediately after September 11.

Subsequently, the U.S. successes against the Taliban in Afghanistan and the absence of further terrorist attacks reduced market fears and uncertainty, causing g to recover and k_e to fall. The denominator in Equation 5 then fell, leading to a recovery in P_0 and the stock market in October and November. However, by the beginning of 2002, the Enron scandal and disclosures that many companies had overstated their earnings caused many investors to doubt the formerly rosy forecast of earnings and dividend growth for corporations. The resulting revision of g downward, and the rise in k_e because of increased uncertainty about the quality of accounting information, should have led to a rise in the denominator in the Gordon Equation 5, thereby lowering P_0 for many companies and hence the overall stock market. As predicted by our analysis, this is exactly what happened. The stock market recovery was aborted and it entered a downward slide.

Stock Market Indexes

A stock market index is used to monitor the behavior of a group of stocks. By reviewing the average behavior of a group of stocks, investors are able to gain some insight as to how a broad group of stocks may have performed. Various stock market indexes are reported to give investors an indication of the performance of different groups of stocks. The most commonly quoted index is the Dow Jones Industrial Average (DJIA), an index based on the performance of the stocks of 30 large companies. The "Mini-Case" box on p. 288 provides more background on this famous index. Table 3 lists the 30 stocks that made up the index in November 2004.

Other indexes, such as Standard and Poor's 500 Index, the NASDAQ composite, and the NYSE composite, may be more useful for following the performance

A wealth of information about the current DJIA and its history can be found at www.djindexes.com

TABLE 3   *The Thirty Companies That Make Up the Dow Jones Industrial Average*

Alcoa Inc.	General Electric Co.	Merck & Co. Inc.
Altria	General Motors Corp.	Microsoft Corp.
American Express Co.	Hewlett-Packard Co.	Minnesota Mining & Manufacturing Co.
American International Group	Home Depot Inc.	
	Honeywell International Inc.	Pfizer
Boeing Co.		Procter & Gamble Co.
Caterpillar Inc.	Intel Corp.	SBC Communications Inc.
Citigroup Inc.	International Business Machines Corp.	United Technologies Corp.
Coca-Cola Co.		Verizon Communications
E.I. DuPont de Nemours & Co.	J. P. Morgan Chase & Co.	Wal-Mart Stores Inc.
	Johnson & Johnson	Walt Disney Co.
Exxon Mobil Corp.	McDonald's Corp.	

 MINI-CASE

History of the Dow Jones Industrial Average

The Dow Jones Industrial Average (DJIA) is an index composed of 30 "blue chip" industrial firms. On May 26, 1896, Charles H. Dow added up the prices of 12 of the best-known stocks and created an average by dividing by the number of stocks. In 1916, eight more stocks were added, and in 1928, the 30-stock average made its debut.

Today the editors of the *Wall Street Journal* select the firms that make up the DJIA. They take a broad view of the type of firm that is considered "industrial": In essence, it is almost any company that is not in the transportation or utility business (because there are also Dow Jones averages for those kinds of stocks). In choosing a new company for DJIA, they look among substantial industrial companies with a history of successful growth and wide interest among investors. The components of the DJIA are changed periodically. For example, in 2004, AT&T, Eastman Kodak, and International Paper were replaced with American International Group, Pfizer, and Verizon Communications.

Most market watchers agree that the DJIA is not the best indicator of the market's overall day-to-day performance. Indeed, it varies substantially from broader-based stock indexes in the short run. It continues to be followed so closely primarily because it is the oldest index and was the first to be quoted by other publications. But it tracks the performance of the market reasonably well over the long run.

of different groups of stocks. The *Wall Street Journal* reports on 23 different indexes in its "Stock Market Daily Data Bank." Figure 2 shows the DJIA since 1980.

Buying Foreign Stocks

In Chapter 4 we learned that diversification of a portfolio reduces risk. In recent years, investors have come to realize that some risk can also be eliminated by diversifying across different countries. When one country is suffering from a recession, others may be booming. If inflationary concerns in the United States cause stock prices to drop, falling inflation in Japan may cause Japanese stocks to rise.

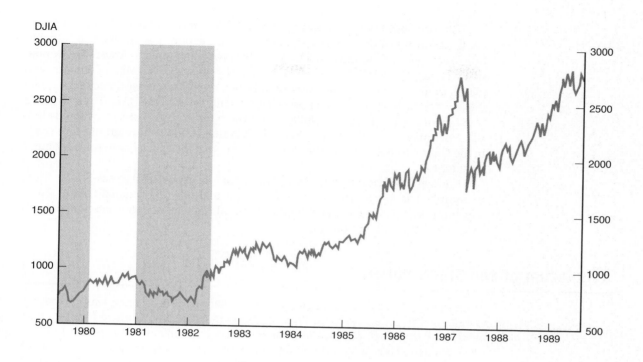

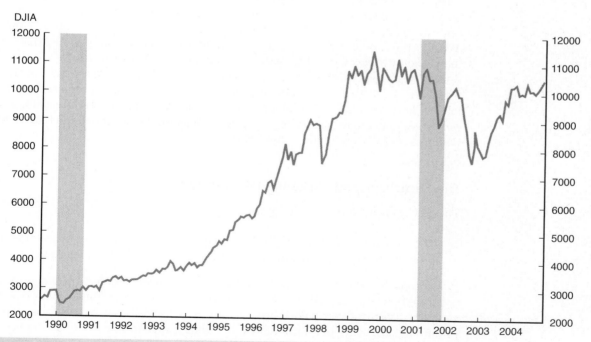

FIGURE 2 *Dow Jones Indusrial Averages, 1980–2004*

Shaded areas indicate periods of recession.

Source: http://finance.yahoo.com/?u.

The problem, with buying foreign stocks is that most foreign companies are not listed on any of the U.S. stock exchanges, so the purchase of shares is difficult. Intermediaries have found a way to solve this problem by selling **American depository receipts (ADRs).** A U.S. bank buys the shares of a foreign company and places them in its vault. The bank then issues receipts against these shares, and these receipts can be traded domestically, usually on the NASDAQ. Trade in ADRs is conducted entirely in U.S. dollars, and the bank converts stock dividends into U.S. currency. One advantage of the ADR is that it allows foreign firms to trade in the United States without the firms having to meet the disclosure rules required by the SEC.

Foreign stock trading has been growing rapidly. Since 1979, cross-border trade in equities has grown at a rate of 28% a year and now exceeds $2 trillion annually. Interest is particularly keen in the stocks of firms in emerging economies such as Mexico, Brazil, and South Korea.

Regulation of the Stock Market

Properly functioning capital markets are a hallmark of an economically advanced economy. For an economy to flourish, firms must be able to raise funds to take advantage of growth opportunities as they become available. Firms raise funds in the capital markets, and for these to function properly investors must be able to trust the information that is released about the firms that are using them. Markets can collapse in the absence of this trust. The most notable example of this in the United States was the Great Depression. During the 1920s about $50 billion in new securities were offered for sale. By 1932 half had become worthless. The public's confidence in the capital markets justifiably plummeted, and lawmakers agreed that for the economy to recover, public faith had to be restored. Following a series of investigative hearings, Congress passed the Securities Act of 1933, and shortly after the Securities Act of 1934. The main purpose of these laws was to (1) require firms to tell the public the truth about their businesses, and (2) require brokers, dealers, and exchanges to treat investors fairly. Congress established the Securities and Exchange Commission (SEC) to enforce these laws.

The Securities and Exchange Commission

The SEC website states the following:

The primary mission of the U.S. Securities and Exchange Commission is to protect investors and maintain the integrity of the securities markets.[3]

It accomplishes this daunting task primarily by assuring a constant, timely, and accurate flow of information to investors, who can then judge for themselves if a company's securities are a good investment. Thus, the SEC is primarily focused on promoting disclosure of information and reducing asymmetric information rather than determining the strength or well-being of any particular firm. The SEC brings

[3]www.sec.gov/about/whatwedo.shtml.

400 to 500 civil enforcement actions against individuals and companies each year in its effort to maintain the quality of the information provided to investors.

The SEC is organized around four divisions and 18 offices and employs about 3100 people. One way to better understand how it accomplishes its goals is to review the duties assigned to each division.

- The Division of Corporate Finance is responsible for collecting the many documents that public companies are required to file. These include annual reports, registration statements, quarterly filings, and many others. The division reviews these filings to check for compliance with the regulations. It does not verify the truth or accuracy of filings. The division staff also provides companies with help interpreting the regulations and recommends new rules for adoption.
- The Division of Market Regulation establishes and maintains standards for an orderly and efficient market by regulating the major securities market participants. This is the division that reviews and approves new rules and changes to existing rules.
- The Division of Investment Management oversees and regulates the investment management industry. This includes oversight of the mutual fund industry. Just as the Division of Market Regulation establishes rules governing the markets, the Division of Investment Management establishes rules governing investment companies.
- The Division of Enforcement investigates violation of any of the rules and regulations established by the other divisions. The Division of Enforcement conducts its own investigations into various types of securities fraud and acts on tips provided by the SEC's other divisions. The SEC itself can only bring civil lawsuits; however, it works closely with various criminal authorities to bring criminal cases when appropriate.

Later, in Chapter 16 and again in Chapter 21, we discuss specific instances where the SEC has addressed fraud and violations of ethical standards.

Summary

1. There are both organized and over-the-counter exchanges. Organized exchanges are distinguished by a physical building where trading takes place. The over-the-counter market operates primarily over phone lines and computer links. Typically, larger firms trade on organized exchanges and smaller firms in the over-the-counter market, though there are many exceptions to this rule. In recent years ECNs have begun to capture a significant portion of business traditionally belonging to the stock exchanges. These electronic networks are likely to become increasingly significant players in the future.

2. Stocks are valued as the present value of the dividends. Unfortunately, we do not know very precisely what these dividends will be. This introduces a great deal of error to the valuation process. The Gordon growth model is a simplified method of computing stock value that depends on the assumption that the dividends are growing at a constant rate forever. Given our uncertainty regarding future dividends, this assumption is often the best we can do.

3. An alternative method for estimating stock price is to multiply the firm's earnings per share times the industry price earnings ratio. This ratio can be adjusted up or down to reflect specific characteristics of the firm.

4. The interaction among traders in the market is what actually sets prices on a day-to-day basis. The trader that values the security the most either because of less uncertainty about the cash flows or because of greater estimated cash flows will be willing to pay the most. As new information is released, investors will revise their estimates of the true value of the security and will either buy or sell

it depending upon how the market price compares to their estimated valuation. Because small changes in estimated growth rates or required return result in large changes in price, it is not surprising that the markets are often volatile.

Key Terms

American depository receipts
(ADRs), *p. 290*
common stock, *p. 274*
generalized dividend model,
p. 281

Gordon growth model, *p. 281*
NASDAQ, *p. 276*
preferred stock, *p. 274*

price earnings ratio (PE),
p. 283

Questions

1. What basic principle of finance can be applied to the valuation of any investment asset?

2. Identify the cash flows available to an investor in stock. How reliably can these cash flows be estimated? Compare the problem of estimating stock cash flows to estimating bond cash flows. Which security would you predict to be more volatile?

3. Discuss the features that differentiate organized exchanges from the over-the-counter market.

4. What is the National Association of Securities Dealers Automated Quotation System (NASDAQ)?

5. What distinguishes stocks from bonds?

6. Review the list of firms now included in the Dow Jones Industrial Average listed in Table 3. How many firms appear to be technology related? Discuss what this means in terms of the risk of the index.

Quantitative Problems

eBay, Inc., went public in September of 1998. The following information on shares outstanding was listed in the final prospectus filed with the SEC.[4]

In the IPO, eBay issued 3,500,000 new shares. The initial price to the public was $18.00 per share. The final first-day closing price was $44.88.

1. If the investment bankers retained $1.26 per share as fees, what was the net proceeds to eBay? What was the market capitalization of the new shares of eBay?

2. Two common statistics in IPOs are *underpricing* and *money left on the table*. Underpricing is defined as percentage change between the offering price and the first day closing price. Money left on the table is the difference between the first day closing price and the offering price, multiplied by the number of shares offered. Calculate the underpricing and money left on the table for eBay. What does this suggest about the efficiency of the IPO process?

3. The shares of Misheak, Inc., are expected to generate the following possible returns over the next 12 months:

Return (%)	Probability
−5	.10
5	.25
10	.30
15	.25
25	.10

If the stock is currently trading at $25 per share, what is the expected price in one year? Assume that the stock pays no dividends.

4. Suppose SoftPeople, Inc., is selling at $19.00 and currently pays an annual dividend of $0.65 per share. Analysts project that the stock will be priced around $23.00 in one year. What is the expected return?

5. In September of 2004, Microsoft, Inc., was trading at $27.29 per share. At that time, Microsoft was paying an annual dividend of $0.32 per share, and

---

[4]This information is summarized from **http://www.sec.gov/Archives/edgar/data/1065088/0001012870-98-002475.txt**.

analysts had set a one-year target price around $33.30 per share. What is the expected return of this stock?

6. LaserAce is selling at $22.00 per share. The most recent annual dividend paid was $0.80. Using the Gordon Growth Model, if the market requires a return of 11%, what is the expected dividend growth rate for LaserAce?

7. Huskie Motors just paid an annual dividend of $1.00 per share. Management has promised shareholders to increase dividends at a constant rate of 5%. If the required return is 12%, what is the current price per share?

8. In September of 2004, Microsoft, Inc., was trading at $27.29 per share. At that time, Microsoft was paying an annual dividend of $0.32 per share, which is double its 2003 dividend of $0.16 per share. If this trend is expected to continue, what is the required return on Microsoft?

9. Gordon & Co.'s stock has just paid its annual dividend of $1.10 per share. Analysts believe that Gordon will maintain its historic dividend growth rate of 3%. If the required return is 8%, what is the expected price of the stock next year?

10. Macro Systems just paid an annual dividend of $0.32 per share. Its dividend is expected to double for the next four years (D_1 through D_4), after which it will grow at a more modest pace of 1% per year. If the required return is 13%, what is the current price?

11. Nat-T-Cat Industries just went public. As a growing firm, it is not expected to pay a dividend for the first five years. After that, investors expect Nat-T-Cat to pay an annual dividend of $1.00 per share (i.e., $D_6 = 1.00$), with no growth. If the required return is 10%, what is the current stock price?

12. Analysts are projecting that CB Railways will have earnings per share of $3.90. If the average industry PE ratio is about 25, what is the current price of CB Railways?

13. For 2003, Microsoft, Inc., reported earnings per share of around $0.75. If Microsoft is in an industry with a PE ratio ranging from 30 to 40, what is a reasonable price range for Microsoft?

14. Consider the following security information for four securities making up an index:

Security	Price Time = 0	Price Time = 1	Shares Outstanding
1	8	13	20 million
2	22	25	50 million
3	35	30	120 million
4	50	55	75 million

What is the change in the value of the index from Time = 0 to Time = 1 if the index is calculated using a value-weighted arithmetic mean?

15. An index had an average (geometric) mean return over 20 years of 3.8861%. If the beginning index value was 100, what was the final index value after 20 years?

16. Compute the price of a share of stock that pays a $1 per year dividend and that you expect to be able to sell in one year for $20, assuming you require a 15% return.

17. The projected earnings per share for Risky Ventures, Inc., is $3.50. The average PE ratio for the industry composed of Risky Ventures' closest competitors is 21. After careful analysis, you decide that Risky Ventures is a little more risky than average, so you decide a PE ratio of 23 better reflects the market's perception of the firm. Estimate the current price of the firm's stock.

Web Exercises

The Stock Market

1. Visit **http://www.forecasts.org/data/index.htm**. Click on "Stock Index" at the very top of the page. Review the indices for the DJIA, the S&P 500, and the NASDAQ composite. Which index appears most volatile? In which index would you have rather invested in 1985 if the investment had been allowed to compound until now?

2. There are a number of indexes that track the performance of the stock market. It is interesting to review how well they track along with each other. Go to **http://bloomberg.com**. Click on the "Charts" tab at the top of the screen. Put checks in the boxes to display the DJIA, S&P 500, NASDAQ, and the Russell 2000. Set the time frame to five years. Click on "Get Chart." You may want to add one index to the chart at a time to keep track of which color corresponds to each index.

a. Which index has been most volatile over the last five years?

b. Which index has posted the greatest gains over the last five years?

c. Now adjust the time frame to intraday. Which index has performed the best today? Which has been most volatile?

CHAPTER 12

The Mortgage Markets

Preview   Part of the classic American dream is to own one's own home. With the price of the average house now over $140,000, few of us could hope to do this until late in life if we were not able to borrow the bulk of the purchase price. Similarly, businesses rely on borrowed capital far more than on equity investment to finance their growth. Many small firms do not have access to the bond market and must find alternative sources of funds. Consider the state of the mortgage loan markets 100 years ago. They were organized mostly to accommodate the needs of businesses and the very wealthy. Much has changed since then. The purpose of this chapter is to discuss these changes.

Chapter 9 discussed the *money markets,* the markets for short-term funds. Chapters 10 and 11 discussed the *bond and stock markets.* This chapter discusses the *mortgage markets,* where borrowers—individuals, businesses, and governments—can obtain long-term collateralized loans. From one perspective, the mortgage markets form a subcategory of the capital markets because mortgages involve long-term funds. But the mortgage markets differ from the stock and bond markets in important ways. First, the usual borrowers in the capital markets are government entities and businesses, whereas the usual borrowers in the mortgage markets are individuals. Second, mortgage loans are made for varying amounts and maturities, depending on the borrowers' needs, features that cause problems for developing a secondary market.

In this chapter we will identify the characteristics of typical residential mortgages, discuss the usual term and types of mortgages available, and review who provides and services these loans. We will also discuss the growth of the mortgage-backed security market.

What Are Mortgages?

A **mortgage** is a long-term loan secured by real estate. A developer may obtain a mortgage loan to finance the construction of an office building, or a family may obtain a mortgage loan to finance the purchase of a home. In either case, the loan is **amortized:** The borrower pays it off over time in some combination of principal and interest payments that result in full payment of the debt by maturity. Table 1 shows the distribution of mortgage loan borrowers. Because over 82% of mortgage loans finance residential home purchases, that will be the primary focus of this chapter.

One way to understand the modern mortgage is to review its history. Originally, many states had laws that prevented banks from funding mortgages so that banks would not tie up their funds in long-term loans. The National Banking Act of 1863 further restricted mortgage lending. As a result, most mortgage contracts in the past were arranged between individuals, usually with the help of a lawyer who brought the parties together and drew up the papers. Such loans were generally available only to the wealthy and socially connected. As the demand for long-term funds increased, however, more mortgage brokers surfaced. They often originated loans in the rapidly developing western part of the country and sold them to savings banks and insurance companies in the East.

By 1880, mortgage bankers had learned to streamline their operations by selling bonds to raise the long-term funds they lent. They would gather a portfolio of mortgage contracts and use them as security for an issue of bonds that were sold publicly. Many of these loans were used to finance agricultural expansion in the Midwest. Unfortunately, an agricultural recession in the 1890s resulted in many defaults. Land prices fell, and a large number of the mortgage bankers went bankrupt.

Thereafter, it was very difficult to obtain long-term loans until after World War I, when national banks were authorized to make mortgage loans. This regulatory change caused a tremendous real estate boom, and mortgage lending expanded rapidly.

The mortgage market was again devastated by the Great Depression in the 1930s. Millions of borrowers were without work and were unable to make their loan payments. This led to foreclosures and land sales that caused property values to collapse. Mortgage-lending institutions were again hit hard, and many failed.

One reason that so many borrowers defaulted on their loans was the type of mortgage loan they had. Most mortgages in this period were **balloon loans:** The borrower paid only interest for three to five years, at which time the entire loan amount became due. The lender was usually willing to renew the debt with some

TABLE 1	*Mortgage Loan Borrowing, 2004*	
Type of Property	Mortgage Loans Issued ($ billions)	Proportion of Total (%)
One- to four-family dwelling	7,324	77.02
Multifamily dwelling	537	5.65
Commercial building	1,516	15.94
Farm	132	1.39

Source: Federal Reserve Bulletin, 2004, Table 1.54.

reduction in principal. However, if the borrower were unemployed, the lender would not renew, and the borrower would default.

As part of the recovery program from the depression, the federal government stepped in and restructured the mortgage market. The government took over delinquent balloon loans and allowed borrowers to repay them over long periods of time. It is no surprise that these new types of loans were very popular. The surviving savings and loans began offering home buyers similar loans, and the high demand contributed to restoring the health of the mortgage industry.

Characteristics of the Residential Mortgage

The modern mortgage lender has continued to refine the long-term loan to make it more desirable to borrowers. Even in the past 20 years, both the nature of the lenders and the instruments have undergone substantial changes. One of the biggest changes is the development of an active secondary market for mortgage contracts. We will examine the nature of mortgage loan contracts and then look at their secondary market.

The mortgage market has become very competitive in recent years. Twenty years ago, savings and loan institutions and the mortgage departments of large banks originated most mortgage loans. Currently, there are many loan production offices that compete in real estate financing. Some of these offices are subsidiaries of banks, and others are independently owned. As a result of the competition for mortgage loans, borrowers can choose from a variety of terms and options.

Mortgage Interest Rates

The interest rate borrowers pay on their mortgages is probably the most important factor in their decision of how much and from whom to borrow. The interest rate on the loan is determined by three factors: current long-term market rates, the life (term) of the mortgage, and the number of discount points paid.

Track mortgage rates and shop for mortgage rates in different geographic areas at www.interest. com

1. *Market rates.* Long-term market rates are determined by the supply of and demand for long-term funds, which are in turn influenced by a number of global, national, and regional factors. As Figure 1 shows, mortgage rates tend to stay above the less risky Treasury bonds most of the time but tend to track along with them.
2. *Term.* Longer-term mortgages have higher interest rates than shorter-term mortgages. The usual mortgage lifetime is either 15 or 30 years. Lenders also offer 20-year loans, though they are not as popular. Because interest-rate risk falls as the term to maturity decreases, the interest rate on the 15-year loan will be substantially less than on the 30-year loan. For example, in August, 2004, the average 30-year mortgage rate was 6.06%, and the 15-year rate was 5.47%.
3. *Discount points.* **Discount points** (or simply *points*) are interest payments made at the beginning of a loan. A loan with one discount point means that the borrower pays 1% of the loan amount at *closing,* the moment when the borrower signs the loan paper and receives the proceeds of the loan. In exchange for the points, the lender reduces the interest rate

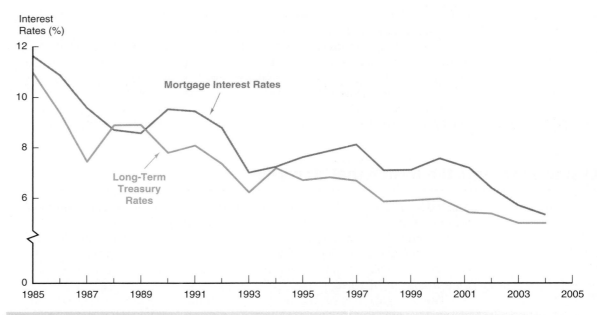

FIGURE 1 *Mortgage Rates and Long-Term Treasury Interest Rates, 1985–2004*

Source: Federal Reserve Bulletin, various issues, Table 1.53 Line 7 and Table 1.35 Line 23.

on the loan. In considering whether to pay points, borrowers must determine whether the reduced interest rate over the life of the loan fully compensates for the increased up-front expense. To make this determination, borrowers must take into account how long they will hold on to the loan. Typically, discount points should not be paid if the borrower will pay off the loan in five years or less. This breakeven point is not surprising since the average home sells every five years.

Case

THE DISCOUNT POINT DECISION

Suppose that you are offered two loan alternatives. In the first, you pay no discount points and the interest rate is 12%. In the second, you pay 2 discount points but receive a lower interest rate of 11.5%. Which alternative do you choose?

To answer this question you must first compute the effective annual rate without discount points. Since the loan is compounded monthly, you pay 1% per month. Because of the compounding, the effective annual rate is greater than the simple annual rate. To compute the effective rate, raise 1 plus the monthly rate to the twelfth power and subtract 1. The effective annual rate on the no-point loan is thus

$$\text{Effective annual rate} = (1.01)^{12} - 1 = 0.1268 = 12.68\%$$

Because of monthly compounding, a 12% annual percentage rate has an effective annual rate of 12.68%. On a 30-year, $100,000 mortgage loan, your payment will be $1028.61 as found on a financial calculator.

TABLE 2 *Effective Rate of Interest on a Loan at 12% with 2 Discount Points*

Year of Prepayment	Effective Rate of Interest (%)	Year of Prepayment	Effective Rate of Interest (%)
1	14.54	6	12.65
2	13.40	7	12.60
3	13.02	10	12.52
4	12.84	15	12.45
5	12.73	30	12.42

Now compute the effective annual rate if you pay 2 discount points. Let's assume that the amount of the loan is still $100,000. If you pay 2 points, instead of receiving $100,000, you will receive only $98,000 ($100,000 − $2000). Your payment is computed on the $100,000, but at the lower interest rate. Using a financial calculator, we find that the monthly payment is $990.29 and your monthly rate is 0.9804%.[1] The effective annual rate after compounding is

$$\text{Effective annual rate} = (1.009804)^{12} - 1 = 0.1242 = 12.42\%$$

As a result of paying the 2 discount points, the effective annual rate has dropped from 12.68% to 12.42%. On the surface, it would seem like a good idea to pay the points. The problem is that these calculations were made assuming the loan would be held for 30 years. What happens if you sell the house before the loan matures?

If the loan is paid off early, the borrower will benefit from the lower interest rate for a shorter length of time, and the discount points are spread over a shorter period of time. The result of these two factors is that the effective interest rate rises the shorter the time the loan is held before being paid. This relationship is demonstrated in Table 2. If the 2-point loan is held for 15 years, the effective rate is 12.45%. At 10 years, the effective rate is up to 12.52%. Even at 6 years, when the effective rate is 12.65%, paying the discount points has saved the borrower money. However, if the loan is paid off at 5 years, the effective rate is 12.73%, which is higher than the 12.68% effective rate if no points were paid.[2]

Loan Terms

Mortgage loan contracts contain many legal and financial terms, most of which protect the lender from financial loss.

Collateral One characteristic common to mortgage loans is the requirement that collateral, usually the real estate being financed, be pledged as security. The

---

[1]The case on p. 301 discusses how mortgage loan payments are computed.

[2]For example, to compute the effective rate if the loan is prepaid after 2 years, find the FV if I = 11.5%, PV = 100,000, N = 360, and PMT = 990.29. Now set PV equal to 98,000 and compute I. Divide this I by 12, add 1, and raise the result to the twelfth power.

lending institution will place a **lien** against the property, and this remains in effect until the loan is paid off. A lien is a public record that attaches to the title of the property, advising that the property is security for a loan, and it gives the lender the right to sell the property if the underlying loan defaults.

No one can buy the property and obtain clear title to it without paying off this lien. For example, if you purchased a piece of property with a loan secured by a lien, the lender would file notice of this lien at the public recorder's office. The lien gives notice to the world that if there is a default on the loan, the lender has the right to seize the property. If you try to sell the property without paying off the loan, the lien would remain attached to the title or deed to the property. Since the lender can take the property away from whoever owns it, no one would buy it unless you paid off the loan. The existence of liens against real estate explains why a title search is an important part of any mortgage loan transaction. During the title search, a lawyer or title company searches the public record for any liens. Title insurance is then sold that guarantees the buyer that the property is free of *encumbrances,* any questions about the state of the title to the property, including the existence of liens.

Down Payments   To obtain a mortgage loan, the lender also requires the borrower to make a **down payment** on the property, that is, to pay a portion of the purchase price. The balance of the purchase price is paid by the *loan proceeds.* Down payments (like liens) are intended to make the borrower less likely to default on the loan. A borrower who does not make a down payment could walk away from the house and the loan and lose nothing. Furthermore, if real estate prices drop even a small amount, the balance due on the loan will exceed the value of the collateral. As we discussed in Chapter 2, the down payment reduces *moral hazard* for the borrower. The amount of the down payment depends on the type of mortgage loan. Many lenders require that the borrower pay 5% of the purchase price; in other situations, up to 20% may be required.

Private Mortgage Insurance   Another way that lenders protect themselves against default is by requiring the borrower to purchase **private mortgage insurance (PMI).** PMI is an insurance policy that guarantees to make up any discrepancy between the value of the property and the loan amount, should a default occur. For example, if the balance on your loan was $120,000 at the time of default and the property was worth only $100,000, PMI would pay the lending institution $20,000. The default still appears on the credit record of the borrower, but the lender avoids sustaining the loss. PMI is usually required on loans that have less than a 20% down payment. If the loan-to-value ratio falls because of payments being made or because the value of the property increases, the borrower can request that the PMI requirement be dropped. PMI usually costs between $20 and $30 per month for a $100,000 loan.

Borrower Qualification   Before granting a mortgage loan, the lender will determine whether the borrower qualifies for it. Qualifying for a mortgage loan is different from qualifying for a bank loan because most lenders sell their mortgage loans to one of a few federal agencies in the secondary mortgage market. These agencies establish very precise guidelines that must be followed before they will accept the loan. If the lender gives a mortgage loan to a borrower who does not fit these guidelines, the lender may not be able to resell the loan. That ties up the lender's funds. Banks can be more flexible with loans that will be kept on the bank's own books.

CHAPTER 12 THE MORTGAGE MARKETS

TABLE 3   *Amortization of a 30-Year, $130,000 Loan at 8.5%*

Payment Number	Beginning Balance of Loan	Monthly Payment	Amount Applied to Interest	Amount Applied to Principal	Ending Balance of Loan
1	130,000.00	999.59	920.83	78.75	129,921.24
24	128,040.25	999.59	906.95	92.66	127,947.62
60	124,256.74	999.59	880.15	119.43	124,137.31
120	115,365.63	999.59	817.17	182.41	115,183.22
180	101,786.23	999.59	720.99	278.60	101,507.63
240	81,046.41	999.59	574.08	425.51	80,620.90
360	991.77	999.59	7.82	991.77	0

The rules for qualifying a borrower are complex and constantly changing, but a rule of thumb is that the loan payment, including taxes and insurance, should not exceed 25% of gross monthly income. Furthermore, the sum of the monthly payments on all loans to the borrower, including car loans and credit cards, cannot exceed 33% of gross monthly income. A borrower who fails this income test can pay off some of the outstanding debt, increase the down payment, or find a less expensive house to buy.

Mortgage Loan Amortization

Mortgage loan borrowers agree to pay a monthly amount of principal and interest that will fully amortize the loan by its maturity. "Fully amortize" means that the payments will pay off the outstanding indebtedness by the time the loan matures. During the early years of the loan, the lender applies most of the payment to the interest on the loan and a small amount to the outstanding principal balance. Many borrowers are surprised to find that after years of making payments, their loan balance has not dropped appreciably.

Table 3 shows the distribution of principal and interest for a 30-year, $130,000 loan at 8.5% interest. Only $78.75 of the first payment is applied to reduce the loan balance. At the end of two years, the balance due is $127,947, and at the end of five years, the balance due is $124,137. Put another way, of $59,975.40 in loan payments made during the first five years, only $5862.69 is applied to the principal. Over the life of the $130,000 loan, a total of $229,850 in interest will be paid.

If the loan in Table 3 had been financed for 15 years instead of for 30, the payment would have increased by about $280 per month to $1279.59, but the interest savings over the life of the loan would be nearly $130,000. It is no wonder why so many borrowers prefer the shorter-term loans.

Case

COMPUTING THE PAYMENT ON MORTGAGE LOANS

We can apply the techniques for computing loan payments introduced in Chapter 3 to computing the payment on mortgage loans. Suppose that you have graduated and want to buy a condominium instead of renting an apartment. The condo costs $100,000, and a 5% down payment is required by your mortgage lender. How much will your monthly loan payment be?

To compute fixed-amount loan payments, we recognize that the lender must equate the present value of the stream of payments you will pay to the amount of the loan. In equation form,

$$\text{Loan amount} = \frac{P}{1+i} + \frac{P}{(1+i)^2} + \frac{P}{(1+i)^3} + \cdots + \frac{P}{(1+i)^n} \quad (1)$$

where

P = fixed payment
i = interest rate on the loan
n = term of the loan

An alternative form for Equation 1, which takes advantage of present value tables included at the end of most introductory finance texts, is

$$\text{Loan amount} = P(PVIFA_{i,n}) \quad (2)$$

where $PVIFA$ is the present value interest factor with an interest rate of i for n periods. P can then be found by looking up the factor for the term and interest rate on the loan you are interested in and dividing this factor into the loan amount. Most factor tables include only 50 or 60 periods, so we cannot use this method to compute the payment on 30-year loans with monthly payments ($30 \times 12 = 360$ periods). Instead, a close approximation of the monthly payment can be found by computing the annual payment and dividing by 12.

EXAMPLE 1

Mortgage Loans

You obtain a 30-year loan at 8% on the $95,000 you need to finance your new condo. The price of the condo is $100,000 minus a $5000 down payment. Use Table 4 and Equation 2 to calculate the fixed payment on the loan.

Solution

The fixed payment on the loan would be $703 per month.

$$\text{Loan amount} = P(PVIFA_{i,n})$$

where

Loan amount = amount loaned by the bank = $95,000
i = interest rate on the loan = 0.08
n = term of the loan = 30

Thus

$$\$95,000 = P_{ann}(PVIFA_{8\%,30})$$

$$\$95,000 = P_{ann}(11.2578)$$

$$P_{ann} = \frac{\$95,000}{11.2578}$$

$$P_{ann} = \$8,439$$

$$P_{mo} = \frac{\$8,439}{12 \text{ months}} = \$703 \text{ per month}$$

TABLE 4 *Present Value Interest Factor at Various Rates of Interest*

Payment Periods	Interest Rate					
	5%	6%	7%	8%	9%	10%
15	10.3797	9.7122	9.1079	8.5595	8.0607	7.6061
20	12.4622	11.4699	10.5940	9.8181	9.1285	8.5136
25	14.0939	12.7834	11.6536	10.6748	9.8226	9.0770
30	15.3725	13.7648	12.4090	11.2578	9.8226	9.0770

To find the present value interest factor in Table 4, pick out the payment period in the left-hand column and then move across the row to the entry in the column for the interest rate on the loan. For a 30-year loan at 8%, the present value interest factor is 11.2578.

To solve using a financial calculator:

N = number of periods = 30 years × 12 months = 360

PV = amount of the loan (LV)   = −95,000

FV = amount of the loan after 30 years   = 0

I = monthly interest rate = 8/12 months   = 0.6667

Then push the PMT button = fixed monthly payment (P) = $697
  (Note: small differences between the table solution and the calculator solution are due to rounding.)

Types of Mortgage Loans

A number of types of mortgage loans are available in the market. Different borrowers may qualify for different ones. A skilled mortgage banker can help find the best type of mortgage loan for each particular situation.

Insured and Conventional Mortgages

Mortgages are classified as either *insured* or *conventional*. **Insured mortgages** are originated by banks or other mortgage lenders but are guaranteed by either the Federal Housing Administration (FHA) or the Veterans Administration (VA). Applicants for FHA and VA loans must meet certain qualifications, such as having served in the military or having income below a given level, and can borrow only up to a certain amount. The FHA or VA then guarantees the bank making the loans against any losses—that is, the agency guarantees that it will pay off the mortgage loan if the borrower defaults. One important advantage to a borrower who qualifies for an FHA or VA loan is that only a very low or zero down payment is required.

Conventional mortgages are originated by the same sources as insured loans but are not guaranteed. Private mortgage companies now insure many conventional loans against default. As we noted, most lenders require the borrower to obtain private mortgage insurance on all loans with a loan-to-value ratio exceeding 80%.

Fixed- and Adjustable-Rate Mortgages

In standard mortgage contracts, borrowers agree to make regular payments on the principal and interest they owe to lenders. As we saw earlier, the interest rate significantly affects the size of this monthly payment. In *fixed-rate mortgages,* the interest rate and the monthly payment do not vary over the life of the mortgage.

The interest rate on *adjustable-rate mortgages (ARMs)* is tied to some market interest rate and therefore changes over time. ARMs usually have limits, called *caps,* on how high (or low) the interest rate can move in one year and during the term of the loan. A typical ARM might tie the interest rate to the average Treasury bill rate plus 2%, with caps of 2% per year and 6% over the lifetime of the mortgage. Caps make ARMs more palatable to borrowers.

Borrowers tend to prefer fixed-rate loans to ARMs because ARMs may cause financial hardship if interest rates rise. However, fixed-rate borrowers do not benefit if rates fall unless they are willing to refinance their mortgage (pay it off by obtaining a new mortgage at a lower interest rate). The fact that individuals are risk-averse means that fear of hardship most often overwhelms anticipation of savings.

Lenders, by contrast, prefer ARMs because ARMs lessen interest-rate risk. Recall from Chapter 3 that interest-rate risk is the risk that rising interest rates will cause the value of debt instruments to fall. The effect on the value of the debt is greatest when the debt has a long term to maturity. Since mortgages are usually long-term, their value is very sensitive to interest-rate movements. Lending institutions can reduce the sensitivity of their portfolios by making ARMs instead of standard fixed-rate loans.

Seeing that lenders prefer ARMs and borrowers prefer fixed-rate mortgages, lenders must entice borrowers by offering lower initial interest rates on ARMs than on fixed-rate loans. For example, in August 2004, the reported interest rate for 30-year fixed-rate mortgage loans was 6.04%. The rate at that time for adjustable-rate mortgages was 3.56%. The rate on the ARM would have to rise 2.48% before the borrower of the ARM would be in a worse position than the fixed-rate borrower.

Other Types of Mortgages

As the market for mortgage loans becomes more competitive, lenders are offering more innovative mortgage contracts in an effort to attract borrowers. We discuss some of these mortgages here.

Graduated-Payment Mortgages (GPMs)   Graduated-payment mortgages are useful for home buyers who expect their incomes to rise. The GPM has lower payments in the first few years; then the payments rise. The early payments may not even be sufficient to cover the interest due, in which case the principal balance increases. As time passes, the borrower expects income to increase so that the higher payment will not be a burden.

The advantage of the GPM is that borrowers will qualify for a larger loan than if they requested a conventional mortgage. This may help buyers purchase adequate housing now and avoid the need to move to more expensive homes as their family size increases. The disadvantage is that the payments escalate whether the borrower's income does or not.

Growing-Equity Mortgages (GEMs)   Lenders designed the growing-equity mortgage loan to help the borrower pay off the loan in a shorter period of time. With a GEM, the payments will initially be the same as on a conventional mortgage. However, over time the payment will increase. This increase will reduce the principal more quickly than the conventional payment stream would. For example, a typical contract may call for level payments for the first two years. The payments may increase by 5% per year for the next five years, then remain the same until maturity. The result is to reduce the life of the loan from 30 years to about 17.

GEMs are popular among borrowers who expect their incomes to rise in the future. It gives them the benefit of a small payment at the beginning while still retiring the debt early. Although the increase in payments is *required* in GEMs, most mortgage loans have no prepayment penalty. This means that a borrower with a 30-year loan could create a GEM by simply increasing the monthly payments beyond what is required and designating that the excess be applied entirely to the principal.

The GEM is similar to the graduated-payment mortgage; the difference is that the goal of the GPM is to help the borrower qualify by reducing the first few years' payments. The loan still pays off in 30 years. The goal of the GEM is to let the borrower pay off early.

Shared-Appreciation Mortgages (SAMs)   When interest rates are high, the monthly payments on mortgage loans are also high. That prevents many borrowers from qualifying for loans. To help borrowers qualify and to keep loan volume high, lenders created the shared-appreciation mortgage. In a SAM, the lender lowers the interest rate on the mortgage in exchange for a share of any appreciation in the real estate (if the property sells for more than a stated amount, the lender is entitled to a portion of the gain). As interest rates and inflation fell in the late 1980s and into the 1990s, the popularity of these loans also diminished.

Equity Participation Mortgages   In a shared-appreciation mortgage, the lender shares in the appreciation of the property. In an equity participation mortgage, an outside investor rather than the lender shares in the appreciation of the property. This investor will either provide a portion of the purchase price of the property or supplement the monthly payments. In return, the investor receives a portion of any appreciation in the property. As with the SAM, the borrower benefits by being able to qualify for a larger loan than without such help.

Second Mortgages   Second mortgages are loans that are secured by the same real estate that is used to secure the first mortgage. The second mortgage is junior to the original loan. This means that should a default occur, the second mortgage holder will be paid only after the original loan has been paid off, if sufficient funds remain.

Second mortgages have two purposes. The first is to give borrowers a way to use the equity they have in their homes as security for another loan. An alternative to the second mortgage would be to refinance the home at a higher loan amount than is currently owed. The cost of obtaining a second mortgage is often much lower than refinancing.

Another purpose of the second mortgage is to take advantage of one of the few remaining tax deductions available to the middle class. The interest on loans secured by residential real estate is tax-deductible (the tax laws allow borrowers to deduct the interest on the primary residence and one vacation home). No other kind of consumer loan has this tax deduction. Many banks now offer lines of credit secured by second mortgages. In most cases, the value of the security

TABLE 5 *Summary of Mortgage Types*

Conventional mortgage	Loan is not guaranteed; usually requires private mortgage insurance; 5% to 20% down payment
Insured mortgage	Loan is guaranteed by FHA or VA; low or zero down payment
Adjustable-rate mortgage (ARM)	Interest rate is tied to some other security and is adjusted periodically; size of adjustment is subject to annual limits
Graduated-payment mortgage (GPM)	Initial low payment increases each year; loan amortizes in 30 years
Growing-equity mortgage (GEM)	Initial payment increases each year; loan amortizes in less than 30 years
Shared-appreciation mortgage (SAM)	In exchange for providing a low interest rate, the lender shares in any appreciation of the real estate
Equity participation mortgage	In exchange for paying a portion of the down payment or for supplementing the monthly payments, an outside investor shares in any appreciation of the real estate
Second mortgage	Loan is secured by a second lien against the real estate; often used for lines of credit or home improvement loans
Reverse annuity mortgage	Lender disburses a monthly payment to the borrower on an increasing-balance loan; loan comes due when the real estate is sold

is not of great interest to the bank. Consumers prefer that the line of credit be secured so that they can deduct the interest on the loan from their taxes.

Reverse Annuity Mortgages (RAMs)   The reverse annuity mortgage is an innovative method for retired people to live on the equity they have in their homes. The contract for a RAM has the bank advancing funds on a monthly schedule. This increasing-balance loan is secured by the real estate. The borrower does not make any payments against the loan. When the borrower dies, the borrower's estate sells the property to retire the debt.

The advantage of the RAM is that it allows retired people to use the equity in their homes without the necessity of selling it. For retirees in need of supplemental funds to meet living expenses, the RAM can be a desirable option.

The various mortgage types are summarized in Table 5.

Mortgage-Lending Institutions

Originally, the thrift industry was established with the mandate from Congress to provide mortgage loans to families. Congress gave these institutions the ability to attract depositors by allowing S&Ls to pay slightly higher interest rates on

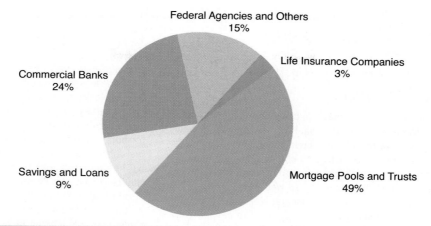

FIGURE 2   *Share of the Mortgage Market Held by Major Mortgage-Lending Institutions*

Source: Federal Reserve Bulletin, 2004, Table 1.54.

deposits. For many years, the thrift industry did its job well. Thrifts raised short-term funds by attracting deposits and used these funds to make long-term mortgage loans. The growth of the housing industry owes much of its success to these institutions. (The thrift industry is discussed further in Chapter 19.)

Until the 1970s, interest rates remained relatively stable, and when fluctuations did occur, they tended to be small and short-lived. But in the 1970s, interest rates rose rapidly, along with inflation, and thrifts became the victims of interest-rate risk. As market interest rates rose, the value of their fixed-rate mortgage loan portfolios fell. Because of the losses the thrifts suffered, they stopped being the primary source of mortgage loans.

Another serious problem with the early mortgage market was that thrift institutions were restricted from nationwide branching by federal and state laws and were forbidden to lend outside of their normal lending territory, about 100 miles from their offices. So even if an institution appeared very diversified, with thousands of different loans, all of the loans were from the same region. When that region had economic problems, many of the loans would default at the same time. For example, Texas and Oklahoma experienced a recession in the mid-1980s due to falling oil prices. Many mortgage loans defaulted because real estate values fell at the same time as the region's unemployment rate rose. That other areas of the country remained healthy was of no help to local lenders.

Figure 2 shows the share of the total mortgage market held by the major mortgage-lending institutions in the United States. (Mortgage pools and trusts are discussed later in this chapter.)

Loan Servicing

Many of the institutions making mortgage loans do not want to hold large portfolios of long-term securities. Commercial banks, for example, obtain their funds from short-term sources. Investing in long-term loans would subject them to unacceptably high interest-rate risk. Commercial banks, thrifts, and most other loan

E-FINANCE

Borrowers Shop the Web for Mortgages

One business area that has been significantly affected by the Web is mortgage banking. Historically, borrowers went to local banks, savings and loans, and mortgage banking companies to obtain mortgage loans. These offices packaged the loans and resold them. In recent years, hundreds of new Web-based mortgage banking companies have emerged.

The mortgage market is well suited to providing on-line service for several reasons. First, it is information-based and no products have to be shipped or inventoried. Second, the product (a loan) is homogeneous across providers. A borrower does not really care who provides the money as long as it is provided efficiently. Third, because home buyers tend not to obtain mortgage loans very often, they have little loyalty to any local lender. Finally, on-line lenders can often offer loans at lower cost because they can operate with lower overhead than firms that must greet the public.

The on-line mortgage market makes it much easier for borrowers to shop interest rates and terms. By filling out one application, a borrower can obtain a number of alternative loan options from various Web service companies. Borrowers can then select the option that best suits their requirements.

On-line mortgage firms, such as Lending Tree, have made mortgage lending more competitive. This may lead to lower rates and better service. It has also led lenders to offer an often confusing array of loan alternatives that most borrowers have difficulty interpreting. This makes comparison shopping more difficult than simply comparing interest rates.

originators do, however, make money through the fees that they earn for packaging loans for other investors to hold. Loan origination fees are typically 1% of the loan amount, though this varies with the market.

Once a loan has been made, many lenders immediately sell the loan to another investor. The borrower may not even be aware that the original lender transferred the loan. By selling the loan, the originator frees up funds that can be lent to another borrower, thereby generating additional fee income.

Some of the originators also provide servicing of the loan. The loan-servicing agent collects payments from the borrower, passes the principal and interest on to the investor, keeps required records of the transaction, and maintains **reserve accounts.** Reserve accounts are established for most mortgage loans to permit the lender to make tax and insurance payments for the borrower. Lenders prefer to make these payments because they protect the security of the loan. Loan-servicing agents usually earn 0.5% per year of the total loan amount for their efforts.

In summary, there are three distinct elements to most mortgage loans:

1. The originator packages the loan for an investor.
2. The investor holds the loan.
3. The servicing agent handles the paperwork.

One, two, or three different intermediaries may provide these functions.

Mortgage loans are increasingly obtained from the Web. The "E-Finance" box discusses this new source of mortgage loans.

Secondary Mortgage Market

The federal government founded the secondary market for mortgages. As we noted earlier, the mortgage market had all but collapsed during the Great Depression. To help spur the nation's economic activity, the government established several agencies to buy mortgages. The Federal National Mortgage Association (Fannie Mae) was set up to buy mortgages from thrifts so that these institutions could make more mortgage loans. This agency would fund these purchases by selling bonds to the public.

At about the same time, the Federal Housing Administration was established to insure certain mortgage contracts. This made it easier to sell the mortgages because the buyer did not have to be concerned with the borrower's credit history or the value of the collateral. A similar insurance program was set up through the Veterans Administration to insure loans to veterans after World War II.

One advantage of the insured loans was that they were required to be written on a standard loan contract. This standardization was an important factor in the growth of the secondary market for mortgages.

As the secondary market for mortgage contracts took shape, a new intermediary, the mortgage bank, emerged. Because this firm did not accept deposits, it was able to open offices across the country. The mortgage bank originated the loans, funding them initially with its own capital. After a group of similar loans were made, they would be bundled and sold, either to one of the federal agencies or to an insurance or pension fund. There were several advantages to the mortgage banks. Because of their size, they were able to capture economies of scale in loan origination and servicing. They were also able to bundle loans from different regions together, which helped reduce their risk. The increased competition for loans among these intermediaries led to lower rates for borrowers.

Securitization of Mortgages

Intermediaries still faced several problems when trying to sell mortgages. The first was that mortgages are usually too small to be wholesale instruments. The average mortgage loan is now about $200,000. This is far below the $5 million round lot established for commercial paper, for example. Many institutional investors do not want to deal in such small denominations.

The second problem with selling mortgages in the secondary market was that they were not standardized. They have different times to maturity, interest rates, and contract terms. That makes it difficult to bundle a large number of mortgages together.

Third, mortgage loans are relatively costly to service. Compare the servicing a mortgage loan requires to that of a corporate bond. The lender must collect monthly payments, often pay property taxes and insurance premiums, and service reserve accounts. None of this is required if a bond is purchased.

Finally, mortgages have unknown default risk. Investors in mortgages do not want to spend a lot of time evaluating the credit of borrowers. These problems inspired the creation of the **mortgage-backed security.**

What Is a Mortgage-Backed Security?

By the late 1960s, the secondary market for mortgages was declining, mostly because fewer veterans were obtaining guaranteed loans. The government reorganized Fannie Mae and also created two new agencies: the Government National Mortgage Association (GNMA, or Ginnie Mae) and the Federal Home Loan Mortgage Corporation (FHLMC, or Freddie Mac). These three agencies were now able

MINI-CASE

Are Fannie Mae and Freddie Mac Getting Too Big for Their Britches?

With the growth of Fannie Mae and Freddie Mac to immense proportions, there are growing concerns that these federally sponsored agencies could pose a threat to the health of the financial system. Fannie Mae and Freddie Mac either own or insure the risk on nearly 75% of America's residential mortgages. In fact, their publicly issued debt is well over half that issued by the federal government. A failure of either of these institutions would therefore pose a grave shock to the financial system. Because the federal government would be unlikely to stand by and just let them fail, there would be substantial costs to the taxpayer, as occurred in the S&L crisis.

Concerns about the safety and soundness of these institutions arise because they have much smaller capital-to-asset ratios than banks. Critics also are concerned that Fannie Mae and Freddie Mac have become so large that they wield too much political influence. In addition, these federally sponsored agencies have conflicts of interest because they have to serve two masters: As publicly traded corporations they are supposed to maximize profits for the shareholders, but as government agencies they are supposed to work in the interests of the public. These concerns have led to calls for reform of these agencies, with many calling for full privatization as was done voluntarily by the Student Loan Market Association (Sallie Mae) in the mid-1990s.

to offer new securities backed by both insured and, for the first time, uninsured mortgages (see the "Mini-Case" box).

An alternative to selling mortgages directly to investors is to create a new security backed by (secured by) a large number of mortgages assembled into what is called a *mortgage pool.* A trustee, such as a bank or a government agency, holds the mortgage pool, which serves as collateral for the new security. This process is called *securitization.* The most common type of mortgage-backed security is the **mortgage pass-through,** a security that has the borrower's mortgage payments pass through the trustee before being disbursed to the investors in the mortgage pass-through. If borrowers prepay their loans, investors receive more principal than expected. For example, investors may buy mortgage-backed securities on which the average interest rate is 9%. If interest rates fall and borrowers refinance at lower rates, the securities will pay off early. The possibility that mortgages will prepay and force investors to seek alternative investments, usually with lower returns, is called *prepayment risk.*

As is evident in Figure 3, the dollar volume of outstanding mortgage pools increased steadily since 1984. The reason that mortgage pools have become so popular is that they permit the creation of new securities (like mortgage pass-throughs) that make investing in mortgage loans much more efficient. For example, an institutional investor can invest in one large mortgage pass-through secured by a mortgage pool rather than investing in many small and dissimilar mortgage contracts.

Types of Pass-Through Securities

There are several types of mortgage pass-through securities: GNMA pass-throughs, FHLMC pass-throughs, and private pass-throughs.

Government National Mortgage Association (GNMA) Pass-Throughs Ginnie Mae began guaranteeing pass-through securities in 1968. Since then, the popularity of these instruments has increased dramatically.

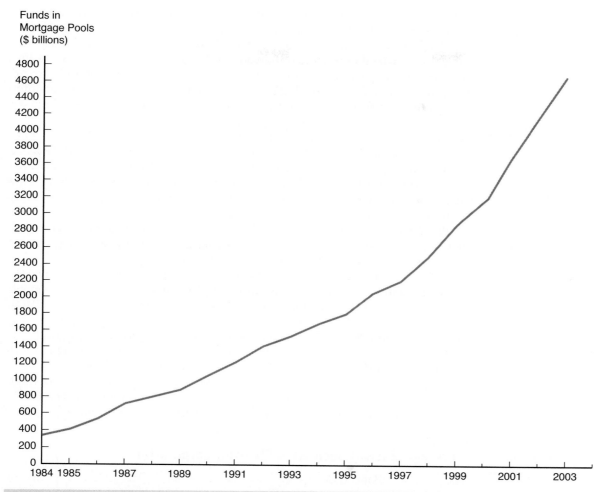

Funds in
Mortgage Pools
($ billions)

FIGURE 3 *Value of Mortgage Principal Held in Mortgage Pools, 1984–2003*
Source: Federal Reserve Bulletin, various issues, Table 1.54, Line 55.

A variety of financial intermediaries, including commercial banks and mortgage companies, originate Ginnie Mae mortgages. Ginnie Mae aggregates these mortgages into a pool and issues pass-through securities that are collateralized by the interest and principal payments from the mortgages. Ginnie Mae also guarantees the pass-through securities against default. The usual minimum denomination for pass-throughs is $25,000. The minimum pool size is $1 million. One pool may back up many pass-through securities.

Federal Home Loan Mortgage Corporation (FHLMC) Pass-Throughs Freddie Mac was created to assist savings and loan associations, which are not eligible to originate Ginnie Mae–guaranteed loans. Freddie Mac purchases mortgages for its own account and also issues pass-through securities similar to those issued by Ginnie Mae. Pass-through securities issued by Freddie Mac are called *participation certificates (PCs)*. Freddie Mac pools are distinct from Ginnie Mae pools in that they contain conventional (nonguaranteed) mortgages, are not federally insured, contain mortgages with different rates, are larger (ranging up to several hundred million dollars), and have a minimum denomination of $100,000.

A relatively recent innovation in the FHLMC pass-through market has been the **collateralized mortgage obligation (CMO).** CMOs are securities classified by when prepayment is likely to occur and are issued by Freddie Mac. These differ from traditional mortgage-backed securities in that they are offered in different maturity groups. These securities help reduce prepayment risk, which is a problem with other types of pass-through securities.

CMOs backed by a particular mortgage pool are divided into classes. When principal is repaid, the investors in the first class are paid first, then those in the second class, and so on. Investors choose a class that matches their maturity requirements. For example, if they will need cash from their investment in a few years, they purchase class 1 or 2 CMOs. If they want the investment to be long-term, they can purchase CMOs from the last class.

Even when an investor purchases a CMO, there are no guarantees about how long the investment will last. If interest rates fall significantly, many borrowers will pay off their mortages early by refinancing at lower rates.

Real estate mortgage investment conduits (REMICs) were authorized by the 1986 Tax Reform Act to allow originators to pass through all interest payments tax-free. Only their legal and tax consequences distinguish REMICs from CMOs.

Private Pass-Throughs (PIPs)   In addition to the agency pass-throughs, intermediaries in the private sector have offered privately issued pass-through securities. The first of these PIPs was offered by BankAmerica in 1977.

One mortgage market opportunity available to private institutions is for mortgages larger than the maximum size set by the government. These so-called *jumbo mortgages* are often bundled into pools to back private pass-throughs.

Mortgage-Backed Securities Clearing Corporation

The homepage of the MBSCC, www.ficc.com, gives information on this provider of automated post-trade comparison, netting, risk management, and pool-notification services to the mortgage-backed securities market.

The Mortgage-Backed Securities Clearing Corporation (MBSCC) was formed by the Midwest Stock Exchange in 1979 to automate the trading of mortgage-backed securities. Both parties to an exchange of mortgage-backed securities submit information to the MBSCC. The computer system checks that the information is in agreement and then confirms the trade.

Mortgage-Backed Mutual Funds   Mortgage-backed mutual funds offer individual investors an opportunity to invest in mortgage-backed securities despite their large denomination. Since mortgage-backed securities offer a higher return than Treasury bonds but are considered only slightly riskier, investors find them attractive. A typical mortgage-backed mutual fund will hold a combination of pass-throughs, CMOs, and Treasury bonds. Investors in these funds must be aware that when interest rates fall, many of the loans will pay off and be replaced with lower-interest mortgages. As a result, the fund's return will fall.

The Impact of Securitized Mortgages on the Mortgage Market

Mortgage-backed securities (also called **securitized mortgages**) have been a very important development in the financial markets in recent years. These new debt instruments compete for funds with government bonds, corporate bonds, and stocks. Securitized mortgages are low-risk securities that have higher yields than comparable government bonds and attract funds from around the world.

One benefit of the securitized mortgage is that it reduces the problems caused by regional lending institutions' sensitivity to local economic fluctuations. Because the loans are sold nationally and internationally, regional variations are no longer as great a source of risk to lenders.

A second benefit of the securitized mortgage is that borrowers now have access to a national capital market. In the early twentieth century, borrowers could choose among mortgages offered by only a few local lenders. The new securitized mortgages function much more like the rest of the capital markets. As a result, rates in the mortgage market follow other capital market rates much more closely.

Another benefit of the securitized mortgages is that an investor can enjoy the low-risk and long-term nature of investing in mortgages without having to service the loan.

A side effect of the development of securitized mortgages has been that mortgage rates are now more open to national and international influences. As a result, mortgage rates are more volatile than they were in the past.

Summary

1. Mortgages are long-term loans secured by real estate. Both individuals and businesses obtain mortgage loans to finance real estate purchases.

2. Mortgage interest rates are relatively low due to competition among various institutions that want to make mortgage loans. In addition to keeping interest rates low, the competition has resulted in a variety of terms and options for mortgage loans. For example, borrowers may choose to obtain a 30-year fixed-rate loan or an adjustable-rate loan that has its interest rate tied to the Treasury bill rate.

3. Several features of mortgage loans are designed to reduce the likelihood that the borrower will default. For example, a down payment is usually required so that the borrower will suffer a loss if the lender repossesses the property. Most lenders also require that the borrower purchase private mortgage insurance unless the loan-to-value ratio drops below 80%.

4. A variety of mortgages are available to meet the needs of most borrowers. The graduated-payment mortgage has low initial payments that increase over time. The growing-equity mortgage has increasing payments that cause the loan to be paid off in a shorter period than a level-payment loan. Shared-appreciation loans were used when interest rates and inflation were high. The lender shared in the increase in the real estate's value in exchange for lower interest rates.

5. Securitized mortgages have been growing in popularity in recent years as institutional investors look for attractive investment opportunities. Securitized mortgages are securities collateralized by a pool of mortgages. The payments on the pool are passed through to the investors. Ginnie Mae, Freddie Mac, and private banks issue pass-through securities.

Key Terms

amortized, *p. 296*

balloon loan, *p. 296*

collateralized mortgage obligation (CMO), *p. 312*

conventional mortgage, *p. 303*

discount points, *p. 297*

down payment, *p. 306*

insured mortgage, *p. 303*

lien, *p. 300*

mortgage, *p. 296*

mortgage-backed security, *p. 309*

mortgage pass-through, *p. 310*

private mortgage insurance (PMI), *p. 300*

reserve account, *p. 308*

securitized mortgage, *p. 312*

Questions

1. What distinguishes the mortgage markets from other capital markets?

2. Most mortgage loans once had balloon payments; now most current mortgage loans fully amortize. What is the difference between a balloon loan and an amortizing loan?

3. What features contribute to keeping long-term mortgage interest rates low?

4. What are discount points, and why do some mortgage borrowers choose to pay them?

5. What is a lien, and when is it used in mortgage lending?

6. What is the purpose of requiring that a borrower make a down payment before receiving a loan?

7. What kind of insurance do lenders usually require of borrowers who have less than an 80% loan-to-value ratio?

8. Lenders tend not to be as flexible about the qualifications required of mortgage customers as they can be for other types of bank loans. Why is this so?

9. Distinguish between conventional mortgage loans and insured mortgage loans.

10. Interpret what is meant when a lender quotes the terms on a loan as "floating with the T-bill plus 2 with caps of 2 and 6."

11. The monthly payments on both graduated-payment loans and growing-equity loans increase over time. Despite this similarity, the two types of loans have different purposes. What is the motivation behind each type of loan?

12. Many banks offer lines of credit that are secured by a second mortgage (or lien) on real property. These loans have been very popular among bank customers. Why are homeowners so willing to pledge their homes as security for these lines of credit?

13. The reverse annuity mortgage (RAM) allows retired people to live off the equity they have in their homes without having to sell the home. Explain how a RAM works.

14. What is a securitized mortgage?

15. Describe how a mortgage pass-through works.

Quantitative Problems

1. Compute the required monthly payment on an $80,000 30-year fixed-rate mortgage with a nominal interest rate of 5.80%. How much of the payment goes toward principal and interest during the first year?

2. Compute the face value of a 30-year fixed-rate mortgage with a monthly payment of $1100, assuming a nominal interest rate of 9%. If the mortgage requires 5% down, what is the maximum house price?

3. Consider a 30-year fixed-rate mortgage for $100,000 at a nominal rate of 9%. If the borrower wants to pay off the remaining balance on the mortgage after making the 12th payment, what is the remaining balance on the mortgage?

4. Consider a 30-year fixed-rate mortgage for $100,000 at a nominal rate of 9%. If the borrower pays an additional $100 with each payment, how fast will the mortgage be paid off?

5. Consider a 30-year fixed-rate mortgage for $100,000 at a nominal rate of 9%. An S&L issues this mortgage on April 1 and retains the mortgage in its portfolio. However, by April 2, mortgage rates have increased to a 9.5% nominal rate. By how much has the value of the mortgage fallen?

6. Consider a 30-year fixed-rate mortgage of $100,000 at a nominal rate of 9%. What is the duration of the loan? If interest rates increase to 9.5% immediately after the mortgage is made, how much is the loan worth to the lender?

7. Consider a 5-year balloon loan for $100,000. The bank requires a monthly payment equal to that of a 30-year fixed-rate loan with a nominal annual rate of 5.5%. How much will the borrower owe when the balloon payment is due?

8. A 30-year variable-rate mortgage offers a first-year teaser rate of 2%. After that, the rate starts at 4.5%, adjusted based on actual interest rates. The maximum rate over the life of the loan is 10.5%, and the rate can increase by no more than 200 basis points a year. If the mortgage is for $250,000, what is the monthly payment during the first year? Second year? What is the maximum payment during the fourth year? What is the maximum payment ever?

9. Consider a 30-year fixed-rate mortgage for $500,000 at a nominal rate of 6%. What is the difference in required payments between a monthly payment and a bimonthly payment (payments made twice a month)?

10. Consider the following options available to a mortgage borrower:

	Loan Amount	Interest Rate (%)	Type of Mortgage	Discount Points
Option 1	$100,000	6.75	30-yr fixed	none
Option 2	$150,000	6.25	30-yr fixed	1
Option 3	$125,000	6.0	30-yr fixed	2

What is the effective annual rate for each option?

11. Two mortgage options are available: a 15-year fixed-rate loan at 6% with no discount points, and a 15-year fixed-rate loan at 5.75% with 1 discount point. Assuming you will not pay off the loan early, which alternative is best for you? Assume a $100,000 mortgage.

12. Two mortgage options are available: a 30-year fixed-rate loan at 6% with no discount points, and a 30-year fixed-rate loan at 5.75% with 1 discount point. How long do you have to stay in the house for the mortgage with points to be a better option? Assume a $100,000 mortgage.

13. Two mortgage options are available: a 30-year fixed-rate loan at 6% with no discount points, and a 30-year fixed-rate loan at 5.75% with points. If you are planning on living in the house for 12 years, what is the most you are willing to pay in points for the 5.75% mortgage? Assume a $100,000 mortgage.

14. A mortgage on a house worth $350,000 requires what down payment to avoid PMI insurance?

15. Consider a shared-appreciation mortgage (SAM) on a $250,000 mortgage with yearly payments. Current market mortgage rates are high, running at 13%, 10% of which is annual inflation. Under the terms of the SAM, a 15-year mortgage is offered at 5%. After 15 years, the house must be sold, and the bank retains $400,000 of the sale price. If inflation remains at 10%, what are the cash flows to the bank? To the owner?

16. Consider a 30-year graduated-payment mortgage on a $250,000 mortgage with yearly payments. The stated interest rate on the mortgage is 6%, but the first annual payment is calculated assuming a 3% rate for the life of the loan. Thereafter, the annual payment will grow by 3.151222%. Develop an amortization table for this loan, assuming the initial payment is based on 30 years and the loan pays off in 15.

17. Consider a growing equity mortgage on a $250,000 mortgage with yearly payments. The stated interest rate on the mortgage is 6%, but this only applies to the first annual payment. Thereafter, the annual payment will grow by 5.5797%. Develop an amortization table for this loan, assuming the initial payment is based on 30 years and the loan pays off in 15 years.

18. Rusty Nail owns his house free and clear, and it's worth $400,000. To finance his retirement, he acquires a reverse annuity mortgage (RAM) from his bank. The RAM provides a fixed monthly payment over 15 years on 70% of the value of his home at 5%. The payments are made at the beginning of the month. How much does Rusty get each month?

19. You are working with a pool of 1000 mortgages. Each mortgage is for $100,000 and has a stated annual interest rate (nominal) of 6.00%. The mortgages are all 30-year fixed rate and fully amortizing. Mortgage servicing fees are currently 0.25% annually. Complete the following table.

	(1)	(2)	(3)	(4)	(5)	(6)	(7)
Month	Beginning Balance	Required Payment	Interest	Principal	Expected Prepayment	Servicing Fees	Ending Balance
1	100,000,000		500,000	99,551	16,665		
2					33,322		99,750,430

Web Exercises

The Mortgage Markets

1. You may be looking into acquiring a home in the near future. One common question you may have is how large a mortgage loan you can afford. Go to **http://interest.com** and click on "Mortgage Calculators." Choose the calculator labeled "How much mortgage loan you can afford to borrow." Input your expected future salary data. How large a mortgage can you afford according to the calculator? Increase your debt to see the impact on the amount of mortgage loan you will qualify for.

2. One of the more difficult decisions faced by homeowners is whether it pays to refinance a mortgage loan when rates have dropped. Go to **http://interest.com** and click on "Mortgage Calculators." Choose the calculator that computes how long it will take to recoup the costs of refinancing your mortgage loan. Assume you obtained a 30-year $130,000 loan four years ago at 7%. Now rates have dropped and your income is higher. Determine how much you will save if you get a new loan for 15 years at 6.25%.

CHAPTER 13

The Foreign Exchange Market

Preview

In the mid-1980s, American businesses became less competitive with their foreign counterparts; subsequently, in the 1990s and 2000s, their competitiveness increased. Did this swing in competitiveness occur primarily because American management fell down on the job in the 1980s and then got its act together afterwards? Not really. American business became less competitive in the 1980s because American dollars become worth more in terms of foreign currencies, making American goods more expensive relative to foreign goods. By the 1990s and 2000s, the value of the U.S. dollar had fallen appreciably from its highs in the mid-1980s, making American goods cheaper and American businesses more competitive.

The price of one currency in terms of another is called the **exchange rate**. It affects the economy and our daily lives, because when the U.S. dollar becomes more valuable relative to foreign currencies, foreign goods become cheaper for Americans and American goods become more expensive for foreigners. When the U.S. dollar falls in value, foreign goods become more expensive for Americans and American goods become cheaper for foreigners. We begin our study of international finance by examining the **foreign exchange market**, the financial market where exchange rates are determined.

As you can see in Figure 1, exchange rates are highly volatile. What factors explain the rise and fall of exchange rates? Why are exchange rates so volatile from day to day?

To answer these questions, we develop a modern view of exchange rate determination that explains recent behavior in the foreign exchange market.

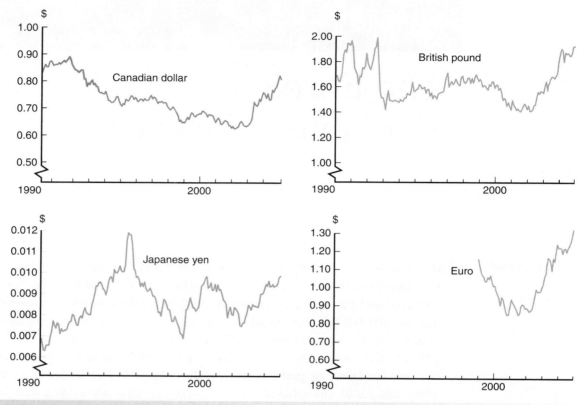

FIGURE 1 *Exchange Rates, 1990–2005*

Dollar prices of selected currencies. Note that a rise in these plots indicates a strengthening of the currency (weakening of the dollar).

Source: Federal Reserve (www.federalreserve.gov/releases/h10/hist).

Foreign Exchange Market

At www.ny.frb.org/ fxc/ you can obtain various reports and documents concerning the foreign exchange market.

Most countries of the world have their own currencies: The United States has its dollar; France, the euro; Brazil, its real; and India, its rupee. Trade between countries involves the mutual exchange of different currencies (or, more usually, bank deposits denominated in different currencies). When an American firm buys foreign goods, services, or financial assets, for example, U.S. dollars (typically, bank deposits denominated in U.S. dollars) must be exchanged for foreign currency (bank deposits denominated in the foreign currency).

The trading of currency and bank deposits denominated in particular currencies takes place in the foreign exchange market. The volume of these transactions worldwide averages over $1 trillion daily. Transactions conducted in the foreign exchange market determine the rates at which currencies are exchanged, which in turn determine the cost of purchasing foreign goods and financial assets.

What Are Foreign Exchange Rates?

There are two kinds of exchange rate transactions. The predominant ones, called **spot transactions,** involve the immediate (two-day) exchange of bank deposits. **Forward transactions** involve the exchange of bank deposits at some specified future date. The **spot exchange rate** is the exchange rate for the spot transaction, and the **forward exchange rate** is the exchange rate for the forward transaction.

When a currency increases in value, it experiences **appreciation;** when it falls in value and is worth fewer U.S. dollars, it undergoes **depreciation.** At the beginning of 1999, for example, the euro was valued at $1.18, and, as indicated in the "Following the News" box, on December 14, 2004, it was valued at $1.33. The euro *appreciated* by 13%: $(1.33 - 1.18)/1.18 = 0.127 = 13\%$. Conversely, we could say that the U.S. dollar, which went from a value of 0.85 euros per dollar in 1999 to a value of 0.75 euros per dollar by December 2004, *depreciated* by 12%: $(0.75 - 0.85)/0.85 = -0.12 = -12\%$.

Why Are Exchange Rates Important?

Exchange rates are important because they affect the relative price of domestic and foreign goods. The dollar price of French goods to an American is determined by the interaction of two factors: the price of French goods in euros and the euro/dollar exchange rate.

Suppose that Wanda the Winetaster, an American, decides to buy a bottle of 1961 (a very good year) Château Lafite Rothschild to complete her wine cellar. If the price of the wine in France is 1000 euros and the exchange rate is $1.33 to the euro, the wine will cost Wanda $1330 (= 1000 euros × $1.33/euro). Now suppose that Wanda delays her purchase by two months, at which time the euro has appreciated to $1.50 per euro. If the domestic price of the bottle of Lafite Rothschild remains 1000 euros, its dollar cost will have risen from $1333 to $1500.

The same currency appreciation, however, makes the price of foreign goods in France less expensive. At an exchange rate of $1.33 per euro, a Dell computer priced at $2000 costs Claude the Programmer 1504 euros; if the exchange rate increases to $1.50 per euro, the computer will cost only 1333 euros.

A depreciation of the euro lowers the cost of French goods in America but raises the cost of American goods in France. If the euro drops in value to $0.50, Wanda's bottle of Lafite Rothschild will cost her only $500 instead of $1330, and the Dell computer will cost Claude 4000 euros rather than 1504.

Such reasoning leads to the following conclusion: ***When a country's currency appreciates (rises in value relative to other currencies), the country's goods abroad become more expensive and foreign goods in that country become cheaper (holding domestic prices constant in the two countries). Conversely, when a country's currency depreciates, its goods abroad become cheaper and foreign goods in that country become more expensive.***

Appreciation of a currency can make it harder for domestic manufacturers to sell their goods abroad and can increase competition at home from foreign goods because they cost less. From 1980 to early 1985, the appreciating dollar hurt U.S. industries. For instance, the U.S. steel industry was hurt not just because sales of the more expensive American steel declined abroad but also because sales of relatively cheap foreign steel in the United States increased. Although appreciation of the U.S. dollar hurt some domestic businesses, American consumers

At http://quotes.ino.com/chart/, click on "Foreign Exchange" to get market rates and time charts for U.S. dollar to major world currencies.

THE *WALL STREET JOURNAL*: FOLLOWING THE NEWS

Foreign Exchange Rates

Foreign exchange rates are published daily and appear in the "Currency Trading" column of the *Wall Street Journal*. The entries from one such column, shown here, are explained in the text.

The first entry for the euro lists the exchange rate for the spot transaction (the spot exchange rate) on December 14, 2004, and is quoted in two ways:

$1.3305 per euro and 0.7516 euros per dollar. Americans generally regard the exchange rate with the euro as $1.3305 per euro, while the Europeans think of it as 0.7516 euros per dollar. The three entries immediately below some spot exchange rates give the rates for forward transactions (the forward exchange rates) that will take place 1 month, 3 months, and 6 months in the future.

CURRENCY TRADING

EXCHANGE RATES

December 14, 2004

The foreign exchange mid-range rates below apply to trading among banks in amounts of $1 million and more, as quoted at 4 P.M. Eastern time by Reuters and other sources. Retail transactions provide fewer units of foreign currency per dollar.

Country	U.S. $ equivalent Mon	Fri	Currency Per U.S. $ Mon	Fri
Argentina (Peso)-y	.3357	.3363	2.9789	2.9735
Australia (Dollar)	.7566	.7588	1.3217	1.3179
Bahrain (Dinar)	2.6525	2.6526	.3770	.3770
Brazil (Real)	.3616	.3627	2.7655	2.7571
Canada (Dollar)	.8095	.8143	1.2353	1.2280
1-month forward	.8094	.8141	1.2355	1.2284
3-months forward	.8092	.8140	1.2358	1.2285
6-months forward	.8097	.8144	1.2350	1.2279
Chile (Peso)	.001715	.001712	583.09	584.11
China (Renminbi)	.1208	.1208	8.2781	8.2781
Columbia (Peso)	.0004202	.0004168	2379.82	2399.23
Czech. Rep. (Koruna)				
Commercial rate	.04347	.04337	23.004	23.057
Denmark (Krone)	.1790	.1791	5.5866	5.5835
Ecuador (US Dollar)	1.0000	1.0000	1.0000	1.0000
Egypt (Pound)-y	.1610	.1606	6.2100	6.2251
Hong Kong (Dollar)	.1286	.1286	7.7760	7.7760
Hungary (Forint)	.005406	.005362	184.98	186.50
India (Rupee)	.02273	.02264	43.995	44.170
Indonesia (Rupiah)	.0001074	.0001078	9311	9276
Israel (Shekel)	.2308	.2299	4.3328	4.3497
Japan (Yen)	.009476	.009537	105.53	104.85
1-month forward	.009496	.009558	105.31	104.62
3-months forward	.009534	.009596	104.89	104.21
6-months forward	.009604	.009665	104.12	103.47
Jordan (Dinar)	1.4104	1.4104	.7090	.7090
Kuwait (Dinar)	3.3927	3.3934	.2948	.2947
Lebanon (Pound)	.0006607	.0006604	1513.55	1514.23
Malaysia (Ringgit)-b	.2632	.2632	3.7994	3.7994
Malta (Lira)	3.0821	3.0818	.3245	.3245
Mexico (Peso)				
Floating rate	.0888	.0888	11.2600	11.2651

Country	U.S. $ equivalent Mon	Fri	Currency Per U.S. $ Mon	Fri
New Zealand (Dollar)	.7090	.7096	1.4104	1.4092
Norway (Krone)	.1617	.1622	6.1843	6.1652
Pakistan (Rupee)	.01682	.01679	59.453	59.559
Peru (new Sol)	.3058	.3051	3.2701	3.2776
Philippines (Peso)	.01777	.01776	56.275	56.306
Poland (Zloty)	.3186	.3172	3.1387	3.1526
Russia (Ruble)-a	.03575	.03558	27.972	28.106
Saudi Arabia (Riyal)	.2667	.2667	3.7495	3.7495
Singapore (Dollar)	.6056	.6072	1.6513	1.6469
Slovak Rep. (Koruna)	.03432	.03416	29.138	29.274
South Africa (Rand)	.1749	.1744	5.7176	5.7339
South Korea (Won)	.0009447	.0009447	1058.54	1058.54
Sweden (Krona)	.1483	.1487	6.7431	6.7249
Switzerland (Franc)	.8664	.8665	1.1542	1.1541
1-month forward	.8677	.8678	1.1525	1.1523
3-months forward	.8701	.8702	1.1493	1.1492
6-months forward	.8746	.8746	1.1434	1.1434
Taiwan (Dollar)	.03076	.03095	32.510	32.310
Thailand (Baht)	.02534	.02536	39.463	39.432
Turkey (Lira)	.00000070	.00000070	1428571	1428571
U.K. (Pound)	1.9288	1.9288	.5185	.5195
1-month forward	1.9246	1.9207	.5196	.5206
3-months forward	1.9181	1.9140	.5213	.5225
6-months forward	1.9090	1.9051	.5238	.5249
United Arab (Dirham)	.2723	.2723	3.6724	3.6724
Uruguay (Peso)				
Financial	.03760	.03760	26.596	26.596
Venezuela (Bolivar)	.000521	.000521	1919.39	1919.39
SDR	1.5343	1.5301	.6518	.6536
Euro	1.3305	1.3306	.7516	.7515

Special Drawing Rights (SDR) are based on exchange rates for the U.S., British, and Japanese currencies. Source: International Monetary Fund.

a-Russian Central Bank rate.　b-Government rate.　y-Floating rate.

REUTERS GROUP PLC is the primary data provider for several statistical tables in The Wall Street Journal, including foreign stock quotations, futures and futures options prices, and foreign exchange tables. Reuters real-time data feeds are used to calculate various Dow Jones Indexes.

benefited because foreign goods were less expensive. Japanese videocassette recorders and cameras and the cost of vacationing in Europe fell in price as a result of the strong dollar.

How Is Foreign Exchange Traded?

You cannot go to a centralized location to watch exchange rates being determined; currencies are not traded on exchanges such as the New York Stock Exchange. Instead, the foreign exchange market is organized as an over-the-counter market in which several hundred dealers (mostly banks) stand ready to buy and sell deposits denominated in foreign currencies. Because these dealers are in constant telephone and computer contact, the market is very competitive; in effect, it functions no differently from a centralized market.

An important point to note is that while banks, companies, and governments talk about buying and selling currencies in foreign exchange markets, they do not take a fistful of dollar bills and sell them for British pound notes. Rather, most trades involve the buying and selling of bank deposits denominated in different currencies. So when we say that a bank is buying dollars in the foreign exchange market, what we actually mean is that the bank is buying deposits *denominated in dollars*.

Trades in the foreign exchange market consist of transactions in excess of $1 million. The market that determines the exchange rates in the "Following the News" box is not where one would buy foreign currency for a trip abroad. Instead, we buy foreign currency in the retail market from dealers such as American Express or from banks. Because retail prices are higher than wholesale, when we buy foreign exchange, we obtain fewer units of foreign currency per dollar than exchange rates in the box indicate.

Exchange Rates in the Long Run

Like the price of any good or asset in a free market, exchange rates are determined by the interaction of supply and demand. To simplify our analysis of exchange rates in a free market, we divide it into two parts. First, we examine how exchange rates are determined in the long run; then we use our knowledge of the long-run determinants of the exchange rate to help us understand how they are determined in the short run.

Law of One Price

The starting point for understanding how exchange rates are determined is a simple idea called the **law of one price:** If two countries produce an identical good, the price of the good should be the same throughout the world no matter which country produces it. Suppose that American steel costs $100 per ton and identical Japanese steel costs 10,000 yen per ton. For the law of one price to hold, the exchange rate between the yen and the dollar must be 100 yen per dollar ($0.01 per yen) so that one ton of American steel sells for 10,000 yen in Japan (the price of Japanese steel) and one ton of Japanese steel sells for $100 in the United States (the price of U.S. steel). If the exchange rate were 200 yen to the dollar, Japanese steel would sell for $50 per ton in the United States, or half the price of American steel, and American steel would sell for 20,000 yen per ton in Japan, twice the price of the Japanese steel. Because American steel is identical to Japanese steel and would be more expensive than Japanese steel in both countries, the demand for American steel would go to zero. Given a fixed dollar price for American steel, the resulting excess supply of American steel will be eliminated only if the exchange rate falls to 100 yen per dollar, making the price of American steel and Japanese steel the same in both countries.

EXAMPLE 1   *Law of One Price*

Recently, the yen price of Japanese steel has increased by 10% (to 11,000 yen) relative to the dollar price of American steel (unchanged at $100). By what amount must the dollar increase or decrease in value for the law of one price to hold true?

Solution

For the law of one price to hold, the exchange rate must rise to 110 yen per dollar, which is a 10% appreciation of the dollar.

The exchange rate rises to 110 yen so that the price of Japanese steel in dollars remains unchanged at $100 (= 11,000 yen/110 yen per dollar). In other words, the 10% depreciation of the yen (10% appreciation of the dollar) just offsets the 10% increase in the yen price of the Japanese steel.

Theory of Purchasing Power Parity

One of the most prominent theories of how exchange rates are determined is the **theory of purchasing power parity (PPP).** It states that exchange rates between any two currencies will adjust to reflect changes in the price levels of the two countries. The theory of PPP is simply an application of the law of one price to national price levels.

As Example 1 illustrates, if the law of one price holds, a 10% rise in the yen price of Japanese steel results in a 10% appreciation of the dollar. Applying the law of one price to the price levels in the two countries produces the theory of purchasing power parity, which maintains that if the Japanese price level rises 10% relative to the U.S. price level, the dollar will appreciate by 10%. As our U.S./Japanese example illustrates, *the theory of PPP suggests that if one country's price level rises relative to another's, its currency should depreciate (the other country's currency should appreciate).*

As you can see in Figure 2, this prediction of the theory of PPP is borne out in the long run. From 1973 to 2004, the British price level rose 85% relative to the U.S. price level, and as the theory of PPP predicts, the dollar appreciated against sterling, though by 37%, an amount smaller than the 85% increase predicted by PPP.

Yet, as the same figure indicates, PPP theory often has little predictive power in the short run. From early 1985 to the end of 1987, for example, the British price level rose relative to that of the United States. Instead of appreciating, as PPP theory predicts, the U.S. dollar actually depreciated by 40%. So even though PPP theory provides some guidance to the long-run movement of exchange rates, it is not perfect and in the short run is a particularly poor predictor. What explains PPP theory's failure to predict well?

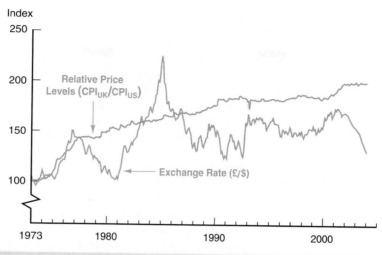

FIGURE 2 *Purchasing Power Parity, United States/United Kingdom, 1973–2004 (Index: March 1973 = 100)*

Source: http://www.statistics.gov.uk/statbase/.

Why the Theory of Purchasing Power Parity Cannot Fully Explain Exchange Rates

The PPP conclusion that exchange rates are determined solely by changes in relative price levels rests on the assumption that all goods are identical in both countries. When this assumption is true, the law of one price states that the relative prices of all these goods (that is, the relative price level between the two countries) will determine the exchange rate. The assumption that goods are identical may not be too unreasonable for American and Japanese steel, but is it a reasonable assumption for American and Japanese cars? Is a Toyota the equivalent of a Chevrolet?

Because Toyotas and Chevys are obviously not identical, their prices do not have to be equal. Toyotas can be more expensive relative to Chevys and both Americans and Japanese will still purchase Toyotas. Because the law of one price does not hold for all goods, a rise in the price of Toyotas relative to Chevys will not necessarily mean that the yen must depreciate by the amount of the relative price increase of Toyotas over Chevys.

PPP theory furthermore does not take into account that many goods and services (whose prices are included in a measure of a country's price level) are not traded across borders. Housing, land, and services such as restaurant meals, haircuts, and golf lessons are not traded goods. So even though the prices of these items might rise and lead to a higher price level relative to another country's, there would be little direct effect on the exchange rate.

Factors That Affect Exchange Rates in the Long Run

Our analysis indicates that relative price levels and additional factors affect the exchange rate. In the long run, there are four major factors: relative price levels, tariffs and quotas, preferences for domestic versus foreign goods, and productivity. We examine how each of these factors affects the exchange rate while holding the others constant.

The basic reasoning proceeds along the following lines: Anything that increases the demand for domestic goods relative to foreign goods tends to appreciate the domestic currency because domestic goods will continue to sell well even when the value of the domestic currency is higher. Similarly, anything that increases the demand for foreign goods relative to domestic goods tends to depreciate the domestic currency because domestic goods will continue to sell well only if the value of the domestic currency is lower.

Relative Price Levels In line with PPP theory, when prices of American goods rise (holding prices of foreign goods constant), the demand for American goods falls and the dollar tends to depreciate so that American goods can still sell well. By contrast, if prices of Japanese goods rise so that the relative prices of American goods fall, the demand for American goods increases, and the dollar tends to appreciate because American goods will continue to sell well even with a higher value of the domestic currency. ***In the long run, a rise in a country's price level (relative to the foreign price level) causes its currency to depreciate, and a fall in the country's relative price level causes its currency to appreciate.***

Trade Barriers Barriers to free trade such as **tariffs** (taxes on imported goods) and **quotas** (restrictions on the quantity of foreign goods that can be imported) can affect the exchange rate. Suppose that the United States imposes a tariff or a quota on Japanese steel. These trade barriers increase the demand for American steel, and the dollar tends to appreciate because American steel will still sell well even with a higher value of the dollar. ***Increasing trade barriers causes a country's currency to appreciate in the long run.***

Preferences for Domestic Versus Foreign Goods If the Japanese develop an appetite for American goods—say, for Florida oranges and American movies—the increased demand for American goods (exports) tends to appreciate the dollar because the American goods will continue to sell well even at a higher value for the dollar. Likewise, if Americans decide that they prefer Japanese cars to American cars, the increased demand for Japanese goods (imports) tends to depreciate the dollar. ***Increased demand for a country's exports causes its currency to appreciate in the long run; conversely, increased demand for imports causes the domestic currency to depreciate.***

Productivity If one country becomes more productive than other countries, businesses in that country can lower the prices of domestic goods relative to foreign goods and still earn a profit. As a result, the demand for domestic goods rises, and the domestic currency tends to appreciate. If, however, its productivity lags behind that of other countries, its goods become relatively more expensive, and the currency tends to depreciate. ***In the long run, as a country becomes more productive relative to other countries, its currency appreciates.***[1]

---

[1]A country might be so small that a change in productivity or the preferences for domestic or foreign goods would have no effect on prices of these goods relative to foreign goods. In this case, changes in productivity or changes in preferences for domestic or foreign goods affect the country's income but will not necessarily affect the value of the currency. In our analysis, we are assuming that these factors can affect relative prices and consequently the exchange rate.

TABLE 1 SUMMARY   *Factors That Affect Exchange Rates in the Long Run*

Factor	Change in Factor	Response of the Exchange Rate, E*
Domestic price level[†]	↑	↓
Trade barriers[†]	↑	↑
Import demand	↑	↓
Export demand	↑	↑
Productivity[†]	↑	↑

*Units of foreign currency per dollar: ↑ indicates currency appreciation; ↓, depreciation.
[†]Relative to other countries.

Note: Only increases (↑) in the factors are shown; the effects of decreases in the variables on the exchange rate are the opposite of those indicated in the "Response" column.

Study Guide

The trick to figuring out what long-run effect a factor has on the exchange rate is to remember the following: *If a factor increases the demand for domestic goods relative to foreign goods, the domestic currency will appreciate, and if a factor decreases the relative demand for domestic goods, the domestic currency will depreciate.* See how this works by explaining what happens to the exchange rate when any of the factors in Table 1 declines rather than increases.

Our long-run theory of exchange rate behavior is summarized in Table 1. We use the convention that the exchange rate E is quoted so that an appreciation of the currency corresponds to a rise in the exchange rate. In the case of the United States, this means that we are quoting the exchange rate as units of foreign currency per dollar (say, yen per dollar).[2]

Exchange Rates in the Short Run

We have developed a theory of the long-run behavior of exchange rates. However, if we are to understand why exchange rates exhibit such large changes (sometimes several percent) from day to day, we must develop a theory of how current exchange rates (spot exchange rates) are determined in the short run.

The key to understanding the short-run behavior of exchange rates is to recognize that an exchange rate is the price of domestic bank deposits (those denominated in the domestic currency) in terms of foreign bank deposits (those denominated in the foreign currency). Because the exchange rate is the price of

---

[2]In professional writing, many economists quote exchange rates as units of domestic currency per foreign currency so that an appreciation of the domestic currency is portrayed as a fall in the exchange rate. The opposite convention is used in the text here because it is more intuitive to think of an appreciation of the domestic currency as a rise in the exchange rate.

one asset in terms of another, the natural way to investigate the short-run determination of exchange rates is through an asset market approach that relies heavily on our analysis of the determinants of asset demand developed in Chapter 4. As you will see, however, the long-run determinants of the exchange rate we have just outlined also play an important role in the short-run asset market approach.[3]

Earlier approaches to exchange rate determination emphasized the role of import and export demand. The more modern asset market approach used here does not emphasize the flows of purchases of exports and imports over short periods because these transactions are quite small relative to the amount of domestic and foreign bank deposits at any given time. For example, foreign exchange transactions in the United States each year are well over 25 times greater than the amount of U.S. exports and imports. Thus over short periods such as a year, decisions to hold domestic or foreign assets play a much greater role in exchange rate determination than the demand for exports and imports does.

Comparing Expected Returns on Domestic and Foreign Deposits

In this analysis, we treat the United States as the home country, so domestic bank deposits are denominated in dollars. For simplicity, we use euros to stand for any foreign country's currency, so foreign bank deposits are denominated in euros. Our analysis of the determinants of asset demand suggests that the most important factor affecting the demand for domestic (dollar) deposits and foreign (euro) deposits is the expected return on these assets relative to each other. When Americans or foreigners expect the return on dollar deposits to be high relative to the return on foreign deposits, there is a higher demand for dollar deposits and a correspondingly lower demand for euro deposits. To understand how the demands for dollar and foreign deposits change, we need to compare the expected returns on dollar deposits and foreign deposits.

To illustrate further, suppose that dollar deposits have an interest rate (expected return payable in dollars) of i^D, and foreign bank deposits have an interest rate (expected return payable in the foreign currency, euros) of i^F. To compare the expected returns on dollar deposits and foreign deposits, investors must convert the returns into the currency unit they use.

First let us examine how François the Foreigner compares the returns on dollar deposits and foreign deposits denominated in his currency, the euro. When he considers the expected return on dollar deposits in terms of euros, he recognizes that it does not equal i^D; instead, the expected return must be adjusted for any expected appreciation or depreciation of the dollar. If the dollar were expected to appreciate by 7%, for example, the expected return on dollar deposits in terms of euros would be 7% higher because the dollar has become worth 7% more in terms of euros. Thus if the interest rate on dollar deposits is 10%, with an expected appreciation of the dollar of 7%, the expected return on dollar deposits in terms of euros is 17%: the 10% interest rate plus the 7% expected appreciation of the dollar. Conversely, if the dollar were expected to depreciate by 7% over the year,

---

[3]For a further description of the modern asset market approach to exchange rate determination that we use here, see Paul Krugman and Maurice Obstfeld, *International Economics*, 4th ed. (Reading, Mass.: Addison Wesley Longman, 1997).

the expected return on dollar deposits in terms of euros would be only 3%: the
10% interest rate minus the 7% expected depreciation of the dollar.

Writing the currency exchange rate (the spot exchange rate) as E_t and the
expected exchange rate for the next period as E_{t+1}^e, we can write the expected
rate of appreciation of the dollar as $(E_{t+1}^e - E_t)/E_t$. Our reasoning indicates that
the expected return on dollar deposits R^D in terms of foreign currency can be written as the sum of the interest rate on dollar deposits plus the expected appreciation of the dollar:[4]

$$R^D \text{ in terms of euros} = i^D + \frac{E_{t+1}^e - E_t}{E_t}$$

However, François's expected return on foreign deposits R^F in terms of euros
is just i^F. Thus in terms of euros, the relative expected return on dollar deposits
(that is, the difference between the expected return on dollar deposits and euro
deposits) is calculated by subtracting i^F from the expression just given to yield

$$\text{Relative } R^D = i^D - i^F + \frac{E_{t+1}^e - E_t}{E_t} \tag{1}$$

As the relative expected return on dollar deposits increases, foreigners will want
to hold more dollar deposits and fewer foreign deposits.

Next let us look at the decision to hold dollar deposits versus euro deposits
from Al the American's point of view. Following the same reasoning we used to
evaluate the decision for François, we know that the expected return on foreign
deposits R^F in terms of dollars is the interest rate on foreign deposits i^F plus the
expected appreciation of the foreign currency, equal to minus the expected appreciation of the dollar, $-(E_{t+1}^e - E_t)/E_t$; that is,

$$R^F \text{ in terms of dollars} = i^F - \frac{E_{t+1}^e - E_t}{E_t}$$

If the interest rate on euro deposits is 5%, for example, and the dollar is
expected to appreciate by 4%, then the expected return on euro deposits in terms
of dollars is 1%. Al earns the 5% interest rate, but he expects to lose 4% because

---

[4]This expression is actually an approximation of the expected return in terms of euros, which
can be more precisely calculated by thinking how a foreigner invests in the dollar deposit. Suppose
that François decides to put one euro into dollar deposits. First he buys $1/E_t$ of U.S. dollar deposits
(recall that E_t, the exchange rate between dollar and euro deposits, is quoted in euros per dollar),
and at the end of the period he is paid $(1 + i^D)(1/E_t)$ in dollars. To convert this amount into the
number of euros he expects to receive at the end of the period, he multiplies this quantity by E_{t+1}^e.
François's expected return on his initial investment of one euro can thus be written as
$(1 + i^D)E_{t+1}^e/E_t)$ minus his initial investment of one euro:

$$(1 + i^D)\left(\frac{E_{t+1}^e}{E_t}\right) - 1$$

which can be rewritten as

$$i^D\left(\frac{E_{t+1}^e}{E_t}\right) + \frac{E_{t+1}^e - E_t}{E_t}$$

which is approximately equal to the expression in the text because E_{t+1}^e/E_t is typically close to 1.

he expects the euro to be worth 4% less in terms of dollars as a result of the dollar's appreciation.

Al's expected return on the dollar deposits R^D in terms of dollars is just i^D. Hence in terms of dollars, the relative expected return on dollar deposits is calculated by subtracting the expression just given from i^D to obtain

$$\text{Relative } R^D = i^D - \left(i^F - \frac{E_{t+1}^e - E_t}{E_t} \right) = i^D - i^F + \frac{E_{t+1}^e - E_t}{E_t}$$

This equation is the same as the one describing François's relative expected return on dollar deposits (calculated in terms of euros). The key point here is that the relative expected return on dollar deposits is the same whether it is calculated by François in terms of euros or by Al in terms of dollars. Thus as the relative expected return on dollar deposits increases, both foreigners and domestic residents respond in exactly the same way—both will want to hold more dollar deposits and fewer foreign deposits.

Interest Parity Condition

We currently live in a world in which there is **capital mobility:** Foreigners can easily purchase American assets such as dollar deposits, and Americans can easily purchase foreign assets such as euro deposits. Because foreign bank deposits and American bank deposits have similar risk and liquidity and because there are few impediments to capital mobility, it is reasonable to assume that the deposits are perfect substitutes (that is, equally desirable). When capital is mobile and when bank deposits are perfect substitutes, if the expected return on dollar deposits is above that on foreign deposits, both foreigners and Americans will want to hold only dollar deposits and will be unwilling to hold foreign deposits. Conversely, if the expected return on foreign deposits is higher than on dollar deposits, both foreigners and Americans will not want to hold any dollar deposits and will want to hold only foreign deposits. For existing supplies of both dollar deposits and foreign deposits to be held, it must therefore be true that there is no difference in their expected returns; that is, the relative expected return in Equation 1 must equal zero. This condition can be rewritten as

$$i^D = i^F - \frac{E_{t+1}^e - E_t}{E_t} \tag{2}$$

This equation is called the **interest parity condition,** and it states that the domestic interest rate equals the foreign interest rate minus the expected appreciation of the domestic currency. Equivalently, this condition can be stated in a more intuitive way: The domestic interest rate equals the foreign interest rate plus the expected appreciation of the foreign currency. If the domestic interest rate is above the foreign interest rate, this means that there is a positive expected appreciation of the foreign currency, which compensates for the lower foreign interest rate.

EXAMPLE 2   *Interest Parity Condition*

If interest rates in the United States and Japan are 6% and 3%, respectively, what is the expected rate of appreciation of the foreign (Japanese) currency?

Solution

The expected appreciation of the foreign currency is 3%.

$$i^D = i^F - \frac{E^e_{t+1} - E_t}{E_t}$$

where

i^D = interest rate on dollars = 6%

i^F = interest rate on foreign currency = 3%

Thus

$$6\% = 3\% - \frac{E^e_{t+1} - E_t}{E_t}$$

$$-\frac{E^e_{t+1} - E_t}{E_t} = \text{rate of appreciation of the foreign currency} = 6\% - 3\% = 3\%$$

There are several ways to look at the interest parity condition. First, we should recognize that interest parity means simply that the expected returns are the same on both dollar deposits and foreign deposits. To see this, note that the left side of the interest parity condition (Equation 2) is the expected return on dollar deposits, while the right side is the expected return on foreign deposits, both calculated in terms of a single currency, the U.S. dollar. Given our assumption that domestic and foreign bank deposits are perfect substitutes (equally desirable), the interest parity condition is an equilibrium condition for the foreign exchange market. Only when the exchange rate is such that expected returns on domestic and foreign deposits are equal—that is, when interest parity holds—will the outstanding domestic and foreign deposits be willingly held.

Equilibrium in the Foreign Exchange Market

To see how the interest parity equilibrium condition works in determining the exchange rate, our first step is to examine how the expected returns on euro and dollar deposits change as the current exchange rate changes.

Expected Return on Euro Deposits   As we demonstrated earlier, the expected return in terms of dollars on foreign deposits R^F is the foreign interest rate minus the expected appreciation of the domestic currency: $i^F - (E^e_{t+1} - E_t)/E_t$. Suppose that the foreign interest rate i^F is 10% and that the expected exchange rate next period E^e_{t+1} is 1 euro per dollar. When the current exchange rate E_t is 0.95 euros per dollar, the expected appreciation of the dollar is $(1 - 0.95)/0.95 = 0.052 = 5.2\%$, so the expected return on euro deposits R^F in terms of dollars is 4.8% (equal to the 10% foreign interest rate minus the 5.2% dollar appreciation). This expected return when $E_t = 0.95$ euros per dollar is plotted as point A in Figure 3. At a higher current exchange rate of $E_t = 1$ euro per dollar, the expected appreciation of the dollar is zero because E^e_{t+1} also equals 1 euro per dollar. Hence R^F, the expected dollar return on euro deposits, is now just $i^F = 10\%$. This expected return on euro deposits when $E_t = 1$ euro per dollar is plotted as point B. At an even higher exchange rate of $E_t = 1.05$ euros per dollar, the expected change in the value of the dollar is now -4.8% [$= (1 - 1.05)/1.05 = -0.048$], so the expected dollar return on foreign deposits R^F has now risen to 14.8%

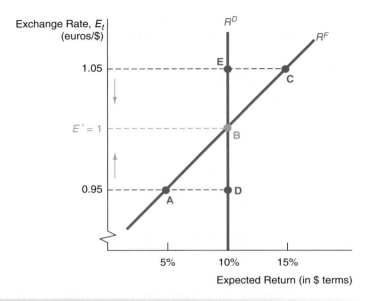

FIGURE 3 *Equilibrium in the Foreign Exchange Market*

Equilibrium in the foreign exchange market occurs at the intersection of the schedules for the expected return on euro deposits R^F and the expected return on dollar deposits R^D at point B. The equilibrium exchange rate is $E^* = 1$ euro per dollar.

[$= 10\% - (-4.8\%)$]. This combination of exchange rate and expected return on euro deposits is plotted as point C.

The curve connecting these points is the schedule for the expected return on euro deposits in Figure 3, labeled R^F, and as you can see, it slopes upward; that is, as the exchange rate E_t rises, the expected return on euro deposits rises. The intuition for this upward slope is that because the expected next-period exchange rate is held constant as the current exchange rate rises, there is less expected appreciation of the dollar. Hence a higher current exchange rate means a greater expected appreciation of the foreign currency in the future, which increases the expected return on foreign deposits in terms of dollars.

Expected Return on Dollar Deposits   The expected return on dollar deposits in terms of dollars R^D is always the interest rate on dollar deposits i^D no matter what the exchange rate is. Suppose that the interest rate on dollar deposits is 10%. The expected return on dollar deposits, whether at an exchange rate of 0.95, 1, or 1.05 euros per dollar, is always 10% (points D, B, and E). The line connecting these points is the schedule for the expected return on dollar deposits, labeled R^D in Figure 3.

Equilibrium   The intersection of the schedules for the expected return on dollar deposits R^D and the expected return on euro deposits R^F is where equilibrium occurs in the foreign exchange market; in other words,

$$R^D = R^F$$

At the equilibrium point B where the exchange rate E^* is 1 euro per dollar, the interest parity condition is satisfied because the expected returns on dollar deposits and on euro deposits are equal.

To see that the exchange rate actually heads toward the equilibrium exchange rate E^*, let's see what happens if the exchange rate is 1.05 euros per dollar, a value above the equilibrium exchange rate. As we can see in Figure 3, the expected return on euro deposits at point C is greater than the expected return on dollar deposits at point E. Since dollar and euro deposits are perfect substitutes, people will not want to hold any dollar deposits, and holders of dollar deposits will try to sell them for euro deposits in the foreign exchange market (which is referred to as "selling dollars" and "buying euros"). However, because the expected return on these dollar deposits is below that on euro deposits, no one holding euros will be willing to exchange them for dollar deposits. The resulting excess supply of dollar deposits means that the price of the dollar deposits relative to euro deposits must fall; that is, the exchange rate (amount of euros per dollar) falls as is illustrated by the downward arrow drawn in the figure at the exchange rate of 1.05 euros per dollar. The decline in the exchange rate will continue until point B is reached at the equilibrium exchange rate of 1 euro per dollar, where the expected return on dollar and euro deposits is now equalized.

Now let us look at what happens when the exchange rate is 0.95 euros per dollar, a value below the equilibrium level. Here the expected return on dollar deposits is greater than that on euro deposits. No one will want to hold euro deposits, and everyone will try to sell them to buy dollar deposits ("sell euros" and "buy dollars"), thus driving up the exchange rate as illustrated by the upward arrow. As the exchange rate rises, there is a smaller expected appreciation of the dollar and so a higher expected appreciation of the euro, thereby increasing the expected return on euro deposits. Finally, when the exchange rate has risen to $E^* = 1$ euro per dollar, the expected return on euro deposits has risen enough so that it again equals the expected return on dollar deposits.

Explaining Changes in Exchange Rates

To explain how an exchange rate changes over time, we have to understand the factors that shift the expected-return schedules for domestic (dollar) deposits and foreign (euro) deposits.

Shifts in the Expected-Return Schedule for Foreign Deposits

As we have seen, the expected return on foreign (euro) deposits depends on the foreign interest rate i^F minus the expected appreciation of the dollar $(E_{t+1}^e - E_t)/E_t$. Because a change in the current exchange rate E_t results in a movement along the expected-return schedule for euro deposits, factors that shift this schedule must work through the foreign interest rate i^F and the expected future exchange rate E_{t+1}^e. We examine the effect of changes in these factors on the expected-return schedule for euro deposits R^F, holding everything else constant.

Study Guide

To grasp how the expected-return schedule for euro deposits shifts, just think of yourself as an investor who is considering putting funds into foreign deposits. When a variable changes (i^F, for example), decide whether at a given level of the current exchange rate, holding all other variables constant, you would earn a higher or lower expected return on euro deposits.

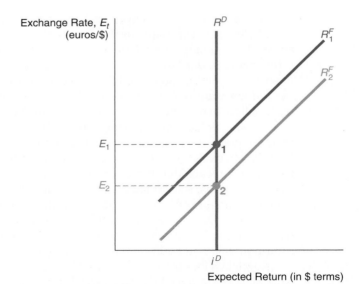

FIGURE 4 *Shifts in the Schedule for the Expected Return on Foreign Deposits R^F*

An increase in the expected return on foreign deposits, which occurs when either the foreign interest rate rises or the expected future exchange rate falls, shifts the schedule for the expected return on foreign deposits from R_1^F to R_2^F, and the exchange rate falls from E_1 to E_2.

Changes in the Foreign Interest Rate.   If the interest rate on foreign deposits i^F increases, holding everything else constant, the expected return on these deposits must also increase. Hence at a given exchange rate, the increase in i^F leads to a rightward shift in the expected-return schedule for euro deposits from R_1^F to R_2^F in Figure 4. As you can see in the figure, the outcome is a depreciation of the dollar from E_1 to E_2. An alternative way to see this is to recognize that the increase in the expected return on euro deposits at the original equilibrium exchange rate resulting from the rise in i^F means that people will want to buy euros and sell dollars, so the value of the dollar must fall. Our analysis thus generates the following conclusion: ***An increase in the foreign interest rate i^F shifts the R^F schedule to the right and causes the domestic currency to depreciate (E↓).***

Conversely, if i^F falls, the expected return on euro deposits falls, the R^F schedule shifts to the left, and the exchange rate rises. This yields the following conclusion: ***A decrease in i^F shifts the R^F schedule to the left and causes the domestic currency to appreciate (E↑).***

Changes in the Expected Future Exchange Rate   Any factor that causes the expected future exchange rate E_{t+1}^e to fall decreases the expected appreciation of the dollar and hence raises the expected appreciation of the euro. The result is a higher expected return on euro deposits, which shifts the schedule for the expected return on euro deposits to the right and leads to a decline in the exchange rate as in Figure 4. Conversely, a rise in E^e_{t+1} raises the expected appreciation of the dollar, lowers the expected return on foreign deposits, shifts the R^F schedule to the left, and raises the exchange rate. To summarize, *a rise in the expected future exchange rate shifts the R^F schedule to the left and causes an appreciation of the domestic currency; a fall in the expected future exchange rate shifts the R^F schedule to the right and causes a depreciation of the domestic currency.*

Summary Our analysis of the long-run determinants of the exchange rate indicates the factors that influence the expected future exchange rate: the relative price level, relative trade barriers, import demand, export demand, and relative productivity (refer to Table 1). The theory of purchasing power parity suggests that if a higher American price level relative to the foreign price level is expected to persist, the dollar will depreciate in the long run. A higher expected relative American price level should thus have a tendency to raise the expected return on euro deposits, shift the R^F schedule to the right, and lower the current exchange rate.

Similarly, the other long-run determinants of the exchange rate we discussed earlier can also influence the expected return on euro deposits and the current exchange rate. Briefly, the following changes will increase the expected return on euro deposits, shift the R^F schedule to the right, and cause a depreciation of the domestic currency, the dollar: (1) expectations of a rise in the American price level relative to the foreign price level, (2) expectations of lower American trade barriers relative to foreign trade barriers, (3) expectations of higher American import demand, (4) expectations of lower foreign demand for American exports, and (5) expectations of lower American productivity relative to foreign productivity.

Shifts in the Expected-Return Schedule for Domestic Deposits

Since the expected return on domestic (dollar) deposits is just the interest rate on these deposits i^D, this interest rate is the only factor that shifts the schedule for the expected return on dollar deposits.

Changes in the Domestic Interest Rate A rise in i^D raises the expected return on dollar deposits, shifts the R^D schedule to the right, and leads to a rise in the exchange rate, as is shown in Figure 5. Another way of seeing this is to recognize that a rise in i^D, which raises the expected return on dollar deposits, creates an excess demand for dollar deposits at the original equilibrium exchange rate, and the resulting purchases of dollar deposits cause an appreciation of the dollar. *A rise in the domestic interest rate i^D shifts the R^D schedule to the right and causes an appreciation of the domestic currency; a fall in i^D shifts the R^D schedule to the left and causes a depreciation of the domestic currency.*

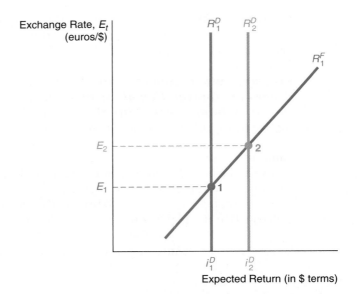

An increase in the expected return on dollar deposits i^D shifts the expected return on domestic (dollar) deposits from R_1^D to R_2^D, and the exchange rate rises from E_1 to E_2.

Study Guide

As a study aid, the factors that shift the R^F and R^D schedules and lead to changes in the current exchange rate E_t are listed in Table 2. The table shows what happens to the exchange rate when there is an increase in each of these variables, holding everything else constant. To give yourself practice, see if you can work out what happens to the R^F and R^D schedules and to the exchange rate if each of these factors falls rather than rises. Check your answers by seeing if you get the opposite change in the exchange rate to those indicated in Table 2.

Case

CHANGES IN THE EQUILIBRIUM EXCHANGE RATE: TWO EXAMPLES

Our analysis has revealed the factors that affect the value of the equilibrium exchange rate. Now we use this analysis to take a close look at the response of the exchange rate to changes in interest rates and money growth.

Changes in Domestic Interest Rates

Changes in domestic interest rates i^D are often cited as a major factor affecting exchange rates. For example, we see headlines in the financial press like this one: "Dollar Recovers As Interest Rates Edge Upward." But is the view presented in this headline always correct?

Not necessarily, because to analyze the effects of interest-rate changes, we must carefully distinguish the sources of the changes. The Fisher equation (Chapter 3) states that a (nominal) interest rate equals the *real* interest

TABLE 2 SUMMARY   *Factors That Shift the R^F and R^D Schedules and Affect the Exchange Rate*

Factor	Change in Factor	Response of the Exchange Rate, E_t	
Domestic interest rate, i^D	↑	↑	
Foreign interest rate, i^F	↑	↓	
Expected domestic price level*	↑	↓	
Expected trade barriers*	↑	↑	
Expected import demand	↑	↓	
Expected export demand	↑	↑	
Productivity*	↑	↑	

*Relative to other countries.

Note: Only increases (↑) in the factors are shown; the effects of decreases in the variables on the exchange rate are the opposite of those indicated in the "Response" column.

rate plus expected inflation: $i = i_r + \pi^e$. The Fisher equation indicates that an interest rate i can change for two reasons: Either the real interest rate i_r changes or the expected inflation rate π^e changes. The effect on the exchange rate is quite different, depending on which of these two factors is the source of the change in the nominal interest rate.

Suppose that the domestic real interest rate increases so that the nominal interest rate i^D rises while expected inflation remains unchanged. In this case, it is reasonable to assume that the expected appreciation of the dollar will be unchanged because expected inflation is unchanged, and so the expected return on foreign deposits will remain unchanged for any given exchange rate. The result is that the R^F schedule stays put and the R^D schedule shifts to the right, and we end up with the situation depicted in Figure 5, which analyzes an increase in i^D, holding everything else constant. Our model of the foreign exchange market produces the following result: **When domestic real interest rates rise, the domestic currency appreciates.**

When the nominal interest rate rises because of an increase in expected inflation, we get a different result from the one shown in Figure 5. The rise in expected domestic inflation leads to a decline in the expected appreciation of the dollar (a higher appreciation of the euro), which is typically thought to be larger than the increase in the domestic interest rate i^D.[5] As a result, at any given exchange rate, the expected return on foreign deposits rises more than the expected return on dollar deposits. Thus, as we see in Figure 6, the R^F schedule shifts to the right more than the R^D schedule, and the exchange rate falls. Our analysis leads to this conclusion: **When domestic interest rates rise due to an expected increase in inflation, the domestic currency depreciates.**

Because this conclusion is completely different from the one reached when the rise in the domestic interest rate is associated with a higher real interest rate, we must always distinguish between *real* and nominal measures when analyzing the effects of interest rates on exchange rates.

Changes in the Money Supply

Suppose that the Federal Reserve decides to increase the level of the money supply in order to reduce unemployment, which it believes to be excessive. The higher money supply will lead to a higher American price level in the long run and hence to a lower expected future exchange rate. The resulting decline in the expected appreciation of the dollar increases the expected return on foreign deposits at any given current exchange rate and so shifts the R^F schedule rightward from R_1^F to R_2^F in Figure 7. In addition, the higher money supply will lead to a higher real money supply M/P because the price level does not immediately increase in the short run. As suggested in Chapter 4, the resulting rise in the real money supply causes the domestic interest

---

[5]This conclusion is standard in asset market models of exchange rate determination; see Rudiger Dornbusch, "Expectations and Exchange Rate Dynamics," *Journal of Political Economy* 84 (1976): 1061–1076. It is also consistent with empirical evidence that suggests that nominal interest rates do not rise one-for-one with increases in expected inflation. See Frederic S. Mishkin, "The Real Interest Rate: An Empirical Investigation," *Carnegie-Rochester Conference Series on Public Policy* 15 (1981): 151–200; and Lawrence Summers, "The Nonadjustment of Nominal Interest Rates: A Study of the Fisher Effect," in *Macroeconomics, Prices and Quantities,* ed. James Tobin (Washington, D.C.: Brookings Institution, 1983), pp. 201–240.

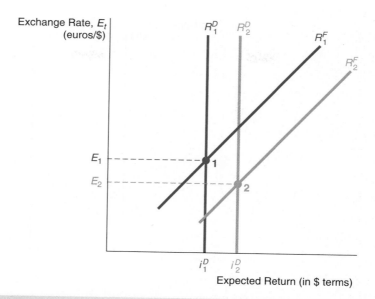

FIGURE 6 *Effect of a Rise in the Domestic Nominal Interest Rate as a Result of an Increase in Expected Inflation*

Because a rise in domestic expected inflation leads to a decline in expected dollar appreciation that is larger than the resulting increase in the domestic interest rate, the expected return on foreign deposits rises by more than the expected return on domestic (dollar) deposits. R^F shifts to the right more than R^D, and the equilibrium exchange rate falls from E_1 to E_2.

rate to fall from i_1^D to i_2^D, which lowers the expected return on domestic (dollar) deposits, shifting the R^D schedule in from R_1^D to R_2^D. As we can see in Figure 7, the result is a decline in the exchange rate from E_1 to E_2. The conclusion is this: ***A higher domestic money supply causes the domestic currency to depreciate.***

Exchange Rate Overshooting

Our analysis of the effect of a money supply increase on the exchange rate is not yet over—we still need to look at what happens to the exchange rate in the long run. A basic proposition in monetary theory, called **monetary neutrality,** states that in the long run, a onetime percentage rise in the money supply is matched by the same onetime percentage rise in the price level, leaving unchanged the real money supply and all other economic variables such as interest rates. An intuitive way to understand this proposition is to think of what would happen if our government announced overnight that an old dollar would now be worth 100 new dollars. The money supply in new dollars would be 100 times its old value and the price level would also be 100 times higher, but nothing in the economy would really have changed; interest rates and the real money supply would remain the same. Monetary neutrality tells us that in the long run, the rise in the money supply would not lead to a change in the domestic interest rate and so it would return to i_1^D in the long run, and the schedule for the expected return on domestic

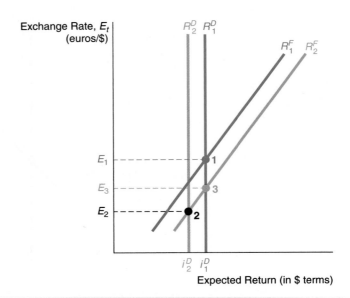

FIGURE 7 *Effect of a Rise in the Money Supply*

A rise in the money supply leads to a higher domestic price level in the long run, which in turn leads to a lower expected future exchange rate. The resulting decline in the expected appreciation of the dollar raises the expected return on foreign deposits, shifting the R^F schedule rightward from R_1^F to R_2^F. In the short run, the domestic interest rate i^D falls, shifting R^D from R_1^D to R_2^D. The short-run outcome is that the exchange rate falls from E_1 to E_2. In the long run, however, the interest rate returns to i_1^D, and R^D returns to R_1^D. The exchange rate thus rises from E_2 to E_3 in the long run.

deposits would return to R_1^D. As we can see in Figure 7, this means that the exchange rate would rise from E_2 to E_3 in the long run.

The phenomenon we have described here in which the exchange rate falls by more in the short run than it does in the long run when the money supply increases is called **exchange rate overshooting.** It is important because, as we will see in the following case, it can help explain why exchange rates exhibit so much volatility.

Another way of thinking about why exchange rate overshooting occurs is to recognize that when the domestic interest rate falls in the short run, equilibrium in the foreign exchange market means that the expected return on foreign deposits must be lower. With the foreign interest rate given, this lower expected return on foreign deposits means that there must be an expected appreciation of the dollar (depreciation of the euro) in order for the expected return on foreign deposits to decline when the domestic interest rate falls. This can occur only if the current exchange rate falls below its long-run value.

Case

WHY ARE EXCHANGE RATES SO VOLATILE?

The high volatility of foreign exchange rates surprises many people. Thirty or so years ago, economists generally believed that allowing exchange rates to be determined in the free market would not lead to large fluctuations in their values. Recent experience has proved them wrong. If we return to Figure 1, we see that exchange rates over the 1980–2004 period have been very volatile.

The asset market approach to exchange rate determination that we have outlined in this chapter gives a straightforward explanation of volatile exchange rates. Because expected appreciation of the domestic currency affects the expected return on foreign deposits, expectations about the price level, inflation, trade barriers, productivity, import demand, export demand, and the money supply play important roles in determining the exchange rate. When expectations about any of these variables change, our model indicates that there will be an immediate effect on the expected return on foreign deposits and therefore on the exchange rate. Since expectations on all these variables change with just about every bit of news that appears, it is not surprising that the exchange rate is volatile. In addition, we have seen that our exchange rate analysis produces exchange rate overshooting when the money supply increases. Exchange rate overshooting is an additional reason for the high volatility of exchange rates.

Because earlier models of exchange rate behavior focused on goods markets rather than asset markets, they did not emphasize changing expectations as a source of exchange rate movements, and so these earlier models could not predict substantial fluctuations in exchange rates. The failure of earlier models to explain volatility is one reason why they are no longer so popular. The more modern approach developed here emphasizes that the foreign exchange market is like any other asset market in which expectations of the future matter. The foreign exchange market, like other asset markets such as the stock market, displays substantial price volatility, and foreign exchange rates are notoriously hard to forecast.

Case

EXPLAINING THE RISE AND FALL OF THE DOLLAR IN THE 1980S

In the chapter preview we mentioned that the dollar was weak in the late 1970s, rose substantially from 1980 to 1985, and declined thereafter. We can use our analysis of the foreign exchange market to understand exchange rate movements and help explain the dollar's rise and fall in the 1980s.

Some important information for tracing the dollar's changing value is presented in Figure 8, which plots measures of real and nominal interest rates and the value of the dollar in terms of a basket of foreign currencies (called an **effective exchange rate index**). We can see that the value of the dollar and the measure of real interest rates rise and fall together. In the late 1970s, real interest rates were at low levels, and so was the value of the dollar. Beginning in 1980, however, real interest rates in the United States began to climb sharply, and at the same time so did the dollar. After 1984, the real interest rate declined substantially, as did the dollar.

Our model of exchange rate determination helps explain the rise and fall in the dollar in the 1980s. As Figure 5 indicates, a rise in the U.S. real interest rate raises the expected return on dollar deposits while leaving the expected return on foreign deposits unchanged. The resulting increased demand for dollar deposits then leads to purchases of dollar deposits (and sales of foreign deposits), which raise the exchange rate. This is exactly what

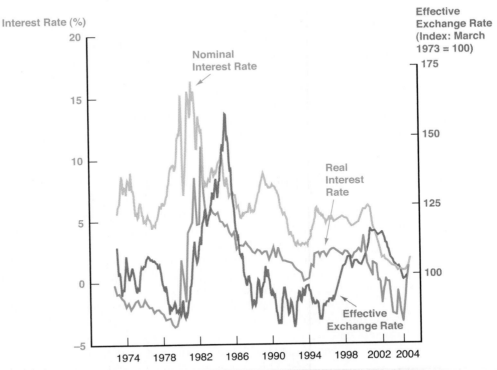

FIGURE 8 *Value of the Dollar and Interest Rates, 1973–2004*

Source: http://www.federalreserve.gov/releases/H10/summary/indexbc_m.txt.

occurred in the 1980–1984 period. The subsequent fall in U.S. real interest rates then lowered the expected return on dollar deposits relative to foreign deposits, and the resulting sales of dollar deposits (and purchases of foreign deposits) lowered the exchange rate.

The plot of *nominal* interest rates in Figure 8 also demonstrates that the correspondence between nominal interest rates and exchange rate movements is not nearly as close as that between *real* interest rates and exchange rate movements. This is also exactly what our analysis predicts. The rise in nominal interest rates in the late 1970s was not reflected in a corresponding rise in the value of the dollar; indeed, the dollar actually fell in the late 1970s. Figure 8 explains why the rise in nominal rates in the late 1970s did not produce a rise in the dollar. As a comparison of the real and nominal interest rates in the late 1970s indicates, the rise in nominal interest rates reflected an increase in expected inflation and not an increase in real interest rates. As our analysis in Figure 6 demonstrates, the rise in nominal interest rates stemming from a rise in expected inflation should lead to a decline in the dollar, and that is exactly what transpired.

If there is a moral to the story, it is that a failure to distinguish between real and nominal interest rates can lead to poor predictions of exchange rate movements: The weakness of the dollar in the late 1970s and the strength of the dollar in the early 1980s can be explained by movements in *real* interest rates but not by movements in *nominal* interest rates.

Case

THE EURO'S FIRST SIX YEARS

With much fanfare, the euro debuted on January 1, 1999, at an exchange rate of 1.18 dollars per euro. Despite initial hopes that the euro would be a strong currency, it actually proved to be weak, declining 30% to a low of 83 cents per euro in October 2000, and then began a steady recovery to around the $1.30 level by the end of 2004. What explains the weakness of the euro in its first two years and the subsequent recovery thereafter?

The previous case showed how changes in real interest rates are an important factor determining the exchange rate. When the domestic real interest rate falls relative to the foreign real interest rate, then the domestic currency declines in value. Indeed, this is exactly what has happened to the euro. While the euro was coming into existence, European economies were experiencing only a slow recovery from recession, thus causing both real and nominal interest rates to fall. In contrast, in 1999 and 2000, the United States experienced very rapid growth, substantially higher than Europe, which kept real and nominal interest rates high and substantially above their European counterparts. As in the analysis of the previous case, the falling, low real interest rates in Europe relative to those in the United States led to a decline in the value of the euro.

With the slowing of the U.S. economy after the recession started in the spring of 2001, both real and nominal interest rates in the United States began to fall to extremely low levels, thereby weakening the dollar relative to the euro.

Case

The *Wall Street Journal*

THE "CURRENCY TRADING" COLUMN

Now that we have an understanding of how exchange rates are determined, we can use our analysis to understand discussions about developments in the foreign exchange market reported in the financial press.

Every day, the *Wall Street Journal* reports on developments in the foreign exchange market on the previous business day in its "Currency Trading" column, an example of which is presented in the "Following the News" box on p. 343.

The column indicates that the dollar fell against the yen but was effectively unchanged against other currencies. Our analysis of the foreign exchange market can explain these developments.

The column indicates that the dollar initially rose relative to European currencies because of soft data in Europe. The view that the economy in Europe would not be strong suggested that interest rates in Europe would be lower, which would lower the expected return on foreign deposits, thereby shifting the R^F curve to the left, which would lead to a rise in the dollar relative to European currencies. Shortly after New York trading got underway, the announcement that retail sales were weak in the United States suggested that interest rates would be lower in the United States, which would shift the R^D curve to the left and cause a fall in the dollar. In addition, announcement of a larger current account deficit indicated that either the demand for U.S. exports had fallen or the demand for foreign imports had risen, both of which indicated that the dollar would fall in the future. The larger current account deficit thus increased the expected return on foreign deposits, thereby shifting the R^F curve to the right, which leads to a decline in the dollar. The announcements of weak retail sales and a larger current account deficit thus worked to lower the value of the dollar, which offset the earlier rise due to the soft data in Europe, leaving the dollar even against the European currencies. However, because there was no announcement of softer data for Japan, the later announcements that led to a fall in the dollar were not offset, and so the dollar ended up lower against the Japanese yen.

The Practicing Manager

PROFITING FROM FOREIGN EXCHANGE FORECASTS

Managers of financial institutions care a great deal about what foreign exchange rates will be in the future because these rates affect the value of assets on their balance sheet that are denominated in foreign currencies. In addition, financial institutions often engage in trading foreign exchange, both for their own account and for their customers. Forecasts of future foreign exchange rates can thus have a big impact on the profits that financial institutions make on their foreign exchange trading operations.

Managers of financial institutions obtain foreign exchange forecasts either by hiring their own staff economists to generate them or by purchasing forecasts from other financial institutions or economic forecasting firms. In predicting exchange rate movements, forecasters look at the factors mentioned in this chapter. For example, if they expect domestic real interest rates to rise, they will predict, in line with our analysis, that the domestic currency will appreciate; conversely, if they expect domestic inflation to increase, they will predict that the domestic currency will depreciate.

Managers of financial institutions, particularly those engaged in international banking, rely on foreign exchange forecasts to make decisions about which assets denominated in foreign currencies they should hold. For example, if a financial institution manager has a reliable forecast that the euro will appreciate in the future but the yen will depreciate, the manager will want to sell off assets denominated in yen and instead purchase assets denominated in euros. Alternatively, the manager might instruct loan officers to make more loans denominated in euros and fewer loans denominated in yen. Likewise, if the yen is forecast to appreciate and the euro to depreciate, the manager would want to switch out of euro-denominated assets into yen-denominated assets and would want to make more loans in yen and fewer in euros.

If the financial institution has a foreign exchange trading operation, a forecast of an appreciation of the yen means that the financial institution manager should tell foreign exchange traders to buy yen. If the forecast turns out to be correct, the higher value of the yen means that the trader can sell the yen in the future and pocket a tidy profit. If the euro is forecast to depreciate, the trader can sell euros and buy them back in the future at a lower price if the forecast turns out to be correct, and again the financial institution will make a profit.

Accurate foreign exchange rate forecasts can thus help a financial institution manager generate substantial profits for the institution. Unfortunately, exchange rate forecasters are no more or less accurate than other economic forecasters, and they often make large errors. Reports on foreign exchange rate forecasts and how well forecasters are doing appear from time to time in the *Wall Street Journal* and in the trade magazine *Euromoney*.

THE *WALL STREET JOURNAL*: FOLLOWING THE NEWS

The "Currency Trading" Column

The "Currency Trading" column appears daily in the *Wall Street Journal*; an example is presented here. It is found in the third section, "Money and Investing."

Dollar Ends Lower Against Yen But Is Even Against Other Rivals

CURRENCY TRADING

By Steven Vames
Dow Jones Newswires

The dollar lost ground against the yen in a reversal of Monday's rally, but remained little changed against the euro and other major currencies.

Though the session was marked by some modest swings for the dollar due to weak economic data first in Germany and the United Kingdom, then in the U.S., currency analysts said that on the whole, the figures didn't lend much clarity to a directionless market.

Gains for the yen were mostly attributable to technical factors, said traders. The dollar had rallied against those currencies Monday, but selling was triggered when the dollar failed to extend its gains above day-earlier highs of 110.37 yen.

Late yesterday afternoon, the euro was at $1.2261, steady from $1.2252 late Monday. The dollar was at 109.60 yen, down from 110.07 yen. The pound traded at $1.7972 from $1.7951, while the dollar fetched 1.2587 Swiss francs, down slightly from 1.2598 francs.

The dollar advanced against the euro and other European currencies overnight, after the German ZEW Index of economic sentiment slipped to 38.4 in September from 45.3 in August to reach its lowest level since June 2003. The pound, too, was hit by soft data in early European trading. U.K. consumer-price inflation came in at 1.3% year-over-year, compared with an expected 1.4%.

But the dollar fell shortly after New York trading got underway when the second-quarter U.S. current-account deficit came in wider than expected and retail sales showed a decline in August.

"It's like we're in a competition to see who has worse news," said Grant Wilson, senior foreign-exchange trader at Mellon Bank in Pittsburgh.

Following the release of the two sets of U.S. data, which came concurrently at 8:30 a.m. EDT, the euro popped to a session high of $1.2295. Its overnight low in London trading had been $1.223.

While the current-account deficit was expected to have widened and retail sales were forecast to be weak, both came in somewhat worse than expected. But the deviation from expectations was generally immaterial and served mainly to validate recent weakness in the dollar, said Mr. Wilson.

"For the most part, the market had been expecting pretty bad numbers. The initial reaction was to sell dollars, but it's since come back a little bit," he added.

The yen had rallied ahead of reports in U.S. and Europe, based on low expectations that were eventually confirmed. Beyond that, technical strength helped it continue to gain ground against the dollar.

Source: Wall Street Journal, September 15, 2004, p. C5.

Summary

1. Foreign exchange rates (the price of one country's currency in terms of another's) are important because they affect the price of domestically produced goods sold abroad and the cost of foreign goods bought domestically.

2. The theory of purchasing power parity suggests that long-run changes in the exchange rate between two countries are determined by changes in the relative price levels of the two countries. Other factors that affect exchange rates in the long run are tariffs and quotas, import demand, export demand, and productivity.

3. Exchange rates are determined in the short run by the interest parity condition, which states that the expected return on domestic deposits is equal to the expected return on foreign deposits.

4. Any factor that changes the expected returns on domestic or foreign deposits will lead to changes in the exchange rate. Such factors include changes in the interest rates on domestic and foreign deposits as well as changes in any of the factors that affect the long-run exchange rate and hence the expected future exchange rate. Changes in the money supply lead to exchange rate overshooting, causing the exchange rate to change by more in the short run than in the long run.

5. The asset market approach to exchange rate determination can explain both the volatility of exchange rates and the rise of the dollar in the 1980–1984 period and its subsequent fall.

6. Forecasts of foreign exchange rates are very valuable to managers of financial institutions because these rates influence decisions about which assets denominated in foreign currencies the institutions should hold and what kinds of trades should be made by their traders in the foreign exchange market.

Key Terms

appreciation, *p. 319*
capital mobility, *p. 328*
depreciation, *p. 319*
effective exchange rate index, *p. 339*
exchange rate, *p. 317*
exchange rate overshooting, *p. 338*

foreign exchange market, *p. 317*
forward exchange rate, *p. 319*
forward transaction, *p. 319*
interest parity condition, *p. 328*
law of one price, *p. 321*

monetary neutrality, *p. 337*
quota, *p. 324*
spot exchange rate, *p. 319*
spot transaction, *p. 319*
tariff, *p. 324*
theory of purchasing power parity (PPP), *p. 322*

Questions

1. When the euro appreciates, are you more likely to drink California or French wine?

2. "A country is always worse off when its currency is weak (falls in value)." Is this statement true, false, or uncertain? Explain your answer.

3. Check in a newspaper the exchange rates for the foreign currencies listed in the "Following the News" box on page 320. Which of these currencies have appreciated and which have depreciated since December 14, 2004?

4. If the European price level rises by 5% relative to the price level in the United States, what does the theory of purchasing power parity predict will happen to the value of the euro in terms of dollars?

5. If the demand for a country's exports falls at the same time that tariffs on imports are raised, will the country's currency tend to appreciate or depreciate in the long run?

6. In the mid- to late 1970s, the yen appreciated relative to the dollar even though Japan's inflation rate was higher than America's. How can this be explained by an improvement in the productivity of Japanese industry relative to American industry?

Predicting the Future

Answer the remaining problems by drawing the appropriate exchange market diagrams.

7. The president of the United States announces that he will reduce inflation with a new anti-inflation program. If the public believes him, predict what will happen to the U.S. exchange rate.

8. If the British central bank prints money to reduce unemployment, what will happen to the value of the pound in the short run and the long run?

9. If several European governments unexpectedly announce that they will be imposing higher tariffs on foreign goods one year from now, what will happen to the value of the euro today?

10. If nominal interest rates in America rise but real interest rates fall, predict what will happen to the U.S. exchange rate.

11. If American auto companies make a breakthrough in automobile technology and are able to produce a car that gets 60 miles to the gallon, what will happen to the U.S. exchange rate?

12. If Americans go on a spending spree and buy twice as much French perfume, Japanese TVs, English sweaters, Swiss watches, and Italian wine, what will happen to the value of the U.S. dollar?

13. If expected inflation drops in Europe so that interest rates fall there, predict what will happen to the U.S. exchange rate.

14. If the European central bank decides to contract the money supply in order to fight inflation, what will happen to the value of the U.S. dollar?

15. If there is a strike in France, making it harder to buy French goods, what will happen to the value of the euro?

Quantitative Problems

1. A German sports car is selling for 70,000 euros. What is the dollar price in the United States for the German car if the exchange rate is 0.90 euros per dollar?

2. An investor in England purchased a 91-day T-bill for $987.65. At that time, the exchange rate was $1.75 per pound. At maturity, the exchange rate was $1.83 per pound. What was the investor's holding period return in pounds?

3. An investor in Canada purchased 100 shares of IBM on January 1 at $93.00 per share. IBM paid an annual dividend of $0.72 on December 31. The stock was sold that day as well for $100.25. The exchange rate was $0.68 per Canadian dollar on January 1 and $0.71 per Canadian dollar on December 31. What is the investor's total return in Canadian dollars?

4. The current exchange rate is 0.93 euro per dollar, but you believe the dollar will decline to 0.85 euro per dollar. If a euro-denominated bond is yielding 2%, what return do you expect in U.S. dollars?

5. The six-month forward rate between the British pound and the U.S. dollar is $1.75 per pound. If six-month rates are 3% in the United States and 150 basis points higher in England, what is the current exchange rate?

6. If the Canadian dollar to U.S. dollar exchange rate is 1.28 and the British pound to U.S. dollar exchange rate is 0.62, what must the Canadian dollar to British pound exchange rate be?

7. The New Zealand dollar to U.S. dollar exchange rate is 1.36, and the British pound to U.S. dollar exchange rate is 0.62. If you find that the British pound to New Zealand dollar were trading at 0.49, what would you do to earn a riskless profit?

8. In 1999, the euro was trading at $0.90 per euro. If the euro is now trading at $1.16 per euro, what is the percentage change in the euro's value? Is this an appreciation or depreciation?

9. The Brazilian real is trading at 0.375 real per U.S. dollar. What is the U.S. dollar per real exchange rate?

10. The Mexican peso is trading at 10 pesos per dollar. If the expected U.S. inflation rate is 2% while the expected Mexican inflation rate is 23% over the next year, what is the expected exchange rate in one year?

11. The current exchange rate between the United States and Britain is $1.825 per pound. The six-month forward rate between the British pound and the U.S. dollar is $1.79 per pound. What is the percentage difference between current six-month U.S. and British interest rates?

12. The current exchange rate between the Japanese yen and the U.S. dollar is 120 yen per dollar. If the dollar is expected to depreciate by 10% relative to the yen, what is the new expected exchange rate?

13. If the price level recently increased by 20% in England while falling by 5% in the United States, how much must the exchange rate change if PPP holds? Assume that the current exchange rate is 0.55 pound per dollar.

14. A one-year CD in Europe is currently paying 5%, and the exchange rate is currently 0.99 euros per dollar. If you believe the exchange rate will be 1.04 euros per dollar one year from now, what is the expected return in terms of dollars?

15. Short-term interest rates are 2% in Japan and 4% in the United States. The current exchange rate is

120 yen per dollar. What is the expected forward exchange rate?

16. Short-term interest rates are 2% in Japan and 4% in the United States. The current exchange rate is 120 yen per dollar. If you can enter into a forward exchange rate of 115 yen per dollar, how can you arbitrage the situation?

17. The interest rate in the United States is 4%, and the euro is trading at 1 euro per dollar. The euro is expected to depreciate to 1.1 euros per dollar. Calculate the interest rate in Germany.

Web Exercises

The Foreign Exchange Market

1. The Federal Reserve maintains a website that lists the exchange rate between the U.S. dollar and many other currencies. Go to **http://www.federal reserve.gov/releases/H10/hist/**. Go to the historical data from 1999 on and find the euro. What has been the annual percentage change in the euro/dollar exchange rate for each year since the euro's introduction?

2. International travelers and businesspeople frequently need to accurately convert from one currency to another. It is often easy to find the rate needed to convert the U.S. dollar into another currency. It can more difficult to find cross-conversion rates. Go to **http://www.oanda.com/convert/ classic**. This site lets you convert from any currency into any other currency. How many Lithuanian litas can you currently buy with one Chilean peso?

CHAPTER 14

The International Financial System

Preview

Thanks to the growing interdependence between the U.S. economy and the economies of the rest of the world, the international financial system now plays a more prominent role in economic events in the United States. In this chapter, we see how fixed and managed exchange rate systems work and how they can provide substantial profit opportunities for financial institutions. We also look at the controversies over what role capital controls and the International Monetary Fund should play in the international financial system.

Intervention in the Foreign Exchange Market

In Chapter 13 we analyzed the foreign exchange market as if it were a completely free market that responds to all market pressures. However, the foreign exchange market, like many others, is not free of government intervention; central banks regularly engage in international financial transactions called **foreign exchange interventions** in order to influence exchange rates. In our current international environment, exchange rates fluctuate from day to day, but central banks attempt to influence their countries' exchange rates by buying and selling currencies. The exchange rate analysis we developed in Chapter 13 is used here to explain the impact that central bank intervention has on the foreign exchange market.

Foreign Exchange Intervention and the Money Supply

The first step in understanding how central bank intervention in the foreign exchange market affects exchange rates is to see the impact on the monetary base and the money supply from a central bank sale in the foreign exchange market of some of its holdings of assets denominated in a foreign currency (called **international reserves**). Suppose that the Fed decides to sell $1 billion of its foreign assets in exchange for $1 billion of U.S. currency. (This transaction is done at the foreign exchange desk at the Federal Reserve Bank of New York—see the "Inside the Fed" box.) The Fed's purchase of dollars has two effects. First, it

347

reduces the Fed's holding of international reserves by $1 billion. Second, because its purchase of currency removes it from the hands of the public, currency in circulation falls by $1 billion. To see this we make use of a simplified balance sheet called a **T-account,** with lines in the form of a T, that lists only the changes that occur in balance sheet items starting from an initial balance sheet position. The T-account for the Federal Reserve illustrating this transaction is as follows:

Federal Reserve System		
Assets	**Liabilities**	
Foreign assets (international reserves) −$1 billion	Currency in circulation	−$1 billion

Because the monetary base is made up of currency in circulation plus reserves, this decline in currency implies that the monetary base has fallen by $1 billion.

   If instead of paying for the foreign assets sold by the Fed with currency, the persons buying the foreign assets pay for them by checks written on accounts at domestic banks, then the Fed deducts the $1 billion from the deposit accounts these banks have with the Fed. The result is that deposits with the Fed (reserves) decline by $1 billion, as shown in the following T-account.

INSIDE THE FED

A Day at the Federal Reserve Bank of New York's Foreign Exchange Desk

Although the U.S. Treasury is primarily responsible for foreign exchange policy, decisions to intervene in the foreign exchange market are made jointly by the U.S. Treasury and the Federal Reserve as represented by the FOMC (Federal Open Market Committee). The actual conduct of foreign exchange intervention is the responsibility of the foreign exchange desk at the Federal Reserve Bank of New York, which is right next to the open market desk.

   Dino Kos, the head of the markets group at the New York Fed, supervises the traders and analysts who follow developments in the foreign exchange market. Every morning at 7:30, a trader on Kos's staff who has arrived at the New York Fed in the predawn hours speaks on the telephone with counterparts at the U.S. Treasury and provides an update on overnight activity in overseas financial and foreign exchange markets. Later in the morning, at 9:30, Kos and his staff hold a conference call with senior staff at the Board of Governors of the Federal Reserve in Washington. In the afternoon, at 2:30, they have a second conference call, which is a joint briefing of officials at the board and the Treasury. Although by statute the Treasury has the lead role in setting foreign exchange policy, it strives to reach a consensus among all three parties—the Treasury, the Board of Governors, and the Federal Reserve Bank of New York. If they decide that a foreign exchange intervention is necessary that day—an unusual occurrence, as a year may go by without a U.S. foreign exchange intervention—Kos instructs his traders to carry out the agreed-on purchase or sale of foreign currencies. Because funds for exchange rate intervention are held separately by the Treasury (in its Exchange Stabilization Fund) and the Federal Reserve, Kos and his staff are not trading the funds of the Federal Reserve Bank of New York; rather they act as an agent for the Treasury and the FOMC in conducting these transactions.

   As part of their duties, before every FOMC meeting, Kos and his staff help prepare a lengthy document full of data for the FOMC members, other Reserve Bank presidents, and Treasury officials that describes developments in the domestic and foreign markets over the previous five or six weeks, a task that keeps them especially busy right before the FOMC meeting.

Federal Reserve System		
Assets	Liabilities	
Foreign assets (international reserves) −$1 billion	Deposits with the Fed (reserves) −$1 billion	

In this case, the outcome of the Fed sale of foreign assets and the purchase of dollar deposits is a $1 billion decline in reserves and a $1 billion decline in the monetary base because reserves are also a component of the monetary base.

We now see that the outcome for the monetary base is exactly the same when a central bank sells foreign assets to purchase domestic bank deposits or domestic currency. This is why when we say that a central bank has purchased its domestic currency, we do not have to distinguish whether it actually purchased currency or bank deposits denominated in the domestic currency. We have thus reached an important conclusion: *A central bank's purchase of domestic currency and corresponding sale of foreign assets in the foreign exchange market leads to an equal decline in its international reserves and the monetary base.*

We could have reached the same conclusion by a more direct route. A central bank sale of a foreign asset is no different from an open market sale of a government bond. We learned in Chapter 8 that an open market sale leads to an equal decline in the monetary base; therefore, a sale of foreign assets also leads to an equal decline in the monetary base. By similar reasoning, a central bank purchase of foreign assets paid for by selling domestic currency, like an open market purchase, leads to an equal rise in the monetary base. Thus we reach the following conclusion: *A central bank's sale of domestic currency to purchase foreign assets in the foreign exchange market results in an equal rise in its international reserves and the monetary base.*

The intervention we have just described, in which a central bank allows the purchase or sale of domestic currency to have an effect on the monetary base and hence on the money supply, is called an **unsterilized foreign exchange intervention.** But what if the central bank does not want the purchase or sale of domestic currency to affect the monetary base and the money supply? All it has to do is to counter the effect of the foreign exchange intervention by conducting an offsetting open market operation in the government bond market. For example, in the case of a $1 billion purchase of dollars by the Fed and a corresponding $1 billion sale of foreign assets, which we have seen would decrease the monetary base by $1 billion, the Fed can conduct an open market purchase of $1 billion of government bonds, which would increase the monetary base by $1 billion. The resulting T-account for the foreign exchange intervention and the offsetting open market operation leaves the monetary base unchanged:

Federal Reserve System		
Assets	Liabilities	
Foreign assets (international reserves) −$1 billion Government bonds +$1 billion	Monetary base (currency in circulation plus reserves) 0	

A foreign exchange intervention with an offsetting open market operation that leaves the monetary base unchanged is called a **sterilized foreign exchange intervention.**

Now that we understand that there are two types of foreign exchange interventions, unsterilized and sterilized, let's look at how each affects the exchange rate.

Unsterilized Intervention

Your intuition might lead you to suspect that if a central bank wants to lower the value of the domestic currency, it should sell its currency in the foreign exchange market and purchase foreign assets. Indeed, this intuition is correct for the case of an unsterilized intervention.

Recall that in an unsterilized intervention, if the Federal Reserve decides to sell dollars in order to buy foreign assets in the foreign exchange market, this works just like an open market purchase of bonds that increases the monetary base and the money supply. Hence we find ourselves analyzing exactly the situation described in Figure 7 of Chapter 13, which is reproduced here as Figure 1. The higher money supply leads to a higher U.S. price level in the long run and so to a lower expected future exchange rate. The resulting decline in the expected appreciation of the dollar increases the expected return on foreign deposits and shifts the R^F schedule to the right. In addition, the increase in the money supply will lead to a higher real money supply in the short run, which causes the interest rate on dollar deposits to fall. The resulting lower expected return on dollar

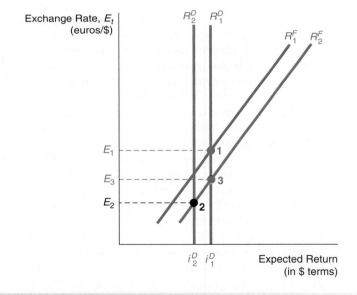

FIGURE 1 *Effect of a Sale of Dollars and a Purchase of Foreign Assets*

A sale of dollars and the consequent open market purchase of foreign assets increase the monetary base. The resulting rise in the money supply leads to a higher domestic price level in the long run, which leads to a lower expected future exchange rate. The resulting decline in the expected appreciation of the dollar raises the expected return on foreign deposits, shifting the R^F schedule rightward from R_1^F to R_2^F. In the short run, the domestic interest rate i^D falls, shifting R^D from R_1^D to R_2^D. The short-run outcome is that the exchange rate falls from E_1 to E_2. In the long run, however, the interest rate returns to i_1^D, and R^D returns to R_1^D. The exchange rate therefore rises from E_2 to E_3 in the long run.

deposits translates as a leftward shift in the R^D schedule. The fall in the expected return on dollar deposits and the increase in the expected return on foreign deposits means that foreign assets have a higher expected return than dollar deposits at the old equilibrium exchange rate. Hence people will try to sell their dollar deposits, and the exchange rate will fall. Indeed, as we saw in Chapter 13, the increase in the money supply will lead to exchange rate overshooting, whereby the exchange rate falls by more in the short run than it does in the long run.

Our analysis leads us to the following conclusion about unsterilized interventions in the foreign exchange market: ***An unsterilized intervention in which domestic currency is sold to purchase foreign assets leads to a gain in international reserves, an increase in the money supply, and a depreciation of the domestic currency.***

The reverse result is found for an unsterilized intervention in which domestic currency is purchased by selling foreign assets. The purchase of domestic currency by selling foreign assets (reducing international reserves) works like an open market sale to reduce the monetary base and the money supply. The decrease in the money supply raises the interest rate on dollar deposits and shifts R^D rightward while causing R^F to shift leftward because it leads to a lower U.S. price level in the long run and thus to a higher expected appreciation of the dollar and hence a lower expected return on foreign deposits. The increase in the expected return on dollar deposits relative to foreign deposits will mean that people will want to buy more dollar deposits, and the exchange rate will rise. ***An unsterilized intervention in which domestic currency is purchased by selling foreign assets leads to a drop in international reserves, a decrease in the money supply, and an appreciation of the domestic currency.***

Sterilized Intervention

The key point to remember about a sterilized intervention is that the central bank engages in offsetting open market operations so that there is no impact on the monetary base and the money supply. In the context of the model of exchange rate determination we have developed here, it is straightforward to show that a sterilized intervention has *no effect* on the exchange rate. Remember that in our model, foreign and domestic deposits are perfect substitutes, so equilibrium in the foreign exchange market occurs when the expected returns on foreign and domestic deposits are equal. A sterilized intervention leaves the money supply unchanged and so has no way of directly affecting interest rates or the expected future exchange rate.[1] Because the expected returns on dollar and foreign deposits are unaffected, the expected return schedules remain at R^D_1 and R^F_1 in Figure 1, and the exchange rate remains unchanged at E_1.

---

[1]Note that a sterilized intervention could indicate what central banks want to happen to the future exchange rate and so might provide a signal about the course of future monetary policy. In this way, a sterilized intervention could lead to shifts in the R^F schedule, but in reality it is the future change in monetary policy, not the sterilized intervention, that is the ultimate source of exchange rate effects. For a discussion of the signaling effect, see Maurice Obstfeld, "The Effectiveness of Foreign Exchange Intervention: Recent Experience, 1985–1988," in *International Policy Coordination and Exchange Rate Fluctuations*, ed. William H. Branson, Jacob A. Frenkel, and Morris Goldstein (Chicago: University of Chicago Press, 1990), pp. 197–237.

At first it might seem puzzling that a central bank purchase or sale of domestic currency that is sterilized does not lead to a change in the exchange rate. A central bank purchase of domestic currency cannot raise the exchange rate because with no effect on the domestic money supply or interest rates, any resulting rise in the exchange rate would mean that the expected return on foreign deposits would be greater than the expected return on domestic deposits. Given our assumption that foreign and domestic deposits are perfect substitutes (equally desirable), this would mean that no one would want to hold domestic deposits.[2] So the exchange rate would have to fall back to its previous level, where the expected returns on domestic and foreign deposits were equal.

Balance of Payments

The site http://research. stlouisFed.org/ Fred2/ contains exchange rates, balance of payments, and trade data.

Because international financial transactions such as foreign exchange interventions have considerable effects on the economy, it is worth knowing how these transactions are measured. This is done using the **balance of payments,** a bookkeeping system for recording all receipts and payments that have a direct bearing on the movement of funds between nations that result from private and government transactions.

Here we examine a few key items in the balance of payments that you often hear about in the media.[3] The number you hear about most often is the **current account,** which shows international transactions that involve currently produced goods and services. The most important item in this account is the **trade balance,** the difference between merchandise exports and imports (i.e., the net receipts from trade). When merchandise imports are greater than exports, which has been the case for the United States in recent years, we have a trade deficit; if exports are greater than imports, we have a trade surplus.

Another important item in the balance of payments is the **capital account,** the net receipts from capital transactions. Flows of capital into a country are registered as receipts, whereas outflows are registered as payments, so that a positive capital account means that, on net, capital is flowing into a country. Because the balance of payments must balance, the net change in government international reserves that a government (as represented by its central bank) uses to finance international transactions equals the current account plus the capital account. That is,

$$\text{Current account} + \text{capital account} = \text{net change in government international reserves}$$

This equation shows us why the current account receives so much attention from economists and the media: It tells us whether the United States (private sector and government combined) is increasing its claims on foreign wealth or whether foreigners are increasing their claims on U.S. wealth. For example, the

---

[2]If domestic and foreign deposits are not perfect substitutes, a sterilized intervention can affect the exchange rate. However, most studies find little evidence to support the position that sterilized intervention has a significant impact on foreign exchange rates. For a further discussion of the effects of sterilized versus unsterilized intervention, see Paul Krugman and Maurice Obstfeld, *International Economics,* 6th ed. (Reading, Mass.: Addison Wesley, 2003).

[3]For more information on how the balance of payments accounts are measured and constructed, see the appendix to this chapter, which can be found on the book's website at **www.aw-bc.com/mishkin_eakins**.

equation tells us that a negative current account balance (i.e., a deficit) must be matched either by a positive capital account (net capital inflow) or a negative net change in international reserves, both of which involve an increase in claims of foreigners on U.S. wealth. Hence, the recent large U.S. current account deficits indicate that foreigners are increasing their claims on our wealth. Countries which, in contrast, have current account surpluses are increasing their claims on foreign wealth.

Exchange Rate Regimes in the International Financial System

Exchange rate regimes in the international financial system are of two basic types: fixed and floating. In a **fixed exchange rate regime,** the values of currencies are kept pegged relative to one currency (called the **anchor currency**) so that exchange rates are fixed. In a **floating exchange rate regime,** the values of currencies are allowed to fluctuate against one another. However, countries often attempt to influence their exchange rates by buying and selling currencies, so in this case the regime is referred to as a **managed float regime** (or a **dirty float**).

Fixed Exchange Rate Regimes

After World War II, the victors set up a fixed exchange rate system that became known as the **Bretton Woods system,** after the town in which the agreement was negotiated, Bretton Woods, New Hampshire. It lasted until 1971.

The Bretton Woods agreement created the **International Monetary Fund (IMF),** headquartered in Washington, D.C., which had 30 original member countries in 1945 and currently has over 150. The IMF was given the task of promoting the growth of world trade by setting rules for the maintenance of fixed exchange rates and by making loans to countries that were experiencing balance-of-payments difficulties. As part of its role of monitoring the compliance of member countries with its rules, the IMF also took on the job of collecting and standardizing international economic data.

The Bretton Woods agreement also set up the International Bank for Reconstruction and Development, commonly referred to as the **World Bank,** also headquartered in Washington, which provides long-term loans to help developing countries build dams, roads, and other physical capital that would contribute to their economic development. The funds for these loans are obtained primarily by issuing World Bank bonds, which are sold in the capital markets of the developed countries. In addition, the General Agreement on Tariffs and Trade (GATT), headquartered in Geneva, was set up to monitor rules for the conduct of trade between countries (tariffs and quotas); this organization has evolved into the **World Trade Organization (WTO).**

Because the United States emerged from World War II as the world's largest economic power, the fixed exchange rates were to be maintained by intervention in the foreign exchange market by central banks in countries besides the United States who bought and sold dollar assets, which they held as international reserves. The U.S. dollar, which was used by other countries to denominate the assets that they held as international reserves, was called the **reserve currency.** Thus an important feature of the Bretton Woods system was the establishment of the United States as the reserve currency country. Even after the breakup of the Bretton Woods system, the U.S. dollar has kept its position as the reserve currency in which most international financial transactions are conducted.

The Euro's Challenge to the Dollar

With the adoption of the euro by countries in the European Monetary System, in the future the U.S. dollar may face a challenge to its position as the key reserve currency in international financial transactions. Adoption of the euro has increased integration of Europe's financial markets, which could help them rival those in the United States. The resulting increase in the use of euros in financial markets is making it more likely that international transactions are carried out in the euro. The economic clout of the European Union rivals that of the United States: Both have a similar share of world GDP (around 20%) and world exports (around 15%). If the European Central Bank can make sure that inflation remains low so that the euro becomes a sound currency, this should bode well for the euro.

However, for the euro to eat significantly into the dollar's position as a reserve currency, the European Union must function as a cohesive political entity that is able to exert its influence on the world stage. There are serious doubts on this score, and most analysts think that it will be a long time before the euro beats out the dollar in international financial transactions.

However, with the creation of the euro in 1999, the U.S. dollar may be subject to a serious challenge to its supremacy (see the "Global" box above).

The fixed exchange rate Bretton Woods system was abandoned in 1971, but in the period from 1979 to 1990, the European Union instituted among its members a fixed exchange rate system known as the European Monetary System (EMS). In the so-called exchange rate mechanism (ERM) in this system, the exchange rate between any pair of currencies of the participating countries was not allowed to fluctuate outside narrow limits, called the *snake*. However, in practice, all the countries in the EMS pegged their currencies to the German mark.

How a Fixed Exchange Rate Regime Works   Figure 2 shows how a fixed exchange rate regime works in practice using the model of exchange rate determination we learned in Chapter 13. Panel (a) describes a situation in which the domestic currency is fixed relative to an anchor currency and is initially overvalued: The schedule for the expected return on foreign deposits R_1^F intersects the schedule for the expected return on domestic deposits R_1^D at exchange rate E_1, which is lower than the par (fixed) value of the exchange rate E_{par}. To keep the exchange rate at E_{par}, the central bank must intervene in the foreign exchange market to purchase domestic currency by selling foreign assets, and this action, like an open market sale, means that the monetary base and the money supply decline. Because the exchange rate will continue to be fixed at E_{par}, the expected future exchange rate remains unchanged, and so the schedule for the expected return on foreign deposits remains at R_1^F. However, the purchase of domestic currency, which leads to a fall in the money supply, also causes the interest rate on domestic deposits i^D to rise. This increase in turn shifts the expected return on domestic deposits R^D to the right. The central bank will continue purchasing domestic currency and selling foreign assets until the R^D curve reaches R_2^D and the equilibrium exchange rate is at E_{par} at point 2 in panel (a).

We have thus come to the conclusion that ***when the domestic currency is overvalued, the central bank must purchase domestic currency to keep the exchange rate fixed, but as a result it loses international reserves.***

Panel (b) in Figure 2 shows how a central bank intervention keeps the exchange rate fixed at E_{par} when the exchange rate is initially undervalued, that is, when R_1^F and the initial R_1^D intersect at exchange rate E_1, which is above E_{par}.

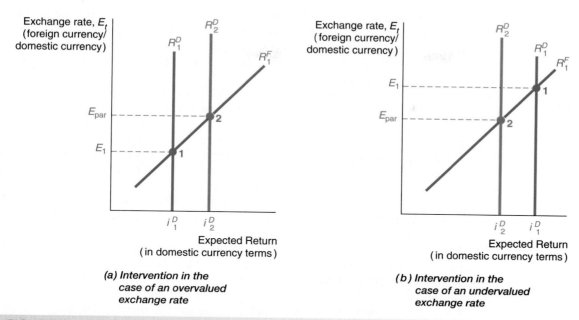

**(a) Intervention in the
case of an overvalued
exchange rate**

**(b) Intervention in the
case of an undervalued
exchange rate**

FIGURE 2 *Intervention in the Foreign Exchange Market under a Fixed Exchange Rate Regime*

In panel (a), the exchange rate at E_{par} is overvalued. To keep the exchange rate at E_{par} (point 2), the central bank must purchase domestic currency to shift the schedule for the expected return on domestic deposits to R_2^D. In panel (b), the exchange rate at E_{par} is undervalued, so a central bank sale of domestic currency is needed to shift R^D to R_2^D to keep the exchange rate at E_{par} (point 2).

Here the central bank must sell domestic currency and purchase foreign assets, and this works like an open market purchase to raise the money supply and to lower the interest rate on domestic deposits i^D. The central bank keeps selling domestic currency and lowers i^D until R^D shifts all the way to R_2^D, where the equilibrium exchange rate is at E_{par}—point 2 in panel (b). Our analysis thus leads us to the following result: **When the domestic currency is undervalued, the central bank must sell domestic currency to keep the exchange rate fixed, but as a result it gains international reserves.**

As we have seen, if a country's currency has an overvalued exchange rate, its central bank's attempts to keep the currency from depreciating will result in a loss of international reserves. If the country's central bank eventually runs out of international reserves, it cannot keep its currency from depreciating, and a **devaluation** must occur, meaning that the par exchange rate is reset at a lower level.

If, by contrast, a country's currency has an undervalued exchange rate, its central bank's intervention to keep the currency from appreciating leads to a gain of international reserves. Because, as we will see shortly, the central bank might not want to acquire these international reserves, it might want to reset the par value of its exchange rate at a higher level (a **revaluation**).

Note that if domestic and foreign deposits are perfect substitutes, as is assumed in the model of exchange rate determination used here, a sterilized exchange rate intervention would not be able to keep the exchange rate at E_{par} because, as we have seen in Chapter 13, neither R^F nor R^D will shift. For example, if the exchange rate is overvalued, a sterilized purchase of domestic currency will still leave the expected return on domestic deposits below the expected return on foreign deposits at the par exchange rate—so pressure for a depreciation of the domestic currency is not removed. If the central bank keeps on purchasing its domestic currency but continues to sterilize, it will just keep on losing international reserves until it finally runs out of them and is forced to let the value of the currency seek a lower level.

One implication of the foregoing analysis is that a country that ties its exchange rate to an anchor currency of a larger country loses control of its monetary policy. If the larger country pursues a more contractionary monetary policy and decreases its money supply, this would lead to lower expected inflation in the larger country, thus causing an appreciation of the larger country's currency and a depreciation of the smaller country's currency. The smaller country, having locked its exchange rate to the anchor currency, will now find its currency overvalued and will therefore have to sell the larger country's currency and buy its own to keep its currency from depreciating. The result of this foreign exchange intervention will then be a decline in the smaller country's international reserves, a contraction of the monetary base, and thus a decline in its money supply. Sterilization of this foreign exchange intervention is not an option because this would just lead to a continuing loss of international reserves until the smaller country was forced to devalue. The smaller country no longer controls its monetary policy because movements in its money supply are completely determined by movements in the larger country's money supply.

Smaller countries are often willing to tie their exchange rate to that of a larger country in order to inherit the more disciplined monetary policy of their bigger neighbor, thus ensuring a lower inflation rate. An extreme example of such a strategy is the currency board, which has been used by Hong Kong and has recently been adopted by countries such as Argentina (see the "Global" box), Latvia, and Estonia. An even more extreme strategy is **dollarization,** in which a country abandons its currency altogether and adopts that of another country, typically the U.S. dollar (see the "Global" box on page 357).

A serious shortcoming of fixed exchange rate systems such as the Bretton Woods system or the European Monetary System is that they can lead to foreign exchange crises involving a "speculative attack" on a currency—massive sales of a weak currency or purchases of a strong currency to cause a sharp change in the exchange rate. In the following case, we use our model of exchange rate determination to understand how the September 1992 exchange rate crisis that rocked the European Monetary System came about.

Case

THE FOREIGN EXCHANGE CRISIS OF SEPTEMBER 1992

In the aftermath of German reunification in October 1990, the German central bank, the Bundesbank, faced rising inflationary pressures, with inflation having accelerated from below 3% in 1990 to near 5% by 1992. To get monetary growth under control and to dampen inflation, the Bundesbank raised German interest rates to near double-digit levels. Figure 3 shows the consequences of these actions by the Bundesbank in the foreign exchange market for sterling. Note that in the diagram, the pound sterling is the domestic currency and R^D is the expected return on sterling deposits, while the foreign currency is the German mark (deutsche mark, DM), so R^F is the expected return on mark deposits.

GLOBAL

Argentina's Currency Board

Argentina has a long history of monetary instability, with inflation rates fluctuating dramatically and sometimes surging beyond 1000% a year. To end this cycle of inflationary surges, Argentina decided to adopt a currency board in April 1991. A *currency board system* is one in which the domestic currency has 100% backing in foreign reserves and in which the note-issuing authority, whether the central bank or the government, adopts a fixed exchange rate against a particular foreign currency and then stands ready to exchange domestic currency for foreign currency at that rate whenever the public requests it.

The Argentine currency board worked as follows. Under Argentina's convertibility law, the peso/dollar exchange rate was fixed at one to one, and a member of the public could go to the Argentine central bank and exchange a peso for a dollar, or vice versa, at any time. A currency board is just a variant of a fixed exchange rate regime in which the commitment to the fixed exchange rate is especially strong because the conduct of monetary policy is in effect put on autopilot and is completely taken out of the hands of the central bank and the government. The money supply could expand only when dollars were exchanged for pesos at the central bank, meaning that the increased amount of pesos was matched by an equal increase in foreign exchange reserves. The central bank therefore no longer had the ability to print money and thereby cause inflation.

The early years of Argentina's currency board looked stunningly successful. Inflation, which had been running at an 800% rate in 1990, fell below 5% by the end of 1994, and economic growth was rapid, averaging almost 8% annually from 1991 to 1994. However, a currency board is not without problems. In the aftermath of the Mexican peso crisis, concern about the health of the Argentine economy resulted in the public's pulling money out of the banks (deposits fell by 18%) and exchanging pesos for dollars, thus causing a contraction of the Argentine money supply. The result was a sharp decline in Argentine economic activity, with real GDP down more than 5% in 1995 and the unemployment rate jumping above 15%. Only in 1996 did the economy begin to recover.

However, in 1998 Argentina entered another recession which was both severe and very long lasting. By the end of 2001, unemployment reached nearly 20%, a level comparable to that experienced in the United States during the Great Depression of the 1930s. The result was civil unrest and the fall of the elected government, as well as a major banking crisis and a default on nearly $150 billion of government debt. Because the Central Bank of Argentina had no control over monetary policy under the currency board system, it was unable to use monetary policy to expand the economy and get out of its recession. Furthermore, because the currency board did not allow the central bank to create pesos and lend them to banks, it had very little capability to act as a lender of last resort. In January 2002, the currency board finally collapsed and the peso depreciated by more than 70%. The result was the full-scale financial crisis described in Chapter 15, with inflation shooting up and an extremely severe depression. Clearly, the Argentina public is not as enamored of its currency board as it once was.

The increase in German interest rates i^F shifted the R^F schedule rightward to R_2^F in Figure 3, so that the intersection of the R_1^D and the R_2^F schedules at point 1' was below the lower exchange rate limit (2.778 marks per pound, denoted E_{par}) under the exchange rate mechanism. To lower the value of the mark relative to the pound and restore the pound/mark exchange rate to within the ERM limits, either the Bank of England had to pursue a contractionary monetary policy, thereby raising British interest rates to i_2^D and shifting the R_1^D schedule to the right to point 2, or the Bundesbank could pursue an expansionary monetary policy, thereby lowering German interest rates, which would shift the R^F schedule to the left to move back to point 1. (The shift in R^D to point 2 or R^F to point 1 are not shown in the figure.)

The catch was that the Bundesbank, whose primary goal is fighting inflation, was unwilling to pursue an expansionary monetary policy, while the

GLOBAL

Dollarization

Dollarization, which involves the adoption of another country's currency, usually the U.S. dollar (but other sound currencies like the euro or the yen are also possibilities), is a more extreme version of fixed exchange rate than is a currency board. A currency board can be abandoned, allowing a change in the value of the currency, but a change of value is impossible with dollarization: A dollar bill is always worth one dollar whether it is held in the United States or outside of it. Panama has been dollarized since the inception of the country in the early twentieth century, while El Salvador and Ecuador have recently adopted dollarization.

Dollarization, like a currency board, prevents a central bank from creating inflation. Another key advantage is that it completely avoids the possibility of a speculative attack on the domestic currency (because

there is none) that is still a danger even under a currency board arrangement. However, like a currency board, dollarization does not allow a country to pursue its own monetary policy or have a lender of last resort. Dollarization has one additional disadvantage not characteristic of a currency board: Because a country adopting dollarization no longer has its own currency, it loses the revenue that a government receives by issuing money, which is called *seigniorage*. Because governments (or their central banks) do not have to pay interest on their currency, they earn revenue (seigniorage) by using this currency to purchase income-earning assets such as bonds. In the case of the Federal Reserve in the United States, this revenue is on the order of $20 billion dollars per year. If an emerging-market country dollarizes and give up its currency, it needs to make up this loss of revenue somewhere, which is not always easy for a poor country.

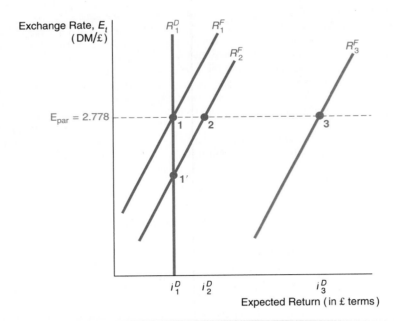

FIGURE 3 *Foreign Exchange Market for British Pounds in 1992*

The realization by speculators that the United Kingdom would soon devalue the pound increased the expected return on foreign (German mark, DM) deposits and shifted R_2^F rightward to R_3^F. The result was the need for a much greater purchase of pounds by the British central bank to raise the interest rate to i_3^D to keep the exchange rate at DM 2.778 per pound.

British, who were facing their worst recession in the postwar period, were unwilling to pursue a contractionary monetary policy to prop up the pound. This impasse became clear when in response to great pressure from other members of the EMS, the Bundesbank was willing to lower its lending rates by only a token amount on September 14 after a speculative attack was mounted on the currencies of the Scandinavian countries. So at some point in the near future, the value of the pound would have to decline to point 1′. Speculators now knew that the appreciation of the mark was imminent and hence that the value of foreign (mark) deposits would rise in value relative to the pound. As a result, the expected return on mark deposits increased sharply, shifting the R^F schedule to R_3^F in Figure 3.

The huge potential losses on pound deposits and potential gains on mark deposits caused a massive sell-off of pounds (and purchases of marks) by speculators. The need for the British central bank to intervene to raise the value of the pound now became much greater and required a huge rise in British interest rates, all the way to i_3^D. After a major intervention effort on the part of the Bank of England, which included a rise in its lending rate from 10% to 15% that still wasn't enough, the British were finally forced to give up on September 16: They pulled out of the ERM indefinitely, allowing the pound to depreciate by 10% against the mark.

Speculative attacks on other currencies forced devaluation of the Spanish peseta by 5% and the Italian lira by 15%. To defend its currency, the Swedish central bank was forced to raise its daily lending rate to the astronomical level of 500%! By the time the crisis was over, the British, French, Italian, Spanish, and Swedish central banks had intervened to the tune of $100 billion; the Bundesbank alone had laid out $50 billion for foreign exchange intervention. Because foreign exchange crises lead to large changes in central banks' holdings of international reserves and thus affect the official reserve asset items in the balance of payments, these crises are also referred to as **balance-of-payments crises.**

The attempt to prop up the European Monetary System was not cheap for these central banks. It is estimated that they lost $4 to $6 billion as a result of exchange rate intervention during the crisis.

**The
Practicing
Manager**

PROFITING FROM A FOREIGN EXCHANGE CRISIS

Large banks and other financial institutions often conduct foreign exchange trading operations that generate substantial profits for their parent institution. When a foreign exchange crisis like the one that occurred in September 1992 comes along, foreign exchange traders and speculators are presented with a golden opportunity. The foregoing analysis of this crisis helps explain why.

As we saw in Figure 3, the high German interest rates resulted in a situation in which the British pound was overvalued, in that the equilibrium exchange rate in the absence of intervention by the British and German central banks was below the lower exchange rate limit of 2.778 German marks per British pound. Once foreign exchange traders realized that the central banks would not be willing to intervene sufficiently or alter their policies to keep the value of the pound above the 2.778-mark-per-pound lower limit, the traders were presented with a "heads I win, tails you lose" bet. They knew that there was only one direction in which the exchange rate could go—down—and so they were almost sure to make money by buying marks and selling pounds. Our analysis of Figure 3 reflects this state of affairs; another way of looking at this one-sided bet is to recognize that it implies that the expected return on mark-denominated deposits increased sharply, shifting the R^F schedule to R_3^F in Figure 3.

Savvy foreign exchange traders, who read the writing on the wall early in September 1992, sold pounds and bought marks. When the pound depreciated 10% against the mark after September 16, they made huge profits because the marks they had bought could now be sold at a price 10% higher. Foreign exchange traders at Citibank are reported to have made $200 million in the week of the September 1992 exchange rate crisis—not bad for a week's work! But these profits pale in comparison to those made by George Soros, an investment fund manager whose funds are reported to have run up profits of $1 billion during the crisis. (However, Soros gave some of these profits back in 1994 when he acknowledged that he had suffered a $600 million loss from trades on the yen.) Clearly, foreign exchange trading can be a highly profitable enterprise for financial institutions, particularly during foreign exchange rate crises.

Case

RECENT FOREIGN EXCHANGE CRISES IN EMERGING MARKET COUNTRIES: MEXICO 1994, EAST ASIA 1997, BRAZIL 1999, AND ARGENTINA 2002

Major currency crises in emerging market countries have been a common occurrence in recent years. We can use Figure 3 to understand the sequence of events during the currency crises in Mexico in 1994, East Asia in 1997, Brazil in 1999, and Argentina in 2002. To do so, we just need to recognize that dollars are the foreign currency, so that R^F is the expected return on dollar deposits, while R^D is the expected return on deposits denominated in the domestic currency, whether it was pesos, baht, or reals. (Note that the exchange rate label on the vertical axis would be in terms of dollars/domestic currency and that the label on the horizontal axis would be expected return in the domestic currency—say, pesos.)

In Mexico in March 1994, political instability (the assassination of the ruling party's presidential candidate) sparked investors' concerns that the peso might be devalued. The result was that the expected return on dollar deposits rose, thus moving the R^F schedule from R_1^F to R_2^F in Figure 3. In the case of Thailand in May 1997, the large current account deficit and the weakness of the Thai financial system raised similar concerns about the devaluation of the domestic currency, with the same effect on the R^F schedule. In Brazil in late 1998 and Argentina in 2001, concerns about fiscal situations that could lead to the printing of money to finance the deficit, and thereby raise inflation, also meant that a devaluation was more likely to occur. The concerns thus raised the expected return on dollar deposits and shifted the R^F schedule from R_1^F to R_2^F. In all of these cases, the result was that the intersection of the R_1^D and R_2^F curves was below the pegged value of the domestic currency at E_{par}.

To keep their domestic currencies from falling below E_{par}, these countries' central banks needed to buy the domestic currency and sell dollars to raise interest rates to i_2^D and shift the R^D curve to the right, in the process losing international reserves. At first, the central banks were successful in containing this speculative attack. However, when more bad news broke, speculators became even more confident that these countries could not defend their currencies. (The bad news was everywhere: in Mexico, with an uprising in Chiapas and revelations about problems in the banking system; in Thailand, there was a major failure of a financial institution; in Brazil, a worsening fiscal situation was reported, along with a threat by a governor to default on his state's debt; and in Argentina, a full-scale bank panic and an actual default on the government debt occurred.) As a result, the expected returns on dollar deposits shot up further, and R^F moved much farther to the right, to R_3^F; and the central banks lost even more international reserves. Given the stress on the economy from rising interest rates and the loss of reserves, eventually the monetary authorities could no longer continue to defend the currency and were forced to give up and let their currencies depreciate. This scenario happened in Mexico in December 1994, in Thailand in July 1997, in Brazil in January 1999, and in Argentina in January 2002.

Concerns about similar problems in other countries then triggered speculative attacks against them as well. This contagion occurred in the aftermath of the Mexican crisis (jauntily referred to as the "Tequila effect") with speculative attacks on other Latin American currencies, but there were no further currency collapses. In the East Asian crisis, however, fears of devaluation spread throughout the region, leading to a scenario akin to that depicted in Figure 3. Consequently, one by one, Indonesia, Malaysia, South Korea, and the Philippines were forced to devalue sharply. Even Hong Kong, Singapore, and Taiwan were subjected to speculative attacks, but because these countries had healthy financial systems, the attacks were successfully averted.

The sharp depreciations in Mexico, East Asia, and Argentina led to full-scale financial crises that severely damaged these countries' economies. The foreign exchange crisis that shocked the European Monetary System in September 1992 cost central banks a lot of money, but the public in European countries were not seriously affected. By contrast, the public in Mexico, Argentina, and the crisis countries of East Asia were not so lucky: The collapse of these currencies triggered by speculative attacks led to financial crises, producing severe depressions that caused hardship and political unrest.

Managed Float

Although exchange rates are currently allowed to change daily in response to market forces, central banks have not been willing to give up their option of intervening in the foreign exchange market. Preventing large changes in exchange rates makes it easier for firms and individuals purchasing or selling goods abroad to plan into the future. Furthermore, countries with surpluses in their balance of payments frequently do not want to see their currencies appreciate because it makes their goods more expensive abroad and foreign goods cheaper in their country. Because an appreciation might hurt sales for domestic businesses and increase unemployment, surplus countries have often sold their currency in the foreign exchange market and acquired international reserves.

Countries with balance-of-payments deficits do not want to see their currency lose value because it makes foreign goods more expensive for domestic consumers and can stimulate inflation. To keep the value of the domestic currency high, deficit countries have often bought their own currency in the foreign exchange market and given up international reserves.

The current international financial system is a hybrid of a fixed and a flexible exchange rate system. Rates fluctuate in response to market forces but are not determined solely by them. Furthermore, many countries continue to keep the value of their currency fixed against other currencies.

The IMF continues to function as a data collector and international lender but does not attempt to encourage fixed exchange rates. The IMF's role of international lender has also become important recently because of situations like the third-world debt crisis of the 1980s and the more recent Mexican, East Asian, Brazilian, and Argentinian foreign exchange crises. The IMF has been directly involved in helping developing countries with difficulties in repaying their loans and provided large loans to Mexico and other countries in the aftermath of the Mexican peso crisis.

Capital Controls

Because capital flows have been an important element in the currency crises in Mexico and East Asia, politicians and some economists have advocated that capital mobility in emerging market countries should be restricted with capital controls in order to avoid financial instability. Are capital controls a good idea?

Controls on Capital Outflows

Capital outflows can promote financial instability in emerging market countries because when domestic residents and foreigners pull their capital out of a country, the resulting capital outflow forces a country to devalue its currency. This is why recently some politicians in emerging market countries have found capital controls particularly attractive. For example, Prime Minister Mahathir of Malaysia instituted capital controls in 1998 to restrict outflows in the aftermath of the East Asian crisis.

Although these controls sound like a good idea, they suffer from several disadvantages. First, empirical evidence indicates that controls on capital outflows are seldom effective during a crisis because the private sector finds ingenious ways to evade them and has little difficulty moving funds out of the country.[4] Second, the evidence suggests that capital flight may even increase after controls are put into place because confidence in the government is weakened. Third, controls on capital outflows often lead to corruption, as government officials get paid off to look the other way when domestic residents are trying to move funds

---

[4]See Sebastian Edwards, "How Effective Are Capital Controls?" *Journal of Economic Perspectives*, 13 (Winter 2000): 65–84.

abroad. Fourth, controls on capital outflows may lull governments into thinking they do not have to take the steps to reform their financial systems to deal with the crisis, with the result that opportunities are lost to improve the functioning of the economy.

Controls on Capital Inflows

Although most economists find the arguments against controls on capital outflows persuasive, controls on capital inflows receive more support. Supporters reason that if speculative capital cannot come in, then it cannot go out suddenly and create a crisis. Our analysis of the financial crises in East Asia in Chapter 15 provides support for this view by suggesting that capital inflows can lead to a lending boom and excessive risk taking on the part of banks, which then helps trigger a financial crisis.

However, controls on capital inflows have the undesirable feature that they may block from entering a country funds that would be used for productive investment opportunities. Although such controls may limit the fuel supplied to lending booms through capital flows, over time they produce substantial distortions and misallocation of resources as households and businesses try to get around them. Indeed, just as with controls on capital outflows, controls on capital inflows can lead to corruption. There are serious doubts whether capital controls can be effective in today's environment, in which trade is open and where there are many financial instruments that make it easier to get around these controls.

On the other hand, there is a strong case for improving bank regulation and supervision so that capital inflows are less likely to produce a lending boom and encourage excessive risk taking by banking institutions. For example, restricting banks in how fast their borrowing could grow might have the impact of substantially limiting capital inflows. Supervisory controls of this type, focusing on the sources of financial fragility rather than the symptoms, can enhance the efficiency of the financial system rather than hampering it.

The Role of the IMF

The International Monetary Fund was originally set up under the Bretton Woods system to help countries deal with balance-of-payments problems and stay with the fixed exchange rate by lending to deficit countries. With the collapse of the Bretton Woods system of fixed exchange rates in 1971, the IMF has taken on new roles.

Although the IMF no longer attempts to encourage fixed exchange rates, its role as an international lender has become more important recently. This role first came to the fore in the 1980s during the third-world debt crisis, in which the IMF assisted developing countries in repaying their loans. The financial crises in Mexico in 1994–95 and in East Asia in 1997–98 led to huge loans by the IMF to these and other affected countries to help them recover from their financial crises and to prevent the spread of these crises to other countries. This role, in which the IMF acts like an international lender of last resort to cope with financial instability, is indeed highly controversial.

Should the IMF Be an International Lender of Last Resort?

As we saw in Chapter 8, in industrialized countries when a financial crisis occurs and the financial system threatens to seize up, domestic central banks can address matters with a lender-of-last-resort operation to limit the degree of instability in the banking system. In emerging markets, however, where the credibility of the central bank as an inflation-fighter may be in doubt and debt contracts are typically short-term and in foreign currencies, a lender-of-last-resort operation becomes a two-edged sword—as likely to exacerbate the financial crisis as to alleviate it. For example, when the U.S. Federal Reserve engaged in a lender-of-last-resort operation during the 1987 stock market crash (Chapter 8), there was almost no sentiment in the markets that there would be substantially higher inflation. However, for a central bank having less inflation-fighting credibility than the Fed, central bank lending to the financial system in the wake of a financial crisis—even under the lender-of-last-resort rhetoric—may well arouse fears of inflation spiraling out of control, causing an even greater currency depreciation and still greater deterioration of balance sheets. The resulting increase in moral hazard and adverse selection problems in financial markets, along the lines discussed in Chapter 15, would only make the financial crisis worse.

Central banks in emerging market countries therefore have only a very limited ability to successfully engage in a lender-of-last-resort operation. However, liquidity provided by an international lender of last resort does not have these undesirable consequences, and in helping to stabilize the value of the domestic currency it strengthens domestic balance sheets. Moreover, an international lender of last resort may be able to prevent contagion, the situation in which a successful speculative attack on one emerging market currency leads to attacks on other emerging market currencies, spreading financial and economic disruption as it goes. Since a lender of last resort for emerging market countries is needed at times, and since it cannot be provided domestically, there is a strong rationale for an international institution to fill this role. Indeed, since Mexico's financial crisis in 1994, the International Monetary Fund and other international agencies have stepped into the lender-of-last-resort role and provided emergency lending to countries threatened by financial instability.

However, support from an international lender of last resort brings risks of its own, especially the risk that the perception it is standing ready to bail out irresponsible financial institutions may lead to excessive risk taking of the sort that makes financial crises more likely. In the Mexican and East Asian crises, governments in the crisis countries have used IMF support to protect depositors and other creditors of banking institutions from losses. This safety net creates a well-known moral hazard problem because the depositors and other creditors have less incentive to monitor these banking institutions and withdraw their deposits if the institutions are taking on too much risk. The result is that these institutions are encouraged to take on excessive risks. Indeed, critics of the IMF, most prominently the Congressional Commission headed by Professor Alan Meltzer of Carnegie-Mellon University, contend that its lending in the Mexican crisis, which was used to bail out foreign lenders, set the stage for the East Asian crisis because these lenders expected to be bailed out if things went wrong and thus provided funds that were used to fuel excessive risk taking.[5]

---

[5]See International Financial Institution Advisory Commission, *Report* (IFIAC: Washington, D.C., 2000).

An international lender of last resort must find ways to limit this moral hazard problem, or it can actually make the situation worse. The international lender of last resort can make it clear that it will extend liquidity to governments that put the proper measures in place to prevent excessive risk taking. In addition, it can reduce the incentives for risk taking by restricting the ability of governments to bail out stockholders and large uninsured creditors of domestic financial institutions.

One problem that arises for international organizations like the IMF engaged in lender-of-last-resort operations is that they know that if they don't come to the rescue, the emerging market country will suffer extreme hardship and possible political instability. Politicians in the crisis country may exploit these concerns and engage in a game of chicken with the international lender of last resort: They resist necessary reforms, hoping that the IMF will cave in. Elements of this game were present in the Mexico crisis of 1995 and were also a particularly important feature of the negotiations between the IMF and Indonesia during the Asian crisis.

The IMF would produce better outcomes if it makes it clear that it will not play this game. Just as giving in to ill-behaved children may be the easy way out in the short run, but supports a pattern of poor behavior in the long run, some critics worry that the IMF may not be tough enough when confronted by short-run humanitarian concerns. For example, these critics have been particularly critical of the IMF's lending to the Russian government, which has resisted adopting appropriate reforms to stabilize its financial system.

The IMF has also been criticized for imposing on the East Asian countries so-called austerity programs that focus on tight macroeconomic policies rather than on microeconomic policies to fix the crisis-causing problems in the financial sector. Such programs are likely to increase resistance to IMF recommendations, particularly in emerging market countries. Austerity programs allow these politicians to label institutions such as the IMF as being anti-growth, rhetoric that helps the politicians to mobilize the public against the IMF and avoid doing what they really need to do to reform the financial system in their country. IMF programs focused instead on microeconomic policies related to the financial sector would increase the likelihood that the IMF would be seen as a helping hand in the creation of a more efficient financial system.

An important historical feature of successful lender-of-last-resort operations is that the faster the lending is done, the lower is the amount that actually has to be lent. An excellent example occurred in the aftermath of the stock market crash on October 19, 1987 (Chapter 8). At the end of that day, in order to service their customers' accounts, securities firms needed to borrow several billion dollars to maintain orderly trading. However, given the unprecedented developments, banks were very nervous about extending further loans to these firms. Upon learning this, the Federal Reserve engaged in an immediate lender-of-last-resort operation, with the Fed making it clear that it would provide liquidity to banks making loans to the securities industry. Indeed, what is striking about this episode is that the extremely quick intervention of the Fed resulted not only in a negligible impact of the stock market crash on the economy, but also meant that the amount of liquidity that the Fed needed to supply to the economy was not very large.

The ability of the Fed to engage in a lender-of-last-resort operation within a day of a substantial shock to the financial system is in sharp contrast to the amount of time it has taken the IMF to supply liquidity during the recent crises in Mexico and Asian countries. Because IMF lending facilities were originally designed to provide funds after a country was experiencing a balance-of-payments crisis and because the conditions for the loan had to be negotiated, it took several months before the IMF made funds available. By this time, the crisis had gotten much worse—and over $50 billion was needed to cope with the crisis, often stretching the resources of the IMF. One reason that central banks can lend so much more quickly than the IMF is that they have set up procedures in advance to provide loans, with the terms and conditions for this lending agreed upon beforehand. The need for quick provision of liquidity to keep the loan amount manageable argues for similar credit facilities at the international lender of last resort so that funds can be provided quickly as long as the borrower meets conditions such as properly supervising its banks or keeping budget deficits low. A step in this direction was made in 1999 when the IMF set up a new lending facility, the Contingent Credit Line, so it can provide liquidity faster during a crisis.

The debate on whether the world will be better off with the IMF operating as an international lender of last resort is currently a hot one. Much attention is being focused on making the IMF more effective in performing this role, and redesign of the IMF is at the center of proposals for a new international financial architecture to help reduce international financial instability.

Summary

1. An unsterilized central bank intervention in which the domestic currency is sold to purchase foreign assets leads to a gain in international reserves, an increase in the money supply, and a depreciation of the domestic currency. Available evidence suggests, however, that sterilized central bank interventions have little long-term effect on the exchange rate.

2. The balance of payments is a bookkeeping system for recording all payments between a country and foreign countries that have a direct bearing on the movement of funds between them. Because the balance of payments must balance, the net change in government international reserves that a government (as represented by its central bank) uses to finance international transactions equals the current account plus the capital account.

3. After World War II, the Bretton Woods system and the IMF were established to promote a fixed exchange rate system in which the U.S. dollar was convertible into gold. The Bretton Woods system collapsed in 1971. We now have an international financial system that has elements of a managed float and a fixed exchange rate system. Some exchange rates fluctuate from day to day, although central banks intervene in the foreign exchange market, while other exchange rates are fixed.

4. Controls on capital outflows receive support because they might prevent domestic residents and foreigners from pulling capital out of a country during a crisis and make devaluation less likely. Controls on capital inflows make sense under the theory that if speculative capital cannot flow in, then it cannot go out suddenly and create a crisis. However, capital controls suffer from several disadvantages: They are seldom effective, they lead to corruption, and they may allow governments to avoid taking the steps to reform their financial systems to deal with the crisis.

5. The IMF has recently taken on the role of an international lender of last resort. Because central banks in emerging market countries are unlikely to be able to perform a lender-of-last-resort operation successfully, an international lender of last resort like the IMF is needed to prevent financial instability. However, the IMF's role as an international lender of last resort creates a serious moral hazard problem that can encourage excessive risk taking and make a financial crisis more likely. The IMF thus needs to limit the moral hazard created by its lender-of-last-resort role, but it may find this politically hard to do. In addition, it needs to be able to provide liquidity quickly during a crisis in order to keep manageable the amount of funds lent.

Key Terms

anchor currency, *p. 353*

balance of payments, *p. 352*

balance-of-payments crisis, *p. 359*

Bretton Woods system, *p. 353*

capital account, *p. 352*

current account, *p. 352*

devaluation, *p. 355*

dollarization, *p. 356*

fixed exchange rate regime, *p. 353*

floating exchange rate regime, *p. 353*

foreign exchange intervention, *p. 347*

International Monetary Fund (IMF), *p. 353*

international reserves, *p. 347*

managed float regime (dirty float), *p. 353*

reserve currency, *p. 353*

revaluation, *p. 355*

sterilized foreign exchange intervention, *p. 349*

T-account, *p. 348*

trade balance, *p. 352*

unsterilized foreign exchange intervention, *p. 349*

World Bank, *p. 353*

World Trade Organization (WTO), *p. 353*

Questions

1. If the Federal Reserve buys dollars in the foreign exchange market but conducts an offsetting open market operation to sterilize the intervention, what will be the impact on international reserves, the money supply, and the exchange rate?

2. If the Federal Reserve buys dollars in the foreign exchange market but does not sterilize the intervention, what will be the impact on international reserves, the money supply, and the exchange rate?

3. For each of the following, identify in which part of the balance-of-payments account it appears (current account, capital account, or method of financing) and whether it is a receipt or a payment.

   a. A British subject's purchase of a share of Johnson & Johnson stock

   b. An American's purchase of an airline ticket from Air France

   c. The Swiss government's purchase of U.S. Treasury bills

   d. A Japanese's purchase of California oranges

   e. $50 million of foreign aid to Honduras

   f. A loan by an American bank to Mexico

   g. An American bank's borrowing of Eurodollars

4. Why does a balance-of-payments deficit for the United States have a different effect on its international reserves than a balance-of-payments deficit for the Netherlands?

5. Under the gold standard, if Britain became more productive relative to the United States, what would happen to the money supply in the two countries? Why would the changes in the money supply help preserve a fixed exchange rate between the United States and Britain?

6. What is the exchange rate between dollars and euros if one dollar is convertible into $\frac{1}{20}$ ounce of gold and one euro is convertible into $\frac{1}{40}$ ounce of gold?

7. If a country's par exchange rate was undervalued during the Bretton Woods fixed exchange rate regime, what kind of intervention would that country's central bank be forced to undertake, and what effect would it have on its international reserves and the money supply?

8. How can a large balance-of-payments surplus contribute to the country's inflation rate?

9. "If a country wants to keep its exchange rate from changing, it must give up some control over its money supply." Is this statement true, false, or uncertain? Explain your answer.

10. Why can balance-of-payments deficits force some countries to implement a contractionary monetary policy?

11. "Balance-of-payments deficits always cause a country to lose international reserves." Is this statement true, false, or uncertain? Explain your answer.

12. How can persistent U.S. balance-of-payments deficits stimulate world inflation?

13. "Inflation is not possible under the gold standard." Is this statement true, false, or uncertain? Explain your answer.

14. Why is it that in a pure flexible exchange rate system, the foreign exchange market has no direct effects on the money supply? Does this mean that the foreign exchange market has no effect on monetary policy?

15. "The abandonment of fixed exchange rates after 1973 has meant that countries have pursued more independent monetary policies." Is this statement true, false, or uncertain? Explain your answer.

16. Are capital controls on capital outflows a good idea? Why or why not?

17. Discuss the pros and cons of capital controls on capital inflows.

18. Why might central banks in emerging-market countries find that engaging in a lender-of-last resort operation might be counterproductive? Does this provide a rationale for having an international lender of last resort like the IMF?

19. Has the IMF done a good job in performing the role of the international lender of last resort?

20. What steps should an international lender of last resort take to limit moral hazard?

Quantitative Problems

1. The Federal Reserve purchases $1,000,000 of foreign assets for $1,000,000. Show the effect of this open market operation using T-accounts.

2. Again, the Federal Reserve purchases $1,000,000 of foreign assets. However, to raise the funds, the trading desk sells $1,000,000 in T-bills. Show the effect of this open market operation using T-accounts.

3. If the interest rate is 4% on euro deposits and 2% on dollar deposits, while the euro is trading at $1.30 per euro, what does the market expect the exchange rate to be one year from now?

4. If the dollar begins trading at $1.30 per euro, with the same interest rates given in Problem 3, and the ECB raises interest rates so that the rate on euro deposits rises by 1 percentage point, what will happen to the exchange rate (assuming that the expected future exchange rate is unchanged)?

5. If the balance in the current account increases by $2 billion while the capital account is off $3.5 billion, what is the impact on governmental international reserves?

Web Exercises

The International Financial System

1. The Federal Reserve publishes information on-line that explains the workings of the foreign exchange market. One such publication can be found at **http://www.ny.frb.org/education/addpub/ usfxm/**. Review the table of contents and open Chapter 10, "The Evolution of the International Monetary System." Read this chapter and write a one-page summary that discusses why each monetary standard was dropped in favor of the succeeding one.

2. The International Monetary Fund stands ready to help nations facing monetary crises. Go to **http://www.imf.org**. Click on the tab labeled "About IMF." What is the stated purpose of the IMF? How many nations participate, and when was it established?

Web Appendices

Please visit our Web site at **www.aw-bc.com/mishkin _eakins** to read the Web appendix to Chapter 14, *Balance of Payments*

PART 5

Fundamentals of Financial Institutions

CHAPTER 15

Why Do Financial Institutions Exist?

Preview

A healthy and vibrant economy requires a financial system that moves funds from people who save to people who have productive investment opportunities. But how does the financial system make sure that your hard-earned savings get channeled to those with productive investment opportunities?

This chapter answers that question by providing a theory for understanding why financial institutions exist to promote economic efficiency. The theoretical analysis focuses on a few simple but powerful economic concepts that enable us to explain features of our financial markets such as why financial contracts are written as they are, why financial intermediaries are more important than securities markets for getting funds to borrowers, and why financial crises occur and have such severe consequences for the health of the economy.

Basic Facts About Financial Structure Throughout the World

The financial system is complex in structure and function throughout the world. There are many different types of institutions: banks, insurance companies, mutual funds, stock and bond markets, and so on—all of which are regulated by government. The financial system channels billions of dollars per year from savers to people with productive investment opportunities. If we take a close look at financial structure all over the world, we need to explain eight basic (and sometimes surprising) facts in order to understand how the financial system works.

The pie chart in Figure 1 indicates how American businesses financed their activities using external funds (those obtained from outside the business itself) in the period 1970–1996. The *Bank loans* category is made up primarily of bank loans; *Nonbank loans* is made up primarily of loans by other financial intermediaries. The *Bonds* category includes marketable debt securities such as corporate bonds and commercial paper. *Stock* consists of issues of new equity (stock market shares). Figure 2 uses the same classifications as Figure 1, and compares the U.S. data to those of Germany and Japan.

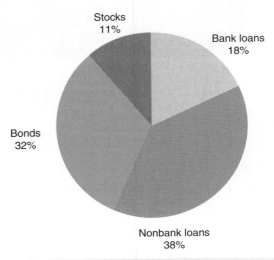

FIGURE 1   *Sources of External Funds for Nonfinancial Businesses in the United States*

The categories of external funds are as follows: *Bank loans,* which is made up primarily of bank loans; *Nonbank loans,* which includes loans from other financial intermediaries; *Bonds,* which includes marketable debt such as corporate bonds; and *Stocks,* which consists of issues of new equity (stock market shares). The data are from 1970–2000 and are gross flows as percentage of the total, not including trade and other credit data, which are not available.

Source: Andreas Hackethal and Reinhard H. Schmidt, "Financing Patterns: Measurement Concepts and Empirical Results," Johann Wolfgang Goethe-Universitat Working Paper No. 125, January 2004.

Now let us explore the eight basic facts.

1. ***Stocks are not the most important source of external financing for businesses.*** Because so much attention in the media is focused on the stock market, many people have the impression that stocks are the most important sources of financing for American corporations. However, as we can see from the pie chart in Figure 1, the stock market accounted for only a small fraction of the external financing of American businesses in the 1970–2000 period, 11%.[1] Similarly small figures apply in the other countries presented in Figure 2 as well. Why is the stock market less important than other sources of financing in the United States and other countries?

---

[1]The 11% figure for the percentage of external financing provided by stocks is based on the flows of external funds to corporations. However, this flow figure is somewhat misleading because when a share of stock is issued, it raises funds permanently, whereas when a bond is issued, it raises funds only temporarily until they are paid back at maturity. To see this, suppose that a firm raises $1000 by selling a share of stock and another $1000 by selling a $1000 one-year bond. In the case of the stock issue, the firm can hold on to the $1000 it raised this way, but to hold on to the $1000 it raised through debt, it has to issue a new $1000 bond every year. If we look at the flow of funds to corporations over a 26-year period, as in Figure 1, the firm will have raised $1000 with a stock issue only once in the 26-year period, while it will have raised $1000 with debt 26 times, once in each of the 26 years. Thus it will look like debt is 26 times more important than stocks in raising funds, even though our example indicates that they are actually equally important for the firm.

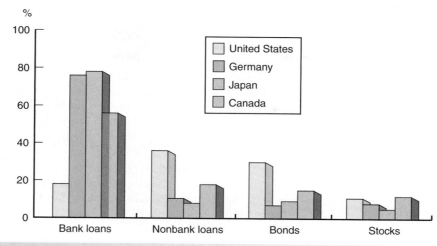

FIGURE 2 *Sources of External Funds for Nonfinancial Businesses: A Comparison of the United States with Germany, Japan, and Canada*

The categories of external funds are the same as in Figure 1, and the data are for the period 1970–2000.

Source: Andreas Hackethal and Reinhard H. Schmidt, "Financing Patterns: Measurement Concepts and Empirical Results," Johann Wolfgang Goethe-Universitat Working Paper No. 125, January 2004, and Apostolos Serletis and Karl Pinno, "Corporate Financing in Canada," University of Calgary, mimeograph, February 2004.

2. ***Issuing marketable debt and equity securities is not the primary way in which businesses finance their operations.*** Figure 1 shows that bonds are a far more important source of financing than stocks in the United States (32% versus 11%). However, stocks and bonds combined (43%), which make up the total share of marketable securities, still supply less than one-half of the external funds corporations need to finance their activities. The fact that issuing marketable securities is not the most important source of financing is true elsewhere in the world as well. Indeed, as we see in Figure 2, most countries have a much smaller share of external financing supplied by marketable securities than the United States. Why don't businesses use marketable securities more extensively to finance their activities?

3. ***Indirect finance, which involves the activities of financial intermediaries, is many times more important than direct finance, in which businesses raise funds directly from lenders in financial markets.*** Direct finance involves the sale to households of marketable securities such as stocks and bonds. The 43% share of stocks and bonds as a source of external financing for American businesses actually greatly overstates the importance of direct finance in our financial system. Since 1970, less than 5% of newly issued corporate bonds and commercial paper and around 50% of stocks have been sold directly to American households. The rest of these securities have been bought primarily by financial intermediaries such as insurance companies, pension funds, and mutual funds. These figures indicate that direct finance is used in less than 5% of the external funding of American business. Because in most countries

marketable securities are an even less important source of finance than in the United States, direct finance is also far less important than indirect finance in the rest of the world. Why have financial intermediaries and indirect finance been so important in financial markets? In recent years, indirect finance has been declining in importance. Why is this happening?

4. *Financial intermediaries, particularly banks, are the most important source of external funds used to finance businesses.* As we can see in Figures 1 and 2, the primary source of external funds for businesses throughout the world are loans made by financial intermediaries (56% in the United States, but over 70% in Japan, Germany, and Canada). In other industrialized countries, bank loans are by far the largest category of sources of external finance (over 70% in Japan and Germany and over 50% in Canada), and so the data suggest that banks in these countries have the most important role in financing business activities. Although in the United States bank loans are no longer larger than loans from other financial intermediaries combined as they once were, banks are still the most important financial intermediary. In developing countries banks play an even more important role in the financial system than they do in the industrialized countries. What makes banks so important to the workings of the financial system? Although banks are very important, their share of external funds for businesses has been declining in recent years. What is driving this decline?

5. *The financial system is among the most heavily regulated sectors of the economy.* You learned in Chapter 2 that the financial system is heavily regulated, not only in the United States but in all other developed countries as well. Governments regulate financial markets primarily to promote the provision of information in part to protect consumers, and to ensure the soundness (stability) of the financial system. Why are financial markets so extensively regulated throughout the world?

6. *Only large, well-established corporations have easy access to securities markets to finance their activities.* Individuals and smaller businesses that are not well established are less likely to raise funds by issuing marketable securities. Instead, they most often obtain their financing from banks. Why do only large, well-known corporations find it easier to raise funds in securities markets?

7. *Collateral is a prevalent feature of debt contracts for both households and businesses.* **Collateral** is property that is pledged to the lender to guarantee payment in the event that the borrower should be unable to make debt payments. Collateralized debt (which is also known as **secured debt** to contrast it with **unsecured debt,** such as credit card debt, which is not collateralized) is the predominant form of household debt and is widely used in business borrowing as well. The majority of household debt in the United States consists of collateralized loans: Your automobile is collateral for your auto loan, and your house is collateral for your mortgage. Commercial and farm mortgages, for which property is pledged as collateral, make up one-quarter of borrowing by nonfinancial businesses; corporate bonds and other bank loans also often involve pledges of collateral. Why is collateral such an important feature of debt contracts?

8. *Debt contracts are typically extremely complicated legal documents that place substantial restrictions on the behavior of the*

borrower. Many students think about a debt contract as a simple IOU that can be written on a single piece of paper. The reality of debt contracts is far different, however. In all countries, bond or loan contracts are typically long legal documents with provisions (called **restrictive covenants**) that restrict and specify certain activities that the borrower can engage in. Restrictive covenants are not just a feature of debt contracts for businesses; for example, personal automobile loan and home mortgage contracts have restrictive covenants that require the borrower to maintain sufficient insurance on the automobile or house purchased with the loan. Why are debt contracts so complex and restrictive?

As you may recall from Chapter 2, an important feature of financial markets is that they have substantial transaction and information costs. A theoretical analysis of how these costs affect financial markets provides us with solutions to the eight basic facts, which in turn provide us with a much deeper understanding of how our financial system works. In the next section we examine the impact of transaction costs on the structure of our financial system. Then we turn to how information costs affect financial structure.

Transaction Costs

Transaction costs are a major problem in financial markets. An example will make this clear.

How Transaction Costs Influence Financial Structure

Say you have $5000 you would like to invest, and you think about investing in the stock market. Because you have only $5000, you can buy only a small number of shares. Even if you use on-line trading, your purchase is so small that the brokerage commission for buying the stock you picked will be a significant percentage of the purchase price of the shares. If instead you decide to buy a bond, the problem is even worse because the smallest denomination for some bonds you might want to buy is as much as $10,000 and you do not have that much to invest. Indeed, the broker may not even be interested in your business at all because the small size of your account doesn't make spending time on it worthwhile. You are disappointed and realize that you will not be able to use financial markets to earn a return on your hard-earned savings. You can take some consolation, however, in the fact that you are not alone in being stymied by high transaction costs. This is a fact of life for most of us: Most American households never own any securities.

You also face another problem because of transaction costs. Because you have only a small amount of funds available, you can make only a restricted number of investments. That is, you have to put all your eggs in one basket, and your inability to diversify will subject you to a lot of risk.

How Financial Intermediaries Reduce Transaction Costs

This example of the problems posed by transaction costs and the example outlined in Chapter 2 in which legal costs kept you from making a loan to Carl the Carpenter illustrate that small savers like you are frozen out of financial markets and are unable to benefit from them. Fortunately, financial intermediaries, an important part of the financial structure, have evolved to reduce transaction costs and allow small savers and borrowers to benefit from the existence of financial markets.

Economies of Scale   One solution to the problem of high transaction costs is to bundle the funds of many investors together so that they can take advantage of *economies of scale,* the reduction in transaction costs per dollar of investment as the size (scale) of transactions increases. By bundling investors' funds together, transaction costs for each individual investor are far smaller. Economies of scale exist because the total cost of carrying out a transaction in financial markets increases only a little as the size of the transaction grows. For example, the cost of arranging a purchase of 10,000 shares of stock is not much greater than the cost of arranging a purchase of 50 shares of stock.

The presence of economies of scale in financial markets helps explain why financial intermediaries developed and are such an important part of our financial structure. The clearest example of a financial intermediary that arose because of economies of scale is a mutual fund. A *mutual fund* is a financial intermediary that sells shares to individuals and then invests the proceeds in bonds or stocks. Because it buys large blocks of stocks or bonds, a mutual fund can take advantage of lower transaction costs. These cost savings are then passed on to individual investors after the mutual fund has taken its cut in the form of management fees for administering their accounts. An additional benefit for individual investors is that a mutual fund is large enough to purchase a widely diversified portfolio of securities. The increased diversification for individual investors reduces their risk, thus making them better off.

Economies of scale are also important in lowering the costs of things, such as computer technology, that financial institutions need to accomplish their tasks. Once a large mutual fund has invested a lot of money in setting up a telecommunications system, for example, it can be used for a huge number of transactions at a low cost per transaction.

Expertise   Financial intermediaries also arise because they are better able to develop expertise to lower transaction costs. Mutual funds, banks, and other financial intermediaries develop expertise in computer technology so that they can cheaply provide convenient services such as toll-free numbers that allow you to check on how well your investments are doing or the ability to write checks on your account.

An important outcome of a financial intermediary's low transaction costs is that they allow a financial intermediary to provide its customers with *liquidity services,* services that make it easier for customers to conduct transactions. Money market mutual funds, for example, allow shareholders to write checks that enable them to pay their bills easily while at the same time paying them high interest rates.

Asymmetric Information: Adverse Selection and Moral Hazard

The presence of transaction costs in financial markets explains in part why financial intermediaries and indirect finance play such an important role in financial markets (fact 3). To understand financial structure more fully, however, we turn to the role of information in financial markets.[2]

---

[2]An excellent survey of the literature on information and financial structure that expands on the topics discussed in the rest of this chapter is contained in Mark Gertler, "Financial Structure and Aggregate Economic Activity: An Overview," *Journal of Money, Credit and Banking* 20 (1988): 559–588.

Asymmetric information—one party having insufficient knowledge about the other party involved in a transaction to make accurate decisions—is an important aspect of financial markets. For example, managers of a corporation know whether they are honest or have better information about how well their business is doing than the stockholders do. The presence of asymmetric information leads to adverse selection and moral hazard problems, which were introduced in Chapter 2.

Adverse selection is an asymmetric information problem that occurs *before* the transaction occurs: Potential bad credit risks are the ones who most actively seek out loans. Thus the parties who are the most likely to produce an undesirable outcome are most likely to want to engage in the transaction. For example, big risk takers or outright crooks might be the most eager to take out a loan because they know that they are unlikely to pay it back. Because adverse selection increases the chances that a loan might be made to a bad credit risk, lenders may decide not to make any loans even though there are good credit risks in the marketplace.

Moral hazard arises *after* the transaction occurs: The lender runs the risk that the borrower will engage in activities that are undesirable from the lender's point of view because they make it less likely that the loan will be paid back. For example, once borrowers have obtained a loan, they may take on big risks (which have possible high returns but also run a greater risk of default) because they are playing with someone else's money. Because moral hazard lowers the probability that the loan will be repaid, lenders may decide that they would rather not make a loan.

The analysis of how asymmetric information problems affect economic behavior is called **agency theory.** We will apply this theory here to explain why financial structure takes the form it does, thereby explaining the facts described at the beginning of the chapter.

The Lemons Problem: How Adverse Selection Influences Financial Structure

A particular characterization of the adverse selection problem and how it interferes with the efficient functioning of a market was outlined in a famous article by George Akerlof, a Nobel prize-winner. It is referred to as the "lemons problem" because it resembles the problem created by lemons in the used-car market.[3] Potential buyers of used cars are frequently unable to assess the quality of the car; that is, they can't tell whether a particular used car is a good car that will run well or a lemon that will continually give them grief. The price that a buyer pays must therefore reflect the *average* quality of the cars in the market, somewhere between the low value of a lemon and the high value of a good car.

The owner of a used car, by contrast, is more likely to know whether the car is a peach or a lemon. If the car is a lemon, the owner is more than happy to sell it at the price the buyer is willing to pay, which, being somewhere between the value of a lemon and a good car, is greater than the lemon's value. However, if

---

[3]George Akerlof, "The Market for 'Lemons': Quality, Uncertainty and the Market Mechanism," *Quarterly Journal of Economics* 84 (1970): 488–500. Two important papers that have applied the lemons problem analysis to financial markets are Stewart Myers and N. S. Majluf, "Corporate Financing and Investment Decisions When Firms Have Information That Investors Do Not Have," *Journal of Financial Economics* 13 (1984): 187–221, and Bruce Greenwald, Joseph E. Stiglitz, and Andrew Weiss, "Information Imperfections in the Capital Market and Macroeconomic Fluctuations," *American Economic Review* 74 (1984): 194–199.

the car is a peach, the owner knows that the car is undervalued by the price the buyer is willing to pay, and so the owner may not want to sell it. As a result of this adverse selection, very few good used cars will come to the market. Because the average quality of a used car available in the market will be low and because very few people want to buy a lemon, there will be few sales. The used-car market will then function poorly, if at all.

Lemons in the Stock and Bond Markets

A similar lemons problem arises in securities markets, that is, the debt (bond) and equity (stock) markets. Suppose that our friend Irving the Investor, a potential buyer of securities such as common stock, can't distinguish between good firms with high expected profits and low risk and bad firms with low expected profits and high risk. In this situation, Irving will be willing to pay only a price that reflects the *average* quality of firms issuing securities—a price that lies between the value of securities from bad firms and the value of those from good firms. If the owners or managers of a good firm have better information than Irving and *know* that they are a good firm, they know that their securities are undervalued and will not want to sell them to Irving at the price he is willing to pay. The only firms willing to sell Irving securities will be bad firms (because the price is higher than the securities are worth). Our friend Irving is not stupid; he does not want to hold securities in bad firms, and hence he will decide not to purchase securities in the market. In an outcome similar to that in the used-car market, this securities market will not work very well because few firms will sell securities in it to raise capital.

The analysis is similar if Irving considers purchasing a corporate debt instrument in the bond market rather than an equity share. Irving will buy a bond only if its interest rate is high enough to compensate him for the average default risk of the good and bad firms trying to sell the debt. The knowledgeable owners of a good firm realize that they will be paying a higher interest rate than they should, and so they are unlikely to want to borrow in this market. Only the bad firms will be willing to borrow, and because investors like Irving are not eager to buy bonds issued by bad firms, they will probably not buy any bonds at all. Few bonds are likely to sell in this market, and so it will not be a good source of financing.

The analysis we have just conducted explains fact 2—why marketable securities are not the primary source of financing for businesses in any country in the world. It also partly explains fact 1—why stocks are not the most important source of financing for American businesses. The presence of the lemons problem keeps securities markets such as the stock and bond markets from being effective in channeling funds from savers to borrowers.

Tools to Help Solve Adverse Selection Problems

In the absence of asymmetric information, the lemons problem goes away. If buyers know as much about the quality of used cars as sellers so that all involved can tell a good car from a bad one, buyers will be willing to pay full value for good used cars. Because the owners of good used cars can now get a fair price, they will be willing to sell them in the market. The market will have many transactions and will do its intended job of channeling good cars to people who want them.

Similarly, if purchasers of securities can distinguish good firms from bad, they will pay the full value of securities issued by good firms, and good firms will sell their securities in the market. The securities market will then be able to move funds to the good firms that have the most productive investment opportunities.

Private Production and Sale of Information   The solution to the adverse selection problem in financial markets is to eliminate asymmetric information by furnishing people supplying funds with full details about the individuals or firms seeking to finance their investment activities. One way to get this material to saver-lenders is to have private companies collect and produce information that distinguishes good from bad firms and then sell it. In the United States, companies such as Standard and Poor's, Moody's, and Value Line gather information on firms' balance sheet positions and investment activities, publish these data, and sell them to subscribers (individuals, libraries, and financial intermediaries involved in purchasing securities).

The system of private production and sale of information does not completely solve the adverse selection problem in securities markets, however, because of the so-called **free-rider problem.** The free-rider problem occurs when people who do not pay for information take advantage of the information that other people have paid for. The free-rider problem suggests that the private sale of information will be only a partial solution to the lemons problem. To see why, suppose that you have just purchased information that tells you which firms are good and which are bad. You believe that this purchase is worthwhile because you can make up the cost of acquiring this information, and then some, by purchasing the securities of good firms that are undervalued. However, when our savvy (free-riding) investor Irving sees you buying certain securities, he buys right along with you, even though he has not paid for any information. If many other investors act as Irving does, the increased demand for the undervalued good securities will cause their low price to be bid up immediately to reflect the securities' true value. As a result of all these free riders, you can no longer buy the securities for less than their true value. Now because you will not gain any profits from purchasing the information, you realize that you never should have paid for this information in the first place. If other investors come to the same realization, private firms and individuals may not be able to sell enough of this information to make it worth their while to gather and produce it. The weakened ability of private firms to profit from selling information will mean that less information is produced in the marketplace, and so adverse selection (the lemons problem) will still interfere with the efficient functioning of securities markets.

Government Regulation to Increase Information   The free-rider problem prevents the private market from producing enough information to eliminate all the asymmetric information that leads to adverse selection. Could financial markets benefit from government intervention? The government could, for instance, produce information to help investors distinguish good from bad firms and provide it to the public free of charge. This solution, however, would involve the government in releasing negative information about firms, a practice that might be politically difficult. A second possibility (and one followed by the United States and most governments throughout the world) is for the government to regulate securities markets in a way that encourages firms to reveal honest information about themselves so that investors can determine how good or bad the firms are. In the United States, the Securities and Exchange Commission (SEC) is the government agency that requires firms selling their securities in public markets to have independent **audits,** in which accounting firms certify that the firm is adhering to standard accounting principles, and to disclose information about their sales, assets, and earnings. Similar regulations are found in other countries. However, disclosure requirements do not always work well, as the recent collapse of Enron and accounting scandals at other corporations, such as WorldCom and Parmalat (an Italian company) suggest (see the "Conflicts of Interest" box below).

The asymmetric information problem of adverse selection in financial markets helps explain why financial markets are among the most heavily regulated sectors in the economy (fact 5). Government regulation to increase information for investors is needed to reduce the adverse selection problem, which interferes with the efficient functioning of securities (stock and bond) markets.

Although government regulation lessens the adverse selection problem, it does not eliminate it. Even when firms provide information to the public about their sales, assets, or earnings, they still have more information than investors: There is a lot more to knowing the quality of a firm than statistics can provide. Furthermore, bad firms have an incentive to make themselves look like good firms because this would enable them to fetch a higher price for their securities. Bad firms will slant the information they are required to transmit to the public, thus making it harder for investors to sort out the good firms from the bad.

Financial Intermediation   So far we have seen that private production of information and government regulation to encourage provision of information lessen but do not eliminate the adverse selection problem in financial markets. How, then, can the financial structure help promote the flow of funds to people with productive investment opportunities when there is asymmetric information? A clue is provided by the structure of the used-car market.

An important feature of the used-car market is that most used cars are not sold directly by one individual to another. An individual considering buying a used car might pay for privately produced information by subscribing to a magazine like *Consumer Reports* to find out if a particular make of car has a good repair record.

CONFLICTS OF INTEREST

The Enron Implosion

Until 2001, Enron Corporation, a firm that specialized in trading in the energy market, appeared to be spectacularly successful. It had a quarter of the energy-trading market and was valued as high as $77 billion in August 2000, just a little over a year before its collapse, making it the seventh largest corporation in the United States at that time. However, toward the end of 2001, Enron came crashing down. In October 2001 Enron announced a big third-quarter loss of $618 million and disclosed accounting "mistakes." The SEC then engaged in a formal investigation of Enron's financial dealings with partnerships led by its former finance chief. It then became clear that Enron was engaged in a complex set of transactions that enabled it to keep substantial amounts of debt and financial contracts off of its balance sheet, thus enabling the company to act in its own interest and hide its financial difficulties from stockholders and lenders. Despite securing as much as $1.5 billion of new financing from J.P. Morgan Chase and Citigroup in December, the company was forced to declare bankruptcy, making it the largest in U.S. history.

The Enron collapse illustrates that although government regulation lessens asymmetric information problems, it cannot eliminate them. When a firm is in trouble, its management has tremendous incentives to hide its problems, making it hard for investors to know the true value of the firm.

Nevertheless, reading *Consumer Reports* does not solve the adverse selection problem because even if a particular make of car has a good reputation, the specific car someone is trying to sell could be a lemon. The prospective buyer might also bring the used car to a mechanic for a once-over. But what if the prospective buyer doesn't know a mechanic who can be trusted or if the mechanic would charge a high fee to evaluate the car?

Because these roadblocks make it hard for individuals to acquire enough information about used cars, most used cars are not sold directly by one individual to another. Instead, they are sold by an intermediary, a used-car dealer who purchases used cars from individuals and resells them to other individuals. Used-car dealers produce information in the market by becoming experts in determining whether a car is a peach or a lemon. Once they know that a car is good, they can sell it with some form of a guarantee: either a guarantee that is explicit, such as a warranty, or an implicit guarantee in which they stand by their reputation for honesty. People are more likely to purchase a used car because of a dealer's guarantee, and the dealer is able to make a profit on the production of information about automobile quality by being able to sell the used car at a higher price than the dealer paid for it. If dealers purchase and then resell cars on which they have produced information, they avoid the problem of other people free-riding on the information they produced.

Just as used-car dealers help solve adverse selection problems in the automobile market, financial intermediaries play a similar role in financial markets. A financial intermediary such as a bank becomes an expert in the production of information about firms so that it can sort out good credit risks from bad ones. Then it can acquire funds from depositors and lend them to the good firms. Because the bank is able to lend mostly to good firms, it is able to earn a higher return on its loans than the interest it has to pay to its depositors. As a result, the bank earns a profit, which allows it to engage in this information production activity.

An important element in the ability of the bank to profit from the information it produces is that it avoids the free-rider problem by primarily making private loans rather than by purchasing securities that are traded in the open market. Because a private loan is not traded, other investors cannot watch what the bank is doing and bid up the loan's price to the point that the bank receives no compensation for the information it has produced. The bank's role as an intermediary that holds mostly nontraded loans is the key to its success in reducing asymmetric information in financial markets.

Our theoretical analysis of adverse selection indicates that financial intermediaries in general, and banks in particular because they hold a large fraction of nontraded loans, should play a greater role in moving funds to corporations than securities markets do. Our analysis thus explains facts 3 and 4: why indirect finance is so much more important than direct finance and why banks are the most important source of external funds for financing businesses.

Another important fact that is explained by the analysis here is the greater importance of banks in the financial systems of developing countries. As we have seen, when the quality of information about firms is better, asymmetric information problems will be less severe, and it will be easier for firms to issue securities. Information about private firms is even harder to collect in developing countries than in industrialized countries; therefore, the smaller role played by securities markets leaves a greater role for financial intermediaries such as banks. A corollary of this analysis is that as information about firms becomes easier to acquire, the role of banks should decline. A major development in the past 20 years in the United States has been huge improvements in information technology. Thus the analysis here suggests that the lending role of financial institutions such as banks in the United States should have declined, and this is exactly what has occurred (see Chapter 18).

Our analysis of adverse selection also explains fact 6, which describes which firms are more likely to obtain funds from securities markets, a direct route, rather than from banks and financial intermediaries, an indirect route. The better known a corporation is, the more information about its activities is available in the marketplace. Thus it is easier for investors to evaluate the quality of the corporation and determine whether it is a good firm or a bad one. Because investors have fewer worries about adverse selection with well-known corporations, they will be willing to invest directly in their securities. Our adverse selection analysis thus suggests that there should be a pecking order for which firms can issue securities. The larger and more established a corporation is, the more likely it will be to issue securities to raise funds, a view that is known as the **pecking order hypothesis.** This hypothesis is supported in the data and is what fact 6 describes.

Collateral and Net Worth Adverse selection interferes with the functioning of financial markets only if a lender suffers a loss when a borrower is unable to make loan payments and thereby defaults. Collateral, property promised to the lender if the borrower defaults, reduces the consequences of adverse selection because it reduces the lender's losses in the event of a default. If a borrower defaults on a loan, the lender can sell the collateral and use the proceeds to make up for the losses on the loan. For example, if you fail to make your mortgage payments, the lender can take title to your house, auction it off, and use the receipts to pay off the loan. Lenders are thus more willing to make loans secured by collateral, and borrowers are willing to supply collateral because the reduced risk for the lender makes it more likely they will get the loan in the first place and perhaps at a better loan rate. The presence of adverse selection in credit markets thus provides an explanation for why collateral is an important feature of debt contracts (fact 7).

Net worth (also called **equity capital**), the difference between a firm's assets (what it owns or is owed) and its liabilities (what it owes), can perform a similar role to collateral. If a firm has a high net worth, then even if it engages in investments that cause it to have negative profits and so defaults on its debt payments, the lender can take title to the firm's net worth, sell it off, and use the proceeds to recoup some of the losses from the loan. In addition, the more net worth a firm has in the first place, the less likely it is to default because the firm has a cushion of assets that it can use to pay off its loans. Hence when firms seeking credit have high net worth, the consequences of adverse selection are less important and lenders are more willing to make loans. This analysis lies behind the often-heard lament, "Only the people who don't need money can borrow it!"

Summary So far we have used the concept of adverse selection to explain seven of the eight basic facts about financial structure introduced earlier: The first four emphasize the importance of financial intermediaries and the relative unimportance of securities markets for the financing of corporations; the fifth, that financial markets are among the most heavily regulated sectors of the economy; the sixth, that only large, well-established corporations have access to securities markets; and the seventh, that collateral is an important feature of debt contracts.

In the next section we will see that the other asymmetric information concept of moral hazard provides additional reasons for the importance of financial intermediaries and the relative unimportance of securities markets for the financing of corporations, the prevalence of government regulation, and the importance of collateral in debt contracts. In addition, the concept of moral hazard can be used to explain our final basic fact (fact 8) of why debt contracts are complicated legal documents that place substantial restrictions on the behavior of the borrower.

How Moral Hazard Affects the Choice Between Debt and Equity Contracts

Moral hazard is the asymmetric information problem that occurs after the financial transaction takes place, when the seller of a security may have incentives to hide information and engage in activities that are undesirable for the purchaser of the security. Moral hazard has important consequences for whether a firm finds it easier to raise funds with debt than with equity contracts.

Moral Hazard in Equity Contracts: The Principal-Agent Problem

Equity contracts, such as common stock, are claims to a share in the profits and assets of a business. Equity contracts are subject to a particular type of moral hazard called the **principal-agent problem.** When managers own only a small fraction of the firm they work for, the stockholders who own most of the firm's equity (called the *principals*) are not the same people as the managers of the firm, who are the *agents* of the owners. This separation of ownership and control involves moral hazard in that the managers in control (the agents) may act in their own interest rather than in the interest of the stockholder-owners (the principals) because the managers have less incentive to maximize profits than the stockholder-owners do.

To understand the principal-agent problem more fully, suppose that your friend Steve asks you to become a silent partner in his ice-cream store. The store requires an investment of $10,000 to set up, but Steve has only $1000. So you purchase an equity stake (stock shares) for $9000, which entitles you to 90% of the ownership of the firm, while Steve owns only 10%. If Steve works hard to make tasty ice cream, keeps the store clean, smiles at all the customers, and hustles to wait on tables quickly, after all expenses (including Steve's salary), the store will have $50,000 in profits per year, of which Steve receives 10% ($5000) and you receive 90% ($45,000).

But if Steve doesn't provide quick and friendly service to his customers, uses the $50,000 in income to buy artwork for his office, and even sneaks off to the beach while he should be at the store, the store will not earn any profit. Steve can only earn the additional $5000 (his 10% share of the profits) over his salary if he works hard and forgoes unproductive investments (such as art for his office). Steve might decide that the extra $5000 just isn't enough to make him want to expend the effort to be a good manager; he might decide that it would be worth his while only if he earned an extra $10,000. If Steve feels this way, he does not have enough incentive to be a good manager and will end up with a beautiful office, a good tan, and a store that doesn't show any profits. Because the store won't show any profits, Steve's decision not to act in your interest will cost you $45,000 (your 90% of the profits if he had chosen to be a good manager instead).

The moral hazard arising from the principal-agent problem might be even worse if Steve were not totally honest. Because his ice-cream store is a cash business, Steve has the incentive to pocket $50,000 in cash and tell you that the profits were zero. He now gets a return of $50,000, but you get nothing. The moral hazard incentive to underreport profits is illustrated by the experience with accounting practices in the movie industry described in the "Conflicts of Interest" box below.

Further indications that the principal-agent problem created by equity contracts can be severe are provided by examples of managers who build luxurious offices for themselves or drive high-priced corporate automobiles. Besides pursuing personal benefits, managers might also pursue corporate strategies (such as the acquisition of other firms) that enhance their personal power but do not increase the corporation's profitability.

The principal-agent problem would not arise if the owners of a firm had complete information about what the managers were up to and could prevent wasteful expenditures or fraud. The principal-agent problem, which is an example of moral hazard, arises only because a manager, like Steve, has more information about his activities than the stockholder does—that is, there is asymmetric information. The principal-agent problem would also not arise if Steve alone owned the store and there was no separation of ownership and control. If this were the case, Steve's hard work and avoidance of unproductive investments would yield him a profit (and extra income) of $50,000, an amount that would make it worth his while to be a good manager.

Tools to Help Solve the Principal-Agent Problem

Production of Information: Monitoring   You have seen that the principal-agent problem arises because managers have more information about their activities and actual profits than stockholders do. One way for stockholders to reduce this moral

CONFLICTS OF INTEREST

"Hollywood Accounting": Was Forrest Gump a Money Loser?

Accounting practices in the movie industry are notorious, giving the phrase "Hollywood accounting" a dubious reputation. A standard practice at movie studios is to keep two sets of books, a practice that might not be tolerated in other businesses but is in the movie business. One set is maintained according to the generally accepted accounting principles in other industries; that set is used to report profits to management and to shareholders. The second set of books, referred to as "contractual accounting," is used when a studio commits to paying out percentages of a movie's "net profits" among actors, directors, writers, and other parties as part of contractual arrangements. Given that the movie studios have a moral hazard incentive to

minimize these "net profits," not surprisingly they are rarely positive. For example, Forrest Gump, which took in over $600 million at the box office, did not show any profits according to Paramount, the filmmaker. The same has also been the case for other blockbusters such as the first Batman movie, J.F.K., and Coming to America. Can we really believe that Forrest Gump, one of the most successful movies of all time, was a money loser, or is this just an example of the principal-agent problem at work?

The dubious accounting practices of the movie industry have been coming under attack as a result of numerous lawsuits. In addition, the squeaky-clean Walt Disney Company is trying to change industry practices by going on record that it will not use contractual accounting and a second set of books when it compensates movie actors, directors, and writers.

hazard problem is for them to engage in a particular type of information production, the monitoring of the firm's activities: auditing the firm frequently and checking on what the management is doing. The problem is that the monitoring process can be expensive in terms of time and money, as reflected in the name financial economists give it, **costly state verification.** Costly state verification makes the equity contract less desirable, and it explains, in part, why equity is not a more important element in our financial structure.

As with adverse selection, the free-rider problem decreases the amount of information production that would reduce the moral hazard (principal-agent) problem. In this example, the free-rider problem decreases monitoring. If you know that other stockholders are paying to monitor the activities of the company you hold shares in, you can take a free ride on their activities. Then you can use the money you save by not engaging in monitoring to vacation on a Caribbean island. If you can do this, though, so can other stockholders. Perhaps all the stockholders will go to the islands, and no one will spend any resources on monitoring the firm. The moral hazard problem for shares of common stock will then be severe, making it hard for firms to issue them to raise capital (providing an additional explanation for fact 1).

Government Regulation to Increase Information

As with adverse selection, the government has an incentive to try to reduce the moral hazard problem created by asymmetric information, which provides another reason why the financial system is so heavily regulated (fact 5). Governments everywhere have laws to force firms to adhere to standard accounting principles that make profit verification easier. They also pass laws to impose stiff criminal penalties on people who commit the fraud of hiding and stealing profits. However, these measures can only be partly effective. Catching this kind of fraud is not easy; fraudulent managers have the incentive to make it very hard for government agencies to find or prove fraud.

Financial Intermediation

Financial intermediaries have the ability to avoid the free-rider problem in the face of moral hazard, which is another reason why the financial system is so heavily regulated (fact 5). One financial intermediary that helps reduce the moral hazard arising from the principal-agent problem is the **venture capital firm.** Venture capital firms pool the resources of their partners and use the funds to help budding entrepreneurs start new businesses. In exchange for the use of the venture capital, the firm receives an equity share in the new business. Because verification of earnings and profits is so important in eliminating moral hazard, venture capital firms usually insist on having several of their own people participate as members of the managing body of the firm, the board of directors, so that they can keep a close watch on the firm's activities. When a venture capital firm supplies start-up funds, the equity in the firm is not marketable to anyone *but* the venture capital firm. Thus other investors are unable to take a free ride on the venture capital firm's verification activities. As a result of this arrangement, the venture capital firm is able to garner the full benefits of its verification activities and is given the appropriate incentives to reduce the moral hazard problem.

Debt Contracts

Moral hazard arises with an equity contract, which is a claim on profits in all situations, whether the firm is making or losing money. If a contract could be structured so that moral hazard would exist only in certain situations, there would be a reduced need to monitor managers, and the contract would be more attractive than the equity contract. The debt contract has exactly these attributes because it is a contractual agreement by the borrower to pay the lender *fixed* dollar amounts at periodic intervals. When the firm has high profits, the lender receives the contractual payments and does not need to know the exact profits of the firm. If the managers are hiding profits or are pursuing activities that are personally beneficial but don't increase profitability, the lender doesn't care as long as these activities do not interfere with the ability of the firm to make its debt payments on time. Only when the firm cannot meet its debt payments, thereby being in a state of default, is there a need for the lender to verify the state of the firm's profits. Only in this situation do lenders involved in debt contracts need to act more like equity holders; now they need to know how much income the firm has in order to get their fair share.

The advantage of a less frequent need to monitor the firm, and thus a lower cost of state verification, helps explain why debt contracts are used more frequently than equity contracts to raise capital. The concept of moral hazard thus helps explain fact 1, why stocks are not the most important source of financing for businesses.[4]

How Moral Hazard Influences Financial Structure in Debt Markets

Even with the advantages just described, debt contracts are still subject to moral hazard. Because a debt contract requires the borrowers to pay out a fixed amount and lets them keep any profits above this amount, the borrowers have an incentive to take on investment projects that are riskier than the lenders would like.

For example, suppose that because you are concerned about the problem of verifying the profits of Steve's ice-cream store, you decide not to become an equity partner. Instead, you lend Steve the $9000 he needs to set up his business and have a debt contract that pays you an interest rate of 10%. As far as you are concerned, this is a surefire investment because there is a strong and steady demand for ice cream in your neighborhood. However, once you give Steve the funds, he might use them for purposes other than you intended. Instead of opening up the ice-cream store, Steve might use your $9000 loan to invest in chemical research equipment because he thinks he has a 1-in-10 chance of inventing a diet ice cream that tastes every bit as good as the premium brands but has no fat or calories.

Obviously, this is a very risky investment, but if Steve is successful, he will become a multimillionaire. He has a strong incentive to undertake the riskier investment with your money because the gains to him would be so large if he succeeded. You would clearly be very unhappy if Steve used your loan for the riskier investment because if he were unsuccessful, which is highly likely, you would lose most, if not all, of the money you gave him. And if he were successful, you wouldn't share in his success—you would still get only a 10% return on the loan because the principal and interest payments are fixed. Because of the potential moral hazard (Steve might use your money to finance a very risky venture), you would probably not make the loan to Steve, even though an ice-cream store in the neighborhood is a good investment that would provide benefits for everyone.

---

[4]Another factor that encourages the use of debt contracts rather than equity contracts in the United States is our tax code. Debt interest payments are a deductible expense for American firms, whereas dividend payments to equity shareholders are not.

Tools to Help Solve Moral Hazard in Debt Contracts

Net Worth   When borrowers have more at stake because their *net worth* (the difference between their assets and their liabilities) is high, the risk of moral hazard—the temptation to act in a manner that lenders find objectionable—will be greatly reduced because the borrowers themselves have a lot to lose. Let's return to Steve and his ice-cream business. Suppose that the cost of setting up either the ice-cream store or the research equipment is $100,000 instead of $10,000. So Steve needs to put $91,000 of his own money into the business (instead of $1000) in addition to the $9000 supplied by your loan. Now if Steve is unsuccessful in inventing the no-calorie nonfat ice cream, he has a lot to lose, the $91,000 of net worth ($100,000 in assets minus the $9000 loan from you). He will think twice about undertaking the riskier investment and is more likely to invest in the ice-cream store, which is more of a sure thing. Hence when Steve has more of his own money (net worth) in the business, you are more likely to make him the loan.

One way of describing the solution that high net worth provides to the moral hazard problem is to say that it makes the debt contract **incentive-compatible;** that is, it aligns the incentives of the borrower with those of the lender. The greater the borrower's net worth, the greater the borrower's incentive to behave in the way that the lender expects and desires, the smaller the moral hazard problem in the debt contract is, and the easier it is for the firm to borrow. Conversely, when the borrower's net worth is lower, the moral hazard problem is greater, and it is harder for the firm to borrow.

Monitoring and Enforcement of Restrictive Covenants   As the example of Steve and his ice-cream store shows, if you could make sure that Steve doesn't invest in anything riskier than the ice-cream store, it would be worth your while to make him the loan. You can ensure that Steve uses your money for the purpose *you* want it to be used for by writing provisions (restrictive covenants) into the debt contract that restrict his firm's activities. By monitoring Steve's activities to see whether he is complying with the restrictive covenants and enforcing the covenants if he is not, you can make sure that he will not take on risks at your expense.

Restrictive covenants are directed at reducing moral hazard either by ruling out undesirable behavior or by encouraging desirable behavior. There are four types of restrictive covenants that achieve this objective:

1. *Covenants to discourage undesirable behavior.* Covenants can be designed to lower moral hazard by keeping the borrower from engaging in the undesirable behavior of undertaking risky investment projects. Some such covenants mandate that a loan can be used only to finance specific activities, such as the purchase of particular equipment or inventories. Others restrict the borrowing firm from engaging in certain risky business activities, such as purchasing other businesses.

2. *Covenants to encourage desirable behavior.* Restrictive covenants can encourage the borrower to engage in desirable activities that make it more likely that the loan will be paid off. One restrictive covenant of this type requires the breadwinner in a household to carry life insurance that pays off the mortgage upon that person's death. Restrictive covenants of this type for businesses focus on encouraging the borrowing firm to keep its net worth high because higher borrower net worth reduces moral hazard and makes it less likely that the lender will suffer losses. These restrictive

covenants typically specify that the firm must maintain minimum holdings of certain assets relative to the firm's size.

3. *Covenants to keep collateral valuable.* Because collateral is an important protection for the lender, restrictive covenants can encourage the borrower to keep the collateral in good condition and make sure that it stays in the possession of the borrower. This is the type of covenant ordinary people encounter most often. Automobile loan contracts, for example, require the car owner to maintain a minimum amount of collision and theft insurance and prevent the sale of the car unless the loan is paid off. Similarly, the recipient of a home mortgage must have adequate insurance on the home and must pay off the mortgage when the property is sold.

4. *Covenants to provide information.* Restrictive covenants also require a borrowing firm to provide information about its activities periodically in the form of quarterly accounting and income reports, thereby making it easier for the lender to monitor the firm and reduce moral hazard. This type of covenant may also stipulate that the lender has the right to audit and inspect the firm's books at any time.

We now see why debt contracts are often complicated legal documents with numerous restrictions on the borrower's behavior (fact 8): Debt contracts require complicated restrictive covenants to lower moral hazard.

Financial Intermediation   Although restrictive covenants help reduce the moral hazard problem, they do not eliminate it completely. It is almost impossible to write covenants that rule out *every* risky activity. Furthermore, borrowers may be clever enough to find loopholes in restrictive covenants that make them ineffective.

Another problem with restrictive covenants is that they must be monitored and enforced. A restrictive covenant is meaningless if the borrower can violate it knowing that the lender won't check up or is unwilling to pay for legal recourse. Because monitoring and enforcement of restrictive covenants are costly, the free-rider problem arises in the debt securities (bond) market just as it does in the stock market. If you know that other bondholders are monitoring and enforcing the restrictive covenants, you can free-ride on their monitoring and enforcement. But other bondholders can do the same thing, so the likely outcome is that not enough resources are devoted to monitoring and enforcing the restrictive covenants. Moral hazard therefore continues to be a severe problem for marketable debt.

As we have seen before, financial intermediaries, particularly banks, have the ability to avoid the free-rider problem as long as they primarily make private loans. Private loans are not traded, so no one else can free-ride on the intermediary's monitoring and enforcement of the restrictive covenants. The intermediary making private loans thus receives the benefits of monitoring and enforcement and will work to shrink the moral hazard problem inherent in debt contracts. The concept of moral hazard has provided us with additional reasons why financial intermediaries play a more important role in channeling funds from savers to borrowers than marketable securities do, as described in facts 3 and 4.

Summary

The presence of asymmetric information in financial markets leads to adverse selection and moral hazard problems that interfere with the efficient functioning of those markets. Tools to help solve these problems involve the private production and sale of information, government regulation to increase information in financial markets, the importance of collateral and net worth to debt contracts, and the use of monitoring and restrictive covenants. A key finding from our theoretical analysis is that the existence of the free-rider problem for traded securities such as stocks and bonds indicates that financial intermediaries, particularly banks, should play a greater role than securities markets in financing the activities of businesses. Theoretical analysis of the consequences of adverse selection and moral hazard has helped elucidate the basic features of our financial system and has provided explanations for the eight basic facts about our financial structure outlined at the beginning of this chapter.

Study Guide

To help you keep track of all the tools that help solve asymmetric information problems, summary Table 1 provides a listing of the asymmetric information problems and what tools can help solve them. In addition, it lists how these tools and asymmetric information problems explain the eight facts of financial structure described at the beginning of the chapter.

TABLE 1 SUMMARY *Asymmetric Information Problems and Tools to Solve Them*

Asymmetric Information Problem	Tools to Solve It	Explains Fact No.
Adverse selection	Private production and sale of information	1, 2
	Government regulation to increase information	5
	Financial intermediation	3, 4, 6
	Collateral and net worth	7
Moral hazard in equity contracts (Principal-agent problem)	Production of information: monitoring	1
	Government regulation to increase information	5
	Financial intermediation	3
	Debt contracts	1
Moral hazard in debt contracts	Net worth	
	Monitoring and enforcement of restrictive covenants	8
	Financial intermediation	3, 4

Note: List of facts:
1. Stocks are not the most important source of external financing.
2. Marketable securities are not the primary source of finance.
3. Indirect finance is more important than direct finance.
4. Financial intermediaries, especially banks, are the most important source of external funds.
5. The financial system is heavily regulated.
6. Only large, well-established firms have access to securities markets.
7. Collateral is prevalent in debt contracts.
8. Debt contracts have numerous restrictive covenants.

Case

FINANCIAL DEVELOPMENT AND ECONOMIC GROWTH

Recent research has found that an important reason why many developing countries or ex-communist countries like Russia experience very low rates of growth is that their financial systems are underdeveloped (a situation referred to as *financial repression*).[5] The theoretical analysis of financial structure helps explain how an underdeveloped financial system leads to a low state of economic development and economic growth.

The financial systems in developing and ex-communist countries face several difficulties that keep them from operating efficiently. As we have seen, two important tools used to help solve adverse selection and moral hazard problems in credit markets are collateral and restrictive covenants. In many developing countries, the legal system functions poorly, making it hard to make effective use of these two tools. In these countries, bankruptcy procedures are often extremely slow and cumbersome. For example, in many countries, **creditors** (holders of debt) must first sue the defaulting debtor for payment, which can take several years, and then once a favorable judgment has been obtained, the creditor has to sue again to obtain title to the collateral. The process can take in excess of five years, and by the time the lender acquires the collateral, it well may have been neglected and thus have little value. In addition, governments often block lenders from foreclosing on borrowers in politically powerful sectors such as agriculture. Where the market is unable to use collateral effectively, the adverse selection problem will be worse because the lender will need even more information about the quality of the borrower in order to screen out a good loan from a bad one. The result is that it will be harder for lenders to channel funds to borrowers with the most productive investment opportunities, thereby leading to less productive investment and hence a slower-growing economy. Similarly, a poorly developed legal system may make it extremely difficult for borrowers to enforce restrictive covenants. Thus they may have a much more limited ability to reduce moral hazard on the part of borrowers and so will be less willing to lend. Again the outcome will be less productive investment and a lower growth rate for the economy.

Governments in developing and ex-communist countries have also often decided to use their financial systems to direct credit to themselves or to favored sectors of the economy by setting interest rates at artificially low levels for certain types of loans, by creating so-called development finance institutions to make specific types of loans, or by directing existing institutions to lend to certain entities. As we have seen, private institutions have an incentive to solve adverse selection and moral hazard problems and lend to borrowers with the most productive investment opportunities. Governments have less incentive to do so because they are not driven by the profit motive and so their directed credit programs may not channel funds to sectors that will produce high growth for the economy. The outcome is again likely to result in less efficient investment and slower growth.

In addition, banks in many developing and ex-communist countries have been nationalized by their governments. Again because of the absence of the profit motive, these nationalized banks have little incentive to allocate their

[5]World Bank, *Finance for Growth: Policy Choices in a Volatile World* (Oxford: World Bank and Oxford University Press, 2001) for a survey of this literature and a list of further references.

capital to the most productive uses. Indeed, the primary loan customer of these nationalized banks is often the government, which does not always use the funds wisely.

We have seen that government regulation can increase the amount of information in financial markets to make them work more efficiently. Many developing and ex-communist countries have an underdeveloped regulatory apparatus that retards the provision of adequate information to the marketplace. For example, these countries often have weak accounting standards, making it very hard to ascertain the quality of a borrower's balance sheet. As a result, asymmetric information problems are more severe, and the financial system is severely hampered in channeling funds to the most productive uses.

The institutional environment of a poor legal system, weak accounting standards, inadequate government regulation, and government intervention through directed credit programs and nationalization of banks all help explain why many countries stay poor while others grow richer.

Financial Crises and Aggregate Economic Activity

Our theoretical analysis of the effects of adverse selection and moral hazard can help us understand **financial crises,** major disruptions in financial markets that are characterized by sharp declines in asset prices and the failures of many financial and nonfinancial firms. Financial crises have been common in most countries throughout modern history. The United States experienced major financial crises in 1819, 1837, 1857, 1873, 1884, 1893, 1907, and 1930–1933 but has not had full-scale financial crises since then.[6] Studying financial crises is worthwhile because they have led to severe economic downturns in the past and have the potential for doing so in the future.

Financial crises occur when there is a disruption in the financial system that causes such a sharp increase in adverse selection and moral hazard problems in financial markets that the markets are unable to channel funds efficiently from savers to people with productive investment opportunities. As a result of this inability of financial markets to function efficiently, economic activity contracts sharply.

Factors Causing Financial Crises

To understand why banking and financial crises occur and more specifically how they lead to contractions in economic activity, we need to examine the factors that cause them. Four categories of factors can trigger financial crises: increases in interest rates, increases in uncertainty, asset market effects on balance sheets, and bank panics.

Increases in Interest Rates   As we saw earlier, individuals and firms with the riskiest investment projects are exactly those who are willing to pay the highest interest rates. If market interest rates are driven up sufficiently because of increased

---

[6]Although we in the United States have not experienced any financial crises since the Great Depression, we have had several close calls—the October 1987 stock market crash, for example. An important reason why we have escaped financial crises is the timely action of the Federal Reserve to prevent them during episodes like that of October 1987. The Fed's role in preventing financial crises is discussed in Chapter 8.

demand for credit or because of a decline in the money supply, good credit risks are less likely to want to borrow while bad credit risks are still willing to borrow. Because of the resulting increase in adverse selection, lenders will no longer want to make loans. The substantial decline in lending will lead to a substantial decline in investment and aggregate economic activity.

Increases in Uncertainty   A dramatic increase in uncertainty in financial markets, due perhaps to the failure of a prominent financial or nonfinancial institution, a recession, or a stock market crash, makes it harder for lenders to screen good from bad credit risks. The resulting inability of lenders to solve the adverse selection problem makes them less willing to lend, which leads to a decline in lending, investment, and aggregate activity.

Asset Market Effects on Balance Sheets   The state of firms' balance sheets has important implications for the severity of asymmetric information problems in the financial system. A sharp decline in the stock market is one factor that can cause a serious deterioration in firms' balance sheets that can increase adverse selection and moral hazard problems in financial markets and provoke a financial crisis. A decline in the stock market means that the net worth of corporations has fallen because share prices are the valuation of a corporation's net worth. The decline in net worth as a result of a stock market decline makes lenders less willing to lend because, as we have seen, the net worth of a firm plays a role similar to that of collateral. When the value of collateral declines, it provides less protection to lenders, meaning that losses on loans are likely to be more severe. Because lenders are now less protected against the consequences of adverse selection, they decrease their lending, which in turn causes investment and aggregate output to decline. In addition, the decline in corporate net worth as a result of a stock market decline increases moral hazard by providing incentives for borrowing firms to make risky investments, as they now have less to lose if their investments go sour. The resulting increase in moral hazard makes lending less attractive—another reason why a stock market decline and hence a decline in net worth leads to decreased lending and economic activity.

In economies in which inflation has been moderate, which characterizes most industrialized countries, many debt contracts are typically of fairly long maturity with fixed interest rates. In this institutional environment, unanticipated declines in the aggregate price level also decrease the net worth of firms. Because debt payments are contractually fixed in nominal terms, an unanticipated decline in the price level raises the value of firms' liabilities in *real* terms (increases the burden of the debt) but does not raise the real value of firms' assets. The result is that net worth in *real* terms (the difference between assets and liabilities in *real* terms) declines. A sharp drop in the price level therefore causes a substantial decline in real net worth and an increase in adverse selection and moral hazard problems facing lenders. An unanticipated decline in the aggregate price level thus leads to a drop in lending and economic activity.

Because of uncertainty about the future value of the domestic currency in developing countries (and in some industrialized countries), many nonfinancial firms, banks, and governments in these countries find it easier to issue debt denominated in foreign currencies. This can lead to a financial crisis in a fashion similar to an unanticipated decline in inflation. With debt contracts denominated in foreign currency, when there is an unanticipated fall in the value of the domestic currency, the debt burden of domestic firms increases. Since assets are typically denominated in domestic currency, there is a resulting deterioration in firms' balance sheets and a decline in net worth, which then increases adverse selection and moral hazard problems along the lines just described. The increase in asymmetric information problems leads to a decline in investment and economic activity.

Although we have seen that increases in interest rates have a direct effect on increasing adverse selection problems, increases in interest rates also play a role in promoting a financial crisis through their effect on both firms' and households' balance sheets. A rise in interest rates and therefore in households' and firms' interest payments decreases firms' **cash flow,** the difference between cash receipts and cash expenditures. The decline in cash flow causes a deterioration in the balance sheet because it decreases the liquidity of the household or firm and thus makes it harder for lenders to know whether the firm or household will be able to pay its bills. As a result, adverse selection and moral hazard problems become more severe for potential lenders to these firms and households, leading to a decline in lending and economic activity. There is thus an additional reason why sharp increases in interest rates can be an important factor leading to financial crises.

Problems in the Banking Sector   Banks play a major role in financial markets since they are well positioned to engage in information-producing activities that facilitate productive investment for the economy. The state of banks' balance sheets has an important effect on bank lending. If banks suffer a deterioration in their balance sheets and so have a substantial contraction in their capital, they will have fewer resources to lend, and bank lending will decline. The contraction in lending then leads to a decline in investment spending, which slows economic activity.

If the deterioration in bank balance sheets is severe enough, banks will start to fail, and fear can spread from one bank to another, causing even healthy banks to go under. The multiple bank failures that result are known as a **bank panic.** The source of the contagion is again asymmetric information. In a panic, depositors, fearing the safety of their deposits (in the absence of deposit insurance) and not knowing the quality of banks' loan portfolios, withdraw their deposits from other banks to the point that the banks fail. The disappearance of a large number of banks in a short period of time means that there is a loss of information production in financial markets and hence a direct loss of financial intermediation by the banking sector. The decrease in bank lending during a financial crisis also decreases the supply of funds to borrowers, which leads to higher interest rates. The outcome is an increase in adverse selection and moral hazard problems in credit markets; this produces an even sharper decline in lending to facilitate productive investments and a strong contraction in economic activity.

Government Fiscal Imbalances   In emerging market countries (Argentina, Brazil, and Turkey are recent examples), government fiscal imbalances may create fears of default on the government debt. As a result, the government may have trouble getting people to buy its bonds and so it might force banks to purchase them. If the debt then declines in price—which, as we have seen in Chapter 5, will occur if a government default is likely—this can substantially weaken bank balance sheets and lead to a contraction in lending for the reasons described earlier. Fears of default on the government debt can also spark a foreign exchange crisis in which the value of the domestic currency falls sharply because investors pull their money out of the country. The decline in the domestic currency's value will then lead to the destruction of the balance sheets of firms with large amounts of debt denominated in foreign currency. These balance sheet problems lead to an increase in adverse selection and moral hazard problems, a decline in lending, and a contraction of economic activity.

Case

FINANCIAL CRISES IN THE UNITED STATES

As mentioned, the United States has a long history of banking and financial crises, such crises having occurred every 20 years or so in the nineteenth and early twentieth centuries—in 1819, 1837, 1857, 1873, 1884, 1893, 1907, and 1930–1933. Our analysis of the factors that lead to a financial crisis can explain why these crises took place and why they were so damaging to the U.S. economy.

Study Guide

To understand fully what took place in a U.S. financial crisis, make sure that you can state the reasons why each of the factors—increases in interest rates, increases in uncertainty, asset market effects on balance sheets, and bank panics—increases adverse selection and moral hazard problems, which in turn lead to a decline in economic activity. To help you understand these crises, you might want to refer to Figure 3, a diagram that traces the sequence of events in a U.S. financial crisis.

As shown in Figure 3, most financial crises in the United States have begun with a deterioration in banks' balance sheets, a sharp rise in interest rates (frequently stemming from increases in interest rates abroad), a steep stock market decline, and an increase in uncertainty resulting from a failure of major financial or nonfinancial firms (the Ohio Life Insurance & Trust Company in 1857, the Northern Pacific Railroad and Jay Cooke & Company in 1873, Grant & Ward in 1884, the National Cordage Company in 1893, the Knickerbocker Trust Company in 1907, and the Bank of the United States in 1930). During these crises, deterioration in banks' balance sheets, the increase in uncertainty, the rise in interest rates, and the stock market decline increased the severity of adverse selection problems in credit markets; the stock market decline, the deterioration in banks' balance sheets, and the rise in interest rates, which decreases firms' cash flow, also increased moral hazard problems. The rise in adverse selection and moral hazard problems then made it less attractive for lenders to lend and led to a decline in investment and aggregate economic activity.

Because of the worsening business conditions and uncertainty about their bank's health (perhaps banks would go broke), depositors began to withdraw their funds from banks, and the massive withdrawal of deposits led to bank failures, which, if they snowballed, led to a full-scale bank panic. The resulting decline in the number of banks raised interest rates even further and decreased the amount of financial intermediation by banks. Worsening of the problems created by adverse selection and moral hazard led to further economic contraction.

Finally, there was a sorting out of firms that were **insolvent** (that had a negative net worth and hence were bankrupt) from healthy firms by bankruptcy proceedings. The same process occurred for banks, often with the help of public and private authorities. Once this sorting out was complete, uncertainty in financial markets declined, the stock market underwent a recovery, and interest rates fell. The overall result was that adverse selection

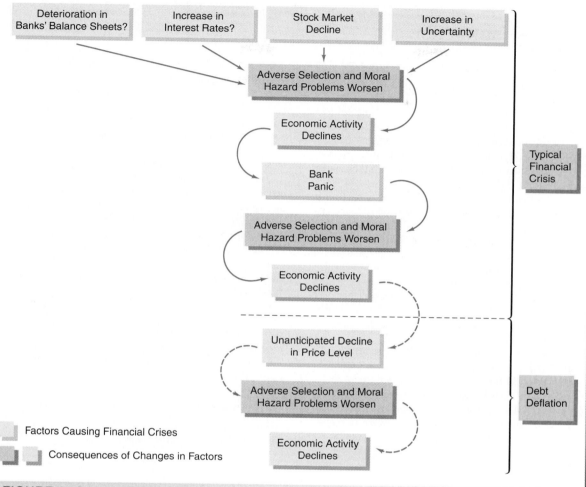

FIGURE 3 *Sequence of Events in U.S. Financial Crises*

The solid arrows trace the sequence of events in a typical financial crisis; the dotted arrows show the additional set of events that occurs if the crisis develops into a debt deflation.

and moral hazard problems diminished and the financial crisis subsided. With the financial markets able to operate well again, the stage was set for the recovery of the economy.

If, however, the economic downturn led to a sharp decline in prices, the recovery process was short-circuited. In this situation, shown in Figure 3, a process called **debt deflation** occurred, in which a substantial decline in the price level set in, leading to a further deterioration in firms' net worth because of the increased burden of indebtedness. When debt deflation set in, the adverse selection and moral hazard problems continued to increase so that lending, investment spending, and aggregate economic activity remained depressed for a long time. The most significant financial crisis that included debt deflation was the Great Depression, the worst economic contraction in U.S. history (see the "Mini-Case" box).

MINI-CASE

Case Study of a Financial Crisis: The Great Depression

Federal Reserve officials viewed the stock market boom of 1928 and 1929, during which stock prices doubled, as excessive speculation. To curb it, they pursued a tight monetary policy to raise interest rates. The Fed got more than it bargained for when the stock market crashed in October 1929.

Although the 1929 crash had a great impact on the minds of a whole generation, most people forget that by the middle of 1930, more than half of the stock market decline had been reversed. What might have been a normal recession turned into something far different, however, with adverse shocks to the agricultural sector, a continuing decline in the stock market after the middle of 1930, and a sequence of bank collapses from October 1930 until March 1933 in which over one-third of the banks in the United States went out of business.

The continuing decline in stock prices after mid-1930 (by mid-1932 stocks had declined to 10% of their value at the 1929 peak) and the increase in uncertainty from the unsettled business conditions created by the economic contraction made adverse selection and moral hazard problems worse in the credit markets. The loss of one-third of the banks

reduced the amount of financial intermediation. This intensified adverse selection and moral hazard problems, thereby decreasing the ability of financial markets to channel funds to firms with productive investment opportunities. As our analysis predicts, the amount of outstanding commercial loans fell by half from 1929 to 1933, and investment spending collapsed, declining by 90% from its 1929 level.

The short-circuiting of the process that kept the economy from recovering quickly, which it does in most recessions, occurred because of a fall in the price level by 25% in the 1930–1933 period. This huge decline in prices triggered a debt deflation in which net worth fell because of the increased burden of indebtedness borne by firms. The decline in net worth and the resulting increase in adverse selection and moral hazard problems in the credit markets led to a prolonged economic contraction in which unemployment rose to 25% of the labor force. The financial crisis in the Great Depression was the worst ever experienced in the United States, and it explains why this economic contraction was also the most severe one ever experienced by the nation.*

---

*See Ben Bernanke, "Nonmonetary Effects of the Financial Crisis in the Propagation of the Great Depression," *American Economic Review* 73 (1983): 257–276, for a discussion of the role of asymmetric information problems in the Great Depression period.

Case

FINANCIAL CRISES IN EMERGING MARKET COUNTRIES: MEXICO, 1994–1995, EAST ASIA, 1997–1998, AND ARGENTINA, 2001–2002

In recent years, many emerging market countries have experienced financial crises, the most dramatic of which were the Mexican crisis, which started in December 1994, and the East Asian crisis, which started in July 1997. An important fact is how a developing country can shift dramatically from a path of high growth before a financial crisis—as was true for Mexico and particularly the East Asian countries of Thailand, Malaysia, Indonesia, the Philippines, and South Korea—to a sharp decline in economic activity, damaging both the economy and the social fabric of the country. We can again apply our asymmetric information analysis of financial crises to explain this fact and to understand the Mexican and East Asian situations.

Because of the different institutional features of emerging market countries' debt markets, the sequence of events in the Mexican and East Asian crises is different from what occurred in the United States in the nineteenth and early twentieth centuries. Figure 4 diagrams the sequence of events that occurred in Mexico and East Asia.

An important factor leading up to both financial crises was the deterioration in banks' balance sheets because of increasing loan losses. When financial markets were deregulated, a lending boom ensued in which bank credit to the private nonfinancial business sector accelerated sharply. Because of weak supervision by bank regulators and a lack of expertise in screening and monitoring borrowers at banking institutions, losses on the loans began to mount, causing an erosion of banks' net worth (capital). As we have seen, this would mean that the banks would have fewer resources to lend, and this lack of lending would eventually lead to a contraction in economic activity.

Argentina also experienced a deterioration in bank balance sheets leading up to its crisis, but the source of this deterioration was quite different. In contrast to Mexico and the East Asian crisis countries, Argentina had a well-supervised banking system, and a lending boom did not occur before the crisis. On the other hand, in 1998 Argentina entered a recession that

Find out about the East Asian financial crisis at **www.worldbank. org/data**, *which provides background information, speeches and articles, and press releases.*

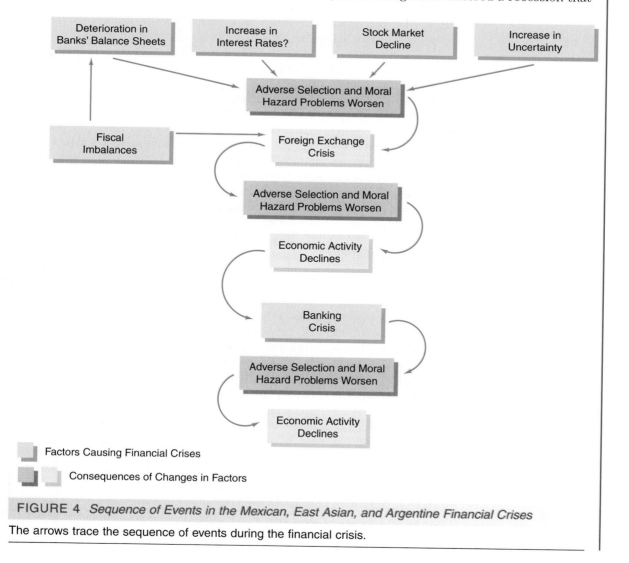

FIGURE 4 *Sequence of Events in the Mexican, East Asian, and Argentine Financial Crises*

The arrows trace the sequence of events during the financial crisis.

led to some loan losses. However, it was the fiscal problems of the Argentine government that led to severe weakening of bank balance sheets. Again in contrast to Mexico and the East Asian countries before their crises, Argentina was running substantial budget deficits that could not be financed by foreign borrowing. To solve its fiscal problems, the Argentine government coerced banks into absorbing large amounts of government debt. When investors lost confidence in the ability of the Argentine government to repay this debt, the price of this debt plummeted, leaving big holes in commercial banks' balance sheets. This weakening in bank balance sheets, as in Mexico and East Asia, helped lead to a contraction of economic activity.

Consistent with the U.S. experience in the nineteenth and early twentieth centuries, another precipitating factor in the Mexican and Argentine (but not East Asian) financial crises was a rise in interest rates abroad. Before the Mexican crisis, in February 1994, and before the Argentine crisis, in mid-1999, the Federal Reserve began a cycle of raising the federal funds rate to head off inflationary pressures. Although the monetary policy moves by the Fed were quite successful in keeping inflation in check in the United States, they put upward pressure on interest rates in both Mexico and Argentina. The rise in interest rates in Mexico and Argentina directly added to increased adverse selection in their financial markets because, as discussed earlier, it was more likely that the parties willing to take on the most risk would seek loans.

Also consistent with the U.S. experience in the nineteenth and early twentieth centuries, stock market declines and increases in uncertainty occurred prior to and contributed to full-blown crises in Mexico, Thailand, South Korea, and Argentina. (The stock market declines in Malaysia, Indonesia, and the Philippines, on the other hand, occurred simultaneously with the onset of the crisis.) The Mexican economy was hit by political shocks in 1994 (specifically, the assassination of the ruling party's presidential candidate and an uprising in the southern state of Chiapas) that created uncertainty, while the ongoing recession increased uncertainty in Argentina. Right before their crises, Thailand and Korea experienced major failures of financial and nonfinancial firms that increased general uncertainty in financial markets.

As we have seen, an increase in uncertainty and a decrease in net worth as a result of a stock market decline increase asymmetric information problems. It becomes harder to screen out good from bad borrowers, and the decline in net worth decreases the value of firms' collateral and increases their incentives to make risky investments because there is less equity to lose if the investments are unsuccessful. The increase in uncertainty and stock market declines that occurred before the crisis, along with the deterioration in banks' balance sheets, worsened adverse selection and moral hazard problems (shown at the top of the diagram in Figure 4) and made the economies ripe for a serious financial crisis.

At this point, full-blown speculative attacks developed in the foreign exchange market, plunging these countries into a full-scale crisis. With the Colosio assassination, the Chiapas uprising, and the growing weakness in the banking sector, the Mexican peso came under attack. Even though the Mexican central bank intervened in the foreign exchange market and raised interest rates sharply, it was unable to stem the attack and was forced to devalue the peso on December 20, 1994. In the case of Thailand, concerns about the large current account deficit and weakness in the Thai financial system, culminating with the failure of a major finance company, Finance One, led to a successful speculative attack that forced the Thai central bank to allow the baht to float downward in July 1997. Soon thereafter, speculative attacks developed against the other countries in the region, leading to the collapse of the Philippine peso, the Indonesian rupiah, the Malaysian ringgit, and the South Korean won. In Argentina, a full-scale banking panic began in Octo-ber–November 2001. This, along with realization that the government was going to default on its debt, also led to a speculative attack on the Argen-tine peso, resulting in its collapse on January 6, 2002.

The institutional structure of debt markets in Mexico and East Asia now interacted with the currency devaluations to propel the economies into full-fledged financial crises. Because so many firms in these countries had debt denominated in foreign currencies like the dollar and the yen, depreciation of their currencies resulted in increases in their indebtedness in domestic currency terms, even though the value of their assets remained unchanged. When the peso lost half its value by March 1995 and the Thai, Philippine, Malaysian, and South Korean currencies lost between a third and half of their value by the beginning of 1998, firms' balance sheets took a big negative hit, causing a dramatic increase in adverse selection and moral hazard prob-lems. This negative shock was especially severe for Indonesia and Argentina, which saw the value of their currencies fall by over 70%, resulting in insol-vency for firms with substantial amounts of debt denominated in foreign currencies.

The collapse of currencies also led to a rise in actual and expected infla-tion in these countries, and market interest rates rose sky-high (to around 100% in Mexico and Argentina). The resulting increase in interest payments caused reductions in households' and firms' cash flow, which led to further deterioration in their balance sheets. A feature of debt markets in emerging-market countries, like those in Mexico, East Asia, and Argentina is that debt contracts have very short durations, typically less than one month. Thus the rise in short-term interest rates in these countries meant that the effect on cash flow and hence on balance sheets was substantial. As our asymmetric information analysis suggests, this deterioration in households' and firms' balance sheets increased adverse selection and moral hazard problems in the credit markets, making domestic and foreign lenders even less willing to lend.

Consistent with the theory of financial crises outlined in this chapter, the sharp decline in lending helped lead to a collapse of economic activity, with real GDP growth falling sharply.

As shown in Figure 4, further deterioration in the economy occurred because the collapse in economic activity and the deterioration in the cash flow and balance sheets of both firms and households led to worsening bank-ing crises. The problems of firms and households meant that many of them were no longer able to pay off their debts, resulting in substantial losses for the banks. Even more problematic for the banks was that they had many short-term liabilities denominated in foreign currencies, and the sharp increase in the value of these liabilities after the devaluation led to a fur-ther deterioration in the banks' balance sheets. Under these circumstances, the banking system would have collapsed in the absence of a government safety net—as it did in the United States during the Great Depression—but with the assistance of the International Monetary Fund, these coun-tries were in some cases able to protect depositors and avoid a bank panic.

However, given the loss of bank capital and the need for the government to intervene to prop up the banks, the banks' ability to lend was nevertheless sharply curtailed. As we have seen, a banking crisis of this type hinders the ability of the banks to lend and also makes adverse selection and moral hazard problems worse in financial markets, because banks are less capable of playing their traditional financial intermediation role. The banking crisis, along with other factors that increased adverse selection and moral hazard problems in the credit markets of Mexico, East Asia, and Argentina, explains the collapse of lending and hence economic activity in the aftermath of the crisis.

In the aftermath of their crises, Mexico began to recover in 1996, while the crisis countries in East Asia saw the glimmer of recovery in 1999. Argentina started to recover in 2003 but is still in bad shape. In all these countries, the economic hardship caused by the financial crises was tremendous. Unemployment rose sharply, poverty increased substantially, and even the social fabric of the society was stretched thin. For example, Mexico City and Buenos Aires have become crime-ridden, while Indonesia has experienced waves of ethnic violence.

Summary

1. There are eight basic facts about our financial structure. The first four emphasize the importance of financial intermediaries and the relative unimportance of securities markets for the financing of corporations; the fifth recognizes that financial markets are among the most heavily regulated sectors of the economy; the sixth states that only large, well-established corporations have access to securities markets; the seventh indicates that collateral is an important feature of debt contracts; and the eighth presents debt contracts as complicated legal documents that place substantial restrictions on the behavior of the borrower.

2. Transaction costs freeze many small savers and borrowers out of direct involvement with financial markets. Financial intermediaries can take advantage of economies of scale and are better able to develop expertise to lower transaction costs, thus enabling their savers and borrowers to benefit from the existence of financial markets.

3. Asymmetric information results in two problems: adverse selection, which occurs before the transaction, and moral hazard, which occurs after the transaction. Adverse selection refers to the fact that bad credit risks are the ones most likely to seek loans, and moral hazard refers to the risk of the borrower's engaging in activities that are undesirable from the lender's point of view.

4. Adverse selection interferes with the efficient functioning of financial markets. Tools to help reduce the adverse selection problem include private production and sale of information, government regulation to increase information, financial intermediation, and collateral and net worth. The free-rider problem occurs when people who do not pay for information take advantage of information that other people have paid for. This problem explains why financial intermediaries, particularly banks, play a more important role in financing the activities of businesses than securities markets do.

5. Moral hazard in equity contracts is known as the principal-agent problem because managers (the agents) have less incentive to maximize profits than stockholders (the principals). The principal-agent problem explains why debt contracts are so much more prevalent in financial markets than equity contracts. Tools to help reduce the principal-agent problem include monitoring, government regulation to increase information, and financial intermediation.

6. Tools to reduce the moral hazard problem in debt contracts include net worth, monitoring and enforcement of restrictive covenants, and financial intermediaries.

7. Financial crises are major disruptions in financial markets. They are caused by increases in adverse selection and moral hazard problems that prevent financial markets from channeling funds to people with productive investment opportunities, leading to a sharp contraction in economic activity. The four types of factors that lead to financial crises are increases in interest rates, increases in uncertainty, asset market effects on balance sheets, and bank panics.

Key Terms

agency theory, *p. 377*

audit, *p. 380*

bank panic, *p. 393*

cash flow, *p. 393*

collateral, *p. 374*

costly state verification, *p. 385*

creditor, *p. 390*

debt deflation, *p. 395*

equity capital, *p. 382*

financial crisis, *p. 391*

free-rider problem, *p. 379*

incentive-compatible, *p. 387*

insolvent, *p. 394*

net worth, *p. 382*

pecking order hypothesis,
    p. 382

principal-agent problem, *p. 383*

restrictive covenants, *p. 375*

secured debt, *p. 374*

unsecured debt, *p. 374*

venture capital firm, *p. 385*

Questions

1. How can economies of scale help explain the existence of financial intermediaries?

2. Describe two ways in which financial intermediaries help lower transaction costs in the economy.

3. Would moral hazard and adverse selection still arise in financial markets if information were not asymmetric? Explain your answer.

4. How do standard accounting principles required by the government help financial markets work more efficiently?

5. Do you think the lemons problem would be more severe for stocks traded on the New York Stock Exchange or for those traded over-the-counter? Explain your answer.

6. Which firms are most likely to use bank financing rather than to issue bonds or stocks to finance their activities? Why?

7. How can the existence of asymmetric information provide a rationale for government regulation of financial markets?

8. Would you be more willing to lend to a friend if she put all of her life savings into her business than you would if she had not done so? Why?

9. Rich individuals often worry that people will seek to marry them only for their money. Is this a problem of adverse selection?

10. "The more collateral there is backing a loan, the less the lender has to worry about adverse selection." Is this statement true, false, or uncertain? Explain your answer.

11. How does the free-rider problem aggravate adverse selection and moral hazard problems in financial markets?

12. Explain how the separation of ownership and control in American corporations might lead to poor management.

13. Is a financial crisis more likely to occur when the economy is experiencing deflation or inflation? Explain your answer.

14. How can a stock market crash provoke a financial crisis?

15. How can a sharp rise in interest rates provoke a financial crisis?

Quantitative Problems

1. You are in the market for a used car. At a used car lot, you know that the blue book value for the cars you are looking at is between $20,000 and $24,000. If you believe the dealer knows *as much* about the car as you, how much are you willing to pay? Why? Assume that you only care about the expected value of the car you buy and that the car values are symmetrically distributed.

2. Now, you believe the dealer knows *more* about the cars than you. How much are you willing to pay? Why? How can this be resolved in a competitive market?

3. You wish to hire Ricky to manage your Dallas operations. The profits from the operations depend partially on how hard Ricky works, as follows.

	Probabilities	
	Profit = $10,000	Profit = $50,000
Lazy	60%	40%
Hard worker	20%	80%

If Ricky is lazy, he will surf the Internet all day, and he views this as a zero cost opportunity. However,

Ricky would view working hard as a "personal cost" valued at $1000. What fixed percentage of the profits should you offer Ricky? Assume Ricky only cares about his expected payment less any "personal cost."

4. You own a house worth $400,000 on a river. If the river floods moderately, the house will be completely destroyed. This happens about once every 50 years. If you build a seawall, the river would have to flood heavily to destroy your house, which only happens about once every 200 years. What would be the annual premium for an insurance policy that offers full insurance? For a policy that only pays 75% of the home value, what are your expected costs with and without a seawall? Do the different policies provide an incentive to be safer (i.e., to build the seawall)?

Web Exercises

Why Do Financial Institutions Exist?

1. In this chapter we discuss the lemons problem and its effect on the efficient functioning of a market. This theory was initially developed by George Akerlof. Go to **http://www.nobel.se/economics/laureates/2001/public.html**. This site reports that Akerlof, Michael Spence, and Joseph Stiglitz were awarded the Nobel Prize in Economics in 2001 for their work. Read this report down through the section on George Akerlof. Summarize his research ideas in a one-page report.

2. This chapter discusses how an understanding of adverse selection and moral hazard can help us better understand financial crises. The greatest financial crisis faced by the United States was during the Great Depression from 1929 to 1933. Go to **http://education.yahoo.com/reference/encyclopedia/**. Type "Great Depression" in the search blank. This site contains a brief discussion of the factors that led to this depression. Write a one-page summary explaining how adverse selection and moral hazard were responsible for the depression.

CHAPTER 16

What Should Be Done About Conflicts of Interest in the Financial Industry?

Preview

Since the end of the stock market boom in 2000, financial markets have been jolted by one corporate scandal after another. The cycle began in December 2001 with the spectacular bankruptcy of Enron Corporation, which was once valued as the seventh-largest corporation in the United States, and the indictment of Enron's auditor, Arthur Andersen, one of the big five accounting firms. Subsequently, revelations of misleading accounting statements at numerous other corporations, including WorldCom, Tyco Industries, and Fannie Mae, have increased investors' doubts about the quality of information in the corporate sector. Criminal cases have been filed against investment banks that encouraged their stock analysts to hype dubious stocks, which later proved to be disastrous investments.

These scandals have attracted tremendous public attention for several reasons. First, the resulting bankruptcies cost employees of these firms their jobs, their pensions, or both. Second, these activities may have been a factor in the stock market crash after March 2000 and the subsequent 50% decline from the peak to the trough in the S&P 500 index and 75% decline in the NASDAQ. Third, they have created doubts about the ethics of those working in the financial service industry. Conflicts of interest, a manifestation of the moral hazard problem, may be responsible for these scandals. In each case, people who were supposed to act in the investing public's best interests by providing them with reliable information were given incentives to deceive the public. What are these conflicts of interest, and how serious are they? Where do they occur? Have they been the source of the woes in financial markets recently? What should we do about them?

This chapter provides a framework for answering these questions. It first explains what conflicts of interest are, why we should care about them, and why they raise ethical issues. It then surveys the different types of conflicts of

To review the timing of the stock market declines, you can go to http://stock charts.com/ charts/ historical/, where a variety of stock market indexes are graphed for easy viewing.

interest in the financial industry and discusses policies to remedy them.[1] We are addressing these issues at this point in the book because conflicts of interest are a pervasive problem in the financial institutions industry that we will examine further in the following chapters.

What Are Conflicts of Interest and Why Are They Important?

In the previous chapter, we saw how financial institutions play an important role in the financial system. Specifically, their expertise in interpreting signals and collecting information from their customers gives them a cost advantage in the production of information. Furthermore, because they are collecting, producing, and distributing this information, the financial institutions have the advantage of being able to use the information over and over again in as many ways as they would like, thereby obtaining economies of scale. Thus, not only are they lower-cost producers of information for one type of financial service, but by providing multiple financial services to their customers, they can also obtain **economies of scope**—that is, lower the costs of information production for each service by applying one information resource to many different services. Additionally, by providing multiple financial services to their customers, financial institutions can develop broader and longer-term relationships with firms, which further reduce the cost of producing information, and thus further increase economies of scope.

Although the presence of economies of scope may substantially benefit financial institutions, it also creates potential costs in the form of conflicts of interest. Although conflicts of interest arise in almost all aspects of our lives, we need to be precise about the conflicts of interest that concern us here. Given the crucial role of information in financial markets, we are focusing on the conflicts of interest that arise when financial service providers or their employees have the opportunity to serve their own interests, rather than those of their customers, by misusing information, providing false information, or concealing information.

Conflicts of interest may occur within financial institutions that provide a specialized service. However, conflicts of interest stand out most sharply when an institution provides multiple financial services. The potentially competing interests of these services may lead to the concealment of information or dissemination of misleading information. Combinations of services that bring together any group of depository intermediaries, nondepository intermediaries, or brokers, or allow any of these to invest directly in business attract the greatest criticism for apparent conflicts of interest.

We care about these conflicts of interest because a substantial reduction in the quality of information in financial markets increases the presence of asymmetric information, which prevents financial markets from channeling funds into productive investment opportunities. Consequently, the financial markets and the economy become less efficient.

---

[1]The analysis in this chapter is based on Andrew Crockett, Trevor Harris, Frederic S. Mishkin, and Eugene N. White, *Conflicts of Interest in the Financial Services Industry: What Should We Do About Them?* Geneva Reports on the World Economy 4 (Geneva and London: International Center for Monetary and Banking Studies and Centre for Economic Policy Research, 2003).

Ethics and Conflicts of Interest

Conflicts of interest also raise ethical dilemmas for those engaged in the financial service business. Conflicts of interest generate incentives for financial service providers or their employees to conceal or provide misleading information, thereby hurting the customers they work for. Conflicts of interest thus tempt financial service providers to engage in unethical behavior. The growing synergies in the financial industry that have led financial institutions to offer more services under one roof have increased conflicts of interest; not surprisingly, this has led to numerous instances of unethical behavior, as we will see in the next section. One way to limit these conflicts of interest is to make those working in the financial industry aware of the ethical issues that arise when they exploit conflicts of interest, so that they are less likely to do so. This is why business schools are now bringing the discussion of ethics into the classroom. Policies that make it harder for individuals to exploit conflicts of interest, which we will discuss later, can also help to limit unethical behavior.

Types of Conflicts of Interest

Four areas of financial service activities harbor the greatest potential for generating conflicts of interest that ultimately reduce the amount of information available in financial markets. The four areas are as follows:

- Underwriting and research in investment banking
- Auditing and consulting in accounting firms
- Credit assessment and consulting in credit-rating agencies
- Universal banking

Underwriting and Research in Investment Banking

Investment banks both *research* companies issuing securities and *underwrite* these securities by selling them to the public on behalf of the issuing corporations. Investment banks often combine these distinct financial services in order to create information synergies. A conflict of interest arises between the brokerage and underwriting services because the bank is attempting to serve two client groups—the issuing firms and the investors to whom it sells securities. These client groups have different information needs. Issuers benefit from optimistic research, whereas investors desire unbiased research. However, due to economies of scope, both groups will receive the same information. When the potential revenues from underwriting greatly exceed brokerage commissions, there will be a strong incentive to alter the information provided to both clients to favor the issuing firms' needs or risk losing the former to competitors. For example, an internal Morgan Stanley memo excerpted in the *Wall Street Journal* on July 14, 1992, stated: "Our objective . . . is to adopt a policy, fully understood by the entire firm, including the Research Department, that we do not make negative or controversial comments about our clients as a matter of sound business practice."

Because of directives like this, analysts in investment banks might distort their research to please issuers (and their employers). Their actions undermine the reliability of the information that investors use to make their financial decisions and,

CONFLICTS OF INTEREST

The King, Queen, and Jack of the Internet

The King, Queen, and Jack of the Internet are the nicknames of a trio of bullish technology analysts who were very influential during the tech boom of the late 1990s: Henry Blodgett at Merrill Lynch, Jack Grubman at Salomon Smith Barney (Citigroup), and Mary Meeker at Morgan Stanley. Their stories reveal a lot about how conflicts of interest may have influenced analysts' recommendations during the tech boom.*

In late 1998, Henry Blodgett, then at Oppenheimer and Company, recommended a price target of $400 per share for Amazon.com. At the time, most analysts believed that Amazon.com was overvalued at $240 per share. In particular, Jonathan Cole of Merrill Lynch indicated that $50 was a more reasonable price. When Amazon.com rose above $400 per share, Blodgett was hailed as a guru and hired by Merrill Lynch, while Cole left the firm. Clearly, Blodgett saw that he could reap benefits by hyping tech stocks. A subsequent investigation by the New York Attorney General's office found that Blodgett issued very positive reports on certain Internet stocks while privately deriding them in emails. Blodgett was accused of issuing favorable research reports for InfoSpace because he knew that it was planning to buy Go2Net, one of Merrill Lynch's clients. Similarly, Blodgett was alleged to have maintained a positive recommendation for GoTo.com, even though it was not doing well, at a time when Merrill Lynch was competing to manage a new stock issue for the company. He only downgraded GoTo.com's rating when it chose Credit Suisse First Boston as its underwriter instead.

The New York Attorney General's office accused Jack Grubman of engaging in similar questionable behavior. Although he expressed doubts in private, Grubman made wildly bullish recommendations about several telecom companies—including WorldCom Inc., Global Crossing Ltd., and Winstar Communications—that were spiraling toward bankruptcy. In 1999, he upgraded his rating of AT&T when Salomon Smith Barney was competing for a new issue of AT&T's spin-off of its cellular division. Six months after his firm, along with Goldman Sachs and Merrill Lynch, was awarded AT&T's business, Grubman downgraded AT&T's rating.

Blodgett and Grubman have faced criminal charges for their actions, whereas Mary Meeker has not. Like Blodgett and Grubman, Mary Meeker kept her ratings of tech stocks high after their prices plummeted. However, unlike Blodgett and Grubman, there was no evidence that Meeker did not believe her ratings, and she did discourage many Internet issues when the companies had poor outlooks. Morgan Stanley argued on her behalf that "research analysts helped screen out IPO candidates such that Morgan Stanley rejected five Internet IPOs for every one the firm underwrote. Mary Meeker was an integral part of this screening process, which benefited the firm's investor clients." Despite the New York Attorney General's office's criticisms of some of Morgan Stanley practices, Mary Meeker was not subjected to criminal charges because she did provide some screening and there was no evident exploitation of conflicts of interest.

---

*For more detail, see Andrew Crockett, Trevor Harris, Frederic S. Mishkin, and Eugene N. White, *Conflicts of Interest in the Financial Services Industry: What Should We Do About Them?* Geneva Reports on the World Economy 4 (Geneva and London: International Center for Monetary and Banking Studies and Centre for Economic Policy Research, 2003).

as a result, diminish the efficiency of securities markets. A similar chain of events precipitated the tech boom of the 1990s (see the first "Conflicts of Interest" box above).

Another common practice that exploits conflicts of interest is **spinning.** Spinning occurs when investment banks allocate hot, but underpriced, **initial public offerings (IPOs),** shares of newly issued stock, to executives of other companies in return for their companies' future business with the investment banks (see the "Conflicts of Interest" box on page 407). Because hot IPOs typically immediately rise in price after they are first purchased, spinning is a form of kickback that might influence executives not to use the investment bank that can get the highest price for the company's securities. This may raise the cost of capital for the firm, and therefore hinder the efficiency of the capital market.

CONFLICTS OF INTEREST

Frank Quattrone and Spinning

Frank Quattrone of Credit Suisse First Boston was a highly regarded investment banker specializing in technology companies when in March 2003 the National Association of Securities Dealers (NASD) filed a complaint against him for improperly pressuring his analysts to provide favorable coverage in order to solicit customers for his firm. Allegedly, Quattrone linked his analysts' bonuses to their investment banking work and permitted executives of companies whose stock he handled to make changes in his staff's draft research reports.

NASD also accused Quattrone of spinning because he maintained more than 300 "Friends of Frank" accounts for executives of technology companies that were active or prospective clients of the bank. These "friends" were allocated hot shares at his discretion. Spinning was not isolated to Quattrone's firm; it was actually quite common on Wall Street. Salomon Smith Barney also allocated hard-to-get IPO shares to a number of executives, including Bernard Ebbers of World-Com, Philip Anshutz and Joe Nacchio of Qwest, Stephen Garfalo of Metromedia, and Clark McLeod of McLeodUSA. The bank claimed that it issued shares to these executives because they were among the firm's best individual customers and not because it wanted to get these executives to channel their companies' investment banking business to Salomon Smith Barney. This claim was dubious, at best. Quattrone was convicted in 2004 of obstructing the investigation into his activities and was sentenced to 18 months of prison.

Auditing and Consulting in Accounting Firms

Traditionally, an auditor checks the books of companies and monitors the quality of the information produced by firms in order to reduce the inevitable information asymmetry between the firm's managers and its shareholders. In auditing, threats to truthful reporting arise from several potential conflicts of interest. The conflict of interest that has received the most attention in the media occurs when an accounting firm provides its client with both auditing services and nonaudit consulting services—commonly known as **management advisory services**—such as tax advice, accounting or management information systems, and strategic advice. These purveyors of multiple services enjoy economies of scale and scope, but create two potential sources of conflicts of interest. First, clients may be able to pressure auditors into skewing their judgments and opinions in order to limit any loss of fees for the other accounting services. Second, auditors may be auditing information systems or structuring (tax and financial) advice put in place by their nonaudit counterparts within the firm and may be reluctant to criticize this advice or systems. In both ways these conflicts may lead to biased audits, with the result that less information is available in financial markets and it is more difficult for investors to efficiently allocate capital.

Another conflict of interest arises when an auditor provides an overly favorable audit view in order to solicit or retain audit business. The unfortunate demise of Arthur Andersen—once of the five largest accounting firms in the United States—suggests that this may be the most dangerous conflict of interest (see the "Conflicts of Interest" box on page 408).

Credit Assessment and Consulting in Credit-Rating Agencies

Investors use debt ratings to determine the creditworthiness of the issuers. Therefore, the debt ratings play a major role in the pricing of debt securities and in the regulatory process. Conflicts of interest can arise when multiple users, who have

CONFLICTS OF INTEREST

The Demise of Arthur Andersen

In 1913, Arthur Andersen, a young accountant who had denounced the slipshod and deceptive practices that enabled companies to fool the investing public, founded his own firm. Up until the early 1980s, auditing was the most important source of profits within this firm. However, by the late 1980s, the consulting part of the business experienced high revenue growth with high profit margins, while audit profits slumped in a more competitive market. Consulting partners began to assert more power within the firm, and the resulting internal conflicts split the firm in two. Arthur Andersen (the auditing service) and Andersen Consulting were established as separate companies in 2000.

During the period of increasing conflict before the split, Andersen's audit partners had been under increasing pressure to focus on boosting revenue and profits from audit services. Many of Arthur Andersen's clients who later went bust—Enron, WorldCom, Qwest, and Global Crossing—were also the largest clients in Arthur Andersen's regional offices. The combination of intense pressure to generate revenue and profits from auditing and the fact that some clients dominated regional offices translated into tremendous incentives for regional office managers to provide favorable audit stances for these large clients. The loss of a client like Enron or WorldCom would have been devastating for a regional office and its partners, even if that client contributed only a small fraction of the overall revenue and profits of Arthur Andersen.

The Houston office of Arthur Andersen, for example, ignored problems in Enron's reporting. Arthur Andersen was indicted in March 2002 and then convicted in June 2002 for obstruction of justice for impeding the SEC's investigation of the Enron collapse. Its conviction—the first ever against a major accounting firm—barred Arthur Andersen from conducting audits of publicly traded firms. This development contributed to the firm's demise.

---

divergent interests (at least in the short term), depend on the credit ratings. The investors and regulators are interested in a well-researched, impartial assessment of credit quality; the issuer needs a favorable rating. In the credit-rating industry, the issuers of securities pay to have their securities rated (see the "Mini-Case" box). The investors and regulators are obviously concerned that credit-rating agencies may bias their ratings upwards in order to attract more business.

Conflicts of interest are affecting this industry in other ways: Credit-rating agencies have recently begun to provide ancillary consulting services. Rating agencies are increasingly asked to advise firms on the structuring of debt issues, usually to help the firms secure a favorable rating. In this situation, the credit-rating agencies would be in the position of "auditing their own work," thus introducing a conflict of interest similar to the one present in accounting firms that provide both auditing and consulting services. Furthermore, credit-rating agencies may deliver favorable ratings in order to garner new clients for the ancillary consulting business. The possible decline in the quality of credit assessments issued by rating agencies could increase asymmetric information in financial markets, thereby reducing their ability to allocate credit.

Moodys is a major rating agency for company debt. To view the Moodys website and to learn more about how it evaluates company credit, go to http://www. moodys.com/ cust/default.as. You will have to register to view Moodys Web materials.

Universal Banking

Commercial banks, investment banks, and insurance companies arose as distinct financial institutions, but soon recognized that combinations of these activities would provide economies of scope. However, in 1933 the Glass-Steagall Act halted the development of universal banking by banning the consolidation of these services under one organization. When the Glass-Steagall Act was repealed by Congress in 1999, universal banking reappeared. Given that activities within universal

MINI-CASE

Why Do Issuers of Securities Pay to Have Their Securities Rated?

Prior to the 1970s, credit-rating agencies earned their revenue by having subscribers pay to receive information about securities ratings. However, in the early 1970s, the major rating agencies switched to having issuers of securities pay for their ratings. Why would they have done this when it appears to set up an obvious conflict of interest?

The answer is provided by the asymmetric information framework, which was discussed in the previous

chapter. By the early 1970s, technological changes, such as the advent of cheap photocopying, made it easier to disseminate information. Market participants were able to get information on securities ratings without paying for it. The free-rider problem became more widespread. As a result, the credit-rating agencies were no longer able to earn enough revenue from selling ratings information. The solution was to have the issuers of securities pay for the ratings, and this is the business model that we see currently.

banks serve multiple clients, there are many potential conflicts of interest. If the potential for revenues in one department increases, employees will have an incentive to distort information to the advantage of their clients and the profit of their department.

Several types of conflicts of interest can arise in universal banks.

- Issuers served by the underwriting department will benefit from aggressive sales to customers of the bank, whereas these customers are hoping to get unbiased investment advice.
- A bank manager may push the affiliate's products to the disadvantage of the customer or limit losses from a poor public offering by placing them in the bank's managed trust accounts.
- A bank with a loan to a firm whose credit or bankruptcy risk has increased has private knowledge that may encourage it to use the bank's underwriting department to sell bonds to the unsuspecting public, thereby paying off the loan and earning a fee.
- A bank may make loans on overly favorable terms in order to obtain fees from activities such as underwriting securities.
- To sell its insurance products, a bank may try to influence or coerce a borrowing or investing customer.

All of these conflicts of interest may lead to a decrease in accurate information production by the universal bank, thereby hindering its ability to promote efficient credit allocation. Although there have not been any recent banking scandals involving conflicts of interest, they did surface in the aftermath of the stock market crash of 1929 (see the "Conflicts of Interest" box on page 410).

When Are Conflicts of Interest a Serious Problem?

As our analysis in the previous chapter indicated, conflicts of interest present their main problem for the financial system when they lead to a decrease in the flow of reliable information, either because information is concealed or because misleading information is disseminated. The decline in the flow of reliable information then makes it harder for the financial system to solve adverse selection and moral

CONFLICTS OF INTEREST

Banksters

Just as in the aftermath of the collapse of the tech bubble in 2000, the stock market crash of 1929 led many investors to question why they had been encouraged to purchase so many securities that so quickly declined in value. The public blamed the universal banks for hyping securities, and bankers were pejoratively referred to as "banksters." Public pressure led the Senate Banking and Currency Committee to set up hearings to investigate potential abuses by the universal banks. These hearings, which became known as the Pecora hearings after the chief counsel who led them, were as famous in their day as the Watergate hearings that led to President Nixon's resignation in 1974 or the hearings of the 9/11 Commission in 2004.

The Pecora hearings turned up several cases of apparently severe abuses of conflicts of interest in the banking industry. An affiliate of National City Bank (the precursor to Citibank) was accused of selling "unsound

and speculative securities" to the bank's customers, particularly bonds from the Republic of Peru that went into default. Chase National Bank and National City Bank were accused of converting bad loans to companies such as General Theaters and Equipment and the General Sugar Company into securities that were sold to the public and investment trusts managed by these banks. The president of National City Bank, Charles E. Mitchell, and the head of Chase National Bank, Albert H. Wiggin, were accused of setting up so-called pool operations in which resources from the banks were used to prop up the bank's stock price for the benefit of these executives and their associates.

The resulting scandals led to passage of the Glass-Steagall Act (discussed more extensively in Chapter 18) in 1933, which eliminated the possibility of these conflicts of interest by enforcing complete separation of commercial banking from investment banking activities. It was not until 1999 that this act was repealed by Congress to enable banks to be more competitive.

hazard problems, which can slow the flow of credit to parties with productive investment opportunities.

Even though conflicts of interest exist, they do not necessarily reduce the flow of reliable information because the incentives to exploit the conflict of interest may not be very high. When an exploitation of a conflict of interest is visible to the market, the reputation of the financial firm is jeopardized. Given the importance of maintaining and enhancing reputation, exploiting the conflict of interest would then decrease the future profitability of the firm because it would have greater difficulty selling its services in the future. In this way the firm actually has incentives to prevent exploitation of the conflict of interest. These incentives constrain conflicts of interest in the long run, but they may not be effective in the short run depending on structural factors within the firm, such as a lack of transparency and inappropriate monetary incentives.

One enlightening example occurs in credit-rating agencies. At first glance, the fact that rating agencies are paid by the firms issuing securities to produce ratings for these securities looks like a serious conflict of interest. Rating agencies would seem to have incentives to gain business by providing firms issuing securities with higher credit ratings than they deserve, making it easier for them to sell these securities at higher prices. However, there is little evidence that rating agencies take advantage of this conflict of interest, despite prominent examples such as Enron.[2]

---

[2]See the survey in Bank for International Settlements, "Credit Ratings and Complementary Sources of Credit Quality Information," Basel Committee on Banking Supervision Working Papers No. 3, August 2000, and the discussion in Andrew Crockett, Trevor Harris, Frederic S. Mishkin, and Eugene N. White, *Conflicts of Interest in the Financial Services Industry: What Should We Do About Them?* Geneva Reports on the World Economy 4 (Geneva and London: International Center for Monetary and Banking Studies and Centre for Economic Policy Research, 2003).

Much research has shown that there is a reasonably close correlation between ratings and default probabilities. Ratings agencies don't exploit the conflict of interest because giving higher credit ratings to firms that pay for the ratings would result in decreased credibility of the ratings, thus making them less valuable to the market. The market is eventually able to assess the quality of biased ratings down the road because it can observe poorer performance by individual securities. Furthermore, credit-rating agencies themselves provide evidence on the relationship between their ratings and subsequent default history. Therefore, the resulting loss of trust in the information provided by the rating agency if this conflict were to be exploited would lead to a costly decline in its reputation, thus providing incentives for the agency not to exploit this conflict of interest.

Commercial banks that underwrote securities before the Glass-Steagall Act was enacted do not appear to have exploited this conflict of interest. When a commercial bank underwrites securities, the bank may have an incentive to market the securities of financially troubled firms to the public because the firms will then be able to pay back the loans they owe to the bank, while the bank earns fees from the underwriting services. The evidence suggests that in the 1920s markets found securities underwritten by bond departments within a commercial bank to be less attractive than securities underwritten in separate affiliates where the conflict of interest was more transparent. In order to maintain the bank's reputation, commercial banks shifted their underwriting to separate affiliates over time, with the result that securities underwritten by banks were valued as highly as those underwritten by independent investment banks.[3] When affiliates were unable to certify the absence of conflicts, they focused on more senior securities where there was less of an information asymmetry and conflicts of interest were less pronounced. Again, the market provided incentives to control potential conflicts of interest. However, it is important to note that the market solution was not immediate, but took some time to develop.

The responsiveness of the market is also evident in the apparent conflict of interest present in investment banks when underwriters who have incentives to favor issuers over investors pressure research analysts to provide more favorable assessments of issuers' securities. Lead underwriters make more buy recommendations for IPOs than other firms' analysts for the same securities, yet the stock prices of firms recommended by lead underwriting investment banks declined during the SEC's 25-day quiet period (which restricts the release of information from when the IPO is registered with the SEC until the SEC declares the registration is effective) while other investment banks' picks rose. Over a two-year period the performance of other analysts' recommended issues was 50% better than the performance of underwriters' recommendations. The market appears to recognize the difference in the quality of information when there is a potential conflict of interest.[4]

---

[3]See Randall S. Kroszner and Raghuram G. Rajan, "Is the Glass-Steagall Act Justified? A Study of the US Experience with Universal Banking Before 1933," *American Economic Review* 84 (1994): 810–832 and "Organization, Structure, and Credibility: Evidence from Commercial Bank Securities Activities Before the Glass-Steagall Act," *Journal of Monetary Economics* 39 (1997); James S. Ang and Terry Richardson, "The Underwriting Experience of Commercial Bank Affiliates Prior to the Glass-Steagall Act," *Journal of Banking and Finance* 18 (March 1994): 351–395, and Manu Pari, "Commercial Banks in Investment Banking: Conflict of Interest or Certification Role?" *Journal of Financial Economics* 40 (1996).

[4]Rani Micaela and Kent L. Womack, "Conflict of Interest and the Credibility of Underwriter Analyst Recommendations," *Review of Financial Studies* 12, no. 4 (Special Issue 1999): 653–686.

There are fewer empirical studies in auditing, but even the limited evidence available suggests that the market adjusts for potential conflicts of interest. There is evidence that clients, who are concerned that conflicts of interest arise from the joint provision of auditing and management advisory services, will reduce the value of their audit opinions and limit nonaudit purchases from incumbent auditors.[5]

These examples do not indicate that the market can always restrain the incentives to exploit conflicts of interest. In order for the market to prevent exploitation of conflicts of interest, the market needs to have information to assess whether an exploitation of conflicts of interest might be occurring. In some cases, those who want to take advantage of conflicts of interest will try to hide these circumstances from the market. In other cases, alerting the market to potential conflicts of interest would reveal proprietary information that would help a financial firm's competitors, thus reducing the firm's incentives to reveal its true position.

The recent scandals described in this chapter demonstrate that the exploitation of a conflict of interest often leads to large gains for some members of the financial firm even while it reduces the value of the whole firm. Compensation mechanisms inside a firm, if inappropriately designed, may lead to conflicts of interest that not only reduce the flow of reliable information to credit markets but end up destroying the firm. In other words, damaging conflicts of interest are likely to arise from poor management. Indeed, the story of the demise of Arthur Andersen illustrates how the compensation arrangements for one line of business, like auditing, can create serious conflicts of interest. In this case, the partners in regional offices had incentives to please their largest clients even if their actions were detrimental to the firm as a whole. The conflict of interest problem can become even more hazardous when several lines of business are combined and the returns from one of the activities—such as underwriting or consulting—are very high for only a brief amount of time. A compensation scheme that works reasonably well in the short term might become poorly aligned over time.

The extraordinary surge in the stock market created huge temporary rewards, permitting well-positioned analysts, underwriters, or audit firm partners to exploit the conflicts before incentives could be realigned. The conflicts of interest are dangerous because they are not readily visible to the market and may not even be visible to the top management of the firm. In the most severe cases, opportunistic individuals were able to capture the firm's **reputational rents,** profits that the firm earns because it is trusted by the marketplace. The exploitation of conflicts of interest clearly damaged the reputation of such investment banks as Merrill Lynch, Salomon Smith Barney of Citigroup, and Credit Suisse First Boston—and perhaps the credibility of analysts in general. Audit firms have lost much of their nonaudit business, while Arthur Andersen was destroyed.

What Has Been Done to Remedy Conflicts of Interest?

Two major policy measures have been implemented to deal with conflicts of interest: the Sarbanes-Oxley Act and the Global Legal Settlement.

---

[5]Mohinder Parkas and Carol F. Venable, "Auditee Incentives for Auditor Independence: The Case of Non Audit Services," *The Accounting Review* 68 (1993): 113–133.

Sarbanes-Oxley Act of 2002

In 2002, the public outcry over the corporate and accounting scandals led to the passage of the Public Accounting Reform and Investor Protection Act, more commonly referred to as the Sarbanes-Oxley Act after its two principal authors in Congress. This act has six major components.

Go to http://www.sarbanes-oxley.com/ to view a website devoted to discussion and dissemination of information about the Sarbanes-Oxley Act.

1. It established a Public Company Accounting Oversight Board (PCAOB), overseen by the SEC, to supervise accounting firms and ensure that audits are both independent and controlled for quality. The PCAOB registers public accounting firms and establishes rules for auditing, quality control, ethics, independence, and other standards. In addition, it conducts inspections of accounting firms and, when needed, carries out investigations and disciplinary proceedings and imposes sanctions.

2. It made it unlawful for a registered public accounting firm to provide any nonaudit service to a client contemporaneously with the audit. Nonaudit services include bookkeeping; financial information systems design; appraisals; actuarial services; internal audit outsourcing; management functions; broker, dealer, investment advisor, investment banker, and legal services; and any other services that the PCAOB determines are impermissible. The PCAOB is empowered to allow for case-by-case exceptions if nonaudit services constitute less than 5% of the total amount of revenues paid to the auditor by a client.

3. It required that members of the audit committee (the subcommittee of the board of directors that oversees the company's audit) be independent; that is, they cannot be managers in the company or receive any consulting or advisory fees from the company. In addition, the chief executive officer (CEO) and chief financial officer (CFO) must certify that periodic financial statements and disclosures of the firm fairly represent the operations and financial condition of the firm.

4. Every annual and quarterly financial report must disclose all material off-balance sheet transactions and other relationships with off-balance sheet entities, commonly known as special-purpose entities.

5. It increased the appropriation for the SEC in 2003 to $776 million to be used to hire an additional 200 employees to supervise securities markets.

6. It beefed up criminal charges for white-collar crime and obstruction of official investigations.

Global Legal Settlement of 2002

The second policy arose out of a lawsuit brought by New York Attorney General Elliott Spitzer against the ten largest investment banks (Bear Stearns, Credit Suisse First Boston, Deutsche Bank, Goldman Sachs, J. P. Morgan, Lehman Brothers, Merrill Lynch, Morgan Stanley, Salomon Smith Barney, and UBS Warburg). Spitzer alleged that these firms allowed their investment banking departments to have inappropriate influence over their research analysts, thereby creating a conflict of interest. On December 20, 2002, the SEC, the New York Attorney General, NASD, NASAA, NYSE, and state regulators reached a global agreement with these investment banks. The five key terms of the agreement are as follows:

- Firms are required to sever the links between their research and investment banking divisions. This includes ending analyst compensation for equity research and the practice of analysts accompanying investment banking personnel to road shows and pitches.
- The practice of spinning is banned.
- Each firm is required to make public its analysts' recommendations, including their ratings and price target forecasts.
- For a five-year period, each of the brokerage firms will be required to contract with no less than three independent research firms that will provide research to the brokerage firms' customers. An independent consultant—a "monitor"—for each firm will be chosen by regulators to procure independent research from independent providers to ensure that investors get objective investment advice.
- The investment banks paid fines, which in total amounted to more than $1.4 billion, part of which will be used to fund independent research and investor education.

A Framework for Evaluating Policies to Remedy Conflicts of Interest

The information view of conflicts of interest developed in this chapter provides a framework for evaluating whether conflicts of interest require public policy actions to eliminate or reduce them. Some combination of financial service activities may result in incentives for agents to conceal information, but they may also result in synergies that make it easier to produce information. Thus, preventing the combination of activities to eliminate the conflicts of interest may actually make financial markets less efficient. This reasoning suggests that there are two propositions critical to evaluating what should be done about conflicts of interest:

1. *The fact that a conflict of interest exists does not mean that the conflict will have serious adverse consequences.* Even though a conflict of interest exists, the incentives to exploit the conflict of interest may not be very high. An exploitation of a conflict of interest that is visible to the market will typically result in a decrease in the reputation of the financial firm where it takes place. Given the importance of maintaining and enhancing reputation, exploiting the conflict of interest would decrease the future profitability of the firm because it would have greater difficulty selling its services in the future. Therefore firms create their own incentives to avoid the exploitation of the conflict of interest. Hence, the marketplace may be able to control conflicts of interest because there is a high value to financial firms' reputations. When evaluating the need for remedies, this proposition raises the issue of whether the market has the information and incentives to control conflicts of interest.
2. *Even if incentives to exploit conflicts of interest remain strong, eliminating the economies of scope that create the conflicts of interest may be harmful because it will reduce the flow of reliable information.* Thus in evaluating possible remedies, we also need to examine whether imposing the remedy will do more harm than good by reducing the flow of reliable information in financial markets.

Approaches to Remedying Conflicts of Interest

In thinking about remedies for specific conflicts, it is worthwhile discussing five generic approaches to reconciling conflicts of interest. These approaches are discussed in the order of their intrusiveness, from least intrusive to most intrusive.

Leave It to the Market This approach has a powerful appeal to many economists and may be a sufficient response in many cases. Market forces can work through two mechanisms. They can penalize the financial service provider if it exploits conflicts of interest. For example, a penalty may be imposed by the market in the form of higher funding costs or lower demand for its services, in varying degrees, even to the point of forcing demise of the firm. Second, market forces can promote new institutional means to contain conflicts of interest. For example, they can generate a demand for information from nonconflicted organizations. This is exactly what happened in the United States in the 1920s when security affiliates took preeminence over in-house bond departments in universal banks.

One of the advantages of market-driven solutions is that they can hit where it hurts most, through pecuniary penalties. Moreover, they may help avoid the risk of overreaction. It can be hard to resist the temptation to adopt nonmarket solutions to appease public opinion that may reduce information production in financial markets. On the other hand, market-based solutions may not always work if the market cannot obtain sufficient information to appropriately punish financial firms that are exploiting conflicts of interest. Memories may be short in financial markets, as is suggested by the new field of behavioral finance discussed in Chapter 6. Once a triggering event has faded from memory, conflicts may creep back in unless reforms have been "hard-wired."

Regulate for Transparency A competitive market structure does not always adequately reduce information asymmetries. The gathering of information is costly, and any individual economic agent will only gather information if the private benefit outweighs the cost. When the information collected becomes available to the market immediately, the free-rider problem may become serious. Information has the attribute of a public good, which will be undersupplied in the absence of some public intervention. To some extent, mandatory information disclosure can alleviate information asymmetries and is a key element of regulation of the financial system.

When mandatory disclosure of information reveals whether a conflict of interest exists, the market is able to discipline the financial firm that engages in conflicts of interest. In addition, if a financial institution is required to provide information about potential conflicts of interest, the user of the institution's information services may be able to judge how much weight to place on the information this institution supplies.

On the other hand, mandatory disclosure could create problems if it reveals so much proprietary information that the financial institution is unable to profitably engage in the information production business. The result could then be less information production rather than more. Also, mandatory disclosure may not work if financial firms are able to avoid the regulation and continue to hide relevant information about potential conflicts of interest. The free-rider problem might also result in insufficient monitoring of conflicts of interest because the benefits of monitoring and constraining these conflicts accrue only partially to the monitors.

Finally, complying with regulations requiring information disclosure may be costly for financial firms, and could possibly be higher than the costs due to conflicts of interest.

Supervisory Oversight   If mandatory disclosure does not work because firms are still able to hide relevant information, because the free-rider problem is severe, or because mandatory disclosure would reveal proprietary information, supervisory oversight can come to the rescue and contain conflicts of interest. Supervisors can observe proprietary information about conflicts of interest without revealing it to a financial firm's competitors so that the firm can continue to profitably engage in information production activities. Supplied with this information, the supervisor can take actions to prevent financial firms from exploiting conflicts of interest. As part of this supervisory oversight, standards of practice can be developed, either by the supervisor or by the firms engaged in a specific information production activity. Enforcement of these standards would then be in the hands of the supervisor.

As we will see in Chapter 20, supervisory oversight of this type is very common in the banking industry. In recent years, bank supervisors have increased their focus on risk management. They examine bank's risk management procedures to ensure that the appropriate internal controls on risk-taking are in place at the bank. In a similar fashion, supervisors can examine the internal procedures and controls to restrict conflicts of interest. When they find weak internal controls, they can require the financial institution to modify them so that incentives to engage in conflicts of interest are eliminated.

Although supervisory oversight has been successful in improving internal controls in financial firms in recent years, if the incentives to engage in conflicts of interest are sufficiently strong, financial institutions may be able to hide conflicts of interest from the supervisors. Furthermore, supervisors have not always done their job well, as we will also see in Chapter 20.

Separation of Functions   Where the market cannot get sufficient information to constrain conflicts of interest—because there is no satisfactory way of inducing information disclosure by market discipline or supervisory oversight—the incentives to exploit conflicts of interest may be reduced or eliminated by regulations enforcing separation of functions. There are several degrees of separation. First, activities may be separated into different in-house departments with firewalls between them. Second, the firms may conduct different activities in separately capitalized affiliates. Third, regulations may prohibit the combination of activities in any organizational form.

The goal of separation of functions is to ensure that agents are not placed in the position of responding to multiple principals. Moving from relaxed to more stringent separation of functions, conflicts of interest are reduced. However, more stringent separation of functions reduces synergies of information collection, thereby preventing financial firms from taking advantage of economies of scope in information production. The resulting increased cost of producing information could then lead to a decreased flow of reliable information because it becomes more expensive to produce it. Deciding on the appropriate amount of separation thus involves a tradeoff between the benefits of reducing conflicts of interest and the cost of reducing economies of scope in producing information.

The SEC is primarily responsible for preventing fraud in the securities markets. Go to http://www.sec.gov/ and click on "What we do." This discussion highlights the role the SEC envisions for itself in the securities industry.

Socialization of Information Production   The most radical response to conflicts generated by asymmetric information is the socialization of the provision or the funding source of the relevant information. For example, much macroeconomic information is provided by publicly funded agencies because this particular public good is likely to be undersupplied if left to private provision. It is conceivable that other information-providing functions, for example credit ratings and auditing, could also be publicly supplied. Alternatively, if the information-generating services are left to the private sector, they could be funded by public sources or by a publicly mandated levy to help ensure that information production is not tainted by obligations to fee-paying entities with special interests.

Of course, the problem with this approach is that a government agency or publicly funded entity may not have the same strong incentives as private financial institutions to produce high-quality information. Forcing information production to be conducted by a government or quasi-government entity—although it may reduce conflicts of interest—may also end up reducing the flow of reliable information to financial markets. Furthermore, government agencies may have difficulty paying market wages to attract the best people. This problem may be even more serious if there are economies of scope. For example, analysts in an investment banking firm are likely to receive additional compensation when their research has multiple uses. A government agency only interested in one use of research may not provide a level of compensation adequate to produce high-quality information. In addition, the government might not provide sufficient funds for information collection. Indeed, this has happened with macroeconomic data, where government provision of important series has been discontinued because of a lack of funding.

Case

EVALUATING SARBANES-OXLEY AND THE GLOBAL SETTLEMENT

Using the analytic framework discussed earlier, we now can turn to evaluating the Sarbanes-Oxley Act and the Global Settlement.

We have seen that policies that regulate conflicts of interest can help to increase the amount of information in financial markets. Sarbanes-Oxley does exactly this when it requires that the CEO and the CFO certify the periodic financial statements and disclosures of the firm. It increases the likelihood that these statements will provide reliable information. In addition, Sarbanes-Oxley requires disclosure of off-balance sheet transactions and other relationships with special-purpose entities. Again this can help increase information in the marketplace because these off-balance sheet transactions were often used, as in the Enron case, to hide what was going on inside the firm. However, the costs of complying with the new regulations imposed by Sarbanes-Oxley are not cheap. A survey by Financial Executives International found that these costs would be over $3 million for the average public corporation.

We have also seen that the market is often able to constrain conflicts of interest when it has sufficient information to do so. The Global Settlement includes a provision that requires investment banking firms to make their analyst recommendations public. This part of the policy helps the market to assess whether the analysts are acting in good faith. The SEC also requires increased disclosure by investment analysts, credit-rating agencies, and auditors to reveal any interests they have in the firms they analyze. Provision of this information makes it more likely that financial institutions will develop internal rules to ensure that conflicts of interest are minimized, so that their reputations remain high and thereby the firms are kept profitable.

We have also seen that disclosure may not be enough to get markets to control conflicts of interest because firms still have incentives to hide information so that they can profitably exploit conflicts of interest. Disclosure may also reveal so much proprietary information that the financial institution is unable to profitably engage in the information production business. In addition, as we have seen, some of the most damaging conflicts of interest arose from poorly designed, internal compensation mechanisms that are difficult for markets to observe. Supervisory oversight can focus on exactly these issues.

Increased supervisory oversight is a key feature of Sarbanes-Oxley. First, it establishes the PCAOB to supervise accounting firms. The PCAOB monitors compensation mechanisms to make sure that they are in accord with best practice to control conflicts of interest. Second, Sarbanes-Oxley provides for substantially more resources for the SEC. A supervisory agency cannot do its job properly without resources. Indeed, one of the reasons why the SEC may have failed to provide adequate supervisory oversight during the boom of the 1990s is because it was starved for resources. As we will see in Chapter 19, a similar problem occurred for the supervisors of the savings and loan industry, and this helped lead to scandals and a bailout that cost taxpayers over a hundred billion dollars.

By making the audit committee independent of management, Sarbanes-Oxley eliminates the conflict of interest that occurs when the management of the firm hires the auditor. Sarbanes-Oxley also sets up the PCAOB, which will be instrumental in writing the regulations to ensure that auditors will report to, be hired by, and be compensated by an independent audit committee that is supposed to represent shareholders other than management. The Global Settlement also directly eliminates one Wall Street practice that led to obvious conflicts of interest—spinning, in which executives received hot IPO shares in return for their companies' future business with the investment bank. The Global Settlement also punished investment banks by imposing a fine of over $1.4 billion. This punishment, along with the increase in criminal penalties established by Sarbanes-Oxley, provides incentives for investment banking firms to avoid taking advantage of conflicts of interest in the future.

The more radical parts of Sarbanes-Oxley and the Global Settlement involve separation of functions and socialization of information. Sarbanes-Oxley makes it illegal for accounting firms to provide nonaudit consulting services to their audit customers. This law will potentially reduce the economies of scope available to auditing firms that provide consulting services to their clients. It is unlikely that the proscription of nonauditing services in this situation, as envisioned by Sarbanes-Oxley, would have prevented the recent audit failures. However, greater transparency about the nature and role of nonaudit services would be valuable to control a firm's temptation to exploit this conflict of interest. Similarly, the Global Settlement requires investment banking firms to sever the link between research and investment banking. This also has the potential to eliminate economies of scope in information production. Analysts may get much more information on firms they cover when the investment banking arm of the firm can share information with them.

The Global Settlement requires that for a five-year period, brokerage firms contract with independent research firms to provide information to their customers. In addition, part of the $1.4 billion fine paid by the investment banks is to be used to fund independent research and investor education. While it remains to be seen how the terms of this agreement are implemented, there are both positive and potentially negative features. Independent research may produce unbiased information. However, by socializing research, firms can no longer compete for customers on the basis of the quality of their research. Because they are being taxed to fund independent research, firms may decrease their investment in their own research analysis. If the investment banks do not control the information that they are being forced to acquire, the analysis produced may be of a lower quality.

Summary

1. Conflicts of interest arise when financial service providers or their employees are serving multiple interests and develop incentives to misuse or conceal information needed for the effective functioning of financial markets. We care about conflicts of interest because if taking advantage of them substantially reduces the amount of reliable information in financial markets, asymmetric information increases and prevents financial markets from channeling funds to those with productive investment opportunities.

2. Four types of financial service activities have the greatest potential for conflicts of interest that reduce reliable information in financial markets: (1) underwriting and research in investment banking, (2) auditing and consulting in accounting firms, (3) credit assessment and consulting in credit-rating agencies, and (4) universal banking.

3. Even though conflicts of interest exist, they do not necessarily reduce the flow of reliable information because there may be a stronger incentive to avoid damaging the reputation of the firm. The evidence suggests that the market is often able to contain the incentives to exploit conflicts of interest. However, conflicts of interest still pose a threat to the efficiency of financial markets.

4. Two major policy measures deal with conflicts of interest: the Sarbanes-Oxley Act of 2002 and the Global Legal Settlement arising from the lawsuit by the New York Attorney General against the ten largest investment banks.

5. There are two basic propositions that are critical to evaluating what should be done about conflicts of interest: (1) The fact that a conflict of interest exists does not mean that the conflict will have serious adverse consequences. (2) Even if incentives to exploit conflicts of interest remain strong, eliminating the conflict of interest may be harmful if doing so destroys economies of scope, thereby reducing the flow of reliable information. There are five generic approaches to remedying conflicts of interest, going from least intrusive to most intrusive: (1) leave it to the market, (2) regulate for transparency, (3) supervisory oversight, (4) separation of functions, and (5) socialization of information.

6. Sarbanes-Oxley and the Global Settlement help increase the flow of reliable information in financial markets by requiring the CEO and CFO to certify financial statements, corporations to disclose off-balance sheet transactions and entities, and investment banks to make public their analysts' recommendations, and requiring increased disclosure of potential conflicts of interest. Sarbanes-Oxley increases supervisory oversight by establishing the Public Company Accounting Oversight Board (PCAOB) and by increasing resources for the SEC. Sarbanes-Oxley also reduces conflicts of interest in auditing by making the audit committee independent of management, while the Global Settlement eliminates the conflict of interest inherent in spinning. The $1.4 billion fine and increased criminal penalties in Sarbanes-Oxley provide incentives for investment banks not to exploit conflicts of interest again. The more radical parts of Sarbanes-Oxley and the Global Settlement, which involve separation of functions (research from underwriting and auditing from nonaudit consulting) and socialization of research information, may end up reducing rather than increasing information in financial markets.

Key Terms

conflicts of interest, *p. 403*
economies of scope, *p. 404*
initial public offerings (IPOs),
   p. 406

management advisory services,
   p. 407
reputational rents, *p. 412*
spinning, *p. 406*

Questions

1. Why can provision of several types of financial services by one firm lead to a lower cost of information production?

2. How does the provision of several types of financial services by one firm lead to conflicts of interest?

3. How can conflicts of interest make financial markets less efficient?

4. How can conflicts of interest lead to unethical behavior?

5. Describe two conflicts of interest that occur when underwriting and research are provided by a single investment banking firm.

6. How does spinning lead to a less efficient financial market?

7. Describe two conflicts of interest that occur in accounting firms.

8. Some commentators have attributed the demise of Arthur Andersen to the combining of auditing and consulting activities in the firm. Is this correct?

9. Describe two conflicts of interest that occur in credit-rating agencies.

10. Describe two conflicts of interest that occur in universal banks.

11. True, False, or Uncertain: Conflicts of interest always reduce the flow of reliable information.

12. Give two examples of conflicts of interest that do not seem to have been exploited and thus did not lead to a reduction of reliable information in the financial markets.

13. When is it more likely that conflicts of interest will be exploited?

14. How can compensation schemes in firms lead to conflicts of interest?

15. What are the advantages and disadvantages of mandatory disclosure in dealing with conflicts of interest?

16. How can supervisory oversight help reduce conflicts of interest?

17. What are the disadvantages of separating financial activities into different firms in order to deal with conflicts of interest?

18. What are the advantages and disadvantages of government provision of information as a solution to the problems created by conflicts of interest?

19. Which provisions of the Sarbanes-Oxley Act do you think are beneficial and which ones are not?

20. Which provisions of the Global Settlement do you think are beneficial and which ones are not?

Quantitative Problems

Bsquare Corporation went public on October 20, 1999. Its lead underwriter was Credit Suisse First Boston. The prospectus listed the following information about shares outstanding prior to the IPO:

	Shares Purchased	
	Number	Percent
Existing shareholders	28,076,916	87.5
New investors	4,000,000	12.5
Total	32,076,916	100

Bsquare issued 4,000,000 shares at a price to the public of $15.00 per share, with the underwriting syndicate retaining $1.05 as fees. The final price at the end of the first day was $25.625.

1. What were the total proceeds from this offering? What proceeds were retained by Bsquare? By the investment banker?

2. In percentage terms, what was the first-day return? If you were on the "Friends of Frank" list and received 100 shares, how much cash could you walk away with after the first day?

3. How much total wealth was available in this IPO for underwriters to dole out to their best clients, future clients, and so forth? Another way of asking this is, how much money was left on the table?

4. Based on what we know following the first day of trading, how many shares and at what price could Bsquare have gone public? Based on this, how efficient does the process appear?

5. How much in commissions can brokers and dealers expect during the first several months? How does this compare with the money left on the table?

6. Examine the prospectus at the SEC website (**http://www.sec.gov/Archives/edgar/data/1054 721/0000891020-99-001742-index.html**). How much were the various original owners worth when Bsquare went public? Do you think they care that the process was somewhat inefficient? How does this affect the process in the long run?

Web Exercises

What Should Be Done About Conflicts of Interest in the Financial Industry?

1. Go to **http://www.sarbanes-oxley.com/**. This site tracks issues and news related to the Sarbanes-Oxley Act.

   a. Summarize in two or three sentences the primary reason for passage of the Sarbanes-Oxley Act.

   b. Go to the above website and summarize one of the articles discussed under the news/current events section. Address how this article relates to conflicts of interest in the financial markets.

2. Go to **http://www.sec.gov/** and click on "Press releases."

   a. Summarize the major types of issues that the SEC addresses in these press releases.

   b. Look over the last three months of releases and count how many appear to be enforcement actions aimed at firms or individuals who have violated SEC regulations. From this review, does the SEC appear to be active in its effort to prevent fraud and misrepresentation in the securities industry?

PART 6

The Financial Institutions Industry

CHAPTER 17

Banking and the Management of Financial Institutions

Preview

Because banking plays such a major role in channeling funds to borrowers with productive investment opportunities, this financial activity is important in ensuring that the financial system and the economy run smoothly and efficiently. In the United States, banks (depository institutions) supply over $5 trillion of credit annually. They provide loans to businesses, help us finance our college educations or the purchase of a new car or home, and provide us with services such as checking and savings accounts.

   In this chapter we examine how banking is conducted to earn the highest profits possible: how and why banks make loans, how they acquire funds and manage their assets and liabilities (debts), and how they earn income. Although we focus on commercial banking because this is the most important financial intermediary activity, many of the same principles are applicable to other types of financial institutions.

The Bank Balance Sheet

To understand how banking works, first we need to examine the **balance sheet,** a list of the bank's assets and liabilities. As the name implies, this list balances; that is, it has the characteristic that

$$\text{Total assets} = \text{total liabilities} + \text{capital}$$

   Furthermore, a bank's balance sheet lists *sources* of bank funds (liabilities) and *uses* to which they are put (assets). Banks obtain funds by borrowing and by issuing other liabilities such as deposits. They then use these funds to acquire assets such as securities and loans. Banks make profits by charging an interest rate on their holdings of securities and loans that is higher than the expenses on their liabilities. The balance sheet of all commercial banks at the end of 2004 appears in Table 1.

A sample bank balance sheet is available at www.bankof america.com/ investor. Click on "annual report" in the left margin.

TABLE 1 *Balance Sheet of All Commercial Banks (items as a percentage of the total, end of 2004; amounts in billions of dollars)*

Assets (Uses of Funds)*		Liabilities (Sources of Funds)	
Reserves and cash items	1	Checkable deposits	9
Securities		Nontransaction deposits	
U.S. government and agency	15	Small-denomination time deposits	
State and local government and other securities	8	(<$100,000) + savings deposits	46
		Large-denomination time deposits	15
Loans			
Commercial and industrial	8	Borrowings	24
Real estate	29	Bank capital	6
Interbank	16		
Other	3		
Other assets (for example, physical capital)	20		
Total	100	Total	100

*In order of decreasing liquidity.
Source: http://www.federalreserve.gov/releases/Z1/Current/z1r-4.pdf

Liabilities

A bank acquires funds by issuing (selling) liabilities, which are consequently also referred to as *sources of funds*. The funds obtained from issuing liabilities are used to purchase income-earning assets.

Checkable Deposits Checkable deposits are bank accounts that allow the owner of the account to write checks to third parties. Checkable deposits include all accounts on which checks can be drawn: non-interest-bearing checking accounts (demand deposits), interest-bearing NOW (negotiable order of withdrawal) accounts, and money market deposit accounts (MMDAs). Introduced with the Depository Institutions Act in 1982, MMDAs have features similar to money market mutual funds and are included in the checkable deposits category. However, MMDAs differ from checkable deposits in that they are not subject to reserve requirements (discussed later in the chapter) like checkable deposits. Table 1 shows that the category of checkable deposits is an important source of bank funds, making up 9% of bank liabilities. Once checkable deposits were the most important source of bank funds (over 60% of bank liabilities in 1960), but with the appearance of new, more attractive financial instruments such as money market mutual funds, the share of checkable deposits in total bank liabilities has shrunk over time.

Checkable deposits and money market deposit accounts are payable on demand; that is, if a depositor shows up at the bank and requests payment by making a withdrawal, the bank must pay the depositor immediately. Similarly, if a person who receives a check written on an account from a bank presents that check at the bank, it must pay the funds out immediately (or credit them to that person's account).

A checkable deposit is an asset for the depositor because it is part of his or her wealth. Conversely, because the depositor can withdraw funds from an account that the bank is obligated to pay, checkable deposits are a liability for the bank. They are usually the lowest-cost source of bank funds because depositors are willing to forgo some interest in order to have access to a liquid asset that can be used to make purchases. The bank's costs of maintaining checkable deposits include interest payments and the costs incurred in servicing these accounts—processing and storing canceled checks, preparing and sending out monthly statements, providing efficient tellers (human or otherwise), maintaining an impressive building and conveniently located branches, and advertising and marketing to entice customers to deposit their funds with a given bank. In recent years, interest paid on deposits (checkable and time) has accounted for around 25% of total bank operating expenses, while the costs involved in servicing accounts (employee salaries, building rent, and so on) have been approximately 65% of operating expenses.

Nontransaction Deposits Nontransaction deposits are the primary source of bank funds (61% of bank liabilities in Table 1). Owners cannot write checks on nontransaction deposits, but the interest rates are usually higher than those on checkable deposits. There are two basic types of nontransaction deposits: savings accounts and time deposits (also called certificates of deposit, or CDs).

Savings accounts were once the most common type of nontransaction deposit. In these accounts, to which funds can be added or from which funds can be withdrawn at any time, transactions and interest payments are recorded in a monthly statement or in a small book (the passbook) held by the owner of the account.

Time deposits have a fixed maturity length, ranging from several months to over five years, and have substantial penalties for early withdrawal (the forfeiture of several months' interest). Small-denomination time deposits (deposits of less than $100,000) are less liquid for the depositor than passbook savings, earn higher interest rates, and are a more costly source of funds for the banks.

Large-denomination time deposits (CDs) are available in denominations of $100,000 or over and are typically bought by corporations or other banks. Large-denomination CDs are negotiable; like bonds, they can be resold in a secondary market before they mature. For this reason, negotiable CDs are held by corporations, money market mutual funds, and other financial institutions as alternative assets to Treasury bills and other short-term bonds. Since 1961, when they first appeared, negotiable CDs have become an important source of bank funds (15%).

Borrowings Banks obtain funds by borrowing from the Federal Reserve System, the Federal Home Loan Banks, other banks, and corporations. Borrowings from the Fed are called **discount loans** (also known as *advances*). Banks also borrow reserves overnight in the federal (fed) funds market from other U.S. banks and financial institutions. Banks borrow funds overnight in order to have enough deposits at the Federal Reserve to meet the amount required by the Fed. (The *federal funds* designation is somewhat confusing because these loans are not made by the federal government or by the Federal Reserve but rather by banks to other banks.) Other sources of borrowed funds are loans made to banks by their parent companies (bank holding companies), loan arrangements with corporations (such as repurchase agreements), and borrowings of Eurodollars (deposits denominated in U.S. dollars residing in foreign banks or foreign branches of U.S. banks). Borrowings have become a more important source of bank funds over time: In 1960, they made up only 2% of bank liabilities; currently, they are 24% of bank liabilities.

Bank Capital   The final category on the liabilities side of the balance sheet is bank capital, the bank's net worth, which equals the difference between total assets and liabilities (6% of total bank assets in Table 1). The funds are raised by selling new equity (stock) or from retained earnings. Bank capital is a cushion against a drop in the value of its assets, which could force the bank into insolvency (when the value of bank assets falls below its liabilities, meaning that the bank can be forced into liquidation).

Assets

A bank uses the funds that it has acquired by issuing liabilities to purchase income-earning assets. Bank assets are thus naturally referred to as *uses of funds*, and the interest payments earned on them are what enable banks to make profits.

Reserves   All banks hold some of the funds they acquire as deposits in an account at the Fed. **Reserves** are these deposits plus currency that is physically held by banks (called **vault cash** because it is stored in bank vaults overnight). Although reserves currently do not pay any interest, banks hold them for two reasons. First, some reserves, called **required reserves,** are held because of **reserve requirements,** the regulation that for every dollar of checkable deposits, a certain fraction (say, 10 cents, for example) must be kept as reserves at the Fed. This fraction (10% in the example) is called the **required reserve ratio.** Banks hold additional reserves, called **excess reserves,** because they are the most liquid of all bank assets and can be used by a bank to meet its obligations when funds are withdrawn, either directly by a depositor or indirectly when a check is written on an account.

Cash Items in Process of Collection   Suppose that a check written on an account at another bank is deposited in your bank and the funds for this check have not yet been received (collected) from the other bank. The check is classified as a cash item in process of collection, and it is an asset for your bank because it is a claim on another bank for funds that will be paid within a few days.

Securities   A bank's holdings of securities are an important income-earning asset: Securities (made up entirely of debt instruments for commercial banks because banks are not allowed to hold stock) account for 23% of bank assets in Table 1, and they provide commercial banks with about 10% of their revenue. These securities can be classified into three categories: U.S. government and agency securities, state and local government (municipal) securities, and other securities. U.S. government and agency securities are the most liquid because they can be easily traded and converted into cash with low transaction costs. Because of their high liquidity, short-term U.S. government securities are called **secondary reserves.**

State and local government securities are desirable for banks to hold primarily because state and local governments are more likely to do business with banks that hold their securities. In addition, state and local government securities purchased before August 1986 have substantial tax advantages for banks because their interest payments are deductible from income taxes, and 80% of the interest costs associated with the funding of their purchase is deductible. State and local government and other securities are less marketable (hence less liquid) and are also riskier than U.S. government securities, primarily because of default risk: There is some possibility that the issuer of the securities may not be able to make its interest payments or pay back the face value of the securities when they mature.

Loans Banks make their profits primarily by issuing loans. In Table 1, some 56% of bank assets are in the form of loans, and in recent years they have generally produced more than half of bank revenues. A loan is a liability for the individual or corporation receiving it but an asset for a bank because it provides income to the bank. Loans are typically less liquid than other assets because they cannot be turned into cash until the loan matures. If the bank makes a one-year loan, for example, it cannot get its funds back until the loan comes due in one year. Loans also have a higher probability of default than other assets. Because of the lack of liquidity and higher default risk, the bank earns its highest return on loans.

As you can see in Table 1, the largest categories of loans for commercial banks are commercial and industrial loans made to businesses and real estate loans. Commercial banks also make consumer loans and lend to each other. The bulk of these interbank loans are overnight loans lent in the federal funds market. The major difference in the balance sheets of the various depository institutions is primarily in the type of loan in which they specialize. Savings and loans and mutual savings banks, for example, specialize in residential mortgages, while credit unions tend to make consumer loans.

Other Assets The physical capital (bank buildings, computers, and other equipment) owned by the banks is included in this category.

Basics of Banking

Before proceeding to more detailed study of how a bank manages its assets and liabilities in order to make the highest profit, you should understand the basic operation of a bank.

In general terms, banks make profits by selling liabilities with one set of characteristics (a particular combination of liquidity, risk, size, and return) and using the proceeds to buy assets with a different set of characteristics. This process is often referred to as *asset transformation*. Instead of making a mortgage loan directly to a neighbor, a person can hold a savings deposit that enables a bank to use the funds provided by the deposit to make the loan to the neighbor. The bank has, in effect, transformed the savings deposit (an asset held by the depositor) into a mortgage loan (an asset held by the bank). Another way this process of asset transformation is described is to say that the bank "borrows short and lends long" because it makes long-term loans and funds them by issuing short-dated deposits.

The process of transforming assets and providing a set of services (check clearing, record keeping, credit analysis, and so forth) is like any other production process in a firm. If the bank produces desirable services at low cost and earns substantial income on its assets, it earns profits; if not, the bank suffers losses.

To make our analysis of the operation of a bank more concrete, we use a tool called a **T-account.** A T-account is a simplified balance sheet, with lines in the form of a T, that lists only the changes that occur in balance sheet items starting from some initial balance sheet position. Let's say that Jane Brown has heard that the First National Bank provides excellent service, so she opens a checking account with a $100 bill. She now has a $100 checkable deposit at the bank, which shows up as a $100 liability on the bank's balance sheet. The bank now puts her $100 bill into its vault so that the bank's assets rise by the $100 increase in vault cash. The T-account for the bank looks like this:

First National Bank

Assets		Liabilities	
Vault Cash	+$100	Checkable deposits	+$100

Since vault cash is also part of the bank's reserves, we can rewrite the T-account as follows:

Assets		Liabilities	
Reserves	+$100	Checkable deposits	+$100

Note that Jane Brown's opening of a checking account leads to *an increase in the bank's reserves equal to the increase in checkable deposits.*

If Jane had opened her account with a $100 check written on an account at another bank, say, the Second National Bank, we would get the same result. The initial effect on the T-account of the First National Bank is as follows:

Assets		Liabilities	
Cash items in process of collection	+$100	Checkable deposits	+$100

Checkable deposits increase by $100 as before, but now the First National Bank is owed $100 by the Second National Bank. This asset for the First National Bank is entered in the T-account as $100 of cash items in process of collection because the First National Bank will now try to collect the funds that it is owed. It could go directly to the Second National Bank and ask for payment of the funds, but if the two banks are in separate states, that would be a time-consuming and costly process. Instead, the First National Bank deposits the check in its account at the Fed, and the Fed collects the funds from the Second National Bank. The result is that the Fed transfers $100 of reserves from the Second National Bank to the First National Bank, and the final balance sheet positions of the two banks are as follows:

First National Bank				**Second National Bank**			
Assets		Liabilities		Assets		Liabilities	
Reserves	+$100	Checkable deposits	+$100	Reserves	−$100	Checkable deposits	−$100

The process initiated by Jane Brown can be summarized as follows: When a check written on an account at one bank is deposited in another, the bank receiving the deposit gains reserves equal to the amount of the check, while the bank on which the check is written sees its reserves fall by the same amount. Therefore, **when a bank receives additional deposits, it gains an equal amount of reserves; when it loses deposits, it loses an equal amount of reserves.**

Study Guide

T-accounts are used to study various topics throughout this text. Whenever you see a T-account, try to analyze what would happen if the opposite action were taken; for example, what would happen if Jane Brown decided to close her $100 account at the First National Bank by writing a $100 check and depositing it in a new checking account at the Second National Bank?

Now that you understand how banks gain and lose reserves, we can examine how a bank rearranges its balance sheet to make a profit when it experiences a change in its deposits. Let's return to the situation when the First National Bank has just received the extra $100 of checkable deposits. As you know, the bank is obliged to keep a certain fraction of its checkable deposits as required reserves. If the fraction (the required reserve ratio) is 10%, the First National Bank's required reserves have increased by $10, and we can rewrite its T-account as follows:

First National Bank			
Assets		**Liabilities**	
Required reserves	+$10	Checkable deposits	+$100
Excess reserves	+$90		

Let's see how well the bank is doing as a result of the additional checkable deposits. Because reserves pay no interest, it has no income from the additional $100 of assets. But servicing the extra $100 of checkable deposits is costly because the bank must keep records, pay tellers, return canceled checks, pay for check clearing, and so forth. The bank is making a loss! The situation is even worse if the bank makes interest payments on the deposits, as with NOW accounts. If it is to make a profit, the bank must put to productive use all or part of the $90 of excess reserves it has available.

Let us assume that the bank chooses not to hold any excess reserves but to make loans instead. The T-account then looks like this:

Assets		**Liabilities**	
Required reserves	+$10	Checkable deposits	+$100
Loans	+$90		

The bank is now making a profit because it holds short-term liabilities such as checkable deposits and uses the proceeds to buy longer-term assets such as loans with higher interest rates. As mentioned earlier, this process of asset transformation is frequently described by saying that banks are in the business of "borrowing short and lending long." For example, if the loans have an interest rate of 10% per year, the bank earns $9 in income from its loans over the year. If the $100 of checkable deposits is in a NOW account with a 5% interest rate and it costs another $3 per year to service the account, the cost per year of these deposits is $8. The bank's profit on the new deposits is then $1 per year (a 1% return on assets).

General Principles of Bank Management

Now that you have some idea of how a bank operates, let's look at how a bank manages its assets and liabilities in order to earn the highest possible profit. The bank manager has four primary concerns. The first is to make sure that the bank has enough ready cash to pay its depositors when there are **deposit outflows,** that is, when deposits are lost because depositors make withdrawals and demand payment. To keep enough cash on hand, the bank must engage in **liquidity management,** the acquisition of sufficiently liquid assets to meet the bank's obligations to depositors. Second, the bank manager must pursue an acceptably low level of risk by acquiring assets that have a low rate of default and by diversifying asset holdings (**asset management**). The third concern is to acquire funds at low cost (**liability management**). Finally, the manager must decide the amount of capital the bank should maintain and then acquire the needed capital (**capital adequacy management**).

To understand bank management fully, we must go beyond the general principles of bank asset and liability management described next and look in more detail at how a bank manages its assets. In Chapter 24 we look at how managers of financial institutions such as banks manage risk, specifically, **credit risk,** the risk arising because borrowers may default, and **interest-rate risk,** the riskiness of earnings and returns on bank assets that results from fluctuations in interest rates.

Liquidity Management and the Role of Reserves

Let us see how a typical bank, the First National Bank, can deal with deposit outflows that occur when its depositors withdraw cash from checking or savings accounts or write checks that are deposited in other banks. In the example that follows, we assume that the bank has ample excess reserves and that all deposits have the same required reserve ratio of 10% (the bank is required to keep 10% of its time and checkable deposits as reserves). Suppose that the First National Bank's initial balance sheet is as follows:

Assets		Liabilities	
Reserves	$20 million	Deposits	$100 million
Loans	$80 million	Bank capital	$ 10 million
Securities	$10 million		

The bank's required reserves are 10% of $100 million, or $10 million. Since it holds $20 million of reserves, the First National Bank has excess reserves of $10 million. If a deposit outflow of $10 million occurs, the bank's balance sheet becomes

Assets		Liabilities	
Reserves	$10 million	Deposits	$90 million
Loans	$80 million	Bank capital	$10 million
Securities	$10 million		

The bank loses $10 million of deposits *and* $10 million of reserves, but since its required reserves are now 10% of only $90 million ($9 million), its reserves still exceed this amount by $1 million. In short, *if a bank has ample reserves, a deposit outflow does not necessitate changes in other parts of its balance sheet.*

The situation is quite different when a bank holds insufficient excess reserves. Let's assume that instead of initially holding $10 million in excess reserves, the First National Bank makes loans of $10 million, so that it holds no excess reserves. Its initial balance sheet would be

Assets		Liabilities	
Reserves	$10 million	Deposits	$100 million
Loans	$90 million	Bank capital	$ 10 million
Securities	$10 million		

When it suffers the $10 million deposit outflow, its balance sheet becomes

Assets		Liabilities	
Reserves	$ 0	Deposits	$90 million
Loans	$90 million	Bank capital	$10 million
Securities	$10 million		

After $10 million has been withdrawn from deposits and hence reserves, the bank has a problem: It has a reserve requirement of 10% of $90 million, or $9 million, but it has no reserves! To eliminate this shortfall, the bank has four basic options. One is to acquire reserves to meet a deposit outflow by borrowing them from other banks in the federal funds market or by borrowing from corporations.[1] If the First National Bank acquires the $9 million shortfall in reserves by borrowing it from other banks or corporations, its balance sheet becomes

Assets		Liabilities	
Reserves	$ 9 million	Deposits	$90 million
Loans	$90 million	Borrowings from other	
Securities	$10 million	banks or corporations	$ 9 million
		Bank capital	$10 million

The cost of this activity is the interest rate on these loans, such as the federal funds rate.

A second alternative is for the bank to sell some of its securities to help cover the deposit outflow. For example, it might sell $9 million of its securities and deposit the proceeds with the Fed, resulting in the following balance sheet:

Assets		Liabilities	
Reserves	$ 9 million	Deposits	$90 million
Loans	$90 million	Bank capital	$10 million
Securities	$ 1 million		

The bank incurs some brokerage and other transaction costs when it sells these securities. The U.S. government securities that are classified as secondary reserves are very liquid, so the transaction costs of selling them are quite modest. However, the other securities the bank holds are less liquid and the transaction costs can be appreciably higher.

A third way that the bank can meet a deposit outflow is to acquire reserves by borrowing from the Fed. In our example, the First National Bank could leave its security and loan holdings the same and borrow $9 million in discount loans from the Fed. Its balance sheet would be

Assets		Liabilities	
Reserves	$ 9 million	Deposits	$90 million
Loans	$90 million	Discount loans from	
Securities	$10 million	the Fed	$ 9 million
		Bank capital	$10 million

The cost of taking out a discount loan is the interest rate that must be paid to the Fed (called the **discount rate**).

Finally, a bank can acquire the $9 million of reserves to meet the deposit outflow by reducing its loans by this amount and depositing the $9 million it then

[1]One way that the First National Bank can borrow from other banks and corporations is by selling negotiable certificates of deposit. This method for obtaining funds is discussed in the section on liability management.

receives with the Fed, thereby increasing its reserves by $9 million. This trans-
action changes the balance sheet as follows:

Assets		Liabilities	
Reserves	$ 9 million	Deposits	$90 million
Loans	$81 million	Bank capital	$10 million
Securities	$10 million		

The First National Bank is once again in good shape because its $9 million of
reserves satisfies the reserve requirement.

However, this process of reducing its loans is the bank's costliest way of acquiring reserves when there is a deposit outflow. If the First National Bank has numerous short-term loans renewed at fairly short intervals, it can reduce its total
amount of loans outstanding fairly quickly by *calling in* loans—that is, by not
renewing some loans when they come due. Unfortunately for the bank, this is likely
to antagonize the customers whose loans are not being renewed because they have
not done anything to deserve such treatment. Indeed, they are likely to take their
business elsewhere in the future, a very costly consequence for the bank.

A second method for reducing its loans is for the bank to sell them off to other
banks. Again, this is very costly because other banks do not personally know the
customers who have taken out the loans and so may not be willing to buy the loans
at their full value.

The foregoing discussion explains why banks hold excess reserves even
though loans or securities earn a higher return. When a deposit outflow occurs,
holding excess reserves allows the bank to escape the costs of (1) borrowing from
other banks or corporations, (2) selling securities, (3) borrowing from the Fed,
or (4) calling in or selling off loans. ***Excess reserves are insurance against
the costs associated with deposit outflows. The higher the costs associated with deposit outflows, the more excess reserves banks will want
to hold.***

Just as you and I would be willing to pay an insurance company to insure us
against a casualty loss such as the theft of a car, a bank is willing to pay the cost
of holding excess reserves (the opportunity cost, which is the earnings forgone by
not holding income-earning assets such as loans or securities) in order to insure
against losses due to deposit outflows. Because excess reserves, like insurance,
have a cost, banks also take other steps to protect themselves; for example, they
might shift their holdings of assets to more liquid securities (secondary reserves).

Study Guide

Bank management is easier to grasp if you put yourself in the banker's shoes and imagine what
you would do in the situations described. To understand a bank's possible responses to deposit
outflows, imagine how you as a banker might respond to two successive deposit outflows of
$10 million.

Asset Management

Now that you understand why a bank has a need for liquidity, we can examine
the basic strategy a bank pursues in managing its assets. To maximize its profits,
a bank must simultaneously seek the highest returns possible on loans and

securities, reduce risk, and make adequate provisions for liquidity by holding liquid assets. Banks try to accomplish these three goals in four basic ways.

First, banks try to find borrowers who will pay high interest rates and are unlikely to default on their loans. They seek out loan business by advertising their borrowing rates and by approaching corporations directly to solicit loans. It is up to the bank's loan officer to decide if potential borrowers are good credit risks who will make interest and principal payments on time. Typically, banks are conservative in their loan policies; the default rate is usually less than 1%. It is important, however, that banks not be so conservative that they miss out on attractive lending opportunities that earn high interest rates.

Second, banks try to purchase securities with high returns and low risk. Third, in managing their assets, banks must attempt to lower risk by diversifying. They accomplish this by purchasing many different types of assets (short- and long-term, U.S. Treasury, and municipal bonds) and approving many types of loans to a number of customers. Banks that have not sufficiently sought the benefits of diversification often come to regret it later. For example, banks that had overspecialized in making loans to energy companies, real estate developers, or farmers suffered huge losses in the 1980s with the slump in energy, property, and farm prices. Indeed, many of these banks went broke because they had put too many eggs in one basket.

Finally, the bank must manage the liquidity of its assets so that it can satisfy its reserve requirements without bearing huge costs. This means that it will hold liquid securities even if they earn a somewhat lower return than other assets. The bank must decide, for example, how much excess reserves must be held to avoid costs from a deposit outflow. In addition, it will want to hold short-term U.S. government securities as secondary reserves so that even if a deposit outflow forces some costs on the bank, these will not be terribly high. Again, it is not wise for a bank to be too conservative. If it avoids all costs associated with deposit outflows by holding only excess reserves, losses are suffered because reserves earn no interest, while the bank's liabilities are costly to maintain. The bank must balance its desire for liquidity against the increased earnings that can be obtained from less liquid assets such as loans.

Liability Management

Before the 1960s, liability management was a staid affair: For the most part, banks took their liabilities as fixed and spent their time trying to achieve an optimal mix of assets. There were two main reasons for the emphasis on asset management. First, over 60% of the sources of bank funds was obtained through checkable (demand) deposits that by law could not pay any interest. Thus banks could not actively compete with one another for these deposits, and so their amount was effectively a given for an individual bank. Second, because the markets for making overnight loans between banks were not well developed, banks rarely borrowed from other banks to meet their reserve needs.

Starting in the 1960s, however, large banks (called **money center banks**) in key financial centers, such as New York, Chicago, and San Francisco, began to explore ways in which the liabilities on their balance sheets could provide them with reserves and liquidity. This led to an expansion of overnight loans markets, such as the federal funds market, and the development of new financial instruments such as negotiable CDs (first developed in 1961), which enabled money center banks to acquire funds quickly.[2]

This new flexibility in liability management meant that banks could take a different approach to bank management. They no longer needed to depend on checkable deposits as the primary source of bank funds and as a result no longer treated their sources of funds (liabilities) as given. Instead, they aggressively set target goals for their asset growth and tried to acquire funds (by issuing liabilities) as they were needed.

For example, today, when a money center bank finds an attractive loan opportunity, it can acquire funds by selling a negotiable CD. Or if it has a reserve shortfall, funds can be borrowed from another bank in the federal funds market without incurring high transaction costs. The federal funds market can also be used to finance loans.

The emphasis on liability management explains some of the important changes over the past three decades in the composition of banks' balance sheets. While negotiable CDs and bank borrowings have greatly increased in importance as a source of bank funds in recent years (rising from 2% of bank liabilities in 1960 to 39% by the end of 2004), checkable deposits have decreased in importance (from 61% of bank liabilities in 1960 to 9% by the end of 2004). Newfound flexibility in liability management and the search for higher profits have also stimulated banks to increase the proportion of their assets held in loans, which earn higher income (from 46% of bank assets in 1960 to 56% by the end of 2004).

Capital Adequacy Management

Banks have to make decisions about the amount of capital they need to hold for three reasons. First, bank capital helps prevent *bank failure*, a situation in which the bank cannot satisfy its obligations to pay its depositors and other creditors and so goes out of business. Second, the amount of capital affects returns for the owners (equity holders) of the bank. And third, a minimum amount of bank capital (bank capital requirements) is required by regulatory authorities.

How Bank Capital Helps Prevent Bank Failure   Let's consider two banks with identical balance sheets, except that the High Capital Bank has a ratio of capital to assets of 10% while the Low Capital Bank has a ratio of 4%.

High Capital Bank				Low Capital Bank			
Assets		Liabilities		Assets		Liabilities	
Reserves	$10 million	Deposits	$90 million	Reserves	$10 million	Desposits	$96 million
Loans	$90 million	Bank capital	$10 million	Loans	$90 million	Bank capital	$ 4 million

Suppose that both banks got caught up in the euphoria of the real estate market in the 1980s, only to find that $5 million of their real estate loans became worthless in the 1990s. When these bad loans are written off (valued at zero), the total value of assets declines by $5 million, and so bank capital, which equals total assets minus liabilities, also declines by $5 million. The balance sheets of the two banks now look like this:

---

[2]Because small banks are not as well known as money center banks and so might be a higher credit risk, they find it harder to raise funds in the negotiable CD market. Hence they do not engage nearly as actively in liability management.

High Capital Bank				Low Capital Bank			
Assets		Liabilities		Assets		Liabilities	
Reserves	$10 million	Deposits	$90 million	Reserves	$10 million	Desposits	$96 million
Loans	$85 million	Bank capital	$ 5 million	Loans	$85 million	Bank capital	−$1 million

The High Capital Bank takes the $5 million loss in stride because its initial cushion of $10 million in capital means that it still has a positive net worth (bank capital) of $5 million after the loss. The Low Capital Bank, however, is in big trouble. Now the value of its assets has fallen below its liabilities, and its net worth is now −$1 million. Because the bank has a negative net worth, it is insolvent: It does not have sufficient assets to pay off all holders of its liabilities (creditors). When a bank becomes insolvent, government regulators close the bank, its assets are sold off, and its managers are fired. Since the owners of the Low Capital Bank will find their investment wiped out, they would clearly have preferred the bank to have had a larger cushion of bank capital to absorb the losses, as was the case for the High Capital Bank. We therefore see an important rationale for a bank to maintain a high level of capital: ***A bank maintains bank capital to lessen the chance that it will become insolvent.***

How the Amount of Bank Capital Affects Returns to Equity Holders   Because owners of a bank must know whether their bank is being managed well, they need good measures of bank profitability. A basic measure of bank profitability is the **return on assets (ROA),** the net profit after taxes per dollar of assets:

$$ROA = \frac{\text{net profit after taxes}}{\text{assets}}$$

The return on assets provides information on how efficiently a bank is being run because it indicates how much profits are generated on average by each dollar of assets.

However, what the bank's owners (equity holders) care about most is how much the bank is earning on their equity investment. This information is provided by the other basic measure of bank profitability, the **return on equity (ROE),** the net profit after taxes per dollar of equity capital:

$$ROE = \frac{\text{net profit after taxes}}{\text{equity capital}}$$

There is a direct relationship between the return on assets (which measures how efficiently the bank is run) and the return on equity (which measures how well the owners are doing on their investment). This relationship is determined by the so-called **equity multiplier (EM),** which is the amount of assets per dollar of equity capital:

$$EM = \frac{\text{assets}}{\text{equity capital}}$$

To see this, we note that

$$\frac{\text{Net profit after taxes}}{\text{Equity capital}} = \frac{\text{net profit after taxes}}{\text{assets}} \times \frac{\text{assets}}{\text{equity capital}}$$

which, using our definitions, yields

$$ROE = ROA \times EM \tag{1}$$

The formula in Equation 1 tells us what happens to the return on equity when a bank holds a smaller amount of capital (equity) for a given amount of assets. As we have seen, the High Capital Bank initially has $100 million of assets and $10 million of equity, which gives it an equity multiplier of 10 (= $100 million/$10 million). The Low Capital Bank, by contrast, has only $4 million of equity, so its equity multiplier is higher, equaling 25 (= $100 million/$4 million). Suppose that these banks have been equally well run so that they both have the same returns on assets of 1%. The return on equity for the High Capital Bank equals 1% × 10 = 10%, while the return on equity for the Low Capital Bank equals 1% × 25 = 25%. The equity holders in the Low Capital Bank are clearly a lot happier than the equity holders in the High Capital Bank because they are earning more than twice as high a return. We now see why owners of a bank may not want it to hold a lot of capital. ***Given the return on assets, the lower the bank capital, the higher the return for the owners of the bank.***

Trade-off Between Safety and Returns to Equity Holders   We now see that bank capital has benefits and costs. Bank capital benefits the owners of a bank in that it makes their investment safer by reducing the likelihood of bankruptcy. But bank capital is costly because the higher it is, the lower will be the return on equity for a given return on assets. In determining the amount of bank capital, managers must decide how much of the increased safety that comes with higher capital (the benefit) they are willing to trade off against the lower return on equity that comes with higher capital (the cost).

In more uncertain times, when the possibility of large losses on loans increases, bank managers might want to hold more capital to protect the equity holders. Conversely, if they have confidence that loan losses won't occur, they might want to reduce the amount of bank capital, have a high equity multiplier, and thereby increase the return on equity.

Bank Capital Requirements   Banks also hold capital because they are required to do so by regulatory authorities. Because of the high costs of holding capital for the reasons just described, bank managers often want to hold less bank capital than is required by the regulatory authorities. In this case, the amount of bank capital is determined by the bank capital requirements. We discuss the details of bank capital requirements and why they are such an important part of bank regulation in Chapter 20.

The Practicing Manager

STRATEGIES FOR MANAGING BANK CAPITAL

Mona, the manager of the First National Bank, has to make decisions about the appropriate amount of bank capital. Looking at the balance sheet of the bank, which has a ratio of bank capital to assets of 10% ($10 million of capital and $100 million of assets), Mona is concerned that the large amount of bank capital is causing the return on equity to be too low. She concludes that the bank has a capital surplus and should increase the equity multiplier to increase the return on equity. To lower the amount of capital relative to assets and raise the equity multiplier, she can do any of three things: (1) She can reduce the amount of bank capital by buying back some of the bank's stock. (2) She can reduce the bank's capital by paying out higher dividends to its stockholders, thereby reducing the bank's retained earnings. (3) She can keep bank capital constant but increase the bank's assets by acquiring new funds, say, by issuing CDs, and then seeking out loan business or purchasing more securities with these new funds. Because the bank manager feels that she will enhance her position with the stockholders, she decides to pursue the second alternative and raises the dividends on First National Bank stock.

Now suppose that the First National Bank is in a situation similar to that of the Low Capital Bank and has a ratio of bank capital to assets of 3%. The bank manager now might worry that the bank is short on capital relative to assets because it does not have a sufficient cushion to prevent bank failure. To raise the amount of capital relative to assets, she now has the following three choices: (1) She can raise capital for the bank by having it issue equity (common stock). (2) She can raise capital by reducing the bank's dividends to shareholders, thereby increasing retained earnings that it can put into its capital account. (3) She can keep capital at the same level but reduce the bank's assets by making fewer loans or by selling off securities and then using the proceeds to reduce its liabilities. Suppose that raising bank capital is not easy to do at the current time because capital markets are tight or because shareholders will protest if their dividends are cut. Then Mona might have to choose the third alternative and decide to shrink the size of the bank.

In recent years, many banks have experienced capital shortfalls and have had to restrict asset growth, as Mona did, when the bank is short of capital. The important consequences of this for the credit markets are discussed in the case that follows.

Case

DID THE CAPITAL CRUNCH CAUSE A CREDIT CRUNCH IN THE EARLY 1990s?

During the 1990–1991 recession and the year following, there occurred a slowdown in the growth of credit that was unprecedented in the post-World War II era. Many economists and politicians have claimed that there was a "credit crunch" during this period in which credit was hard to get, and as a result the performance of the economy in 1990–1992 was very weak. Was the slowdown in credit growth a manifestation of a credit crunch, and if so, what caused it?

Our analysis of how a bank manages bank capital suggests that a credit crunch was likely to have occurred in 1990–1992 and that it was caused at least in part by the so-called capital crunch in which shortfalls of bank capital led to slower credit growth.

The period of the late 1980s saw a boom and then a major bust in the real estate market that led to huge losses for banks on their real estate loans. As our example on how bank capital helps prevent bank failures demonstrates, the loan losses caused a substantial fall in the amount of bank capital. At the same time, regulators were raising capital requirements (a subject we will discuss in Chapter 20). The resulting capital shortfalls meant that banks had either to raise new capital or to restrict their asset growth by cutting back on lending. Because of the weak economy at the time, raising new capital was extremely difficult for banks, so they chose the latter course. Banks did restrict their lending, and borrowers found it harder to obtain loans, leading to complaints from banks' customers.[3] Only with the stronger recovery of the economy in 1993, helped by a low-interest-rate policy at the Federal Reserve, did these complaints subside.

Off-Balance-Sheet Activities

Although asset and liability management has traditionally been the major concern of banks, in the more competitive environment of recent years banks have been aggressively seeking out profits by engaging in off-balance-sheet activities. **Off-balance-sheet activities** involve trading financial instruments and generating income from fees and loan sales, activities that affect bank profits but do not appear on bank balance sheets. Indeed, off-balance-sheet activities have been growing in importance for banks: The income from these activities as a percentage of assets has nearly doubled since 1980.

Loan Sales

One type of off-balance-sheet activity that has grown in importance in recent years involves income generated by loan sales. A **loan sale,** also called a *secondary loan participation*, involves a contract that sells all or part of the cash stream from a specific loan and thereby removes the loan from the bank's balance sheet. Banks earn profits by selling loans for an amount slightly greater than the amount of the original loan. Because the high interest rate on these loans makes them attractive, institutions are willing to buy them even though the higher price means that they earn a slightly lower interest rate than the original interest rate on the loan, usually on the order of 0.15 percentage point.

Generation of Fee Income

Another type of off-balance-sheet activity involves the generation of income from fees that banks receive for providing specialized services to their customers, such as making foreign exchange trades on a customer's behalf, servicing a mortgage-backed security by collecting interest and principal payments and then paying them out, guaranteeing debt securities such as banker's acceptances (the bank promises to make interest and principal payments if the party issuing the security

---

[3]As we will see in Chapter 20, not only were capital requirements raised, but also risk-based capital requirements were imposed that required even more capital if loans were made but not if banks bought government securities. The risk-based capital requirements thus encouraged banks to switch out of loans and into government securities, and this was an additional factor that led to a decline in bank lending. For a discussion of the evidence on how the capital crunch caused the credit crunch of 1990–1992, see "The Role of the Credit Slowdown in the Recent Recession," *Federal Reserve Bank of New York Quarterly Review*, Spring 1993.

cannot), and providing backup lines of credit. There are several types of backup lines of credit. The most important is the **loan commitment,** under which for a fee the bank agrees to provide a loan at the customer's request, up to a given dollar amount, over a specified period of time. Credit lines are also now available to bank depositors with "overdraft privileges"—these bank customers can write checks in excess of their deposit balances and, in effect, write themselves a loan. Other lines of credit for which banks get fees include standby letters of credit to back up issues of commercial paper and other securities, and credit lines—called **note issuance facilities (NIFs)** and **revolving underwriting facilities (RUFs)**—for underwriting Euronotes, which are medium-term Eurobonds.

Off-balance-sheet activities involving guarantees of securities and backup credit lines increase the risk a bank faces. Even though a guaranteed security does not appear on a bank balance sheet, it still exposes the bank to default risk: If the issuer of the security defaults, the bank is left holding the bag and must pay off the security's owner. Backup credit lines also expose the bank to risk because the bank may be forced to provide loans when it does not have sufficient liquidity or when the borrower is a very poor credit risk.

Trading Activities and Risk Management Techniques

Banks' attempts to manage interest-rate risk led them to trading in financial futures, options for debt instruments, and interest-rate swaps. Banks engaged in international banking also conduct transactions in the foreign exchange market. All transactions in these markets are off-balance-sheet activities because they do not have a direct effect on the bank's balance sheet. Although bank trading in these markets is often directed toward reducing risk or facilitating other bank business, banks also try to outguess the markets and engage in speculation. This speculation can be a very risky business and indeed has led to bank insolvencies, the most dramatic being the failure of Barings, a British bank, in 1995.

Trading activities, although often highly profitable, are dangerous because they make it easy for financial institutions and their employees to make huge bets both easily and quickly. A particular problem for management of trading activities is that the principal-agent problem, discussed in Chapter 15, is especially severe. Given the ability to place large bets, a trader (the agent), whether she trades in bond markets, in foreign exchange markets, or in financial derivatives, has an incentive to take on excessive risks: If her trading strategy leads to large profits, she is likely to receive a high salary and bonuses, but if she takes large losses, the financial institution (the principal) will have to cover them. As the Barings Bank failure in 1995 so forcefully demonstrated, a trader subject to the principal-agent problem can take a bank that is quite healthy and drive it into insolvency very fast (see the "Conflicts of Interest" box).

To reduce the principal-agent problem, bank management must set up internal controls to prevent debacles like the one at Barings. Such controls include the complete separation of the people in charge of trading activities and those in charge of the bookkeeping for trades. In addition, bank management must set limits on the total amount of traders' transactions and on the bank's risk exposure. Bank management must also scrutinize risk assessment procedures using the latest computer technology. One such method involves the so-called value-at-risk approach. In this approach, the bank develops a statistical model with which it can calculate the maximum loss that its portfolio is likely to sustain over a given time interval, dubbed the value at risk, or VAR. For example, a bank might estimate that

Available at www.federalre serve.gov/ boarddocs/ SupManual/ default.htm# trading, the Federal Reserve Bank "Trading and Capital Market Activities Manual" offers an in-depth discussion of a wide range of risk management issues encountered in trading operations.

CONFLICTS OF INTEREST

Barings, Daiwa, and Sumitomo: Rogue Traders and the Principal-Agent Problem

The demise of Barings, a venerable British bank over a century old, is a sad morality tale of how the principal-agent problem operating through a rogue trader can take a financial institution that has a healthy balance sheet one month and turn it into an insolvent tragedy the next.

In July 1992, Nick Leeson, Barings's new head clerk at its Singapore branch, began to speculate on the Nikkei, the Japanese version of the Dow Jones index. By late 1992, Leeson had suffered losses of $3 million, which he hid from his superiors by stashing the losses in a secret account. He even fooled his superiors into thinking he was generating large profits, thanks to a failure of internal controls at his firm, which allowed him to execute trades on the Singapore exchange and oversee the bookkeeping of those trades. (As anyone who runs a cash business, such as a bar, knows, there is always a lower likelihood of fraud if more than one person handles the cash. Similarly for trading operations, you never mix management of the back room with management of the front room; this principle was grossly violated by Barings management.) Things didn't get better for Leeson, who by late 1994 had losses exceeding $250 million. In January and February 1995, he bet the bank. On January 17, 1995, the day of the Kobe earthquake, he lost $75 million, and by the end of the week had lost more than $150 million. When the stock market declined on February 23, leaving him with a further loss of $250 million, he called it quits and fled Singapore. Three days later, he turned himself in at the Frankfurt airport. By the end of his wild ride, Leeson's losses, $1.3 billion in all, ate up Barings's capital and caused the bank to fail.

Our asymmetric information analysis of the principal-agent problem explains Leeson's behavior and the danger of Barings's management lapse. By letting Leeson control both his own trades and the back room, it increased asymmetric information because it reduced the principal's (Barings's) knowledge about Leeson's trading activities. This lapse increased the moral hazard incentive for him to take risks at the bank's expense, as he was now less likely to be caught. Furthermore, once he had experienced large losses, he had even greater incentives to take on even higher risk because if his bets worked out, he could reverse his losses and keep in good standing with the company, whereas if his bets soured, he had little to lose since he was out of a job anyway. Indeed, the bigger his losses, the more he had to gain by bigger bets, which explains the escalation of the amount of his trades as his losses mounted. If Barings's managers had understood the principal-agent problem, they would have been more vigilant in learning what Leeson was up to, and the bank might still be here today.

Unfortunately, Nick Leeson is no longer a rarity in the rogue traders' billionaire club, those who have lost more than $1 billion. Over 11 years, Toshihide Iguchi, an officer in the New York branch of Daiwa Bank, also had control of both the bond trading operation and the back room, and he racked up $1.1 billion in losses over the period. In July 1995, Iguchi disclosed his losses to his superiors, but the management of the bank did not disclose them to its regulators. The result was that Daiwa was slapped with a $340 million fine and the bank was thrown out of the country by U.S. bank regulators. Yasuo Hamanaka is the latest member of the billionaire club. In July 1996, he topped Leeson's and Iguchi's record, losing $2.6 billion for his employer, the Sumitomo Corporation, one of Japan's top trading companies. The moral of these stories is that management of firms engaged in trading activities must reduce the principal-agent problem by closely monitoring their traders' activities.

the maximum loss that it would be likely to sustain over one day with a probability of 1 in 100 is $1 million; the $1 million figure is the bank's calculated value at risk. Another approach is called "stress testing." In this approach, the bank asks models what would happen if a doomsday scenario occurs; that is, it looks at the losses it would sustain if an unusual combination of bad events occurred. With the value-at-risk approach and stress testing, a bank can assess its risk exposure and take steps to reduce it.

U.S. bank regulators have become concerned about increased risk from banks' off-balance-sheet activities and, as we will see in Chapter 20, are encouraging banks to pay increased attention to risk management. In addition, the Bank for

International Settlements is developing additional bank capital requirements based on value-at-risk calculations for a bank's trading activities.

Measuring Bank Performance

To understand how well a bank is doing, we need to start by looking at a bank's income statement, the description of the sources of income and expenses that affect the bank's profitability.

Bank's Income Statement

The end of year 2003 income statement for all federally insured commercial banks appears in Table 2.

Operating Income **Operating income** is the income that comes from a bank's ongoing operations. Most of a bank's operating income is generated by interest on its assets, particularly loans. As we see in Table 2, in 2003 interest income represented 64.3% of commercial banks' operating income. Interest income fluctuates with the level of interest rates, and so its percentage of operating income is highest when interest rates are at peak levels. That is exactly what happened in 1981, when interest rates rose above 15% and interest income rose to 93% of total bank operating income.

Noninterest income, which made up 35.7% of operating income in 2003, is generated partly by service charges on deposit accounts, but the bulk of it comes from the off-balance-sheet activities mentioned earlier, which generate fees or trading profits for the bank. The importance of these off-balance-sheet activities to bank profits has been growing in recent years. Whereas in 1980 other noninterest income from off-balance-sheet activities represented only 5% of operating income, it reached 29.6% in 2003.

Operating Expenses **Operating expenses** are the expenses incurred in conducting the bank's ongoing operations. An important component of a bank's operating expenses is the interest payments that it must make on its liabilities, particularly on its deposits. Just as interest income varies with the level of interest rates, so do interest expenses. Interest expenses as a percentage of total operating expenses reached a peak of 74% in 1981, when interest rates were at their highest, and fell to 25.4% in 2003 as interest rates moved lower. Noninterest expenses include the costs of running a banking business: salaries for tellers and officers, rent on bank buildings, purchases of equipment such as desks and vaults, and servicing costs of equipment such as computers.

The final item listed under operating expenses is provisions for loan losses. When a bank has a bad debt or anticipates that a loan might become a bad debt in the future, it can write up the loss as a current expense in its income statement under the "provision for loan losses" heading. Provisions for loan losses are directly related to loan loss reserves. When a bank wants to increase its loan loss reserves account by, say, $1 million, it does this by adding $1 million to its provisions for loan losses. Loan loss reserves rise when this is done because by increasing expenses when losses have not yet occurred, earnings are being set aside to deal with the losses in the future.

TABLE 2   *Income Statement for All Federally Insured Commercial Banks, 2003*

	Amount ($ billions)	Share of Operating Income or Expenses (%)
Operating Income		
Interest income	335.7	64.3
Interest on loans	265.9	50.9
Interest on securities	54.1	10.4
Other interest	15.7	3.0
Noninterest income	186.5	35.7
Service charges on deposit accounts	31.7	6.1
Other noninterest income	154.8	29.6
Total operating income	522.2	100.0
Operating Expenses		
Interest expenses	95.7	25.4
Interest on deposits	63.0	16.7
Interest on fed funds and repos	8.1	2.2
Other	24.6	6.5
Noninterest expenses	246.0	65.3
Salaries and employee benefits	107.8	28.6
Premises and equipment	31.3	8.3
Other	106.9	28.4
Provisions for loan losses	34.8	9.3
Total operating expense	376.5	100.0
Net Operating Income	145.7	
Gains (losses) on securities	5.6	
Extraordinary items, net	0.0	
Income taxes	−49.2	
Net Income	102.1	

Source: www.fdic.gov/banks/statistical/statistics/0106/cbr

Provisions for loan losses have been a major element in fluctuating bank profits in recent years. The 1980s brought the third-world debt crisis mentioned in Chapter 20; a sharp decline in energy prices in 1986, which caused substantial losses on loans to energy producers; and a collapse in the real estate market. As a result, provisions for loan losses were particularly high in the late 1980s, reaching a peak of 13% of operating expenses in 1987. Since then, losses on loans have begun to subside, and in 2003 provisions for loan losses dropped to only 9.3% of operating expenses.

Income   Subtracting the $376.5 billion in operating expenses from the $522.2 billion of operating income in 2003 yields net operating income of $145.7 billion.

Net operating income is closely watched by bank managers, bank shareholders, and bank regulators because it indicates how well the bank is doing on an ongoing basis.

Two items, gains (or losses) on securities sold by banks ($5.6 billion) and net extraordinary items, which are events or transactions that are both unusual and infrequent (insignificant), are added to the $145.7 billion net operating income figure to get the $151.3 billion figure for net income before taxes. Net income before taxes is more commonly referred to as profits before taxes. Subtracting the $49.2 billion of income taxes then results in $102.1 billion of net income. Net income, more commonly referred to as profits after taxes, is the figure that tells us most directly how well the bank is doing because it is the amount that the bank has available to keep as retained earnings or to pay out to stockholders as dividends.

Measures of Bank Performance

Although net income gives us an idea of how well a bank is doing, it suffers from one major drawback: It does not adjust for the bank's size, thus making it hard to compare how well one bank is doing relative to another. A basic measure of bank profitability that corrects for the size of the bank is the return on assets (ROA), mentioned earlier in the chapter, which divides the net income of the bank by the amount of its assets. ROA is a useful measure of how well a bank manager is doing on the job because it indicates how well a bank's assets are being used to generate profits. At the beginning of 2004, the assets of all federally insured commercial banks amounted to $7292.8 billion, so using the $102.1 billion net income figure from Table 2 gives us a return on assets of

$$\text{ROA} = \frac{\text{net income}}{\text{assets}} = \frac{102.1}{7292.8} = 0.014 = 1.4\%$$

Although ROA provides useful information about bank profitability, we have already seen that it is not what the bank's owners (equity holders) care about most. They are more concerned about how much the bank is earning on their equity investment, an amount that is measured by the return on equity (ROE), the net income per dollar of equity capital. At the beginning of 2004, equity capital for all federally insured commercial banks was $667.32 billion, so the ROE was therefore

$$\text{ROE} = \frac{\text{net income}}{\text{capital}} = \frac{102.1}{667.32} = 0.153 = 15.3\%$$

Another commonly watched measure of bank performance is called the **net interest margin (NIM)**, the difference between interest income and interest expenses as a percentage of total assets:

$$\text{NIM} = \frac{\text{interest income} - \text{interest expenses}}{\text{assets}}$$

As we have seen earlier in the chapter, one of a bank's primary intermediation functions is to issue liabilities and use the proceeds to purchase income-earning assets. If a bank manager has done a good job of asset and liability management such that the bank earns substantial income on its assets and has low costs on its liabilities, profits will be high. How well a bank manages its assets and liabilities is affected by the spread between the interest earned on the bank's assets and the interest costs on its liabilities. This spread is exactly what the net interest margin measures. If the bank is able to raise funds with liabilities that have low interest costs and is able to acquire assets with high interest income, the net interest margin will be high, and the bank is likely to be highly profitable. If the interest cost of its liabilities rises relative to the interest earned on its assets, the net interest margin will fall, and bank profitability will suffer.

Recent Trends in Bank Performance Measures

Table 3 provides measures of return on assets (ROA), return on equity (ROE), and the net interest margin (NIM) for all federally insured commercial banks from 1980 to 2004. Because the relationship between bank equity capital and total assets

TABLE 3   *Measures of Bank Performance, 1980–2004*

Year	Return on Assets (ROA) (%)	Return on Equity (ROE) (%)	Net Interest Margin (NIM)(%)
1980	0.77	13.38	3.33
1981	0.79	13.68	3.31
1982	0.73	12.55	3.39
1983	0.68	11.60	3.34
1984	0.66	11.04	3.47
1985	0.72	11.67	3.62
1986	0.64	10.30	3.48
1987	0.09	1.54	3.40
1988	0.82	13.74	3.57
1989	0.50	7.92	3.58
1990	0.49	7.81	3.50
1991	0.53	8.25	3.60
1992	0.94	13.86	3.89
1993	1.23	16.30	3.97
1994	1.20	15.00	3.95
1995	1.17	14.66	4.29
1996	1.19	14.45	4.27
1997	1.23	14.69	4.21
1998	1.18	13.30	3.47
1999	1.31	15.31	4.07
2000	1.19	14.02	3.95
2001	1.15	13.09	3.90
2002	1.33	14.47	4.09
2003	1.40	15.31	3.83
2004*	1.36	14.84	3.70

*Projected by FDIC.

Source: http://www2.fdic.gov/qbp

for all commercial banks remained fairly stable in the 1980s, both the ROA and ROE measures of bank performance move closely together and indicate that from the early to the late 1980s, there was a sharp decline in bank profitability. The rightmost column, net interest margin, indicates that the spread between interest income and interest expenses remained fairly stable throughout the 1980s and even improved in the late 1980s and early 1990s, which should have helped bank profits. The NIM measure thus tells us that the poor bank performance in the late 1980s was not the result of interest-rate movements.

The explanation of the weak performance of commercial banks in the late 1980s is that they had made many risky loans in the early 1980s that turned sour. The resulting huge increase in loan loss provisions in that period directly decreased net income and hence caused the fall in ROA and ROE. (Why bank profitability deteriorated and the consequences for the economy are discussed in Chapters 18 and 20.)

Beginning in 1992, bank performance improved substantially. The return on equity rose to nearly 14% in 1992 and remained above 13% in the 1993–2004 period. Similarly, the return on assets rose from the 0.5% level in the 1990–1991 period to well over the 1% level in 1993–2004. The performance measures in Table 3 suggest that the banking industry has returned to health.

Summary

1. The balance sheet of commercial banks can be thought of as a list of the sources and uses of bank funds. The bank's liabilities are its sources of funds, which include checkable deposits, time deposits, discount loans from the Fed, borrowings from other banks and corporations, and bank capital. The bank's assets are its uses of funds, which include reserves, cash items in process of collection, deposits at other banks, securities, loans, and other assets (mostly physical capital).

2. Banks make profits through the process of asset transformation: They borrow short (accept deposits) and lend long (make loans). When a bank takes in additional deposits, it gains an equal amount of reserves; when it pays out deposits, it loses an equal amount of reserves.

3. Although more liquid assets tend to earn lower returns, banks still desire to hold them. Specifically, banks hold excess and secondary reserves because they provide insurance against the costs of a deposit outflow. Banks manage their assets to maximize profits by seeking the highest returns possible on loans and securities while at the same time trying to lower risk and making adequate provisions for liquidity. Although liability management was once a staid affair, large (money center) banks now actively seek out sources of funds by issuing liabilities such as negotiable CDs or by actively borrowing from other banks and corporations. Banks manage the amount of capital they hold to prevent bank failure and to meet bank capital requirements set by the regulatory authorities. However, they do not want to hold too much capital because by so doing they will lower the returns to equity holders.

4. Off-balance-sheet activities consist of trading financial instruments and generating income from fees and loan sales, all of which affect bank profits but are not visible on bank balance sheets. Because these off-balance-sheet activities expose banks to increased risk, bank management must pay particular attention to risk assessment procedures and internal controls to restrict employees from taking on too much risk.

5. A bank's net operating income equals operating income minus operating expenses. Adding gains (or losses) on securities and net extraordinary items to net operating income and then subtracting taxes yields net income (profits after taxes). Additional measures of bank performance include the return on assets (ROA), the return on equity (ROE), and the net interest margin (NIM).

Key Terms

asset management, *p. 432*

balance sheet, *p. 425*

capital adequacy management, *p. 432*

credit risk, *p. 432*

deposit outflows, *p. 431*

discount loans, *p. 427*

discount rate, *p. 433*

equity multiplier (EM), *p. 437*

excess reserves, *p. 428*

interest-rate risk, *p. 432*

liability management, *p. 432*

liquidity management, *p. 431*

loan commitment, *p. 441*

loan sale, *p. 440*

money center banks, *p. 435*

net interest margin (NIM), *p. 445*

note issuance facilities (NIFs), *p. 441*

off-balance-sheet activities, *p. 440*

operating expenses, *p. 443*

operating income, *p. 443*

required reserve ratio, *p. 428*

required reserves, *p. 428*

reserve requirement, *p. 428*

reserves, *p. 428*

return on assets (ROA), *p. 437*

return on equity (ROE), *p. 437*

revolving underwriting facilities (RUFs), *p. 441*

secondary reserves, *p. 428*

T-account, *p. 429*

vault cash, *p. 428*

Questions

1. Rank the following bank assets from most to least liquid:

   a. Commercial loans

   b. Securities

   c. Reserves

   d. Physical capital

2. If the president of a bank told you that the bank was so well run that it has never had to call in loans, sell securities, or borrow as a result of a deposit outflow, would you be willing to buy stock in that bank? Why or why not?

3. If the bank you own has no excess reserves and a sound customer comes in asking for a loan, should you automatically turn the customer down, explaining that you don't have any excess reserves to loan out? Why or why not? What options are available for you to provide the funds your customer needs?

4. Why has the development of overnight loan markets made it more likely that banks will hold fewer excess reserves?

5. If you are a banker and expect interest rates to rise in the future, would you want to make short-term or long-term loans?

6. "Bank managers should always seek the highest return possible on their assets." Is this statement true, false, or uncertain? Explain your answer.

7. "Banking has become a more dynamic industry because of more active liability management." Is this statement true, false, or uncertain? Explain your answer.

8. Why has noninterest income been growing as a source of bank operating income?

9. Which components of operating expenses experience the greatest fluctuations? Why?

10. Why do equity holders care more about ROE than about ROA?

11. What does the net interest margin measure, and why is it important to bank managers?

12. If a bank doubles the amount of its capital and ROA stays constant, what will happen to ROE?

13. If a bank finds that its ROE is too low because it has too much bank capital, what can it do to raise its ROE?

14. What are the benefits and costs for a bank when it decides to increase the amount of its bank capital?

15. If a bank is falling short of meeting its capital requirements by $1 million, what four things can it do to rectify the situation?

Quantitative Problems

1. The balance sheet of TriBank starts with an allowance for loan losses of $1.33 million. During the year, TriBank charges off worthless loans of $0.84 million, recovers $0.22 million on loans previously charged off, and charges current income for a $1.48 million provision for loan losses. Calculate the end-of-year allowance for loan losses.

2. X-Bank reported an ROE of 15% and an ROA of 1%. How well capitalized is this bank?

3. In mid-1978, Wiggley S&L issued a standard 30-year fixed rate mortgage at 7.8% for $150,000. Thirty-six months later, mortgage rates jumped to 13%. If the S&L sells the mortgage, how much of a loss is expected?

4. Refer to the previous question. In 1981 Congress allowed S&Ls to sell mortgages at a loss and to amortize the loss over the remaining life of the mortgage. If this were used for the previous question, how would the transaction have been recorded? What would be the annual adjustment? When would that end?

5. For the upcoming week, Nobel National Bank plans to issue $25 million in mortgages and purchase $100 million 31-day T-bills. New deposits of $35 million are expected, and other sources will generate $15 million in cash. What is Nobel's estimate of funds needed?

6. A bank estimates that demand deposits are, on average, $100 million with a standard deviation of $5 million. The bank wants to maintain a minimum of 8% of deposits in reserves at all times. What is the highest expected level of deposits during the month? What reserves do they need to maintain? Use a 99% confidence level.

The remaining questions relate to the first month's operations of NewBank.

7. NewBank started its first day of operations with $6 million in capital. $100 million in checkable deposits is received. The bank issues a $25 million commercial loan and another $25 million in mortgages, with the following terms:

   - Mortgages: 100 standard 30-year fixed-rate mortgages with a nominal annual rate of 5.25% each for $250,000
   - Commercial loan: 3-year loan, simple interest paid monthly at 0.75% per month

   If required reserves are 8%, what does the bank balance sheets look like? Ignore any loan loss reserves.

8. NewBank decides to invest $45 million in 30-day T-bills. The T-bills are currently trading at $4986.70 (including commissions) for a $5000 face value instrument. How many do they purchase? What does the balance sheet look like?

9. On the third day of operations, deposits fall by $5 million. What does the balance sheet look like? Are there any problems?

10. To meet any shortfall in the previous question, NewBank will borrow the cash in the federal funds market. Management decides to borrow the needed funds for the remainder of the month (now 29 days). The required yield on a discount basis is 2.9%. What does the balance sheet look like after this transaction?

11. The end of the month finally arrives for NewBank, and it receives all the required payments from its mortgages, commercial loans, and T-bills. How much cash was received? How are these transactions recorded?

12. NewBank also pays off its federal funds borrowed. How much cash is owed? How is this recorded?

13. What does the month-end balance sheet for NewBank look like? Calculate this before any income tax consideration.

14. Calculate NewBank's ROA and NIM for its first month. Assume that net interest equals EBT, and that NewBank is in the 34% tax bracket.

15. Calculate NewBank's ROE and final balance sheet, including its tax liabilities.

16. If NewBank were required to establish a loan loss reserve at 0.25% of the loan value for commercial loans, how would this be recorded? Recalculate NewBank's ROE and final balance sheet, including its tax liabilities.

17. If NewBank's target ROE is 4.5%, how much net fee income must it generate to meet this target?

18. After making payments for three years, one of the mortgage borrowers defaults on the mortgage. NewBank immediately takes possession of the house and sells it at auction for $175,000. Legal fees amount to $25,000. If no loan loss reserve was established for the mortgage loans, how is this event recorded?

Web Exercises

Banking and the Management of Financial Institutions

1. Table 1 reports the balance sheet of all commercial banks based on aggregate data found in the Federal Reserve website. Compare this table to the balance sheet reported by Wachovia: Go to **http://www.wachovia.com/investor/**. and then click on "Financial Reports." Does Wachovia have more or less of its portfolio in loans than the average bank? What types of loans does it hold the most of?

2. It is relatively easy to find up-to-date information on banks because of their extensive reporting requirements. Go to **http://www2.fdic.gov/qbp/**. Sponsored by the Federal Deposit Insurance Corporation, this site offers summary data on financial institutions. Go to the most recent Quarterly Banking Profile. Scroll to the bottom and open Table 1-A.

   a. Have banks' return on assets been increasing or decreasing over the last few years?

   b. Has the core capital been increasing, and how does it compare to the capital ratio reported in Table 1 in the text?

   c. How many institutions are currently reporting to the FDIC?

CHAPTER 18

Commercial Banking Industry: Structure and Competition

Preview

The operations of individual banks (how they acquire, use, and manage funds to make a profit) are roughly similar throughout the world. In all countries, banks are financial intermediaries in the business of earning profits. When you consider the structure and operation of the banking industry as a whole, however, the United States is in a class by itself. In most countries, four or five large banks typically dominate the banking industry, but in the United States there are on the order of 8000 commercial banks.

Is more better? Does this diversity mean that the American banking system is more competitive and therefore more economically efficient and sound than banking systems in other countries? What in the American economic and political system explains this large number of banking institutions? In this chapter we try to answer these questions by examining the historical trends in the commercial banking industry and its overall structure.

We start by examining the historical development of the banking system and how financial innovation has increased the competitive environment for the banking industry and is causing fundamental changes in it. We then go on to look at the commercial industry in detail. In addition to looking at our domestic banking system, we also examine the forces behind the growth in international banking to see how it has affected us in the United States. Finally, we examine how financial innovation has increased the competitive environment for the banking industry and is causing fundamental changes in it.

Historical Development of the Banking System

The modern commercial banking industry began when the Bank of North America was chartered in Philadelphia in 1782. With the success of this bank, other banks opened for business, and the American banking industry was off and running. (As

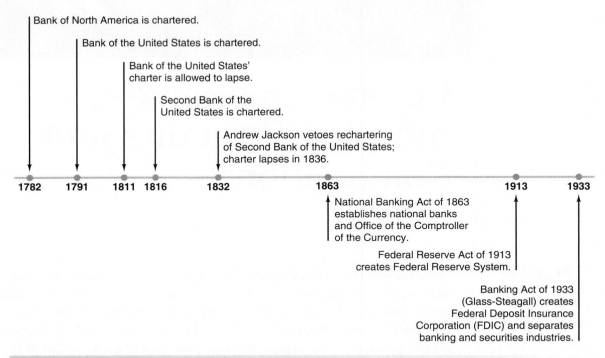

FIGURE 1 *Time Line of the Early History of Commercial Banking in the United States*

a study aid, Figure 1 provides a time line of the most important dates in the history of American banking before World War II.)

A major controversy involving the industry in its early years was whether the federal government or the states should charter banks. The Federalists, particularly Alexander Hamilton, advocated greater centralized control of banking and federal chartering of banks. Their efforts led to the creation in 1791 of the Bank of the United States, which had elements of both a private and a central bank, a government institution that has responsibility for the amount of money and credit supplied in the economy as a whole. Agricultural and other interests, however, were quite suspicious of centralized power and hence advocated chartering by the states. Furthermore, their distrust of moneyed interests in the big cities led to political pressures to eliminate the Bank of the United States, and in 1811 their efforts met with success when its charter was not renewed. Because of abuses by state banks and the clear need for a central bank to help the federal government raise funds during the War of 1812, Congress was stimulated to create the Second Bank of the United States in 1816. The tensions between advocates and opponents of centralized banking power were a recurrent theme during the operation of this second attempt at central banking in the United States, and with the election of Andrew Jackson, a strong advocate of states' rights, the fate of the Second Bank was sealed. After the election in 1832, Jackson vetoed the rechartering of the Second Bank of the United States as a national bank, and its charter lapsed in 1836.

Until 1863, all commercial banks in the United States were chartered by the banking commission of the state in which each operated. No national currency existed, and banks obtained funds primarily by issuing *banknotes* (currency circulated by the banks that could be redeemed for gold). Because banking regulations were extremely lax in many states, banks regularly failed due to fraud or lack of sufficient bank capital; their banknotes became worthless.

To eliminate the abuses of the state-chartered banks (called **state banks**), the National Banking Act of 1863 (and subsequent amendments to it) created a new banking system of federally chartered banks (called **national banks**), supervised by the Office of the Comptroller of the Currency, a department of the U.S. Treasury. This legislation was originally intended to dry up sources of funds to state banks by imposing a prohibitive tax on their banknotes while leaving the banknotes of the federally chartered banks untaxed. The state banks cleverly escaped extinction by acquiring funds by offering checking accounts. As a result, today the United States has a **dual banking system** in which banks supervised by the federal government and banks supervised by the states operate side by side.

Central banking did not reappear in this country until the Federal Reserve System (the Fed) was created in 1913 to promote an even safer banking system. All national banks were required to become members of the Federal Reserve System and became subject to a new set of regulations issued by the Fed. State banks could choose (but were not required) to become members of the system, and most did not because of the high costs of membership stemming from the Fed's regulations.

During the Great Depression years 1930–1933, some 9000 bank failures wiped out the savings of many depositors at commercial banks. To prevent future depositor losses from such failures, banking legislation in 1933 established the Federal Deposit Insurance Corporation (FDIC), which provided federal insurance on bank deposits. Member banks of the Federal Reserve System were required to purchase FDIC insurance for their depositors, and non–Federal Reserve commercial banks could choose to buy this insurance (almost all of them did). The purchase of FDIC insurance made banks subject to another set of regulations imposed by the FDIC.

The FDIC gathers data about individual financial institutions and the banking industry that you can access at www.fdic.gov/bank/

Because investment banking activities of the commercial banks were blamed for many bank failures, provisions in the banking legislation of 1933 (also known as the Glass-Steagall Act) prohibited commercial banks from underwriting or dealing in corporate securities (commercial banks were allowed to sell new issues of government securities, however) and limited banks to the purchase of debt securities approved by the bank regulatory agencies. Likewise it prohibited investment banks from engaging in commercial banking activities. In effect, the Glass-Steagall Act separated the activities of commercial banks from those of the securities industry.

Under the conditions of the Glass-Steagall Act, commercial banks had to sell off their investment banking operations. The First National Bank of Boston, for example, spun off its investment banking operations into the First Boston Corporation, now one of the most important investment banking firms in America. Investment banking firms typically discontinued their deposit business, although J. P. Morgan discontinued its investment banking business and reorganized as a commercial bank; however, some senior officers of J. P. Morgan went on to organize Morgan Stanley, another one of the largest investment banking firms today.

Multiple Regulatory Agencies

Commercial bank regulation in the United States has developed into a crazy-quilt system of multiple regulatory agencies with overlapping jurisdictions. The Office of the Comptroller of the Currency has the primary supervisory responsibility for the 3000 national banks that own more than half of the assets in the commercial banking system. The Federal Reserve and the state banking authorities have joint primary responsibility for the 1000 state banks that are members of the Federal Reserve System. The Fed also has sole regulatory responsibility over companies that own one or more banks (called **bank holding companies**) and secondary responsibility for the national banks. The FDIC and the state banking authorities jointly supervise state banks that have FDIC insurance but are not members of the Federal Reserve System. The state banking authorities have sole jurisdiction over the fewer than 500 state banks without FDIC insurance. (Such banks hold less than 0.2% of the deposits in the commercial banking system.)

If you find the U.S. bank regulatory system confusing, imagine how confusing it is for the banks, which have to deal with multiple regulatory agencies. Several proposals have been raised by the U.S. Treasury to rectify this situation by centralizing the regulation of all depository institutions under one independent agency. However, none of these has been successful in Congress, and whether there will be regulatory consolidation in the future is highly uncertain.

Financial Innovation and the Evolution of the Banking Industry

To understand how the banking industry has evolved over time, we must first understand the process of financial innovation, which has transformed the entire financial system. Like other industries, the financial industry is in business to earn profits by selling its products. If a soap company perceives that there is a need in the marketplace for a laundry detergent with fabric softener, it develops a product to fit the need. Similarly, to maximize their profits, financial institutions develop new products to satisfy their own needs as well as those of their customers; in other words, innovation—which can be extremely beneficial to the economy—is driven by the desire to get (or stay) rich. This view of the innovation process leads to the following simple analysis: *A change in the financial environment will stimulate a search by financial institutions for innovations that are likely to be profitable.*

Starting in the 1960s, individuals and financial institutions operating in financial markets were confronted with drastic changes in the economic environment: Inflation and interest rates climbed sharply and became harder to predict, a situation that changed demand conditions in financial markets. Computer technology advanced rapidly, which changed supply conditions. In addition, financial regulations became more burdensome. Financial institutions found that many of the old ways of doing business were no longer profitable; the financial services and products they had been offering to the public were not selling. Many financial intermediaries found that they were no longer able to acquire funds with their traditional financial instruments, and without these funds they would soon be out of business. To survive in the new economic environment, financial institutions had to research and develop new products and services that would meet customer needs and prove profitable, a process referred to as **financial engineering.** In their case, necessity was the mother of innovation.

Our discussion of why financial innovation occurs suggests that there are three basic types of financial innovations: responses to changes in demand conditions, responses to changes in supply conditions, and avoidance of regulations. Now that we have a framework for understanding why financial institutions such as banks produce innovations, let's look at examples of how financial institutions in their search for profits have produced financial innovations of the three basic types.

Responses to Changes in Demand Conditions

The most significant change in the economic environment that altered the demand for financial products in recent years has been the dramatic increase in the volatility of interest rates. In the 1950s, the interest rate on three-month Treasury bills fluctuated between 1.0% and 3.5%; in the 1970s, it fluctuated between 4.0% and 11.5%. This volatility became even more pronounced in the 1980s, during which the three-month T-bill rate ranged from 5% to over 15%. We have seen in Chapter 3 (Table 2) that a rise in the interest rate from 10% to 20% would result in a capital loss of nearly 50% on a 30-year bond and a negative return of almost 40%. Large fluctuations in interest rates lead to substantial capital gains or losses and greater uncertainty about returns on investments. Recall that the risk that is related to the uncertainty about interest-rate movements and returns is called *interest-rate risk,* and high volatility of interest rates, such as we saw in the 1970s and 1980s, leads to a higher level of interest-rate risk.

We would expect the increase in interest-rate risk to increase the demand for financial products and services that could reduce that risk. This change in the economic environment would thus stimulate a search for profitable innovations by financial institutions that meet this new demand and would spur the creation of new financial instruments that help lower interest-rate risk. Two financial innovations in the banking industry that appeared in the 1970s confirm this prediction: the development of adjustable-rate mortgages and financial derivatives.

Adjustable-Rate Mortgages Like other investors, financial institutions find that lending is more attractive if interest-rate risk is lower. They would not want to make a mortgage loan at a 10% interest rate and two months later find that they could obtain a 12% interest rate on the same mortgage. To reduce interest-rate risk, in 1975 savings and loans in California began to issue adjustable-rate mortgages, mortgage loans on which the interest rate changes when a market interest rate (usually the Treasury bill rate) changes. Initially, an adjustable-rate mortgage might have a 5% interest rate. In six months, this interest rate might increase or decrease by the amount of the increase or decrease in, say, the six-month Treasury bill rate, and the mortgage payment would change. Because adjustable-rate mortgages allow mortgage-issuing institutions to earn higher interest rates on mortgages when rates rise, profits are kept higher during these periods.

This attractive feature of adjustable-rate mortgages has encouraged mortgage-issuing institutions to issue adjustable-rate mortgages with lower initial interest rates than on conventional fixed-rate mortgages, making them popular with many households. However, because the mortgage payment on a variable-rate mortgage can increase, many households continue to prefer fixed-rate mortgages. Hence both types of mortgages are widespread.

Financial Derivatives Given the greater demand for the reduction of interest-rate risk, commodity exchanges such as the Chicago Board of Trade recognized that if they could develop a product that would help investors and financial institutions to protect themselves from, or **hedge,** interest-rate risk, then they could make profits by selling this new instrument. **Futures contracts,** in which the seller agrees to provide a certain standardized commodity to the buyer on a specific future date at an agreed-on price, had been around for a long time. Officials at the Chicago Board of Trade realized that if they created futures contracts in financial instruments, which are called **financial derivatives** because their payoffs are linked to previously issued securities, they could be used to hedge risk. Thus in 1975, financial derivatives were born. We will study financial derivatives later in the book, in Chapter 25.

Responses to Changes in Supply Conditions

The most important source of the changes in supply conditions that stimulate financial innovation has been the improvement in computer and telecommunications technology. This technology, called *information technology*, has had two effects. First, it has lowered the cost of processing financial transactions, making it profitable for financial institutions to create new financial products and services for the public. Second, it has made it easier for investors to acquire information, thereby making it easier for firms to issue securities. The rapid developments in information technology have resulted in many new financial products and services that we examine here.

Bank Credit and Debit Cards   Credit cards have been around since well before World War II. Many individual stores (Sears, Macy's, Goldwater's) institutionalized charge accounts by providing customers with credit cards that allowed them to make purchases at these stores without cash. Nationwide credit cards were not established until after World War II, when Diners Club developed one to be used in restaurants all over the country (and abroad). Similar credit card programs were started by American Express and Carte Blanche, but because of the high cost of operating these programs, cards were issued only to selected persons and businesses who could afford expensive purchases.

A firm issuing credit cards earns income from loans it makes to credit card holders and from payments made by stores on credit card purchases (a percentage of the purchase price, say, 5%). A credit card program's costs arise from loan defaults, stolen cards, and the expense involved in processing credit card transactions.

Bankers saw the success of Diners Club, American Express, and Carte Blanche and wanted to share in the profitable credit card business. Several commercial banks attempted to expand the credit card business to a wider market in the 1950s, but the cost per transaction when running these programs was so high that their early attempts failed.

In the late 1960s, improved computer technology, which lowered the transaction costs for providing credit card services, made it more likely that bank credit card programs would be profitable. The banks tried to enter this business again, and this time their efforts led to the creation of two successful bank credit card programs: BankAmericard (originally started by the Bank of America but now an independent organization called Visa) and MasterCharge (now MasterCard, run by the Interbank Card Association). These programs have become phenomenally successful; more than 200 million of their cards are in use. Indeed, bank credit cards have been so profitable that nonfinancial institutions such as Sears (which launched the Discover Card), General Motors, and AT&T have also entered the credit card business. Consumers have benefited because credit cards are more widely accepted than checks when paying for purchases (particularly abroad), and they allow consumers to take out loans more easily.

The success of bank credit cards has led these institutions to come up with a new financial innovation, *debit cards*. Debit cards often look just like credit cards and can be used to make purchases in an identical fashion. However, in contrast to credit cards, which extend the purchaser a loan that does not have to be paid off immediately, a debit card purchase is immediately deducted from the card holder's bank account. Debit cards depend even more on low costs of processing transactions, since their profits are generated entirely from the fees paid by merchants on debit card purchases at their stores. Debit cards have been growing increasingly popular in recent years.

Electronic Banking The wonders of modern computer technology have also enabled banks to lower the cost of bank transactions by having the customer interact with an electronic banking facility rather than with a human being. One important form of an e-banking facility is the **automated teller machine (ATM),** an electronic machine that allows customers to get cash, make deposits, transfer funds from one account to another, and check balances. The ATM has the advantage that it does not have to be paid overtime and never sleeps, thus being available for use 24 hours a day. Not only does this result in cheaper transactions for the bank, but it also provides more convenience for the customer. Furthermore, because of its low cost, ATMs can be put at locations other than a bank or its branches, further increasing customer convenience. The low cost of ATMs has meant that they have sprung up everywhere and now number over 250,000 in the United States alone. Furthermore, it is now as easy to get foreign currency from an ATM when you are traveling in Europe as it is to get cash from your local bank. In addition, transactions with ATMs are so much cheaper for the bank than ones conducted with human tellers that some banks charge customers less if they use the ATM than if they use a human teller.

With the drop in the cost of telecommunications, banks have developed another financial innovation, home banking. It is now cost-effective for banks to set up an electronic banking facility in which the bank's customer is linked up with the bank's computer to carry out transactions by using either a telephone or a personal computer. Now a bank's customers can conduct many of their bank transactions without ever leaving the comfort of home. The advantage for the customer is the convenience of home banking, while banks find that the cost of transactions is substantially less than having the customer come to the bank. The success of ATMs and home banking has led to another innovation, the **automated banking machine (ABM),** which combines in one location an ATM, an Internet connection to the bank's website, and a telephone link to customer service.

With the decline in the price of personal computers and their increasing presence in the home, we have seen a further innovation in the home banking area, the appearance of a new type of banking institution, the **virtual bank,** a bank that has no physical location but rather exists only in cyberspace. In 1995, Security First Network Bank, based in Atlanta but now owned by Royal Bank of Canada, became the first virtual bank, planning to offer an array of banking services on the Internet—accepting checking account and savings deposits, selling certificates of deposit, issuing ATM cards, providing bill-paying facilities, and so on. The virtual bank thus takes home banking one step further, enabling the customer to have a full set of banking services at home 24 hours a day. In 1996, Bank of America and Wells Fargo entered the virtual banking market, to be followed by many others, with Bank of America now being the largest Internet bank in the United States. Will virtual banking be the predominant form of banking in the future (see the "E-Finance" box below)?

Electronic Payment   The development of inexpensive computers and the spread of the Internet now makes it very cheap for banks to allow their customers to make bill payments electronically. Whereas in the past you had to pay your bills by mailing a check, now banks provide a website in which you just log on, make a few clicks, and your payment is transmitted electronically. You not only save the cost of the stamp, but paying bills now becomes (almost) a pleasure, requiring little effort. Electronic payment systems provided by banks now even allow you to avoid the step of having to log on to pay the bill. Instead, recurring bills can be automatically deducted from your bank account without your having to do a thing. Providing these services increases profitability for banks in two ways. First, payment of a bill electronically means that banks don't need people to process what would have otherwise been a paper transaction. Estimates of the cost savings for banks when a bill is paid electronically rather than by a check exceed one dollar. Second, the extra convenience for you, the customer, means that you are more likely to open an account with the bank. Electronic payment is thus becoming far more common in the United States, but Americans are far behind Europeans, particularly Scandinavians, in their use of electronic payments (see the "E-Finance" box on page 459).

E-Money   Electronic payments technology can not only substitute for checks but can, in the form of **electronic money** (or **e-money**), money that exists only

---

E-FINANCE

Will "Clicks" Dominate "Bricks" in the Banking Industry?

With the advent of virtual banks ("clicks") and the convenience they provide, a key question is whether they will become the primary form in which banks do their business, eliminating the need for physical bank branches ("bricks") as the main delivery mechanism for banking services. Indeed, will stand-alone Internet banks be the wave of the future?

The answer seems to be no. Internet-only banks such as Wingspan (owned by Bank One), First-e (Dublin-based), and Egg (a British Internet-only bank owned by Prudential) have had disappointing revenue growth and profits. The result is that pure on-line banking has not been the success that proponents had hoped for. Why has Internet banking been a disappointment?

There have been several strikes against Internet banking. First, bank depositors want to know that their savings are secure, so are reluctant to put their money into new institutions without a long track record. Second, customers worry about the security of their on-line transactions and whether their transactions will truly be kept private. Traditional banks are viewed as being more secure and trustworthy in terms of releasing private information. Third, customers may prefer services provided by physical branches. For example, banking customers seem to prefer to purchase long-term savings products face-to-face. Fourth, Internet banking still has run into technical problems—server crashes, slow connections over phone lines, mistakes in conducting transactions—that will probably diminish over time as technology improves.

The wave of the future thus does not appear to be pure Internet banks. Instead it looks like "clicks and bricks" will be the predominant form of banking, in which on-line banking is used to complement the services provided by traditional banks. Nonetheless, the delivery of banking services is undergoing massive changes, with more and more banking services delivered over the Internet and the number of physical bank branches likely to decline in the future.

in electronic form, substitute for cash as well. The first form of e-money is a stored-value card. The simplest form of stored-value card is purchased for a preset dollar amount that the consumer spends down. The more sophisticated stored-value card is known as a **smart card.** It contains its own computer chip so that it can be loaded with digital cash from the owner's bank account whenever needed. Smart cards can be loaded either from ATM machines, personal computers with a smart card reader, or from specially equipped telephones.

A second form of electronic money is often referred to as **e-cash,** and it is used on the Internet to purchase goods or services. A consumer gets e-cash by setting up an account with a bank that has links to the Internet and then has the e-cash transferred to her PC. When she wants to buy something with e-cash, she surfs to a store on the Web, clicks the "buy" option for a particular item, whereupon the e-cash is automatically transferred from her computer to the merchant's computer. The merchant can then have the funds transferred from the consumer's bank account to his before the goods are shipped.

Given the convenience of e-money, you might think that we would move quickly to the cashless society in which all payments were made electronically. However, this hasn't happened, as discussed in the "E-Finance" box on page 460.

E-FINANCE

Why Are Scandinavians so Far Ahead of Americans in Using Electronic Payments and On-Line Banking?

Americans are the biggest users of checks in the world. Close to 100 billion checks are written every year in the United States, and over three-quarters of noncash transactions are conducted with paper. In contrast, in most countries of Europe, over two-thirds of noncash transactions are electronic, with Finland and Sweden having the greatest proportion of on-line banking customers of any countries in the world. Indeed, if you were Finnish or Swedish, instead of writing a check, you would be far more likely to pay your bills on-line, not only through a personal computer, but even with your mobile phone. Why are Europeans and especially Scandinavians so far ahead of Americans in the use of electronic payments and on-line banking?

First, Europeans got used to making payments without checks, even before the advent of the personal computer. Europeans have made use of so-called *giro* payments for a long time, in which banks and post offices transfer funds for customers to pay bills. Second, Europeans, and particularly Scandinavians, are much greater users of mobile phones and the Internet than are Americans. Finland has the highest per capita

use of mobile phones in the world, while Finland and Sweden lead the world in the percentage of the population that accesses the Internet. Maybe this is because of the low population densities of their countries and the fact that it is so cold and dark during the winter that Scandinavians prefer to stay inside at their PCs. Scandinavians would rather take the view that the reason for their being more high-tech is their good education systems and the resulting high degree of computer literacy, the presence of top technology companies such as Finland's Nokia and Sweden's Ericsson, and government policies to increase the use of personal computers, such as Sweden's giving companies tax incentives to provide their employees with home computers. The result of their wired population is that the Finns (and to a lesser extent Swedes) are percentagewise the biggest users of on-line banking in the world.

Americans are clearly behind the curve in their use of electronic payments, and this has imposed a high cost on the economy. Switching from checks to electronic payments might save the U.S. economy tens of billions of dollars per year, according to some estimates. Indeed, the U.S. federal government is trying to switch all its payments to electronic ones by directly depositing them into bank accounts in order to reduce its expenses. Can Americans be weaned from paper checks in the future and fully embrace the world of high-tech banking?

E-FINANCE

Are We Headed for a Cashless Society?

Predictions of a cashless society have been around for decades, but they have not come to fruition. For example, *Business Week* predicted in 1975 that electronic means of payment "would soon revolutionize the very concept of money itself," only to reverse itself several years later. Pilot projects in recent years with smart cards to convert consumers to the use of e-money have not been a success. Mondex, one of the widely touted, early stored-value cards that was launched in Britain in 1995, is only used on a few British university campuses. In Germany and Belgium, millions of people carry bank cards with computer chips embedded in them that enable them to make use of e-money, but very few use them. Why has the movement to a cashless society been so slow in coming?

Although e-money might be more convenient and may be more efficient than a payments system based on paper, several factors work against the disappearance of the paper system. First, it is very expensive to set up the computer, card reader, and telecommunications networks necessary to make electronic money the dominant form of payment. Second, electronic means of payment may raise security and privacy concerns. We often hear media reports that an unauthorized hacker has been able to access a computer database and to alter information stored there. The fact that this is not an uncommon occurrence means that unscrupulous persons might be able to access bank accounts in electronic payments systems and steal funds by moving them from someone else's accounts into their own. The prevention of this type of fraud is no easy task, and a whole new field of computer science is developing to cope with security issues. A further concern is that the use of electronic means of payment leaves an electronic trail that contains a large amount of personal data on buying habits. There are worries that government, employers, and marketers might be able to access these data, thereby encroaching on our privacy.

The conclusion from this discussion is that although the use of e-money will surely increase in the future, to paraphrase Mark Twain, "the reports of cash's death are greatly exaggerated."

Junk Bonds   Before the advent of computers and advanced telecommunications, it was difficult to acquire information about the financial situation of firms that might want to sell securities. Because of the difficulty in screening out bad from good credit risks, the only firms that were able to sell bonds were very well established corporations that had high credit ratings.[1] Before the 1980s, then, only corporations that could issue bonds with ratings of Baa or above could raise funds by selling newly issued bonds. Some firms that had fallen on bad times, so-called *fallen angels,* had previously issued long-term corporate bonds that now had ratings that had fallen below Baa, bonds that were pejoratively dubbed "junk bonds."

With the improvement in information technology in the 1970s, it became easier for investors to screen out bad from good credit risks, thus making it more likely that they would buy long-term debt securities from less well known corporations with lower credit ratings. With this change in supply conditions, we would expect that some smart individual would pioneer the concept of selling new public issues of junk bonds, not for fallen angels but for companies that had not yet achieved investment-grade status. This is exactly what Michael Milken of Drexel Burnham, an investment banking firm, started to do in 1977. Junk bonds became an important factor in the corporate bond market, with the amount outstanding exceeding $200 billion by the late 1980s. Although there was a sharp slowdown

---

[1]The discussion of adverse selection problems in Chapter 15 provides a more detailed analysis of why only well-established firms with high credit ratings were able to sell securities.

in activity in the junk bond market after Milken was indicted for securities law violations in 1989, it heated up again in the 1990s.

Commercial Paper Market *Commercial paper* is a short-term debt security issued by large banks and corporations. The commercial paper market has undergone tremendous growth since 1970, when there was $33 billion outstanding, to over $1.3 trillion outstanding at the end of 2004. Indeed, commercial paper has been one of the fastest-growing money market instruments.

Improvements in information technology also help provide an explanation for the rapid rise of the commercial paper market. We have seen that the improvement in information technology made it easier for investors to screen out bad from good credit risks, thus making it easier for corporations to issue debt securities. Not only did this make it easier for corporations to issue long-term debt securities as in the junk bond market, but it also meant that they could raise funds by issuing short-term debt securities like commercial paper more easily. Many corporations that used to do their short-term borrowing from banks now frequently raise short-term funds in the commercial paper market instead.

The development of money market mutual funds has been another factor in the rapid growth in the commercial paper market. Because money market mutual funds need to hold liquid, high-quality, short-term assets such as commercial paper, the growth of assets in these funds to around $2.0 trillion has created a ready market in commercial paper. The growth of pension and other large funds that invest in commercial paper has also stimulated the growth of this market.

Securitization An important example of a financial innovation arising from improvements in both transaction and information technology is securitization, one of the most important financial innovations in the past two decades. **Securitization** is the process of transforming otherwise illiquid financial assets (such as residential mortgages, auto loans, and credit card receivables), which have typically been the bread and butter of banking institutions, into marketable capital market securities. As we have seen, improvements in the ability to acquire information have made it easier to sell marketable capital market securities. In addition, with low transaction costs because of improvements in computer technology, financial institutions find that they can cheaply bundle together a portfolio of loans (such as mortgages) with varying small denominations (often less than $100,000), collect the interest and principal payments on the mortgages in the bundle, and then "pass them through"(pay them out) to third parties. By dividing the portfolio of loans into standardized amounts, the financial institution can then sell the claims to these interest and principal payments to third parties as securities. The standardized amounts of these securitized loans make them liquid securities, and the fact that they are made up of a bundle of loans helps diversify risk, making them desirable. The financial institution selling the securitized loans makes a profit by servicing the loans (collecting the interest and principal payments and paying them out) and charging a fee to the third party for this service.

Avoidance of Existing Regulations

The process of financial innovation we have discussed so far is much like innovation in other areas of the economy: It occurs in response to changes in demand and supply conditions. However, because the financial industry is more heavily regulated than other industries, government regulation is a much greater spur to innovation in this industry. Government regulation leads to financial innovation by creating incentives for firms to skirt regulations that restrict their ability to earn profits. Edward Kane, an economist at Boston College, describes this process of avoiding regulations as "loophole mining." The economic analysis of innovation suggests that when the economic environment changes such that regulatory constraints are so burdensome that large profits can be made by avoiding them, loophole mining and innovation are more likely to occur.

Because banking is one of the most heavily regulated industries in America, loophole mining is especially likely to occur. The rise in inflation and interest rates from the late 1960s to 1980 made the regulatory constraints imposed on this industry even more burdensome, leading to financial innovation.

Two sets of regulations have seriously restricted the ability of banks to make profits: reserve requirements that force banks to keep a certain fraction of their deposits as reserves (vault cash and deposits in the Federal Reserve System) and restrictions on the interest rates that can be paid on deposits. For the following reasons, these regulations have been major forces behind financial innovation.

1. *Reserve requirements*. The key to understanding why reserve requirements led to financial innovation is to recognize that they act, in effect, as a tax on deposits. Because the Fed does not pay interest on reserves, the opportunity cost of holding them is the interest that a bank could otherwise earn by lending the reserves out. For each dollar of deposits, reserve requirements therefore impose a cost on the bank equal to the interest rate, i, that could be earned if the reserves could be lent out times the fraction of deposits required as reserves, r. The cost of $i \times r$ imposed on the bank is just like a tax on bank deposits of $i \times r$.

   It is a great tradition to avoid taxes if possible, and banks also play this game. Just as taxpayers look for loopholes to lower their tax bills, banks seek to increase their profits by mining loopholes and by producing financial innovations that allow them to escape the tax on deposits imposed by reserve requirements.

2. *Restrictions on interest paid on deposits*. Until 1980, legislation prohibited banks in most states from paying interest on checking account deposits, and through Regulation Q, the Fed set maximum limits on the interest rate that could be paid on time deposits. To this day, banks are not allowed to pay interest on corporate checking accounts. The desire to avoid these **deposit rate ceilings** also led to financial innovations.

   If market interest rates rose above the maximum rates that banks paid on time deposits under Regulation Q, depositors withdrew funds from banks to put them into higher-yielding securities. This loss of deposits from the banking system restricted the amount of funds that banks could lend (called **disintermediation**) and thus limited bank profits. Banks had an incentive to get around deposit rate ceilings, because by so doing, they could acquire more funds to make loans and earn higher profits.

   We can now look at how the desire to avoid restrictions on interest payments and the tax effect of reserve requirements led to two important financial innovations.

Money Market Mutual Funds   Money market mutual funds issue shares that are redeemable at a fixed price (usually $1) by writing checks. For example, if you buy 5000 shares for $5000, the money market fund uses these funds to invest in short-term money market securities (Treasury bills, certificates of deposit, commercial paper) that provide you with interest payments. In addition, you are able to write checks up to the $5000 held as shares in the money market fund. Although money market fund shares effectively function as checking account deposits that earn interest, they are not legally deposits and so are not subject to reserve requirements or prohibitions on interest payments. For this reason, they can pay higher interest rates than deposits at banks.

The first money market mutual fund was created by two Wall Street mavericks, Bruce Bent and Henry Brown, in 1971. However, the low market interest rates from 1971 to 1977 (which were just slightly above Regulation Q ceilings of 5.25 to 5.5%) kept them from being particularly advantageous relative to bank deposits. In early 1978, the situation changed rapidly as market interest rates began to climb over 10%, well above the 5.5% maximum interest rates payable on savings accounts and time deposits under Regulation Q. In 1977, money market mutual funds had assets under $4 billion; in 1978, their assets climbed to close to $10 billion; in 1979, to over $40 billion; and in 1982, to $230 billion. Currently, their assets are around $2 trillion. To say the least, money market mutual funds have been a successful financial innovation, which is exactly what we would have predicted to occur in the late 1970s and early 1980s when interest rates soared beyond Regulation Q ceilings.

Sweep Accounts   Another innovation that enables banks to avoid the "tax" from reserve requirements is the **sweep account.** In this arrangement, any balances above a certain amount in a corporation's checking account at the end of a business day are "swept out" of the account and invested in overnight securities that pay the corporation interest. Because the "swept out" funds are no longer classified as checkable deposits, they are not subject to reserve requirements and thus are not "taxed." They also have the advantage that they allow banks in effect to pay interest on these corporate checking accounts, which otherwise is not allowed under existing regulations. Because sweep accounts have become so popular, they have lowered the amount of required reserves to the degree that most banking institutions do not find reserve requirements binding: In other words, they voluntarily hold more reserves than they are required to.

The financial innovation of sweep accounts is particularly interesting because it was stimulated not only by the desire to avoid a costly regulation, but also by a change in supply conditions: in this case, information technology. Without low-cost computers to process inexpensively the additional transactions required by these accounts, this innovation would not have been profitable and therefore would not have been developed. Technological factors often combine with other incentives, such as the desire to get around a regulation, to produce innovation.

Conclusion   Our discussion of financial innovation and the challenges that are facing managers of banks indicates that banking is no longer the staid profession it once was, prompting one banker to state, "Despite all the dark suits worn by its leaders, banking is a very dynamic industry."[2]

---

[2]"Banking Takes a Beating," *Time,* December 3, 1984, p. 49.

PROFITING FROM A NEW FINANCIAL PRODUCT: A CASE STUDY OF TREASURY STRIPS

We have seen that the advent of high-speed computers, which lowered the cost of processing financial transactions, led to such financial innovations as bank credit and debit cards. Because there is money to be made from financial innovation, it is important for managers of financial institutions to understand the thinking that goes into producing new, highly profitable financial products that take advantage of computer technology. To illustrate how financial institution managers can figure out ways to increase profits through financial innovation, we look at Treasury strips, a financial instrument first developed in 1982 by Salomon Brothers and Merrill Lynch. (Indeed, this innovation was so successful that the U.S. Treasury copied it when they issued STRIPS in 1985, as discussed in Chapter 10.)

One problem for investors in long-term coupon bonds, even when investors have a long holding period, is that there is some uncertainty in their returns arising from what is called *reinvestment risk*. Even if an investor holding a long-term coupon bond has a holding period of ten years, the return on the bond is not certain. The problem is that coupon payments are made before the bond matures in ten years, and these coupon payments must be reinvested. Because the interest rates at which the coupon payments will be reinvested fluctuate, the eventual return on the bond fluctuates as well. In contrast, long-term zero-coupon bonds have no reinvestment risk because they make no cash payments before the bond matures. The return on a zero-coupon bond if it is held to maturity is known at the time of purchase. The absence of reinvestment risk is an attractive feature of zero-coupon bonds, and as a result, investors are willing to accept a slightly lower interest rate on them than on coupon bonds, which do bear some reinvestment risk.

The fact that zero-coupon bonds have lower interest rates, along with the ability to use computers to create so-called hybrid securities, which are securities derived from other underlying securities, gave employees of Salomon Brothers and Merrill Lynch a brilliant idea for making profits. They could use computers to separate ("strip") a long-term Treasury coupon bond into a set of zero-coupon bonds. For example, a $1 million ten-year Treasury bond might be stripped into ten $100,000 zero-coupon bonds, which, naturally enough, are called *Treasury strips*. The lower interest rates on the more desirable Treasury strip zero-coupon bonds would mean that the value of these bonds would exceed the price of the underlying long-term Treasury bond, allowing Salomon Brothers and Merrill Lynch to make a profit by purchasing the long-term Treasury bond, separating it into Treasury strips, and selling them off as zero-coupon bonds.

To see in more detail how their thinking worked, let's look more closely at a $1 million ten-year Treasury bond with a coupon rate of 10% whose yield to maturity is also 10%, so it is selling at par. The cash payments for this bond are listed in the second column of Table 1. To make things simple, let's assume that the yield curve is absolutely flat so that the interest rate used to discount all the future cash payments is the same. Because zero-coupon bonds, which have no reinvestment risk, are more desirable than the ten-year Treasury coupon bond, the interest rate on the zero-coupon bonds is 9.75%, a little lower than the 10% interest rate on the coupon bond.

TABLE 1   *Market Value of Treasury Strip Zero-Coupon Bonds Derived from a $1 Million Ten-Year Treasury Bond with a 10% Coupon Rate and Selling at Par*

(1)	(2)	(3)	(4)
Year	Cash Payment ($)	Interest Rate on Zero-Coupon Bond (%)	Present Discounted Value of Zero-Coupon Bond ($)
1	100,000	9.75	91,116
2	100,000	9.75	83,022
3	100,000	9.75	75,646
4	100,000	9.75	68,926
5	100,000	9.75	62,802
6	100,000	9.75	57,223
7	100,000	9.75	52,140
8	100,000	9.75	47,508
9	100,000	9.75	43,287
10	100,000	9.75	39,442
10	1,000,000	9.75	394,416
Total			$1,015,528

How would Fran, a smart and sophisticated financial institution manager, figure out if she could make a profit from creating and selling the Treasury strips? Her first step is to figure out what the zero-coupon Treasury strips would sell for. She would find this easy to do if she had read Chapter 3 of this book: Using Equation 1 in that chapter, she would figure out that each of the Treasury strip zero-coupon bonds would sell for its present discounted value:

$$\frac{\text{Cash payment in year } n}{(1 + 0.0975)^n}$$

The results of this calculation for each year are listed in column (4) of Table 1. When Fran adds up the values of the collection of the Treasury strip zero-coupon bonds, she gets a figure of $1,015,528, which is greater than the $1 million purchase price of the Treasury bond. As long as it costs less than $15,528 to collect the payments from the Treasury and then pass them through to the owners of the zero-coupon strips, which is likely to be the case since computer technology makes the cost of conducting these financial transactions low, the zero-coupon strips will be profitable for her financial institution. Fran would thus recommend that her firm go ahead and market the new financial product. Because the financial institution can now generate much higher profits by selling substantial numbers of Treasury strips, it would amply reward Fran with a spanking new red BMW and a $100,000 bonus!

Financial Innovation and the Decline of Traditional Banking

The traditional financial intermediation role of banking has been to make long-term loans and to fund them by issuing short-term deposits, a process of asset transformation commonly referred to as "borrowing short and lending long." Here we examine how financial innovations have created a more competitive environment for the banking industry, causing the industry to change dramatically, with its traditional banking business going into decline.

In the United States, the importance of commercial banks as a source of funds to nonfinancial borrowers has shrunk dramatically. As we can see in Figure 2, in 1974 commercial banks provided 35% of these funds; yet by 2004, their market share was down to near 27%. The decline in market share for thrift institutions has been even more precipitous: from over 20% in the late 1970s to below 10% today. Another way of viewing the declining role of banking in traditional financial intermediation is to look at the size of banks' balance sheet assets relative to those of other financial intermediaries. Commercial banks' share of total financial intermediary assets has fallen from around 40% in the 1960–1980 period to below 30% by the end of 2004. Similarly, the share of total financial intermediary assets held by thrift institutions has declined even more from the 20% level of the 1960–1980 period to below 10% by 2004.

Clearly, the traditional financial intermediation role of banking, whereby banks make loans that are funded with deposits, is no longer as important in our financial system. However, the decline in the market share of banks in total lending and total financial intermediary assets does not necessarily indicate that the banking industry is in decline. There is no evidence of a declining trend in bank profitability. However, overall bank profitability is not a good indicator of the profitability of traditional banking, because it includes an increasing amount of income from nontraditional off-balance-sheet activities, discussed in Chapter 17. Noninterest income derived from off-balance-sheet activities, as a share of total banking income, increased from around 7% in 1980 to more than 45% of total bank income today.

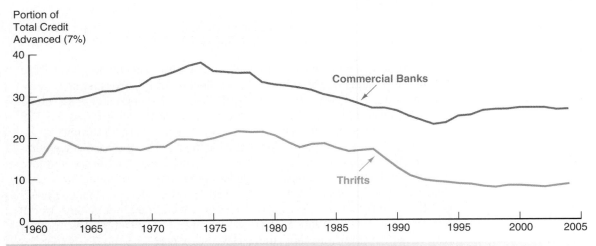

FIGURE 2 *Bank Share of Total Nonfinancial Borrowing, 1960–2004*

Source: Federal Reserve Flow of Funds, Table L1, Lines 2, 37, 42, 43

Given that the overall profitability of banks has not risen, the increase in income from off-balance-sheet activities implies that the profitability of traditional banking business has declined. This decline in profitability then explains why banks have been reducing their traditional business.

To understand why traditional banking business has declined in both size and profitability, we need to look at how the financial innovations described earlier have caused banks to suffer declines in their cost advantages in acquiring funds, that is, on the liabilities side of their balance sheet, while at the same time they have lost income advantages on the assets side of their balance sheet. The simultaneous decline of cost and income advantages has resulted in reduced profitability of traditional banking and an effort by banks to leave this business and engage in new and more profitable activities.

Decline in Cost Advantages in Acquiring Funds (Liabilities)   Until 1980, banks were subject to deposit rate ceilings that restricted them from paying any interest on checkable deposits and (under Regulation Q) limited them to paying a maximum interest rate of a little over 5% on time deposits. Until the 1960s, these restrictions worked to the banks' advantage because their major source of funds (over 60%) was checkable deposits, and the zero interest cost on these deposits meant that the banks had a very low cost of funds. Unfortunately, this cost advantage for banks did not last. The rise in inflation from the late 1960s on led to higher interest rates, which made investors more sensitive to yield differentials on different assets. The result was the so-called disintermediation process in which people began to take their money out of banks, with their low interest rates on both checkable and time deposits, and began to seek out higher-yielding investments. Also, as we have seen, at the same time, attempts to get around deposit rate ceilings and reserve requirements led to the financial innovation of money market mutual funds, which put the banks at an even further disadvantage because depositors could now obtain checking account-like services while earning high interest on their money market mutual fund accounts. One manifestation of these changes in the financial system was that the low-cost source of funds, checkable deposits, declined dramatically in importance for banks, falling from over 60% of bank liabilities to 10% today.

The growing difficulty for banks in raising funds led to their supporting legislation in the 1980s that eliminated Regulation Q ceilings on time deposit interest rates and allowed checkable deposits like NOW accounts that paid interest. Although these changes in regulation helped make banks more competitive in their quest for funds, it also meant that their cost of acquiring funds had risen substantially, thereby reducing their earlier cost advantage over other financial institutions.

Our discussion of international banking later in this chapter documents the encroachment of foreign (particularly Japanese) banks in U.S. financial markets. The loss of cost advantages of American banks helps explain this trend. With the high savings by the Japanese public, Japanese banks were able to tap a large savings pool and thus had access to a cheaper source of funds than American banks. This cost advantage for Japanese banks meant that they could more aggressively seek out loan business in the United States, which is exactly what they did. As a result, they grew at the expense of American banks. This explains why only two of the top ten banks are U.S.

Decline in Income Advantages on Uses of Funds (Assets)   The loss of cost advantages on the liabilities side of the balance sheet for American banks is one reason that they have become less competitive, but they have also been hit by a decline in income advantages on the assets side from the financial innovations we discussed earlier, junk bonds, securitization, and the rise of the commercial paper market.

We have seen that improvements in information technology have made it easier for firms to issue securities directly to the public. This has meant that instead of going to banks to finance short-term credit needs, many of the banks' best business customers now find it cheaper to go to the commercial paper market for funds instead. The loss of this competitive advantage for banks is evident in the fact that before 1970, nonfinancial commercial paper equaled less than 5% of commercial and industrial bank loans, whereas the figure has risen to over 20% today. In addition, this growth in the commercial paper market has allowed finance companies, which depend primarily on commercial paper to acquire funds, to expand their operations at the expense of banks. Finance companies, which lend to many of the same businesses that borrow from banks, have increased their market share relative to banks: Before 1980, finance company loans to business equaled around 30% of commercial and industrial bank loans; currently, they are 60%.

The rise of the junk bond market has also eaten into banks' loan business. Improvements in information technology have made it easier for corporations to sell their bonds to the public directly, thereby bypassing banks. Although Fortune 500 companies started taking this route in the 1970s, now lower-quality corporate borrowers are using banks less often because they have access to the junk bond market.

We have also seen that improvements in computer technology have led to securitization, whereby illiquid financial assets such as bank loans or mortgages are transformed into marketable securities. Computers enable other financial institutions to originate loans because they can now accurately evaluate credit risk with statistical methods, while computers have lowered transaction costs, making it possible to bundle these loans and sell them as securities. As a result, banks no longer have an advantage in making loans when default risk can be easily evaluated with computers. Without their former advantages, banks have lost loan business to other financial institutions even though the banks themselves are involved in the process of securitization. Securitization has been a particular problem for mortgage-issuing institutions such as S&Ls because most residential mortgages are now securitized.

Banks' Responses   In any industry, a decline in profitability usually results in exit from the industry (often due to widespread bankruptcies) and a shrinkage of market share. This occurred in the banking industry in the United States during the 1980s via consolidations and bank failures (discussed in the next two chapters).

In the attempt to survive and maintain adequate profit levels, many U.S. banks face two alternatives. First, they can attempt to maintain their traditional lending activity by expanding into new and riskier areas of lending. For example, U.S. banks have increased their risk taking by placing a greater percentage of their total funds in commercial real estate loans, traditionally a riskier type of loan. In addition, they have increased lending for corporate takeovers and leveraged buyouts, which are highly leveraged transaction loans. The decline in the profitability of banks' traditional business may thus have helped lead to the crisis in banking that we discuss in Chapter 20.

The second way banks have sought to maintain former profit levels is to pursue new off-balance-sheet activities that are more profitable. U.S. commercial banks did this during the early 1980s, nearly doubling the share of their income coming from off-balance-sheet, noninterest-income activities. This strategy, however, has generated concerns about what are proper activities for banks and about whether nontraditional activities might be riskier and result in banks' taking excessive risks.

The decline of banks' traditional business has thus meant that the banking industry has been driven to seek out new lines of business. This could be beneficial because by so doing, banks can keep vibrant and healthy. Indeed, bank profitability has been high in recent years, and nontraditional, off-balance-sheet activities have been playing an important role in the resurgence of bank profits. However, there is a danger that the new directions in banking could lead to increased risk taking, and thus the decline in traditional banking requires regulators to be more vigilant. It also poses new challenges for bank regulators, who, as we will see in Chapter 20, must now be far more concerned about banks' off-balance-sheet activities.

Decline of Traditional Banking in Other Industrialized Countries Forces similar to those in the United States have been leading to the decline of traditional banking in other industrialized countries. The loss of banks' monopoly power over depositors has occurred outside the United States as well. Financial innovation and deregulation are occurring worldwide and have created attractive alternatives for both depositors and borrowers. In Japan, for example, deregulation has opened a wide array of new financial instruments to the public, causing a disintermediation process similar to that in the United States. In European countries, innovations have steadily eroded the barriers that have traditionally protected banks from competition.

In other countries, banks have also faced increased competition from the expansion of securities markets. Both financial deregulation and fundamental economic forces in other countries have improved the availability of information in securities markets, making it easier and less costly for firms to finance their activities by issuing securities rather than going to banks. Further, even in countries where securities markets have not grown, banks have still lost loan business because their best corporate customers have had increasing access to foreign and offshore capital markets, such as the Eurobond market. In smaller economies, like Australia, which still do not have well-developed corporate bond or commercial paper markets, banks have lost loan business to international securities markets. In addition, the same forces that drove the securitization process in the United States are at work in other countries and will undercut the profitability of traditional banking in these countries as well. The United States is not unique in seeing its banks face a more difficult competitive environment. Thus, although the decline of traditional banking has occurred earlier in the United States than in other countries, the same forces are causing a decline in traditional banking abroad.

Structure of the U.S. Commercial Banking Industry

There are around 8000 commercial banks in the United States, far more than in any other country in the world. As Table 2 indicates, we have an extraordinary number of small banks: 49.1% of the banks have less than $100 million in assets. Far more typical is the size distribution in Canada or the United Kingdom, where five or fewer banks dominate the industry. The five largest commerical banks in the United States (listed in Table 3) together hold 50.6% of the assets in their industry.

TABLE 2   *Size Distribution of Insured Commercial Banks, December 31, 2003*

Assets	Number of Banks	Share of Banks (%)	Share of Assets Held (%)
Less than $100 million	3755	49.1	2.3
$100 million–$1 billion	3458	45.1	11.3
$1–$10 billion	360	4.7	11.8
$10 billion or more	87	1.1	74.6
Total	7660	100	100

Source: http://www.fdic.gov/bank/statistical/statistics/0109/allstru.html

Most industries in the United States have far fewer firms than the commerical banking industry; typically, large firms tend to dominate these industries to a greater extent than in the commercial banking industry. (Consider the computer software industry, which is dominated by Microsoft, or the automobile industry, which is dominated by General Motors, Ford, Chrysler, Toyota, and Honda.) Does the large number of banks in the commercial banking industry and the absence of a few dominant firms suggest that commercial banking is more competitive than other industries?

Restrictions on Branching

The presence of so many commercial banks in the United States actually reflects past regulations that restricted the ability of these financial institutions to open **branches** (additional offices for the conduct of banking operations). Each state had its own regulations on the type and number of branches that a bank could

TABLE 3   *Ten Largest U.S. Banks, 2003*

Bank	Assets ($ billions)	Share of All Commercial Bank Assets (%)
1. Citicorp, New York, NY	1264	17.0
2. Bank of America (& Fleet), Charlotte, NC	937	12.6
3. J.P. Morgan Chase, New York, NY	771	10.4
4. Wachovia, Charlotte, NC	401	5.4
5. Wells Fargo, San Francisco, CA	388	5.2
6. Bank One, Columbus, OH	327	4.4
7. Washington Mutual, Seattle, WA	235	3.2
8. U.S. Bancorp, Minneapolis, MN	189	2.5
9. Sun Trust Bank, Atlanta, GA	125	1.7
10. HSBC Holding, London	93	1.3
Total	4730	63.7

Source: http://www.onlinebankingreport.com/resources/100.html

open. Regulations on both coasts, for example, tended to allow banks to open branches throughout a state; in the middle part of the country, regulations on branching were more restrictive. The McFadden Act of 1927, which was designed to put national banks and state banks on an equal footing (and the Douglas Amendment of 1970, which closed a loophole in the McFadden Act) effectively prohibited banks from branching across state lines and forced all national banks to conform to the branching regulations in the state of their location.

The McFadden Act and state branching regulations constituted strong anti-competitive forces in the commercial banking industry, allowing many small banks to stay in existence. If competition is beneficial to society, why have regulations restricting branching arisen in America? The simplest explanation is that the American public has historically been hostile to large banks. States with the most restrictive branching regulations were typically ones in which populist antibank sentiment was strongest in the nineteenth century. (These states usually had large farming populations whose relations with banks periodically became tempestuous when banks would foreclose on farmers who couldn't pay their debts.) The legacy of nineteenth-century politics was a banking system with restrictive branching regulations and hence an inordinate number of small banks. However, as we will see later in this chapter, branching restrictions are being eliminated, and we are heading toward nationwide banking.

Response to Branching Restrictions

An important feature of the U.S. banking industry is that competition can be repressed by regulation but not completely quashed. As we saw earlier in this chapter, the existence of restrictive regulation will stimulate banking institutions to go "loop-hole mining," coming up with financial innovations that get around these regulations in the banks' search for profits. Regulations restricting branching have stimulated similar economic forces and have promoted the development of such financial innovations as bank holding companies and automated teller machines.

Bank Holding Companies A holding company is a corporation that owns several different companies. This form of corporate ownership has important advantages for banks. It has allowed them to circumvent restrictive branching regulations, because the holding company can own a controlling interest in several banks even if branching is not permitted. Furthermore, a bank holding company can engage in other activities related to banking, such as the provision of investment advice, data processing and transmission services, leasing, credit card services, and servicing of loans in other states.

The growth of bank holding companies has been dramatic over the past three decades. Today bank holding companies own almost all large banks, and over 90% of all commercial bank deposits are held in banks owned by holding companies.

Automated Teller Machines Another financial innovation that avoided the restrictions on branching is the electronic banking facility known as the automated teller machine (ATM). Banks realized that if they did not own or rent the ATM, but instead let it be owned by someone else and paid for each transaction with a fee, the ATM would probably not be considered a branch of the bank and thus would not be subject to branching regulations. This is exactly what the regulatory agencies and courts in most states concluded. Because they enable banks to widen their markets, a number of these shared facilities (such as Cirrus and NYCE) have been established nationwide. Furthermore, even when an ATM is owned by a bank, states typically have special provisions that allow wider establishment of ATMs than is permissible for traditional "brick and mortar" branches.

As we saw earlier in this chapter, avoiding regulation was not the only reason for the development of the ATM. The advent of cheaper computer and telecommunications technology enabled banks to provide ATMs at low cost, making them a profitable innovation. This example further illustrates that technological factors often combine with incentives such as the desire to avoid restrictive regulations like branching restrictions to produce financial innovation.

Bank Consolidation and Nationwide Banking

As we can see in Figure 3, after a remarkable period of stability from 1934 to the mid-1980s, the number of commercial banks has begun to fall dramatically. Why is this sudden decline taking place?

The banking industry hit some hard times in the 1980s and early 1990s, with bank failures running at a rate of over 100 per year from 1985 to 1992 (more on this in Chapter 20). But bank failures are only part of the story. In the years 1985–1992, the number of banks declined by 3000—more than double the number of failures. And in the period 1992–2004, when the banking industry returned to health, the number of commercial banks declined by over 3700, less than 5 percent of which were bank failures, and most of those were of small banks. Thus we see that bank failures played an important, though not predominant, role in the decline in the number of banks in the 1985–2004 period and an almost negligible role in the decline in the number of banks since then.

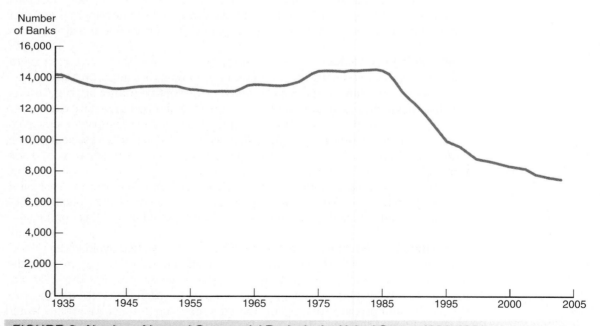

FIGURE 3 *Number of Insured Commercial Banks in the United States, 1934–2004*

Source: http://www2.fdic.gov/qbp.

So what explains the rest of the story? The answer is bank consolidation. Banks have been merging to create larger entities or have been buying up other banks. This gives rise to a new question: Why has bank consolidation been taking place in recent years?

As we have seen, loophole mining by banks has reduced the effectiveness of branching restrictions, with the result that many states have recognized that it would be in their best interest if they allowed ownership of banks across state lines. The result has been the formation of reciprocal and regional compacts in which banks in one state are allowed to own banks in other states in the region. In 1975, Maine enacted the first interstate banking legislation that allowed out-of-state bank holding companies to purchase banks in that state. In 1982, Massachusetts enacted a regional compact with other New England states to allow interstate banking, and many other regional compacts were adopted thereafter until, by the early 1990s, almost all states allowed some form of interstate banking.

With the barriers to interstate banking breaking down in the early 1980s, banks recognized that they could gain the benefits of diversification because they would now be able to make loans in many states rather than in just one. This gave them the advantage that if one state's economy was weak, another in which they operated might be strong, thus decreasing the likelihood that loans in different states would default at the same time. In addition, allowing banks to own banks in other states meant that they could take advantage of economies of scale by increasing their size through out-of-state acquisition of banks or by merging with banks in other states. Mergers and acquisitions explain the first phase of banking consolidation which has played such an important role in the decline in the number of banks since 1985. Another result of the loosening of restrictions on interstate branching is the development of a new class of bank, the so-called **superregional banks,** bank holding companies that have begun to rival the money center banks in size but whose headquarters are not based in one of the money center cities (New York, Chicago, and San Francisco). Examples of these superregional banks are NationsBank of Charlotte, North Carolina, and Banc One of Columbus, Ohio.

Not surprisingly, the advent of the Web and improved computer technology is another factor driving bank consolidation. Economies of scale have increased because large upfront investments are required to set up many information technology platforms for financial institutions (see the "E-Finance" box on page 474). To take advantage of these economies of scale, banks have needed to get bigger, and this development has led to additional consolidation. Information technology has also been increasing **economies of scope,** the ability to use one resource to provide many different products and services. For example, details about the quality and creditworthiness of firms not only inform decisions about whether to make loans to them, but also can be useful in determining at what price their shares should trade. Similarly, once you have marketed one financial product to an investor, you probably know how to market another. Business people describe economies of scope by saying that there are "synergies" between different lines of business, and information technology is making these synergies more likely. The result is that consolidation is taking place not only to make financial institutions bigger, but also to increase the combination of products and services they can provide. This consolidation has had two consequences. First, different types of financial intermediaries are encroaching on each other's territory, making them more alike. Second, consolidation has led to the development of what the Federal Reserve has named **large, complex banking organizations (LCBOs).** This development has been facilitated by the repeal of the Glass-Steagall restrictions on combinations of banking and other financial service industries discussed in the next section.

Riegle-Neal Interstate Banking and Branching Efficiency Act of 1994

Banking consolidation has been given further stimulus by the passage in 1994 of the Riegle-Neal Interstate Banking and Branching Efficiency Act. This legislation expanded the regional compacts to the entire nation and overturned the McFadden Act and Douglas Amendment's prohibition of interstate banking. Not only did this act allow bank holding companies to acquire banks in any other state, notwithstanding any state laws to the contrary, but it allowed interstate branching by allowing bank holding companies to merge the banks they own into one bank with branches in different states beginning June 1, 1997. States did have the option of allowing interstate branching to occur earlier than this date, and several did so; they also had the option of opting out of interstate branching, a choice only Texas made.

The Riegle-Neal Act finally established the basis for a true nationwide banking system. Although interstate banking was accomplished previously by out-of-state purchase of banks by bank holding companies, up until 1994 interstate branching was virtually nonexistent because very few states had enacted interstate branching legislation. Allowing banks to conduct interstate banking through branching is especially important because many bankers feel that economies of scale cannot be fully exploited through the bank holding company structure; they can be fully exploited only through branching networks in which all of the bank's operations are fully coordinated.

E-FINANCE

Information Technology and Bank Consolidation

Achieving low costs in banking requires huge investments in information technology. In turn, such enormous investments require a business line of very large scale. This has been particularly true in the credit card business in recent years, in which huge technology investments have been made to provide customers with convenient websites and to develop better systems to handle processing and risk analysis for both credit and fraud risk. The result has been substantial consolidation: As recently as 1995, the top five banking institutions issuing credit cards held less than 40% of total credit card debt, while today this number is above 60%.

Information technology has also spurred increasing consolidation of the bank custody business. Banks hold the actual certificate for investors when they purchase a stock or bond and provide data on the value of these securities and how much risk an investor is facing. Because this business is also computer-intensive, it also requires very large-scale investments in computer technology in order for the bank to offer these services at competitive rates. The percentage of assets at the top ten custody banks has therefore risen from 40% in 1990 to more than 90% today.

The increasing importance of e-finance, in which the computer is playing a more central role in delivering financial services, is bringing tremendous changes to the structure of the banking industry. Although banks are more than willing to offer a full range of products to their customers, they no longer find it profitable to produce all of them. Instead, they are contracting out the business, a practice that will lead to further consolidation of technology-intensive banking businesses in the future.

Nationwide banks are now beginning to emerge. With the merger in 1998 of BankAmerica and NationsBank, which created the first bank with branches on both coasts, consolidation in the banking industry should eventually lead to banking organizations with operations in almost all of the 50 states.

What Will the Structure of the U.S. Banking Industry Look Like in the Future?

With true nationwide banking becoming a reality, the benefits of bank consolidation for the banking industry have increased substantially, thus driving the next phase of mergers and acquisitions and accelerating the decline in the number of commercial banks. Great changes are occurring in the structure of this industry, and the natural question arises: What will the industry look like in, say, ten years?

One view is that the industry will become more like that in many other countries (see the "Global" box) and we will end up with only a couple of hundred banks. A more extreme view is that it will look like that of Canada or the United Kingdom, with a few large banks dominating the industry. Research on this question, however, comes up with a different answer. The structure of the U.S. banking industry will still be unique, but not as unique as it once was. Most experts predict that the consolidation surge will settle down as the U.S. banking industry approaches several thousand, rather than several hundred, banks. One simple way of seeing why the number of banks will continue to be substantial is to recognize that California, which has unrestricted branching throughout the state, has close to 400 commercial banks. Blowing up the number of banks by the share of banking assets in California relative to the whole country produces an estimate of the number of banks with unrestricted nationwide branching on the order of 4000. More sophisticated research suggests that the number of banks in the United States will ultimately be somewhat fewer than this, but not much.[3]

Banking consolidation will result in not only a smaller number of banks, but as the mergers between Chase Manhattan Bank and Chemical Bank and between BankAmerica and NationsBank suggest, a shift in assets from smaller banks to larger banks as well. Within ten years, the share of bank assets in banks with less than $100 million in assets is expected to halve, while the amount at the so-called megabanks, those with over $100 billion in assets, is expected to more than double. Indeed, we now have trillion dollar banks (e.g., Citibank).

Are Bank Consolidation and Nationwide Banking Good Things?

Advocates of nationwide banking believe that it will produce more efficient banks and a healthier banking system less prone to bank failures. However, critics of bank consolidation fear that it will eliminate small banks, referred to as *community banks,* and that this will result in less lending to small businesses. In addition, they

---

[3]For example, see Allen N. Berger, Anil K. Kashyap, and Joseph Scalise, "The Transformation of the U.S. Banking Industry: What a Long, Strange Trip It's Been," *Brookings Papers on Economic Activity* 2 (1995): 55–201, and Timothy Hannan and Stephen Rhoades, "Future U.S. Banking Structure, 1990–2010," in *Antitrust Bulletin* 37 (1992): 737–798. For a more detailed treatment of the bank consolidation process taking place in the United States, see Frederic S. Mishkin, "Bank Consolidation: A Central Banker's Perspective," National Bureau Working Paper No. 5849, December 1996.

GLOBAL

Comparison of Banking Structures in the United States and Abroad

The structure of the commercial banking industry in the United States is radically different from that in other industrialized nations. The United States is the only country that is just now developing a true national banking system in which banks have branches throughout the country. One result is that there are many more banks in the United States than in other industrialized countries. In contrast to the United States, which has on the order of 8000 commercial banks, every other industrialized country has well under 1000. Japan, for example, has fewer than 100 commercial banks—a mere fraction of the number in the United States, even though its economy and population are half the size of the United States. Another result of the past restrictions on branching in the United States is that our banks tend to be much smaller than those in other countries.

worry that a few banks will come to dominate the industry, making the banking business less competitive.

Most economists are skeptical of these criticisms of bank consolidation. As we have seen, research indicates that even after bank consolidation is completed, the United States will still have plenty of banks. Furthermore, megabanks will not dominate the banking industry. This research suggests that there will be more than ten banks with assets over $100 billion, and their collective share of bank assets will be less than 50%. The banking industry will thus remain highly competitive, probably even more so than now considering that banks that have been protected from competition from out-of-state banks will now have to compete with them vigorously to stay in business.

It also does not look as though community banks will disappear. When New York State liberalized branching laws in 1962, there were fears that community banks upstate would be driven from the market by the big New York City banks. Not only did this not happen, but some of the big boys found that the small banks were able to run rings around them in the local markets. Similarly, California, which has had unrestricted statewide branching for a long time, continues to have a thriving collection of community banks.

Economists see some important benefits of bank consolidation and nationwide banking. The elimination of geographic restrictions on banking will increase competition and drive inefficient banks out of business, thus raising the efficiency of the banking sector. The move to larger banking organizations is also being driven by advances in computer technology, and it also means that there will be some increase in efficiency because of economies of scale. The increased diversification of banks' loan portfolios may lower the probability of a banking crisis in the future. In the 1980s and early 1990s, bank failures were often concentrated in states with weak economies. For example, after the decline in oil prices in 1986, all the major commercial banks in Texas, which had been very profitable, now found themselves in trouble. At that time, banks in New England were doing fine. However, when the 1990–1991 recession hit New England hard, New England banks started failing. With nationwide banking, a bank could make loans in both New England and Texas and would thus be less likely to fail because when the loans were going sour in one location, they would likely be doing well in the other. Thus nationwide banking is seen as a major step toward creating a healthy banking system that is less prone to banking crises.

Two concerns remain about the effects of bank consolidation—that it may lead to a reduction in lending to small businesses and that banks rushing to expand into new geographic markets may take increased risks leading to bank failures. The jury is still out on these concerns, but most economists see the benefits of bank consolidation and nationwide banking as outweighing the costs.

Separation of Banking and Other Financial Service Industries

Another important feature of the structure of the banking industry in the United States until recently was the separation of banking and other financial services industries—such as securities, insurance, and real estate—mandated by the Glass-Steagall Act of 1933. Glass-Steagall allowed commercial banks to sell new offerings of government securities but prohibited them from underwriting corporate securities or from engaging in brokerage activities. It also prevented banks from engaging in insurance and real estate activities. In turn, it prevented investment banks and insurance companies from engaging in commercial banking activities, and thus protected banks from competition.

Erosion of Glass-Steagall

Despite the Glass-Steagall prohibitions, the pursuit of profits and financial innovation stimulated both banks and other financial institutions to bypass the intent of the Glass-Steagall Act and encroach on each other's traditional territory. Brokerage firms engaged in the traditional banking business of issuing deposit instruments with the development of money market mutual funds and cash management accounts. After the Federal Reserve used a loophole in Section 20 of the Glass-Steagall Act in 1987 to allow bank holding companies to underwrite previously prohibited classes of securities, banks began to enter this business. The loophole allowed affiliates of approved commercial banks to engage in underwriting activities as long as the revenue didn't exceed a specified amount, which started at 10% but was raised to 25%, of the affiliates' total revenue. After the U.S. Supreme Court validated the Fed's action in July 1988, the Federal Reserve allowed J. P. Morgan, a commercial bank holding company, to underwrite corporate debt securities (in January 1989) and to underwrite stocks (in September 1990), with the privilege extended to other bank holding companies. The regulatory agencies later allowed banks to engage in some real estate and some insurance activities.

The Gramm-Leach-Bliley Financial Services Modernization Act of 1999: Repeal of Glass-Steagall

Because restrictions on commercial banks' securities and insurance activities put American banks at a competitive disadvantage relative to foreign banks, bills to overturn Glass-Steagall appeared in almost every session of Congress in the 1990s. With the merger in 1998 of Citicorp, the second-largest bank in the United States, and Travelers Group, an insurance company that also owned the third-largest securities firm in the country (Salomon Smith Barney), the pressure to abolish Glass-Steagall became overwhelming. Legislation to eliminate Glass-Steagall finally came to fruition in 1999. This legislation, the Gramm-Leach-Bliley Financial Services

Modernization Act of 1999, allows securities firms and insurance companies to purchase banks, and allows banks to underwrite insurance and securities and engage in real estate activities. Under this legislation, states retain regulatory authority over insurance activities while the Securities and Exchange Commission will continue oversight of securities activities. The Office of the Comptroller of the Currency has the authority to regulate bank subsidiaries engaged in securities underwriting, but the Federal Reserve continues to have the authority to oversee bank holding companies under which all real estate and insurance activities and large securities operations will be housed.

Implications for Financial Consolidation

As we have seen, the Riegle-Neal Interstate Banking and Branching Efficiency Act of 1994 has stimulated consolidation of the banking industry. The financial consolidation process will be even further speeded up by the Gramm-Leach-Bliley Act of 1999, because the way is now open to consolidation in terms not only of the number of banking institutions but also across financial service activities. Given that information technology is increasing economies of scope, mergers of banks with other financial service firms like that of Citicorp and Travelers are becoming increasingly common, and more mega-mergers are likely to be on the way. Banking institutions will become not only larger but increasingly complex organizations, engaging in the full gamut of financial service activities.

Separation of Banking and Other Financial Services Industries Throughout the World

Not many other countries in the aftermath of the Great Depression followed the lead of the United States in separating the banking and other financial services industries. In fact, in the past this separation was the most prominent difference between banking regulation in the United States and in other countries. Around the world, there are three basic frameworks for the banking and securities industries.

The first framework is *universal banking,* which exists in Germany, the Netherlands, and Switzerland. It provides no separation at all between the banking and securities industries. In a universal banking system, commercial banks provide a full range of banking, securities, and insurance services, all within a single legal entity. Banks are allowed to own sizable equity shares in commercial firms, and often they do.

The British-style universal banking system, the second framework, is found in the United Kingdom and countries with close ties to it, such as Canada and Australia. The British-style universal bank engages in securities underwriting, but it differs from the German-style universal bank in three ways: Separate legal subsidiaries are more common, bank equity holdings of commercial firms are less common, and combinations of banking and insurance firms are less common.

The third framework features legal separation of the banking and securities industries, as in the United States and Japan. A major difference between the U.S. and Japanese banking systems is that Japanese banks are allowed to hold substantial equity stakes in commercial firms, whereas American banks cannot. In addition, most American banks use a bank-holding-company structure, but bank holding companies are illegal in Japan. Although the banking and securities industries were legally separated under the Glass-Steagall Act in the United States and Section 65 of the Japanese Securities Act, in both countries commercial banks are increasingly being allowed to engage in securities activities and are thus becoming more like British-style universal banks.

International Banking

In 1960, only eight U.S. banks operated branches in foreign countries, and their total assets were less than $4 billion. Currently, around 100 American banks have branches abroad, with assets totaling over $1.5 trillion. The spectacular growth in international banking can be explained by three factors.

First is the rapid growth in international trade and multinational (worldwide) corporations that has occurred since 1960. When American firms operate abroad, they need banking services in foreign countries to help finance international trade. For example, they might need a loan in a foreign currency to operate a factory abroad. And when they sell goods abroad, they need to have a bank exchange the foreign currency they have received for their goods into dollars. Although these firms could use foreign banks to provide them with these international banking services, many of them prefer to do business with the U.S. banks with which they have established long-term relationships and which understand American business customs and practices. As international trade has grown, international banking has grown with it.

Second, when American banks go abroad, they are allowed to pursue activities that are prohibited in the United States under the Glass-Steagall Act. American banks are very active in global investment banking, in which they underwrite foreign securities. They also sell insurance abroad, and they derive substantial profits from these investment banking and insurance activities. The desire to escape burdensome regulations, an important factor that has stimulated financial innovations, has therefore also been a major spur to international banking.

Third, American banks have wanted to tap into the large pool of dollar-denominated deposits in foreign countries known as Eurodollars. To understand the structure of U.S. banking overseas, let us first look at the Eurodollar market, an important source of growth for international banking.

Eurodollar Market

Eurodollars are created when deposits in accounts in the United States are transferred to a bank outside the country and are kept in the form of dollars. For example, if Rolls-Royce PLC deposits a $1 million check, written on an account at an American bank, in its bank in London—specifying that the deposit is payable in dollars—$1 million in Eurodollars is created.[4] Over 90% of Eurodollar deposits are time deposits, more than half of them certificates of deposit with maturities of 30 days or more. The total amount of Eurodollars outstanding is on the order of $5 trillion, making the Eurodollar market one of the most important financial markets in the world economy.

---

[4]Note that the London bank has acquired the deposit at the American bank formerly owned by Rolls-Royce, so the creation of Eurodollars has not caused a reduction in the amount of bank deposits in the United States.

Why would companies like Rolls-Royce want to hold dollar deposits outside the United States? First, the dollar is the most widely used currency in international trade, so Rolls-Royce might want to hold deposits in dollars to conduct its international transactions. Second, Eurodollars are "offshore" deposits—they are held in countries that will not subject them to regulations such as reserve requirements or restrictions (called *capital controls*) on taking the deposits outside the country.[5]

The main center of the Eurodollar market is London, a major international financial center for hundreds of years. Eurodollars are also held outside of Europe in locations that provide offshore status to these deposits—for example, Singapore, the Bahamas, and the Cayman Islands.

The minimum-sized transaction in the Eurodollar market is typically $1 million, and approximately 75% of Eurodollar deposits are held by banks. Plainly, you and I are unlikely to come into direct contact with Eurodollars. The Eurodollar market is, however, an important source of funds to U.S. banks, whose borrowing of these deposits is over $700 billion. Rather than using an intermediary and borrowing all the deposits from foreign banks, American banks decided that they could earn higher profits by opening their own branches abroad to attract these deposits. Consequently, the Eurodollar market has been an important stimulus to U.S. banking overseas.

Structure of U.S. Banking Overseas

U.S. banks have most of their foreign branches in Latin America, the Far East, the Caribbean, and London. The largest volume of assets is held by branches in London because it is a major international financial center and the central location for the Eurodollar market. Latin America and the Far East have many branches because of the importance of U.S. trade with these regions. Parts of the Caribbean (especially the Bahamas and the Cayman Islands) have become important as tax havens, with minimal taxation and few restrictive regulations. In actuality, the bank branches in the Bahamas and the Cayman Islands are "shell operations" because they function primarily as bookkeeping centers and do not provide normal banking services.

An alternative corporate structure for U.S. banks that operate overseas is the **Edge Act corporation,** which is a special subsidiary engaged primarily in international banking. This corporate structure, created by the Edge Act of 1919, allows American banks to compete more effectively against foreign banks by exempting Edge Act corporations from certain U.S. banking regulations. For example, Edge Act corporations are exempt from the prohibition on branching across state lines; they can have branches in different states to facilitate the financing of trade with different parts of the world—an office on the West Coast to handle the financing of trade with Japan, an office in Miami to handle the financing of trade with Latin America, and so forth.

U.S. banks (through their holding companies) can also own a controlling interest in foreign banks and in foreign companies that provide financial services, such as finance companies. The international activities of member banks of the Federal Reserve System, bank holding companies, and Edge Act corporations (which

---

[5]Although most offshore deposits are denominated in dollars, some are also denominated in other currencies. Collectively, these offshore deposits are referred to as Eurocurrencies.

account for almost all international banking conducted by U.S. banks) are governed by the Federal Reserve's Regulation K. As in the case of bank holding companies, these international activities must be "closely related to banking."

In late 1981, the Federal Reserve approved the creation of **international banking facilities (IBFs)** within the United States that can accept time deposits from foreigners but are not subject to either reserve requirements or restrictions on interest payments. IBFs are also allowed to make loans to foreigners, but they are not allowed to make loans to domestic residents. States have encouraged the establishment of IBFs by exempting them from state and local taxes. In essence, IBFs are treated like foreign branches of U.S. banks and are not subject to domestic regulations and taxes. The purpose of establishing IBFs is to encourage American and foreign banks to do more banking business in the United States rather than abroad. From this point of view, IBFs have been a success: Their assets climbed to nearly $200 billion in the first two years and currently exceed that amount.

Foreign Banks in the United States

The growth in international trade has not only encouraged U.S. banks to open offices overseas but also encouraged foreign banks to establish offices in the United States. Foreign banks have been extremely successful in the United States. Over the past 20 years, foreign banks have more than doubled their market share in the United States. Currently, they hold more than 20% of total U.S. bank assets and do almost as much commercial lending as U.S.-owned banks, with nearly a 50% share of the market lending to U.S. corporations.

Foreign banks engage in banking activities in the United States by operating an agency office of the foreign bank, a subsidiary U.S. bank, or a branch of the foreign bank. An agency office can lend and transfer funds in the United States, but it cannot accept deposits from domestic residents. Agency offices have the advantage of not being subject to regulations that apply to full-service banking offices (such as requirements for FDIC insurance and restrictions on branching). A subsidiary U.S. bank is just like any other U.S. bank (it may even have an American-sounding name) and is subject to the same regulations, but it is owned by the foreign bank. A branch of a foreign bank bears the foreign bank's name and is usually a full-service office. Foreign banks may also form Edge Act corporations and IBFs.

Before 1978, foreign banks were not subject to many regulations that applied to domestic banks: They could open branches across state lines and were not expected to meet reserve requirements, for example. The passage of the International Banking Act of 1978, however, put foreign and domestic banks on a more equal footing. Now foreign banks may open new full-service branches only in the state they designate as their home state or in states that allow the entry of out-of-state banks. Limited-service branches and agency offices in any other state are permitted, however, and foreign banks are allowed to retain any full-service branches opened before ratification of the International Banking Act of 1978.

The internationalization of banking, both by U.S. banks going abroad and by foreign banks entering the United States, has meant that financial markets throughout the world have become more integrated. As a result, there is a growing trend toward international coordination of bank regulation, one example of which is the 1988 Basel agreement to standardize minimum capital requirements in industrialized countries, discussed in Chapter 20. Financial market integration has also encouraged bank consolidation abroad, culminating in trillion dollar banks. Another development has been the importance of foreign banks in international banking. As shown in Table 4, in 2003, nine of the ten largest banks in the world were foreign.

TABLE 4 *Ten Largest Banks in the World, 2003*

Bank	Assets (U.S. $ billions)
1. Citigroup (U.S.)	1,264,032
2. Mizuho Financial Group (Japan)	1,223,478
3. UBS (Switzerland)	1,116,215
4. Groupe Credit Agricole (France)	1,098,669
5. HSBC (U.K.)	1,034,216
6. Deutsche Bank (Germany)	1,008,696
7. BNP Paribas (France)	982,917
8. Sumitomo Mitsui Banking (Japan)	863,507
9. Mitsubishi Tokyo FG (Japan)	836,358
10. Royal Bank of Scotland (U.K.)	809,433

Source: *Euromoney*, June 2004, vol. 35 (422), p.176.

Summary

1. The history of banking in the United States has left us with a dual banking system, with commercial banks chartered by the states and the federal government. Multiple agencies regulate commercial banks: the Office of the Comptroller, the Federal Reserve, the FDIC, and the state banking authorities.

2. A change in the economic environment will stimulate financial institutions to search for financial innovations. Changes in demand conditions, especially the rise in interest-rate risk; changes in supply conditions, especially improvements in information technology; and the desire to avoid costly regulations have been major driving forces behind financial innovation. Financial innovation has caused banks to suffer declines in cost advantages in acquiring funds and in income advantages on their assets. The resulting squeeze has hurt profitability in banks' traditional lines of business and has led to a decline in traditional banking.

3. Restrictive state branching regulations and the McFadden Act, which prohibits branching across state lines, have led to a large number of small commercial banks. The large number of commercial banks in the United States reflects the past *lack* of competition, not the presence of vigorous competition. Bank holding companies and ATMs were important responses to branching restrictions that have weakened the restrictions' anticompetitive effect.

4. Since the mid-1980s, bank consolidation has been occurring at a rapid pace. The first phase of bank consolidation was the result of bank failures and the reduced effectiveness of branching restrictions. The second phase has been stimulated by the Riegle-Neal Interstate Banking and Branching Efficiency Act of 1994, which establishes the basis for a nationwide banking system. Once banking consolidation has settled down, we are likely to be left with a banking system with several thousand banks. Most economists believe that the benefits of bank consolidation and nationwide banking will outweigh the costs.

5. The Glass-Steagall Act separated commercial banking from the securities industry. With competitive forces causing bypass of the intent of the act, the Gramm-Leach-Bliley legislation of 1999 repealed Glass-Steagall and removed the separation of these industries.

6. With the rapid growth of world trade since 1960, international banking has grown dramatically. U.S. banks engage in international banking activities by opening branches abroad, owning controlling interests in foreign banks, forming Edge Act corporations, and operating international banking facilities (IBFs) located in the United States. Foreign banks operate in the United States by owning a subsidiary American bank or by operating branches or agency offices in the United States.

Key Terms

automated banking machine, (ABM) *p. 457*

automated teller machine (ATM), *p. 457*

bank holding companies, *p. 454*

branches, *p. 470*

deposit rate ceilings, *p. 462*

disintermediation, *p. 462*

dual banking system, *p. 453*

e-cash, *p. 459*

economies of scope, *p. 473*

Edge Act corporation, *p. 480*

electronic money (e-money), *p. 458*

financial derivatives, *p. 456*

financial engineering, *p. 454*

futures contracts, *p. 456*

hedge, *p. 455*

international banking facilities (IBFs), *p. 481*

large, complex banking organizations (LCBOs), *p. 473*

national banks, *p. 453*

securitization, *p. 461*

smart card, *p. 459*

state banks, *p. 453*

sweep account, *p. 463*

superregional banks, *p. 473*

virtual bank, *p. 457*

Questions

1. Why was the United States one of the last of the major industrialized countries to have a central bank?

2. Which regulatory agency has the primary responsibility for supervising the following categories of commercial banks?

   a. National banks

   b. Bank holding companies

   c. Non–Federal Reserve member state banks

   d. Federal Reserve member state banks

3. "The commercial banking industry in Canada is less competitive than the commercial banking industry in the United States because in Canada only a few large banks dominate the industry, while in the United States there are around 8,175 commercial banks." Is this statement true, false, or uncertain? Explain your answer.

4. Why has new technology made it harder to enforce limitations on bank branching?

5. Why has there been such a dramatic increase in bank holding companies?

6. What incentives have regulatory agencies created to encourage international banking? Why have they done this?

7. How could the approval of international banking facilities (IBFs) by the Fed in 1981 have reduced employment in the banking industry in Europe?

8. If the bank at which you keep your checking account is owned by Saudi Arabians, should you worry that your deposits are less safe than if the bank were owned by Americans?

9. If reserve requirements were eliminated in the future, as some economists advocate, what effects would this have on the size of money market mutual funds?

10. Why have banks been losing cost advantages in acquiring funds in recent years?

11. "If inflation had not risen in the 1960s and 1970s, the banking industry might be healthier today." Is this statement true, false, or uncertain? Explain your answer.

12. Why have banks been losing income advantages on their assets in recent years?

13. "The invention of the computer is the major factor behind the decline of the banking industry." Is this statement true, false, or uncertain? Explain your answer.

14. How did competitive forces lead to the repeal of the Glass-Steagall Act's separation of the banking and the securities industries?

15. What will be the likely effect of the Gramm-Leach-Bliley Act on financial consolidation?

Web Exercises

Commercial Banking Industry: Structure and Competition

1. Go to **http://www2.fdic.gov/SDI/SOB**. Select "Historical Statistics on Banking," then "Commercial Bank Reports." Finally, choose "Number of Institutions, Branches, and Total Offices." Looking at the trend in bank branches, does the public appear to have more or less access to banking facilities? How many banks were there in 1934, and how many are there now? Does the graph indicate that the trend toward consolidation is continuing?

2. Despite the regulations that protect banks from failure, some do fail. Go to **http://www2.fdic.gov/hsob/**. Select the tab labeled "Bank and Thrift Failures." How many bank failures occurred in the United States during the most recent complete calendar year? What were the total assets held by the banks that failed? How many banks failed in 1937?

Savings Associations and Credit Unions

Preview

Suppose that you are a typical middle-class worker in New York in 1820. You work hard and earn fair wages as a craftsman. You are married and about to have a child, so you decide that you would like to own your own home. There are many commercial banks in the city, but as their name implies, these institutions exist to serve commerce, not the working class, because that is where the profits are. Where could you go to borrow the money to buy a home? Your options at that time would have been very limited. Later in the century, however, a new institution emerged that opened the possibility of home ownership to more than the very wealthy. That institution was the savings and loan association.

The middle class also had problems finding financial institutions willing to offer small consumer-type loans. Again, banks had determined that loans to these customers were not profitable. Another type of institution, the credit union, emerged at about the same time as savings and loans to service the borrowing needs of this segment of the economy.

In Chapters 17 and 18 we discussed commercial banks, the largest of the depository institutions. Though smaller, savings and loan associations, mutual savings banks, and credit unions, collectively called thrift institutions or thrifts, are important to the servicing of consumer borrowing needs. Thrifts are primarily concerned with lending to individuals and households, as opposed to banks, which still tend to be more concerned with lending to businesses. We begin our discussion by reviewing the history of the thrift industry. We then describe the nature of the industry today and project where it might be in the future.

Mutual Savings Banks

The first pure savings banks were established by philanthropists in Scotland and England to encourage saving by the poor. The founders of the institutions would often provide subsidies that allowed the institution to pay interest rates above the current market level. Because of the nature of the savings banks' customers, the institutions were very conservative with their funds and placed most of them in commercial banks. The first savings banks in the United States were chartered by Congress and founded in the Northeast in 1816. These institutions quickly lost their distinction of being strictly for the poor and instead became a popular place for members of the middle class to store their excess money.

Savings banks were originally organized as **mutual banks,** meaning that the depositors were the owners of the firm. This form of ownership led to a conservative investment posture, which prevented many of the mutual savings banks from failing during the recession at the end of the nineteenth century or during the Great Depression in the 1930s. In fact, between 1930 and 1937, deposits in mutual savings banks grew while those in commercial banks actually shrank. Following World War II, savings banks made mortgage lending their primary business. This focus made them similar to savings and loans.

Mutual ownership means that no stock in the bank is issued or sold; the depositors own a share of the bank in proportion to their deposits. There are currently 367 mutual savings banks, primarily concentrated on the eastern seaboard. Most are state chartered. (Federal chartering of savings banks did not begin until 1978.) Because they are state chartered, they are regulated and supervised by the state as well as the federal government.

The mutual form of ownership has both advantages and disadvantages. On the one hand, since the capital of the institution is contributed by the depositors, more capital is available because all deposits represent equity. This leads to greater safety in that mutual savings banks have far fewer liabilities than other banking organizations. On the other hand, the mutual form of ownership accentuates the principal-agent problem that exists in corporations. In corporations, managers are hired by the board of directors, who are in turn elected by the shareholders. Because most shareholders do not own a very large percentage of the firm, when there is a disagreement with management, it makes more sense to sell shares than to try to change policy. This problem also exists for the mutual form of ownership. Most depositors do not have a large enough stake in the firm to make it cost-effective for them to monitor the firm's managers closely.

The corporation, however, has alternative methods of aligning managers' goals with those of shareholders. For example, managers can be offered a stake in the firm, or stock options can be part of their compensation package. Similarly, managers of corporations are always under the threat of takeover by another firm if they fail to manage effectively. These alternatives are not available in the mutual form of ownership. As a result, there may be less control over management.

An advantage to the mutual form of ownership is that managers are more risk-averse than in the corporate form. This is because mutual managers gain nothing if the firm does very well, since they do not own a stake in the firm, but they lose everything if the firm fails. This incentive arrangement appeals to the very risk-averse investor, but its importance has diminished now that the government provides deposit insurance.

Savings and Loan Associations

In the early part of the nineteenth century, commercial banks focused on short-term loans to businesses, so it was very difficult for families to obtain loans for the purchase of a house. In 1816, Congress decided that home ownership was part of the American dream, and to make that possible, Congress passed regulations creating savings and loans and mutual savings institutions. Congress chartered the first savings and loans 15 years after the first mutual savings banks received their charters. The original mandate to the industry was to provide a source of funds for families wanting to buy a home.

These institutions were to aggregate depositors' funds and use the money to make long-term mortgage loans. The institutions were not to take in demand deposits but instead were authorized to offer savings accounts that paid slightly higher interest than that offered by commercial banks.

There were about 12,000 savings and loans in operation by the 1920s. Mortgages accounted for about 85% of their total assets. The rest of their assets were usually deposited in commercial banks. One of every four mortgages in the country was held by a savings and loan institution, making S&Ls the single largest provider of mortgage loans in the country.

Despite the large number of separate savings and loan institutions, they were not an integrated industry. Each state regulated its own S&Ls, and regulations differed substantially from state to state. In 1913, Congress created the Federal Reserve System to regulate and help commercial banks. No such system existed for savings and loans.

Before any significant legislation could be passed, the Great Depression caused the failure of thousands of thrift institutions. In response to the problems facing the industry and to the loss of $200 million in savings, Congress passed the **Federal Home Loan Bank Act of 1932.** This act created the **Federal Home Loan Bank Board (FHLBB)** and a network of regional home loan banks, similar to the organization of the Federal Reserve System. The act gave thrifts the choice of being state or federally chartered. In 1934, Congress continued its efforts to support savings and loans by establishing the **Federal Savings and Loan Insurance Corporation (FSLIC),** which insured deposits in much the same way as the FDIC did for commercial banks.

Savings and loans were successful, low-risk businesses for many years following these regulatory changes (see Chapter 20). Their main source of funds was individual savings accounts, which tended to be stable and low-cost, and their primary assets (about 60% of their total assets) were mortgage loans (see Figure 1). Since real estate secured virtually all of these loans and since real estate values increased steadily through the mid-1970s, loan losses were very small. Thrifts

Information about savings institutions is available on-line; for example, the Wisconsin Department of Financial Institutions website, www.wdfi.org/fi/, gives lists of savings institutions, statutes, rules and financial data of the institutions.

www2.fdic.gov/qbp/ provides a source of tools and charts related to savings and loans. Most current data in this chapter comes from this source.

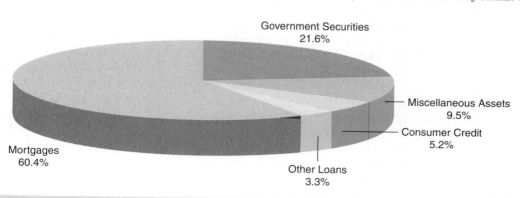

FIGURE 1 *Distribution of Savings and Loan Assets, 2004*

Source: http://www2.fdic.gov/qbp/2004mar/sav2.html.

provided the fuel for the home-building boom that for almost half a century, from 1934 to 1978, was the centerpiece of America's domestic economy.

Mutual Savings Banks and Savings and Loans Compared

Mutual savings banks and savings and loan associations are similar in many ways; however, they do differ in ways other than ownership structure.

- Mutual savings banks are concentrated in the northeastern United States; savings and loans are located throughout the country.
- Mutual savings banks may insure their deposits with the state or with the Federal Deposit Insurance Corporation; S&Ls may not.
- Mutual savings banks are not as heavily concentrated in mortgages and have had more flexibility in their investing practices than savings and loans.

Because the similarities between mutual savings banks and savings and loans are more important than the differences, the focus of this chapter will be more on savings and loans.

Savings and Loans in Trouble: The Thrift Crisis

As part of the regulatory changes following the Great Depression, Congress imposed a cap on the rate of interest that savings and loans could pay on savings accounts. The theory was that if S&Ls obtained funds at a low cost, they could make loans to home borrowers at a low cost. The interest-rate caps became a serious problem for savings and loans in the 1970s when inflation rose. Chapters 17 and 18 provide an in-depth discussion of the capital adequacy and interest-rate problems depository institutions faced at that time.

By 1979, inflation was running at 13.3%, but savings and loans were restricted to paying a maximum of 5.5% on deposits. These rates did not even maintain depositors' purchasing power with inflation running almost 8% higher than their interest return—in effect, the real interest rate they were earning was –7.8%. They were actually losing spending power leaving money in savings and loans.

At this same time, securities houses began offering a new product that circumvented interest-rate caps. *Money market accounts* paid market rates on short-term funds. Though not insured, the bulk of the cash placed in money market funds was in turn invested in low-risk securities such as Treasury securities or commercial paper. Because the savings and loan customers were not satisfied with the low returns they were earning on their funds, they left S&Ls in droves for the high returns these accounts offered.

Financial innovation and deregulation in the permissive atmosphere of the 1980s led to expanded powers for the S&L industry that led to several problems. First, many S&L managers did not have the required expertise to manage risk appropriately in these new lines of business. Second, the new expanded powers meant that there was a rapid growth in new lending, particularly to the real estate sector. Even if the required expertise was available initially, rapid credit growth might outstrip the available information resources of the banking institution, resulting in excessive risk taking. Third, these new powers of the S&Ls and the lending boom meant that their activities were expanding in scope and were becoming more complicated, requiring an expansion of regulatory resources to monitor these activities appropriately. Unfortunately, regulators of the S&Ls at the Federal Savings and Loan Insurance Corporation (FSLIC) had neither the expertise nor the resources that would have enabled them to monitor these new activities sufficiently. Given the lack of expertise in both the S&L industry and the FSLIC, the weakening of the regulatory apparatus, and the moral hazard incentives provided by deposit insurance, it is no surprise that S&Ls took on excessive risks, which led to huge losses on bad loans.

In addition, the incentives of moral hazard were increased dramatically by a historical accident: the combination of the sharp increases in interest rates from late 1979 until 1981 and a severe recession in 1981–1982, both of which were engineered by the Federal Reserve to bring down inflation. The sharp rises in interest rates produced rapidly rising costs of funds for the savings and loans that were not matched by higher earnings on the S&Ls' principal asset, long-term residential mortgages (whose rates had been fixed at a time when interest rates were far lower). The 1981–1982 recession and a collapse in the prices of energy and farm products hit the economies of certain parts of the country, such as Texas, very hard. As a result, there were defaults on many S&Ls' loans. Losses for savings and loan institutions mounted to $10 billion in 1981–1982, and by some estimates over half of the S&Ls in the United States had a negative net worth and were thus insolvent by the end of 1982.

Later Stages of the Crisis: Regulatory Forbearance

At this point, a logical step might have been for the S&L regulators—the Federal Home Loan Bank Board and its deposit insurance subsidiary, the Federal Savings and Loan Insurance Fund (FSLIC), both now abolished—to close the insolvent S&Ls. Instead, these regulators adopted a stance of **regulatory forbearance:** They refrained from exercising their regulatory right to put the insolvent S&Ls out of business. To sidestep their responsibility to close ailing S&Ls, they adopted irregular regulatory accounting principles that in effect substantially lowered capital requirements. For example, they allowed S&Ls to include in their capital calculations a high value for intangible capital, called *goodwill*.

There were three main reasons why the Federal Home Loan Bank Board and FSLIC opted for regulatory forbearance. First, the FSLIC did not have sufficient funds in its insurance fund to close the insolvent S&Ls and pay off their deposits. Second, the Federal Home Loan Bank Board was established to encourage the growth of the savings and loan industry, so the regulators were probably too close to the people they were supposed to be regulating. Third, because bureaucrats do not like to admit that their own agency is in trouble, the Federal Home Loan Bank Board and the FSLIC preferred to sweep their problems under the rug in the hope that they would go away.

Regulatory forbearance increases moral hazard dramatically because an operating but insolvent S&L (nicknamed a "zombie S&L" by Edward Kane of Ohio State University because it is the "living dead") has almost nothing to lose by taking on great risk and "betting the bank": If it gets lucky and its risky investments pay off, it gets out of insolvency. Unfortunately, if, as is likely, the risky investments don't pay off, the zombie S&L's losses will mount, and the deposit insurance agency will be left holding the bag.

This strategy is similar to the "long bomb" strategy in football. When a football team is almost hopelessly behind and time is running out, it often resorts to a high-risk play: the throwing of a long pass to try to score a touchdown. Of course, the long bomb is unlikely to be successful, but there is always a small chance that it will work. If it doesn't, the team is no worse off, since it would have lost the game anyway.

Given the sequence of events we have discussed here, it should be no surprise that savings and loans began to take huge risks: They built shopping centers in the desert, bought manufacturing plants to convert manure to methane, and purchased billions of dollars of high-risk, high-yield junk bonds. The S&L industry was no longer the staid industry that once operated on the so-called *3–6–3 rule*: You took in money at 3%, lent it at 6%, and played golf at 3 P.M. Although many savings and loans were making money, losses at other S&Ls were colossal.

Another outcome of regulatory forbearance was that with little to lose, zombie S&Ls attracted deposits away from healthy S&Ls by offering higher interest rates. Because there were so many zombie S&Ls in Texas pursuing this strategy, above-market interest rates on deposits at Texas S&Ls were said to have a "Texas premium." Potentially healthy S&Ls now found that to compete for deposits, they had to pay higher interest rates, which made their operations less profitable and frequently pushed them into the zombie category. Similarly, zombie S&Ls in pursuit of asset growth made loans at below-market interest rates, thereby lowering loan interest rates for healthy S&Ls, and again made them less profitable. The zombie S&Ls had actually taken on attributes of vampires—their willingness to pay above-market rates for deposits and take below-market interest rates on loans was sucking the lifeblood (profits) out of healthy S&Ls.

Competitive Equality in Banking Act of 1987

Toward the end of 1986, the growing losses in the savings and loan industry were bankrupting the insurance fund of the FSLIC. The Reagan administration sought $15 billion in funds for the FSLIC, a completely inadequate sum considering that many times this amount was needed to close down insolvent S&Ls. The legislation passed by Congress, the Competitive Equality in Banking Act (CEBA) of 1987, did not even meet the administration's requests. It allowed the FSLIC to borrow only $10.8 billion through a subsidiary corporation called Financing Corporation (FICO) and, what was worse, included provisions that directed the Federal Home Loan Bank Board to continue to pursue regulatory forbearance (allow insolvent institutions to keep operating), particularly in economically depressed areas such as Texas.

The failure of Congress to deal with the savings and loan crisis was not going to make the problem go away, and consistent with our analysis, the situation deteriorated rapidly. Losses in the savings and loan industry surpassed $10 billion in 1988 and approached $20 billion in 1989. The crisis was reaching epidemic proportions. The collapse of the real estate market in the late 1980s led to additional huge loan losses that greatly exacerbated the problem.

Political Economy of the Savings and Loan Crisis

Although we now have a grasp of the regulatory and economic forces that created the S&L crisis, we still need to understand the political forces that produced the regulatory structure and activities that led to it. The key to understanding the political economy of the S&L crisis is to recognize that the relationship between voter-taxpayers and the regulators and politicians creates a particular type of moral hazard problem, discussed in Chapter 15: the *principal-agent problem*, which occurs when representatives (agents) such as managers have incentives that differ from those of their employer (the principal) and so act in their own interest rather than in the interest of the employer.

Principal-Agent Problem for Regulators and Politicians

Regulators and politicians are ultimately agents for voter-taxpayers (principals) because in the final analysis, taxpayers bear the cost of any losses by the deposit insurance agency. The principal-agent problem occurs because the agent (a politician or regulator) does not have the same incentives to minimize costs to the economy as the principal (the taxpayer).

To act in the taxpayer's interest and lower costs to the deposit insurance agency, regulators have several tasks, as we have seen. They must set tight restrictions on holding assets that are too risky, must impose high capital requirements, and must not adopt a stance of regulatory forbearance, which allows insolvent institutions to continue to operate. However, because of the principal-agent problem, regulators have incentives to do the opposite. Indeed, as our sad saga of the S&L debacle indicates, they have at times loosened capital requirements and restrictions on risky asset holdings and pursued regulatory forbearance. One important incentive for regulators that explains this phenomenon is their desire to escape blame for poor performance by their agency. By loosening capital requirements and pursuing regulatory forbearance, regulators can hide the problem of an insolvent bank and hope that the situation will improve. Edward Kane characterizes such behavior on the part of regulators as "bureaucratic gambling."

Another important incentive for regulators is that they want to protect their careers by acceding to pressures from the people who most influence their careers. These people are not the taxpayers but the politicians who try to keep regulators from imposing tough regulations on institutions that are major campaign contributors. Members of Congress have often lobbied regulators to ease up on a particular S&L that contributed large sums to their campaigns (as we see in the following case). Regulatory agencies that have little independence from the political process are more vulnerable to these pressures.

In addition, both Congress and the presidential administration promoted banking legislation in 1980 and 1982 that made it easier for savings and loans to engage in risk-taking activities. After the legislation passed, the need for monitoring the S&L industry increased because of the expansion of permissible activities. The S&L regulatory agencies needed more resources to carry out their monitoring activities properly, but Congress (successfully lobbied by the S&L industry) was unwilling to allocate the necessary funds. As a result, the S&L regulatory agencies became so shortstaffed that they actually had to cut back on their on-site examinations just when these were needed most. In the period from January 1984 to July 1986, for example, several hundred S&Ls were not examined even once. Worse yet, spurred on by the intense lobbying efforts of the S&L industry, Congress passed the Competitive Equality in Banking Act of 1987, which provided inadequate funding to close down the insolvent S&Ls and also hampered the S&L regulators from doing their job properly by including provisions encouraging regulatory forbearance.

As these examples indicate, the structure of our political system has created a serious principal-agent problem: Politicians have strong incentives to act in their own interests rather than in the interests of taxpayers. Because of the high cost of running campaigns, American politicians must raise substantial contributions. This situation may provide lobbyists and other campaign contributors with the opportunity to influence politicians to act against the public interest, as we see in the following case.

Case

PRINCIPAL-AGENT PROBLEM IN ACTION: CHARLES KEATING AND THE LINCOLN SAVINGS AND LOAN SCANDAL

We see that the principal-agent problem for regulators and politicians creates incentives that may cause excessive risk taking on the part of banking institutions, which then cause substantial losses to the taxpayer. The scandal associated with Charles H. Keating Jr. and the Lincoln Savings and Loan Association provides a graphic example of the principal-agent problem at work. As Edwin Gray, a former chairman of the Federal Home Loan Bank Board, stated, "This is a story of incredible corruption. I can't call it anything else."[1]

Charles Keating was allowed to acquire Lincoln Savings and Loan of Irvine, California, in early 1984, even though he had been accused of fraud by the SEC less than five years earlier. For Keating, whose construction firm, American Continental, planned to build huge real estate developments in Arizona, the S&L was a gold mine: In the lax regulatory atmosphere at the time, controlling the S&L gave his firm easy access to funds without being scrutinized by outside bankers. Within days of acquiring control, Keating got rid of Lincoln's conservative lending officers and internal auditors, even though he had promised regulators he would keep them. Lincoln then plunged into high-risk investments such as currency futures, junk bonds, common stock, hotels, and vast tracts of desert land in Arizona.

Because of a shortage of savings and loan examiners at the time, Lincoln was able to escape a serious examination until 1986, whereupon examiners from the Federal Home Loan Bank of San Francisco discovered that Lincoln had exceeded the 10% limit on equity investments by $600 million. Because of these activities and some evidence that Lincoln was deliberately trying to mislead the examiners, the examiners recommended federal seizure of the bank and all its assets. Keating was not about to take this lying down; he engaged hordes of lawyers—eventually 77 law firms—and accused the bank examiners of bias. He also sued unsuccessfully to overturn the 10% equity limit. Keating is said to have bragged that he spent $50 million fighting regulators.

Lawyers were not Keating's only tactic for keeping regulators off his back. After receiving $1.3 million of contributions to their campaigns from Keating, five senators—Dennis De Concini and John McCain of Arizona, Alan Cranston of California, John Glenn of Ohio, and Donald Riegle of Michigan (subsequently nicknamed the "Keating Five")—met with Edwin Gray, the

[1]Quoted in Tom Morganthau, Rich Thomas, and Eleanor Clift, "The S&L Scandal's Biggest Blowout," *Newsweek*, November 6, 1989, p. 35.

CHAPTER 19 SAVINGS ASSOCIATIONS AND CREDIT UNIONS

chairman of the Federal Home Loan Board, and later with four top regulators from San Francisco in April 1987. They complained that the regulators were being too tough on Lincoln and urged the regulators to quit dragging out the investigation. After Gray was replaced by M. Danny Wall, Wall took the unprecedented step of removing the San Francisco examiners from the case in September 1987 and transferred the investigation to the bank board's headquarters in Washington. No examiners called on Lincoln for the next ten months, and as one of the San Francisco examiners described it, Lincoln dropped into a "regulatory black hole."

Lincoln Savings and Loan finally failed in April 1989, with estimated costs to taxpayers of $2.6 billion, making it possibly the most costly S&L failure in history. Keating was convicted for abuses (such as having Lincoln pay him and his family $34 million), but after serving four and a half years in jail, his conviction was overturned in 1996. Wall was forced to resign as head of the Office of Thrift Supervision because of his involvement in the Keating scandal. As a result of their activities on behalf of Keating, the Keating Five senators were made the object of a congressional ethics investigation, but given Congress's propensity to protect its own, they were subjected only to minor sanctions.

Savings and Loan Bailout: Financial Institutions Reform, Recovery, and Enforcement Act of 1989

Immediately after taking office, the Bush administration proposed new legislation to provide adequate funding to close down the insolvent S&Ls. The resulting legislation, the **Financial Institutions Reform, Recovery, and Enforcement Act (FIRREA),** was signed into law on August 9, 1989. It was the most significant legislation to affect the thrift industry since the 1930s. FIRREA's major provisions were as follows: The regulatory apparatus was significantly restructured without the Federal Home Loan Bank Board and the FSLIC, both of which had failed in their regulatory tasks. The regulatory role of the Federal Home Loan Bank Board was relegated to the Office of Thrift Supervision (OTS), a bureau within the U.S. Treasury Department, whose responsibilities are similar to those that the Office of the Comptroller of the Currency has over the national banks. The regulatory responsibilities of the FSLIC were given to the FDIC, and the FDIC became the sole administrator of the federal deposit insurance system with two separate insurance funds: the Bank Insurance Fund (BIF) and the Savings Association Insurance Fund (SAIF). Another new agency, the **Resolution Trust Corporation (RTC),** was established to manage and resolve insolvent thrifts placed in conservatorship or receivership. It was made responsible for selling more than $450 billion of real estate owned by failed institutions. After seizing the assets of about 750 insolvent S&Ls, over 25% of the industry, the RTC sold over 95% of them, with a recovery rate of over 85%. After this success, the RTC went out of business on December 31, 1995.

Initially, the total cost of the bailout was estimated to be $159 billion over the ten-year period through 1999, but more recent estimates indicated that the cost would be far higher. Indeed, the General Accounting Office placed a cost for the bailout at more than $500 billion over 40 years. However, as pointed out in Chapter 3, this estimate was misleading because, for example, the value of a payment 30 years from now is worth much less in today's dollars. The present value

The Office of Thrift Supervision website, www.ots.treas.gov/, contains quarterly industry information, statistical reports, and laws and regulations. The OTS 2003 Fact Book, www.ots.treas.gov/docs/4/480149.pdf, offers a statistical profile of the thrift industry.

of the bailout cost actually ended up being on the order of $150 billion. The funding for the bailout came partly from capital in the Federal Home Loan Banks (owned by the S&L industry) but mostly from the sale of government debt by both the Treasury and the Resolution Funding Corporation (RefCorp).

To replenish the reserves of the Savings Association Insurance Fund, insurance premiums for S&Ls were increased from 20.8 cents per $100 of deposits to 23 cents and can rise as high as 32.5 cents. Premiums for banks immediately rose from 8.3 cents to 15 cents per $100 of deposits and were raised further to 23 cents in 1991.

FIRREA also imposed new restrictions on thrift activities that in essence reregulated the S&L industry to the asset choices it had before 1982. S&Ls can no longer purchase junk bonds and had to sell their holdings by 1994. Commercial real estate loans are restricted to four times capital rather than the previous limit of 40% of assets, and so this new restriction is a reduction for all institutions whose capital is less than 10% of assets. S&Ls must also hold at least 70%—up from 60%—of their assets in investments that are primarily housing-related. Among the most important provisions of FIRREA was the increase in the core capital leverage requirement from 3% to 8% and the eventual adherence to the same risk-based capital standards imposed on commercial banks.[2]

FIRREA also enhanced the enforcement powers of thrift regulators by making it easier for them to remove managers, issue cease and desist orders, and impose civil penalties. The Justice Department was also given $75 million per year for three years to uncover and prosecute fraud in the banking industry, and maximum fines rose substantially.

As a result of the failure of savings and loans and the passage of FIRREA, the total assets of savings and loans fell between 1988 and 1998. Figure 2 shows the total assets of savings and loans between 1979 and 2004; note the rapid decrease between 1988 and 1992. Since 1997, the assets of S&Ls have been increasing slowly.

The Savings and Loan Industry Today

Despite the problems and turmoil surrounding the industry in the 1980s, the savings and loan industry managed to survive, although somewhat changed. In this section we review the current state of the industry.

Number of Institutions

The savings and loan industry has witnessed a substantial reduction in the number of institutions. Many failed or were taken over by the RTC; others merged with stronger institutions to avoid failure. The number of S&Ls declined by more than half between the end of 1986, when there were 3600 of them, and 2004, when there were only 1404. As shown in Figure 3, the number of savings institutions

---

[2]Thrifts are now prohibited from accepting brokered deposits, short-term large-denomination deposits placed in thrifts by funds managers. Brokered deposits are discussed further in Chapter 20.

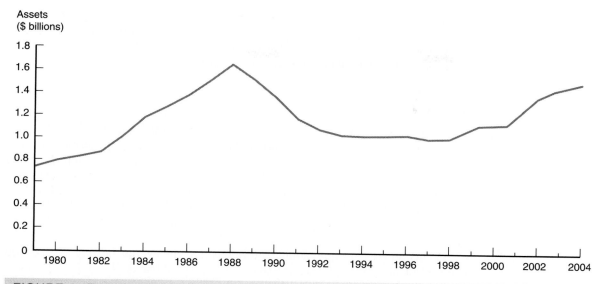

FIGURE 2 *Total Assets of Savings and Loan Associations, 1979–2004*

Source: http://www2.fdic.gov/qbp.

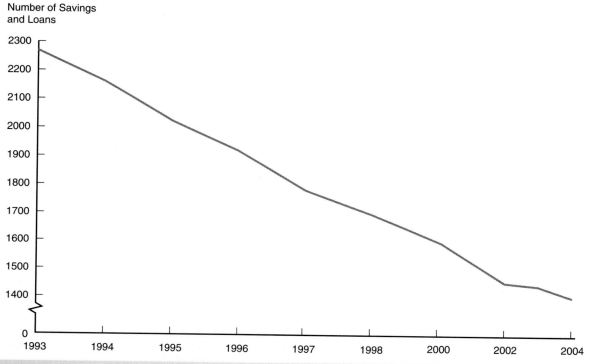

FIGURE 3 *Number of Savings and Loans in the United States, 1993–2004*

Source: http://www2.fdic.gov/qbp/2004mar/sav1.html.

continues to decline. Although new S&Ls continue to open, existing ones convert to commercial banks or credit unions or merge with other savings banks. It is interesting to note that consolidation in the savings industry has not been as dramatic as in commercial banking in recent years.

S&L Size

Figure 4 shows the average total assets for savings and loans since 1984. When viewed along with Figure 3, the graph indicates that the industry has consolidated in recent years. Between 1988 and 1991, the average size of S&Ls fell. This was likely due to the 1989 passage of FIRREA, which required S&Ls to increase their capital-to-asset ratio. Many institutions met the new standard by decreasing their assets rather than by increasing their capital. From 1992 to 2004, total S&L assets increased, even though the number of institutions decreased. The result is fewer but larger institutions.

A second point to note about Figure 4 is that the average size of savings and loans is substantially greater than that of commercial banks. Recall from Chapter 18 that the growth of commercial banks was often constrained by restrictive banking regulations. As a result, the average size of commercial banks at the end of 2004 was over $1 billion in assets. Thus the size of the average commercial bank is less than that of the average savings and loan. Now that Congress has removed most of the restrictions on interstate branching by commercial banks, many industry observers expect a period of rapid consolidation in that industry.

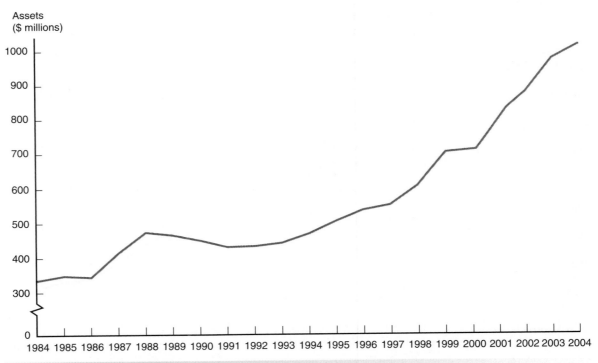

FIGURE 4 *Average Assets per Savings and Loan Association, 1984–2004*

Source: http://www2.fdic.gov/qbp/2004mar/sav3.html.

TABLE 1   *Consolidated Balance Sheet for Savings and Loan Associations ($ billions, first quarter, 2004)*

Savings and Loan Associations

Assets		Liabilities	
Cash and reserves	64.3	Deposits	946.7
Securities	312.1	Other borrowed funds	281.4
Mortgage loans	927.5	All other liabilities	209.7
Commercial loans	49.6	Equity	118.7
Consumer credit	81.3	Total liabilities and equities	1556.5
Corporate equities	28.2		
Miscelleneous	93.5		
Total assets	1556.5		

Sources: Flow of Funds, Table L114 and www.federalreserve.gov/releases/z1

S&L Assets

Table 1 provides a consolidated balance sheet for the savings and loan industry. Let us first discuss the assets side.

The 1982 reforms allowed S&Ls to make consumer and commercial loans. The intent of this legislation was to give S&Ls a source of assets with short maturities. The problem was that commercial loans are far riskier and require lending expertise that many S&Ls did not possess. FIRREA severely curtailed S&Ls' commercial lending. In the four years following passage of the law, the number of loans made for commercial purposes dropped by about 50%. Currently, nearly 90% of all S&L loans are secured by real estate, and 62% are for residential mortgages. Clearly, the industry has returned to its original mandate of financing home ownership.

Savings and loans are subject to reserve requirements, just like banks. Recall from Chapter 17 that reserve requirements are cash deposits that must be held in the vault or at the Federal Reserve in non-interest-bearing accounts. The purpose of reserve requirements is to limit the expansion of the money supply and to ensure adequate liquidity for the institutions. About 4% of total S&L assets are kept in cash.

In addition to cash, savings and loans hold securities, such as corporate, Treasury, and government agency bonds. Unlike reserve deposits, these assets earn interest. The 1982 legislation allowed savings and loans to hold up to 11% of their assets in junk bonds. S&Ls were a major source of funds during the mid-1980s for corporations looking for capital to use in acquiring other firms. In 1989, the FIRREA required that savings and loans divest themselves of these high-risk securities. Currently, only relatively safe securities can be purchased.

S&L Liabilities and Net Worth

Now let's look at the right-hand side of the balance sheet in Table 1. The primary liabilities of savings and loans are deposits and borrowed funds.

The largest liability of savings and loans are customer funds held on deposit. In the past, the bulk of the deposits were from **passbook savings accounts,** interest-bearing savings accounts. In the past, banks issued small books to savers to use for keeping track of their savings balances. The customer would present this book to the teller every time a deposit or withdrawal was made, and the teller would validate the entry. The physical passbook has almost been phased out over the years and replaced with computerized record keeping.

The second major liability is *borrowings*, funds obtained in either the money or capital markets. Since savings and loan deposits are typically short-term, one way to lengthen their average maturity is to borrow long-term funds. Borrowed funds have become a major source of funds for savings and loans, now accounting for over 18% of total assets, up from 11% in 1990.

Capital

The capital of financial institutions is often measured by the *net worth ratio*, total equity (also known as *net worth*) divided by total assets. This figure is closely watched by regulators for indications that a financial institution may be undercapitalized. The average net worth-to-assets ratio was about 3% in 1984. Many institutions had a negative net worth at this time. Since 1989, the average net worth ratio has improved. At the end of 2003, it stood at 7.6%. This is now about the same as the 6% average net worth ratio for commercial banks. One reason for the improvement in the capital of savings and loans is that FIRREA mandated that it be increased. (We discussed the importance of capital in the functioning of a financial institution in Chapter 17.)

The accounting for savings and loans permitted extensive use of goodwill, an asset account on the balance sheet that supposedly reflects the value of a firm's good name and reputation. For example, in 1987, goodwill accounted for $29.6 billion of savings and loan assets. This represented more than half of the $53.8 billion in total capital. If we removed goodwill from capital before calculating the net worth-to-assets ratio in 1987, we find that the ratio is only 1.6%, not the 3.7% it was when including goodwill. The value of goodwill fell steadily since its high that year. Listing large amounts of goodwill as an asset was another way that savings and loans were able to hide the fact that they were insolvent.

Profitability and Health

One indication that the health of savings and loans has improved in recent years is that their earnings have increased. From 1987 through 1990, the industry suffered net losses. But in 1991, net after-tax income for the industry was $859 million, and by 2000, it had reached $10.7 billion (see Figure 5).

A better measure of a firm's health than net income is its return on equity (ROE). Figure 6 shows that there was a steady increase in S&Ls' ROE from 1993 to 2003, when it was over 12%. S&L profits for 2003 were the highest ever reported by the industry. Over 94% of all S&Ls were profitable. Part of this income was due to the sale of mortgage loans that had increased in value when interest rates fell.

Only eight S&Ls have failed since 1995. Furthermore, the number of "problem" thrifts is down to 13, compared to 146 in 1993. The percentage of loans being charged off as losses is also at a low 0.25%.

In summary, savings institutions, which were in grave condition a decade ago, have returned to robust health. They are providing fair returns to their shareholders and are not in any danger of causing additional taxpayer losses. The industry's equity-to-capital ratio is now the highest it has ever been.

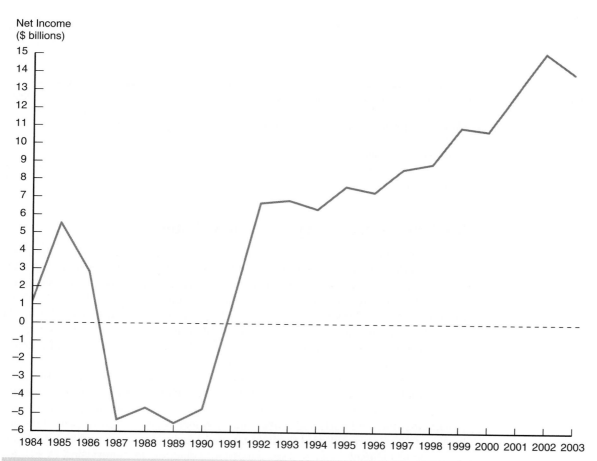

FIGURE 5 *Net Income of Savings and Loan Associations, 1984–2003*

Source: http://www2.fdic.gov/qbp/.

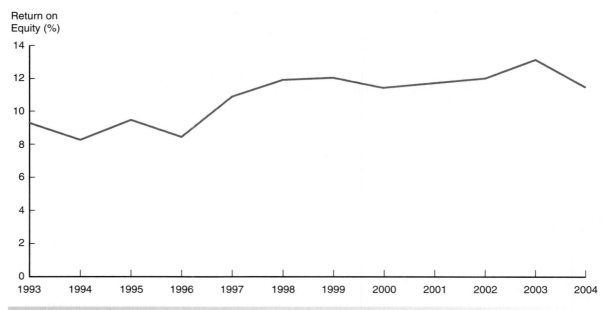

FIGURE 6   *Average Return on Equity for Savings and Loan Institutions, 1993–2004*

Source: http://www2.fdic.gov/qbp/2004mar/sav1.html.

The Future of the Savings and Loan Industry

One issue that has received considerable attention in recent years is whether the savings and loan industry is still needed. Observers who favor eliminating S&L charters altogether point out that there is now a large number of alternative mortgage loan outlets available for home buyers. In Chapter 12 we introduced the securitized mortgage. This new instrument has provided the majority of the funds needed by the mortgage market. A reasonable question to ask is whether there is a need for an industry dedicated exclusively to providing a service efficiently provided elsewhere in the financial system.

Let us review the history of the savings and loan industry for a moment. S&Ls were established to provide mortgages to home buyers. The industry was healthy until interest rates increased and they were stuck holding low-interest fixed-rate mortgages financed with high-cost funds. Congress attempted to provide relief by giving S&Ls a great deal of flexibility in their capital structure and lending functions. Due to abuses, poor market conditions, inadequate supervision by FSLIC, and fraud, tremendous losses accrued. Finally, Congress reregulated the industry and again required that its primary business be mortgage lending. The only trouble now is that mortgage loans are available from many other sources (see Chapter 12).

Just as efficient markets develop new securities and services when the need for them arises, efficient markets should eliminate unneeded institutions when they are no longer required. Many industry analysts expect the savings and loan industry to disappear, perhaps by existing savings and loans being acquired by other institutions or by commercial banks. We can examine the evidence to see if this is beginning to happen.

We noted earlier that the number of savings and loans has decreased by 56% since its high in 1986. There were fewer S&Ls in 2004 than in 1994. However, the drop in the number of institutions could be due to consolidation within the industry, much like what is happening in commercial banking. A better indication of the future of the industry may be provided by the trend in total assets. Figure 2 shows that the total assets of savings and loans have increased since 1993. This suggests that there is at least not a rapid trend to eliminate these institutions. It may be that they will continue to be a provider of mortgage loans along with a number of other sources.

Congress will be pressured again to deregulate the industry to allow S&Ls to perform more of the functions allowed by commercial banks. Although this may happen, the losses sustained as a result of the last attempt at deregulation are still fresh in the minds of regulators. It is unlikely that we will again witness an attempt at rapid deregulation. Instead, we can expect to see gradual changes in the industry that will continue to blur the distinction between savings and loans and commercial banks.

Credit Unions

The third type of thrift institution is the **credit union,** a financial institution that focuses on servicing the banking and lending needs of its members. These institutions are also designed to service the needs of consumers, not businesses, and are distinguished by their ownership structure and their "common bond" membership requirement. Most credit unions are relatively small.

History and Organization

In the early 1900s, commercial banks focused most of their attention on the business borrower. This left the small consumer without a ready source of funds. Because Congress was concerned that commercial banks were not meeting the needs of consumers, it established savings banks and savings and loan associations to help consumers obtain mortgage loans. In the early 1900s, the credit union was established to help consumers with *other* types of loans. A secondary purpose was to provide a place for small investors to place their savings.

The concept behind credit unions originated in Germany in the nineteenth century. A group of consumers would pool their assets as collateral for a loan from a bank. The funds so raised were then loaned to the members of the group, and each member of the group was personally liable for repayment of the loan. Defaults were very rare because members knew one another well.

The first two credit unions in the United States were established in Massachusetts in 1910. The Massachusetts Credit Union (MCU) was organized in 1914 as a functioning credit union but with the additional purpose of encouraging the formation of additional credit unions. The MCU evolved into a kind of central credit union facility. In 1921, the MCU was reorganized as the **Credit Union National Extension Bureau (CUNEB),** which worked to have credit unions established in every state. In 1935, CUNEB was replaced by the **Credit Union National Association (CUNA).**

In 1934, Congress passed the **Federal Credit Union Act,** which allowed federal chartering of credit unions in all states. Prior to this, most credit unions were chartered by the state in which they operated. Currently, about 40% of credit unions have state charters and 60% have federal charters.

One reason for the growth of credit unions has been the support they received from employers. They realized that employee morale could be raised and time saved if banking-type facilities were readily available. In many cases, employers donated space on business property for the credit union to operate. The convenience of this institution soon attracted a large number of customers.

Mutual Ownership   Credit unions are organized as *mutuals*; that is, they are owned by their depositors. A customer receives shares when a deposit is made. Rather than earning interest on deposited funds, the customer earns dividends. The amount of the dividend is not guaranteed, like the interest rate earned on accounts at banks. Instead, the amount of the dividend is estimated in advance and is paid if at all possible.

Each depositor has one vote, regardless how much money he or she may have with the institution. Depositors vote for directors, who in turn hire managers to run the credit union.

Because credit unions are cooperative businesses, they are managed somewhat differently from other businesses. For example, many credit unions make extensive use of volunteer help to reduce their costs. Since any cost reductions are passed on to the depositors, volunteers feel that they are working for the common good. Similarly, as noted, operating facilities may be donated.

Common Bond Membership   The single most important feature of credit unions that distinguishes them from other depository institutions is the common bond member rule. The idea behind **common bond membership** is that only members of a particular association, occupation, or geographic region are permitted to join the credit union. A credit union's common bonds define its field of membership.

The most frequent type of common bond applies to employees of a single occupation or employer. For example, most state employees are eligible to join their state credit union. Similarly, the Navy Credit Union is open to all U.S. Navy personnel. Other credit unions accept members from the same religious or professional background.

One problem with the common bond membership rule is that it prevents credit unions from diversifying their risk. If most of a credit union's members are employed by one business and that business is forced to lay off workers, it is likely that the credit union will have high default rates on loans. A recent trend among credit unions has been for several to merge, a move that helps reduce the risk of having all members linked by a single bond. To make mergers easier, regulators have interpreted the common bond requirement less strictly. For example, most credit unions now let members of the immediate family of an eligible member join, and many credit unions have adopted a "once a member, always a member" policy. In 1982, regulators ruled that credit unions could accept members from several employee groups instead of just one. In 1988, regulators determined that the bond between members of the American Association of Retired People was sufficient and authorized the organization to open its own credit union. The American Automobile Association, however, was rejected.

The commercial bank lobby violently disagrees with relaxed membership rules for credit unions that in some instances have allowed them to admit virtually everyone in a community. Commercial banks view credit unions as unfair competitors due to the government support they receive in the form of tax advantages (to be discussed shortly). Many bankers feel that the threat posed by credit unions could cause more vulnerable banks to fail.

To curb this threat, a group of Tennessee bankers sued to change the regulators' stance that federal law allows multiple occupational groups, each of which independently shares a common bond, to join a single credit union. In April 1997, an appeals court ruled in favor of the bankers, saying that the restrictions on common bond membership should be left intact.

On February 24, 1997, the U.S. Supreme Court reviewed a different lower court ruling on the AT&T Family Federal Credit Union that placed sharp limits on membership in federally chartered credit unions. It ruled that bankers have the right to sue about the field-of-membership issue and that the credit union regulator, the National Credit Union Administration, can no longer allow federal credit unions to expand outside of their original memberships.

This ruling resulted in intense congressional lobbying by credit union supporters that led to the passage of the Credit Union Membership Access Act on August 7, 1998. The intent of this law was to preserve the right of all consumers to choose the credit union alternative. It maintains the concept of common bond membership but allows for the combining of groups with different common bonds in a single credit union. This act became effective on January 1, 1999.

Nonprofit, Tax-Exempt Status   The Federal Credit Union Act of 1934 contained the provision that credit unions were to be nonprofit and consequently exempt from federal taxation. All of the income earned by the institutions is to be spent on their members. Credit unions are currently the only financial institutions that are tax-exempt. This makes it easier for them to accumulate retained earnings than it is for other institutions. Banks and S&Ls are questioning this tax-exempt status as credit unions become larger and more significant competitors. Savings and loans lost their tax-exempt status in 1951. The American Bankers Association estimates that the subsidy reduces the cost of funds to credit unions by almost 2.5% and gives them a cost advantage of $1 billion per year. The credit unions dispute this number and assign their cost advantage to their use of volunteer help. It remains a question how long the favorable tax treatment for credit unions can be maintained.

Partly as a result of being nonprofit and partly due to the cost advantage of being tax-exempt, credit union fees tend to be lower than those of banks.

Regulation and Insurance   The **National Credit Union Act of 1970** established the **National Credit Union Administration (NCUA).** This independent federal agency is charged with the task of regulating and supervising federally chartered credit unions and state-chartered credit unions that receive federal deposit insurance. The remaining credit unions are regulated by state credit union or banking departments, which generally follow federal practices.

The National Credit Union Act of 1970 also established the **National Credit Union Share Insurance Fund (NCUSIF),** to be controlled by the NCUA. This fund insures the deposits of all nationally chartered credit unions and most state-chartered credit unions for up to $100,000 per account. The remaining state-chartered credit unions are insured by one of the state insurance systems. Since the savings and loan crisis, most states are eager to get out of the insurance business. It is likely that in the future, all credit union deposit insurance will be provided by the NCUSIF.

The National Credit Union Administration site, www.ncua.gov/, includes general information about credit unions and credit union data.

Central Credit Unions   Because many credit unions are small and have very little diversification, they are often susceptible to seasonal cash flow problems. Most credit unions also lack the size needed to support large administrative staffs. One way they overcome these problems is with "state central" or "corporate" credit unions, which service the credit unions in their area by providing computer and financial assistance. There are currently 44 state central credit unions, which provide a number of valuable services, including these:

- They may help with member institutions' credit needs. The state central can invest excess funds and make loans to cover short-term shortages.
- They can invest excess funds with the **U.S. Central Credit Union,** which in turn can invest in the financial markets.
- They can hold clearing balances.
- They can provide educational services.

The U.S. Central Credit Union was organized in 1974 to act as a central bank for credit unions. It is chartered as a commercial bank in Kansas, and its primary function is to provide banking services to the 44 state central credit unions. It allows these institutions access to the money markets and to long-term capital markets. Most individual credit unions and even most state central credit unions lack sufficient size and transaction volume to operate efficiently in these wholesale markets.

In 1978, the **Financial Institutions Reform Act** created the **Central Liquidity Facility (CLF)** as the lender of last resort for credit unions. This agency provides many of the same functions for credit unions that the Federal Reserve provides for commercial banks. Although most day-to-day liquidity needs of credit unions are met by the state central organizations, in the event of a national liquidity crisis, a federal agency can raise far more funds. For example, in a crisis, the CLF can borrow directly from the Federal Reserve.

Membership in the CLF is voluntary, and any state or federally chartered credit union may join the CLF by pledging 0.5% of capital. Most of the funds in the CLF are borrowed from the federal government.

Credit Union Size   Credit unions are small relative to other depository financial institutions. The industry accounts for only about 10% of all consumer deposits and about 15% of all consumer loans. One reason for credit unions' limited size is the common bond restraint. Because credit unions can enroll only members who satisfy the common bond, their growth potential is severely restricted. Nevertheless, some credit unions have grown quite large. The Navy Credit Union dwarfs the others, with over $19 billion in total assets. However, most credit unions have less than $1 billion in assets, and many have less than $5 million. Table 2 lists the largest credit unions.

As discussed earlier, mergers between credit unions help them capture economies of scale and diversify their risk. This trend has resulted in fewer but larger credit unions. Figure 7 reports the number of credit unions active from 1933 to 2003. The number has fallen steadily since 1970 as credit unions merged.

TABLE 2 *Ten Largest Federally Insured Credit Unions, June 30, 2003*

Current Rank	Name of Credit Union	Rank 1 Year Ago	City	State	Year Chartered	Assets ($)
1	Navy	1	Merrifield	VA	1947	19,349,783,090
2	State Employees'	2	Raleigh	NC	1937	10,807,516,707
3	Pentagon	3	Alexandria	VA	1935	5,868,211,924
4	The Golden 1	5	Sacramento	CA	1933	4,598,975,035
5	Boeing Employees	4	Tukwila	WA	1935	4,526,390,803
6	United Airlines Employees'	6	Chicago	IL	1935	4,467,797,816
7	Orange County Teachers	7	Santa Ana	CA	1934	4,435,148,462
8	American Airlines	8	DFW Airport	TX	1982	3,967,563,080
9	Suncoast Schools	9	Tampa	FL	1978	3,823,838,611
10	Security Service	12	San Antonio	TX	1956	3,022,998,145

Source: http://www.ncua.gov/ReportsAndPlans/statistics/midyear2003.pdf

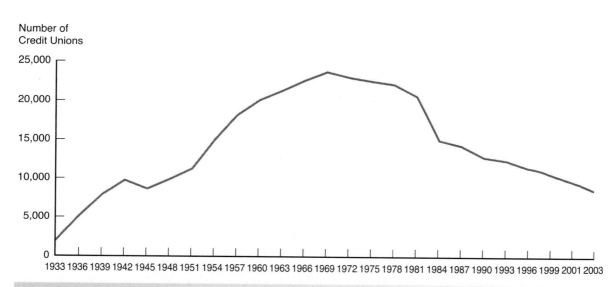

FIGURE 7 *Number of Credit Unions, 1933–2003*

Source: http://ncua.gov/ref/statistics/midyear2003.pdf.

Trade Associations   Because credit unions are so small, they often lack the economies of scale necessary to service their customers at competitive costs. For example, a credit union with only $5 million of deposits cannot afford the costs of maintaining a computer center for processing checks and sending out statements. Similarly, most credit unions cannot afford to maintain their own automated teller machine network. One solution to this problem is the use of **trade associations,** groups of credit unions that have organized together. These associations provide services to large numbers of credit unions.

The largest of the trade associations is the Credit Union National Association. CUNA has a number of affiliations that provide specific services:

- CUNA Service Group provides new products for credit unions.
- CUNA Supply, Inc., provides for bulk purchases of supplies to lower supply costs.
- ICU Services, Inc., provides various investment options, automated payment services, credit card programs, and IRA plans.
- CUNA Mortgage provides a liquidity facility for mortgage lending by credit unions.

In addition to using trade associations, many credit unions contract with commercial banks for data processing services. Checks written by credit union customers are automatically routed to the bank, which takes the funds out of a credit union account. The bank then provides a transaction history in electronic form that is given to the credit union. The tie-in with the servicing bank may be so close that the credit union's teller terminals are linked to the bank's computer system, just like the bank's own teller terminals. The credit union customer may never be aware that a bank is involved in the process.

Sources of Funds

Over 72% of credit union funds come from customer savings and share draft accounts. Unlike commercial banks, credit unions seldom purchase funds in the capital or money markets. Four main types of accounts are offered by credit unions: regular share accounts, share certificates, share draft accounts, and money market accounts. Figure 8 shows the distribution of funds among the share accounts.

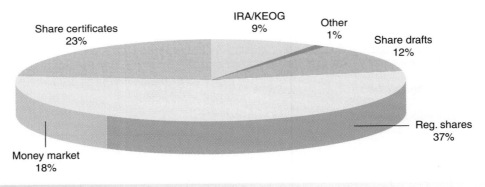

FIGURE 8   *Share Distribution*

Source: http://www.ncua.gov/ref/statistics/midyear2004.pdf.

Regular Share Accounts   Regular share accounts are savings accounts. Customers cannot write checks against these accounts, although they can withdraw funds without giving prior notice or incurring any penalties. These accounts make up about 37% of total deposits. Customers do not receive interest on these accounts. Instead they receive dividends that are not guaranteed in advance but are estimated. The credit union tries to pay the estimated amount.

Share Certificates   Share certificates are comparable to CDs offered by commercial banks. The customer agrees to leave the funds on deposit with the credit union for a specified length of time and in exchange receives a higher return.

Share Draft Accounts   Share drafts were first developed in 1974 and made legal nationally in 1980. They are virtually identical to the checks written by customers of commercial banks. Share draft accounts usually pay interest and permit depositors to write share drafts against them. These accounts represent about 12% of credit union liabilities.

Capital   Credit union capital cannot be measured in the usual way because credit union share accounts are in fact equity accounts. A more meaningful approach is to measure capital as the difference between total assets and total liabilities, where liabilities include all share accounts. Using this approach, the average capital-to-asset ratio was 10.5% in June 2003. One reason for this strong capital position is that regulations require a capital-to-loan ratio of at least 10% for credit unions.

Uses of Funds

In June 2003, 61.4% of credit union assets were invested in loans. Most credit union loans are relatively small. For example, the average credit union loan in 2004 was $12,900. This is in keeping with the mission of credit unions to provide loans to small borrowers. Credit union loan losses are usually quite small. The average ratio of delinquent loans to total loans was under .75% in 2004, the lowest rate ever. This compares closely to the loan loss ratio for commercial banks. The rate of charged off loans was .72% in 2004.

The mix of loans made by credit unions demonstrates that credit unions are indeed providing a service directed at consumers. Figure 9 shows the loan distribution of the industry. We see that auto loans make up about 40% of the total loans volume.

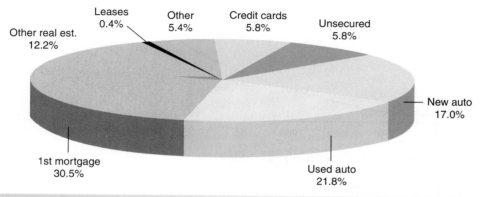

FIGURE 9 *Loan Distribution*

Source: http://www.ncua.gov/ref/statistics/midyear2004.pdf.

The balance of credit union assets are in cash, government securities, deposits at other institutions, and fixed assets. Credit unions tend not to make risky investments and are limited by regulations to certain types of investment securities that assure low risk.

Advantages and Disadvantages of Credit Unions

Figure 10 traces the membership in credit unions from 1933 to 2003. The steady increase is expected to continue because credit unions enjoy several advantages over other depository institutions. These advantages have contributed toward their growth and popularity.

- *Employer support.* Many employers recognize that it is in their own best interest to help their employees manage their funds. This motivates the firm to support the employee credit union. Businesses will frequently provide free office space, utilities, and other help to the credit unions.
- *Tax advantage.* Because credit unions are exempt from paying taxes by federal regulation, this savings can be passed on to the members in the form of higher dividends or lower account-servicing costs.
- *Strong trade associations.* Credit unions have formed many trade associations, which lower their costs and provide the means to offer services the institutions could not otherwise offer.

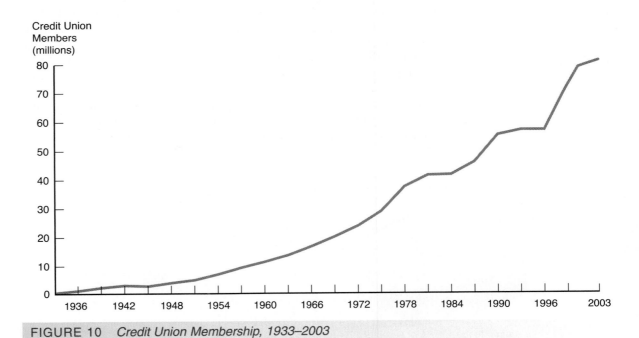

FIGURE 10   *Credit Union Membership, 1933–2003*

Source: http://www.ncua.gov/ref/statistics/midyear2004.pdf.

The main disadvantage of credit unions is that the common bond requirement keeps many of them very small. The cost disadvantage can prevent them from offering the range of services available from larger institutions. This disadvantage is not entirely equalized by the use of trade associations.

The Future of Credit Unions

Credit unions are well positioned to continue their growth as a significant provider of financial services to consumers. Figure 11 shows that credit union assets increased from $282 billion to $599.2 billion over a ten-year period, a 7.8% compounded annual growth rate. Though credit unions are likely to remain small compared to other financial institutions, their cost advantages give them a competitive edge that will continue to attract consumer business.

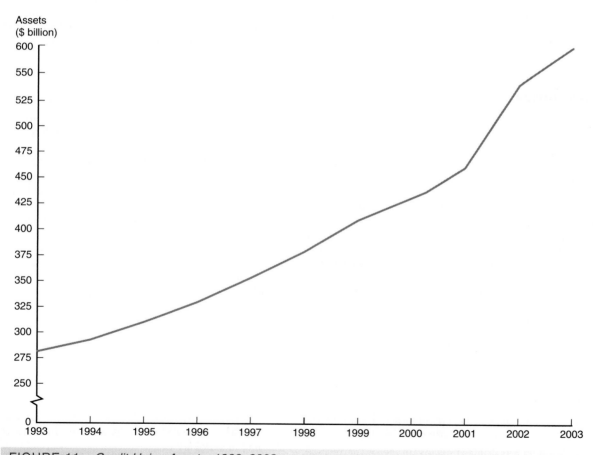

FIGURE 11 *Credit Union Assets, 1993–2003*

Source: http://www.ncua.gov/ref/statistics/midyear2004.pdf.

Summary

1. Congress mandated that savings and loans and mutual savings banks provide mortgage loan opportunities for consumers. For most of the twentieth century, they profitably satisfied this need.

2. In the late 1970s and the 1980s, savings and loans lost money because interest rates on their deposits rose while the return on their mortgage portfolios was fixed. These losses initially led to deregulation. Savings and loans continued to lose money despite regulatory reform.

3. Due to mounting losses among savings and loans the industry was reregulated in 1987. It has since recovered in terms of both profitability and net worth. The industry continues to consolidate, though total assets are remaining about constant. It is too early to determine whether the industry will simply merge with commercial banks or remain independent.

4. Credit unions were established to serve the public's demand for consumer-type loans. They are unique because members must satisfy a common bond requirement to join. This common bond requirement has restricted the growth of credit unions. Most are small compared to savings and loans and commercial banks.

5. Because of their small size, credit unions have benefited by forming cooperative organizations. These coops, such as CUNA, provide technical, liquidity, mortgage, and insurance services that would be impossible for the individual credit unions to have otherwise.

6. Credit unions enjoy several advantages that should keep them viable in the future. First, as nonprofit organizations, they are exempt from federal taxation. Second, many have strong support from a sponsoring company or business, which lowers the operating cost of the institution. The use of volunteers also helps keep costs low.

Key Terms

Central Liquidity Facility (CLF), *p. 504*

common bond membership, *p. 502*

credit union, *p. 501*

Credit Union National Association (CUNA), p. 501

Credit Union National Extension Bureau (CUNEB), *p. 501*

Federal Credit Union Act, *p. 501*

Federal Home Loan Bank Act of 1932, *p. 487*

Federal Home Loan Bank Board (FHLBB), *p. 487*

Federal Savings and Loan Insurance Corporation (FSLIC), *p. 487*

Financial Institutions Reform Act, *p. 504*

Financial Institutions Reform, Recovery, and Enforcement Act (FIRREA), *p. 493*

mutual bank, *p. 486*

National Credit Union Act of 1970, *p. 503*

National Credit Union Administration (NCUA), *p. 503*

National Credit Union Share Insurance Fund (NCUSIF), *p. 503*

passbook savings account, *p. 497*

regulatory forbearance, *p. 489*

Resolution Trust Corporation (RTC), *p. 493*

trade association, *p. 506*

U.S. Central Credit Union, *p. 504*

Questions

1. How does the mutual form of ownership differ from the typical corporate form of ownership?

2. What is the primary disadvantage of the mutual form of ownership?

3. What are the primary assets of savings and loan institutions?

4. Name three factors that led to the thrift crisis.

5. Why did depositors not object to the risky loans and investments made by savings and loans in the early and mid-1980s?

6. How was the thrift crisis ended?

7. What is the most common measure of the capital adequacy of a financial institution?

8. What has been the trend in S&L net income since the mid-1990s?

9. What type of customers are credit unions focused on servicing?

10. What is the purpose of the Credit Union National Association (CUNA)?

11. Describe the common bond membership rule.

12. Why does the commercial banking lobby object to the nonprofit, tax-exempt status enjoyed by credit unions?

13. Are most credit unions larger or smaller than commercial banks? Why?

14. What are share accounts, share certificates, and share drafts?

15. What are the primary advantages enjoyed by credit unions?

16. Why is regulatory forbearance a dangerous strategy for a deposit insurance agency?

17. Why did the S&L crisis not occur unitl the 1980s?

18. The FIRREA legislation in 1989 is the most comprehensive thrift legislation since the 1930s. Describe its major features.

19. Some advocates of campaign finance reform believe that government funding of political campaigns and restrictions on campaign financing might reduce the principal-agent problem in our political system. Do you agree?

20. How can the S&L crisis be blamed on the principal-agent problem?

Web Exercises

Savings Associations and Credit Unions

1. Like banks, thrifts provide a great deal of summary information to the public. One of the most extensive sites for thrift information is at **http://www. ots.treas.gov/**. Select "Industry Performance" under "Data and Research" on the left margin of the site. Now go to "Select Indicator" on the site to answer the following questions.

   a. What is the return on average assets for the most recent time period?

   b. What is the return on average equity for the most recent time period?

   c. How many thrift institutions are reporting to the OTS during the most recent time period?

2. Go to **http://www.ncua.gov/**. This is the home page of the National Credit Union Administration. Click on the history of the credit union industry.

   a. According to the NCUA, what features define a credit union?

   b. What was the name of the first credit union opened in the United States in 1909?

   c. In what year was the Federal Credit Union Act signed into law?

CHAPTER 20

Banking Regulation

Preview

As we have seen in earlier chapters, the financial system is among the most heavily regulated sectors of the economy, and banks are among the most heavily regulated of financial institutions. In this chapter we develop an economic analysis of why regulation of banking takes the form it does.

Unfortunately, the regulatory process may not always work very well, as evidenced by recent crises in the banking systems, not only in the United States but in many countries throughout the world. Here we also use our analysis of banking regulation to explain the worldwide crises in banking and how the regulatory system can be reformed to prevent future disasters.

Asymmetric Information and Bank Regulation

Bank regulation information is available at www.ny.frb.org/ Pihome/regs. html. You can access regulatory publications of the Federal Reserve Board at www.federalre serve.gov/Regu lations/default. htm

In earlier chapters we have seen how asymmetric information, the fact that different parties in a financial contract do not have the same information, leads to adverse selection and moral hazard problems that have an important impact on our financial system. The concepts of asymmetric information, adverse selection, and moral hazard are especially useful in understanding why government has chosen the form of banking regulation we see in the United States and in other countries. There are seven basic categories of banking regulation: the government safety net, restrictions on bank asset holdings and capital requirements, chartering and bank examination, disclosure requirements, consumer protection, restrictions on competition, and separation of the banking and securities industries.

Government Safety Net: Deposit Insurance and the FDIC

As we saw in Chapter 15, banks are particularly well suited to solving adverse selection and moral hazard problems because they make private loans that help avoid the free-rider problem. However, this solution to the free-rider problem creates another asymmetric information problem because depositors lack information about the quality of these private loans. This asymmetric information problem leads to two reasons why the banking system might not function well.

First, before the FDIC started operations in 1934, a bank failure (in which a bank is unable to meet its obligations to pay its depositors and other creditors and so must go out of business) meant that depositors would have to wait to get their deposit funds until the bank was liquidated (until its assets had been turned into cash); at that time, they would be paid only a fraction of the value of their deposits. Unable to learn if bank managers were taking on too much risk or were outright crooks, depositors would be reluctant to put money in the bank, thus making banking institutions less viable. Second is that depositors' lack of information about the quality of bank assets can lead to bank panics, which, as we saw in Chapter 15, can have serious harmful consequences for the economy. To see this, consider the following situation. There is no deposit insurance, and an adverse shock hits the economy. As a result of the shock, 5% of the banks have such large losses on loans that they become insolvent (have a negative net worth and so are bankrupt). Because of asymmetric information, depositors are unable to tell whether their bank is a good bank or one of the 5% that are insolvent. Depositors at bad *and* good banks recognize that they may not get back 100 cents on the dollar for their deposits and will want to withdraw them. Indeed, because banks operate on a "sequential service constraint" (a first-come, first-served basis), depositors have a very strong incentive to show up at the bank first because if they are last in line, the bank may run out of funds and they will get nothing. Uncertainty about the health of the banking system in general can lead to runs on banks both good and bad, and the failure of one bank can hasten the failure of others (referred to as the *contagion effect*). If nothing is done to restore the public's confidence, a bank panic can ensue.

Indeed, bank panics were a fact of American life in the nineteenth and early twentieth centuries, with major ones occurring every 20 years or so in 1819, 1837, 1857, 1873, 1884, 1893, 1907, and 1930–1933. Bank failures were a serious problem even during the boom years of the 1920s, when the number of bank failures averaged around 600 per year.

A government safety net for depositors can short-circuit runs on banks and bank panics, and by providing protection for the depositor, it can overcome reluctance to put funds in the banking system. One form of the safety net is deposit insurance, a guarantee such as that provided by the Federal Deposit Insurance Corporation (FDIC) in the United States in which depositors are paid off in full on the first $100,000 they have deposited in the bank no matter what happens to the bank. With fully insured deposits, depositors don't need to run to the bank to make withdrawals—even if they are worried about the bank's health—because their deposits will be worth 100 cents on the dollar no matter what. From 1930 to 1933, the years immediately preceding the creation of the FDIC, the number of bank failures averaged over 2000 per year. After the establishment of the FDIC in 1934, bank failures averaged fewer than 15 per year until 1981.

The FDIC uses two primary methods to handle a failed bank. In the first, called the *payoff method*, the FDIC allows the bank to fail and pays off deposits up to the $100,000 insurance limit (with funds acquired from the insurance premiums paid by the banks that have bought FDIC insurance). After the bank has been liquidated, the FDIC lines up with other creditors of the bank and is paid its share of the proceeds from the liquidated assets. Typically, when the payoff method is used, account holders with deposits in excess of the $100,000 limit get back more than 90 cents on the dollar, although the process can take several years to complete.

In the second method, called the *purchase and assumption method*, the FDIC reorganizes the bank, typically by finding a willing merger partner who assumes (takes over) all of the failed bank's deposits so that no depositor loses a penny. The FDIC may help the merger partner by providing it with subsidized loans or by buying some of the failed bank's weaker loans. The net effect of the purchase and assumption method is that the FDIC has guaranteed *all* deposits, not just those under the $100,000 limit. The purchase and assumption method was the FDIC's most common procedure for dealing with a failed bank before new banking legislation in 1991.

Deposit insurance is not the only way in which governments provide a safety net for depositors. In other countries, governments have often stood ready to provide support to domestic banks when they face runs even in the absence of explicit deposit insurance. This support is sometimes provided by lending from the central bank to troubled institutions and is often referred to as the "lender of last resort" role of the central bank. In other cases, funds are provided directly by the government to troubled institutions, or these institutions are taken over by the government and the government then guarantees that depositors will receive their money in full. However, in recent years, government deposit insurance has been growing in popularity and has spread to many countries throughout the world. Whether this trend is desirable is discussed in the "Global" box.

Moral Hazard and the Government Safety Net   Although a government safety net has been successful at protecting depositors and preventing bank panics, it is a mixed blessing. The most serious drawback of the government safety net stems from moral hazard, the incentives of one party to a transaction to engage in activities detrimental to the other party. Moral hazard is an important concern in insurance

GLOBAL

The Spread of Government Deposit Insurance Throughout the World: Is This a Good Thing?

For the first 30 years after federal deposit insurance was established in the United States, only 6 countries emulated the United States and adopted deposit insurance. However, this began to change in the late 1960s, with the trend accelerating in the 1990s, when the number of countries adopting deposit insurance doubled to over 70. Government deposit insurance has taken off throughout the world because of growing concern about the health of banking systems, particularly after the increasing number of banking crises in recent years (documented at the end of the chapter). Has this spread of deposit insurance been a good thing? Has it helped improve the performance of the financial system and prevent banking crises?

The answer seems to be no under many circumstances. Research at the World Bank has found that on average, the adoption of explicit government deposit insurance is associated with less banking sector stability and a higher incidence of banking crises.* Furthermore, on average it seems to retard financial development. However, the negative effects of deposit insurance appear only in countries with weak institutional environments: an absence of rule of law, ineffective regulation and supervision of the financial sector, and high corruption. This is exactly what might be expected because, as we will see later in this chapter, a strong institutional environment is needed to limit the incentives for banks to engage in excessively risky behavior created by deposit insurance. The problem is that developing a strong institutional environment may be very difficult to achieve in many emerging market countries. This leaves us with the following conclusion: Adoption of deposit insurance may be exactly the wrong medicine for promoting stability and efficiency of banking systems in emerging market countries.

_____

*See World Bank, *Finance for Growth: Policy Choices in a Volatile World* (Oxford: World Bank and Oxford University Press, 2001).

arrangements in general because the existence of insurance provides increased incentives for taking risks that might result in an insurance payoff. For example, some drivers with automobile collision insurance that has a low deductible might be more likely to drive recklessly because if they get into an accident, the insurance company pays most of the costs for damage and repairs.

Moral hazard is a prominent concern in government arrangements to provide a safety net. Because with a safety net depositors know that they will not suffer losses if a bank fails, they do not impose the discipline of the marketplace on banks by withdrawing deposits when they suspect that the bank is taking on too much risk. Consequently, banks with a government safety net have an incentive to take on greater risks than they otherwise would.

Adverse Selection and the Government Safety Net   A further problem with a government safety net like deposit insurance arises because of adverse selection, the fact that the people who are most likely to produce the adverse outcome insured against (bank failure) are those who most want to take advantage of the insurance. For example, bad drivers are more likely than good drivers to take out automobile collision insurance with a low deductible. Because depositors protected by a government safety net have little reason to impose discipline on the bank, risk-loving entrepreneurs might find the banking industry a particularly attractive one to enter—they know that they will be able to engage in highly risky activities. Even worse, because protected depositors have so little reason to monitor the bank's activities, without government intervention outright crooks might also find banking an attractive industry for their activities because it is easy for them to get away with fraud and embezzlement.

"Too Big to Fail"   The moral hazard created by a government safety net and the desire to prevent bank failures have presented bank regulators with a particular quandary. Because the failure of a very large bank makes it more likely that a major financial disruption will occur, bank regulators are naturally reluctant to allow a big bank to fail and cause losses to its depositors. Indeed, consider Continental Illinois, one of the ten largest banks in the United States when it became insolvent in May 1984. Not only did the FDIC guarantee depositors up to the $100,000 insurance limit, but it also guaranteed accounts exceeding $100,000 and even prevented losses for Continental Illinois bondholders. Shortly thereafter, the Comptroller of the Currency (the regulator of national banks) testified to Congress that the FDIC's policy was to regard the 11 largest banks as "too big to fail"—in other words, the FDIC would bail them out so that no depositor or creditor would suffer a loss. The FDIC would do this by using the purchase and assumption method, giving the insolvent bank a large infusion of capital and then finding a willing merger partner to take over the bank and its deposits. The too-big-to-fail policy has been extended to big banks that are not even among the 11 largest. (Note that "too big to fail" is somewhat misleading because when a bank is closed or merged into another bank, the managers are usually fired, and the stockholders in the bank lose their investment.)

One problem with the too-big-to-fail policy is that it increases the moral hazard incentives for big banks. If the FDIC were willing to close a bank using the alternative payoff method, paying depositors only up to the $100,000 limit, large depositors with more than $100,000 would suffer losses if the bank failed. Thus they would have an incentive to monitor the bank by examining the bank's activities closely and pulling their money out if the bank was taking on too much risk.

To prevent such a loss of deposits, the bank would be more likely to engage in less risky activities. However, once large depositors know that a bank is too big to fail, they have no incentive to monitor the bank and pull out their deposits when it takes on too much risk: No matter what the bank does, large depositors will not suffer any losses. The result of the too-big-to-fail policy is that big banks might take on even greater risks, thereby making bank failures more likely.[1]

Financial Consolidation and the Government Safety Net With the passage of the Riegle-Neal Interstate Banking and Branching and Efficiency Act of 1994 and the Gramm-Leach-Bliley Financial Services Modernization Act in 1999, financial consolidation has been proceeding at a rapid pace, leading to both larger and more complex banking organizations. Financial consolidation poses two challenges to banking regulation because of the existence of the government safety net. First, the increased size of banks as a result of financial consolidation increases the too-big-to-fail problem because there will now be more large institutions whose failure exposes the financial system to systemic (systemwide) risk. Thus, more banking institutions are likely to be treated as too big to fail, and the increased moral hazard incentives for these large institutions to take on greater risk can then increase the fragility of the financial system. Second, financial consolidation of banks with other financial service firms means that the government safety net may be extended to new activities such as securities underwriting, insurance, or real estate activities, thereby increasing incentives for greater risk taking in these activities, which can also weaken the fabric of the financial system. Limiting the moral hazard incentives for larger, more complex, financial organizations that are resulting from recent changes in legislation will be one of the key issues facing banking regulators in the future.

Restrictions on Asset Holdings and Bank Capital Requirements

As we have seen, the moral hazard associated with a government safety net encourages too much risk taking on the part of banks. Bank regulations that restrict asset holdings and bank capital requirements are directed at minimizing this moral hazard, which can cost the taxpayers dearly.

Even in the absence of a government safety net, banks still have the incentive to take on too much risk. Risky assets may provide the bank with higher earnings when they pay off; but if they do not pay off and the bank fails, depositors are left holding the bag. If depositors were able to monitor the bank easily by acquiring information on its risk-taking activities, they would immediately withdraw their deposits if the bank was taking on too much risk. To prevent such a loss of deposits, the bank would be more likely to reduce its risk-taking activities. Unfortunately, acquiring information on a bank's activities to learn how much risk the bank is taking can be a difficult task. Hence most depositors are incapable of imposing discipline that might prevent banks from engaging in risky activities. A strong

---

[1]Recent evidence reveals, as our analysis predicts, that large banks have taken on riskier loans than smaller banks and that this has led to higher loan losses for big banks; see John Boyd and Mark Gertler, "U.S. Commercial Banking: Trends, Cycles and Policy," *NBER Macroeconomics Annual*, 1993, pp. 319–368.

rationale for government regulation to reduce risk taking on the part of banks therefore existed even before the establishment of federal deposit insurance.

Bank regulations that restrict banks from holding risky assets such as common stock are a direct means of making banks avoid too much risk. Bank regulations also promote diversification, which reduces risk by limiting the amount of loans in particular categories or to individual borrowers. Requirements that banks have sufficient bank capital are another way to change the bank's incentives to take on less risk. When a bank is forced to hold a large amount of equity capital, the bank has more to lose if it fails and is thus more likely to pursue less risky activities.

Bank capital requirements take three forms. The first type is based on the so-called **leverage ratio,** the amount of capital divided by the bank's total assets. To be classified as well capitalized, a bank's leverage ratio must exceed 5%; a lower leverage ratio, especially one below 3%, triggers increased regulatory restrictions on the bank. Throughout most of the 1980s, minimum bank capital in the United States was set solely by specifying a minimum leverage ratio.

In the wake of the Continental Illinois and savings and loans bailouts, regulators in the United States and the rest of the world have become increasingly worried about banks' holdings of risky assets and about the increase in banks' **off-balance-sheet activities,** activities that involve trading financial instruments and generating income from fees, which do not appear on bank balance sheets but nevertheless expose banks to risk. An agreement among banking officials from industrialized nations has set up the **Basel Committee on Banking Supervision** (because it meets under the auspices of the Bank for International Settlements in Basel, Switzerland), which has implemented the so-called **Basel Accord** on risk-based capital requirements. The Basel Accord, which required that banks hold as capital at least 8% of their risk-weighted assets, has been adopted by over 100 countries, including the United States. Assets and off-balance-sheet activities were allocated into four categories, each with a different weight to reflect the degree of credit risk. The first category carried a zero weight and included items that have little default risk, such as reserves and government securities in the OECD (industrialized) countries. The second category had a 20% weight and included claims on banks in OECD countries. The third category had a weight of 50% and included municipal bonds and residential mortgages. The fourth category had the maximum weight of 100% and included loans to consumers and corporations. Off-balance-sheet activities are treated in a similar manner by assigning a credit-equivalent percentage that converts them to on-balance-sheet items to which the appropriate risk weight applies. The 1996 Market Risk Amendment to the Accord set minimum capital requirements for risks in banks' trading accounts.

Over time, limitations of the Accord have become apparent because the regulatory measure of bank risk as stipulated by the risk weights can differ substantially from the actual risk the bank faces. This has resulted in what is known as **regulatory arbitrage,** in which banks keep on their books assets that have the same risk-based capital requirement but are relatively risky, such as a loan to a company with a very low credit rating, while taking off their books low-risk assets such as a loan to a company with a very high credit rating. The Basel Accord could thus lead to increased risk taking, the opposite of its intent. To address these limitations, the Basel Committee on Bank Supervision has released proposals for a new capital accord, often referred to as Basel 2, but it is not clear if it is workable and when it will be implemented (see the "Mini-Case" box).

MINI-CASE

Basel 2: Is It Spinning Out of Control?

Starting in June 1999, the Basel Committee on Banking Supervision has released several proposals to reform the original 1988 Basel Accord. Basel 2 is based on three pillars.

Pillar 1 intends to link capital requirements more closely to actual risk. It does this by specifying many more categories of risk with different weights in its so-called standardized approach and allows sophisticated banks to instead pursue an internal ratings-based approach that allows banks to use their own models of credit risk. Pillar 2 focuses on strengthening the supervisory process, particularly in assessing the quality of risk management in banking institutions and whether these institutions have adequate procedures to determine how much capital they need. Pillar 3 focuses on improving market discipline by increased disclosure such as details about the bank's credit exposures, its amount of reserves and capital, who controls the bank, and how a well a bank's internal ratings system operates.

Although Basel 2 makes great strides in the direction of limiting excessive risk taking by banking institutions, it has come at a cost of greatly increasing the complexity of the Accord. The document describing the original Basel Accord was 26 pages, while the second draft of Basel 2 issued in January 2001 is over 500 pages long. The original timetable was for the final round of consultation to be finished by the end of May 2001, with the new rules taking effect by 2004. However, criticism from banks, trade associations and national regulators has led to several postponements, with the Accord now scheduled to be implemented by the end of 2006. Will the increasing complexity of the Basel Accord lead to further postponements, raising the question of whether Basel 2 will actually be put into operation?

The Basel Committee's work on bank capital requirements is never ending. As the banking industry changes, the regulation of bank capital must change with it to ensure the safety and soundness of the banking institutions.

Bank Supervision: Chartering and Examination

Overseeing who operates banks and how they are operated, referred to as **bank supervision** or more generally as **prudential supervision,** is an important method for reducing adverse selection and moral hazard in the banking business. Because banks can be used by crooks or overambitious entrepreneurs to engage in highly speculative activities, such undesirable people would be eager to run a bank. (Charles Keating Jr., discussed in Chapter 19, was one such person.) Chartering banks is one method for preventing this adverse selection problem; through chartering, proposals for new banks are screened to prevent undesirable people from controlling them.

Regular on-site bank examinations, which allow regulators to monitor whether the bank is complying with capital requirements and restrictions on asset holdings, also function to limit moral hazard. Bank examiners give banks a so-called *CAMELS rating* (the acronym is based on the six areas assessed: capital adequacy, asset quality, management, earnings, liquidity, and sensitivity to market risk). With this information about a bank's activities, regulators can enforce regulations by taking such formal actions as *cease and desist orders* to alter the bank's behavior or even close a bank if its CAMELS rating is sufficiently low. Actions taken to reduce moral hazard by restricting banks from taking on too much risk help reduce the adverse selection problem further because with less opportunity for risk taking, risk-loving entrepreneurs will be less likely to be attracted to the banking industry.

Note that the methods regulators use to cope with adverse selection and moral hazard have their counterparts in private financial markets (see Chapter 15). Chartering is similar to the screening of potential borrowers, regulations restricting risky asset holdings are similar to restrictive covenants that prevent borrowing firms from engaging in risky investment activities, bank capital requirements act like restrictive covenants that require minimum amounts of net worth for borrowing firms, and regular bank examinations are similar to the monitoring of borrowers by lending institutions.

A commercial bank obtains a charter either from the Comptroller of the Currency (in the case of a national bank) or from a state banking authority (in the case of a state bank). To obtain a charter, the people planning to organize the bank must submit an application that shows how they plan to operate the bank. In evaluating the application, the regulatory authority looks at whether the bank is likely to be sound by examining the quality of the bank's intended management, the likely earnings of the bank, and the amount of the bank's initial capital. Before 1980, the chartering agency typically explored the issue of whether the community needed a new bank. Often a new bank charter would not be granted if existing banks in a community would be severely hurt by its presence. Today this anticompetitive stance (justified by the desire to prevent bank failures of existing banks) is no longer as strong in the chartering agencies.

Once a bank has been chartered, it is required to file periodic (usually quarterly) *call reports* that reveal the bank's assets and liabilities, income and dividends, ownership, foreign exchange operations, and other details. The bank is also subject to examination by the bank regulatory agencies to ascertain its financial condition at least once a year. To avoid duplication of effort, the three federal agencies work together and usually accept each other's examinations. This means that, typically, national banks are examined by the Office of the Comptroller of the Currency, the state banks that are members of the Federal Reserve System are examined by the Fed, and nonmember state banks are examined by the FDIC.

Bank examinations are conducted by bank examiners, who sometimes make unannounced visits to the bank (so that nothing can be "swept under the rug" in anticipation of their examination). The examiners study a bank's books to see whether it is complying with the rules and regulations that apply to its holdings of assets. If a bank is holding securities or loans that are too risky, the bank examiner can force the bank to get rid of them. If a bank examiner decides that a loan is unlikely to be repaid, the examiner can force the bank to declare the loan worthless (to write off the loan). If, after examining the bank, the examiner feels that it does not have sufficient capital or has engaged in dishonest practices, the bank can be declared a "problem bank" and will be subject to more frequent examinations.

A New Trend in Bank Supervision: Assessment of Risk Management

Traditionally, on-site bank examinations have focused primarily on assessment of the quality of the bank's balance sheet at a point in time and whether it complies with capital requirements and restrictions on asset holdings. Although the traditional focus is important for reducing excessive risk taking by banks, it is no longer felt to be adequate in today's world in which financial innovation has produced new markets and instruments that make it easy for banks and their employees to make huge bets easily and quickly. In this new financial environment, a bank that is quite healthy at a particular point in time can be driven into insolvency extremely rapidly from trading losses, as forcefully demonstrated by the failure of Barings in 1995 (discussed in Chapter 17). Thus an examination that focuses only on a bank's position at a point in time may not be effective in indicating whether a bank will in fact be taking on excessive risk in the near future.

This change in the financial environment for banking institutions has resulted in a major shift in thinking about the bank supervisory process throughout the world. Bank examiners are now placing far greater emphasis on evaluating the soundness of a bank's management processes with regard to controlling risk. This shift in thinking was reflected in a new focus on risk management in the Federal Reserve System's 1993 guidelines to examiners on trading and derivatives activities. The focus was expanded and formalized in the Trading Activities Manual issued early in 1994, which provided bank examiners with tools to evaluate risk management systems. In late 1995, the Federal Reserve and the Comptroller of the Currency announced that they would be assessing risk management processes at the banks they supervise. Now bank examiners give a separate risk management rating from 1 to 5 that feeds into the overall management rating as part of the CAMELS system. Four elements of sound risk management are assessed to come up with the risk management rating: (1) The quality of oversight provided by the board of directors and senior management, (2) the adequacy of policies and limits for all activities that present significant risks, (3) the quality of the risk measurement and monitoring systems, and (4) the adequacy of internal controls to prevent fraud or unauthorized activities on the part of employees.

This shift toward focusing on management processes is also reflected in recent guidelines adopted by the U.S. bank regulatory authorities to deal with interest-rate risk. At one point, U.S. regulators were contemplating requiring banks to use a standard model to calculate the amount of capital a bank would need to have to allow for the interest-rate risk it bears. Because coming up with a one-size-fits-all model that would work for all banks has proved difficult, the regulatory agencies have instead decided to adopt guidelines for the management of interest-rate risk, although bank examiners will continue to consider interest-rate risk in deciding on the bank's capital requirements. These guidelines require the bank's board of directors to establish interest-rate risk limits, appoint officials of the bank to manage this risk, and monitor the bank's risk exposure. The guidelines also require that senior management of a bank develop formal risk management policies and procedures, to ensure that the board of directors' risk limits are not violated and to implement internal controls to monitor interest-rate risk and compliance with the board's directives.

Disclosure Requirements

The free-rider problem described in Chapter 15 indicates that individual depositors and other bank creditors will not have enough incentive to produce private information about the quality of a bank's assets. To ensure that there is better information for depositors and the marketplace, regulators can require that banks adhere to certain standard accounting principles and disclose a wide range of information that helps the market assess the quality of a bank's portfolio and the amount of the bank's exposure to risk. More public information about the risks incurred by banks and the quality of their portfolio can better enable stockholders, creditors, and depositors to evaluate and monitor banks and so act as a deterrent to excessive risk taking. This view is consistent with a recent position paper issued by the Eurocurrency Standing Committee of the G-10 Central Banks, which recommends that estimates of financial risk generated by firms' own internal risk management systems be adapted for public disclosure purposes.[2] Such information would supplement disclosures based on traditional accounting conventions by providing information about risk exposure and risk management that is not normally included in conventional balance sheet and income statement reports.

Consumer Protection

The existence of asymmetric information also suggests that consumers may not have enough information to protect themselves fully. Consumer protection regulation has taken several forms. First is "truth in lending," mandated under the Consumer Protection Act of 1969, which requires all lenders, not just banks, to provide information to consumers about the cost of borrowing including a standardized interest rate (called the annual percentage rate, or APR) and the total finance charges on the loan. The Fair Credit Billing Act of 1974 requires creditors, especially credit card issuers, to provide information on the method of assessing finance charges and requires that billing complaints be handled quickly. Both of these acts are administered by the Federal Reserve System under Regulation Z.

Congress has also passed legislation to reduce discrimination in credit markets. The Equal Credit Opportunity Act of 1974 and its extension in 1976 forbid discrimination by lenders based on race, gender, marital status, age, or national origin. It is administered by the Federal Reserve under Regulation B. The Community Reinvestment Act (CRA) of 1977 was enacted to prevent "redlining," a lender's refusal to lend in a particular area (marked off by a hypothetical red line on a map). The Community Reinvestment Act requires that banks show that they lend in all areas in which they take deposits, and if banks are found to be in noncompliance with the act, regulators can reject their applications for mergers, branching, or other new activities.

Restrictions on Competition

Increased competition can also increase moral hazard incentives for banks to take on more risk. Declining profitability as a result of increased competition could tip the incentives of bankers toward assuming greater risk in an effort to maintain former profit levels. Thus governments in many countries have instituted regulations to protect banks from competition. These regulations have taken two forms in the United States. First are restrictions on branching, such as those described in Chapter 18, which reduce competition between banks. The second form involves preventing nonbank institutions from competing with banks by engaging in banking business.

Although restricting competition may prop up the health of banks, restrictions on competition can also have serious disadvantages: They can lead to higher charges to consumers and can decrease the efficiency of banking institutions,

---

[2]See Eurocurrency Standing Committee of Central Banks of Group of Ten Countries (Fisher Group), "Discussion Paper on Public Disclosure of Markets and Credit Risks by Financial Intermediaries," September 1994, and a companion piece to this report, Federal Reserve Bank of New York, "A Discussion Paper on Public Disclosure of Risks Related to Market Activity," September 1994.

E-FINANCE

Electronic Banking: New Challenges for Bank Regulation

The advent of electronic banking has raised new concerns for banking regulation, specifically about security and privacy.

Worries about the security of electronic banking and e-money are an important barrier to their increased use. With electronic banking, you might worry that criminals might access your bank account and steal your money by moving your balances to someone else's account. Indeed, a notorious case of this happened in 1995, when a Russian computer programmer got access to Citibank's computers and moved funds electronically into his and his conspirators' accounts. Private solutions to deal with this problem have arisen with the development of more secure encryption technologies to prevent this kind of fraud. However, because bank customers are not knowledgeable about computer security issues, there is a role for the government to regulate electronic banking to make sure that encryption procedures are adequate. Similar encryption issues apply to e-money, so requirements that banks make it difficult for criminals to engage in digital counterfeiting make sense. To meet these challenges, bank examiners in the United States assess how a bank deals with the special security issues raised by electronic banking and also

oversee third-party providers of electronic banking platforms. Also, because consumers want to know that electronic banking transactions are executed correctly, bank examiners also assess the technical skills of banks in setting up electronic banking services and the bank's capabilities for dealing with problems. Another security issue of concern to bank customers is the validity of digital signatures. The Electronic Signatures in Global and National Commerce Act of 2000 makes electronic signatures as legally binding as written signatures in most circumstances.

Electronic banking also raises serious privacy concerns. Because electronic transactions can be stored on databases, banks are able to collect a huge amount of information about their customers—their assets, creditworthiness, what they purchase, and so on—that can be sold to other financial institutions and businesses. This potential invasion of our privacy rightfully makes us very nervous. To protect customers' privacy, the Gramm-Leach-Bliley Act of 1999 has limited the distribution of these data, but it does not go as far as the European Data Protection Directive, which prohibits the transfer of information about on-line transactions. How to protect consumers' privacy in our electronic age is one of the great challenges our society faces, so privacy regulations for electronic banking are likely to evolve over time.

which do not have to compete as hard. Thus although the existence of asymmetric information provides a rationale for anticompetitive regulations, it does not mean that they will be beneficial. Indeed, in recent years, the impulse of governments in industrialized countries to restrict competition has been waning. Electronic banking has raised a new set of concerns for regulators to deal with. See the "E-Finance" box for a discussion of this challenge.

Study Guide

Because so many laws regulating banking have been passed in the United States, it is hard to keep track of them all. As a study aid, Table 1 lists the major banking legislation in the twentieth century and its key provisions.

International Banking Regulation

Because asymmetric information problems in the banking industry are a fact of life throughout the world, bank regulation in other countries is similar to that in the United States. Banks are chartered and supervised by government regulators, just

The most important laws that have affected the banking industry in the United States are described at www.fdic.gov/ regulations/ laws/important/

TABLE 1   *Major Banking Legislation in the United States in the Twentieth Century*

Federal Reserve Act (1913)
Created the Federal Reserve System

McFadden Act of 1927
Put national and state banks on equal footing regarding branching
Effectively prohibited banks from branching across state lines

Banking Acts of 1933 (Glass-Steagall) and 1935
Created the FDIC
Separated commercial banking from the securities industry
Prohibited interest on checkable deposits and restricted such deposits to commercial banks
Put interest-rate ceilings on other deposits

Bank Holding Company Act (1956) and Douglas Amendment (1970)
Clarified the status of bank holding companies (BHCs)
Gave the Federal Reserve regulatory responsibility for BHCs

Depository Institutions Deregulation and Monetary Control Act (DIDMCA) of 1980
Gave thrift institutions wider latitude in activities
Approved NOW and ATS accounts nationwide
Phased out interest-rate ceilings on deposits
Imposed uniform reserve requirements on depository institutions
Eliminated usury ceilings on loans
Increased deposit insurance to $100,000 per account

Depository Institutions Act of 1982 (Garn-St Germain)
Gave the FDIC and the FSLIC emergency powers to merge banks and thrifts across state lines
Allowed depository institutions to offer money market deposit accounts (MMDAs)
Granted thrifts wider latitude in commercial and consumer lending

Competitive Equality in Banking Act (CEBA) of 1987
Provided $10.8 billion to the FSLIC
Made provisions for regulatory forbearance in depressed areas

Financial Institutions Reform, Recovery, and Enforcement Act (FIRREA) of 1989
Provided funds to resolve S&L failures
Eliminated the FSLIC and the Federal Home Loan Bank Board
Created the Office of Thrift Supervision to regulate thrifts
Created the Resolution Trust Corporation to resolve insolvent thrifts
Raised deposit insurance premiums
Reimposed restrictions on S&L activities

Federal Deposit Insurance Corporation Improvement Act (FDICIA) of 1991
Recapitalized the FDIC
Limited brokered deposits and the too-big-to-fail policy
Set provisions for prompt corrective action
Instructed the FDIC to establish risk-based premiums
Increased examinations, capital requirements, and reporting requirements
Included the Foreign Bank Supervision Enhancement Act (FBSEA), which strengthened the Fed's authority to
   supervise foreign banks

Riegle-Neal Interstate Banking and Branching Efficiency Act of 1994
Overturned prohibition of interstate banking
Allowed branching across state lines

Gramm-Leach-Bliley Financial Services Modernization Act of 1999
Repeals Glass-Steagall separation of the banking and securities industry
Allows security firms and insurance companies to purchase banks
Allows banks to underwrite securities and insurance and engage in real estate activities

as they are in the United States. Deposit insurance is also a feature of the regulatory systems in most other developed countries, although its coverage is often smaller than in the United States and is purposely not advertised. We have also seen that bank capital requirements are in the process of being standardized across countries with agreements like the Basel Accord.

Problems in Regulating International Banking

Particular problems in bank regulation occur when banks are engaged in international banking and thus can readily shift their business from one country to another. Bank regulators closely examine the domestic operations of banks in their country, but they often do not have the knowledge or ability to keep a close watch on bank operations in other countries, either by domestic banks' foreign affiliates or by foreign banks with domestic branches. In addition, when a bank operates in many countries, it is not always clear which national regulatory authority should have primary responsibility for keeping the bank from engaging in overly risky activities. The difficulties inherent in regulating international banking were highlighted by the collapse of the Bank of Credit and Commerce International (BCCI). BCCI, which was operating in more than 70 countries, including the United States and the United Kingdom, was supervised by Luxembourg, a tiny country unlikely to be up to the task. When massive fraud was discovered, the Bank of England closed BCCI down, but not before depositors and stockholders were exposed to huge losses. Cooperation among regulators in different countries and standardization of regulatory requirements provide potential solutions to the problems of regulating international banking. The world has been moving in this direction through agreements like the Basel Accords and oversight procedures announced by the Basel Committee in July 1992, which require a bank's worldwide operations to be under the scrutiny of a single home-country regulator with enhanced powers to acquire information on the bank's activities. Also, the Basel Committee ruled that regulators in other countries can restrict the operations of a foreign bank if they feel that it lacks effective oversight. Whether agreements of this type will solve the problem of regulating international banking in the future is an open question.

Summary

Asymmetric information analysis explains what types of banking regulations are needed to reduce moral hazard and adverse selection problems in the banking system. However, understanding the theory behind regulation does not mean that regulation and supervision of the banking system are easy in practice. Getting bank regulators and supervisors to do their job properly is difficult for several reasons. First, as we learned in the discussion of financial innovation in Chapter 18, in their search for profits, financial institutions have strong incentives to avoid existing regulations by loophole mining. Thus regulation applies to a moving target: Regulators are continually playing cat and mouse with financial institutions—financial institutions think up clever ways to avoid regulations, which then causes regulators to modify their regulation activities. Regulators continually face new challenges in a dynamically changing financial system, and unless they can respond rapidly to change, they may not be able to keep financial institutions from taking on excessive risk. This problem can be exacerbated if regulators and supervisors do not have the resources or expertise to keep up with clever people in financial institutions who think up ways to hide what they are doing or ways to get around the existing regulations.

Bank regulation and supervision are difficult for two other reasons. In the regulation and supervision game, the devil is in the details. Subtle differences in the details may have unintended consequences; unless regulators get the regulation and supervision just right, they may be unable to prevent excessive risk taking. In addition, regulators and supervisors may be subject to political pressure not to do their jobs properly. For all these reasons, there is no guarantee that bank regulators and supervisors will be successful in promoting a healthy financial system. Indeed, as we will see, bank regulation and supervision have not always worked well, leading to banking crises in the United States and throughout the world.

The 1980s U.S. Banking Crisis

Before the 1980s, federal deposit insurance seemed to work exceedingly well. In contrast to the pre-1934 period, when bank failures were common and depositors frequently suffered losses, the period from 1934 to 1980 was one in which bank failures were a rarity, averaging about 15 a year for commercial banks. After 1981, this rosy picture changed dramatically. Failures of commercial banks climbed to levels more than ten times greater than in earlier years, as can be seen in Figure 1. Why did this happen? How did a deposit insurance system that seemed to be working well for half a century find itself in so much trouble?

The story starts with the burst of financial innovation in the 1960s, 1970s, and early 1980s. As we saw in Chapter 18, financial innovation decreased the profitability of certain traditional business for commercial banks. Banks now faced

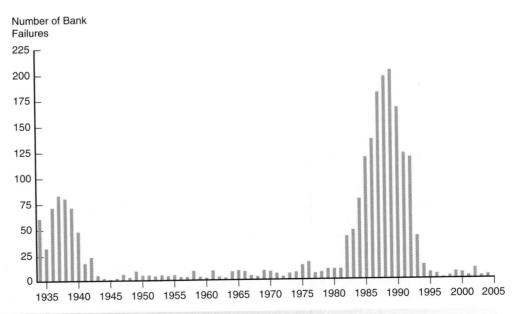

FIGURE 1   *Bank Failures in the United States, 1934–2004*

Source: www2.fdic.gov/book/historical/index.html

increased competition for their sources of funds from new financial institutions such as money market mutual funds while they were losing commercial lending business to the commercial paper market and securitization.

With the decreasing profitability of their traditional business, by the mid-1980s commercial banks were forced to seek out new and potentially risky business to keep their profits up, by placing a greater percentage of their total loans in real estate and in credit extended to assist corporate takeovers and leveraged buyouts (called *highly leveraged transaction loans*).

The existence of deposit insurance increased moral hazard for banks because insured depositors had little incentive to keep the banks from taking on too much risk. Regardless of how much risk banks were taking, deposit insurance guaranteed that depositors would not suffer any losses.

Adding fuel to the fire, financial innovation produced new financial instruments that widened the scope for risk taking. New markets in financial futures, junk bonds, swaps, and other instruments made it easier for banks to take on extra risk—making the moral hazard problem more severe.

In addition, the Depository Institutions Deregulation and Monetary Control Act of 1980 increased the mandated amount of federal deposit insurance from $40,000 per account to $100,000 and phased out Regulation Q deposit-rate ceilings. Banks that wanted to pursue rapid growth and take on risky projects could now attract the necessary funds by issuing larger-denomination insured certificates of deposit with interest rates much higher than those being offered by their competitors. Without deposit insurance, high interest rates would not have induced depositors to provide the high-rolling banks with funds because of the realistic expectation that they might not get the funds back. But with deposit insurance, the government was guaranteeing that the deposits were safe, so depositors were more than happy to make deposits in banks with the highest interest rates.

As a result of these forces, commercial banks did take on excessive risks and began to suffer substantial losses. The outcome was that bank failures rose to a level of 200 per year by the late 1980s. The resulting losses for the FDIC meant that it would have depleted its Bank Insurance Fund by 1992, requiring that this fund be recapitalized. Although the Financial Institutions Reform, Recovery, and Enforcement Act (FIRREA) of 1989 (described in Chapter 19) did not focus on the underlying adverse selection and moral hazard problems created by deposit insurance, it did, however, mandate that the U.S. Treasury produce a comprehensive study and plan for reform of the federal deposit insurance system. After this study appeared in 1991, Congress passed the Federal Deposit Insurance Corporation Improvement Act (FDICIA), which engendered major reforms in the bank regulatory system.

Federal Deposit Insurance Corporation Improvement Act of 1991

FDICIA's provisions were designed to serve two purposes: to recapitalize the Bank Insurance Fund of the FDIC and to reform the deposit insurance and regulatory system so that taxpayer losses would be minimized.

FDICIA recapitalized the Bank Insurance Fund by increasing the FDIC's ability to borrow from the Treasury and mandated that the FDIC assess higher deposit insurance premiums until it could pay back its loans and achieve a level of reserves in its insurance funds that would equal 1.25% of insured deposits.

The bill reduced the scope of deposit insurance in several ways, but the most important one is that the too-big-to-fail doctrine has been substantially limited: The FDIC must now close failed banks using the least-costly method, thus making it far more likely that uninsured depositors will suffer losses. An exception to this provision, whereby a bank would be declared too big to fail so that all depositors, both insured and uninsured, would be fully protected, would be allowed only if not doing so would "have serious adverse effects on economic conditions or financial stability." Furthermore, to invoke the too-big-to-fail policy, a two-thirds majority of both the Board of Governors of the Federal Reserve System and the directors of the FDIC, as well as the approval of the secretary of the Treasury, would be required. Furthermore, FDICIA requires that the Fed share in the FDIC's losses if long-term Fed lending to a bank that fails increases the FDIC's losses.

Probably the most important feature of FDICIA is its prompt corrective action provisions, which require the FDIC to intervene earlier and more vigorously when a bank gets into trouble. Banks are now classified into five groups based on bank capital. Group 1, classified as "well capitalized," are banks that significantly exceed minimum capital requirements and are allowed privileges such as insurance on brokered deposits and the ability to do some securities underwriting. Banks in group 2, classified as "adequately capitalized," meet minimum capital requirements and are not subject to corrective actions but are not allowed the privileges of the well-capitalized banks. Banks in group 3, "undercapitalized," fail to meet capital requirements. Banks in groups 4 and 5 are "significantly undercapitalized" and "critically undercapitalized," respectively, and are not allowed to pay interest on their deposits at rates that are higher than average. In addition, for group 3 banks, the FDIC is required to take prompt corrective actions such as requiring them to submit a capital restoration plan, restrict their asset growth, and seek regulatory approval to open new branches or develop new lines of business. Banks that are so undercapitalized as to have equity capital less than 2% of assets fall into group 5, and the FDIC must take steps to close them down.

FDICIA also instructed the FDIC to come up with risk-based insurance premiums. The system that the FDIC has put in place, however, has not worked very well, because it resulted in more than 90% of the banks with over 95% of the deposits paying the same premium. Other provisions of FDICIA are listed in Table 1 on page 524.

FDICIA is an important step in the right direction, because it increases the incentives for banks to hold capital and decreases their incentives to take on excessive risk. However, concerns that it has not adequately addressed risk-based premiums or the too-big-to-fail problem have led economists to continue to search for further reforms that might help promote the safety and soundness of the banking system.[3]

Banking Crises Throughout the World

Because misery likes company, it might make you feel better to know that the United States has by no means been alone in suffering a banking crisis. Indeed, as Figure 2 and Table 2 illustrate, banking crises have struck a large number of countries throughout the world, and many of them have been substantially worse than ours. We will examine what took place in several of these other countries and see that the same forces that produced a banking crisis in the United States have been at work elsewhere too.

---

[3]A further discussion of how well FDICIA has worked and other proposed reforms of the banking regulatory system appears in an appendix to this chapter that can be found on this book's website at **www.aw-bc.com/mishkin_eakins**.

FIGURE 2 *Banking Crises Throughout the World Since 1970*

Legend:
- Systemic bank crisis
- Borderline and smaller banking crisis
- No bank crisis or insufficient information

Source: Gerard Caprio Jr. and Daniela Klingbiel, "Bank Insolvency: Bad Luck, Bad Policy, or Bad Banking?" Paper prepared for the World Bank's Annual Bank Conference on Development Economics, Washington, D.C., April 25–26, 1996.

Scandinavia

As in the United States, an important factor in the banking crises in Norway, Sweden, and Finland was the financial liberalization that occurred in the 1980s. Before the 1980s, banks in the Scandinavian countries were highly regulated and subject to restrictions on the interest rates they could pay to depositors and on the interest rates they could earn on loans. In this noncompetitive environment, and with artificially low rates on both deposits and loans, these banks lent only to the best credit risks, and both banks and their regulators had little need to develop expertise in screening and monitoring borrowers. With the deregulated environment, a lending boom ensued, particularly in the real estate sector. Given the lack of expertise in both the banking industry and its regulatory authorities in keeping risk taking in check, banks engaged in risky lending. When real estate prices collapsed in the late 1980s, massive loan losses resulted. The outcome of this process was similar to what happened in the savings and loan industry in the United States. The government was forced to bail out almost the entire banking industry in these countries in the late 1980s and early 1990s on a scale that was even larger relative to GDP than in the United States (see Table 2).

TABLE 2   *The Cost of Rescuing Banks in Several Countries*

Date	Country	Cost as a Percentage of GDP
1980–1982	Argentina	55
1997–	Indonesia	50–55
1981–1983	Chile	41
1997–	Thailand	33
1997–	South Korea	27
1997–	Malaysia	21
1994–ongoing	Venezuela	20+
1995	Mexico	20
1990's	Japan	12+
1989–ongoing	Czech Republic	12+
1991–1994	Finland	11
1991–1995	Hungary	10
1994–1995	Brazil	5–10
1987–1993	Norway	8
1998	Russia	5–7
1991–1994	Sweden	4
1984–1991	United States	3

Source: Gerard Caprio Jr. and Daniela Klingbiel, "Episodes of Systemic and Borderline Financial Crises" mimeograph, World Bank, October 1999.

Latin America

The Latin American banking crises show a similar pattern to those in the United States and in Scandinavia. Before the 1980s, banks in many Latin American countries were owned by the government and were subject to interest-rate restrictions as in Scandinavia. Their lending was restricted to the government and other low-risk borrowers. With the deregulation trend that was occurring worldwide, many of these countries liberalized their credit markets and privatized their banks. We then see the same pattern we saw in the United States and Scandinavia, a lending boom in the face of inadequate expertise on the part of both bankers and regulators. The result was again massive loan losses and the inevitable government bailout.

The Argentine banking crisis of 2001, which is ongoing, differed from those typically seen in Latin America. Argentina's banks were well supervised and in relatively good shape before the government coerced them into purchasing large amounts of Argentine government debt in order to help solve the government's fiscal problem. However, when market confidence in the government plummeted, spreads between Argentine government debt and U.S. Treasuries soared to more than 2500 basis points (25 percentage points), leading to a sharp fall in the price of these securities. The losses on their holdings of government debt and rising bad loans because of the ongoing severe recession increased doubts about the solvency of the banking system.

A banking panic erupted in October and November 2001, with the Argentine public rushing to withdraw their deposits. On December 1, after losing more than $8 billion of deposits, the government imposed a $1000 monthly limit on deposit withdrawals. Then with the collapse of the peso and the requirement that the banks must pay back their dollar deposits at a higher exchange value than they would be paid back on their dollar loans, banks' balance sheets went even further in the hole. The cost of the recent Argentine banking crisis is not yet clear, but it could very well be as large as the previous banking crisis in Argentina in the 1980–1982 period listed in Table 2 and could exceed 50% of GDP.

What is particularly striking about the Latin American experience is that the cost of the bailouts relative to GDP dwarfs that in the United States. The cost to the taxpayer of the government bailouts in Latin America has been anywhere from around 20% to more than 50% of GDP, in contrast to the 3% figure for the United States.

Russia and Eastern Europe

Before the end of the Cold War, in the communist countries of Eastern Europe and the Soviet Union, banks were owned by the state. When the downfall of communism occurred, banks in these countries had little expertise in screening and monitoring loans. Furthermore, bank regulatory and supervisory apparatus that could rein in the banks and keep them from taking on excessive risk barely existed. Given the lack of expertise on the part of regulators and banks, not surprisingly, substantial loan losses ensued, resulting in the failure or government bailout of many banks. For example, in the second half of 1993, eight banks in Hungary with 25% of the financial system's assets were insolvent, and in Bulgaria, an estimated 75% of all loans in the banking system were estimated to be substandard in 1995. On August 24, 1995, a bank panic requiring government intervention occurred in Russia when the interbank loan market seized up and stopped functioning because of concern about the solvency of many new banks. This was not the end of troubles in the Russian banking system. On August 17, 1998, the Russian government announced that Russia would impose a moratorium on the repayment of foreign debt because of insolvencies in the banking system. In November, the Russian central bank announced that nearly half of the country's 1500 commercial banks might go under and that the cost of the bailout would be on the order of $15 billion.

Japan

Japan was a latecomer to the banking crisis game. Before 1990, the vaunted Japanese economy looked unstoppable. Unfortunately, it has recently experienced many of the same pathologies that we have seen in other countries. Before the 1980s, Japan's financial markets were among the most heavily regulated in the world, with very strict restrictions on the issuing of securities and interest rates. Financial deregulation and innovation produced a more competitive environment that set off a lending boom, with banks lending aggressively in the real estate sector. As in the other countries we have examined here, financial disclosure and monitoring by regulators did not keep pace with the new financial environment. The result was that banks could and did take on excessive risks, and when property values collapsed in the early 1990s, the banks were left holding massive amounts of bad loans. For example, Japanese banks decided to get into the mortgage lending market by setting up the so-called jusen, home mortgage lending companies that raised funds by borrowing from banks and then loaned these funds out to households. Seven of these *jusen* became insolvent, leaving banks with $60 billion or so of bad loans.

As a result, the Japanese have experienced their first bank failures since World War II. In July 1995, Tokyo-based Cosmo Credit Corporation, Japan's fifth-largest credit union, failed, and on August 30, the Osaka authorities announced the imminent closing of Kizu Credit Cooperative, Japan's second-largest credit union. (Kizu's story is remarkably similar to that of many U.S. savings and loans. Kizu, like many American S&Ls, began offering high rates on large time deposits and grew at a blistering pace, with deposits rising from $2.2 billion in 1988 to $12 billion by 1995 and real estate loans growing by a similar amount. When the property market collapsed, so did Kizu.) On the same day, the Ministry of Finance announced that it was liquidating Hyogo Bank, a midsize Kobe bank that was the first commercial bank to fail. Larger banks now began to follow the same path. In late 1996, the Hanwa Bank, a large regional bank, was liquidated, and this was followed in 1997 by a government-assisted restructuring of the Nippon Credit Bank, Japan's seventeenth-largest bank. In November 1997, Hokkaido Takushoku Bank was forced to go out of business, making it in the first city bank (a large commercial bank) to be closed during the crisis.

The Japanese have been going through the same cycle of regulatory forbearance as occurred in the United States in the 1980s. The Japanese regulators in the Ministry of Finance enabled banks to meet capital standards and to keep operating by allowing them to inflate the value of their assets. For example, they were allowed to value their large holdings of equities at historical value, rather than market value, which was much lower. Inadequate amounts were allocated for recapitalization of the banking system, and the extent of the problem was grossly underestimated by government officials. Furthermore, until the closing of the Hokkaido Takushoku Bank, the bank regulators in the Ministry of Finance were unwilling to close down city banks and impose any losses on stockholders or uninsured creditors.

By the middle of 1998, the Japanese government began to take some steps to clean up the banking mess. In June, the supervision authority over financial institutions was taken away from the Ministry of Finance and transferred to the Financial Supervisory Agency (FSA), which reports directly to the prime minister. This was the first instance in half a century in which the all-powerful Ministry of Finance was stripped of some of its authority. In October, the parliament passed a bailout package of $500 billion. However, disbursement of the funds depended on the voluntary cooperation of the banks: The law did not require insolvent banks to close or to accept the funds if they were insolvent. Indeed, acceptance of the funds required the bailed-out bank to open its books and reveal its true losses, and thus many banks remain very undercapitalized. The banking sector in Japan thus remains in very poor shape: It is burdened with bad loans and poor profitability. Indeed, in 2001, new data from the Financial Supervisory Agency (FSA) indicated that bad loans had reached a level of 150 trillion yen (over $1 trillion), almost double the previous amount estimated by the FSA.

There has been some progress in cleaning up the banking mess: Immediately after the 1998 banking law was passed, one of the ailing city banks, Long-Term Credit Bank of Japan, was taken over by the government and declared insolvent, and in December 1998, the Nippon Credit Bank was finally put out of its misery and closed down by the government. After this, the cleanup process stalled and the economy remained weak, with a growth rate from 1991 to 2002 averaging an anemic 1%. A new, reform-oriented minister, Junichiro Koizumi, who pledged to clean up the banking system, came into office in 2001; however, the Japanese government has been slow to come to grips with the banking problem, and the amount of nonperforming loans is still estimated to be over $1 trillion. In 2003, the fifth-largest bank, Resona, was kept afloat only with a 23 trillion yen ($17 billion) bailout, and a large regional bank, Ashigara, was declared insolvent and nationalized. However, with the pickup of the Japanese economy in 2003, bad loans in the Japanese banks finally seem to be falling. Another sign of optimism is the successful initial public offering of shares in Shinsei ("rebirth" in Japanese), which was formerly the Long-Term Credit Bank that was nationalized in 1998 and then sold to an American venture capital firm, Ripplewood. Despite these encouraging signs, the Japanese banking system still has a long way to go before it is returned to health, and until it does so it will continue to be a serious drag on the economy.

China

Despite China's rapid economic growth, which has been near 10% per year, China has a banking problem nearly as severe as in Japan. Estimates of nonperforming loans are currently around $500 billion. In 1998, the Chinese government injected $30 billion into the four largest banks, all state-owned—Industrial and Commercial Bank of China, Agricultural Bank of China, Bank of China, and China Reconstruction Bank—with another $170 billion injection in 2000–2001. In 2004, the Chinese government entered into its third bailout, with an initial capital injection of over $100 billion that is expected to reach as much as $200 billion. The state-owned banks have gotten into trouble because they have lent massively to unprofitable state-owned enterprises and are notoriously inefficient: The so-called big four have over 1 million employees and over 100,000 branches. The government hopes that the third try at a bailout will be a charm, and is attempting to do this one differently. This bailout is part of a plan to prepare the so-called big four to become partially privatized by having them issue shares overseas, while these banks are being encouraged to speed up the disposal of nonperforming loans, to close unprofitable branches, and to lay off unproductive employees. The Chinese government is aware that it needs to reform the banking sector so that capital can be allocated to private borrowers with good investment opportunities rather than to inefficient state-owned enterprises, but this is a daunting task. How successful the Chinese government will be in this endeavor is far from clear.

East Asia

The banking and financial crisis in the East Asian countries (Thailand, Malaysia, Indonesia, the Philippines, and South Korea) was discussed in Chapter 15. Due to inadequate supervision of the banking system, the lending booms that arose in the aftermath of financial liberalization led to substantial loan losses, which became huge after the currency collapses that occurred in the summer of 1997. An estimated 15% to 35% of all bank loans are now nonperforming in Thailand, Indonesia, and South Korea, and estimates of the cost of the bailout for the banking system in these countries is more than 20% of GDP. The cost of the bailout in Malaysia may also exceed 20%; the Philippines are expected to fare somewhat better.

"Déjà Vu All Over Again"

What we see in banking crises in these different countries is that history has kept on repeating itself. The parallels between the banking crisis episodes in all these countries are remarkably similar, leaving us with a feeling of déjà vu. Although financial liberalization is generally a good thing because it promotes competition and can make a financial system more efficient, as we have seen in the countries examined here, it can lead to an increase in moral hazard risk taking on the part of banks if there is lax regulation and supervision; the result can then be banking crises. However, these episodes do differ in that deposit insurance has not played an important role in many of the countries experiencing banking crises. For example, the size of the Japanese equivalent of the FDIC, the Deposit Insurance Corporation, was so tiny relative to the FDIC that it did not play a prominent role in the banking system and exhausted its resources almost immediately with the first bank failures. This means that deposit insurance is not to blame for some of these banking crises. However, what is common to all the countries discussed here is the existence of a government safety net, in which the government stands ready to bail out banks whether deposit insurance is an important feature of the regulatory environment or not. It is the existence of a government safety net, and not deposit insurance per se, that increases moral hazard incentives for excessive risk taking on the part of banks.

Summary

1. The concepts of asymmetric information, adverse selection, and moral hazard help explain the seven types of banking regulation that we see in the United States and other countries: the government safety net, restrictions on bank asset holdings and capital requirements, bank supervision, disclosure requirements, consumer protection, restrictions on competition, and the separation of the banking and securities industries.

2. Because asymmetric information problems in the banking industry are a fact of life throughout the world, bank regulation in other countries is similar to that in the United States. It is particularly problematic to regulate banks engaged in international banking because they can readily shift their business from one country to another.

3. Because of financial innovation and deregulation, adverse selection and moral hazard problems increased in the 1980s and resulted in a banking crisis in the United States.

4. The Federal Deposit Insurance Corporation Improvement Act (FDICIA) of 1991 recapitalized the Bank Insurance Fund of the FDIC and included reforms for the deposit insurance and regulatory system so that taxpayer losses would be minimized. This legislation limited the use of the too-big-to-fail policy, mandated prompt corrective action to deal with troubled banks, and instituted risk-based deposit insurance premiums. These provisions have helped reduce the incentives of banks to take on excessive risk and so should help reduce taxpayer exposure in the future.

5. The parallels between the banking crisis episodes that have occurred in other countries are striking, indicating that similar forces are at work.

Key Terms

bank supervision, *p. 519*

Basel Accord, *p. 518*

Basel Committee on Banking Supervision, *p. 518*

leverage ratio, *p. 518*

off-balance-sheet activities, *p. 518*

prudential supervision, *p. 519*

regulatory arbitrage, *p. 518*

Questions

1. Give one example each of moral hazard and adverse selection in private insurance arrangements.

2. If casualty insurance companies provided fire insurance without any restrictions, what kind of adverse selection and moral hazard problems might result?

3. What bank regulation is designed to reduce adverse selection problems for deposit insurance? Will it always work?

4. What bank regulations are designed to reduce moral hazard problems created by deposit insurance? Will they completely eliminate the moral hazard problem?

5. What are the costs and benefits of a too-big-to-fail policy?

6. What special problem do off-balance-sheet activities present to bank regulators, and what have they done about it?

7. Why does imposing bank capital requirements on banks help limit risk taking?

8. What forms does bank supervision take, and how does it help promote a safe and sound banking system?

9. What steps were taken in the FDICIA legislation of 1991 to improve the functioning of federal deposit insurance?

10. Why has the trend in bank supervision moved away from a focus on capital requirements to a focus on risk management?

11. How do disclosure requirements help limit excessive risk taking by banks?

12. Do you think that eliminating or limiting the amount of deposit insurance would be a good idea? Explain your answer.

13. Do you think that removing the impediments to a nationwide banking system will be beneficial to the economy? Explain.

14. How could higher deposit insurance premiums for banks with riskier assets benefit the economy?

15. How could market-value accounting for bank capital requirements benefit the economy? How difficult would it be to implement?

Quantitative Problems

1. Consider a failing bank. A deposit of $150,000 is worth how much if the FDIC uses the *payoff* method? The *purchase and assumption* method? Which is more costly to taxpayers?

2. Consider a bank with the following balance sheet:

Assets		Liabilities	
Required		Checkable	
Reserves	$8 million	Deposits	$100 million
Excess		Bank Capital	$6 million
Reserves	$3 million		
T-bills	$45 million		
Mortgages	$40 million		
Commercial			
Loans	$10 million		

Calculate the bank's risk-weighted assets.

3. Consider a bank with the following balance sheet:

Assets		Liabilities	
Required		Checkable	
Reserves	$8 million	Deposits	$100 million
Excess		Bank Capital	$6 million
Reserves	$3 million		
T-bills	$45 million		
Commercial			
Loans	$50 million		

The bank commits to a loan agreement for $10 million to a commercial customer. Calculate the bank's capital ratio before and after the agreement. Calculate the bank's risk-weighted assets before and after the agreement.

Problems 4 through 11 relate to a sequence of transactions at Oldhat Financial.

4. Oldhat Financial started its first day of operations with $9 million in capital. $130 million in checkable deposits are received. The bank issues a $25 million commercial loan and another $50 million in mortgages, with the following terms:

   - Mortgages: 200 standard 30-year, fixed-rate with a nominal annual rate of 5.25% each for $250,000.
   - Commercial loan: Three-year loan, simple interest paid monthly at 0.75% per month.

   If required reserves are 8%, what does the bank balance sheet look like? Ignore any loan loss reserves. How well capitalized is the bank?

5. Calculate the risk-weighted assets and risk-weighted capital ratio of Oldhat's first day.

6. The next day, terrible news hits the mortgage markets, and mortgage rates jump to 13%. What is the

market value of Oldhat's mortgages? What is Old-hat's "market value" capital ratio?

7. Bank regulators force Oldhat to sell its mortgages to recognize the fair market value. What is the accounting transaction? How does this affect its capital position?

8. Congress allowed Oldhat to amortize the loss over the remaining life of the mortgage. If this technique was used in the sale, how would the transaction have been recorded? What would be the annual adjustment? What does Oldhat's balance sheet look like? What is the capital ratio?

9. Oldhat decides to invest the $77 million in excess reserves in commercial loans. What will be the impact on its capital ratio? Its risk-weighted capital ratio?

10. The bad news about the mortgages is featured in the local newspaper, causing a minor bank run. $6 million in deposits is withdrawn. Examine the bank's condition.

11. Oldhat borrows $5.5 million in the overnight federal funds market to meet its resources requirement. What is the new balance sheet for Oldhat? How well capitalized is the bank?

Web Exercises

Banking Regulation

1. Go to **http://www.fdic.gov/regulations/laws/important/**. This site reports on the most significant pieces of legislation affecting banks since the 1800s. Summarize the most recently enacted bank regulation on this site.

2. The Office of the Comptroller of the Currency is responsible for many of the regulations affecting bank operations. Go to **http://www.occ.treas.gov/**. Click on "Regulatory Information." Now click on the 12 CFR Parts 1 to 199. What does Part 1 cover? How many parts are there in 12 CFR? Open Part 18. What topic does it cover? Summarize its purpose.

Web Appendices

Please visit our Web site at **www.aw-bc.com/mishkin_eakins** to read the Web appendix to Chapter 20, *Evaluating FDICIA and Other Proposed Reforms of the Banking Regulatory System*.

CHAPTER 21

The Mutual Fund Industry

Preview   Suppose that you decide that you want to begin investing for retirement. You would probably want to hold some money in a diversified portfolio of stocks. You might want to put some money in bonds. You might even want to hold stock in some foreign companies. Now suppose your budget will only let you invest $25 per week. How are you going to build this retirement fund? You will probably not want to buy individual stocks, and with only $25 to spend at a time, you will not be able to buy bonds. The solution to your problem is to invest in mutual funds.

Mutual funds pool the resources of many small investors by selling them shares in the fund and use the proceeds to buy securities. Through the asset transformation process of issuing shares in small denominations and buying large blocks of securities, mutual funds can take advantage of volume discounts on brokerage commissions and can purchase diversified portfolios of securities. Mutual funds allow small investors to obtain the benefits of lower transaction costs in purchasing securities and to take advantage of a reduction in risk by diversifying their portfolios.

In this chapter we will study why mutual funds have become so popular in recent years, the types of mutual funds, how mutual funds are regulated, and finally, how conflicts of interest in the mutual fund industry have led to many scandals, fines, and indictments since 2001.

The Growth of Mutual Funds

Mutual funds have become the investment vehicle of choice for many investors. At the beginning of 2004 nearly 16% of all assets in intermediaries were held by mutual funds. Twenty-two percent of the entire retirement market was invested in mutual funds by the beginning of 2004, and almost 50% of all U.S. households held stock in them. Given the pervasive nature of this intermediary, we should wonder exactly what service they provide that has caused them to grow from $292 billion in assets to $7.4 trillion in assets over just the last 20 years.

The First Mutual Funds

The origins of mutual funds can be traced back to the mid to late 1800s in England and Scotland. Investment companies were formed that pooled the funds of investors with modest resources and used the money to invest in a number of different securities. These investment companies became more popular when they began investing in the economic growth of the United States, mostly by purchasing American railroad bonds.

The first fund in which new shares were issued as new money was invested—the dominant structure seen today—was introduced in Boston in 1824. This fund allowed for continuous offering of shares, the ability to cash out of the fund at any time, and a set of restrictions on investments aimed at protecting investors from losses.

The stock market crash of 1929 set mutual fund growth back for several decades because small investors distrusted stock investments generally and mutual funds in particular. The Investment Company Act of 1940, which required much more disclosure of fees and investment policies, reinvigorated the industry, and mutual funds began a steady growth.

Benefits of Mutual Funds

There are five principal benefits that attract investors to mutual funds:

1. Liquidity intermediation
2. Denomination intermediation
3. Diversification
4. Cost advantages
5. Managerial expertise

Liquidity intermediation means that investors can convert their investments into cash quickly and with low cost. If you buy a CD or a bond, there can be early redemption penalties or transaction fees imposed if you need your funds before the securities mature. Additionally, if you bought a $10,000 CD, you must redeem the whole security even if you only require $5000 to meet your current needs. Mutual funds allow investors to buy and redeem at any time and in any amount. Some funds are designed especially to meet short-term transaction requirements and have no fees associated with redemption, whereas others are designed for longer-term investment and may have redemption fees if they are held only a short time.

Denomination intermediation allows small investors access to securities they would be unable to purchase without the mutual fund. For example, in Chapter 9 we learned that most money market securities are only available in large denominations, often in excess of $100,000. By pooling money, the mutual fund can purchase these securities on behalf of investors.

Diversification is an important advantage to investing in mutual funds. As we learned in Chapter 4, your risk can be lowered by holding a portfolio of diversified securities rather than a limited number. Small investors buying stocks individually may find it difficult to acquire enough securities in enough different industries to capture this benefit. Additionally, mutual funds provide a low-cost way to diversify into foreign stocks. It can be difficult and expensive to invest in a foreign security not listed on U.S. exchanges. The net assets in world equity funds totaled $517 billion in 2003, representing over 7% of all mutual fund investments.

Significant *cost advantages* may accrue to mutual fund investors. Institutional investors negotiate much lower transaction fees than are available to individual investors. Additionally, large block trades of 100,000 shares or more trade according to a different fee structure than do smaller trades. By buying securities through a mutual fund, investors can share in these lower fees.

One of the main features that has driven mutual fund growth has been access to *managerial expertise*. Despite the fact that research discussed in Chapter 6 has consistently demonstrated that mutual funds do not outperform a random pick from the market, many investors prefer to rely on professional money managers to select their stocks. The failure of mutual funds to post greater-than-average returns should not come as a surprise given our discussion of market efficiency. Still, the financial markets remain something of a mystery to a large number of investors. These investors are willing to pay fees to let someone else choose their stocks.

The increase in the number of defined-contribution pension plans has also been a factor in mutual fund growth. In the past, most pension plans either invested on behalf of the employee and guaranteed a return or required employees to invest in company stock. Now, most new pension plans require the employee to invest his or her own pension dollars. With pension investments being made every payday, the mutual fund provides the perfect pension conduit. Currently, over 22% of all pension dollars are invested in mutual funds. This amount is likely to grow as more pension plans convert to the defined-contribution structure.

Table 1 shows the total net assets, number of funds, and number of mutual funds accounts since 1970. There are currently over 8100 separate mutual funds for investors to choose among. It is interesting to note that this means there are more separate mutual funds than there are stocks trading on the New York, American, and NASDAQ stock exchanges combined.

In 33 years the amount invested in mutual funds has increased from $47 billion to over $7.4 trillion. To put this figure in perspective, this is about the same as the total assets of all commercial banks in the United States at the beginning of 2004.

Ownership of Mutual Funds

An estimated 53.3 million, or 48%, of households own mutual funds. By the beginning of 2004, 80% of mutual fund shares were owned by households, with the rest held by fiduciaries and other business organizations. This represents a tremendous increase since 1980, when only 5.7% of households held mutual fund shares (see Figure 1). The median mutual fund investor is middle class, 48 years old, married, employed, and possesses financial assets of $125,000. About 25% are retired, and fully 84% cite preparing for retirement as one of their main reasons for holding shares.

Mutual funds accounted for $2.7 trillion, or 22%, of the $12.0 trillion U.S. retirement market at the beginning of 2004. This represents 33% of all mutual fund assets.

TABLE 1   *Total Industry Net Assets, Number of Funds, and Number of Shareholder Accounts*

Year	Net Assets (millions)	Number of Funds	Number of Accounts (thousands)
1970	47,618	361	10,690
1971	55,045	392	10,901
1972	59,830	410	10,635
1973	46,518	421	10,330
1974	35,776	431	10,074
1975	45,874	426	9,876
1976	51,276	452	9,060
1977	48,936	477	8,692
1978	55,837	505	8,658
1979	94,511	524	9,790
1980	134,760	564	12,087
1981	241,365	665	17,499
1982	296,678	857	21,448
1983	292,985	1,026	24,604
1984	370,680	1,241	28,268
1985	495,385	1,527	34,762
1986	715,667	1,835	46,012
1987	769,171	2,312	54,421
1988	809,370	2,708	54,676
1989	980,671	2,900	58,135
1990	1,065,194	3,081	61,948
1991	1,393,189	3,405	68,334
1992	1,642,543	3,826	79,932
1993	2,070,023	4,538	93,217
1994	2,155,396	5,330	114,388
1995	2,811,484	5,728	131,231
1996	3,526,270	6,254	150,176
1997	4,468,200	6,684	170,521
1998	5,525,209	7,314	193,854
1999	6,846,339	7,791	226,872
2000	6,965,249	8,171	243,518
2001	6,974,950	8,305	248,809
2002	6,390,360	8,244	251,224
2003	7,414,080	8,126	260,650

Source: Investment Company Institute, *2004 Mutual Fund Fact Book*, 44th ed. (Washington, DC: ICI), p. 105.

Deposits into retirement mutual funds come from two sources: employer-sponsored defined-contribution plans, especially 401(k) plans, and individual retirement accounts (IRAs). Figure 2 shows the average asset allocation of all 401(k)

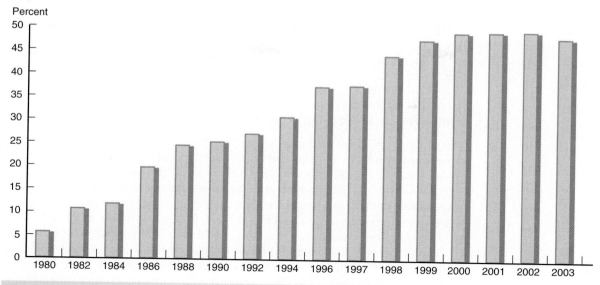

FIGURE 1 *Household Ownership of Mutual Funds, 1980–2003*

Source: Investment Company Institute, *2004 Mutual Fund Fact Book,* 44th ed. (Washington, DC: ICI).

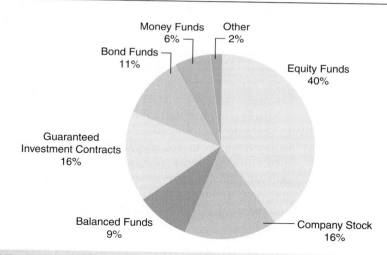

FIGURE 2 *Average Asset Allocation for All 401(k) Plan Balances*

Source: Investment Company Institute, *2004 Mutual Fund Fact Book,* 44th ed. (Washington, DC: ICI).

mutual fund accounts. The bulk of retirement assets are in equity funds, followed by company stock, guaranteed investment contracts, and bond funds.

Mutual Fund Structure

Mutual fund companies frequently offer a number of separate mutual funds. They are called *complexes* and are defined as a group of funds under substantially common management, composed of one or more families of funds. The advantage to investors of fund complexes is that investments can usually be transferred among different funds within a family very easily and quickly. Additionally, account information can be summarized by the complex to help investors keep their assets organized.

In this section we will look at how mutual funds are structured and at the types of investments the funds hold.

Open- Versus Closed-End Funds

Mutual funds are structured in two ways. The first funds were what are now called **closed-end funds.** In a closed-end fund, a fixed number of nonredeemable shares are sold at an initial offering and are then traded in the over-the-counter market like common stock. The market price of these shares fluctuates with the value of the assets held by the funds. The market value of the shares may be above or below the value of the assets held by the fund, depending on the market's assessment of how likely managers are to pick stocks that will increase fund value.

The problem with closed-end funds is that once shares have been sold, the fund cannot take in any more investment dollars. Thus, to grow the fund managers must start a whole new fund. The advantage of closed-end funds to managers is that investors cannot make withdrawals. The only way investors have of getting money out of their investment in the fund is to sell shares.

Today, the closed-end fund has been largely replaced with the **open-end fund.** Investors can contribute to an open-end fund at any time. The fund simply increases the number of shares outstanding. Another feature of open-end funds is that the fund agrees to buy back shares from investors at any time. Each day the fund net asset value is computed based on the number of shares outstanding and the net assets of the fund. All shares bought and sold that day are traded at the same net asset value. See the case for a complete discussion of computing the net asset value.

Open-end mutual funds have a couple of advantages that have contributed to the growth of mutual funds. First, because the fund agrees to redeem shares at any time, the investment is very liquid. As discussed earlier, this liquidity intermediation has great value to investors. Second, the open-end structure allows mutual funds to grow unchecked. As long as investors want to put money into the fund, it can expand to accommodate them. For example, the Vanguard S&P 500 index fund has holdings of about $100 billion.

Organizational Structure

Regardless of whether a fund is organized as a closed- or an open-end fund, it will have the same basic organizational structure. The investors in the fund are the shareholders. In the same way that shareholders of corporations receive the residual income of a company, the shareholders of a mutual fund receive the earnings, after expenses, of the mutual fund.

The board of directors oversees the fund's activities and sets policy. They are also responsible for appointing the investment advisor, usually a separate company, to manage the portfolio of investments and a principal underwriter, who sells the fund shares. SEC regulation requires that a majority of the directors be independent of the mutual fund.

The investment advisors manage the fund in accordance with the fund's stated objectives and policies. The investment advisors actually pick the securities that will be held by the fund and make both buy and sell decisions. It is their expertise that determines the success of the fund.

Case

CALCULATING A MUTUAL FUND'S NET ASSET VALUE

If you invest in a mutual fund, you will receive periodic statements summarizing the activity in your account. The statement will show funds that were added to your investment balance, funds that were withdrawn, and any earnings that have accrued. One term on the statement that is critical to understanding the investment's performance is the **net asset value (NAV).** The net asset value is the total value of the mutual fund's stocks, bonds, cash, and other assets minus any liabilities such as accrued fees, divided by the number of shares outstanding. An example will make this clear.

Suppose that a mutual fund has the following assets and liabilities:

Stock (at current market value)	$20,000,000
Bonds (at current market value)	$10,000,000
Cash	$ 500,000
Total value of assets	$30,500,000
Liabilities	−$ 300,000
Net worth	$30,200,000

The net asset value is computed by dividing the net worth by the number of shares outstanding. If 10 million shares are outstanding, the net asset value is $3.02 ($30,200,000/10,000,000 = $3.02).

The net asset value rises and falls as the value of the underlying assets changes. For example, suppose that the value of the stock portfolio held by the mutual fund rises by 10% and the value of the bond portfolio falls by 2% over the course of a year. If the cash and liabilities are unchanged, the new net asset value will be

Stock (at current market value)	$22,000,000
Bonds (at current market value)	$9,800,000
Cash	$ 500,000
Total value of assets	$32,300,000
Liabilities	−$ 300,000
Net worth	$32,000,000

$$\text{NAV} = \frac{\$32,000,000}{10,000,000} = \$3.20$$

The yield on your investment in the mutual fund is then

$$\text{Yield} = \frac{\$3.20 - \$3.02}{\$3.02} = \frac{\$0.18}{\$3.02} = 5.96\%$$

When you buy and sell shares in the mutual fund, you do so at the current NAV.

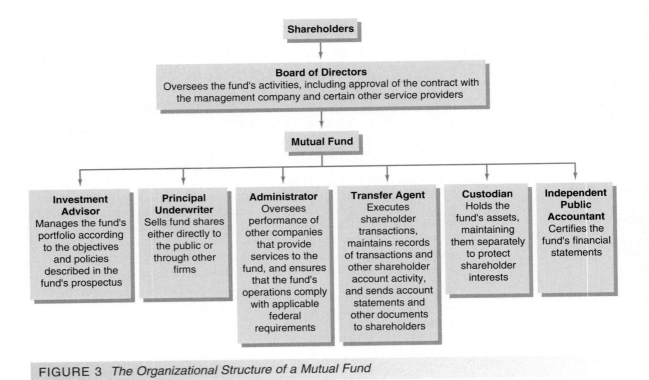

FIGURE 3 *The Organizational Structure of a Mutual Fund*

Source: Investment Company Institute, www.ici.org.

In addition to the investment advisors, the fund will contract with other firms to provide additional services. These will include underwriters, transfer agents, and custodians. Contracts will also be arranged with an independent public accountant. Large funds may arrange for some of these functions to be done in-house, whereas other funds will use all outside companies. Figure 3 shows the organizational structure of a mutual fund.

Investment Objective Classes

Four primary classes of mutual funds are available to investors. They are (1) stock funds (also called equity funds), (2) bond funds, (3) hybrid funds, and (4) money market funds. Figure 4 shows the distribution of assets among these types of funds at the beginning of 2004. The largest class is the equity funds, followed by the money market, bond, and hybrid funds.

Equity Funds

Equity funds share a common theme in that they all invest in stock. After that, they can have very different objectives. The three classes reported by the Investment Company Institute are capital appreciation funds, world funds, and total return funds. Capital appreciation funds are the largest, with about 25% of all mutual fund assets. These funds seek rapid capital appreciation (increases in share

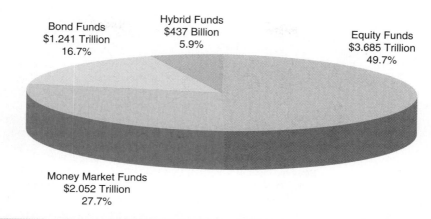

Bond Funds
$1.241 Trillion
16.7%

Hybrid Funds
$437 Billion
5.9%

Equity Funds
$3.685 Trillion
49.7%

Money Market Funds
$2.052 Trillion
27.7%

FIGURE 4 *Distribution of Assets Among Types of Mutual Funds, 2004*

Source: Investment Company Institute, *2004 Mutual Fund Fact Book,* 44th ed. (Washington, DC: ICI).

prices) and are not concerned with dividends. Many of these funds are relatively risky in that the fund managers are attempting to select companies incurring rapid growth. For example, many capital appreciation mutual funds invested heavily in high technology and Internet stocks during the 1990s.

Total return funds represent about 18% of total mutual fund assets. The goal of these funds is to seek a combination of current income and capital appreciation. They will include both mature firms that are paying dividends and growth companies that are expected to post large stock price increases. Total return funds are expected to be less risky than capital appreciation funds since they will include more large established firms. This was borne out in 2000 when capital appreciation funds lost 16.5% of their assets and total return funds only lost 5.7%.

World equity funds invest primarily in stocks of foreign companies. These funds allow investors easy access to international diversification. Many financial planners recommend that investors hold at least a small portion of their investments in foreign stocks. These world funds provide the primary vehicle.

The three types of equity funds presented here oversimplify the range of stock mutual funds available to investors. For example, the Vanguard family of mutual funds offers 62 different stock funds. Each one differs in its stated goals. Some hold stock from specific industries; others hold stock with certain historical growth rates. Others are chosen by their PE ratio. Mutual fund companies try to offer a fund that will appeal to every investor's needs.

Bond Funds

Figure 5 shows the major types of bond funds tracked by the Investment Company Institute. Strategic income bonds are the most popular and invest in a combination of U.S. corporate bonds to provide a high level of current income. The quality of the bonds in these funds will often be lower than in some other classes, but their yields will be higher. Investors are trading safety for greater returns.

Government bonds make up the next most popular class. These are essentially default risk free, but will have relatively low returns. The state and national municipal (muni) bonds are tax free.

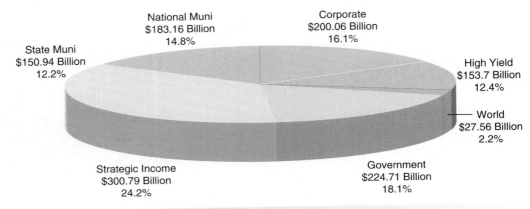

FIGURE 5   *Assets Invested in Different Types of Bond Mutual Funds*

Source: Investment Company Institute, *2004 Mutual Fund Fact Book,* 44th ed. (Washington, DC: ICI).

Bonds are not as risky as stocks, and so it is not usually as important that investors diversify across a large number of different bonds. Additionally, it is relatively easy to buy and sell bonds through the secondary market. As a result, it is not surprising that bond mutual funds hold only about a third of the assets held by stock mutual funds. Still, many investors value the liquidity intervention and automatic reinvestment features provided by bond mutual funds.

Hybrid Funds

Hybrid funds combine stocks and bonds into one fund. The idea is to provide an investment that diversifies across different types of securities as well as across different issuers of a particular type of security. Thus, if an investor found a hybrid fund that held the percentage of stocks and bonds he wanted, he could own just one fund instead of several. Despite this apparent convenience, most investors still prefer to choose separate funds. Only about 7% of all mutual fund accounts are hybrid accounts.

Money Market Funds

Money market mutual funds (MMMFs) have existed since the early 1970s; however, the low market interest rates before 1977 (which were either below or just slightly above the Regulation Q ceiling of 5.25% to 5.5%) kept them from being particularly advantageous relative to bank deposits. In 1978, Merrill Lynch recognized that it could provide better service to its customers if it offered an account that customers could use to warehouse money. Prior to the introduction of MMMFs as a small-investor account, customers had to bring in checks to the brokerage house when they wanted to invest and had to pick up checks when they sold securities. Customers who had MMMF accounts, however, could simply direct the broker to take funds out of this account to buy stocks or to deposit funds in this account when they sold securities. Initially, Merrill Lynch did not look on the MMMF as a major source of income.

In the early 1980s, inflation and interest rates skyrocketed. Regulation Q restricted banks from paying more than 5.25% in interest on savings accounts.

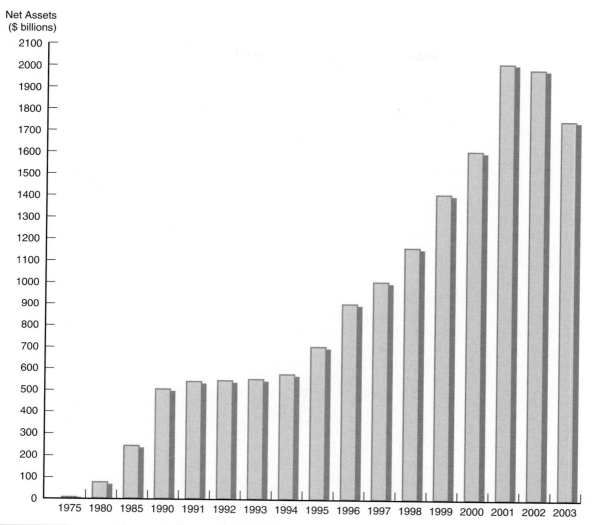

FIGURE 6 *Net Assets of Money Market Mutual Funds, 1975–2003*

Source: Investment Company Institute, *2004 Mutual Fund Fact Book,* 44th ed. (Washington, DC: ICI), Table 4.

The most recent statistics on the net assets of money market mutual funds can be found at www.ici.org/stats/index.html by clicking on "Money Market Mutual Fund Assets."

With interest rates in the money markets exceeding 15%, investors flocked to MMMFs. Figure 6 shows the growth of MMMFs since 1975.

All MMMFs are open-end investment funds that invest only in money market securities. Most funds do not charge investors any fee for purchasing or redeeming shares. The funds usually have a minimum initial investment of $500 to $2000. The funds' yields depend entirely on the performance of the securities purchased.

An important feature of MMMFs is that many have check-writing privileges. They often do not charge a fee for writing checks or have any minimum check amount as long as the balance in the account is above the stated level. This convenience, along with market interest rates, makes the accounts very popular with small investors.

Investors often take their money out of federally insured banks and thrifts and put it into uninsured MMMFs. An important question is why they are so willing to take this extra level of risk. The reason is that the extra risk is really very small. The money invested in MMMFs is in turn invested in money market instruments. Commercial paper is by far the largest component of these funds, followed by U.S. Treasury securities and repurchase agreements. Figure 7 shows the distribution of money market fund assets. Because the risk of default on these securities is very low, the risk of MMMFs is very low. Investors recognize this and so are willing to abandon the safety of banks for higher returns.

Legislation in 1980 and 1982 removed most of the restrictions on bank interest-rate ceilings. These changes were aimed at reducing the flow of funds out of banks and into brokerage houses. Currently investors earn 0.5% to 1% higher return by investing in MMMFs than by putting their money in banks. While MMMFs are still very popular, the low interest rates in recent years have caused total MMMF assets to fall slightly. Any significant increase in short-term rates would likely reverse this trend.

Index Funds

A special kind of mutual fund that does not fit any of the classes discussed previously, yet which represents an alternative investment style, is the index fund. Traditional funds employ investment managers who select stocks and bonds for the fund's portfolio. If we believe the lessons about market efficiency discussed in Chapter 6, we would conclude that investment managers are not likely to pick stocks any better than could a dart thrown at the stock pages of the *Wall Street Journal*. If investment managers are not superior stock pickers, then we might ask why one should pay them a fee to provide a service that may not have any marginal benefit.

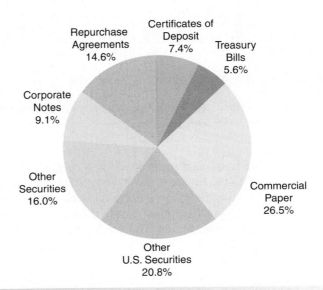

FIGURE 7　*Average Distribution of Money Market Fund Assets, 2004*

Source: Investment Company Institute, *2004 Mutual Fund Fact Book*, 44th ed. (Washington, DC: ICI).

Many investors want the benefits of mutual fund investing without the cost of paying for investment manager services. The answer is the index fund. An index fund contains the stocks in an index. For example, the mammoth Vanguard S&P 500 index fund contains the 500 stocks in that index. The stocks are held in a proportion such that changes to the fund value closely match changes to the index level. There are many other index funds available that mimic the behavior of various stock and bond indexes.

Index funds do not require managers to choose securities. As a result, these funds tend to have far lower fees than other actively managed funds. Some financial experts even argue that these funds will outperform most fund managers because they will ignore the fads, trends, emotions, and hysteria that often cloud investment advisor and individual investor judgment. In an interesting admission, the recently retired founder and former CEO of the Vanguard Group of mutual funds, John Bogle, stated he was an "index investor."[1]

Fee Structure of Investment Funds

Originally, most shares of mutual funds were sold by brokers who received a commission for their efforts. Because this commission was paid at the time of the purchase and immediately subtracted from the redemption value of the shares, these funds were called **load funds.** If the fee is charged when the funds are deposited, it is a front-end load. Most front-end loads are between 4% and 5%. If a fee is charged when funds are taken out (usually a declining fee over 5 years), it is a **deferred load.** The primary purpose of loads is to provide compensation for sales brokers. An alternative motivation, especially for deferred-load funds, is to discourage early withdrawal of deposits.

Beginning in the 1980s, funds that did not charge a direct load (or fee) appeared. These are called **no-load funds.** Most no-load funds can be purchased directly by individual investors, and no middleman is required. Currently about 55% of equity funds and 65% of bond funds are no load. Many investors have realized that when the initial deposit is immediately reduced, it can take a long time to catch up to the returns offered by no-load funds. The shares of front-end loaded funds are termed Class A shares. Shares in deferred-load funds are termed Class B shares. Class C shares are issued for no-load funds.

Regardless whether a load is charged, all mutual fund accounts are subject to a variety of fees. One of the primary factors that an investor should consider before choosing a mutual fund is the level of fees the fund charges. The fees are taken out of portfolio income before it is passed on to the investor. Since the investor is not directly charged the fees, many will not realize that they have even been subtracted. The usual fees charged by mutual funds are the following:

- A *contingent deferred sales charge* imposed at the time of redemption is an alternative way to compensate financial professionals for their services. This fee typically applies for the first few years of ownership and then disappears.

---

[1]Keynote speech by John Bogle, founder and former CEO of the Vanguard Group, before the American Business Editors and Writers Personal Finance Workshop, Denver, Colorado, October 27, 2003.

- A *redemption fee* is a back-end charge for redeeming shares. It is expressed as a dollar amount or a percentage of the redemption price.
- An *exchange fee* may be charged when transferring money from one fund to another within the same fund family.
- An *account maintenance fee* is charged by some funds to maintain low balance accounts.
- *12b-1 fees*, if any, are deducted from the fund's assets to pay marketing and advertising expenses or, more commonly, to compensate sales professionals. By law, 12b-1 fees cannot exceed 1% of the fund's average net assets per year.

Clearly, there are many opportunities for mutual fund managers to charge investors for the right to invest. Investors should very carefully evaluate a mutual fund's fee structure before investing, since these fees can range from 0.25% to as much as 8% per year. No research supports the argument that investors get better returns by investing in funds that charge higher fees. On the contrary, most high-fee mutual funds fail to do as well, after expenses, as low-fee funds.

Over the last 20 years, competition within the mutual fund industry has produced substantially lower costs. Between 1980 and 2004, the average total shareholder cost of equity mutual funds decreased by 40%. The cost of bond and money market funds dropped by 29% and 24%, respectively. One factor undoubtedly contributing to this reduction is the requirement by the SEC that mutual funds clearly disclose all fees and costs that investors will incur. The SEC further requires mutual funds to include in their prospectus a standardized sample account where $10,000 is invested for one, three, five, and ten years. The analysis shows investors exactly what fees they will be subject to if they choose the fund. The fee disclosure requirement makes it very easy for investors to compare funds, and therefore increases competition among them.

Regulation of Mutual Funds

Mutual funds are regulated under four federal laws designed to protect investors. The Securities Act of 1933 mandates that funds make certain disclosures. The Securities Exchange Act of 1934 set out antifraud rules covering the purchase and sale of fund shares. The Investment Company Act of 1940 requires all funds to register with the SEC and to meet certain operating standards. Finally, the Investment Advisers Act of 1940 regulates fund advisers.

As part of this government regulation, all funds must provide two types of documents free of charge: a prospectus and a shareholder report. A mutual fund's prospectus describes the fund's goals, fees and expenses, and investment strategies and risks; it also gives information on how to buy and sell shares. The SEC requires a fund to provide a full prospectus either before an investment or together with the confirmation statement of an initial investment.

Annual and semiannual shareholder reports discuss the fund's recent performance and include other important information, such as the fund's financial statements. By examining these reports, an investor can learn if a fund has been effective in meeting the goals and investment strategies described in the fund's prospectus.

In addition, investors are sent a yearly statement detailing the federal tax status of distributions received from the fund. Mutual fund shareholders are taxed on the fund's income directly, as if the shareholders held the underlying securities themselves. Similarly, any tax-exempt income received by a fund is generally passed on to the shareholders as tax-exempt.

Investment funds are run by brokerage houses and by institutional investors, who now control over 50% of the outstanding stock in the United States. Over 70% of the total daily volume in stocks is due to institutions initiating trades. Many of the mutual funds are run by brokerage houses; others are run by independent investment advisers. Because of the volume of stock controlled by these investors, there is tremendous competition for their business. This has led to significant cost cutting and to the proliferation of alternative methods of trading. For example, computerized trading that eliminates the broker from the transaction accounts for a growing percentage of the activity in stocks.

Mutual funds are the only companies in America that are required by law to have independent directors. The SEC believes that independent directors play a critical role in the governance of mutual funds. In January 2001, the SEC adopted substantive rule amendments designed to enhance the independence of investment company directors and provide investors with more information to assess directors' independence. These rules require that:

- Independent directors constitute at least a majority of the fund's board of directors,
- Independent directors select and nominate other independent directors, and
- Any legal counsel for the fund's independent directors be an independent legal counsel.

In addition, SEC rules require that mutual funds publish extensive information about directors, including their business experience and fund shares held. This system of overseeing the interests of mutual fund shareholders has helped the industry avoid systemic problems and contributed significantly to public confidence in mutual funds.

Hedge Funds

Hedge funds are a special type of mutual fund that have received considerable attention recently due to the near collapse of Long Term Capital Management. In Chapter 24 we discuss how financial markets can use hedges to reduce risk in a wide variety of situations. These risk-reducing strategies should not be confused with hedge funds. Although hedge funds often attempt to be market-neutral, protected from changes in the overall market, they are not riskless.

To illustrate a typical type of transaction conducted by hedge funds, consider a trade made by Long Term Capital Management in 1994. The fund managers noted that $29\frac{1}{2}$-year U.S. Treasury bonds seemed cheap relative to 30-year Treasury securities. The managers figured that the value of the two bonds would converge over time. After all, these securities have nearly identical risk since the maturity risk difference between $29\frac{1}{2}$-year securities and 30-year securities is insignificant. To make money from the temporary divergence of the bond prices, the fund bought $2 billion of the $29\frac{1}{2}$-year bonds and sold short $2 billion of the 30-year bonds. (Selling short means that the fund borrowed bonds it did not own and sold them. Later the fund must cover its short position by buying the bonds back, hopefully at a lower price.) The net investment by Long Term Capital was

$12 million. Six months later, the fund covered its short position by buying 30-year bonds and sold its $29\frac{1}{2}$-year bonds. This transaction yielded a $25 million profit.[2]

In the transaction, the managers did not care whether the overall bond market rose or fell. In this sense, the transaction was market-neutral. All that was required for a profit was that the prices of the bonds converge, an event that occurred as predicted. Hedge fund managers scour the world in their search for pricing anomalies between related securities. Figure 8 shows a situation where hedge funds could invest. Securities A and B move in lockstep over time. At some point they diverge, creating an opportunity. The hedge fund would buy security B, because it is expected to increase relative to A, and would sell A short. The fund managers hope that the gain on security B will be greater than the loss on security A. At times, the search for opportunities leads hedge funds to adopt exotic approaches that are not easily available elsewhere, from investing in distressed securities to participating in venture-capital financing.

In addition to investing money contributed by individuals and institutions, hedge funds often set up lines of credit to use to leverage their investments. For instance, in our example, Long Term Capital earned $25 million on an investment of $12 million, a 108% return [($25 million − $12 million)/$12 million = 1.08 = 108%]. Suppose that half of the $12 million had been borrowed funds. Ignoring interest cost, the return on invested equity would then be 317% ($25 million − $6 million/$6 million = 3.17 = 317%). Long Term Capital advertised that it was leveraged 20 to 1; however, by the time of the crisis, the figure was actually closer to 50 to 1. The "Mini-Case" box discusses how Long Term Capital eventually required a private rescue plan to prevent its failure.

Hedge funds accumulate money from many people and invest on their behalf, but several features distinguish them from traditional mutual funds. First, hedge

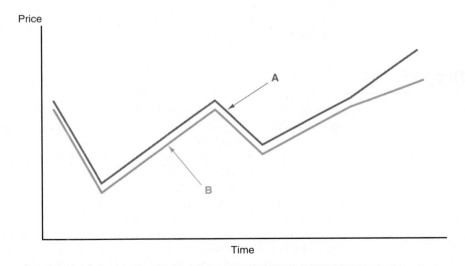

FIGURE 8 *The Price of Two Similar Securities*

Hedge funds search for related securities that historically move in lockstep but have temporarily diverted. In this example, the hedge fund would sell security A short and buy security B.

---

[2]*Wall Street Journal*, November 16, 1998, p. A18.

MINI-CASE

The Long Term Capital Debacle

Long Term Capital Management was a hedge fund managed by a group that included two Nobel Prize winners and 25 other Ph.D.s. It made headlines in September 1998 because it required a private rescue plan organized by the Federal Reserve Bank of New York.

The experience of Long Term Capital Management demonstrates that hedge funds are not risk-free, despite their being market-neutral. Long Term Capital expected that the spread between long-term Treasury bonds and long-term corporate bonds would narrow. Many stock markets around the world plunged, causing a flight to quality. Investors bid up the price of Treasury securities while the price of corporate securities fell. This is exactly the opposite of what Long Term Capital Management had predicted. As losses mounted, Long Term Capital's lenders required that the fund increase its equity position.

By mid-September, the fund was unable to raise sufficient equity to meet the demands of its creditors. Faced with the potential collapse of the fund, together with its highly leveraged investment portfolio consisting of nearly $80 billion in equities and over $1 trillion of notional value in derivatives, the Federal Reserve stepped in to prevent the fund from failing. The Fed's rationale was that a sudden liquidation of the Long Term Capital Management portfolio would create unacceptable systemic risk. Tens of billions of dollars worth of illiquid securities would be dumped on an already jittery market, causing potentially huge losses to numerous lenders and other institutions. A group consisting of banks and brokerage firms contributed $3.6 billion to a rescue plan that prevented the fund's failure.

The Fed's involvement in organizing the rescue of Long Term Capital is controversial, despite no public funds being expended. Some critics argue that the intervention increases moral hazard by weakening the discipline imposed by the market on fund managers. However, others say that the tremendous economic damage the fund's failure would have caused was unacceptable. This debate is likely to rage for some time.

funds have a minimum investment requirement of between $100,000 and $20 million, with the typical minimum investment being $1 million. Long Term Capital Management required a $10 million minimum investment. Most hedge funds are set up as limited partnerships. Federal law limits hedge funds to no more than 99 limited partners with steady annual incomes of $200,000 or more or a net worth of $1 million, excluding their homes. Funds may have up to 499 limited partners if each has $5 million in invested assets. All of these restrictions are aimed at allowing hedge funds to exist largely unregulated, on the theory that the rich can look out for themselves. Many of the 4000 funds are domiciled offshore to escape all regulatory restrictions.

Second, hedge funds are unique in that they usually require that investors commit their money for long periods of time, often several years. The purpose of this requirement is to give managers breathing room to attempt long-range strategies.

Hedge funds often charge large fees to investors. The typical fund charges a 1% annual asset management fee plus 20% of profits. Some charge significantly more. For example, Long Term Capital Management charged investors a 2% management fee and took 25% of profits.

The head of the SEC introduced regulation to Congress in 2004 to increase oversight of the hedge fund industry. He argued that at times, one hedge fund manager can be responsible for 5% of the New York Stock Exchange's daily volume. With the industry fast approaching $1 trillion in assets, he felt the SEC should step in to anticipate potential market problems before they arise. These regulations for increased disclosure are being aggressively opposed by the industry, and their passage is still very uncertain.

Conflicts of Interest in the Mutual Fund Industry

In Chapter 16 we discussed conflicts of interest in the financial industry. We concluded that many of the corporate governance breakdowns observed recently were due to the principal-agent relationship. This section extends that discussion to mutual funds, which have been subject to scandals, fines, and indictments. Several top mutual funds managers and CEOs have even been sentenced to jail time.

Investor confidence in the stability and integrity of the mutual fund industry is critical. A large portion of the population is now responsible for planning their own retirement, and most of these investments are being funneled into various funds. If these funds take advantage of investors or fail to provide the returns they should, people will find themselves unable to retire or having to scale back their retirement plans. No one argues that mutual funds can or should guarantee any specific return. They should, however, treat all investors equally and accurately disclose risk and fees. They must also follow the policies and rules they publish as governing the management of each fund.

Sources of Conflicts of Interest

Conflicts of interest arise when there is asymmetric information and the principal's and agent's interests are not closely aligned. The governance structure of mutual funds creates such a situation. Investors in a mutual fund are the shareholders. They elect directors, who are supposed to look out for their interest. The directors in turn select investment advisors, who actually run the mutual fund. However, given the large number of shareholders in the typical fund, there is a free-rider problem that prevents them from monitoring either the directors or the investment advisors.

Shareholders depend on directors to monitor investment advisors. Unfortunately, recent evidence demonstrates that directors' efforts have not been sufficient to prevent abuses. The incentive structure for compensating investment advisors does not assure that they will be motivated to maximize shareholder wealth. In the absence of monitoring, investment advisors will attempt to increase their own fees and income, even at the expense of shareholders. For example, suppose an institutional investor offers to make a large deposit into the fund in exchange for special trading privileges not afforded other investors. Since investment advisors are compensated as a percentage of the funds under management, they may choose to provide the special treatment because it increases their income. The recent negative publicity about mutual funds is due to this type of misaligned interest. The "Conflicts of Interest" box on page 555 discusses some of the better-known mutual fund scandals.

Mutual Fund Abuses

Until 2001, the mutual fund industry could brag that it had been "untainted by major scandal for more than 60 years."[3] This changed when the New York attorney general began investigating tips that mutual funds were engaging in various activities that undermined their fiduciary duty to shareholders, violated their own policies, and

---

[3]Terry Glenn, head of the mutual funds industry's Investment Company Institute, quoted in the *Wall Street Journal*, September 4, 2003, p. C1.

CONFLICTS OF INTEREST

Many Mutual Funds Are Caught Ignoring Ethical Standards

Some of the best-known names in the mutual fund industry have come under attack by the New York attorney general's office and the SEC. Over 300 lawsuits against 18 different firms were filed and consolidated in federal court in Baltimore. The mutual funds are eager to settle the suits and to get the bad publicity behind them. By mid-2004, nine firms had agreed to pay $1.6 billion in restitution to investors and an additional $855 million in fee reductions. Among the larger settlements were the following:

- The Alliance Capital Management Corp. was charged with allowing traders to engage in market timing. The firm will cut fees by $350 million and pay $250 million in fines and restitution to shareholders.

- Bank of America, which was implicated along with Canary Capital Partners in late trading and market timing, agreed to fee reductions of $160 million and fines and restitution of $375 million.
- Janus Capital Management LLC will reduce fees by $125 million and pay fines and restitution of $100 million.
- Putnam Investments, the fifth-largest family of funds, agreed to pay $10 million in fee reductions and $100 million in fines and restitution.

In addition to the fines, restitution, and fee reductions, some individual investment managers are being charged with criminal activity. The vice-chairperson of Fred Alger & Company, James Connelly Jr., was sentenced to one to three years in jail for his involvement in preferential treatment and self-dealing in the mutual fund.

Source: Wall Street Journal, July 14, 2004, p. C1.

in some cases broke SEC laws. Most of the abuses centered around two activities: late trading and market timing, both of which take advantage of the structure of open-end mutual funds that provide daily liquidity to shareholders by marking all trades to the NAV as of the close of business at 4:00 P.M.

1. *Late trading*. Late trading refers to the practice of allowing trades that are received after 4:00 P.M. to trade at the 4:00 price when they should trade at the next day's price. Suppose that on Wednesday at 4:00 P.M. the NAV for a technology fund is $20. Now suppose that news is received by traders at 6:00 P.M. that HP, Intel, and Microsoft have reported their income surged 50% over the last quarter. Traders, knowing the industry impact this will have, may want to enter buy orders for the fund at the $20 price. They are sure the NAV on Thursday will be substantially higher and they can earn a quick profit. A late trader can trade at the stale 4:00 P.M. price and buy or sell the funds the next day at a profit.

   The attorney general reported in hearings before Congress that "late trading is like betting on a horse race after the horses have crossed the finish line." It is illegal under SEC regulations. The reason it went undetected for many years is that certain late trades were regularly accepted and were legal. If a broker received a buy order from a client at 2:00, the order might not get consolidated with other orders and transmitted to the fund by 4:00. Since the investor placed the order before the market closed, the investor could not benefit from the late trade. Late trades were simply an opportunity to catch up with order processing. It was when large investors took advantage of their special arrangements at the expense of other shareholders that the legal line was crossed.

2. *Market timing*. Market timing, though technically legal, is considered unethical and is expressly forbidden by virtually all mutual funds' policy

standards. Market timing involves taking advantage of time zone differences that allow arbitrage opportunities, especially in foreign stocks. Mutual funds will set their 4:00 closing NAV using the most recent available foreign prices. However, these prices may be very stale. Japan, for example, closes nine hours earlier. If news is released in Japan that is not reflected in their closing prices, arbitrage opportunities exist by buying at the stale prices embedded in the NAV.

Most mutual funds have fees that are supposed to discourage these kinds of rapid in-and-out trades. However, if an investor such as Bank of America places large deposits in the fund, these fees can be waived. This is exactly what Edward J. Stern and his hedge fund Canary Capital Partners LLC did. In September 2003, Stern settled with the attorney general for $40 million in fines for allowing both late trading and market timing by Bank of America.

To better understand how shareholders in mutual funds are hurt by market timing and late trading, suppose a technology fund holds stock in various firms with a total current market value of $350. Further suppose you own one of ten shares outstanding in the fund. The NAV of the fund will be $35 per share ($350/10). Now suppose that after the market closes the tech industry announces better-than-expected earnings that everyone agrees will drive the value of shares held by the fund to $400 when the market opens the next morning. The NAV of your share would be $40 ($400/10). However, if another investor with special privileges is allowed to buy a share in the fund for $35 after hours, your NAV will be diluted. The $35 received by the fund from the privileged investor will have to be held as cash since the market is closed and no additional stock can be purchased by the fund. As a result, the value of the fund's assets the next morning will be $435 ($400 in stock and $35 in cash). The NAV will be $435/11 = $39.54 instead of $40. All of the original investors in the fund will have lost $0.46 per share, while the privileged investor will have gained $4.54 ($39.54 − $35.00).

The costs to investors of market timing and late trading are very hard to estimate since no reliable statistics are available on how frequently these abuses were practiced. Recent academic studies have estimated the losses to long-term investors to be as high as $4.9 billion.[4] See the "Conflicts of Interest" box on page 557 for a discussion of how widespread mutual fund abuses may be.

Government Response to Abuses

Arthur Levitt, former chairman of the SEC, admitted, "I believe this is the worst scandal we have seen in 50 years and I can't say that I saw it coming."[5] In fact the SEC, which is supposed to watch the mutual fund industry, was not the agency that initially investigated the abuses. It was New York State Attorney General Eliot Spitzer who caught the SEC unaware by filing indictments against many of the major players in the mutual fund industry. Now that the issues are commonly recognized, both the SEC and Congress are attempting to assure the safety of these funds.

---

[4]See Eric Zitzewitz, *Journal of Law, Economics & Organization* 19, no. 2 (2003): 245–280; Jason Greene and Charles Hodges, *Journal of Financial Economics* 65 (2002): 131–158; and Goetzmann, Ivkovic, and Rouwenhorst, *Journal of Financial and Quantitative Analysis* 36, no. 3 (September 2001): 287–309.

[5]*New York Times*, November 16, 2003, p. A1.

CONFLICTS OF INTEREST

SEC Survey Reports Mutual Fund Abuses Widespread

When the New York attorney general announced that his office was going to indict a number of mutual fund managers in September 2003, he caught many regulators off guard. Their focus had been on security abuses by corporations. The revelation that the mutual fund industry might also be dirty resulted in rapidly called hearings before Congress. At these hearings Stephen Cutler, the chief of enforcement for the SEC, presented results that showed that illegal trading in mutual funds was more widespread than anyone had imagined. In a sample of the largest 88 mutual fund companies, which represented 90% of the industry's assets, the SEC said that about 25% of the broker-dealers were allowed to make illegal late trades. Additionally, half the funds let some privileged shareholders engage in market timing trades. Finally, the research showed that more than 30% of the funds admitted that their managers had shared sensitive portfolio information with favored shareholders.

- *More independent directors.* One proposal being considered is to require that a greater percentage of mutual fund directors be independent from fund ownership and management. This is expected to increase their willingness to provide meaningful oversight. New regulations are also under consideration that more strictly define the term "independent" to better assure that conflicts of interest do not exist between directors and managers.
- *Hardening of the 4:00 P.M. valuation rule.* By more strictly enforcing the rule that trades received after 4:00 be traded at the next day's NAV rather than at the stale NAV, late trading activities should be prevented. These proposals, however, are controversial because they penalize investors whose trades do not get completed due to trading backlogs. They also fail to prevent market timing arbitrage across time zones.
- *Increased and enforced redemption fees.* Most funds already have a policy against market timing and have a redemption fee that is imposed for shares that are sold within 60 or 90 days of purchase. These fees are usually discretionary and were waived in the cases where abuses occurred. One recommendation under consideration by the SEC is to make these fees mandatory. The problem with mandatory fees is that they may penalize the investor who needs to make an unexpected withdrawal due to an emergency. This penalty makes mutual funds less attractive and, critics contend, would reduce their popularity.
- *Increased transparency.* Other regulations follow the most common approach taken by the SEC—increased disclosure of operating practices to the public. Directors would be required to more clearly and openly reveal any relationships that exist between fund owners or investment managers. Investment managers would be required to more clearly disclose compensation arrangements and how fees are charged. Additionally, more information would be required about compensation arrangements between the mutual fund and sales brokers. This strategy leaves it to the market to discipline any firms that seek to exploit any conflicts of interest.

In 2004 half a dozen separate bills were pending in Congress related to mutual funds. Additionally, a large number of SEC regulation changes were under review and were receiving comments from the industry. It will be interesting to watch how regulators choose to assure the security of mutual funds and control problems due to conflicts of interest in the industry.

Summary

1. Mutual funds have grown rapidly over the last two decades. The growth has been partly fueled by the increase in the number of investors who are responsible for managing their own retirement. Increased liquidity and diversification, among other factors, have also been important. There are currently over 8100 separate mutual funds with $7.1 trillion in net assets.

2. Mutual funds can be organized as either open- or closed-end funds. Closed-end funds issue stock in the fund at an initial offering and do not accept additional funds. Most new funds are organized as open-end funds and issue additional shares when new money is received. The net asset value (NAV) of the shares is computed each day. All trades conducted that day are at the NAV.

3. The primary classes of mutual funds are stock funds, bond funds, hybrid funds, and money market funds. Stock and bond funds can be either actively managed by investment managers or can be structured as index funds that contain the securities in some index, such as the S&P 500.

4. Hedge funds attempt to earn returns by trading on deviations between historical security relationships and current market conditions.

5. The mutual fund industry has been subject to widely publicized scandals for violating SEC regulations and internal policy. Most abuses centered on market timing and late trading by investors receiving privileged treatment in exchange for large deposits with the funds. Conflicts of interest created by fee structures that reward investment managers more for total assets than for returns are partly responsible.

Key Terms

closed-end fund, *p. 542*
deferred load, *p. 549*
diversification, *p. 538*

hedge fund, *p. 551*
load fund, *p. 549*
net asset value (NAV), *p. 543*

no-load fund, *p. 549*
open-end fund, *p. 542*

Questions

1. What features of mutual funds and the investment environment have led to mutual funds' rapid growth in the last two decades?

2. What is meant by liquidity intermediation?

3. Considering the discussion of market efficiency from Chapter 6, discuss whether you should be willing to pay high fees to mutual fund investment managers.

4. Distinguish between an open- and closed-end mutual fund.

5. Discuss why a mutual fund family may find it beneficial to offer 50 or 60 different stock mutual funds.

6. How does an index fund differ from an actively managed fund?

7. What is a load fund?

8. How are deferred loads usually structured?

9. What distinguishes a hedge fund from other types of mutual funds?

10. What prompted the growth of money market mutual funds?

11. What do 12b-1 fees pay and what is the maximum amount these fees can be?

12. What is the primary source of the conflict of interest between shareholders and investment managers?

13. What is *late trading* when referred to by mutual funds?

14. What is *market timing* when referred to by mutual funds?

15. What regulatory changes are being considered to deal with abuses in the mutual fund industry?

Quantitative Problems

1. On January 1, the shares and prices for a mutual fund at 4:00 P.M. are as follows:

Stock	Shares owned	Price
1	1000	$1.92
2	5000	$51.18
3	2800	$29.08
4	9200	$67.19
5	3000	$4.51
Cash	n.a.	$5353.40

Stock 3 announces record earnings, and the price of stock 3 jumps to $32.44 in after-market trading. If the fund (illegally) allows investors to buy at the current NAV, how many shares will $25,000 buy? If the fund waits until the price adjusts, how many shares can be purchased? What is the gain to such illegal trades? Assume 5000 shares are outstanding.

2. A mutual fund charges a 5% upfront load plus reports an expense ratio of 1.34%. If an investor plans on holding a fund for 30 years, what is the average annual fee, as a percent, paid by the investors?

3. A mutual fund offers "A" shares, which have a 5% upfront load and an expense ratio of 0.76%. The fund also offers "B" shares, which have a 3% back-end load and an expense ratio of 0.87%. Which shares make more sense for an investor looking over an 18-year horizon?

4. A mutual fund reported year-end total assets of $1508 million and an expense ratio of 0.90%. What total fees is the fund charging each year?

5. A $1 million fund is charging a back-end load of 1%, 12b-1 fees of 1%, and an expense ratio of 1.9%. Prior to deducting expenses, what must the fund value be at the end of the year for investors to break even?

Questions 6–12 trace a sequence of transactions involving a single mutual fund.

6. On January 1, a mutual fund has the following assets and prices at 4:00 P.M.

Stock	Shares owned	Price
1	1000	$1.97
2	5000	$48.26
3	1000	$26.44
4	10000	$67.49
5	3000	$2.59

Calculate the net asset value (NAV) for the fund. Assume that 8000 shares are outstanding for the fund.

7. An investor sends the fund a check for $50,000. If there is no front-end load, calculate the new number of shares and price per share. Assume the manager purchases 1800 shares of stock 3, and the rest is held as cash.

8. On January 2, the prices at 4:00 P.M. are as follows:

Stock	Shares owned	Price
1	1000	$2.03
2	5000	$51.37
3	2800	$29.08
4	10000	$67.19
5	3000	$4.42
Cash	n.a.	$2408.00

Calculate the net asset value (NAV) for the fund.

9. Assume the new investor then sells the 420 shares. What is his profit? What is the annualized return? The fund sells 800 shares of stock 4 to raise the needed funds. Assume 250 trading days per year.

10. To discourage short-term investing in its fund, the fund now charges a 5% upfront load and a 2% back-end load. The same investor decides to put $50,000 back into the fund. Calculate the new number of shares outstanding. Assume the fund manager buys back as many round-lot shares of stock 4 with the cash.

11. On January 3, the prices at 4:00 P.M. are as follows:

Stock	Shares owned	Price
1	1000	$1.92
2	5000	$51.18
3	2800	$29.08
4	9900	$67.19
5	3000	$4.51
Cash	n.a.	$5353.40

Calculate the new NAV.

12. Unhappy with the results, the new investor then sells the 389.09 shares. What is his profit? What is the new fund value?

Web Exercises

Investment Banks, Brokerage Firms, and Mutual Funds

1. Morningstar is the best-known company that specializes in analysis and review of mutual funds. There are a number of websites that report Morningstar's results. Go to **www.quicken.com/ investments/mutualfunds/finder**. Perform the EasyStep Search according to your own preferences for investment. Can you find funds that provide the return you want with the expense ratio you are willing to pay?

2. The mutual fund industry publishes a fact book containing exhaustive data on the historic and current state of mutual funds. Go to **http://www.ici. org/aboutfunds/factbook_toc.html**.

   a. According to Chapter 3, did the terrorist attack in September 2001 cause an obvious decrease in mutual funds assets?

   b. According to Chapter 4, what percentage of mutual funds assets are currently owned by households?

   c. According to Chapter 4, what is the average annual income of an investor in mutual funds?

CHAPTER 22

Insurance Companies and Pension Funds

Preview

In this chapter we continue our discussion of financial institutions by looking at two nonbank institutions: insurance companies and pension funds. Insurance is an important industry in the United States. Most people hold one or more types of insurance policies (health, life, homeowners, automobile, disability, and so on), and the annual revenues of insurance companies exceed $600 billion. Insurance companies are also a major employer, especially of business majors. Figure 1 shows the number of persons employed by the insurance industry between 1960 and 2002. The numbers rose rapidly during the 1960s, 1970s, and early 1980s. (Currently, well over 2 million Americans are employed in the insurance industry.) In recent years, the rate of growth has slowed, however. There are a couple of possible explanations for this. First, technology has streamlined claims processing so that fewer back-office workers are needed. Second, competition by other financial institutions such as commercial banks and brokerage houses may be cutting into some of the business traditionally reserved for insurance companies.

One major competitor to insurance has been the private, company-sponsored pension plan. Better-educated and longer-lived workers are putting more money into pension funds than ever before. Over 65 million individuals are now invested in a private pension fund. These plans are also reviewed in this chapter.

Insurance companies and pension funds are considered financial intermediaries for several reasons. First, they receive investment funds from their customers. For example, when a person buys a whole life insurance policy, the person receives a life insurance benefit and accumulates a cash balance. Many people use insurance companies as their primary investment avenue. Similarly, private pension funds also take in investment dollars from their customers. Second, both of these institutions place their money in a variety of money-earning investments. Insurance companies and pension funds make large commercial mortgage loans, invest in stocks, and buy bonds. Thus these institutions are financial intermediaries in that they take in funds from one sector and invest it in another.

Insurance Companies

Insurance companies are in the business of assuming risk on behalf of their customers in exchange for a fee, called a *premium*. Insurance companies make a profit by charging premiums that are sufficient to pay the expected claims to the company plus a profit. Why do people pay for insurance when they know that over the lifetime of their policy, they will probably pay more in premiums than the expected amount of any loss they will suffer? Because most people are risk-averse: They would rather pay a **certainty equivalent** (the insurance premium) than accept the gamble that they will lose their house or their car. Thus it is because people are risk-averse that they prefer to buy insurance and know with certainty what their wealth will be (their current wealth minus the insurance premium) than to incur the risk and run the chance that their wealth may fall.

Consider how people's lives would change if insurance were not available. Instead of knowing that the insurance company would help if an emergency occurred, everyone would have to set aside reserves. These reserves could not be invested long-term but would have to be kept in an extremely liquid form. Furthermore, people would be constantly worried that their reserves would be inadequate to pay for catastrophic events such as the loss of their house to fire, the theft of their car, or the death of the family breadwinner. Insurance allows us the peace of mind that a single event can have only a limited financial impact on our lives.

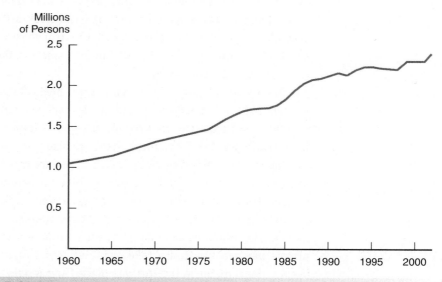

FIGURE 1 *Number of Persons Employed in the U.S. Insurance Industry, 1960–2002*

Source: Life Insurance Fact Book, 2003 (American Council of Life Insurers).

Fundamentals of Insurance

Although there are many types of insurance and insurance companies, all insurance is subject to several basic principles.

1. There must be a relationship between the *insured* (the party covered by insurance) and the *beneficiary* (the party who receives the payment should a loss occur). In addition, the beneficiary must be someone who may suffer potential harm. For example, you could not take out a policy on your neighbor's teenage driver because you are unlikely to suffer harm if the teenager gets into an accident. The reason for this rule is that insurance companies do not want people to buy policies as a way of gambling.
2. The insured must provide full and accurate information to the insurance company.
3. The insured is not to profit as a result of insurance coverage.
4. If a third party compensates the insured for the loss, the insurance company's obligation is reduced by the amount of the compensation.
5. The insurance company must have a large number of insureds so that the risk can be spread out among many different policies.
6. The loss must be quantifiable. For example, an oil company could not buy a policy on an unexplored oil field.
7. The insurance company must be able to compute the probability of the loss occurring.

The purpose of these principles is to maintain the integrity of the insurance process. Without them, people may be tempted to use insurance companies to gamble or speculate on future events. Taken to an extreme, this behavior could undermine the ability of insurance companies to protect persons in real need. In addition, these principles provide a way to spread the risk among many policies and to establish a price for each policy that will provide an expectation of a profitable return. Despite following these guidelines, insurance companies suffer greatly from the problems of asymmetric information that we first described in Chapter 2.

Adverse Selection and Moral Hazard in Insurance

Recall that adverse selection occurs when the individuals most likely to benefit from a transaction are the ones who most actively seek out the transaction and are thus most likely to be selected. In Chapter 2 we discussed adverse selection in the context of borrowers with the worst credit being the ones who most actively seek loans. The problem also occurs in the insurance market. Who is more likely to apply for health insurance, someone who is seldom sick or someone with chronic health problems? Who is more likely to buy flood insurance, someone who lives on a mountain or someone who lives in a river valley? In both cases, the party more likely to suffer a loss is the party likely to seek insurance. The implication of adverse selection is that loss probability statistics gathered for the entire population may not accurately reflect the loss potential for the persons who actually want to buy policies.

The adverse selection problem raises the issue of which policies an insurance company should accept. Because someone in poor health is more likely to buy a supplemental health insurance policy than someone in perfect health, we might predict that insurance companies should turn down anyone who applies. Since this does not happen, insurance companies must have found alternative solutions. For example, most insurance companies require physical exams and may examine previous medical records before issuing a health or life insurance policy. If some previous illness is found to be a factor in the person's health, the company may issue the policy but exclude this preexisting condition. Insurance firms often offer better rates to insure groups of people, such as everyone working at a particular business, because the adverse selection problem is then avoided.

In addition to the adverse selection problem, moral hazard plagues the insurance industry. Moral hazard occurs when the insured fails to take proper precautions to avoid losses because losses are covered by insurance. For example, moral hazard may cause you not to lock your car doors if you will be reimbursed by insurance if the car is stolen. When Hurricane Isabel approached the North Carolina coast in 2003, many yacht owners did not take down their old canvas covers because they hoped the covers would be destroyed by the hurricane, in which case the owners could file a claim with the insurance company and get money to buy new covers.

One way that insurance companies combat moral hazard is by requiring a **deductible.** A deductible is the amount of any loss that must be paid by the insured before the insurance company will pay anything. For example, if new canvas yacht covers cost $5000 and the yacht owner has $1000 deductible, the owner will pay the first $1000 of the loss and the insurance company will pay $4000. In addition to deductibles, there may be other terms in the insurance contract aimed at reducing risk. For example, a business insured against fire may be required to install and maintain a sprinkler system on its premises to reduce the loss should a fire occur.

Although contract terms and deductibles help with the moral hazard problem, these issues remain a constant difficulty for insurance companies. The insurance industry's reaction to moral hazard and adverse selection are discussed in greater detail in "The Practicing Manager" later in this chapter.

Selling Insurance

Another problem common to insurance companies is that people often fail to seek as much insurance as they actually need. Human nature tends to cause people to ignore their mortality, for example. For this reason, insurance, unlike many banking services, does not sell itself. Instead, insurance companies must hire large sales forces to sell their products. The expense of marketing may account for up to 20% of the total cost of a policy. A good sales force can convince people to buy insurance coverage that they never would have pursued on their own yet may have a need for.

Insurance is unique in that agents sell a product that commits the company to a risk. The relationship between the agent and the company varies: *Independent agents* may sell insurance for a number of different companies. They do not have any particular loyalty to any one firm and simply try to find the best product for their customer. There are in excess of 60,000 independent agents in the United States. *Exclusive agents* sell the insurance products for only one insurance company.

Most agents, whether independent or exclusive, are compensated by being paid a commission. The agents themselves are usually not at all concerned with the level of risk of any one policy because they have little to lose if a loss occurs. (Rarely are commissions influenced by the claims submitted by an agent's customers.) To keep control of the risk that agents are incurring on behalf of the company, insurance companies employ **underwriters,** people who review and sign off on each policy an agent writes and who have the authority to turn down a policy if they deem the risk unacceptable. If underwriters have questions about the quality of customers, they may order an independent inspector to review the property being insured or request additional medical information. A final decision to accept the policy may depend on the inspector's report (see the "Mini-Case" box below).

Growth and Organization of Insurance Companies

Figure 2 shows the number of life insurance companies from 1950 to 2002. There was a steady increase in the number until 1988. Since then the number has fallen steadily. Another interesting point to note about Figure 2 is that insurance companies can be organized as either *stock* or *mutual* firms. A **stock company** is owned by stockholders and has the objective of making a profit.

Mutual insurance companies are owned by the policyholders. The objective of mutual insurance firms is to provide insurance at the lowest possible cost to the insured. Policyholders are paid dividends that reflect the surplus of premiums over costs. Because the policyholders share in reducing the cost of insurance, there may be some reduction in the moral hazard that most insurance companies face. A unique feature of mutual insurance dividends is that they are not taxed like dividends received from other types of corporations. The Internal Revenue Service regards the dividends as refunds of overcharges on insurance premiums.

Most new insurance companies organize as stock corporations. As Figure 2 shows, at the end of 2002, only 83 of 1159 insurance companies were organized as mutuals. (See the "Global" box for a description of a unique form of insurance ownership.)

Types of Insurance

Insurance is classified by which type of undesirable event is insured. The most common types are life insurance and property and casualty insurance. In its simplest form, life insurance provides income for the heirs of the deceased. Many

MINI-CASE

Insurance Agent: The Customer's Ally

An underwriter working for Prudential Insurance was responsible for a number of agents selling property insurance in Southern California in 1985. One agent sold a large number of fire insurance policies and was always careful to document clearly when a fire hydrant was on the property by including it in a photograph attached to the policy application. The agent made a mistake on one policy, however, when he included his car in a picture of a different view of the property. The picture showed a plastic fire hydrant lying in the open trunk of his car. He had been putting this fire hydrant on property for years when he needed to give a low quote to get business.

The agent was neither fired nor sued. He was simply advised to halt the practice, and his policies continued to be accepted by the company.

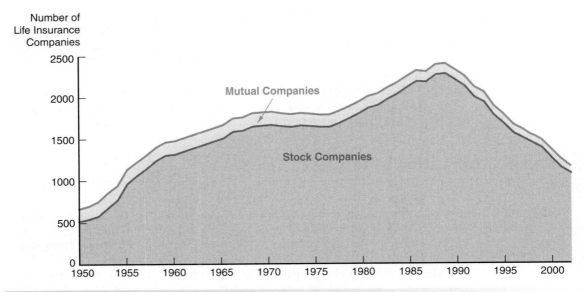

FIGURE 2   *Number of Life Insurance Companies in the United States, 1950–2002*

Source: Life Insurance Fact Book, 2003, Table 1.1 (American Council of Life Insurers).

insurance companies offer policies that provide retirement benefits as well as life insurance. In this case, the premium combines the cost of the life insurance with a savings program. The cost of life insurance depends on such factors as the age of the insured, average life expectancies, the health and lifestyle of the insured (whether the insured smokes, engages in a dangerous hobby such as skydiving, and so on), and the insurance company's operating costs.

Property and casualty insurance protects property (houses, cars, boats, and so on) against losses due to accidents, fire, disasters, and other calamities. Marine insurance, for example, which insures against the loss of a ship and its cargo, is the oldest form of insurance, predating even life insurance. Property and casualty policies tend to be short-term contracts subject to frequent renewal. Another significant distinction between life insurance policies and property and casualty policies is that the latter do not have a savings component. Property and casualty premiums are based simply on the probability of sustaining the loss. That is why car insurance premiums are higher if a driver has had speeding tickets, has caused accidents, or lives in a high-crime area. Each of these events increases the likelihood that the insurance company will have to pay a claim.

Life Insurance

Life is assumed to unfold in a predictable sequence: You work for a number of years while saving for retirement; then you retire, live off the fruits of your earlier labor, and die at a ripe old age. The problem is that you could die too young and not have time to provide for your loved ones, or you could live too long and run out of retirement assets. Either option is very unappealing to most people. The purpose of life insurance is to relieve some of the concern associated with either eventuality. Although insurance cannot make you comfortable with the idea of a premature

GLOBAL

The Woes of Lloyd's of London

In June 1993, Lloyd's of London announced the biggest loss in its history, $4.33 billion for the year 1990 (Lloyd's waits three years to allow all claims to be processed before reporting profits or losses). The chairman of Lloyd's stated that the 1990 deficit "represents in every way the low point of Lloyd's history in the last 305 years."* Things continued to get worse for Lloyd's, with losses continuing until 1992, for a cumulative amount of more than $12 billion over the five-year period 1988–1992.

Lloyd's began in 1688 in a London coffeehouse owned by Edward Lloyd, which was a meeting place for merchants, shipowners, and sea captains. Lloyd's became a marketplace in which members, known as "names," trade pieces of insurance policies in order to spread the risk, a process called *reinsurance*. An unusual feature of Lloyd's is that names are directly exposed to losses because they accept unlimited personal liability for any claims they have to pay. Many of those participating in Lloyd's have come to regret it in recent years, having lost their entire personal fortunes. Indeed, the average loss per name was over $150,000 in 1990. The losses at Lloyd's have also resulted in a slew of lawsuits, with members suing each other right and left over who should be responsible for paying claims.

To survive, the basic structure of Lloyd's has had to change. Lloyd's has opened itself up to corporate capital with only limited liability, has taken measures to lower central spending by the organization, and has altered the way it is governed. In 1996, Lloyd's was able to announce record profits for the year 1993. However, to settle its lawsuits, Lloyd's offered a $4.8 billion rescue package to its 34,000 names, including the creation of a new corporation called Equitas that took over Lloyd's liabilities incurred before 1993, and profits were high for the next few years.

The swings in profits continue to plague Lloyd's. After four years of profitability in the mid-1990s, it suffered four subsequent years of losses. In 2001 alone it lost 3.1 billion pounds. Profitability returned in 2002, and the firm is attempting to take action to mitigate the painful ups and downs it has suffered. In 2003 it hired a new overseer of the 71 insurance groups that make up Lloyd's, who is charged with stabilizing its future. However, since Lloyd's is a market more than a firm, it is difficult to control risk taking and competitive pricing practices.

Whether the changes it has made and the painful lessons it learned in the past will be effective remains to be seen.

---

*"Lloyd's of London Posts Big Loss, Raising Fears on Market's Viability," *Wall Street Journal*, June 23, 1993, p. A10.

---

death, it can at least allow you the peace of mind that comes with knowing that you have provided for your heirs. Life insurance companies also want to help people save for their retirement. In this way, the insurance company provides for the customer's whole life.

The basic products of life insurance companies are life insurance proper, disability insurance, annuities, and health insurance. Life insurance pays off if you die, protecting those who depend on your continued earnings. As mentioned, the person who receives the insurance payment after you die is called the *beneficiary* of the policy. Disability insurance replaces part of your income should you become unable to continue working due to illness or an accident. An **annuity** is an insurance product that will help if you live longer than you expect. For an initial fixed sum or stream of payments, the insurance company agrees to pay you a fixed amount for as long as you live. If you live a short life, the insurance company pays out less than expected. Conversely, if you live unusually long, the insurance company may pay out much more than expected.

Notice one curiosity among these various types of insurance: Although predicting any one individual's life expectancy or probability of being disabled is very difficult, when many people are insured, the actual amount to be paid out by the insurance company can be predicted very accurately. Insurance companies collect and analyze statistics on life expectancies, health claims, disability claims, and other relevant matters.

For example, a life insurance company can predict with a high degree of accuracy when death benefits must be paid by using *actuarial tables* that predict life expectancies. Table 1 lists the expected life of persons at various ages. A 25-year-old female can expect to live another 55.7 years; a 25-year-old male, however, can expect to live only another 50.9 years.

The **law of large numbers** says that when many people are insured, the probability distribution of the losses will assume a normal probability distribution, a distribution that allows accurate predictions. This distribution is important: Because insurance companies insure so many millions of people, the law of large numbers tends to make the company's predictions quite accurate and allows companies to price the policies so that they can earn a profit.

Life insurance policies protect against an interruption in the family's stream of income. The broad categories of life insurance products are *term, whole life*, and *universal life*.

Term Life   The simplest form of life insurance is the *term insurance policy*, which pays out if the insured dies while the policy is in force. This form of policy contains no savings element. Once the policy period expires, there are no residual benefits.

As the insured ages, the probability of death increases, so the cost of the policy rises. For example, Table 2 shows the estimated premiums for a 40-year-old male nonsmoker for $100,000 of term life insurance from a major insurance company. The premium for the first year is $134. This rises to $147 when the insured is 41 years old, $153 when the insured is 42, and so on. By the time the insured is 60 years old, $100,000 of life insurance costs $810 per year. Of course, rates vary among insurance companies, but these sample rates demonstrate how the annual cost of a term policy rises with the age of the insured.

TABLE 1   *Life Expectancy at Various Ages in the United States, 2003*

Age	Male	Female	Total Population
0	74.4	79.8	77.2
1	74.0	79.3	76.7
5	70.1	75.4	72.8
15	60.2	65.5	62.9
25	50.9	55.7	53.4
35	41.5	46.0	43.9
45	32.5	36.6	34.7
55	24.0	27.7	26.0
65	16.4	19.4	18.1
75	10.2	12.3	11.5
85	5.7	6.9	6.5
100	2.5	2.8	2.7

Source: Life Insurance Fact Book, 2003, Table 11.2 (American Council of Life Insurers).

TABLE 2 *Typical Annual Premiums on a $100,000 Term Policy for a 40-Year-Old Male Nonsmoker*

Age of Insured	Cost ($)
40	134
41	147
42	153
45	192
50	286
55	461
60	810

Some term policies fix the premiums for a set number of years, usually five or ten. Alternatively, *decreasing term policies* have a constant premium, but the amount of the insurance coverage declines each year.

Term policies have been historically hard to sell because once they expire, the policyholder has nothing to show for the premium paid. This problem is solved with whole life policies.

Whole Life   A *whole life insurance* policy pays a death benefit if the policyholder dies. Whole life policies usually require the insured to pay a level premium for the duration of the policy. In the beginning, the insured pays more than if a term policy had been purchased. This overpayment accumulates as a cash value that can be borrowed by the insured at reasonable rates.

Survivorship benefits also contribute to the accumulated cash values. When members of the insured pool die, any remaining cash values are divided among the survivors. If the policyholder lives until the policy matures, it can be surrendered for its cash value. This cash value can be used to purchase an annuity. In this way, the whole life policy is advertised as covering the insured for the duration of his or her life.

Universal Life   In the late 1970s, whole life policies fell into disfavor because the rates of return earned on the policy premiums were well below rates available on other investments. For example, say that an investor bought a term policy instead of a whole life policy and invested the difference in the premiums. If she did this each year for the term of the whole life policy, she would be able to pay for term insurance and still have a much greater amount in her investment account than if she had initially purchased the whole life policy. Investment advisers and insurance agents began steering customers away from whole life policies. The sales pitch became "buy term and invest the difference." Because the agents were also selling other investments, they did not suffer from this change in insurance plans. To combat the flow of funds out of their companies, insurance firms introduced the *universal life policy*.

Universal life policies combine the benefits of the term policy with those of the whole life policy. The major benefit of the universal life policy is that the cash value accumulates at a much higher rate.

The universal life policy is structured to have two parts, one for the term life insurance and one for savings. One important advantage that universal life policies have over many alternative investment plans is that the interest earned on the savings portion of the account is tax-exempt until withdrawn. To keep this favorable tax treatment, the cash value of the policy cannot exceed the death benefit.

Universal life policies were introduced in the early 1980s when interest rates were at record high levels. They immediately became very popular and by 1984 accounted for 32% of the volume of life insurance sold. Later, as interest rates fell, their popularity ebbed.

Annuities If we think of term life insurance as insuring against death, the annuity can be viewed as insuring against life. As we noted earlier, one risk people have is outliving their retirement funds. If they live longer than they projected when they initially retired, they could spend all of their money and end up in poverty. One way to avoid this outcome is by purchasing annuities. Once an annuity has been purchased for a fixed amount, it makes payments as long as the beneficiary lives.

Annuities are particularly susceptible to the adverse selection problem. When people retire, they know more about their life expectancy than the insurance company knows. People who are in good health, have a family history of longevity, and have attended to their health all of their lives are more likely to live longer and hence to want to buy an annuity than people in poor or average health. To avoid this problem, insurance companies tend to price individual annuities expensively. Most annuities are sold to members of large groups where all employees covered by a particular pension plan automatically receive their benefit distribution by purchasing an annuity from the insurance company. Because the annuity is automatic, the adverse selection problem is eliminated.

Assets and Liabilities of Life Insurance Companies Life insurance companies derive funds from two sources. First, they receive premiums that represent future obligations that must be met when the insured dies. Second, they receive premiums paid into pension funds managed by the life insurance company. These funds are long-term in nature.

Since life insurance liabilities are predictable and long-term, life insurance companies can invest in long-term assets. Figure 3 shows the distribution of assets

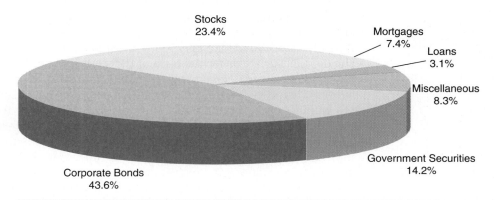

FIGURE 3 *Distribution of Life Insurance Company Assets (beginning of 2003)*

Source: Life Insurance Company Fact Book, 2003, Table 2.4 (American Council of Life Insurers).

of the average life insurance company at the beginning of 2003. Most of the assets are in long-term investments such as corporate stocks and bonds.

Insurance companies have also invested heavily in mortgages and real estate over the years. In 2004, about 6.6% of life insurance assets were invested either in mortgage loans or directly in real estate. This percentage is down substantially from historic levels. Figure 4 displays the percentage of assets invested in mortgages from 1920 to 2004. The decline in mortgage investment, which represents a shift to lower-risk assets, has been offset by increased investment in corporate bonds and government securities.

The shift to less risky securities may be the result of losses suffered by some insurance companies in the late 1980s. As insurance companies competed against mutual funds and money market funds for retirement dollars, they found that they needed higher-return investments. This led some insurance companies to invest in real estate and junk bonds. Deteriorating real estate values brought on by overbuilding during the 1980s caused some firms to suffer large losses. The combination of large real estate losses and junk bond investment contributed to the failure of several large firms in 1991, including Executive Life, with assets of $15 billion, and Mutual Benefit Life, with assets of $14 billion.

Health Insurance

Individual health insurance coverage is very vulnerable to adverse selection problems. People who know that they are likely to get ill are the most likely to seek health insurance coverage. This causes individual health insurance to be very

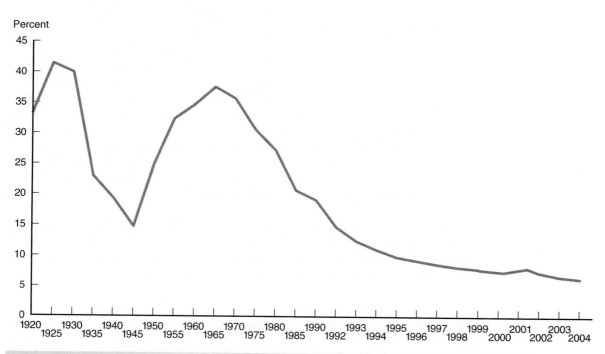

FIGURE 4 *Percentage of Life Insurance Company Assets Invested in Mortgages, 1920–2004*

Source: Federal Reserve Flow of Funds Accounts, Table L117 .

expensive. Most policies are offered through company-sponsored programs in which the company pays all or part of the employee's policy premium.

Most life insurance companies also offer health insurance. Health insurance premiums account for about 25% of total premium income. Life insurance companies compete with Blue Cross and Blue Shield organizations, nonprofit firms that are sponsored by hospitals. Blue Cross usually covers hospital care, and Blue Shield, doctors' services. One national agency coordinates and monitors the 73 Blue Cross/Blue Shield organizations.

The government is also involved in health insurance through Medicare and Medicaid. Medicare provides medical coverage for the elderly, and Medicaid provides coverage for people on welfare.

Health insurance was a major political issue in the 1992 presidential election and continues to be the subject of regulation. In 1996, Congress passed legislation making it more difficult for insurance companies to refuse to insure a person with a preexisting medical problem.

One reason for the extensive debate over medical insurance has been the spiraling costs of health care. For most of the past decade, the cost of health care has risen much faster than the cost of living and real wages. One factor contributing to this increase is the more sophisticated and expensive treatments constantly being offered. For example, studies have shown that cholesterol-reducing drugs can reduce the likelihood of cardiovascular trouble across a broad portion of the population. These drugs cost about $3 per day and did not even exist 15 years ago. Insurance companies have dealt with these rising costs in a number of ways. For example, today the risk of most company-sponsored plans is borne by the company, with the insurance company administering the plan and covering catastrophic expenses. This increases the sponsoring company's incentive to maintain a healthy workforce and to encourage responsible use of medical facilities by its employees. For example, many large firms have found it cost-effective to employ physician assistants on site to reduce medical fees and absenteeism.

Another way that insurance companies are attempting to deal with increased medical costs is by controlling them. This is done by negotiating contracts with physician groups to provide services at reduced cost and through *managed care*, where approval is required before services can be rendered. *Health maintenance organizations (HMOs)* shift the risk from the insurance company to the provider. The insurance company pays the HMO a fixed payment per person covered in exchange for medical services. One problem many people find with the HMO form of health care is that the provider has an incentive to limit medical services. Regulation was required, for example, to ensure mothers at least 48 hours in the hospital following a delivery.

Though it appears that a national health insurance overhaul is not going to come out of Congress, the attention focused on the problem has prompted many changes at the state and local levels. These changes are likely to continue in the future, due largely to pressure from insurance companies.

Property and Casualty Insurance

Property and casualty insurance was the earliest form of insurance. It began in the Middle Ages when merchants sent ships off to foreign ports to trade. A merchant, though willing to accept the risk that the trading might not turn a profit, was often unwilling to accept the risk that the ship might sink or be captured by pirates.

To reduce such risks, merchants began to band together and insure each other's ships against loss. The process became more sophisticated as time went on, and insurance policies were written that were then traded in the major commercial centers of the time.

In 1666, the Great Fire of London did much to advance the case for fire insurance. The first fire insurance company was founded in London in 1680. In the United States, the first fire insurance company was formed by a group led by Benjamin Franklin in 1752. By the beginning of the nineteenth century, the assets of property and casualty insurance firms exceeded even those of commercial banks, making these firms the most important financial intermediary. The invention of the automobile did a great deal to spur the growth of property and casualty insurance companies during the twentieth century.

Property and Casualty Insurance Today   Property and casualty insurance protects against losses from fire, theft, storm, explosion, and even neglect. **Property insurance** protects businesses and owners from the impact of risk associated with owning property. This includes replacement and loss of earnings from income-producing property as well as financial losses to owners of residential property. **Casualty insurance** (or **liability insurance**) protects against liability for harm the insured may cause to others as a result of product failure or accidents. For example, part of your car insurance is property insurance (which pays if your car is damaged), and part is casualty insurance (which pays if you cause an accident).

Property and casualty insurance is different from life insurance. First, policies tend to be short-term, usually for one year or less. Second, whereas life insurance is limited to insuring against one event, property and casualty companies insure against many different events. Finally, the amount of the potential loss is much more difficult to predict than for life insurance. These characteristics cause property and casualty companies to hold more liquid assets than those of life insurance companies. The wide range of losses means that property and casualty firms must maintain substantial liquidity.

Property insurance can be provided in either **named-peril policies** or **open-peril policies.** Named-peril policies insure against loss only from perils that are specifically named in the policy, whereas open-peril policies insure against all perils except those specifically excluded by the policy. For example, many homeowners in low-lying areas are required to buy flood insurance. This insurance covers only losses due to flooding, so it is a named-peril policy. A homeowner's insurance policy, which protects the house from fire, hurricane, tornado, and other damage, is an example of an open-peril policy.

Casualty or liability insurance protects against financial losses because of a claim of negligence. Liability insurance is bought not only by manufacturers who might be sued because of product defects but also by many types of professionals, including physicians, lawyers, and building contractors. Whereas the risk exposure in property insurance policies is relatively easy to predict, since it is usually limited to the value of the property, liability risk exposure is much more difficult to determine.

Liability risk exposure can have long lag times (often referred to as "tails"). This means that a liability claim may be filed long after the policy expires. Consider liability claims filed against the manufacturers of light airplanes. In the 1950s, 1960s, and 1970s, Cessna and Piper produced airplanes that are still being used today. The companies often get sued when one of these 30- or 40-year-old planes crashes. Insurance premiums grew so large in the 1980s due to the extensive lag time that both Cessna and Piper had to stop producing private airplanes. The cost of the liability insurance put the price of the planes out of reach of most private pilots.

There has been extensive publicity about high liability awards given by juries. These awards have often been well above what the insurance companies could have predicted. Liability insurance premiums continue to rise as a result. Some states have attempted to limit liability awards in an effort to contain these insurance costs.

Reinsurance   One way that insurance companies may reduce their risk exposure is to obtain **reinsurance.** Reinsurance allocates a portion of the risk to another company in exchange for a portion of the premium. Reinsurance allows insurance companies to write larger policies because a portion of the policy is actually held by another firm.

About 10% of all property and casualty insurance is reinsured. Smaller insurance firms obtain reinsurance more frequently than large firms. You can think of it as insurance for the insurance company.

Since the originator of the policy usually has more to lose than the reinsurer, the moral hazard and adverse selection problems are small. This means that little specific information about the risk being reinsured is required. As a result of the simplified information requirements, the reinsurance market consists of relatively standardized contracts. One problem with the market is the risk that the reinsurer can fail. For example, in 1990, insurance firms were owed about $20 billion in unrecovered reinsurance.

Terrorism Risk Insurance Act of 2002   The September 11, 2001, terrorist attacks led the insurance industry to rethink its exposure to losses that could potentially destroy even the best-capitalized insurance company. Following an intensive lobbying effort by the insurance industry, new legislation was passed on November 26, 2002, limiting the amount insurance firms would be required to pay out in the event of future attacks. The Terrorism Risk Insurance Act of 2002 is limited to acts of international terrorism in which losses exceed $5 million. Should an act of terrorism occur, as defined in the legislation, the government will pay 90% of the losses. Losses in excess of $100 billion are not covered.

Insurance Regulation

Insurance companies are subject to less federal regulation than many other financial institutions. In fact, the McCarran-Ferguson Act of 1945 explicitly exempts insurance from federal regulation. The primary federal regulator is the Internal Revenue Service, which administers special taxation rules.

Most insurance regulation occurs at the state level. Not only must an insurance company follow the standards set by the state in which it is chartered, but it must also comply with the regulations set in any state in which it does business. New York requires that any insurance company doing business in the state comply with its investment standards. Because New York is such a big market, virtually every company complies. This makes the New York State regulations almost the same as national regulations.

The purpose of most regulations is to protect policyholders from losses due to the insolvency of the company. To accomplish this, insurance companies are restricted as to their asset composition and minimum capital ratio. All states also

CONFLICTS OF INTEREST

Insurance Behemoth Charged with Conflicts of Interest Violations

In October 2004, New York Attorney General Eliot Spitzer charged Marsh & McLennan Cos. (MMC), a $12 billion financial-services company, with fraud related to its insurance brokerage business. This initial attack is likely to have far-reaching effects on an industry that has so far remained removed from the scandals that have plagued other financial service firms.

Companies hire insurance brokers to help them control risk in a cost-effective manner. An insurance broker is hired to use its expertise and influence to search for the best possible prices from the insurance industry. The broker receives a fee for providing this service.

In the complaint filed against MMC, Spitzer charges that the insurance firm engaged in bid-rigging and accepted payoffs from insurance companies in exchange for directing business their way. In practicing bid-rigging, MMC required some insurance companies to submit abnormally high bids. This allowed another favored insurer to receive the business at a price fixed by MMC. The insurance companies were told by MCC that if they did not follow MMC's directions they would lose future business.

MMC also required insurers to pay contingent commissions—payments to MMC for steering clients to them. These pay-to-play revenues amounted to $800 million per year to MMC, or about half of the firm's 2003 net income. An email Spitzer obtained from a senior MMC executive reads, "We need to place our business in 2004 with those that . . . pay us the most." MMC, along with other major insurance brokerage firms Aon and Willis Group Holdings, has halted all contingent commissions.

In the aftermath of these conflicts of interest scandals Chairman and CEO Jeffery Greenberg and four other top executives left the firm. A number of other insurance firms and insurance brokerage companies have come under further scrutiny. In the past, the insurance industry has been largely self-regulated. It is likely that the abuses uncovered by the attorney general and their clear costs to consumers will result in additional regulation and oversight.

require that insurance agents and brokers obtain state licenses to sell each kind of insurance: life, property and casualty, and health. These licenses are to ensure that all agents have a minimum level of knowledge about the products they sell.

See the "Conflicts of Interest" box for a discussion of recent scandals affecting a major insurance broker. Such scandals could result in increased insurance industry regulation.

The Practicing Manager

INSURANCE MANAGEMENT

Insurance companies, like banks, are in the financial intermediation business of transforming one type of asset into another for the public. Insurance companies use the premiums paid on policies to invest in assets such as bonds, stocks, mortgages, and other loans; the earnings from these assets are then used to pay out claims on the policies. In effect, insurance companies transform assets such as bonds, stocks, and loans into insurance policies that provide a set of services (for example, claim adjustments, savings plans, friendly insurance agents). If the insurance company's production process of asset transformation efficiently provides its customers with adequate insurance services at low cost and if it can earn high returns on its investments, it will make profits; if not, it will suffer losses.

In Chapters 2 and 15 the concepts of adverse selection and moral hazard allowed us to understand why financial intermediaries such as insurance companies are important in the economy. Here we use the adverse selection and moral hazard concepts to explain many management practices specific to the insurance industry.

In the case of an insurance policy, moral hazard arises when the existence of insurance encourages the insured party to take risks that increase the likelihood of an insurance payoff. For example, a person covered by burglary insurance might not take as many precautions to prevent a burglary because the insurance company will reimburse most of the losses if a theft occurs. Adverse selection holds that the people most likely to receive large insurance payoffs are the ones who will want to purchase insurance the most. For example, a person suffering from a terminal disease would want to take out the biggest life and medical insurance policies possible, thereby exposing the insurance company to potentially large losses. Both adverse selection and moral hazard can result in large losses to insurance companies because they lead to higher payouts on insurance claims. Minimizing adverse selection and moral hazard to reduce these payouts is therefore an extremely important goal for insurance companies, and this goal explains the insurance practices we discuss here.

Screening

To reduce adverse selection, insurance companies try to screen out poor insurance risks from good ones. Effective information collection procedures are therefore an important principle of insurance management.

When you apply for auto insurance, the first thing your insurance agent does is ask you questions about your driving record (number of speeding tickets and accidents), the type of car you are insuring, and certain personal matters (age, marital status). If you are applying for life insurance, you go through a similar grilling, but you are asked even more personal questions about such things as your health, smoking habits, and drug and alcohol use. The life insurance company even orders a medical evaluation (usually done by an independent company) that involves taking blood and urine samples. The insurance company uses the information you provide to allocate you to a risk class—a statistical estimate of how likely you are to have an insurance claim. Based on this information, the insurance company can decide whether to accept you for the insurance or to turn you down because you pose too high a risk and thus would be an unprofitable customer for the insurance company.

Risk-Based Premium

Charging insurance premiums on the basis of how much risk a policyholder poses for the insurance company is a time-honored principle of insurance management. Adverse selection explains why this principle is so important to insurance company profitability.

To understand why an insurance company finds it necessary to have risk-based premiums, let's examine an example of risk-based insurance premiums that at first glance seems unfair. Harry and Sally, both college students with no accidents or speeding tickets, apply for auto insurance. Normally, Harry will be charged a much higher premium than Sally. Insurance companies do this because young males have a much higher accident rate than young females. Suppose, though, that one insurance company did not base its premiums on a risk classification but rather just charged a premium based on the average combined risk for males and females. Then Sally would be charged too much and Harry too little. Sally could go to another insurance company and get a lower rate, while Harry would sign up for the insurance. Because Harry's premium isn't high enough to cover the accidents he is likely to have, on average the company would lose money on Harry. Only with a premium based on a risk classification, so that Harry is charged more, can the insurance company make a profit.[1]

Restrictive Provisions

Restrictive provisions in policies are another insurance management tool for reducing moral hazard. Such provisions discourage policyholders from engaging in risky activities that make an insurance claim more likely. One type of restrictive provision keeps the policyholder from benefiting from behavior that makes a claim more likely. For example, life insurance companies have provisions in their policies that eliminate death benefits if the insured person commits suicide. Restrictive provisions may also require certain behavior on the part of the insured that makes a claim less likely. A company renting motor scooters may be required to provide helmets for renters in order to be covered for any liability associated with the rental. The role of restrictive provisions is not unlike that of restrictive covenants on debt contracts described in Chapter 15: Both serve to reduce moral hazard by ruling out undesirable behavior.

Prevention of Fraud

Insurance companies also face moral hazard because an insured person has an incentive to lie to the company and seek a claim even if the claim is not valid. For example, a person who has not complied with the restrictive provisions of an insurance contract may still submit a claim. Even worse, a person may file claims for events that did not actually occur. Thus an important management principle for insurance companies is conducting investigations to prevent fraud so that only policyholders with valid claims receive compensation.

Cancellation of Insurance

Being prepared to cancel policies is another insurance management tool. Insurance companies can discourage moral hazard by threatening to cancel a policy when the insured person engages in activities that make a claim more likely. If your auto insurance company makes it clear that if a driver gets too many speeding tickets, coverage will be canceled, you will be less likely to speed.

---

[1]You may recognize that the example here is in fact the lemons problem described in Chapter 15.

Deductibles

The deductible is the fixed amount by which the insured's loss is reduced when a claim is paid off. A $250 deductible on an auto policy, for example, means that if you suffer a loss of $1000 because of an accident, the insurance company will pay you only $750. Deductibles are an additional management tool that helps insurance companies reduce moral hazard. With a deductible, you experience a loss along with the insurance company when you make a claim. Because you also stand to lose when you have an accident, you have an incentive to drive more carefully. A deductible thus makes a policyholder act more in line with what is profitable for the insurance company; moral hazard has been reduced. And because moral hazard has been reduced, the insurance company can lower the premium by more than enough to compensate the policyholder for the existence of the deductible.

Another function of the deductible is to eliminate the administrative costs of small losses by forcing the insured to bear these losses.

Coinsurance

When a policyholder shares a percentage of the losses along with the insurance company, their arrangement is called **coinsurance.** For example, some medical insurance plans provide coverage for 80% of medical bills, and the insured person pays 20% after a certain deductible has been met. Coinsurance works to reduce moral hazard in exactly the same way that a deductible does. A policyholder who suffers a loss along with the insurance company has less incentive to take actions, such as going to the doctor unnecessarily, that involve higher claims. Coinsurance is thus another useful management tool for insurance companies.

Limits on the Amount of Insurance

Another important principle of insurance management is that there should be limits on the amount of insurance provided, even though a customer is willing to pay for more coverage. The higher the insurance coverage, the more the insured person can gain from risky activities that make an insurance payoff more likely and hence the greater the moral hazard. For example, if Zelda's car were insured for more than its true value, she might not take proper precautions to prevent its theft, such as making sure that the key is always removed or putting in an alarm system. If her car were stolen, she comes out ahead because the excessive insurance payoff would allow her to buy an even better car. By contrast, when the insurance payment is lower than the value of her car, she will suffer a loss if it is stolen and will thus take the proper precautions to prevent this from happening. Insurance companies must always make sure that their coverage is not so high that moral hazard leads to large losses.

Summary

Effective insurance management requires several practices: information collection and screening of potential policyholders, risk-based premiums, restrictive provisions, prevention of fraud, cancellation of insurance, deductibles, coinsurance, and limits on the amount of insurance. All of these practices reduce moral hazard and adverse selection by making it harder for policyholders to benefit from engaging in activities that increase the amount and likelihood of claims. With smaller benefits available, the poor insurance risks (those who are more likely to engage in the activities in the first place) see less benefit from the insurance and are thus less likely to seek it out.

Pensions

A **pension plan** is an asset pool that accumulates over an individual's working years and is paid out during the nonworking years. Pension plans represent the fastest-growing financial intermediary. There are a number of reasons for this rapid growth.

As the United States became more urban, people realized that they could not rely on their children to care for them in their retirement. In a rural culture, families tend to stay together on the farm. The property passes from generation to generation with an implicit understanding that the younger generations will care for the older ones. When families became more dispersed and moved off farms, both the opportunity for and the expectation of extensive financial support of the older generations declined.

A second factor contributing to the growth of pension plans is that people are living longer and retiring younger. Again, in the rural setting, people often remained productive well into their retirement years. Many companies in urban America, however, encourage older workers to retire. They are often earning high wages as a result of seniority, yet may be less productive than younger workers. The result of this trend toward younger retirement and longer lives is that the average person can expect to spend more years in retirement. These years must be funded somehow, and the pension plan is often the vehicle of choice.

Types of Pensions

Pension plans can be categorized in several ways. They may be defined-benefit or defined-contribution plans, and they may be public or private.

Defined-Benefit Pension Plans

Under a **defined-benefit plan,** the plan sponsor promises the employees a specific benefit when they retire. The payout is usually determined with a formula that uses the number of years worked and the employee's final salary. For example, a pension benefit may be calculated by the following formula:

Annual payment = 2% × average of final 3 years' income × years of service

In this case, if a worker had been employed for 35 years and the average wages during the last three years were $50,000, the annual pension benefit would be

$$0.02 \times \$50,000 \times 35 = \$35,000 \text{ per year}$$

The defined-benefit plan puts the burden on the employer to provide adequate funds to ensure that the agreed payments can be made. External audits of pension plans are required to determine whether sufficient funds have been contributed by the company. If sufficient funds are set aside by the firm for this purpose, the plan is **fully funded.** If more than enough funds are available, the plan is **overfunded.** Often, insufficient funds are available and the fund is **underfunded.** For example, if Jane Brown contributes $100 per year into her pension plan and the interest rate is 10%, after ten years, the contributions and their interest earnings would be worth $1753.[2] If the defined benefit on her pension plan is $1753 or less after ten years, the plan is fully funded because her contributions and earnings will cover this payment in full. But if the defined benefit is $2000, the plan is underfunded because her contributions and earnings do not cover this amount. Underfunding is most common when the employer fails to contribute adequately to the plan. Surprisingly, it is not illegal for a firm to sponsor an underfunded plan. The companies of the S&P 500, for example, have an estimated aggregate pension deficit of about $150 billion.

Defined-Contribution Pension Plans

As the name implies, instead of defining what the pension plan will pay, **defined-contribution plans** specify only what will be contributed into the fund. The retirement benefits are entirely dependent on the earnings of the fund. Corporate sponsors of defined-contribution plans usually put a fixed percentage of each employee's wages into the pension fund each pay period. In some instances, the employee also contributes to the plan. An insurance company or fund manager acts as trustee and invests the fund's assets. Frequently, employees are allowed to specify how the funds in their individual accounts will be invested. For example, an employee who is a conservative investor may prefer government securities, while one who is a more aggressive investor may prefer to have his or her retirement funds invested in corporate stock. When the employee retires, the balance in the pension account can be transferred into an annuity or some other form of distribution.

Defined-contribution pension plans are becoming increasingly popular. Many existing defined-benefit plans are converting to this form, and virtually all new plans are established as defined-contribution. One reason the defined-contribution plan is becoming so popular is that the onus is put on the employee rather than the employer to look out for the pension plan's performance. This reduces the liability of the employer.

One problem is that plan participants may not understand the need to diversify their holdings. For example, many firms actively encourage employees to invest in company stock. The firm's motivation is to better align employee interest with that of stockholders. The downside is that employees suffer twice should the firm fail. First, they lose their jobs, and second, their retirement portfolios evaporate. The recent collapse of Enron Inc. has brought this issue forcibly to public attention.

---

[2]The $100 contributed in year 1 would become worth $100 \times (1 + 0.10)^{10} = \$259.37$ at the end of ten years; the $100 contributed in year 2 would become worth $100 \times (1 + 0.10)^9 = 235.79$; and so on until the $100 contributed in year 10 would become worth $100 \times (1 + 0.10) = \$110$. Adding these together, we get the total value of these contributions and their earnings at the end of ten years as $1753.

Another problem with defined-contribution plans is that many employees are not familiar enough with investments to make wise long-term choices. For example, only 3.7% of plan participants choose to put any more than half of their investment in stocks, even though long-term growth potential is greatest in the stock market.

Private and Public Pension Plans

Private pension plans, sponsored by employers, groups, and individuals, have grown rapidly as people have become more concerned about the viability of Social Security and more sophisticated about preparing for retirement. In the past, private pension plans invested mostly in government securities and corporate bonds. Although these instruments are still important pension plan assets, corporate stocks, mortgages, open market paper, and time deposits now play a significant role. Figure 5 shows the distribution of private pension plan assets. They are now the largest institutional investor in the stock market. This makes pension plan managers a potentially powerful force if they choose to exercise control over firm management (see the "Mini-Case" box on page 582).

An alternative to privately sponsored pension plans is the public plans, though in many cases there is very little difference between the two. A **public pension plan** is one that is sponsored by a governmental body.

The largest of the public plans is the Federal Old Age and Disability Insurance Program (often called simply Social Security). This pension plan was established in 1935 to provide a safety net for aging Americans and is a "pay-as-you-go" system—money that workers contribute today pays benefits to current recipients. Future generations will be called on to pay benefits to the individuals who are currently contributing. Many people fear that the fund will be unable to meet its obligations by the time they retire. This fear is based on problems that the fund encountered in the 1970s and on the realization that a large number of people from the baby boom generation (born between 1946 and 1964) will swell the ranks of retirees in the rapidly approaching future.

Information on your Social Security benefits is available at www.ssa.gov/

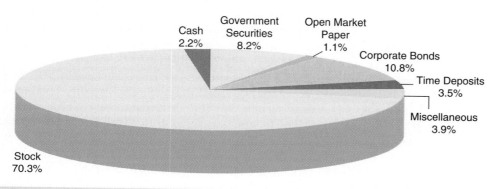

FIGURE 5 *Distribution of Private Pension Plan Assets (end of 2003)*

Source: www.federalreserve.gov/releases/21/current/21.pdf, Table L119.

MINI-CASE

Power to the Pensions

One ramification of the growth of pension plans and other institutional investors is that the managers of these funds have the ability to exercise substantial control over corporate management. Clearly, when a pension fund manager, who controls many thousands of shares, calls a corporate officer, the officer is going to listen. Evidence suggests that fund managers actively apply the power they have to influence corporate management. For example, pension funds recently defeated management-sponsored antitakeover proxy proposals at

Honeywell. And Texaco agreed to name a director from candidates submitted by the huge California Public Employees Retirement System. In addition, the stated mission of the Council of Institutional Investors is to "encourage trustees to take an active role in assuring that corporate actions are not taken at the expense of shareholders." It is possible that these actions will work to benefit shareholders, who do not individually wield enough clout to exert control. However, the clout shareholders wield when their shares are placed into a fund manager's hands may be sufficient to improve corporate management significantly.

The amount of the Social Security benefits a retiree receives is based on the person's earnings history. Workers contribute 6.2% of wages up to a current maximum wage of $87,900 (as of 2004). Employers contribute the same amount. There is a certain amount of redistribution in the benefits, with low-income workers receiving a relatively larger return on their investment than high-income workers. One way to evaluate the amount of the benefits of a pension plan is to determine how the monthly benefits compare to preretirement income. This replacement ratio ranged from 49% for someone earning $15,000 a year to 24% for someone earning $53,400.

Figure 6 shows that the total assets in the Social Security fund decreased in the late 1970s and early 1980s at the same time that the number of insured people was increasing. This situation led to a restructuring that included raising the program's contributions and reducing the program's benefits. To build public confidence, the Social Security system has started accumulating reserves to be used when the baby boom generation begins retiring.

The problem is that the 77 million baby boomers born between 1946 and 1964 will begin reaching their normal retirement ages in 2011. Meanwhile, the number of workers supporting each one of those retirees will fall from 3.3 to 2 by 2038. The government predicts that the Social Security trust fund, built up over the years with excess payroll taxes, will be depleted by that date (see Figure 7). After that, taxes would cover only 75% of benefits. Some experts argue that the crisis will arrive much earlier, as soon as 2018. This is because in 2018 the program will have to start redeeming the trust fund's special Treasury bonds that represent the Social Security surplus. The trouble is that money to redeem these bonds is being spent to run the federal government. By 2030, Social Security will have to redeem $750 billion worth of bonds. "Whether that's a crisis for Social Security, it certainly is a crisis for whoever is around trying to come up with $750 billion," says Michael Tanner, director of the Cato Institute's Project on Social Security Privatization.

A number of proposals are being considered to help keep Social Security viable for the future. The idea that AARP polling finds as the least objectionable is to raise the cap on the maximum amount that workers have to pay into the fund in any given year. The maximum wage that was taxed in 2004 was $87,900, which rep-

www.ssab.gov is the website for the Social Security advisory board. This site will report the most current estimates for when the trust fund will be depleted.

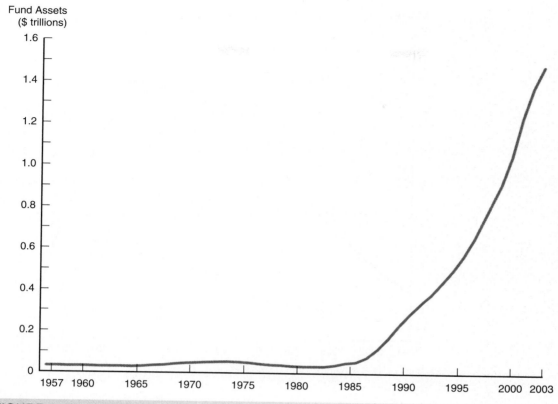

Fund Assets
($ trillions)

FIGURE 6 *Social Security Fund Assets, 1957–2003*

Source: www.ssa.gov/OACT/FACTS/.

resents only 85% of all income. This is down from a tax on 90% of income in 1983. It is likely that this will be one area for change.

Another possible change concerns the minimum age when one can start receiving benefits. This was changed in 1984 to gradually rise so that those born after 1960 cannot start receiving full benefits until they are age 67. The original retirement age of 65 dates back to 1874, when a railroad company established a pension plan. The basis of this decision was that 65 was considered to be the maximum age at which one could safely operate a train. This rule was later incorporated into the Federal Railroad Retirement Act of 1934, which was used to support that retirement age when the Social Security Act was written. Since few Americans are required to operate trains any more, there is some justification for reevaluating the retirement age. The good news is that relatively small changes to the retirement age have a large impact on the Social Security fund balance.

In 2004 Alan Greenspan, the chairman of the Federal Reserve, suggested altering the way that cost of living adjustments to Social Security payments were calculated. Currently the benefit payments are adjusted annually based on the consumer price index (CPI). Greenspan argued that this overstated true inflation because it ignored consumers' switching to less expensive alternatives. While admitting some validity to this, critics argue that the CPI underestimates the increase in medical costs, which make up a large portion of retirees' budgets.

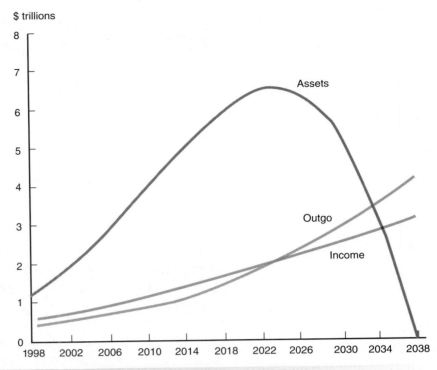

FIGURE 7 *Projected Social Security Trust Fund Assets*

Source: http://www.ssab.gov/actionshouldbetaken.pdf.

Still another suggestion is to recognize that beneficiaries are living longer than in the past and to adjust benefit payments to stretch them over a longer period of time.

Prior to the stock market falling in 2000, many investors were calling for the privatization of Social Security. The biggest obstacle to privatization is that funds diverted into private accounts would not be available to pay current retirees' benefits. This exacerbates the looming problem rather than solving it. Analysts estimate that the cost of transitioning to a fully funded privatized plan would be enormous—about $100 billion. Over time, analysts argue, privatization would gradually transform Social Security from an unfunded, pay-as-you-go system to a fully funded pension with real assets. Workers who retired 20 years ago received all that they paid in, plus interest and much more. But those who retire today will get only about a 2.2% return, adjusted for inflation. A 30-year-old worker will lose money in absolute terms upon retirement. However, falling stock prices in 2000–2002 have reduced support for all privatization options.

In the short term, Social Security reform is more likely to take the form of an increase in tax, a reduction in benefits, a delay in receiving benefits, or all three. For example, the age at which benefits begin is already scheduled to increase from 65 to 67. Some plans suggest delaying benefits until age 70.

If no funding reforms take place and the current estimates regarding the depletion of the Social Security fund are accurate, the payroll tax rate would have to be increased from 12.4% to 18%.

We must remember that these estimates are based on current facts as they are known. Many factors can change to cause the estimates to change. For example, research on cures for cancer has received a great deal of publicity recently. If a cure for any major cause of death is found, the fund will be in greater trouble than currently thought.

www.socialse curity.org/ reformandyou/ sscalc/sscalc. php/ lets you estimate your future Social Security benefits.

Regulation of Pension Plans

For many years, pension plans were relatively free of government regulation. Many companies provided pension benefits as rewards for long years of good service and used the benefits as an incentive. Frequently, pension benefits were paid out of current income. When the firm failed or was acquired by another firm, the benefits ended. During the Great Depression, widespread pension plan failures led to increased regulation and to the establishment of the Social Security system.

A major U.S. Supreme Court decision in 1949 established that pension benefits were a legitimate part of collective bargaining, the negotiation of contracts by unions. This decision led to a great increase in the number of plans in existence as unions pressured employers to establish such plans for union members.

Employee Retirement Income Security Act

The most important and most comprehensive legislation affecting pension funds is the **Employee Retirement Income Security Act (ERISA),** passed in 1974. ERISA set certain standards that must be followed by all pension plans. Failure to follow the provisions of the act may cause a plan to lose its advantageous tax status. The motivation for the act was that many workers who had contributed to plans for many years were losing their benefits when plans failed. The principal features of the act are the following:

- ERISA established guidelines for funding.
- It provided that employees switching jobs may transfer their credits from one employer plan to the next.
- It said that plans must have minimum vesting requirements. *Vesting* refers to how long an employee must work for the company to be eligible for pension benefits. The maximum permissible vesting period is seven years, though most plans allow for vesting in less time. Employee contributions are always immediately vested.
- It increased the disclosure requirements for pension plans, providing employees with more ample information about the health and investments of their pension plans.
- It assigned the responsibility of regulatory oversight to the Department of Labor.

www.pbgc.gov provides additional information about the Pension Benefit Guarantee Corporation.

ERISA also established the **Pension Benefit Guarantee Corporation** (PBGC or simply called **Penny Benny**), a government agency that performs a role similar to that of the FDIC. It insures pension benefits up to a limit (currently just over $44,386 per year per person) if a company with an underfunded pension plan goes bankrupt or is unable to meet its pension obligations for other reasons. Penny Benny charges pension plans a premium to pay for this insurance, but it can also borrow funds up to $100 million from the U.S. Treasury. Penny Benny currently pays benefits to about 460,000 retirees whose pension plans failed.

Almost 60% of defined-benefit pension plan assets are invested in stocks. When the market prices were high, most defined-benefit pension plans were adequately funded. However, the market fall in 2000 along with low interest rates and a weak economy have put many pension plans in jeopardy. As a result, in 2004 PBGC was in the red by $11.2 billion. According to PBGC, there is another $85 billion in pension deficits on the books of weak companies that could end up pushing this deficit far higher.

The accounting for pension plans makes it very difficult to accurately access whether a fund is over- or underfunded. The assumptions behind such calculations are subject to constant revision and argument. Cash-strapped firms have tremendous incentive to underfund their pension plans, and Congress is reluctant to enforce higher payments that could put a firm at greater risk of failure.

The Pension Benefit Guaranty Corporation is rapidly facing a funding crisis that could have far-reaching effects. Many defined-benefit pension funds are in severe trouble due to the increasing life spans of their pensioners, increased medical costs, and weak corporate income that has made it difficult to keep up with funding obligations. For example, United Airlines owes a total of $5.1 billion in benefits between 2004 and 2008 to former employees. Given its poor health, UAL is unlikely to be able to make these payments. Many other pension funds are seriously underfunded. In 2004 Ford's pension plan deficit was $11.7, General Motors' was $8.6 billion, and Delta Airlines' was $5.7 billion.

Many firms with defined-benefit plans find it hard to compete against firms with much lower cost defined-contribution plans. This competitive disadvantage increases the likelihood that the firms may not survive to pay down their deficits. For example, General Motors' profit margin per car in 2003 was 0.5%. Without the burden of pension and retiree health care costs, the margin would have been 5.5%. Morgan Stanley estimates that the benefits cost is $1784 per car for GM, while it is only $200 per car for Toyota.

Firms often fail when they face a cost disadvantage. Due to higher costs, including pension obligations, Bethlehem Steel, LTV, and National Steel all filed for bankruptcy in 2002 and terminated their pension plans. PBGC is now paying over 200,000 former steel workers' benefits. International Steel Group Inc. (ISG) has acquired the mills of these old steel companies and is now the largest steel producer in the country. Its defined-contribution cost for employees was $45 million in 2003. Prior to its bankruptcy, Bethlehem Steel alone was paying out $500 million a year in pension benefits.

If firms with defined benefit plans continue to fail, PBGC will be forced to assume their pension funds' liabilities. These obligations could quickly surpass the financial resources available to PBGC if the economy remains weak. In that event, taxpayers may be called upon to make up the difference.

The government is not strictly responsible for backing up PBGC; however, most observers feel it could not politically allow pensioners to lose their benefits. The temporary fix is to allow firms to use a higher interest rate in their pension calculations so that their pension liability is reduced. The hope is that the economy will continue to revive, stocks will rise, and interest rates increase. Recall from Chapter 19 that this same technique (called regulatory forbearance) was used to prolong the savings and loan crisis. We can only hope it works better this time.

Individual Retirement Plans

The Pension Reform Act of 1978 updated the Self-Employed Individuals Tax Retirement Act of 1962 to authorize **individual retirement accounts (IRAs).** IRAs permitted people (such as those who are self-employed) who are not covered by other pension plans to contribute into a tax-deferred savings account. Legislation in 1981 and 1982 expanded the eligibility of these accounts to make them available to almost everyone. IRAs proved extremely popular, to the extent that their use resulted in significant losses of tax revenues to the government. That led Congress to include provisions in the Tax Reform Act of 1986 sharply curtailing eligibility.

Keogh plans are a retirement savings option for the self-employed. Funds can be deposited with a depository institution, life insurance company, or securities firm. The owner of the Keogh is often allowed some discretion as to how the funds will be invested.

On January 1, 1997, the Small Business Protection Act of 1996 went into effect. This act created simplified retirement plans with so-called SIMPLE IRAs and 401(k) plans for businesses with 100 or fewer employees. SIMPLE retirement plans are becoming significantly more popular, especially among the smallest businesses.

The Future of Pension Funds

We can expect that pension funds will continue their growth and popularity as the population continues to grow and age. Workers in their early years of employment often find discussions of retirement investing creeping into their conversations. This heightened attention to providing for the future will result in an increased number of pension funds as well as a greater variety of pension fund options to choose among. We can also expect to see pension funds gain increased power over corporations as they control increasing amounts of stock.

Summary

1. Insurance companies exist because people are risk-averse and prefer to transfer risk away from themselves. Insurance benefits people's lives by reducing the size of reserves they would have to maintain to cover possible loss of life or property.

2. Adverse selection and moral hazard are problems inherent to the insurance business. Many of the provisions of insurance policies—including deductibles, application screening, and risk-based premiums—are aimed at reducing their effects.

3. Insurance is usually divided into two primary types, life insurance and property and casualty insurance. Many life insurance products also serve as savings vehicles. Property and casualty insurance usually has a much shorter term than most life insurance.

4. Because life insurance liabilities are very predictable, these insurers are able to invest in long-term assets. Property and casualty insurance companies must keep their assets more liquid to pay out on unexpected losses.

5. Pension plans are rapidly growing as a longer-lived generation plans for early retirement.

6. There are two primary types of pension plans: defined-benefit and defined-contribution. Defined-benefit plans pay benefits according to a formula that is established in advance. Defined-contribution plans specify only how much is to be saved; benefits depend on the returns generated by the plans.

7. The largest public pension plan is Social Security, which is a pay-as-you-go system. Current retirees receive payments from current workers. Many people are concerned that as the number of retirees increases, the amount paid in to the Social Security system will not be sufficient to cover the sums being paid out.

8. Most private pension plans are insured by the Pension Benefit Guarantee Corporation, which pays benefits when a plan's sponsor goes bankrupt or is otherwise unable to make payments.

Key Terms

annuity, *p. 567*
casualty (liability) insurance, *p. 573*
certainty equivalent, *p. 562*
coinsurance, *p. 578*
deductible, *p. 564*
defined-benefit plan, *p. 579*
defined-contribution plan, *p. 580*
Employee Retirement Income Security Act (ERISA), *p. 585*
fully funded, *p. 580*

individual retirement account (IRA), *p. 587*
law of large numbers, *p. 568*
mutual insurance company, *p. 565*
named-peril policy, *p. 573*
open-peril policy, *p. 573*
overfunded, *p. 580*
Pension Benefit Guarantee Corporation (Penny Benny), *p. 585*
pension plan, *p. 579*

private pension plan, *p. 581*
property insurance, *p. 573*
public pension plan, *p. 581*
reinsurance, *p. 574*
stock company, *p. 565*
underfunded, *p. 580*
underwriter, *p. 565*

Questions

1. Why do people choose to buy insurance even if their expected loss is less than the payments they will make to the insurance company?

2. Why do insurance companies not allow people to buy insurance on personally unrelated risks?

3. What is information asymmetry, and how does it affect insurance companies?

4. Distinguish between adverse selection and moral hazard as they relate to the insurance industry.

5. How do insurance companies protect themselves against losses due to adverse selection and moral hazard?

6. Distinguish between independent agents and exclusive agents.

7. Are most insurance companies organized as mutuals or stock companies?

8. How are insurance companies able to predict their losses from claims accurately enough to let them price their policies such that they will make a profit?

9. What is the difference between term life insurance and whole life insurance?

10. What risks do property and casualty insurance policies protect against?

11. What is the purpose behind reinsurance?

12. Distinguish between defined-benefit and defined-contribution pension plans.

13. Why have private pension plans grown rapidly in recent years?

14. What is a pay-as-you-go pension plan?

15. Why is Social Security in danger of eventually going bankrupt?

Quantitative Problems

1. Research indicates that the 1,000,000 cars in your city experience unrecoverable losses of $250,000,000 per year from theft, collisions, etc. If 30% of premiums are used to cover expenses, what premium must be charged to car owners?

2. Assume that life expectancy in the United States is normally distributed with a mean of 73 years and a standard deviation of 9 years. What is the probability that you will live to be over 100 years old?

3. Your rich uncle dies, leaving you a life insurance policy worth $100,000. The insurance company also offers you an option to receive $8,225 per year for 20 years, with the first payment due today. Which option should you use?

4. A home products manufacturer estimates that the probability of being sued for product defects is 1% per year per product manufactured. If the firm currently manufactures 20 products, what is the

probability that the firm will experience no lawsuits in a given year?

5. Kio Outfitters estimated the following losses and probabilities from past experience:

Loss	Probability (%)
$30,000	0.25
$15,000	0.75
$10,000	1.50
$5,000	2.50
$1,000	5.00
$250	15.00
$0	75.00

What is the probability Kio will experience a loss of $5000 or greater? If an insurance company offers a loss policy with $1500 deductible, what is the most Kio will pay?

6. A client needs assistance with retirement planning. Here are the facts:

- The client, Dave, is 21 years old. He wants to retire at 65.
- Dave has disposable income of $2,000 per month.
- The IRA Dave has chosen has an average annual return of 8%.

If Dave contributes half of his disposable income to the account, what will it be worth at 65? How much would he need to contribute to have $5,000,000 at 65?

7. When opening an IRA account, investors have two options. With a regular IRA account, funds added are not taxed initially, but are taxed when withdrawn. With a Roth IRA, the funds are taxed initially, but not when withdrawn. If an investor wants to contribute $15,000 before taxes to an IRA, what will be the difference after 30 years between the two options? Assume that the investor is currently in the 25% tax bracket, and that the IRA will earn 6% per year.

8. An employee contributes $200 a year (at the end of the year) to her pension plan. What would be the total contributions and value of the account after five years? Assume that the plan earns 15% per year over the period.

9. Paul's car slid off the icy road, causing $2500 in damage to his car. He was also treated for minor injuries, costing $1300. His car insurance has a $500 deductible, after which the full loss is paid. His health insurance has a $100 deductible and covers 75% of medical cost (total). What was Paul's out-of-pocket costs from the incident?

Web Exercises

Insurance Companies and Pension Funds

1. There are many sites on the Web to help you compute whether you are properly preparing for your retirement. One of the better is offered by Quicken. You will find it at **http://cgi.money.cnn.com/tools/ retirementplanner/retirementplanner.jsp**.

Have you set aside enough retirement money to last your lifetime? The earlier you start, the easier it will be.

In general, your retirement funds will come from four sources:

- Pension plans
- Social Security
- Tax-deferred savings
- Basic (taxable) savings

Use the Retirement Planner to predict the income from the first two, and to determine how much you will need to save to make up the balance for your retirement goals.

2. An alternative to the financial goals calculation in problem 1 is sites that offer calculators that let you input figures to compute your goals. Go to **http://www.financialcalc.com**. Use each of the four calculators provided at this site to solve a sample problem of interest to you.

3. The Internet offers many calculators to help consumers estimate their needs for various financial services. When using these tools, you must remember that they are usually sponsored by financial intermediaries that hope to sell you products. Visit one such site at **www.finaid.org/calculators/ lifeinsuranceneeds.phtml** and calculate how much life insurance you need. Do you have another life insurance policy? Use the calculator to see if that policy is large enough.

CHAPTER 23

Investment Banks, Security Brokers and Dealers, and Venture Capital Firms

Preview

If you decide to take advantage of that hot stock tip you just heard about from your roommate, you may need to interact with a securities company. Similarly, as the new CFO of WWCF, a candy manufacturer, you may need a securities company if you are asked to coordinate a bond sale or to issue additional stock. If your grandfather decides to sell his firm to the public, you may need to help him by working with investment bankers at that securities company. Finally, if you are looking for capital to grow a small, but successful, start-up company, you may need the help of a venture capital firm.

The smooth functioning of securities markets, in which bonds and stocks are traded, involves several financial institutions, including securities brokers and dealers, investment banks, and venture capital firms. None of these institutions were included in our list of financial intermediaries in Chapter 2 because they do not perform the intermediation function of acquiring funds by issuing liabilities and then using the funds to acquire financial assets. Nonetheless, they are important in the process of channeling funds from savers to spenders.

To begin our look at how securities markets work, recall the distinction between primary and secondary securities markets discussed in Chapter 2. In a primary market, new issues of a security are sold to buyers by the corporation or government agency ultimately using the funds. A secondary market then trades the securities that have been sold in the primary market (and so are secondhand). Investment banks assist in the initial sale of securities in the primary market; securities brokers and dealers assist in the trading of securities in the secondary markets. Finally, venture capital firms provide funds to companies not yet ready to sell securities to the public.

Investment Banks

Investment bankers were called "Masters of the Universe" in Tom Wolfe's *The Bonfire of the Vanities*. They are the elite on Wall Street. They have earned this reputation from the types of financial services they provide. Investment banks are best known as intermediaries that help corporations raise funds. However, this definition is far too narrow to accurately explain the many valuable and sophisticated services these companies provide. (Despite its name, an investment bank is not a bank in the ordinary sense; that is, it is not a financial intermediary that takes in deposits and then lends them out.). In addition to underwriting the initial sale of stocks and bonds, **investment banks** also play a pivotal role as deal makers in the mergers and acquisitions area, as intemediaries in the buying and selling of companies, and as private brokers to the very wealthy. Some well-known investment banking firms are Morgan Stanley, Merrill Lynch, Salomon Brothers, First Boston Corporation, and Goldman, Sachs.

One feature of investment banks that distinguishes them from stockbrokers and dealers is that they usually earn their income from fees charged to clients rather than from commissions on stock trades. These fees are often set as a fixed percentage of the dollar size of the deal being worked. Because the deals frequently involve huge sums of money, the fees can be substantial. The percentage fee will be smaller for large deals, in the neighborhood of 3%, and much larger for smaller deals, sometimes exceeding 10%.

Background

In the early 1800s, most American securities had to be sold in Europe. As a result, most securities firms developed from merchants who operated a securities business as a sideline to their primary business. For example, the Morgans built their initial fortune with the railroads. To help raise the money to finance railroad expansion, J. P. Morgan's father resided in London and sold Morgan railroad securities to European investors. Over time, the profitability of the securities businesses became evident and the securities industry expanded.

Prior to the Great Depression, many large, money center banks in New York sold securities and simultaneously conducted conventional banking activities. During the Depression about 10,000 banks failed (about 40 percent of all commercial banks). This led to the passage of the **Glass-Steagall Act,** which separated commercial banking from investment banking.

The Glass-Steagall Act made it illegal for a commercial bank to buy or sell securities on behalf of its customers. The original reasoning behind this legislation was to insulate commercial banks from the greater risk inherent in the securities business. There were also concerns that conflicts of interest might arise that would subject commercial banks to increased risk. For example, suppose that an investment banker working at a commercial bank makes a mistake pricing a new stock offering. After promising the customer that he can sell the stock for $20, no sales materialize. The investment banker might be tempted to go down the hall to the commercial bank's investment department and talk them into bailing him out. This would subject depositors to the risk that the bank could lose money on poor investments.

Regulators thought another problem existed. Suppose the investment banker still cannot sell all of that $20 stock issue. He could call up bank customers and offer to loan them 100% of the funds needed to buy a portion of the stock issue.

This would not cause a problem if the stock price rose in the future, but if it fell, the value of the securities would be less than the amount of the loan and the customer might not feel a great obligation to repay the loan. Many industry observers felt that this practice was partially to blame for some of the bank failures that occurred during the Depression. However, bank lobbyists currently argue that although only large banks were involved in issuing securities, most banks that actually failed were small. There is no evidence that security abuses led directly to any bank failures.

When the Glass-Steagall Act separated commercial banking from investment banking, new securities firms were created, many of which currently offer both investment banking services (selling new securities to the public) as well as brokerage services (selling existing securities to the public).

The legal barriers between commercial and investment banks have been decaying rapidly since the 1980s. One significant trend has been the acquisition of investment banks by commercial banks. For example, in 1997, Bankers Trust acquired Alex Brown, the oldest investment bank in the nation. Bankers Trust was subsequently acquired by Deutsche Banks, which has been spending enormous amounts of money establishing its own investment banking arm. Bank of America bought Roberson Stephens & Co., while NationsBank acquired Montgomery Securities. Subsequent mergers among banks are continuing the consolidation.

Underwriting Stocks and Bonds

When a corporation wants to borrow or raise funds, it may decide to issue long-term debt or equity instruments. It then usually hires an investment bank to facilitate the issuance and subsequent sale of the securities. The investment bank may underwrite the issue. The process of underwriting a stock or bond issue requires that the securities firm *purchase* the entire issue at a predetermined price and then resell it in the market. There are a number of services provided in the process of underwriting.

Giving Advice   Most firms do not issue capital market securities very frequently. Over 80% of all corporate expansion is financed using profits retained from prior-period earnings. As a result, the financial managers at most firms are not familiar with how to proceed with a new security offering. Investment bankers, since they participate in this market daily, can provide advice to firms contemplating a sale. For instance, a firm may not know if it should raise capital by selling stocks or by selling bonds. The investment bankers may be able to help by pointing out, for example, that the market is currently paying high prices for stocks in the firm's industry (historically high PE ratios), while bonds are currently carrying relatively high interest rates (and therefore low prices).

Firms may also need advice as to *when* securities should be offered. If, for example, competitors have recently released earnings reports that show poor profits, it may be better to wait before attempting a sale: Firms want to time the market to sell stock when it will obtain the highest possible price. Again, because of daily interaction with the securities markets, investment bankers should be able to advise firms on the timing of their offerings.

Possibly the most difficult advice an investment banker must give a customer concerns at what *price* the security should be sold. Here the investment banker and the issuing firm have somewhat differing motives. First, consider that the firm wants to sell the stock for the highest price possible. Suppose you started a firm and ran it well for 20 years. You now wish to sell it to the public and retire to Tahiti. If 500,000 shares are to be offered and sold at $10 each, you will receive $5 million for your company. If you can sell the stock for $12, you will receive $6 million.

Investment bankers, however, do not want to overprice the stock because in most underwriting agreements, they will buy the entire issue at the agreed price and then resell it through their brokerage houses. They earn a profit by selling the stock at a slightly higher price than they paid the issuing firm. If the issue is priced too high, the investment bank will not be able to resell, and it will suffer a loss.

Pricing securities is not too hard if the firm has prior issues currently selling in the market, called **seasoned issues.** When a firm issues stock for the first time, called an **initial public offering (IPO),** it is much more difficult to determine what the correct price should be. All of the skill and expertise of the investment banking firm will be used to determine the most appropriate price. If the issuing firm and the investment banking firm can come to agreement on a price, the investment banker can assist with the next stage, filing the required documents.

Filing Documents   In addition to advising companies, investment bankers will assist with making the required **Securities and Exchange Commission (SEC)** filings. The activities of investment banks and the operation of primary markets are heavily regulated by the SEC, which was created by the Securities and Exchange Acts of 1933 and 1934 to ensure that adequate information reaches prospective investors. Issuers of new securities to the general public (for amounts greater than $1.5 million in a year and with a maturity longer than 270 days) must file a **registration statement** with the SEC. This statement contains information about the firm's financial condition, management, competition, industry, and experience. The firm also discloses what the funds will be used for and management's assessment of the risk of the securities. The issuer must then wait 20 days after the registration statement is filed with the SEC before it can sell any of the securities. The SEC will review the registration statement, and if it does not object during a 20-day waiting period, the securities can then be sold.

The SEC review in no way represents an endorsement of the offering by the SEC. Their approval merely means that all of the required statements and disclosures are included in the statement. Nor does SEC approval mean that the information is accurate. Inaccuracies in the registration statement open the issuing firm's management up to lawsuits if it incurs losses. In extreme cases, inaccuracies could result in criminal charges.

A portion of the registration statement is reproduced and made available to investors for review. This widely circulated document is called a **prospectus.** By law, investors must be given a prospectus before they can invest in a new security.

While the registration document is in the process of being approved, the investment banker has other chores to attend to. For issues of debt, the investment banker must:

- Secure a credit rating from one or more of the credit review companies, such as Standard and Poor's or Moody's.
- Hire a bond counsel who will issue a statement attesting to the legality of the issue.
- Select a trustee who is responsible for seeing that the issuer fulfills its obligations as stated in the security's contract.
- Have the securities printed and prepared for distribution.

For equity issues, the investment banker may arrange for the securities to appear on one of the stock exchanges. Clearly, the investment banker can be of great assistance to an issuer well before any securities are actually offered for sale.

Underwriting   Once all of the paperwork has been completed, the investment banker can proceed with the actual underwriting of the issue. At a prespecified time and date, the issuer will sell all of the stock or bond issue to the investment banking firm at the agreed price. The investment banker must now distribute this issue to the public at a greater price to earn its fee. (The ten largest underwriters in the United States are listed in Table 1.)

By agreeing to underwrite an issue, the investment banking firm is certifying the qualify of the issue to the public. We again see how asymmetric information helps justify the need for an intermediary. Investors do not want to put in weeks and weeks of hard technical study of a firm before buying its stock. Nor can they trust the firm's insiders to accurately report its condition. Instead, they rely on the ability of the investment bank to collect information about the firm in order to accurately establish the firm's value. They trust the investment bank's assessment, since it is backing up its opinion by actually purchasing securities in the process of underwriting them. Investment bankers recognize the responsibility they have to report information accurately and honestly, since once they lose investors' confidence, they will no longer be able to market their deals.

The investment banking firm is clearly taking a huge risk at this point. One way that it can reduce the risk is by forming a **syndicate.** A syndicate is a group of investment banking firms each of which buys a portion of the security issue. Each firm in the syndicate is then responsible for reselling its share of the securities. Most securities issues are sold by syndicates because it is such an effective way to spread the risk among many different firms.

Investment banks advertise upcoming securities offerings with ads in the *Wall Street Journal.* The traditional advertisement is a large block ad in the financial section of the paper. These ads are called **tombstones** because of their shape, and

TABLE 1   *Top Ten U.S. Underwriters of Global Debt and Equity Issues, 2004*

Underwriter	Market Share (%)
1. Citigroup	9.4
2. Morgan Stanley	7.3
3. J.P. Morgan	6.8
4. Merrill Lynch	6.6
5. Lehman Brothers	6.5
6. Credit Suisse First Boston	6.4
7. Deutsche Bank	5.9
8. UBS	5.3
9. Goldman Sachs	5.0
10. Bank of America Securities	3.6
Total	62.8

Source: Wall Street Journal, January 3, 2005, section R, p.17.

they list all of the investment banking firms included in the syndicate. Review the tombstone reproduced in the "Following the News" box. The footnote states that this is neither an offer to sell nor will offers to buy be accepted. The actual offer to sell can only be made in the prospectus. Also note the number of different investment banking firms involved in the syndicate.

The longer the investment banker holds the securities before reselling them to the public, the greater the risk that a negative price change will cause losses. One way that the investment banking firm speeds the sale is to solicit offers to buy the securities from investors prior to the date the investment bankers actually take ownership. Then, when the securities are available, the orders are filled and the securities are quickly transferred to the final buyers.

Most investment bankers are attached to larger brokerage houses (multi-function securities firms) that have nationwide sales offices. Each of these offices will be contacted prior to the issue date, and the sales agents will contact their customers to see if they would like to review a prospectus on the new security. The goal is to **fully subscribe** the issue. A fully subscribed issue is one where all of the securities available for sale have been spoken for before the issue date. Security issues may also be **undersubscribed.** In this case, the sales agents have been unable to generate sufficient interest in the security among their customers to sell all of the securities by the issue date. An issue may also be **oversubscribed,** in which case there are more offers to buy than there are securities available.

It is tempting to assume that the best alternative is for an issue to be oversubscribed, but in fact this will alienate the investment banker's customers. Suppose you were issuing a security for the first time and had negotiated with your investment banker to sell the issue of 500 thousand shares of stock at $20. Now you find out that the issue is oversubscribed. You would feel that the investment banker had set the price too low and that you had lost money as a result. Maybe the stock could have sold for $25 and you could have collected an extra $2.5 million [($25 − $20) × 500,000 = $2,500,000]. You, as well as other issuing firms, would be unlikely to use this investment banker in the future.

It is equally serious for an issue to be undersubscribed, since it may be necessary to lower the price below the price the investment bankers paid to the issuer in order to sell all of the securities to the public. The investment banking firm stands to lose extremely large amounts of money because of the volume of securities involved. For example, review the tombstone shown in the "Following the News" box once more. There are over 24 million shares being offered for sale. If the price must be lowered by even $.25 per share, over $6,000,000 would be lost. The high risk taken by investment bankers explains why they tend to be the most elite and highest paid professionals on Wall Street, many earning in the millions of dollars per year.

Best Efforts   An alternative to underwriting a securities offering is to offer the securities under a *best efforts agreement*. In a best efforts agreement the investment banker sells the securities on a commission basis with no guarantee regarding the price the issuing firm will receive. The advantage to the investment banker of a best efforts transaction is that there is no risk of mispricing the security. There is also no need for the time-consuming task of establishing the market value of the security. The investment banker simply markets the security at the price the customer asks. If the security fails to sell, the offering can be canceled.

THE *WALL STREET JOURNAL*: FOLLOWING THE NEWS

New Securities Issues

Information about new securities being issued is presented in distinctive advertisements published in the *Wall Street Journal* and other newspapers. These advertisements, called "tombstones" because of their appearance, are typically found in the "Money and Investing" section of the *Journal*.

The tombstone shown here indicates the number of shares of stock being issued (24,636,659 shares for Google) and the investment banks involved in selling them.

Google™

24,636,659 Shares

Initial Public Offering of Class A Common Stock
(par value $0.001 per share)

Expected Price Range: $108 to $135 per share

You may obtain an electronic copy of the preliminary prospectus from any of the underwriters listed below.

Joint Book-Running Managers

Morgan Stanley   **Credit Suisse First Boston**

Goldman, Sachs & Co.   **Citigroup**

Lehman Brothers   **Allen & Company LLC**

JPMorgan   **UBS Investment Bank**

WRHambrecht+Co   **Thomas Weisel Partners LLC**

Ameritrade   **M.R. Beal & Company**   **William Blair & Company**

Blaylock & Partners, L.P.   **Cazenove Inc.**   **Deutsche Bank Securities**

E*TRADE Securities Inc.   **Epoch Securities, Inc.**   **Fidelity Capital Markets**   **HARRIS***direct*
  (distributed by Charles Schwab & Co., Inc.)   (a division of National Financial, LLC, a Fidelity Investments company)

Lazard   **Needham & Company, Inc.**   **Piper Jaffray**   **Ramirez & Co., Inc.**

Muriel Siebert & Co., Inc.   **Utendahl Capital**   **Wachovia Securities**   **Wells Fargo Securities, LLC**

Source: Wall Street Journal, August 2, 2004 p. C5.

Private Placements   An alternative method of selling securities is called the *private placement.* In a private placement, securities are sold to a limited number of investors rather than to the public as a whole. The advantage of the private placement is that the security does not need to be registered with the SEC as long as certain restrictive requirements are satisfied. Investment bankers are also often involved in private placement transactions. While investment bankers are not required for a private placement, they often facilitate the transaction by advising the issuing firm on the appropriate terms for the issue and by identifying potential purchasers.

The buyers of private placements must be large enough to purchase large amounts of securities at one time. This means that the usual buyers are insurance companies, commercial banks, pension funds, and mutual funds. Private placements are more common for the sale of bonds than for stocks. Goldman Sachs is the most active investment banking firm in the private placement market.

The process of taking a security public is summarized in Figure 1.

Equity Sales

Another service offered by investment banks is to help with the sale of companies or corporate divisions. For example, in 1984, Mattel was dangerously close to having its bank loans called when its electronics subsidiary incurred significant losses. Mattel enlisted the help of the investment banking firm Drexel Burnham Lambert. The first step in the firm's restructuring was to sell off all of its nontoy businesses. Mattel returned to health until it again ran into problems in 1999 due to the acquisition of a software company. In 2000, Mattel again used the services of investment bankers to sell this subsidiary.

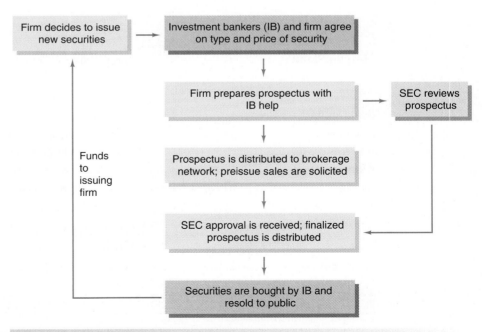

FIGURE 1   *Using Investment Bankers to Distribute Securities to the Public*

The first step in any equity sale will be the seller's determination of the business's worth. The investment banker will provide a detailed analysis of the current market for similar companies and apply various sophisticated models to establish company value. Unlike a box of detergent or bar of candy, a going concern has no set price. The company value is based on the use the buyer intends to make of it. If a buyer is only interested in the physical assets, the firm will be worth one amount. A buyer who sees the firm as an opportunity to take advantage of synergies between this firm and another will have a very different price. Despite the elasticity of the yardstick, investment bankers have developed a number of tools to give business owners a range of values for their firms.

How much cash flows will have to be discounted depends very much on who will be bidding on the firm. Again, investment bankers help. They may make discreet inquiries to feel out who in the market may be interested. Additionally, they will prepare a **confidential memorandum** that presents the detailed financial information required by prospective buyers to make an offer for the company. All prospective buyers must sign a confidentiality agreement stipulating that they will not use the information to compete or share it with third parties. The investment bank will screen prospects to ensure that the information goes only to qualified buyers.

The next step in an equity sale will be the **letter of intent** issued by a prospective buyer. This document signals a desire to go forward with a purchase and outlines preliminary terms. The investment banker will negotiate the terms of the sale on the seller's behalf and will help to analyze and rank competing offers. The investment banker may even help structure financing in order to obtain a better offer.

Once the letter of intent has been accepted by the seller, the **due diligence** period begins. This 20- to 40-day period is used by the buyer to verify the accuracy of the information contained in the confidential memorandum. The findings shape the terms of the **definitive agreement.** This agreement converts information gathered during the due diligence period and the results of subsequent negotiations into a legally binding contract.

As this discussion demonstrates, a wide variety of skills are required to move a typical corporate sale forward. To meet these needs, investment banks often send in multidisciplined teams of experts to work with clients on their projects. These teams include attorneys, financial analysts, accountants, and industry experts.

Mergers and Acquisitions

Investment banks have been active in the **mergers and acquisitions market** since the 1960s. A merger occurs when two firms combine to form one new company. Both firms support the merger, and corporate officers are usually selected so that both companies contribute to the new management team. Stockholders turn in their stock for stock in the new firm. In an acquisition, one firm acquires ownership of another by buying its stock. Often this process is friendly, and the firms agree that certain economies can be captured by combining resources. At other times, the firm being purchased may resist. Resisted takeovers are called *hostile.* In these cases, the acquirer attempts to purchase sufficient shares of the target firm to gain a majority of the seats on the board of directors. Board members are then able to vote to merge the target firm with the acquiring firm.

Investment bankers serve both acquirers and target firms. Acquiring firms require help in locating attractive firms to pursue, soliciting shareholders to sell their shares in a process called a *tender offer* and raising the required capital to complete the transaction. Target firms may hire investment bankers to help ward off undesired takeover attempts.

The mergers and acquisitions markets requires very specialized knowledge and expertise. Investment bankers involved in this market are highly trained (and, not incidentally, highly paid). The best known investment banker involved in mergers and acquisitions was Michael R. Milken, who worked at Drexel Burnham Lambert, Inc. Milken is credited with inventing the junk bond market, which we discussed in Chapter 10. *Junk bonds* are high-risk, high-return debt securities that were used primarily to finance takeover attempts. By allowing companies to raise large amounts of capital, even small firms could pursue and take over large ones. During the 1980s, when Milken was most active in this market, merger and acquisition activity peaked. On February 13, 1990, Drexel Burnham Lambert filed for bankruptcy due to rising default rates on its portfolio of junk bonds, a slow economy, and regulations that forced the savings and loan industry out of the junk bond market. Milken pled guilty to securities fraud and was sent to prison.

As a result of the collapse of Drexel and the junk bond market, merger and acquisitions activity slowed during the early 1990s. A healthy economy and regulatory changes caused a resurgence, especially among commercial banks, in the mid and late 1990s. Mergers and acquisitions again slowed during the recession in 2001.

Securities Brokers and Dealers

Securities brokers and dealers conduct trading in secondary markets. *Brokers* are pure middlemen who act as agents for investors in the purchase or sale of securities. Their function is to match buyers with sellers, a function for which they are paid brokerage commissions.

In contrast to brokers, dealers link buyers and sellers by standing ready to buy and sell securities at given prices. Therefore, dealers hold inventories of securities and make their living by selling these securities for a slightly higher price than they paid for them—that is, on the *spread* between the *bid price,* the price that the broker pays for securities they buy for their inventory, and the *ask price,* the price they receive when they sell the securities. This is a high-risk business because dealers hold securities that can rise or fall in price; in recent years, several firms specializing in bonds have collapsed. Brokers, by contrast, are not as exposed to risk because they do not own the securities involved in their business dealings.[1]

Brokerage Services

Securities brokers offer several types of services.

Securities Orders   If you call a securities brokerage house to buy a stock, you will speak with a broker who will take your order. You have three primary types of transactions available: market orders, limit orders, and short sells.

---

[1]It is easy to remember the distinction between dealers and brokers if you relate to auto dealers and real estate brokers. Auto *dealers* take ownership of the cars and resell them to the public. Real estate *brokers* do not take ownership of the property; they just act as go-betweens.

The two most common types of securities orders are the market order and the limit order. When you place a **market order,** you are instructing your agent to buy or sell the security at the current market price. When placing a market order, there is a risk that the price of the security may have changed significantly from what it was when you made your investment decision. If you are buying a stock and the price falls, no harm is done, but if the price goes up, you may regret your decision. The most notable occasion when prices changed between when orders were placed and when they were filled was during the October 19, 1987, stock crash. Panicked investors told their brokers to sell their stocks, but the transaction volume was so great that day that many orders were not filled until hours after they were placed. By the time they were filled, the price of the stocks had often fallen far below what they were at the time the original orders were placed.

An alternative to the market order is the **limit order.** Here buy orders specify a *maximum* acceptable price, and sell orders specify a *minimum* acceptable price. For example, you could place a limit order to sell your 100 shares of IBM at $100. If the current market price of IBM is less than $100, the order will not be filled. Unfilled limit orders are reported to the stock specialist who works that particular stock on the exchange. When the stock price moves in such a way that limit orders are activated, the stock specialist initiates the trade.

The **stop loss order** is similar to the limit order, but is for stocks you already own. This order tells your broker to sell your stock when it reaches a certain price. For example, suppose you buy a stock for $20 per share. You do not want to suffer a major loss on this stock, so you enter a stop loss order at $18. In the event the stock price falls to $18 the broker will sell the stock. The stop loss order received a great deal of attention in the recent Martha Stewart trial. She was suspected of trading on insider information about ImClone stock. She argued that the reason for the stock sale was because she had a stop loss order on ImClone at $60. Her conviction suggests that the court did not believe this order was truly in place.

When investors believe that the price of a stock will rise in the future, they buy that stock and hold it until the increase occurs. They can then sell at a profit and capture a gain for their effort. What can be done if an investor is convinced that a stock will *fall* in the future? The solution is to sell short. A **short sell** requires that the investor borrow stocks from a brokerage house and sell them today, with the promise of replacing the borrowed stocks by buying them in the future. Suppose that you just tried out the new Apple notebook computer and decided that it would sell poorly (in fact, in 1995, Apple had to recall all of its Powerbook computers to fix problems). You might believe that as the rest of the market learned of the poor product, the price of Apple's stock could decline. To take advantage of this situation, you might instruct your broker to short Apple 100 shares. The broker would then borrow 100 shares from another investor on your behalf and sell them at current market prices. You do not own those shares, of course. They are borrowed and at some point in the future, you would be required to purchase those 100 shares at the new market price to replace them. If you were right and the price of Apple declined, you would buy the shares at a lower price than you received for their earlier sale and would earn a profit. Of course, if you are wrong and the price rises, you will suffer a loss.

Market and limit orders allow you to take advantage of stock price *increases,* and short sells allow you to take advantage of stock price *decreases.* Analysts track the number of short positions taken on a stock as an indicator of the number of investors who feel that a stock's price is likely to fall in the future.

Other Services   In addition to trading in securities, stockbrokers provide a variety of other services. Investors typically leave their securities in storage with the broker for safekeeping. If the securities are left with the broker, they are insured against loss by the Securities Investor Protection Corporation (SIPC), an agency of the federal government. This guarantee is not against loss in value, only against loss of the securities themselves.

Brokers also provide **margin credit.** Margin credit refers to loans advanced by the brokerage house to help investors buy securities. For example, if you are certain that Intel Corporation stock is going to rise rapidly when its latest computer chip is introduced, you could increase the amount of stock you can buy by borrowing from the brokerage house. If you had $5000 and borrowed an additional $5000, you could buy $10,000 worth of stock. Then if the price goes up as you predict, you could earn nearly twice as much as without the loan. The Federal Reserve sets the percentage of the stock purchase price that brokerage houses can lend. Interest rates on margin loans are usually 1 or 2 percentage points above the prime interest rate (the rate charged large, creditworthy corporate borrowers).

As noted in Chapter 18, the forces of competition have led brokerage firms to offer services and engage in activities traditionally conducted by commercial banks. In 1977, Merrill Lynch developed the cash management account (CMA), which provides a package of financial services that includes credit cards, immediate loans, check-writing privileges, automatic investment of proceeds from the sale of securities in a money market mutual fund, and unified record keeping. CMAs were adopted by other brokerage firms and spread rapidly. Many of these accounts allow check-writing privileges and offer ATM and debit cards. In these ways, they compete directly with banks.

As a result of CMAs, the distinction between banking activities and the activities of nonbank financial institutions has become blurred. Walter Wriston, former head of Citicorp (the largest bank holding company in the country), has been quoted as saying, "The bank of the future already exists, and it's called Merrill Lynch."[2]

The advantage of brokerage-based cash management accounts is that they make it easier to buy and sell securities. The stockbroker can take funds out of the account when an investor buys a security and put the money into the account when the investor sells securities.

Full-Service Versus Discount Brokers   Prior to May 1, 1975, virtually all brokerage houses charged the same commissions on trades. Brokerage houses distinguished themselves primarily on the basis of their research and customer relations. In May 1975, Congress determined that fixed commissions were anticompetitive and passed the Securities Acts Amendment of 1975, which abolished fixed commissions. Now brokerage houses may charge whatever fees they choose. This has resulted in two distinct types of brokerage firms: full-service and discount.

Full-service brokers provide research and investment advice to their customers. Full-service brokers will often mail weekly and monthly market reports and recommendations to their customers in an effort to encourage them to invest in certain securities. For example, when the investment banking department of the brokerage house has an initial public offering available, brokers will contact customers they feel may be interested and offer to send a prospectus. Full-service brokers attempt to establish long-term relationships with their customers and to

---

[2]"Banking Takes a Beating," *Time,* December 3, 1984, p. 50.

help them assemble portfolios that are consistent with their financial needs and risk preferences. Of course, this extra attention is costly and must be paid for by requiring higher fees for initiating trades. Merrill Lynch is the biggest of the full-service brokers.

Discount brokers simply execute trades on request. If you want to buy a particular security, you call the discount broker and place your request. No advice or research is typically provided. Because the cost of operating a discount brokerage firm is significantly less than the cost of operating a full-service firm, lower transaction costs are charged. These fees may be a fraction of the fees charged by a full-service broker. Charles Schwab Corp. is the best-known discount broker. Many discount brokerage firms are owned by large commercial banks, which have historically been prohibited from offering full-service brokerage services.

Regardless of which type of brokerage firm you choose, it will own seats on the major exchanges and have computer links to the NASDAQ (National Association of Security Dealers Automated Quotation System). Suppose that you place an order for 100 shares of IBM with your local Merrill Lynch office. Your broker will send an electronic message to the Merrill Lynch traders who work on the floor of the New York Stock Exchange (NYSE) to buy 100 shares of IBM in your name. (Merrill Lynch will have purchased a number of seats on the exchange for its traders, as discussed in Chapter 11.) On the floor of the NYSE, there are circular work areas where specialists in each security that is traded on the exchange stand. Each specialist is responsible for several stocks. The Merrill Lynch floor trader will know where the IBM specialist is and will approach that person to fill your buy order. Confirmation of the purchase will then be communicated back to your local broker, who will inform you that the trade has been completed (see the "Mini-Case" box).

MINI-CASE

Example of Using the Limit-Order Book

Suppose a trader on the New York Stock Exchange was a specialist responsible for Circuit City stock. The limit-order book might look like the following:

Unfilled Circuit City Limit Orders

Buy Orders		Sell Orders	
37	100		
37.12	300		
37.25	100		
		37.37	200
		37.50	500
		37.62	100

Listed under Buy Orders are the highest prices investors are willing to pay to buy the stock. Listed under Sell Orders are the lowest prices investors holding Circuit City are willing to accept to sell. Currently, no transactions occur because there are no cross-over or common prices. In other words, there is currently no one willing to sell Circuit City at a price anyone is willing to pay.

Now suppose the specialist receives a new 200-share market order to buy, an order to be filled at the best market price currently available. The specialist will consult the Sell Orders column and fill the order at 37.37.

Next, the specialist receives a 300-share limit order to sell at 37.12. Again, the specialist will consult the book, but this time will look under the Buy Orders column. The limit order will be filled with 100 shares at 37.25 and 200 shares at 37.12.

Next suppose that a limit order to buy 500 shares at 36.88 is received. Since there is no sell order for this amount, the order is added to the book, which looks as follows at this point.

Unfilled Circuit City Limit Orders

Buy Orders		Sell Orders	
36.88	500		
37	100		
37.12	100		
		37.50	500
		37.62	100

Securities Dealers

Securities dealers hold inventories of securities, which they sell to customers who want to buy. They also hold securities purchased from customers who want to sell.

It is impossible to overemphasize the importance of dealers to the smooth functioning of the U.S. financial markets. Consider what an investor demands before buying a security. In addition to requiring a fair return, the investor wants to know that the investment is *liquid*—that it can be sold quickly if it no longer fits into the investor's portfolio. Consider a small, relatively unknown firm that is trying to sell securities to the public. An investor may be tempted to buy the firm's securities, but if these securities cannot be resold easily, it is unlikely that the investor will take a chance on them. This is where the dealers become crucial. They stand ready to make a market in the security at any time—that is, they make sure that an investor can always sell or buy a security. For this reason, dealers are also called **market makers.** When an investor wishes to sell a thinly traded stock (one without an active secondary market), it is unlikely that another investor is simultaneously seeking to buy that security. This nonsynchronous trading problem is solved when the dealer buys the security from the investor and holds it in inventory until another investor is ready to buy it. The knowledge that dealers will provide this service encourages investors to buy securities that would be otherwise unacceptable. In countries with less well developed financial markets, where dealers will not make a market for less popular securities, it is extremely difficult for small, new, or regional firms to raise funds. Securities market dealers are largely responsible for the health and growth of small businesses in the United States.

Regulation of Securities Firms

Many financial firms engage in all three securities market activities, acting as brokers, dealers, and investment bankers. The largest in the United States is Merrill Lynch; other well-known firms include Paine Webber, Morgan Stanley Dean Witter, and Salomon Smith Barney. The SEC not only regulates the firms' investment banking operations but also restricts brokers and dealers from misrepresenting securities and from trading on *insider information*, unpublicized facts known only to the management of a corporation.

When discussing regulation, it is important to recognize that the public's confidence in the integrity of the financial markets is critical to the growth of our economy and the ability of firms to continue using the markets to raise new capital. If the public believes that there are other powerful players with superior information who can take advantage of smaller investors, the market will be unable to attract funds from these smaller investors. Ultimately, the markets could fail entirely.

The lemons problem introduced in Chapter 15 also applies to the securities markets. Due to asymmetric information, investors will not know as much about securities being offered for sale by firms as firm insiders will. If an average price is set for all securities based on this lack of information, good securities would be withdrawn and only poor and overpriced securities would remain for sale. With only these securities offered, the average price would fall. Now any securities worth more than this new average would be withdrawn. Eventually, the market would fail as the average security offered drops in quality and market prices fall as a result. One solution to the lemons problem is for the government to regulate full disclosure so that asymmetric information is reduced.

The securities laws were designed with two goals: to protect the integrity of the markets and to restrict competition among securities firms so that they would be less likely to fail. Two acts passed in 1933 and 1934 provide the primary basis for regulation of today's securities markets. These acts were passed shortly after the Great Depression and were largely responding to abuses that many people at the time felt were partly responsible for the economic troubles the country was suffering. The principal provisions of the 1933 and 1934 acts are as follows:

- To establish the Securities and Exchange Commission (SEC), which is charged with administering securities laws
- To require that issuers register new securities offerings and that they disclose all relevant information to potential investors
- To require that all publicly held corporations file annual and semiannual reports with the SEC; publicly held corporations must also file a report whenever any event of "significant interest" to investors occurs
- To require that insiders file reports whenever shares are bought or sold
- To prohibit any form of market manipulation

The Securities and Exchange Commission website, www.sec.gov, contains regulatory actions, concept releases, interpretive releases, and more.

Prior to the passage of these acts, the market was subject to much abuse. For example, a study conducted in 1933 showed evidence of 127 "investment pools" operating during 1932 alone. An investment pool is formed to manipulate the market. A group of investors band together and spread false but damaging rumors about the health of a firm. These rumors drive the price of the firm's stock down. When the price is depressed, the members of the pool buy the stock. Once they all hold shares purchased at artificially low prices, the members of the pool release good news about the company so that the price of the stock rises. Obviously, the members of the pool stand to earn huge profits. Small, uninformed investors lose. Practices such as these were outlawed by the securities acts of 1933 and 1934.

As noted in our discussion of private placements, not all securities issues are subject to SEC oversight. SEC registration is not required if less than $1.5 million in securities is issued per year, if the securities mature in less than 270 days, or if the securities are issued by the U.S. government or most municipalities.

Other legislation of significance to securities firms include the Glass-Steagall Act of 1933, which separated commercial and investment banking (mostly repealed by Gramm-Leach-Bliley Act); the Investment Advisers Act of 1940, which required investment advisers to register with the SEC; and the Securities Protection Corporation Act of 1970, which established the Securities Investor Protection Corporation, which insures customers of securities firms from losses to their cash accounts up to $100,000 and from losses of securities documents up to $500,000. Other regulations related specifically to banks but of interest to securities firms are discussed in Chapter 20.

Relationship Between Securities Firms and Commercial Banks

For many years, commercial banks have lobbied for legislative relief to enable them to compete with securities firms. Consider how the business of banking has been eroded. Prior to the introduction of cash management accounts at Merrill Lynch, the only source of checking accounts was a bank. The Merrill Lynch account not only provided low-cost checking but also paid interest that was higher than the law permitted banks to pay. Securities firms were allowed to make loans, offer credit and debit cards, provide ATM access, and, most important, sell securities. In addition, securities firms could sell some types of insurance. It is not hard to understand why bankers were frustrated. Regulations prevented them from competing with securities firms, but no laws restricted securities firms from competing with banks.

Commercial banks clamored on Capitol Hill for a "level playing field." As noted in Chapter 20, regulatory relief in 1980 and 1982 substantially slowed the movement of funds from commercial banks to securities firms; however, banks were still not permitted to sell securities. This is gradually changing.

Venture Capital Firms

So far in this chapter we have discussed investment bankers, who help bring securities to the market for the first time. We then explored the activities of securities firms and brokers and dealers, who facilitate the trading of secondary market securities. In this section we expand our discussion to include venture capital firms, which supply money to firms that are not yet ready to sell securities to the general public. Suppose that you develop and market a new process that you think has a great chance of being a success. However, since it is new and unproven, you cannot get funding from conventional sources. Commercial banks will not loan you money since there is no established cash flow to use to repay the loan. It will be hard to sell stock to the public through investment bankers because the company is so new and has not yet proven that it can be successful. In the absence of alternative sources of funds, your great idea may not have a true chance to be developed. Venture capital firms provide the funds a start-up firm needs to get established.

Description of Industry

Venture capital is usually defined as money supplied to young, start-up firms. This money is most frequently raised by limited partnerships and invested by the general partner in firms showing promise of high returns in the future.

Since the mid-1940s venture capital firms have nurtured the growth of America's high-technology and entrepreneurial communities. Their activities have resulted in job creation, economic growth, and international competitiveness. Venture capitalists backed many of the most successful high-technology companies during the 1980s and 1990s, including Apple Computer, Cisco Systems, Genetech, Microsoft, Netscape, and Sun Microsystems. A number of service firms, such as Staples, Starbucks, and TCBY, also benefited from venture financing. Indeed, much of the growth experienced through the 1980s and 1990s can be traced back to the funding provided by the venture capital industry. Table 2 shows the explosive growth in venture capital funding witnessed during the 1990s and the rapid drop in activity after the market fell in 2000.

TABLE 2   *Venture Capital Investments Made from 1990–2003*

Year	Number of Companies Funded	Investment Total ($ millions)
1990	1317	3,376.21
1991	1088	2,511.43
1992	1294	5,177.56
1993	1151	4,962.87
1994	1191	5,351.18
1995	1327	5,608.30
1996	2004	11,277.67
1997	2696	17,207.05
1998	3155	22,576.49
1999	3956	59,163.93
2000	5458	103,848.59
2001	4609	40,693.00
2002	3033	21,309.00
2003	2739	18,352.00

Source: http://www.NVCA.com/ffax.html

Venture Capitalists Reduce Asymmetric Information

Uncertainty and information asymmetries frequently accompany start-up firms, especially in high-technology communities. Managers of these firms may engage in wasteful expenditures, such as leasing expensive office space, since the manager may benefit disproportionately from them but does not bear their entire cost. The difficulty outside investors have in tracking early-stage high-technology companies leads to other types of costs. For example, a biotechnology company founder may invest in research that brings personal acclaim but little chance for significant returns to investors. As a result of these informational asymmetries, external financing may be costly, difficult, or even impossible to obtain.

Venture capital firms can alleviate the information gap and thus allow firms to receive financing they could not obtain elsewhere. First, as opposed to bank loans or bond financing, venture capital firms hold an equity interest in the firm. The firms are usually privately held, so the stock does not trade publicly. Equity interests in privately held firms are very illiquid. As a result, venture capital investment horizons are long-term. The partners do not expect to earn any return for a number of years, often as long as a decade. In contrast, most investors in stocks are anxious to see annual returns through either stock appreciation or dividend payouts. They are often unwilling to wait years to see if a new idea, process, innovation, or invention will yield profits. Similarly, most investors in bonds are not going to wait years for revenues to grow to a point where interest payments become available. Venture capital financing thus fills an important niche left vacant by alternative sources of capital.

As a second method of addressing the asymmetric information problem, venture capital usually comes with strings attached, the most noteworthy being that the partners in a venture capital firm take seats on the board of directors of the financed firm. Venture capital firms are not passive investors. They actively attempt to add value to the firm through advice, assistance, and business contacts. Venture capitalists may bring together two firms that can complement each other's activities. Venture capital firms will apply their expertise to help the firm solve various financing and growth-related problems. The venture capital partners on the board of directors will carefully monitor expenditures and management to help safeguard the investment in the firm.

One of the most effective ways venture capitalists have of controlling managers is to disburse funds to the company in stages only as the firm demonstrates progress toward its ultimate goal. If development stalls or markets change, funds can be withheld to cut losses.

Implicit to venture capital financing is an expectation of high risk and large compensating returns. Venture capital firms will search very carefully among hundreds of companies to find a few that show real growth potential. Despite this exhaustive search effort, the selected firms usually have little to show initially other than a unique and promising idea. Venture capitalists mitigate the risk by developing a portfolio of young companies within a single fund. Additionally, many venture capital partnerships will manage multiple funds simultaneously. By diversifying the risk among a number of start-up firms, the risk of loss is significantly lowered.

Origins of Venture Capital

The first true venture capital firm was American Research & Development (ARD), established in 1946 by MIT president Karl Compton and local business leaders. The bulk of their success can be traced to one $70,000 investment in a new firm, the Digital Equipment Company. This seed money grew in value to $355 million over the next three decades.[3]

During the 1950s and 1960s most venture capital funding was for the development of real estate and oil fields. By the late 1960s a shift occurred toward financing technology start-ups. High technology remains the dominant area for venture capital funding.

The source of venture capital funding has shifted from wealthy individuals to pension funds and corporations. In 1979, the U.S. Department of labor clarified the **prudent man rule,** which restricted pension funds from making risky investments, to explicitly allow investment in some high-risk assets. This resulted in a surge of pension fund dollars going into venture projects.

Corporate funding of venture capital projects increased when many companies reduced their investment in their own in-house R&D in favor of outside start-up companies. If the project was successful, the company could acquire the

---

[3]Part of this discussion is based on "The Venture Capital Revolution," by Paul Gompers and Josh Lerner, *Journal of Economic Perspectives,* Number 2, Spring 2001, pages 145–168.

start-up. This change was fueled by evidence that many of the best ideas from in-house centralized R&D languished unused or were commercialized in new firms started by defecting employees. Salaried employees tend not to be as motivated as entrepreneurs who stand to capture a large portion of the profits a new idea may generate. By investing in start-up firms, corporations can benefit from new discoveries while supporting the entrepreneurial spirit.

Structure of Venture Capital Firms

Most early venture capital firms were organized as closed-end mutual funds. A closed-end mutual fund sells a fixed number of shares to investors. Once all of the shares have been sold, no additional money can be raised. Instead, a new venture fund is established. The advantage of this organizational structure is that it provides the long-term money required for venture investing. Investors cannot pull money out of the investment as they could from an open-end mutual fund.

In the 1970s and 1980s venture capital firms began organizing as limited partnerships. This organizational structure is exempt from securities regulations, including the burdensome disclosure requirements of the Investment Security Act of 1940. While both organizational forms continue to be used, currently most venture capital firms are limited partnerships.

The Life of a Deal

Most venture capital deals follow a similar life cycle that begins when a limited partnership is formed and funds are raised. In the second phase, the funds are invested in start-up companies. Finally, the venture firm exits the investment.

Next, we take a more detailed look at this process.

Fundraising   A venture firm begins by soliciting commitments of capital from investors. As discussed above, these investors are typically pension funds, corporations, and wealthy individuals. Venture capital firms usually have a portfolio target amount that they attempt to raise. The average venture fund will have from just a few investors up to 100 limited partners. Because the minimum commitment is usually so high, venture capital funding is generally out of reach of most average individual investors.

Once the venture fund begins investing, it will "call" its commitments from the limited partners. These capital calls from the limited partners to the venture fund are sometimes called "takedowns" or "paid-in-capital." Venture firms typically call their capital on an as-needed basis.

The limited partners understand that investments in venture funds are long-term. It may be several years before the first investment starts to pay. In many cases, the capital may be tied up for seven to ten years. The illiquidity of the investment must be carefully considered by the potential investor.

Investing   Once commitments have been received, the venture fund can begin the investment phase. Venture funds may either specialize in one or two industry segments or may generalize, looking at all available opportunities. It is not uncommon for venture funds to focus investments in a limited geographical area to make it easier to review and monitor the firms' activities.

Frequently, venture capitalists invest in a firm before it has a real product or is even clearly organized as a company. This is called **seed investing.** Investing in a firm that is a little further along in its life cycle is known as **early-stage investing.** Finally, some funds focus on **later-stage investing** by providing funds to help the company grow to a critical mass to attract public financing.

Typically, about 60% of venture capital funds go into seed investments, 25% into early-stage investments, and 15% into later-stage investments.

Exiting   The goal of a venture capital investment is to help nurture a firm until it can be funded with alternative capital. Venture firms hope that an exit can be made in no more than seven to ten years. Later-stage investments may take only a few years. Once an exit is made, the partners receive their share of the profits and the fund is dissolved.

There are a number of ways for a venture fund to successfully exit an investment. The most glamorous and visible is through an initial public offering. At the public stock offering, the venture firm is considered an insider and receives stock in the company, but the firm is regulated and restricted in how that stock can be sold or liquidated for several years. Once the stock is freely tradable, usually after two years, the venture fund distributes the stock to its limited partners, who may then hold the stock or sell it. Over the last 25 years, over 3000 companies financed by venture funds have had initial public offerings. During the peak years, there were 258 venture-backed initial public offerings.

While not as visible, an equally common type of successful exit for venture investments is through mergers and acquisitions. In these cases, the venture firm receives stock or cash from the acquiring company. These proceeds are then distributed to the limited partners. There were 269 venture-backed merger and acquisition deals in 2000.

Venture Fund Profitability   Venture investing is extremely high-risk. Most start-up firms do not succeed. Despite the careful monitoring and advice provided by the venture capital firm, there are innumerable hurdles that must be jumped before a new concept or idea yields profits. If venture investing is high-risk then there must also be the possibility of a high return to induce investors to continue supplying funds.

Historically, venture capital firms have been very profitable, despite their high risk. The 20-year average return is 20.3%. Seed investing is the most profitable, with a 20-year average return of 24.5% compared to about 18% for later-stage investing. The 1990s were a wonderful time to be a venture capitalist. The ten-year average return was 30%. From 1995 to 2000, the average return soared to over 50%.

In the late 1990s, venture capital returns continued to be extraordinary. For example, returns exceeded 165% in 1999. Unfortunately, as the market cooled to technology, so too did venture capital returns. By 2000, average returns were 37.5%, and in 2001, venture firms reported a first quarter loss of 8.9%. These losses are likely to extend for a number of years while venture capital firms recover from excessive investment in Web-based technology companies. The "E-Finance" box discusses possible explanations for the losses suffered by venture capital firms.

E-FINANCE

Venture Capitalists Lose Focus with Internet Companies

Table 2 shows that there was a tremendous surge in funds available for venture capitalists in the last half of the 1990s. Much of the investing focus was on the financing of dot-com companies. There are two serious ramifications that result. First, it is likely that there are only a certain number of worthy projects to finance at any one time. When too much money is chasing too few deals, firms are going to obtain financing that would be rejected at other times. As result, the average quality of venture fund portfolios falls.

A second problem caused by the surge of money into venture funds is that the ability of the partners to provide quality monitoring is reduced. Consider the case of Webvan, an Internet grocer that received more than $1 *billion* in venture financing. Even though it was backed by a group of experienced financiers, including Goldman Sachs and Sequoia Capital, its business plan was fundamentally flawed. In its short life, Webvan spent more than $1 billion building automated warehouses and pricey tech gear. This high overhead made it impossible to compete in the grocery business, where average margins are about 1%. Had the investment bankers been actively monitoring the activities of Webvan, they might have balked at developing an infrastructure that required 4000 orders per day per warehouse just to break even. Not surprisingly, Webvan declared bankruptcy in July 2001.

Summary

1. Investment banks are firms that assist in the initial sale of securities in the primary market and, as securities brokers and dealers, assist in the trading of securities in the secondary markets, some of which are organized into exchanges. The Securities and Exchange Commission regulates the financial institutions in the securities markets and ensures that adequate information reaches prospective investors.

2. Underwriting involves the investment banking firm's taking ownership of the stock issue by purchasing all of the shares from the issuer and then reselling them in the market. Issues may be oversubscribed, undersubscribed, or fully subscribed, depending on whether the price is set correctly.

3. Investment bankers assist issuing firms by providing advice, filing documents, and marketing issues. Investment bankers often assist in mergers and acquisitions and in private placements as well.

4. Securities brokers act as go-betweens and do not usually own securities. Securities dealers do buy and sell securities and by doing so make a market. By always having securities to sell and by always being willing to purchase securities, dealers guarantee the liquidity of the market.

5. Investors may place an order, called a *market order,* to buy a security at the current market price. They may also set limits to the lowest price at which they will sell their security or the highest price they will pay for a security. Orders of this type are called *limit orders.*

6. Some brokerage houses provide research and investment advice in addition to conducting trades on behalf of customers. These are called *full-service brokers. Discount brokers* simply place orders. Brokerage houses also store securities, advance loans to buy securities, and offer cash management accounts.

Key Terms

confidential memorandum,
  p. 599
definitive agreement, *p. 599*
due diligence, *p. 599*
early-stage investing, *p. 610*

fully subscribed, *p. 596*
Glass-Steagall Act, *p. 592*
initial public offering (IPO),
  p. 594
investment banks, *p. 592*

later-stage investing, *p. 610*
letter of intent, *p. 599*
limit order, *p. 601*
margin credit, *p. 602*

market maker, *p. 604*
market order, *p. 601*
mergers and acquisitions
   market, *p. 599*
oversubscribed, *p. 596*
primary market, *p. 591*
prospectus, *p. 594*

prudent man rule, *p. 608*
registration statement, *p. 594*
seasoned issues, *p. 594*
secondary market, *p. 591*
Securities and Exchange
   Commission (SEC), *p. 594*
seed investing, *p. 610*

short sell, *p. 601*
stop loss order, *p. 601*
syndicate, *p. 595*
tombstone, *p. 595*
undersubscribed, *p. 596*

Questions

1. What was the motivation behind legislation separating commercial banking from investment banking?

2. What law separated investment banking from commercial banking?

3. What does it mean to say that investment bankers *underwrite* a security offering? How is this different from a best-efforts offering?

4. What are the primary services that an investment banker will provide a firm issuing securities?

5. Does the fact that a security has passed an SEC review mean that investors can buy the security without having to worry about taking a loss on the investment?

6. Why do investment banking firms often form syndicates for selling securities to the public?

7. Is it better for a security issue to be fully subscribed or oversubscribed?

8. Why would an investment banker advise a firm to issue a security using best efforts rather than underwriting?

9. What is the difference between a hostile takeover and a merger?

10. What valuable service do dealers provide that facilitates transaction trading and keeping the markets liquid?

11. What is the difference between a market order and a limit order?

12. Is it possible to make money if you know that the price of a security will *fall* in the future? How?

13. Why do commercial banks object to brokerage houses' being allowed to offer many of the same services traditionally reserved for banks?

Quantitative Problems

Amazon.com issued an initial public offering in May of 1997. Prior to its IPO, the following information on shares outstanding was listed in the final prospectus:

Name and Address	Number of Shares Beneficially Owned	Percentage of Shares Outstanding	
		Prior to Offering	After Offering

Jeffrey P. Bezos
   c/o Amazon.com, Inc.
   1516 Second Avenue, 4th Floor
   Seattle, WA 98101
	9,885,000	47.5%	41.4%

L. John Doerr
   Kleiner Perkins Caufield & Byers
   4 Embarcadero Center, Suite 3520
   San Francisco, CA 94111
	3,401,376	16.4	14.3

Tom A. Alberg	195,000	*	*
Scott D. Cook	75,000	*	*
Patricia Q. Stonesifer	75,000	*	*
All directors and executive officers as a group (14 persons)	15,688,925	72.5	63.5
Total shares outstanding	20,858,702	100.0	—.-

In the IPO, the firm issued 3,000,000 new shares. The initial price was $18.00/share with investment bankers retaining $1.26 as fees. The final first-day closing price was $23.50.

1. What were the total proceeds from this offering? What part was retained by Amazon? What part by the investment bankers? What percent of the offering is this?

2. Mr. Doerr of Kleiner Perkins Caufield & Byers owned a significant number of shares. What was the market value of these shares at the end of the first day of trading?

3. What was the market value of Amazon.com following its first day as a publicly held company?

4. Refer back to the IPO of eBay presented in the problems for Chapter 11. What were the fees for eBay as a percent of funds raised? Does a pattern emerge?

5. To verify this further, examine the IPO for Blue Nile, Inc. It can be found on the SEC's site at **http://www. sec.gov/Archives/edgar/data/1091171/00008916 1804001024/v97093b4e424b4.htm**. What was the offering price? What percent was retained by the underwriter?

6. For Blue Nile, Inc., what are the expected proceeds to the company? Is this certain? What assumptions are you making? How would you verify this?

7. You want to buy 100 shares of a stock currently trading at $50 per share. Your brokerage firm allows margin sales with a 50% opening margin and a maintenance margin of 25%. What does this mean? If you close your position with the shares at $53.50, what is your return?

8. The limit order book for a security is as follows:

Unfilled Limit Orders			
Buy Orders		**Sell Orders**	
25.12	100		
25.20	500		
25.23	200		
		25.36	300
		25.38	200
		25.41	200

The specialist receives the following, in order:

- Market order to sell 300 shares
- Limit order to buy 100 shares at 25.38
- Limit order to buy 500 shares at 25.30

How, if at all, are these orders filled? What does the limit order book look like after these orders?

Web Exercises

Investment Banks, Security Brokers and Dealers, and Venture Capital Firms

1. Initial public offerings (IPOs) are when securities are sold to the public for the first time. Go to **http:// ipohome.com**. This site lists various statistics regarding the IPO market.

   a. What was the largest IPO offered recently, ranked by amount raised?

   b. What is the next IPO that will be offered to the public?

   c. How many IPOs were priced in each of the last four years?

2. The Securities and Exchange Commission is responsible for regulating securities firms. Go to **www.sec.gov**. This is the official home page of the SEC. Use this page to answer the following.

   a. What is EDGAR?

   b. What is the stated purpose of the SEC?

   c. Provide a one-sentence summary of the most recently proposed SEC regulation.

PART 7

The Management of Financial Institutions

CHAPTER 24

Risk Management in Financial Institutions

Preview

Managing financial institutions has never been an easy task, but in recent years it has become even more difficult because of greater uncertainty in the economic environment. Interest rates have become much more volatile, resulting in substantial fluctuations in profits and in the value of assets and liabilities held by financial institutions. Furthermore, as we have seen in Chapter 5, defaults on loans and other debt instruments have also climbed dramatically, leading to large losses at financial institutions. In light of these developments, it is not surprising that financial institution managers have become more concerned about managing the risk their institutions face as a result of greater interest-rate fluctuations and defaults by borrowers.

In this chapter we examine how managers of financial institutions cope with credit risk, the risk arising because borrowers may default on their obligations, and with interest-rate risk, the risk arising from fluctuations in interest rates. We will look at the tools that these managers use to measure risk and the strategies that they employ to reduce it.

The website of the Risk Management Association, www. rmahq.org, offers useful information such as annual statement studies, online publications, and more.

Managing Credit Risk

A major part of the business of financial institutions such as banks, insurance companies, pension funds, and finance companies is making loans. In order for these institutions to earn high profits, they must make successful loans that are paid back in full (and so have low credit risk). The concepts of adverse selection and moral hazard (introduced in Chapter 2) provide a framework for understanding the principles that financial institution managers must follow to minimize credit risk and make successful loans.

Adverse selection is problematic in loan markets because bad credit risks (borrowers most likely to default) are the ones who usually line up for loans—in other words, those who are most likely to produce an *adverse* outcome are the most

617

likely to be *selected.* Borrowers with very risky investment projects in mind have much to gain if their projects are successful, and so they are the most eager to obtain loans. Clearly, however, they are the least desirable borrowers because of the greater possibility that they will be unable to pay back their loans.

Moral hazard is a problem in loan markets because borrowers may have incentives to engage in activities that are undesirable from the lender's point of view. In such situations, it is more likely that the lender will be exposed to the *hazard* of default. Once borrowers have obtained a loan, they are more likely to invest in high-risk investment projects—projects that pay high returns to the borrowers if successful. The high risk, however, makes it less likely that the loan will be paid back.

To be profitable, financial institutions must overcome the adverse selection and moral hazard problems that make loan defaults more likely. The attempts of financial institutions to solve these problems help explain a number of principles for managing credit risk: screening and monitoring, establishment of long-term customer relationships, loan commitments, collateral, compensating balance requirements, and credit rationing.

Screening and Monitoring

Asymmetric information is present in loan markets because lenders have less information about the investment opportunities and activities of borrowers than borrowers do. This situation leads to two information-producing activities by financial institutions: screening and monitoring.

Screening   Adverse selection in loan markets requires that financial institutions screen out the bad credit risks from the good ones so that loans will be profitable. To accomplish effective screening, financial institutions must collect reliable information from prospective borrowers. Effective screening and information collection together form an important principle of credit risk management.

When you go into a bank or a finance company to apply for a consumer loan (such as a car loan or a mortgage to purchase a house), the first thing you are asked to do is fill out forms that elicit a great deal of information about your personal finances. You are asked about your salary, bank accounts, other assets (such as cars, insurance policies, and furnishings), and outstanding loans; your record of loan, credit card, and charge account repayments; and the number of years you've worked and who your employers have been. You also are asked personal questions such as your age, marital status, and number of children. The bank or finance company uses this information to evaluate how good a credit risk you are by calculating your "credit score," a statistical measure derived from your answers that predicts whether you are likely to have trouble making your loan payments. Deciding on how good a risk you are cannot be entirely scientific, so the bank or finance company must also use judgment. A loan officer, whose job is to decide whether you should be given the loan, might call your employer or talk to some of the personal references you supplied. The officer might even make a judgment based on your demeanor or your appearance.

The process of screening and collecting information is similar when a financial institution makes a business loan. The loan officer needs to collect information about the company's profits and losses (income) and about its assets and liabilities. The officer also has to evaluate the likely future success of the business. So in addition to obtaining information such as sales figures, the loan officer might ask questions about the company's future plans, how the loan will be used, and the competition in the industry and might even visit the company to obtain a firsthand look at its operations. The bottom line is that, be it for personal or business loans, financial institutions need to be nosy.

One puzzling feature of lending by financial institutions is that they often specialize in lending to local firms or to firms in particular industries, such as energy. In one sense, this behavior appears surprising because it means that the financial institution is not diversifying its portfolio of loans and is therefore exposing itself to more risk. But from another perspective, such specialization makes perfect sense. Recall that the adverse selection problem requires that financial institutions screen out bad credit risks. It is easier for a financial institution to collect information about local firms and determine their creditworthiness than to collect similar information on firms that are far away. Similarly, by specializing in lending to firms in specific industries, the financial institution becomes more knowledgeable about these industries and is therefore better able to predict whether the firms it lends to will be able to make timely payments on their debt.

Monitoring   After a loan has been obtained, the borrower may have an incentive to take on risky activities that make it less likely that the loan will be paid off. To reduce this moral hazard, financial institution managers must adhere to the principle for managing credit risk of writing provisions (restrictive covenants) into loan contracts that prevent borrowers from engaging in overly risky activities. By monitoring borrowers' activities to see whether they are complying with the restrictive covenants and by enforcing the covenants if they are not, financial institution managers can make sure that borrowers are not taking on risks at the institution's expense. The need for financial institutions to engage in screening and monitoring explains why successful financial institutions spend so much money on auditing and information-collecting activities.

Long-Term Customer Relationships

An additional way for financial institution managers to obtain information about borrowers is to establish long-term customer relationships, another important principle of credit risk management.

If a prospective borrower has had a checking or savings account or loans with the financial institution over a long period of time, a loan officer can look at past activity in the accounts and learn quite a bit about the borrower. The balances in the checking and savings accounts tell the loan officer how liquid the potential borrower is and at what times of the year the borrower has a strong need for cash. A review of the checks the borrower has written reveals the borrower's suppliers. If the borrower has borrowed previously from the financial institution, the institution has a record of the loan payments. Thus long-term customer relationships reduce the costs of information collection and make it easier to screen out bad credit risks.

The need for monitoring by financial institutions adds to the importance of long-term customer relationships. If the borrower has borrowed from the financial institution before, the institution has already established procedures for monitoring that customer. Therefore, the costs of monitoring long-term customers are lower than those for new customers.

Long-term relationships benefit the customers as well as the financial institution. A firm with a previous relationship will find it easier to obtain a loan at a low interest rate because the financial institution has an easier time determining if the prospective borrower is a good credit risk and incurs fewer costs in monitoring the borrower.

A long-term customer relationship has another advantage for the financial institution. No financial institution manager can think of every contingency when the institution writes restrictive covenants into a loan contract; there will always be risky borrower activities that are not ruled out. However, what if a borrower wants to preserve a long-term relationship with the financial institution to make it easier to get future loans at low interest rates? The borrower then has the incentive to avoid risky activities that would upset the financial institution, even if these risky activities are not specifically addressed in the loan contract. Indeed, if the financial institution manager doesn't like what a borrower is doing even when the borrower isn't violating any restrictive covenants, the manager has some power to discourage the borrower from such activity by threatening to refuse new loans in the future. Long-term customer relationships therefore enable financial institution managers to deal with even unanticipated moral hazard contingencies.

Loan Commitments

Banks have a special vehicle for institutionalizing long-term relationships called a **loan commitment.** A loan commitment is a bank's commitment (for a specified future period of time) to provide a firm with loans up to a given amount at a fixed interest rate or, more commonly, at a rate that is tied to some market interest rate. The majority of commercial and industrial loans from banks are made under the loan commitment arrangement. The advantage for the firm is that it has a source of credit when it needs it. The advantage for the bank is that the loan commitment promotes a long-term relationship, which in turn facilitates information collection. In addition, provisions in the loan commitment agreement require that the firm continually supply the bank with information about the firm's income, asset and liability position, business activities, and so on. A loan commitment arrangement is a powerful method for reducing the bank's costs for screening and information collection.

Collateral

Collateral requirements for loans are important credit risk management tools. Loans with these collateral requirements are often referred to as **secured loans.** Collateral, which is property promised to the lender as compensation if the borrower defaults, lessens the consequences of adverse selection because it reduces the lender's losses in the case of a loan default. If a borrower defaults on a loan with collateral, the lender can sell the collateral and use the proceeds to make up for its losses on the loan. Collateral requirements thus offer important protection for financial institutions making loans, and that is why they are extremely common in loans made by financial institutions.

Compensating Balances

One particular form of collateral required when a bank makes commercial loans is called **compensating balances:** A firm receiving a loan must keep a required minimum amount of funds in a checking account at the bank. For example, a business getting a $10 million loan may be required to keep compensating balances of at least $1 million in its checking account at the bank. If the borrower defaults, this $1 million in compensating balances can be taken by the bank to make up some of the losses on the loan.

Besides serving as collateral, compensating balances help increase the likelihood that a loan will be paid off. They do this by helping the bank monitor the borrower and consequently minimize moral hazard. Specifically, by requiring the borrower to use a checking account at the bank, the bank can observe the firm's check payment practices, which may yield a great deal of information about the borrower's financial condition. For example, a sustained drop in the borrower's checking account balance may signal that the borrower is having financial trouble, or account activity may suggest that the borrower is engaging in risky activities; perhaps a change in suppliers means that the borrower is pursuing new lines of business. Any significant change in the borrower's payment procedures is a signal to the bank that it should make inquiries. Compensating balances therefore make it easier for banks to monitor borrowers more effectively and are consequently another important credit risk management tool.

Credit Rationing

Another way in which successful financial institution managers deal with adverse selection and moral hazard is through **credit rationing:** Lenders refuse to make loans even though borrowers are willing to pay the stated interest rate or even a higher rate. Credit rationing takes two forms. The first occurs when a financial institution refuses to make a loan of *any amount* to a borrower, even if the borrower is willing to pay a higher interest rate. The second occurs when the financial institution is willing to make a loan but restricts the size of the loan to less than the borrower would like.

At first you might be puzzled by the first type of credit rationing. After all, even if the potential borrower is a credit risk, why doesn't the financial institution just extend the loan but at a higher interest rate? The answer is that adverse selection rules out this solution. Individuals and firms with the riskiest investment projects are precisely the ones that are willing to pay the highest interest rates. If a borrower took on a high-risk investment and succeeded, the borrower would become extremely rich. But a financial institution wouldn't want to make such a loan precisely because the investment risk is high; the likely outcome is that the borrower will *not* succeed and the financial institution will not be paid back. Charging a higher interest rate just makes adverse selection worse for the financial institution; that is, it increases the likelihood that the financial institution is lending to a bad credit risk. The financial institution would therefore rather not make any loans at a higher interest rate; instead, it would engage in the first type of credit rationing and would turn down loans.

Financial institutions engage in a second type of credit rationing to guard against moral hazard: They grant loans to borrowers, but not loans as large as the borrowers want. Such credit rationing is necessary because the larger the loan, the greater the benefits from moral hazard. For example, if a financial institution gives you a $1000 loan, you are likely to take actions that enable you to pay it back because you don't want to hurt your credit rating for the future. However, if the financial institution lends you $10 million, you are more likely to fly off to Rio to celebrate. The larger your loan, the greater your incentives to engage in activities that make it less likely that you will repay the loan. Because more borrowers repay their loans if the loan amounts are small, financial institutions ration credit by providing borrowers with smaller loans than they seek.

Managing Interest-Rate Risk

As the volatility of interest rates increased in the 1980s, financial institution managers became more concerned about their exposure to interest-rate risk, the riskiness of earnings and returns that is associated with changes in interest rates. Indeed, the S&L debacle, described in Chapter 19, made clearer the dangers of interest-rate risk when many S&Ls went out of business because they had not managed interest-rate risk properly. To see what interest-rate risk is all about, let's take a look at the balance sheet of the First National Bank:

First National Bank			
Assets		**Liabilities**	
Reserves and cash items	$5 million	Checkable deposits	$15 million
Securities		Money market deposit	
Less than 1 year	$5 million	accounts	$5 million
1 to 2 years	$5 million	Savings deposits	$15 million
Greater than 2 years	$10 million	CDs	
Residential mortgages		Variable-rate	$10 million
Variable-rate	$10 million	Less than 1 year	$15 million
Fixed-rate (30-year)	$10 million	1 to 2 years	$5 million
Commercial loans		Greater than 2 years	$5 million
Less than 1 year	$15 million	Fed funds	$5 million
1 to 2 years	$10 million	Borrowings	
Greater than 2 years	$25 million	Less than 1 year	$10 million
Physical capital	$5 million	1 to 2 years	$5 million
		Greater than 2 years	$5 million
		Bank capital	$5 million
Total	$100 million	Total	$100 million

The first step in assessing interest-rate risk is for the bank manager to decide which assets and liabilities are rate-sensitive, that is, which have interest rates that will be reset (repriced) within the year. Note that rate-sensitive assets or liabilities can have interest rates repriced within the year either because the debt instrument matures within the year or because the repricing is done automatically, as with variable-rate mortgages.

For many assets and liabilities, deciding whether they are rate-sensitive is straightforward. In our example, the obviously rate-sensitive assets are securities with maturities of less than one year ($5 million), variable-rate mortgages ($10 million), and commercial loans with maturities less than one year ($15 million), for a total of $30 million. However, some assets that look like fixed-rate assets whose interest rates are not repriced within the year actually have a component that is rate-sensitive. For example, although fixed-rate residential mortgages may have a maturity of 30 years, homeowners can repay their mortgages early by selling their homes or repaying the mortgage in some other way. This means that within the year, a certain percentage of these fixed-rate mortgages will be paid off, and interest rates on this amount will be repriced. From past experience the bank manager knows that 20% of the fixed-rate residential mortgages are repaid within a year, which means that $2 million of these mortgages (20% of $10 million) must be considered rate-sensitive. The bank manager adds this $2 million to the $30 million of rate-sensitive assets already calculated, for a total of $32 million in rate-sensitive assets.

The bank manager now goes through a similar procedure to determine the total amount of rate-sensitive liabilities. The obviously rate-sensitive liabilities are money market deposit accounts ($5 million), variable-rate CDs and CDs with less than one year to maturity ($25 million), federal funds ($5 million), and borrowings with maturities of less than one year ($10 million), for a total of $45 million. Checkable deposits and savings deposits often have interest rates that can be changed at any time by the bank, although banks often like to keep their rates fixed for substantial periods. Thus these liabilities are partially but not fully rate-sensitive. The bank manager estimates that 10% of checkable deposits ($1.5 million) and 20% of savings deposits ($3 million) should be considered rate-sensitive. Adding the $1.5 million and $3 million to the $45 million figure yields a total for rate-sensitive liabilities of $49.5 million.

Now the bank manager can analyze what will happen if interest rates rise by 1 percentage point, say, on average from 10% to 11%. The income on the assets rises by $320,000 (= 1% × $32 million of rate-sensitive assets), while the payments on the liabilities rise by $495,000 (= 1% × $49.5 million of rate-sensitive liabilities). The First National Bank's profits now decline by $175,000 = ($320,000 − $495,000). Another way of thinking about this situation is with the net interest margin concept described in Chapter 17, which is interest income minus interest expense divided by bank assets. In this case, the 1% rise in interest rates has resulted in a decline of the net interest margin by 0.175% (= − $175,000/$100 million). Conversely, if interest rates fall by 1%, similar reasoning tells us that the First National Bank's income rises by $175,000 and its net interest margin rises by 0.175%. This example illustrates the following point: *If a financial institution has more rate-sensitive liabilities than assets, a rise in interest rates will reduce the net interest margin and income, and a decline in interest rates will raise the net interest margin and income.*

Income Gap Analysis

One simple and quick approach to measuring the sensitivity of bank income to changes in interest rates is **gap analysis** (also called **income gap analysis**), in which the amount of rate-sensitive liabilities is subtracted from the amount of rate-sensitive assets. This calculation, *GAP*, can be written as

$$GAP = RSA - RSL \tag{1}$$

where
RSA = rate-sensitive assets
RSL = rate-sensitive liabilities

In our example, the bank manager calculates *GAP* to be

$$GAP = \$32 \text{ million} - \$49.5 \text{ million} = -\$17.5 \text{ million}$$

Multiplying *GAP* times the change in the interest rate immediately reveals the effect on bank income:

$$\Delta I = GAP \times \Delta i \tag{2}$$

where
ΔI = change in bank income
Δi = change in interest rates

EXAMPLE 1   *Income Gap Analysis*

Using the −$17.5 million gap calculated using Equation 1, what is the change in income if interest rates rise by 1%?

Solution

The change in income is −$175,000.

$$\Delta I = GAP \times \Delta i$$

where

$GAP = RSA - RSL \qquad = -\$17.5 \text{ million}$

$\Delta i = \text{change in interest rate} = 0.01$

Thus

$$\Delta I = -\$17.5 \text{ million} \times 0.01 = -\$175,000$$

The analysis we just conducted is known as *basic gap analysis*, and it suffers from the problem that many of the assets and liabilities that are not classified as rate-sensitive have different maturities. One refinement to deal with this problem, the *maturity bucket approach*, is to measure the gap for several maturity subintervals, called maturity buckets, so that effects of interest-rate changes over a multiyear period can be calculated.

EXAMPLE 2   *Income Gap Analysis*

The manager of First National Bank notices that the bank balance sheet allows him to put assets and liabilities into more refined maturity buckets that allow him to estimate the potential change in income over the next one to two years. Rate-sensitive assets in this period consist of $5 million of securities maturing in one to two years, $10 million of commercial loans maturing in one to two years, and an additional $2 million (20% of fixed-rate mortgages) that the bank expects to be repaid. Rate-sensitive liabilities in this period consist of $5 million of one- to two-year CDs, $5 million of one- to two-year borrowings, $1.5 million of checkable deposits (the 10% of checkable deposits that the bank manager estimates are rate-sensitive in this period), and an additional $3 million of savings deposits (the 20% estimate of savings deposits). For the next one to two years, calculate the gap and the change in income if interest rates rise by 1%.

Solution

The gap calculation for the one- to two-year period is $2.5 million.

$$GAP = RSA - RSL$$

where

$RSA = \text{rate-sensitive assets} \quad = \$17 \text{ million}$

$RSL = \text{rate-sensitive liabilities} = \$14.5 \text{ million}$

Thus

$$GAP = \$17 \text{ million} - \$14.5 \text{ million} = \$2.5 \text{ million}$$

If interest rates remain 1% higher, then in the second year income will improve by $25,000.

$$\Delta I = GAP \times \Delta i$$

where

$GAP = RSA - RSL$ $\qquad = \$2.5 \text{ million}$

Δi = change in interest rate = 0.01

Thus

$$\Delta I = \$2.5 \text{ million} \times 0.01 = \$25,000$$

By using the more refined maturity bucket approach, the bank manager can figure out what will happen to bank income over the next several years when there is a change in interest rates.

Duration Gap Analysis

The gap analysis we have examined so far focuses only on the effect of interest-rate changes on income. Clearly, owners and managers of financial institutions care not only about the effect of changes in interest rates on income but also about the effect of changes in interest rates on the market value of the net worth of the financial institution.[1]

An alternative method for measuring interest-rate risk, called **duration gap analysis,** examines the sensitivity of the market value of the financial institution's net worth to changes in interest rates. Duration analysis is based on Macaulay's concept of *duration,* which measures the average lifetime of a security's stream of payments (described in Chapter 3). Recall that duration is a useful concept because it provides a good approximation, particularly when interest-rate changes are small, of the sensitivity of a security's market value to a change in its interest rate using the following formula:

$$\%\Delta P \approx -DUR \times \frac{\Delta i}{1 + i} \qquad (3)$$

where

$\%\Delta P = (P_{t+1} - P_t)/P_t$ = percent change in market value of the security

DUR = duration

i = interest rate

After having determined the duration of all assets and liabilities on the bank's balance sheet, the bank manager could use this formula to calculate how the market

---

[1]Note that accounting net worth is calculated on a historical-cost (book-value) basis, meaning that the value of assets and liabilities is based on their initial price. However, book-value net worth does not give a complete picture of the true worth of the firm; the market value of net worth provides a more accurate measure. This is why duration gap analysis focuses on what happens to the market value of net worth, and not on book value, when interest rates change.

value of each asset and liability changes when there is a change in interest rates and then calculate the effect on net worth. There is, however, an easier way to go about doing this, derived from the basic fact about duration we learned in Chapter 3: Duration is additive; that is, the duration of a portfolio of securities is the weighted average of the durations of the individual securities, with the weights reflecting the proportion of the portfolio invested in each. What this means is that the bank manager can figure out the effect that interest-rate changes will have on the market value of net worth by calculating the average duration for assets and for liabilities and then using those figures to estimate the effects of interest-rate changes.

To see how a bank manager would do this, let's return to the balance sheet of the First National Bank. The bank manager has already used the procedures outlined in Chapter 3 to calculate the duration of each asset and liability, as listed in Table 1. For each asset, the manager then calculates the weighted duration

TABLE 1   *Duration of the First National Bank's Assets and Liabilities*

	Amount ($ millions)	Duration (years)	Weighted Duration (years)
Assets			
Reserves and cash items	5	0.0	0.00
Securities			
Less than 1 year	5	0.4	0.02
1 to 2 years	5	1.6	0.08
Greater than 2 years	10	7.0	0.70
Residential mortgages			
Variable-rate	10	0.5	0.05
Fixed-rate (30-year)	10	6.0	0.60
Commercial loans			
Less than 1 year	15	0.7	0.11
1 to 2 years	10	1.4	0.14
Greater than 2 years	25	4.0	1.00
Physical capital	5	0.0	0.00
Average duration			2.70
Liabilities			
Checkable deposits	15	2.0	0.32
Money market deposit accounts	5	0.1	0.01
Savings deposits	15	1.0	0.16
CDs			
Variable-rate	10	0.5	0.05
Less than 1 year	15	0.2	0.03
1 to 2 years	5	1.2	0.06
Greater than 2 years	5	2.7	0.14
Fed funds	5	0.0	0.00
Borrowings			
Less than 1 year	10	0.3	0.03
1 to 2 years	5	1.3	0.07
Greater than 2 years	5	3.1	0.16
Average duration			1.03

by multiplying the duration times the amount of the asset divided by total assets, which in this case is $100 million. For example, in the case of securities with maturities less than one year, the manager multiplies the 0.4 year of duration times $5 million divided by $100 million to get a weighted duration of 0.02. (Note that physical assets have no cash payments, so they have a duration of zero years.) Doing this for all the assets and adding them up, the bank manager gets a figure for the average duration of the assets of 2.70 years.

The manager follows a similar procedure for the liabilities, noting that total liabilities excluding capital are $95 million. For example, the weighted duration for checkable deposits is determined by multiplying the 2.0-year duration by $15 million divided by $95 million to get 0.32. Adding up these weighted durations, the manager obtains an average duration of liabilities of 1.03 years.

EXAMPLE 3

Duration Gap Analysis

The bank manager wants to know what happens when interest rates rise from 10% to 11%. The total asset value is $100 million, and the total liability value is $95 million. Use Equation 3 to calculate the change in the market value of the assets and liabilities.

Solution

With a total asset value of $100 million, the market value of assets falls by $2.5 million ($100 million $\times$ 0.025 = $2.5 million).

$$\%\Delta P = -DUR \times \frac{\Delta i}{1 + i}$$

where

$$DUR = \text{duration} \qquad\qquad = 2.70$$
$$\Delta i = \text{change in interest rate} = 0.11 - 0.10 = 0.01$$
$$i = \text{interest rate} \qquad\qquad = 0.10$$

Thus

$$\%\Delta P \approx -2.70 \times \frac{0.01}{1 + 0.10} = -0.025 = -2.5\%$$

With total liabilities of $95 million, the market value of liabilities falls by $0.9 million ($95 million $\times$ 0.009 = $-$0.9 million).

$$\%\Delta P \approx -DUR \times \frac{\Delta i}{1 + i}$$

where

$$DUR = \text{duration} \qquad\qquad = 1.03$$
$$\Delta i = \text{change in interest rate} = 0.11 - 0.10 = 0.01$$
$$i = \text{interest rate} \qquad\qquad = 0.10$$

Thus

$$\%\Delta P \approx -1.03 \times \frac{0.01}{1 + 0.10} = -0.009 = -0.9\%$$

The result is that the net worth of the bank would decline by $1.6 million ($-$2.5 million $-$ ($-$0.9 million) = $-$2.5 million + $0.9 million = $-$1.6 million).

The bank manager could have gotten to the answer even more quickly by calculating what is called a *duration gap*, which is defined as follows:

$$DUR_{gap} = DUR_a - \left(\frac{L}{A} \times DUR_l \right) \qquad (4)$$

where
DUR_a = average duration of assets
DUR_l = average duration of liabilities
L = market value of liabilities
A = market value of assets

EXAMPLE 4   *Duration Gap Analysis*

Based on the information provided in Example 3, use Equation 4 to determine the duration gap for First National Bank.

Solution
The duration gap for First National Bank is 1.72 years.

$$DUR_{gap} = DUR_a - \left(\frac{L}{A} \times DUR_l \right)$$

where

DUR_a = average duration of assets   = 2.70

L = market value of liabilities   = 95

A = market value of assets   = 100

DUR_l = average duration of liabilities = 1.03

Thus

$$DUR_{gap} = 2.70 - \left(\frac{95}{100} \times 1.03 \right) = 1.72 \text{ years}$$

To estimate what will happen if interest rates change, the bank manager uses the DUR_{gap} calculation in Equation 4 to obtain the change in the market value of net worth as a percentage of total assets. In other words, the change in the market value of net worth as a percentage of assets is calculated as

$$\frac{\Delta NW}{A} \approx -DUR_{gap} \times \frac{\Delta i}{1 + i} \qquad (5)$$

EXAMPLE 5 *Duration Gap Analysis*

What is the change in the market value of net worth as a percentage of assets if interest rates rise from 10% to 11%? (Use Equation 5.)

Solution

A rise in interest rates from 10% to 11% would lead to a change in the market value of net worth as a percentage of assets of -1.6%

$$\frac{\Delta NW}{A} = -DUR_{gap} \times \frac{\Delta i}{1 + i}$$

where

$$DUR_{gap} = \text{duration gap} \qquad\qquad = 1.72$$
$$\Delta i = \text{change in interest rate} = 0.11 - 0.10 = 0.01$$
$$i = \text{interest rate} \qquad\qquad\qquad = 0.10$$

Thus

$$\frac{\Delta NW}{A} = -1.72 \times \frac{0.01}{1 + 0.10} = -0.016 = -1.6\%$$

With assets totaling $100 million, Example 5 indicates a fall in the market value of net worth of $1.6 million, which is the same figure that we found in Example 3.

As our examples make clear, both income gap analysis and duration gap analysis indicate that the First National Bank will suffer from a rise in interest rates. Indeed, in this example, we have seen that a rise in interest rates from 10% to 11% will cause the market value of net worth to fall by $1.6 million, which is one-third the initial amount of bank capital. Thus the bank manager realizes that the bank faces substantial interest-rate risk because a rise in interest rates could cause it to lose a lot of its capital. Clearly, income gap analysis and duration gap analysis are useful tools for telling a financial institution manager the institution's degree of exposure to interest-rate risk.

Study Guide

To make sure that you understand income gap and duration gap analyses, you should be able to verify that if interest rates fall from 10% to 5%, the First National Bank will find its income increasing and the market value of its net worth rising. For even more practice with these concepts, do some of the problems at the end of this chapter.

Example of a Nonbanking Financial Institution

So far we have focused on an example involving a banking institution that has borrowed short and lent long so that when interest rates rise, both income and the net worth of the institution fall. It is important to recognize that income and duration gap analysis applies equally to other financial institutions. Furthermore, it is important for you to see that some financial institutions have income and duration gaps that are opposite in sign to those of banks, so that when interest rates rise, both income and net worth rise rather than fall. To get a more complete picture of income and duration gap analysis, let us look at a nonbank financial institution, the Friendly Finance Company, which specializes in making consumer loans.

The Friendly Finance Company has the following balance sheet:

Friendly Finance Company			
Assets		**Liabilities**	
Cash and deposits	$3 million	Commercial paper	$40 million
Securities		Bank loans	
Less than 1 year	$5 million	Less than 1 year	$3 million
1 to 2 years	$1 million	1 to 2 years	$2 million
Greater than 2 years	$1 million	Greater than 2 years	$5 million
Consumer loans		Long-term bonds and	
Less than 1 year	$50 million	other long-term debt	$40 million
1 to 2 years	$20 million	Capital	$10 million
Greater than 2 years	$15 million		
Physical capital	$5 million		
Total	$100 million	Total	$100 million

The manager of the Friendly Finance Company calculates the rate-sensitive assets to be equal to the $5 million of securities with maturities less than one year plus the $50 million of consumer loans with maturities of less than one year, for a total of $55 million of rate-sensitive assets. The manager then calculates the rate-sensitive liabilities to be equal to the $40 million of commercial paper, all of which has a maturity of less than one year, plus the $3 million of bank loans maturing in less than a year, for a total of $43 million. The calculation of the income gap is then

$$GAP = RSA - RSL = \$55 \text{ million} - \$43 \text{ million} = \$12 \text{ million}$$

To calculate the effect on income if interest rates rise by 1%, the manager multiplies the *GAP* of $12 million times the change in the interest rate to get the following:

$$\Delta I = GAP \times \Delta i = \$12 \text{ million} \times 1\% = \$120,000$$

Thus the manager finds that the finance company's income will rise by $120,000 when interest rates rise by 1%. The reason that the company has benefited from the interest-rate rise, in contrast to the First National Bank, whose profits suffer from the rise in interest rates, is that the Friendly Finance Company has a positive income gap because it has more rate-sensitive assets than liabilities.

Like the bank manager, the manager of the Friendly Finance Company is also interested in what happens to the market value of the net worth of the company when interest rates rise by 1%. So the manager calculates the weighted duration of each item in the balance sheet, adds them up as in Table 2, and obtains a duration for the assets of 1.16 years and for the liabilities of 2.77 years. The duration gap is then calculated to be

$$DUR_{gap} = DUR_a - \left(\frac{L}{A} \times DUR_l\right) = 1.16 - \left(\frac{90}{100} \times 2.77\right) = -1.33 \text{ years}$$

TABLE 2 *Duration of the Friendly Finance Company's Assets and Liabilities*

	Amount ($ millions)	Duration (years)	Weighted Duration (years)
Assets			
Cash and deposits	3	0.0	0.00
Securities			
Less than 1 year	5	0.5	0.05
1 to 2 years	1	1.7	0.02
Greater than 2 years	1	9.0	0.09
Consumer loans			
Less than 1 year	50	0.5	0.25
1 to 2 years	20	1.5	0.30
Greater than 2 years	15	3.0	0.45
Physical capital	5	0.0	0.00
Average duration			1.16
Liabilities			
Commercial paper	40	0.2	0.09
Bank loans			
Less than 1 year	3	0.3	0.01
1 to 2 years	2	1.6	0.04
Greater than 2 years	5	3.5	0.19
Long-term bonds and other long-term debt	40	5.5	2.44
Average duration			2.77

Since the Friendly Finance Company has a negative duration gap, the manager realizes that a rise in interest rates by 1 percentage point from 10% to 11% will increase the market value of net worth of the firm. The manager checks this by calculating the change in the market value of net worth as a percentage of assets:

$$\frac{\Delta NW}{A} = -DUR_{gap} \times \frac{\Delta i}{1 + i} = -(-1.33) \times \frac{0.01}{1 + 0.10} = 0.012 = 1.2\%$$

With assets of $100 million, this calculation indicates that net worth will rise in market value by $1.2 million.

Even though the income and duration gap analysis indicates that the Friendly Finance Company gains from a rise in interest rates, the manager realizes that if interest rates go in the other direction, the company will suffer a fall in income and market value of net worth. Thus the finance company manager, like the bank manager, realizes that the institution is subject to substantial interest-rate risk.

Some Problems with Income and Duration Gap Analysis

Although you might think that income and duration gap analysis is complicated enough, further complications make a financial institution manager's job even harder.

One assumption that we have been using in our discussion of income and duration gap analysis is that when the level of interest rates changes, interest rates on all maturities change by exactly the same amount. That is the same as saying that we conducted our analysis under the assumption that the slope of the yield curve remains unchanged. Indeed, the situation is even worse for duration gap analysis because the duration gap is calculated assuming that interest rates for all maturities are the same—in other words, the yield curve is assumed to be flat. As our discussion of the term structure of interest rates in Chapter 5 indicated, however, the yield curve is not flat, and the slope of the yield curve fluctuates and has a tendency to change when the level of the interest rate changes. Thus to get a truly accurate assessment of interest-rate risk, a financial institution manager has to assess what might happen to the slope of the yield curve when the level of the interest rate changes and then take this information into account when assessing interest-rate risk. In addition, duration gap analysis is based on the approximation in Equation 3 and thus only works well for small changes in interest rates.

A problem with income gap analysis is that as we have seen, the financial institution manager must make estimates of the proportion of supposedly fixed-rate assets and liabilities that may be rate-sensitive. This involves estimates of the likelihood of prepayment of loans or customer shifts out of deposits when interest rates change. Such guesses are not easy to make, and as a result, the financial institution manager's estimates of income gaps may not be very accurate. A similar problem occurs in calculating durations of assets and liabilities because many of the cash payments are uncertain. Thus the estimate of the duration gap might not be accurate either.

Do these problems mean that managers of banks and other financial institutions should give up on gap analysis as a tool for measuring interest-rate risk? Financial institutions do use more sophisticated approaches to measuring interest-rate risk, such as scenario analysis and value-at-risk analysis, which make greater use of computers to more accurately measure changes in prices of assets when interest rates change. Income and duration gap analyses, however, still provide simple frameworks to help financial institution managers to get a first assessment of interest-rate risk, and they are thus useful tools in the financial institution managers' toolkit.

The Practicing Manager

STRATEGIES FOR MANAGING INTEREST-RATE RISK

Once financial institution managers have done the duration and income gap analyses for their institutions, they must decide which alternative strategies to pursue. If the manager of the First National Bank firmly believes that interest rates will fall in the future, he or she may be willing to take no action knowing that the bank has more rate-sensitive liabilities than rate-sensitive assets and so will benefit from the expected interest-rate decline. However, the bank manager also realizes that the First National Bank is subject to substantial interest-rate risk because there is always a possibility that interest rates will rise rather than fall, and as we have seen, this outcome could bankrupt the bank. The manager might try to shorten the duration of the bank's assets to increase their rate sensitivity either by purchasing assets of shorter maturity or by converting fixed-rate loans into adjustable-rate loans. Alternatively, the bank manager could lengthen the duration of the liabilities. With these adjustments to the bank's assets and liabilities, the bank would be less affected by interest-rate swings.

For example, the bank manager might decide to eliminate the income gap by increasing the amount of rate-sensitive assets to $49.5 million to equal the $49.5 million of rate-sensitive liabilities. Or the manager could reduce rate-sensitive liabilities to $32 million so that they equal rate-sensitive assets. In either case, the income gap would now be zero, so a change in interest rates would have no effect on bank profits in the coming year.

Alternatively, the bank manager might decide to immunize the market value of the bank's net worth completely from interest-rate risk by adjusting assets and liabilities so that the duration gap is equal to zero. To do this, the manager can set DUR_{gap} equal to zero in Equation 4 and solve for DUR_a:

$$DUR_a = \frac{L}{A} \times DUR_l = \frac{95}{100} \times 1.03 = 0.98$$

These calculations reveal that the manager should reduce the average duration of the bank's assets to 0.98 year. To check that the duration gap is set equal to zero, the calculation is

$$DUR_{gap} = 0.98 - \left(\frac{95}{100} \times 1.03 \right) = 0$$

In this case, as in Equation 5, the market value of net worth would remain unchanged when interest rates change. Alternatively, the bank manager could calculate the value of the duration of the liabilities that would produce a duration gap of zero. To do this would involve setting DUR_{gap} equal to zero in Equation 4 and solving for DUR_l:

$$DUR_l = DUR_a \times \frac{A}{L} = 2.70 \times \frac{100}{95} = 2.84$$

This calculation reveals that the interest-rate risk could also be eliminated by increasing the average duration of the bank's liabilities to 2.84 years. The manager again checks that the duration gap is set equal to zero by calculating

$$DUR_{gap} = 2.70 - \left(\frac{95}{100} \times 2.84 \right) = 0$$

Study Guide

To see if you understand how a financial institution manager can protect income and net worth from interest-rate risk, first calculate how the Friendly Finance Company might change the amount of its rate-sensitive assets or its rate-sensitive liabilities to eliminate the income gap. You should find that the income gap can be eliminated either by reducing the amount of rate-sensitive assets to $43 million or by raising the amount of rate-sensitive liabilities to $55 million. Also do the calculations to determine what modifications to the duration of the assets or liabilities would immunize the market value of Friendly Finance's net worth from interest-rate risk. You should find that interest-rate risk would be eliminated if the duration of the assets were set to 2.49 years or if the duration of the liabilities were set to 1.29 years.

One problem with eliminating a financial institution's interest-rate risk by altering the balance sheet is that doing so might be very costly in the short run. The financial institution may be locked into assets and liabilities of particular durations because of its field of expertise. Fortunately, recently developed financial instruments, such as financial futures, options, and interest-rate swaps, help financial institutions manage their interest-rate risk without requiring them to rearrange their balance sheets. We discuss these instruments and how they can be used to manage interest-rate risk in the next chapter.

Summary

1. The concepts of adverse selection and moral hazard explain the origin of many credit risk management principles involving loan activities, including screening and monitoring, development of long-term customer relationships, loan commitments, collateral, compensating balances, and credit rationing.

2. With the increased volatility of interest rates that occurred in recent years, financial institutions became more concerned about their exposure to interest-rate risk. Income gap and duration gap analyses tell a financial institution if it has fewer rate-sensitive assets than liabilities (in which case a rise in interest rates will reduce income and a fall in interest rates will raise it) or more rate-sensitive assets than liabilities (in which case a rise in interest rates will raise income and a fall in interest rates will reduce it). Financial institutions can manage interest-rate risk by modifying their balance sheets and by making use of new financial instruments.

Key Terms

compensating balance, *p. 620*

credit rationing, *p. 621*

duration gap analysis, *p. 625*

gap analysis (income gap analysis), *p. 623*

loan commitment, *p. 620*

secured loan, *p. 620*

Questions

1. Can a financial institution keep borrowers from engaging in risky activities if there are no restrictive covenants written into the loan agreement?

2. Why are secured loans an important method of lending for financial institutions?

3. "If more customers want to borrow funds at the prevailing interest rate, a financial institution can increase its profits by raising interest rates on its loans." Is this statement true, false, or uncertain? Explain your answer.

4. Why is being nosy a desirable trait for a banker?

5. A bank almost always insists that the firms it lends to keep compensating balances at the bank. Why?

6. "Because diversification is a desirable strategy for avoiding risk, it never makes sense for a financial institution to specialize in making specific types of loans." Is this statement true, false, or uncertain? Explain your answer.

Quantitative Problems

1. A bank issues a $100,000 variable-rate 30-year mortgage with a nominal annual rate of 4.5%. If the required rate drops to 4.0% after the first six months, what is the impact on the interest income for the first 12 months?

2. A bank issues a $100,000 fixed-rate 30-year mortgage with a nominal annual rate of 4.5%. If the required rate drops to 4.0% immediately after the mortgage is issued, what is the impact on the value of the mortgage?

3. Calculate the duration of a $100,000 fixed-rate 30-year mortgage with a nominal annual rate of 7.0%. What is the expected percentage change in value if the required rate drops to 6.5% immediately after the mortgage is issued?

4. The value of a $100,000 fixed-rate 30-year mortgage falls to $89,537 when interest rates move from 5% to 6%. What is the approximate duration of the mortgage?

5. Calculate the duration of a commercial loan. The face value of the loan is $2,000,000. It requires simple interest yearly, with an APR of 8%. The loan is due in four years. The current market rate for such loans is 8%.

6. A bank's balance sheet contains interest-sensitive assets of $280 million and interest-sensitive liabilities of $465 million. Calculate the income gap.

7. Calculate the income gap for a financial institution with rate-sensitive assets of $20 million and rate-sensitive liabilities of $48 million. If interest rates rise from 4% to 4.8%, what is the expected change in income?

8. Calculate the income gap given the following items:
   - $8 million in reserves
   - $25 million in variable-rate mortgages
   - $4 million in checkable deposits
   - $2 million in savings deposits
   - $6 million of two-year CDs

9. The following financial statement is for the current year. From the past, you know that 10% of fixed-rate mortgages prepay each year. You also estimate that 10% of checkable deposits and 20% of savings accounts are rate-sensitive.

Second National Bank			
Assets		**Liabilities**	
Reserves	$1,500,000	Checkable deposits	$15,000,000
Securities		Money market	
< 1 year	$6,000,000	deposits	$5,500,000
1 to 2 years	$8,000,000	Savings accounts	$8,000,000
> 2 years	$12,000,000	CDs	
Residential mortgages		Variable-rate	$15,000,000
Variable-rate	$7,000,000	< 1 year	$22,000,000
Fixed-rate	$13,000,000	1 to 2 years	$5,000,000
Commercial loans		> 2 years	$2,500,000
< 1 year	$1,500,000	Federal funds	$5,000,000
1 to 2 years	$18,500,000	Borrowings	
> 2 years	$30,000,000	< 1 year	$12,000,000
Buildings, etc.	$2,500,000	1 to 2 years	$3,000,000
		> 2 years	$2,000,000
		Bank capital	$5,000,000
Total	$100,000,000	Total	$100,000,000

What is the current income gap for Second National Bank? What will happen to the bank's current net interest income if rates fall by 75 basis points?

10. Chicago Avenue Bank has the following assets:

Asset	Value	Duration (in years)
T-bills	$100,000,000	0.55
Consumer loans	$40,000,000	2.35
Commercial loans	$15,000,000	5.90

What is Chicago Avenue Bank's asset portfolio duration?

11. A bank added a bond to its portfolio. The bond has a duration of 12.3 years and cost $1109. Just after buying the bond, the bank discovered that market interest rates are expected to rise from 8% to 8.75%. What is the expected change in the bond's value?

12. Calculate the change in the market value of assets and liabilities when the average duration of assets is 3.60, the average duration of liabilities 0.88, and interest rates increase from 5% to 5.5%.

13. Springer County Bank has assets totaling $180 million with a duration of five years, and liabilities totaling $160 million with a duration of two years. If interest rates drop from 9% by 75 basis points, what is the change in the bank's capitalization ratio?

14. The manager for Tyler Bank and Trust has the following assets to manage:

Asset	Value	Duration (in years)
Bonds	$75,000,000	9.00
Consumer loans	$875,000,000	2.00
Commercial loans	$700,000,000	5.00

Liability	Value	Duration (in years)
Demand deposits	$300,000,000	1.00
Saving accounts	??	0.50

If the manager wants a duration gap of 3.00, what level of saving accounts should the bank raise? Assume that any difference between assets and liabilities is held as cash (duration = 0).

15. The financial statement on page 636 is for the current year. After you review the data, calculate the duration gap for the bank.

	Second National Bank					
Assets		**Duration (in years)**	**Liabilities**			**Duration (in years)**
Reserves	$5,000,000	0.00	Checkable deposits		$15,000,000	2.00
Securities			Money market deposits		5,000,000	0.10
< 1 year	5,000,000	0.40	Savings accounts		15,000,000	1.00
1 to 2 years	5,000,000	1.60	CDs			
> 2 years	10,000,000	7.00	Variable-rate		10,000,000	0.50
Residential mortgages			< 1 year		15,000,000	0.20
Variable-rate	10,000,000	0.50	1 to 2 years		5,000,000	1.20
Fixed-rate	10,000,000	6.00	> 2 years		5,000,000	2.70
Commercial loans			Interbank loans		5,000,000	0.00
< 1 year	15,000,000	0.70	Borrowings			
1 to 2 years	10,000,000	1.40	< 1 year		10,000,000	0.30
> 2 years	25,000,000	4.00	1 to 2 years		5,000,000	1.30
Buildings, etc.	5,000,000	0.00	> 2 years		5,000,000	3.10
			Bank capital		5,000,000	
Total	$100,000,000		Total		$100,000,000	

For Problems 16–23, assume that the First National Bank initially has the balance sheet shown on page 622 and that interest rates are initially at 10%.

16. If the First National Bank sells $10 million of its securities with maturities greater than two years and replaces them with securities maturing in less than one year, what is the income gap for the bank? What will happen to profits next year if interest rates fall by 3 percentage points?

17. If the First National Bank decides to convert $5 million of its fixed-rate mortgages into variable-rate mortgages, what happens to its interest-rate risk? Explain with gap analysis.

18. If the manager of the First National Bank revises the estimate of the percentage of fixed-rate mortgages that are repaid within a year from 20% to 10%, what will be the revised estimate of the interest-rate risk the bank faces? What will happen to profits next year if interest rates fall by 2 percentage points?

19. If the manager of the First National Bank revises the estimate of the percentage of checkable deposits that are rate-sensitive from 10% to 25%, what will be the revised estimate of the interest-rate risk the bank faces? What will happen to profits next year if interest rates rise by 5 percentage points?

20. Given the estimates of duration in Table 1, what will happen to the bank's net worth if interest rates rise by 10 percentage points? Will the bank stay in business? Why or why not?

21. If the manager of the First National Bank revises the estimates of the duration of the bank's assets to four years and liabilities to two years, what is the effect on net worth if interest rates rise by 2 percentage points?

22. Given the estimates of duration in Problem 21, how should the bank alter the duration of its assets to immunize its net worth from interest-rate risk?

23. Given the estimates of duration in Problem 21, how should the bank alter the duration of its liabilities to immunize its net worth from interest-rate risk?

For Problems 24–29, assume that the Friendly Finance Company initially has the balance sheet shown on page 630 and that interest rates are initially at 8%.

24. If the manager of the Friendly Finance Company decides to sell off $10 million of the company's consumer loans, half maturing within one year and half maturing in greater than two years, and uses the resulting funds to buy $10 million of Treasury bills, what is the income gap for the company? What will happen to profits next year if interest rates fall by 5 percentage points? How could the Friendly Finance Company alter its balance sheet to immunize its income from this change in interest rates?

25. If the Friendly Finance Company raises an additional $20 million with commercial paper and uses the funds to make $20 million of consumer loans that mature in less than one year, what happens to its interest-rate risk? In this situation, what additional changes could it make in its balance sheet to eliminate the income gap?

26. Given the estimates of duration in Table 2, what will happen to the Friendly Finance Company's net worth if interest rates rise by 3 percentage points? Will the company stay in business? Why or why not?

27. If the manager of the Friendly Finance Company revises the estimates of the duration of the company's assets to two years and liabilities to four years, what is the effect on net worth if interest rates rise by 3 percentage points?

28. Given the estimates of duration found in Problem 27, how should the Friendly Finance Company alter the duration of its assets to immunize its net worth from interest-rate risk?

29. Given the estimates of duration in Problem 27, how should the Friendly Finance Company alter the duration of its liabilities to immunize its net worth from interest-rate risk?

Web Exercises

Risk Management in Financial Institutions

1. This chapter discussed the need financial institutions have to control credit risk by lending to creditworthy borrowers. If you allow your credit to deteriorate, you may find yourself unable to borrow when you need to. Go to **http://www.quicken.com/cms/viewers/article/banking/39654** and assess your own creditworthiness. What can you do to improve your appeal to lenders?

2. The FDIC is extremely concerned with risk management in banks. High-risk banks are more likely to fail and cost the FDIC money. The FDIC regularly examines banks and rates them using a system called CAMELS. Go to **http://www.fdic.gov/regulations/safety/manual/index.html**. What does the acronym CAMELS stand for? Go to Part VII. 7.1 and review the discussion of Market Risk. Summarize the FDIC interest-rate risk-measurement methods.

CHAPTER 25

Hedging with Financial Derivatives

Preview

Starting in the 1970s and increasingly in the 1980s and 1990s, the world became a riskier place for financial institutions. Swings in interest rates widened, and the bond and stock markets went through some episodes of increased volatility. As a result of these developments, managers of financial institutions have become more concerned with reducing the risk their institutions face. Given the greater demand for risk reduction, the process of financial innovation described in Chapter 18 came to the rescue by producing new financial instruments that help financial institution managers manage risk better. These instruments, called **financial derivatives,** have payoffs that are linked to previously issued securities and are extremely useful risk reduction tools.

In this chapter we look at the most important financial derivatives that managers of financial institutions use to reduce risk: forward contracts, financial futures, options, and swaps. We examine not only how markets for each of these financial derivatives work but also how each can be used by financial institution managers to reduce risk.

Hedging

Financial derivatives are so effective in reducing risk because they enable financial institutions to **hedge,** that is, engage in a financial transaction that reduces or eliminates risk. When a financial institution has bought an asset, it is said to have taken a **long position,** and this exposes the institution to risk if the returns on the asset are uncertain. On the other hand, if it has sold an asset that it has agreed to deliver to another party at a future date, it is said to have taken a **short position,** and this can also expose the institution to risk. Financial derivatives can be used to reduce risk by invoking the following basic principle of hedging: *Hedging risk involves engaging in a financial transaction that offsets a long position by taking an additional short position, or offsets a short position by taking an additional long position.* In other words, if a financial institution has *bought* a security and has therefore taken a long position, it conducts a hedge by contracting to *sell* that security (take a short position) at some future date. Alternatively, if it has taken a short position by *selling* a security that it needs to deliver at a future date, then it conducts a hedge by contracting to *buy* that security (take a long position) at a future date. We first look at how this principle can be applied using forward contracts.

Forward Markets

Forward contracts are agreements by two parties to engage in a financial transaction at a future (forward) point in time. Here we focus on forward contracts that are linked to debt instruments, called **interest-rate forward contracts;** later in the chapter we discuss forward contracts for foreign currencies.

Interest-Rate Forward Contracts

Interest-rate forward contracts involve the future sale of a debt instrument and have several dimensions: (1) specification of the actual debt instrument that will be delivered at a future date, (2) amount of the debt instrument to be delivered, (3) price (interest rate) on the debt instrument when it is delivered, and (4) date on which delivery will take place. An example of an interest-rate forward contract might be an agreement for the First National Bank to sell to the Rock Solid Insurance Company, one year from today, $5 million face value of the 6s of 2023 Treasury bonds (coupon bonds with a 6% coupon rate that mature in 2023) at a price that yields the same interest rate on these bonds as today's, say, 6%. Because Rock Solid will buy the securities at a future date, it has taken a long position, while the First National Bank, which will sell the securities, has taken a short position.

The Practicing Manager

HEDGING INTEREST-RATE RISK WITH FORWARD CONTRACTS

To understand why the First National Bank might want to enter into this forward contract, suppose that you are the manager of the First National Bank and have previously bought $5 million of the 6s of 2023 Treasury bonds, which currently sell at par value and so their yield to maturity is also 6%. Because these are long-term bonds, you recognize that you are exposed to substantial interest-rate risk and worry that if interest rates rise in the future, the price of these bonds will fall, resulting in a substantial capital loss that may cost you your job. How do you hedge this risk?

Knowing the basic principle of hedging, you see that your long position in these bonds must be offset by a short position with a forward contract. That is, you need to contract to sell these bonds at a future date at the current par value price. As a result you agree with another party, in this case, Rock Solid Insurance Company, to sell them the $5 million of the 6s of 2023 Treasury bonds at par one year from today. By entering into this forward contract, you have locked in the future price and so have eliminated the price risk First National Bank faces from interest-rate changes. In other words, you have successfully hedged against interest-rate risk.

Why would the Rock Solid Insurance Company want to enter into the forward contract with the First National Bank? Rock Solid expects to receive premiums of $5 million in one year's time that it will want to invest in the 6s of 2023 but worries that interest rates on these bonds will decline between now and next year. By using the forward contract, it is able to lock in the 6% interest rate on the Treasury bonds (which will be sold to it by the First National Bank).

Pros and Cons of Forward Contracts

The advantage of forward contracts is that they can be as flexible as the parties involved want them to be. This means that an institution like the First National Bank may be able to hedge completely the interest-rate risk for the exact security it is holding in its portfolio, just as it has in our example.

However, forward contracts suffer from two problems that severely limit their usefulness. The first is that it may be very hard for an institution like the First National Bank to find another party (called a *counterparty*) to make the contract with. There are brokers to facilitate the matching up of parties like the First National Bank with the Rock Solid Insurance Company, but there may be few institutions that want to engage in a forward contract specifically for the 6s of 2023. This means that it may prove impossible to find a counterparty when a financial institution like the First National Bank wants to make a specific type of forward contract. Furthermore, even if the First National Bank finds a counterparty, it may not get as high a price as it wants because there may not be anyone else to make the deal with. A serious problem for the market in interest-rate forward contracts, then, is that it may be difficult to make the financial transaction or that it will have to be made at a disadvantageous price; in the parlance of the financial world, this market suffers from a *lack of liquidity*. (Note that this use of the term *liquidity* when it is applied to a market is somewhat broader than its use when it is applied to an asset. For an asset, liquidity refers to the ease with which the asset can be turned into cash, whereas for a market, liquidity refers to the ease of carrying out financial transactions.)

The second problem with forward contracts is that they are subject to default risk. Suppose that in one year's time, interest rates rise so that the price of the 6s of 2023 falls. The Rock Solid Insurance Company might then decide that it would like to default on the forward contract with the First National Bank because it can now buy the bonds at a price lower than the agreed price in the forward contract. Or perhaps Rock Solid may not have been rock solid and will have gone bust during the year and so is no longer available to complete the terms of the forward contract. Because there is no outside organization guaranteeing the contract, the only recourse is for the First National Bank to go to the courts to sue Rock Solid, but this process will be costly. Furthermore, if Rock Solid is already bankrupt, the First National Bank will suffer a loss; the bank can no longer sell the 6s of 2023 at the price it had agreed with Rock Solid but instead will have to sell at a price well below that because the price of these bonds has fallen.

The presence of default risk in forward contracts means that parties to these contracts must check each other out to be sure that the counterparty is both financially sound and likely to be honest and live up to its contractual obligations. Because this is a costly process and because all the adverse selection and moral hazard problems discussed in earlier chapters apply, default risk is a major barrier to the use of interest-rate forward contracts. When the default risk problem is combined with a lack of liquidity, we see that these contracts may be of limited usefulness to financial institutions. Although there is a market for interest-rate forward contracts, particularly in Treasury and mortgage-backed securities, it is not nearly as large as the financial futures market, to which we turn next.

Financial Futures Markets

Given the default risk and liquidity problems in the interest-rate forward market, another solution to hedging interest-rate risk was needed. This solution was provided by the development of financial futures contracts by the Chicago Board of Trade starting in 1975.

Financial Futures Contracts

A **financial futures contract** is similar to an interest-rate forward contract in that it specifies that a financial instrument must be delivered by one party to another on a stated future date. However, it differs from an interest-rate forward contract in several ways that overcome some of the liquidity and default problems of forward markets.

To understand what financial futures contracts are all about, let's look at one of the most widely traded futures contracts, that for Treasury bonds, which are traded on the Chicago Board of Trade. (An illustration of how prices on these contracts are quoted can be found in the "Following the News" box on page 643.) The contract value is for $100,000 face value of bonds. Prices are quoted in points, with each point equal to $1000, and the smallest change in price is one thirty-second of a point ($31.25). This contract specifies that the bonds to be delivered must have at least 15 years to maturity at the delivery date (and must also not be callable, that is, redeemable by the Treasury at its option, in less than 15 years). If the Treasury bonds delivered to settle the futures contract have a coupon rate different from the 6% specified in the futures contract, the amount of bonds to be delivered is adjusted to reflect the difference in value between the delivered bonds and the 6% coupon bond. In line with the terminology used for forward contracts, parties who have bought a futures contract and thereby agreed to buy (take delivery) of the bonds are said to have taken a *long position,* and parties who have sold a futures contract and thereby agreed to sell (deliver) the bonds have taken a *short position.*

To make our understanding of this contract more concrete, let's consider what happens when you buy or sell one of these Treasury bond futures contracts. Let's say that on February 1, you sell one $100,000 June contract at a price of 115 (that is, $115,000). By selling this contract, you agree to deliver $100,000 face value of the long-term Treasury bonds to the contract's counterparty at the end of June for $115,000. By buying the contract at a price of 115, the buyer has agreed to pay $115,000 for the $100,000 face value of bonds when you deliver them at the end of June. If interest rates on long-term bonds rise so that when the contract matures at the end of June the price of these bonds has fallen to 110 ($110,000 per $100,000 of face value), the buyer of the contract will have lost $5000 because he or she paid $115,000 for the bonds but can sell them only for the market price of $110,000. But you, the seller of the contract, will have gained $5000 because you can now sell the bonds to the buyer for $115,000 but have to pay only $110,000 for them in the market.

THE *WALL STREET JOURNAL*: FOLLOWING THE NEWS

Financial Futures

The prices for financial futures contracts for debt instruments are published daily. In the *Wall Street Journal,* these prices are found in the "Commodities" section under the "Interest Rate" heading of the "Futures Prices" columns. An excerpt is reproduced here.

Interest Rate
Treasury Bonds (CBT)-$100,000; pts. 32nds of 100%

	OPEN	HIGH	LOW	SETTLE	CHANGE	LIFETIME HIGH	LIFETIME LOW	OPEN INTEREST
Mar	112-14	113-00	112-06	112-28	17	114-02	100-25	614,170
June	111-19	112-05	111-19	112-02	18	113-07	100-00	20,438

Est vol 238,046; vol Mon 172,561; open int 634,817, +3,526

Information for each contract is presented in columns, as follows. (The Chicago Board of Trade's contract for delivery of long-term Treasury bonds in March 2004 is used as an example.)

Open: Opening price; each point corresponds to $1000 of face value—112 14/32 is $112,437.50 for the March contract

High: Highest traded price that day—113 00/32 is $113,000 for the March contract

Low: Lowest traded price that day—112 06/32 is $112,187.50 for the March contract

Settle: Settlement price, the closing price that day—112 28/32 is $112,875 for the March contract

Chg: Change in the settlement price from the previous trading day—+17/32 is + $531.25 for the March contract

Lifetime High: Highest price ever—114 2/32 is $114,062.50 for the March contract

Lifetime Low: Lowest price ever—100 25/32 is $100,781.25 for the March contract

Open Interest: Number of contracts outstanding—614,170 for the March contract, with a face value of $61.4 billion (614,170 × $100,000)

It is even easier to describe what happens to the parties who have purchased futures contracts and those who have sold futures contracts if we recognize the following fact: ***At the expiration date of a futures contract, the price of the contract is the same as the price of the underlying asset to be delivered.*** To see why this is the case, consider what happens on the expiration date of the June contract at the end of June when the price of the underlying $100,000 face value Treasury bond is 110 ($110,000). If the futures contract is selling below 110, say, at 109, a trader can buy the contract for $109,000, take delivery of the bond, and immediately sell it for $110,000, thereby earning a quick profit of $1000. Because earning this profit involves no risk, it is a great deal that everyone would like to get in on. That means that everyone will try to buy the contract, and as a result, its price will rise. Only when the price rises to 110 will the profit opportunity cease to exist and the buying pressure disappear. Conversely, if the price of the futures contract is above 110, say, at 111, everyone will want to sell the contract. Now the sellers get $111,000 from selling the futures contract but have to pay only $110,000 for the Treasury bonds that they must deliver to the buyer of the contract, and the $1000 difference is their profit. Because this profit involves no risk, traders will continue to sell the futures contract until its price falls back down to 110, at which price there are no longer any profits to be made. The elimination of riskless profit opportunities in the futures market is referred to as **arbitrage,** and it guarantees that the price of a futures contract at expiration equals the price of the underlying asset to be delivered.[1]

Armed with the fact that a futures contract at expiration equals the price of the underlying asset, it is even easier to see who profits and loses from such a contract when interest rates change. When interest rates have risen so that the price of the Treasury bond is 110 on the expiration day at the end of June, the June Treasury bond futures contract will also have a price of 110. Thus if you bought the contract for 115 in February, you have a loss of 5 points, or $5000 (5% of $100,000). But if you sold the futures contract at 115 in February, the decline in price to 110 means that you have a profit of 5 points, or $5000.

The Practicing Manager

HEDGING WITH FINANCIAL FUTURES

As the manager of the First National Bank, you can also use financial futures to hedge the interest-rate risk on its holdings of $5 million of the 6s of 2023.

To see how to do this, suppose that in March 2006, the 6s of 2023 are the long-term bonds that would be delivered in the Chicago Board of Trade's T-bond futures contract expiring one year in the future, in March 2007. Also suppose that the interest rate on these bonds is expected to remain at 6% over the next year so that both the 6s of 2023 and the futures contract are selling at par (i.e., the $5 million of bonds is selling for $5 million and the $100,000 futures contract is selling for $100,000). The basic principle of hedging indicates that you need to offset the long position in these bonds with a short position, so you have to sell the futures contract. But how many contracts should you sell? The number of contracts required to hedge the interest-rate risk is found by dividing the amount of the asset to be hedged by the dollar value of each contract, as is shown in Equation 1 below.

$$NC = VA/VC \tag{1}$$

where

NC = number of contracts for the hedge
VA = value of the asset
VC = value of each contract

EXAMPLE 1   *Hedging with Interest-Rate Futures*

The 6s of 2023 are the long-term bonds that would be delivered in the CBT T-bond futures contract expiring one year in the future in March 2007. The interest rate on these bonds is expected to remain at 6% over the next year so that both the 6s of 2023 and the futures contract are selling at par. How many contracts must First National sell to remove its interest-rate exposure from its $5 million holdings of the 6s of 2023?[2]

---

[1]In actuality, futures contracts sometimes set conditions for delivery of the underlying assets that cause the price of the contract at expiration to differ slightly from the price of the underlying assets. Because the difference in price is extremely small, we ignore it in this chapter.

[2]In the real world, designing a hedge is somewhat more complicated than the example here because the bond that is most likely to be delivered might not be a 6s of 2023.

Solution

$$VA = \$5 \text{ million}$$
$$VC = \$100,000$$

Thus

$$NC = \$5 \text{ million}/\$100,000 = 50$$

You therefore hedge the interest-rate risk by selling 50 of the Treasury Bond futures contracts.

Now suppose that over the next year, interest rates increase to 8% due to an increased threat of inflation. The value of the 6s of 2023 the First National Bank is holding will then fall to $4,039,640 in March 2007.[3] Thus, the loss from the long position in these bonds is $960,360, as shown below:

Value in March 2007 @ 8% interest rate	$4,039,640
Value in March 2006 @ 6% interest rate	−$5,000,000
Loss	−$ 960,360

However, the short position in the 50 futures contracts that obligate you to deliver $5 million of the 6s of 2023 in March 2007 has a value equal to the $5 million of these bonds on that date, after the interest rate has risen to 8%. This value is $4,039,640, as we have seen above. Yet when you sold the futures contract, the buyer was obligated to pay you $5 million on the maturity date. Thus the gain from the short position on these contracts is also $960,360, as shown below:

Amount paid to you in March 2007, agreed in March 2006	$5,000,000
Cost of bonds delivered on March 2007 @ 8% interest rate	−$4,039,640
Gain	$ 960,360

Therefore the net gain for the First National Bank is zero, showing that the hedge has been conducted successfully.

The hedge just described is called a **micro hedge** because the financial institution is hedging the interest-rate risk for a specific asset it is holding. A second type of hedge that financial institutions engage in is called a **macro hedge,** in which the hedge is for the institution's entire portfolio. For example, if a bank has more rate-sensitive liabilities than assets, we have seen in Chapter 24 that a rise in interest rates will cause the value of the bank to decline. By selling interest-rate future contracts that will yield a profit when interest rates rise, the bank can offset the losses on its overall portfolio from an interest-rate rise and thereby hedge its interest-rate risk.[4]

---

[3]The value of the bonds can be calculated using a financial calculator as follows: FV = $5,000,000, PMT = $300,000, I = 8%, N = 19, PV = $4,039,640.

[4]For more details and examples of how interest-rate risk can be hedged with financial futures, see the appendix to this chapter which can be found on the book's website at **www.aw-bc.com/mishkin_eakins**.

Organization of Trading in Financial Futures Markets

Financial futures contracts are traded in the United States on organized exchanges such as the Chicago Board of Trade, the Chicago Mercantile Exchange, the New York Futures Exchange, the MidAmerica Commodity Exchange, and the Kansas City Board of Trade. These exchanges are highly competitive with one another, and each organization tries to design contracts and set rules that will increase the amount of futures trading on its exchange.

The futures exchanges and all trades in financial futures in the United States are regulated by the Commodity Futures Trading Commission (CFTC), which was created in 1974 to take over the regulatory responsibilities for futures markets from the Department of Agriculture. The CFTC oversees futures trading and the futures exchanges to ensure that prices in the market are not being manipulated, and it also registers and audits the brokers, traders, and exchanges to prevent fraud and to ensure the financial soundness of the exchanges. In addition, the CFTC approves proposed futures contracts to make sure that they serve the public interest. The most widely traded financial futures contracts listed in the *Wall Street Journal* and the exchanges where they are traded (along with the number of contracts outstanding, called **open interest,** on January 12, 2005) are listed in Table 1.

Given the globalization of other financial markets in recent years, it is not surprising that increased competition from abroad has been occurring in financial futures markets as well.

Globalization of Financial Futures Markets

Because American futures exchanges were the first to develop financial futures, they dominated the trading of financial futures in the early 1980s. For example, in 1985, all of the top ten futures contracts were traded on exchanges in the United States. With the rapid growth of financial futures markets and the resulting high profits made by the American exchanges, foreign exchanges saw a profit opportunity and began to enter this business. By the 1990s, Eurodollar contracts traded on the London International Financial Futures Exchange, Japanese government bond contracts and Euroyen contracts traded on the Tokyo Stock Exchange, French government bond contracts traded on the Marché à Terme International de France, and Nikkei 225 contracts traded on the Osaka Securities Exchange. All became among the most widely traded futures contracts in the world. Even developing countries are getting into the act. In 1996, seven developing countries (also referred to as *emerging market countries*) established futures exchanges, and this number is expected to double within a few years.

Foreign competition has also spurred knockoffs of the most popular financial futures contracts initially developed in the United States. These contracts traded on foreign exchanges are virtually identical to those traded in the United States and have the advantage that they can be traded when the American exchanges are closed. The movement to 24-hour-a-day trading in financial futures has been further stimulated by the development of the Globex electronic trading system, which allows traders throughout the world to trade futures even when

TABLE 1 *Widely Traded Financial Futures Contracts*

Type of Contract	Contract Size	Exchange*	Open Interest (January 12, 2005)
Interest-Rate Contracts			
Treasury bonds	$100,000	CBT	634,817
Treasury notes	$100,000	CBT	1,685,092
Five-year Treasury notes	$100,000	CBT	1,156,187
Two-year Treasury notes	$200,000	CBT	265,601
Thirty-day Fed funds	$5 million	CBT	117,189
One-month LIBOR	$3 million	CME	46,157
Municipal Bond Index	$1000	CBT	2,822
Eurodollar	$1 million	CME	5,293,924
Euroyen	100 million	CME	30,559
Sterling	£500,000	LIFFE	1,332,204
Long Gilt	£50,000	LIFFE	195,034
Three-month Euribor	1,000,000 euros	LIFFE	2,715,108
Euroswiss franc	SF 1 million	LIFFE	1,318
Euro-Buno	100,000 euros	EUREX	456,981
Canadian banker's acceptance	C$1,000,000	ME	126,948
Stock Index Contracts			
Standard & Poor's 500 Index	$250 × index	CME	685,553
Standard & Poor's MIDCAP 400	$500 × index	CME	13,135
NASDAQ 100	$100 × index	CME	3,500
Nikkei 225 Stock Average	$5 × index	CME	31,146
Financial Times–Stock Exchange 100-Share Index	£10 per index point	LIFFE	464,473
Currency Contracts			
Yen	¥12,500,000	CME	156,574
Euro	E125,000	CME	143,660
Canadian dollar	C$100,000	CME	70,403
British pound	£62,500	CME	67,895
Swiss franc	SF 125,000	CME	53,945
Mexican peso	N$ 500,000	CME	68,161

*Exchange abbreviations: CBT, Chicago Board of Trade; CME, Chicago Mercantile Exchange; LIFFE, London International Financial Futures Exchange; MATIF, Marché à Terme International de France; ME, Montreal Exchange.

the exchanges are not officially open. Financial futures trading is thus well on the way to being completely internationalized, and competition between U.S. and foreign exchanges will continue to be intense in the future.

Explaining the Success of Futures Markets

The tremendous success of the financial futures market in Treasury bonds is evident from the fact that the total open interest of Treasury bond contracts was 634,817 on January 12, 2005, for a total value of over $63 billion (634,817 × $100,000). There are several differences between financial futures and forward contracts and in the organization of their markets that help explain why financial futures markets, like those for Treasury bonds, have been so successful.

Several features of futures contracts were designed to overcome the liquidity problem inherent in forward contracts. The first feature is that, in contrast to forward contracts, the quantities delivered and the delivery dates of futures contracts are standardized, making it more likely that different parties can be matched up in the futures market, thereby increasing the liquidity of the market. In the case of the Treasury bond contract, the quantity delivered is $100,000 face value of bonds, and the delivery dates are set to be the last business days of March, June, September, and December. The second feature is that after the futures contract has been bought or sold, it can be traded (bought or sold) again at any time until the delivery date. In contrast, once a forward contract is agreed on, it typically cannot be traded. The third feature is that in a futures contract, not just one specific type of Treasury bond is deliverable on the delivery date, as in a forward contract. Instead, any Treasury bond that matures in more than 15 years and is not callable for 15 years is eligible for delivery. Allowing continuous trading also increases the liquidity of the futures market, as does the ability to deliver a range of Treasury bonds rather than one specific bond.

Another reason why futures contracts specify that more than one bond is eligible for delivery is to limit the possibility that someone might corner the market and "squeeze" traders who have sold contracts. To corner the market, someone buys up all the deliverable securities so that investors with a short position cannot obtain from anyone else the securities that they contractually must deliver on the delivery date. As a result, the person who has cornered the market can set exorbitant prices for the securities that investors with a short position must buy to fulfill their obligations under the futures contract. The person who has cornered the market makes a fortune, but investors with a short position take a terrific loss. Clearly, the possibility that corners might occur in the market will discourage people from taking a short position and might therefore decrease the size of the market. By allowing many different securities to be delivered, the futures contract makes it harder for anyone to corner the market because a much larger amount of securities would have to be purchased to establish the corner. Corners are more than a theoretical possibility, as the "Mini-Case" box on page 649 indicates, and are a concern to both regulators and the organized exchanges that design futures contracts.

Trading in the futures market has been organized differently from trading in forward markets to overcome the default risk problems arising in forward contracts. In both types, for every contract there must be a buyer who is taking a long position and a seller who is taking a short position. However, the buyer and seller of a futures contract make their contract not with each other but with the

MINI-CASE

The Hunt Brothers and the Silver Crash

In early 1979, two Texas billionaires, W. Herbert Hunt and his brother, Nelson Bunker Hunt, decided that they were going to get into the silver market in a big way. Herbert stated his reasoning for purchasing silver as follows: "I became convinced that the economy of the United States was in a weakening condition. This reinforced my belief that investment in precious metals was wise . . . because of rampant inflation." Although the Hunts' stated reason for purchasing silver was that it was a good investment, others felt that their real motive was to establish a corner in the silver market. Along with other associates, several of them from the Saudi royal family, the Hunts purchased close to 300 million ounces of silver in the form of either actual bullion or silver futures contracts. The result was that the price of silver rose from $6 an ounce to over $50 an ounce by January 1980.

Once the regulators and the futures exchanges got wind of what the Hunts were up to, they decided to take action to eliminate the possibility of a corner by limiting to 2000 the number of contracts that any single trader could hold. This limit, which was equivalent to 10 million ounces, was only a small fraction of what the Hunts were holding, and so they were forced to sell. The silver market collapsed soon afterward, with the price of silver declining back to below $10 an ounce. The losses to the Hunts were estimated to be in excess of $1 billion, and they soon found themselves in financial difficulty. They had to go into debt to the tune of $1.1 billion, mortgaging not only the family's holdings in the Placid Oil Company but also 75,000 head of cattle, a stable of thoroughbred horses, paintings, jewelry, and even such mundane items as irrigation pumps and lawn mowers. Eventually both Hunt brothers were forced into declaring personal bankruptcy, earning them the dubious distinction of declaring the largest personal bankruptcies ever in the United States.

Nelson and Herbert Hunt paid a heavy price for their excursion into the silver market, but at least Nelson retained his sense of humor. When asked right after the collapse of the silver market how he felt about his losses, he said, "A billion dollars isn't what it used to be."

clearinghouse associated with the futures exchange. This setup means that the buyer of the futures contract does not need to worry about the financial health or trustworthiness of the seller, or vice versa, as in the forward market. As long as the clearinghouse is financially solid, buyers and sellers of futures contracts do not have to worry about default risk.

To make sure that the clearinghouse is financially sound and does not run into financial difficulties that might jeopardize its contracts, buyers or sellers of futures contracts must put an initial deposit, called a **margin requirement,** of perhaps $2000 per Treasury bond contract into a margin account kept at their brokerage firm. Futures contracts are then **marked to market** every day. What this means is that at the end of every trading day, the change in the value of the futures contract is added to or subtracted from the margin account. Suppose that after buying the Treasury bond contract at a price of 115 on Wednesday morning, its closing price at the end of the day, the *settlement price,* falls to 114. You now have a loss of 1 point, or $1000, on the contract, and the seller who sold you the contract has a gain of 1 point, or $1000. The $1000 gain is added to the seller's margin account, making a total of $3000 in that account, and the $1000 loss is subtracted from your account, so you now only have $1000 in your account. If the amount in this margin account falls below the maintenance margin requirement (which can be the same as the initial requirement but is usually a little less), the trader is required to add money to the account. For example, if the maintenance margin requirement is also $2000, you would have to add $1000 to your account to bring it up to $2000. Margin requirements and marking to market make it far less likely that a trader will default on a contract, thus protecting the futures exchange from losses.

A final advantage that futures markets have over forward markets is that most futures contracts do not result in delivery of the underlying asset on the expiration date, whereas forward contracts do. A trader who sold a futures contract is allowed to avoid delivery on the expiration date by making an offsetting purchase of a futures contract. Because the simultaneous holding of the long and short positions means that the trader would in effect be delivering the bonds to itself, under the exchange rules the trader is allowed to cancel both contracts. Allowing traders to cancel their contracts in this way lowers the cost of conducting trades in the futures market relative to the forward market in that a futures trader can avoid the costs of physical delivery, which is not so easy with forward contracts.

The Practicing Manager

HEDGING FOREIGN EXCHANGE RISK WITH FORWARD AND FUTURES CONTRACTS

As we discussed in Chapter 13, foreign exchange rates have been highly volatile in recent years. The large fluctuations in exchange rates subject financial institutions and other businesses to significant foreign exchange risk because they generate substantial gains and losses. Luckily for financial institution managers, the financial derivatives discussed in this chapter—forward and financial futures contracts—can be used to hedge foreign exchange risk.

To understand how financial institution managers manage foreign exchange risk, let's suppose that in January, the First National Bank's customer Frivolous Luxuries, Inc., is due a payment of 10 million euros in two months for $10 million worth of goods it has just sold in Germany. Frivolous Luxuries is concerned that if the value of the euro falls substantially from its current value of $1, the company might suffer a large loss because the 10 million euro payment will no longer be worth $10 million. So Sam, the CEO of Frivolous Luxuries, calls up his friend Mona, the manager of the First National Bank, and asks her to hedge this foreign exchange risk for his company. Let's see how the bank manager does this using forward and financial futures contracts.

Hedging Foreign Exchange Risk with Forward Contracts

Forward markets in foreign exchange have been highly developed by commercial banks and investment banking operations that engage in extensive foreign exchange trading and so are widely used to hedge foreign exchange risk. Mona knows that she can use this market to hedge the foreign exchange risk for Frivolous Luxuries. Such a hedge is quite straightforward for her to execute. Because the payment of euros in two months means that at that time Sam would hold a long position in euros, Mona knows that the basic principle of hedging indicates that she should offset this long position by a short position. Thus, she just enters a forward contract that obligates her to sell 10 million euros two months from now in exchange for dollars at the current forward rate of $1 per euro.[5]

In two months, when her customer receives the 10 million euros, the forward contract ensures that it is exchanged for dollars at an exchange rate of $1 per euro, thus yielding $10 million. No matter what happens to future exchange rates, Frivolous Luxuries will be guaranteed $10 million for the goods it sold in Germany. Mona calls up her friend Sam to let him know that his company is now protected from any foreign exchange movements, and he thanks her for her help.

Hedging Foreign Exchange Risk with Futures Contracts

As an alternative, Mona could have used the currency futures market to hedge the foreign exchange risk. In this case, she would see that the Chicago Mercantile Exchange has a euro contract with a contract amount of 125,000 euros and a price of $1 per euro. To do the hedge, Mona must sell euros as with the forward contract, to the tune of 10 million euros of the March futures.

EXAMPLE 2 *Hedging with Foreign Exchange Futures Contracts*

How many of the Chicago Mercantile Exchange March euro contracts must Mona sell in order to hedge the 10 million euro payment due in March?

Solution

Using Equation 1:

VA = 10 million euros

VC = 125,000 euros

Thus

$$NC = 10 \text{ million}/125{,}000 = 40$$

Mona does the hedge by selling 40 of the CME euro contracts.

---

[5]The forward exchange rate will probably differ slightly from the current spot rate of $1 per euro because the interest rates in Europe and the United States may not be equal. In that case, as we saw in Equation 2 in Chapter 13, the future expected exchange rate will not equal the current spot rate and neither will the forward rate. However, since interest differentials have typically been less than 6% at an annual rate (1% bimonthly), the expected appreciation or depreciation of the euro over a two-month period has always been less than 1%. Thus the forward rate is always close to the current spot rate, and so our assumption in the example that the forward rate and the spot rate are the same is a reasonable one.

Given the $1 per euro price, the sale of the contract yields 40 × 125,000 euros = $10 million. The futures hedge thus again enables her to lock in the exchange rate for Frivolous Luxuries so that it gets its payment of $10 million.

One advantage of using the futures market is that the contract size of 125,000 euros, worth $125,000, is quite a bit smaller than the minimum size of a forward contract, which is usually $1 million or more. However, in this case, the bank manager is making a large enough transaction that she can use either the forward or the futures market. Her choice depends on whether the transaction costs are lower in one market than in the other. If the First National Bank is active in the forward market, that market would probably have the lower transaction costs, but if First National rarely deals in foreign exchange forward contracts, the bank manager may do better by sticking with the futures market.

Stock Index Futures

More detailed information about stock index futures is available at www.usafutures. com/stockindex futures.htm

As we have seen, financial futures markets can be useful in hedging interest-rate risk. However, financial institution managers, particularly those who manage mutual funds, pension funds, and insurance companies, also worry about **stock market risk,** the risk that occurs because stock prices fluctuate. Stock index futures were developed in 1982 to meet the need to manage stock market risk, and they have become among the most widely traded of all futures contracts. The futures trading in stock price indexes is now controversial (see the "Mini-Case" box on page 653) because critics assert that it has led to substantial increases in market volatility, especially in such episodes as 1987's stock market crash.

Stock Index Futures Contracts

To understand stock index futures contracts, let's look at the Standard & Poor's 500 Index futures contract (shown in the "Following the News" box on page 654), the most widely traded stock index futures contract in the United States. (The S&P 500 Index measures the value of 500 of the most widely traded stocks.) Stock index futures contracts differ from most other financial futures contracts in that they are settled with a cash delivery rather than with the delivery of a security. Cash settlement gives these contracts the advantage of a high degree of liquidity and also rules out the possibility of anyone's cornering the market. In the case of the S&P 500 Index contract, at the final settlement date, the cash delivery due is $250 times the index, so if the index is at 1000 on the final settlement date, $250,000 would be the amount due. The price quotes for this contract are also quoted in terms of index points, so a change of 1 point represents a change of $250 in the contract's value.

MINI-CASE

Program Trading and Portfolio Insurance: Were They to Blame for the Stock Market Crash of 1987?

In the aftermath of the Black Monday crash on October 19, 1987, in which the stock market declined by over 20% in one day, trading strategies involving stock price index futures markets have been accused (especially by the Brady Commission, which was appointed by President Reagan to study the stock market) of being culprits in the market collapse. One such strategy, called program trading, involves computer-directed trading between the stock index futures and the stocks whose prices are reflected in the stock price index. Program trading is a form of arbitrage conducted to keep stock index futures and stock prices in line with each other. For example, when the price of the stock index futures contract is far below the prices of the underlying stocks in the index, program traders buy index futures, thereby increasing their price, and sell the stocks, thereby lowering their price. Critics of program trading assert that the sharp fall in stock index futures prices on Black Monday led to massive selling in the stock market to keep stock prices in line with the stock index futures prices.

Some experts also blame portfolio insurance for amplifying the crash because they feel that when the stock market started to fall, uncertainty in the market increased, and the resulting increased desire to hedge stocks led to massive selling of stock index futures. The resulting large price declines in stock index futures contracts then led to massive selling of stocks by program traders to keep prices in line.

Because they view program trading and portfolio insurance as causes of the October 1987 market collapse, critics of stock index futures have advocated restrictions on their trading. In response, certain brokerage firms, as well as organized exchanges, have placed limits on program trading. For example, the New York Stock Exchange has curbed computerized program trading when the Dow Jones Industrial Average moves by more than 50 points in one day. However, some prominent finance scholars (among them Nobel laureate Merton Miller of the University of Chicago) do not accept the hypothesis that program trading and portfolio insurance provoked the stock market crash. They believe that the prices of stock index futures primarily reflect the same economic forces that move stock prices—changes in the market's underlying assessment of the value of stocks.

To understand what all this means, let's look at what happens when you buy or sell this futures contract. Suppose that on February 1, you sell one June contract at a price of 1000 (that is, $250,000). By selling the contract, you agree to a delivery amount due of $250 times the S&P 500 Index on the expiration date at the end of June. By buying the contract at a price of 1000, the buyer has agreed to pay $250,000 for the delivery amount due of $250 times the S&P 500 Index at the expiration date at the end of June. If the stock market falls so that the S&P 500 Index declines to 900 on the expiration date, the buyer of the contract will have lost $25,000 because he or she has agreed to pay $250,000 for the contract but has a delivery amount due of $225,000 (900 × $250). But you, the seller of the contract, will have a profit of $25,000 because you agreed to receive a $250,000 purchase price for the contract but have a delivery amount due of only $225,000. Because the amount payable and due are netted out, only $25,000 will change hands; you, the seller of the contract, receive $25,000 from the buyer.

THE *WALL STREET JOURNAL*: FOLLOWING THE NEWS

Stock Index Futures

The prices for stock index futures contracts are published daily. In the *Wall Street Journal,* these prices are found in the section "Futures Prices" under the "Index" heading. An excerpt from this listing is reproduced here.

Index

S&P 500 Index (CME) $250 Times Index

	OPEN	HIGH	LOW	SETTLE	CHANGE	LIFETIME HIGH	LIFETIME LOW	OPEN INTEREST
Mar	119120	119280	118150	118390	−780	122120	84380	665,340
June	119200	119300	118600	118790	−780	122700	95750	11,121
Sept	119250	119720	119120	119240	−780	123000	98970	2,873

Est vol 36,959; vol Mon 42,058; open int 685,553, +1,662.
Idx prl: High 1190.25; Low 1180.43; Close 1182.99, −7.26.

Information for each contract is given in columns, as follows. (The March S&P 500 Index contract is used as an example.)

Open: Opening price; each point corresponds to $250 times the index—1191.20; that is, 1191.20 × $250 = $297,800 per contract

High: Highest traded price that day—1192.80, or $298,200 per contract

Low: Lowest traded price that day—1181.50, or $295,375 per contract

Settle: Settlement price, the closing price that day—1183.90, or $295,975 per contract

Chg: Change in the settlement price from the previous trading day—−7.80 points, or $1,950 per contract

High: High price for the year—1221.20, or $305,300 per contract

Low: Low price for the year—843.80, or $210,950 per contract

Open Interest: Number of contracts outstanding—665,340, or a total value of $197 billion (= 665,340 × $295,975).

The Practicing Manager

HEDGING WITH STOCK INDEX FUTURES

Financial institution managers can use stock index futures contracts to reduce stock market risk.

EXAMPLE 3   *Hedging with Stock Index Futures*

Suppose that in March 2007, Mort, the portfolio manager of the Rock Solid Insurance Company, has a portfolio of stocks valued at $100 million that moves percentagewise one-for-one with the S&P Index. Suppose also that the March 2008 S&P 500 Index contracts are currently selling at a price of 1000. How many of these contracts should Mort sell so that he hedges the stock market risk of this portfolio over the next year?

Solution

Because Mort is holding a long position, using the basic principle of hedging, he must offset it by taking a short position in which he sells S&P futures. To calculate the number of contracts he needs to sell, he uses Equation 1.

VA = $100 million

VC = $250 × 1000 = $250,000

Thus

$$NC = \$100 \text{ million}/\$250,000 = 400$$

Mort's hedge therefore involves selling 400 S&P March 2008 futures contracts.

If the S&P Index falls 10% to 900, the $100 million portfolio will suffer a $10 million loss. At the same time, however, Mort makes a profit of 100 × $250 = $25,000 per contract because he agreed to be paid $250,000 for each contract at a price of 1000, but at a price of 900 on the expiration date he has a delivery amount of only $225,000 (900 × $250). Multiplied by 400 contracts, the $25,000 profit per contract yields a total profit of $10 million. The $10 million profit on the futures contract exactly offsets the loss on Rock Solid's stock portfolio, so Mort has been successful in hedging the stock market risk.

Why would Mort be willing to forego profits when the stock market rises? One reason is that he might be worried that a bear market was imminent, so he wants to protect Rock Solid's portfolio from the coming decline (and so protect his job).[6]

Options

Another vehicle for hedging interest-rate and stock market risk involves the use of options on financial instruments. **Options** are contracts that give the purchaser the option, or *right,* to buy or sell the underlying financial instrument at a specified price, called the **exercise price** or **strike price,** within a specific period of time (the *term to expiration*). The seller (sometimes called the *writer*) of the option is *obligated* to buy or sell the financial instrument to the purchaser if the owner of the option exercises the right to sell or buy. These option contract features are important enough to be emphasized: The *owner* or buyer of an option does not have to exercise the option; he or she can let the option expire without using it. Hence the *owner* of an option is *not obligated* to take any action but

---

[6]For more details of how interest-rate risk can be hedged with futures options, see the appendix to this chapter which can be found on the book's website at **www.aw-bc.com/mishkin_eakins**.

rather has the *right* to exercise the contract if he or she so chooses. The *seller* of an option, by contrast, has no choice in the matter; he or she *must* buy or sell the financial instrument if the owner exercises the option.

Because the right to buy or sell a financial instrument at a specified price has value, the owner of an option is willing to pay an amount for it called a **premium.** There are two types of option contracts: **American options** can be exercised *at any time up to* the expiration date of the contract, and **European options** can be exercised only *on* the expiration date.

Option contracts are written on a number of financial instruments (an example of which is shown in the "Following the News" box below). Options on individual stocks are called **stock options,** and such options have existed for a long time. Option contracts on financial futures called **financial futures options,** or, more commonly, **futures options,** were developed in 1982 and have become the most widely traded option contracts.

You might wonder why option contracts are more likely to be written on financial futures than on underlying debt instruments such as bonds or certificates of deposit. As you saw earlier in the chapter, at the expiration date, the price of the

---

THE *WALL STREET JOURNAL*: FOLLOWING THE NEWS

Futures Options

The prices for financial futures options are published daily. In the *Wall Street Journal,* they are found in the section "Futures Options Prices" under the "Interest Rate" heading. An excerpt from this listing is reproduced here.

Information for each contract is reported in columns, as follows. (The Chicago Board of Trade's option on its Treasury Notes futures contract is used as an example.)

Interest Rate

T-Notes (CBT)
$100,000; points and 64ths of 100%

STRIKE PRICE	CALLS-SETTLE			PUTS-SETTLE		
	Feb	Mar	Apr	Feb	Mar	Apr
110	1-39	1-52	1-29	0-02	0-15	0-49
111	0-45	1-05	0-57	0-08	0-32	1-13
112	0-09	0-34	0-32	0-36	0-61	...
113	0-02	0-13	0-16	1-28	1-40	...
114	0-01	0-04	0-07	...	2-31	...
115	0-01	0-01	0-03	...	3-28	...

Est. vol. 144,154; Mn 54,792 calls; 165,059 puts
Op. Int. Mon 913,156 calls; 1,310,407 puts

Strike Price: Strike (exercise) price of each contract, which runs from 110 to 115

Calls-Settle: Premium (price) at settlement for call options on the Treasury bond futures expiring in the month listed, with each full point representing $1000 and sixty-fourths of a point listed to the right of the hyphen; at a strike price of 111, the February call option's premium is 0-45, or $703.12 per contract

Puts-Settle: Premium (price) at settlement for put options on the Treasury bond futures expiring in the month listed, with each full point representing $1000 and sixty-fourths of a point listed to the right of the hyphen; at a strike price of 111, the February put option's premium is 0-08, or $125.00 per contract

futures contract and of the deliverable debt instrument will be the same because of arbitrage. So it would seem that investors should be indifferent about having the option written on the debt instrument or on the futures contract. However, financial futures contracts have been so well designed that their markets are often more liquid than the markets in the underlying debt instruments. Investors would rather have the option contract written on the more liquid instrument, in this case the futures contract. That explains why the most popular futures options are written on many of the same futures contracts listed in Table 1.

The regulation of option markets is split between the Securities and Exchange Commission (SEC), which regulates stock options, and the Commodity Futures Trading Commission (CFTC), which regulates futures options. Regulation focuses on ensuring that writers of options have enough capital to make good on their contractual obligations and on overseeing traders and exchanges to prevent fraud and ensure that the market is not being manipulated.

Option Contracts

A **call option** is a contract that gives the owner the right to *buy* a financial instrument at the exercise price within a specific period of time. A **put option** is a contract that gives the owner the right to *sell* a financial instrument at the exercise price within a specific period of time.

Study Guide

Remembering which is a call option and which is a put option is not always easy. To keep them straight, just remember that having a *call* option to *buy* a financial instrument is the same as having the option to *call in* the instrument for delivery at a specified price. Having a *put* option to *sell* a financial instrument is the same as having the option to *put up* an instrument for the other party to buy.

Profits and Losses on Option and Futures Contracts

To understand option contracts more fully, let's first examine the option on the June Treasury bond futures contract that we looked at earlier. Recall that if you buy this futures contract at a price of 115 (that is, $115,000), you have agreed to pay $115,000 for $100,000 face value of long-term Treasury bonds when they are delivered to you at the end of June. If you sold this futures contract at a price of 115, you agreed, in exchange for $115,000, to deliver $100,000 face value of the long-term Treasury bonds at the end of June. An option contract on the Treasury bond futures contract has several key features: (1) It has the same expiration date as the underlying futures contract, (2) it is an American option and so can be exercised at any time before the expiration date, and (3) the premium (price) of the option is quoted in points that are the same as in the futures contract, so each point corresponds to $1000. If, for a premium of $2000, you buy one call option contract on the June Treasury bond contract with an exercise price of 115, you have purchased the right to buy (call in) the June Treasury bond futures contract for a price of 115 ($115,000 per contract) at any time through the expiration date of this contract at the end of June. Similarly, when for $2000 you buy a put option on the June Treasury bond contract with an exercise price of 115, you have the right to sell (put up) the June Treasury bond futures contract for a price of 115 ($115,000 per contract) at any time until the end of June.

Futures option contracts are somewhat complicated, so to explore how they work and how they can be used to hedge risk, let's first examine how profits and losses on the call option on the June Treasury bond futures contract occur. In February, our old friend Irving the Investor buys, for a $2000 premium, a call option on the $100,000 June Treasury bond futures contract with a strike price of 115. (We assume that if Irving exercises the option, it is on the expiration date at the end of June and not before.) On the expiration date at the end of June, suppose that the underlying Treasury bond for the futures contract has a price of 110. Recall that on the expiration date, arbitrage forces the price of the futures contract to be the same as the price of the underlying bond, so it too has a price of 110 on the expiration date at the end of June. If Irving exercises the call option and buys the futures contract at an exercise price of 115, he will lose money by buying at 115 and selling at the lower market price of 110. Because Irving is smart, he will not exercise the option, but he will be out the $2000 premium he paid. In such a situation, in which the price of the underlying financial instrument is below the exercise price, a call option is said to be "out of the money." At the price of 110 (less than the exercise price), Irving thus suffers a loss on the option contract of the $2000 premium he paid. This loss is plotted as point A in panel (a) of Figure 1.

On the expiration date, if the price of the futures contract is 115, the call option is "at the money," and Irving is indifferent whether he exercises his option to buy the futures contract or not, since exercising the option at 115 when the market price is also at 115 produces no gain or loss. Because he has paid the $2000 premium, at the price of 115 his contract again has a net loss of $2000, plotted as point B.

If the futures contract instead has a price of 120 on the expiration day, the option is "in the money," and Irving benefits from exercising the option: He would buy the futures contract at the exercise price of 115 and then sell it for 120, thereby earning a 5% gain ($5000 profit) on the $100,000 Treasury bond contract. Because Irving paid a $2000 premium for the option contract, however, his net profit is $3000 ($5000 − $2000). The $3000 profit at a price of 120 is plotted as point C. Similarly, if the price of the futures contract rose to 125, the option contract would yield a net profit of $8000 ($10,000 from exercising the option minus the $2000 premium), plotted as point D. Plotting these points, we get the kinked profit curve for the call option that we see in panel (a).

Suppose that instead of purchasing the futures *option* contract in February, Irving decides instead to buy the $100,000 June Treasury bond *futures* contract at the price of 115. If the price of the bond on the expiration day at the end of June declines to 110, meaning that the price of the futures contract also falls to 110, Irving suffers a loss of 5 percentage points, or $5000. The loss of $5000 on the futures contract at a price of 110 is plotted as point A′ in panel (a). At a price of 115 on the expiration date, Irving would have a zero profit on the futures contract, plotted as point B′. At a price of 120, Irving would have a profit on the contract of 5 percentage points, or $5000 (point C′), and at a price of 125, the profit would be 10 percentage points, or $10,000 (point D′). Plotting these points, we get the linear (straight-line) profit curve for the futures contract that appears in panel (a).

Now we can see the major difference between a futures contract and an option contract. As the profit curve for the futures contract in panel (a) indicates, the futures contract has a linear profit function: Profits grow by an equal dollar amount for every point increase in the price of the underlying financial instrument. By contrast, the kinked profit curve for the option contract is highly nonlinear, meaning that profits do not always grow by the same amount for a given change in the price of the underlying financial instrument. The reason for this nonlinearity

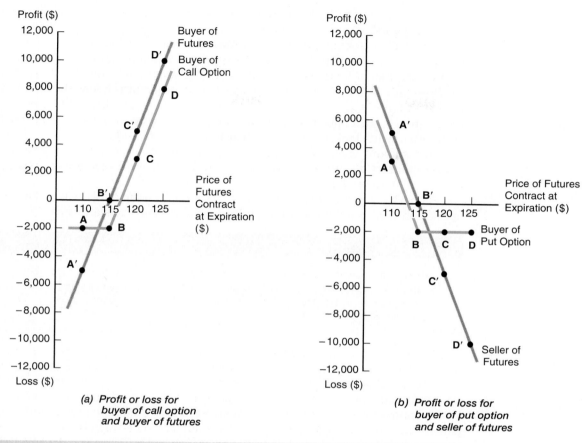

(a) *Profit or loss for buyer of call option and buyer of futures*

(b) *Profit or loss for buyer of put option and seller of futures*

FIGURE 1 *Profits and Losses on Options Versus Futures Contracts*

The futures contract is the $100,000 June Treasury bond contract, and the option contracts are written on this futures contract with an exercise price of 115. Panel (a) shows the profits and losses for the buyer of the call option and the buyer of the futures contract, and panel (b) shows the profits and losses for the buyer of the put option and the seller of the futures contract.

is that the call option protects Irving from having losses that are greater than the amount of the $2000 premium. In contrast, Irving's loss on the futures contract is $5000 if the price on the expiration day falls to 110, and if the price falls even further, Irving's loss will be even greater. This insurance-like feature of option contracts explains why their purchase price is referred to as a premium. Once the underlying financial instrument's price rises above the exercise price, however, Irving's profits grow linearly. Irving has given up something by buying an option rather than a futures contract. As we see in panel (a), when the price of the underlying financial instrument rises above the exercise price, Irving's profits are always less than that on the futures contract by exactly the $2000 premium he paid.

Panel (b) plots the results of the same profit calculations if Irving buys not a call but a put option (an option to sell) with an exercise price of 115 for a premium of $2000 and if he sells the futures contract rather than buying one. In this case, if on the expiration date the Treasury bond futures have a price above the 115 exercise price, the put option is "out of the money." Irving would not want to exercise the put option and then have to sell the futures contract he owns as a result of exercising the put option at a price below the market price and lose money. He would not exercise his option, and he would be out only the $2000 premium he paid. Once the price of the futures contract falls below the 115 exercise price, Irving benefits from exercising the put option because he can sell the futures contract at a price of 115 but can buy it at a price below this. In such a situation, in which the price of the underlying instrument is below the exercise price, the put option is "in the money," and profits rise linearly as the price of the futures contract falls. The profit function for the put option illustrated in panel (b) of Figure 1 is kinked, indicating that Irving is protected from losses greater than the amount of the premium he paid. The profit curve for the sale of the futures contract is just the negative of the profit for the futures contract in panel (a) and is therefore linear.

Panel (b) of Figure 1 confirms the conclusion from panel (a) that profits on option contracts are nonlinear but profits on futures contracts are linear.

Study Guide

To make sure you understand how profits and losses on option and futures contracts are generated, calculate the net profits on the put option and the short position in the futures contract at prices on the expiration day of 110, 115, 120, and 125. Then verify that your calculations correspond to the points plotted in panel (b) of Figure 1.

Two other differences between futures and option contracts must be mentioned. The first is that the initial investment on the contracts differs. As we saw earlier in the chapter, when a futures contract is purchased, the investor must put up a fixed amount, the margin requirement, in a margin account. But when an option contract is purchased, the initial investment is the premium that must be paid for the contract. The second important difference between the contracts is that the futures contract requires money to change hands daily when the contract is marked to market, whereas the option contract requires money to change hands only when it is exercised.

Factors Affecting the Prices of Option Premiums

If we again look closely at the *Wall Street Journal* entry for Treasury bond futures options in the "Following the News" box on page 656, we learn several interesting facts about how the premiums on option contracts are priced. The first thing you might have noticed is that when the strike (exercise) price for a contract is set at a higher level, the premium for the call option is lower and the premium for the put option is higher. For example, in going from a contract with a strike price of 110 to one with 115, the premium for the February call option falls from 1 39/64 to 1/64, and the premium for the February put option rises from 15/64 to 3 28/64.

Our understanding of the profit function for option contracts illustrated in Figure 1 helps explain this fact. As we saw in panel (a), a higher price for the underlying financial instrument (in this case a Treasury bond futures contract) relative to the option's exercise price results in higher profits on the call (buy) option. Thus the lower the strike price, the higher the profits on the call option contract and the greater the premium that investors like Irving are willing to pay. Similarly, we saw in panel (b) that a higher price for the underlying financial instrument relative to the exercise price lowers profits on the put (sell) option, so that a higher strike price increases profits and thus causes the premium to increase.

The second thing you might have noticed in the *Wall Street Journal* entry is that as the period of time over which the option can be exercised (the term to expiration) gets longer, the premiums for both call and put options usually rise. For example, at a strike price of 114, the premium on the call option increases from 1/64 in February to 4/64 in March and to 7/64 in April. Similarly, the premium on the put option at a strike price of 111 increases from 8/64 in February to 32/64 in March and to 1 13/64 in April. The fact that premiums increase with the term to expiration is also explained by the nonlinear profit function for option contracts. As the term to expiration lengthens, there is a greater chance that the price of the underlying financial instrument will be very high or very low by the expiration date. If the price becomes very high and goes well above the exercise price, the call (buy) option will yield a high profit, but if the price becomes very low and goes well below the exercise price, the losses will be small because the owner of the call option will simply decide not to exercise the option. The possibility of greater variability of the underlying financial instrument as the term to expiration lengthens raises profits on average for the call option.

Similar reasoning tells us that the put (sell) option will become more valuable as the term to expiration increases because the possibility of greater price variability of the underlying financial instrument increases as the term to expiration increases. The greater chance of a low price increases the chance that profits on the put option will be very high. But the greater chance of a high price does not produce substantial losses for the put option because the owner will again just decide not to exercise the option.

Another way of thinking about this reasoning is to recognize that option contracts have an element of "heads, I win; tails, I don't lose too badly." The greater variability of where the prices might be by the expiration date increases the value of both kinds of options. Since a longer term to the expiration date leads to greater variability of where the prices might be by the expiration date, a longer term to expiration raises the value of the option contract.

The reasoning that we have just developed also explains another important fact about option premiums. When the volatility of the price of the underlying instrument is great, the premiums for both call and put options will be higher. Higher volatility of prices means that for a given expiration date, there will again be greater variability of where the prices might be by the expiration date. The "heads, I win; tails, I don't lose too badly" property of options then means that the greater variability of possible prices by the expiration date increases average profits for the option and thus increases the premium that investors are willing to pay.

Summary

Our analysis of how profits on options are affected by price movements for the underlying financial instrument leads to the following conclusions about the factors that determine the premium on an option contract:

1. The higher the strike price, everything else being equal, the lower the premium on call (buy) options and the higher the premium on put (sell) options.
2. The greater the term to expiration, everything else being equal, the higher the premiums for both call and put options.
3. The greater the volatility of prices of the underlying financial instrument, everything else being equal, the higher the premiums for both call and put options.

The results we have derived here appear in more formal models, such as the Black-Scholes model, which analyze how the premiums on options are priced. You might study such models in other finance courses.

The Practicing Manager

HEDGING WITH FUTURES OPTIONS

Earlier in the chapter, we saw how a financial institution manager like Mona, the manager of the First National Bank, could hedge the interest-rate risk on its $5 million holdings of 6s of 2023 by selling $5 million of T-bond futures (50 contracts). A rise in interest rates and the resulting fall in bond prices and bond futures contracts would lead to profits on the bank's sale of the futures contracts that would exactly offset the losses on the 6s of 2023 the bank is holding.

As panel (b) of Figure 1 suggests, an alternative way for the manager to protect against a rise in interest rates and hence a decline in bond prices is to buy $5 million of put options written on the same Treasury bond futures. Because the size of the options contract is the same as the futures contract ($100,000 of bonds), the number of put options contracts bought is the same as the number of futures contracts sold, that is, 50. As long as the exercise price is not too far from the current price as in panel (b), the rise in interest rates and decline in bond prices will lead to profits on the futures and the futures put options, profits that will offset any losses on the $5 million of Treasury bonds.

The one problem with using options rather than futures is that the First National Bank will have to pay premiums on the options contracts, thereby lowering the bank's profits in order to hedge the interest-rate risk. Why might the bank manager be willing to use options rather than futures to conduct the hedge? The answer is that the option contract, unlike the futures contract, allows the First National Bank to gain if interest rates decline and bond prices rise. With the hedge using futures contracts, the First National Bank does not gain from increases in bond prices because the profits on the bonds it is holding are offset by the losses from the futures contracts it has sold. However, as panel (b) of Figure 1 indicates, the situation when the hedge is conducted with put options is quite different: Once bond prices rise above the exercise price, the bank does not suffer additional losses on the option contracts. At the same time, the value of the Treasury bonds the bank is holding will increase, thereby leading to a profit for the bank. Thus using options rather than futures to conduct the micro hedge allows the bank to protect itself from rises in interest rates but still allows the bank to benefit from interest-rate declines (although the profit is reduced by the amount of the premium).

Similar reasoning indicates that the bank manager might prefer to use options to conduct the macro hedge to immunize the entire bank portfolio from interest-rate risk. Again, the strategy of using options rather than futures has the disadvantage that the First National Bank has to pay the premiums on these contracts up front. By contrast, using options allows the bank to keep the gains from a decline in interest rates (which will raise the value of the bank's assets relative to its liabilities) because these gains will not be offset by large losses on the option contracts.

In the case of a macro hedge, there is another reason why the bank might prefer option contracts to futures contracts. Profits and losses on futures contracts can cause accounting problems for banks because such profits and losses are not allowed to be offset by unrealized changes in the value of the rest of the bank's portfolio. Consider the case when interest rates fall. If First National sells futures contracts to conduct the macro hedge, then when interest rates fall and the prices of the Treasury bond futures contracts rise, it will have large losses on these contracts. Of course, these losses are offset by unrealized profits in the rest of the bank's portfolio, but the bank is not allowed to offset these losses in its accounting statements. So even though the macro hedge is serving its intended purpose of immunizing the bank's portfolio from interest-rate risk, the bank would experience large accounting losses when interest rates fall. Indeed, bank managers have lost their jobs when perfectly sound hedges with interest-rate futures have led to large accounting losses. Not surprisingly, bank managers might shrink from using financial futures to conduct macro hedges for this reason.

Futures options, however, can come to the rescue of the managers of banks and other financial institutions. Suppose that First National conducted the macro hedge by buying put options instead of selling Treasury bond futures. Now if interest rates fall and bond prices rise well above the exercise price, the bank will not have large losses on the option contracts because it will just decide not to exercise its options. The bank will not suffer the accounting problems produced by hedging with financial futures. Because of the accounting advantages of using futures options to conduct macro hedges, option contracts have become important to financial institution managers as tools for hedging interest-rate risk.[7]

Interest-Rate Swaps

In addition to forwards, futures, and options, financial institutions use one other important financial derivative to manage risk. **Swaps** are financial contracts that obligate each party to the contract to exchange (swap) a set of payments it owns for another set of payments owned by another party. There are two basic kinds of swaps: **Currency swaps** involve the exchange of a set of payments in one currency for a set of payments in another currency. **Interest-rate swaps** involve the exchange of one set of interest payments for another set of interest payments, all denominated in the same currency. We focus on interest-rate swaps.

Interest-Rate Swap Contracts

Interest-rate swaps are an important tool for managing interest-rate risk, and they first appeared in the United States in 1982 when, as we have seen, there was an increase in the demand for financial instruments that could be used to reduce interest-rate risk. The most common type of interest-rate swap (called the *plain vanilla swap*) specifies (1) the interest rate on the payments that are being exchanged; (2) the type of interest payments (variable or fixed-rate); (3) the

---

[7]For more details of how interest-rate risk can be hedged with futures options, see the appendix to this chapter which can be found on the book's website at **www.aw-bc.com/mishkin_eakins**.

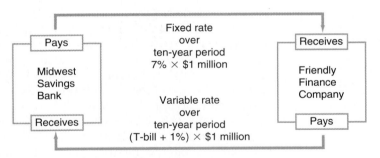

FIGURE 2 *Interest-Rate Swap Payments*

In this swap arrangement, with a notional principal of $1 million and a term of ten years, the Midwest Savings Bank pays a fixed rate of 7% × $1 million to the Friendly Finance Company, which in turn agrees to pay the one-year Treasury bill rate plus 1% × $1 million to the Midwest Savings Bank.

amount of **notional principal,** which is the amount on which the interest is being paid; and (4) the time period over which the exchanges continue to be made. There are many other more complicated versions of swaps, including forward swaps and swap options (called *swaptions*), but here we will look only at the plain vanilla swap. Figure 2 illustrates an interest-rate swap between the Midwest Savings Bank and the Friendly Finance Company. Midwest Savings agrees to pay Friendly Finance a fixed rate of 7% on $1 million of notional principal for the next ten years, and Friendly Finance agrees to pay Midwest Savings the one-year Treasury bill rate plus 1% on $1 million of notional principal for the same period. Thus as shown in Figure 2, every year, the Midwest Savings Bank would be paying the Friendly Finance Company 7% on $1 million while Friendly Finance would be paying Midwest Savings the one-year T-bill rate plus 1% on $1 million.

The Practicing Manager

HEDGING WITH INTEREST-RATE SWAPS

You might wonder why the managers of the two financial institutions find it advantageous to enter into this swap agreement. The answer is that it may help both of them hedge interest-rate risk.

Suppose that the Midwest Savings Bank, which tends to borrow short-term and then lend long-term in the mortgage market, has $1 million less of rate-sensitive assets than it has of rate-sensitive liabilities. As we learned in Chapter 24, this situation means that as interest rates rise, the rise in the cost of funds (liabilities) is greater than the rise in interest payments it receives on its assets, many of which are fixed-rate. The result of rising interest rates is thus a shrinking of Midwest Savings' net interest margin and a decline in its profitability. As we saw in Chapter 24, to avoid this interest-rate risk, the manager of the Midwest Savings would like to convert $1 million of its fixed-rate assets into $1 million of rate-sensitive assets, in effect making rate-sensitive assets equal to rate-sensitive liabilities, thereby eliminating the gap. This is exactly what happens when she engages in the interest-rate swap. By taking $1 million of its fixed-rate income and exchanging it for $1 million of rate-sensitive Treasury bill income, she has converted income on $1 million of fixed-rate assets into income on $1 million of rate-sensitive assets. Now when interest rates increase, the rise in rate-sensitive income on its assets exactly matches the rise in the rate-sensitive cost of funds on its liabilities, leaving the net interest margin and bank profitability unchanged.

The manager of the Friendly Finance Company, which issues long-term bonds to raise funds and uses them to make short-term loans, finds that he is in exactly the opposite situation to Midwest Savings: He has $1 million more of rate-sensitive assets than of rate-sensitive liabilities. He is therefore concerned that a fall in interest rates, which will result in a larger drop in income from its assets than the decline in the cost of funds on its liabilities, will cause a decline in profits. By doing the interest-rate swap, the manager eliminates this interest-rate risk because he has converted $1 million of rate-sensitive income into $1 million of fixed-rate income. Now the manager of the Friendly Finance Company finds that when interest rates fall, the decline in rate-sensitive income is smaller and so is matched by the decline in the rate-sensitive cost of funds on its liabilities, leaving profitability unchanged.[8]

Advantages of Interest-Rate Swaps

To eliminate interest-rate risk, both the Midwest Savings Bank and the Friendly Finance Company could have rearranged their balance sheets by converting fixed-rate assets into rate-sensitive assets, and vice versa, instead of engaging in an interest-rate swap. However, this strategy would have been costly for both financial institutions for several reasons. The first is that financial institutions incur substantial transaction costs when they rearrange their balance sheets. Second, different financial institutions have informational advantages in making loans to certain customers who may prefer certain maturities. Thus, adjusting the balance sheet to eliminate interest-rate risk may result in a loss of these informational advantages, which the financial institution is unwilling to give up. Interest-rate swaps solve these problems for financial institutions because in effect they allow the institutions to convert fixed-rate assets into rate-sensitive assets without affecting the balance sheet. Large transaction costs are avoided, and the financial institutions can continue to make loans where they have an informational advantage.

We have seen that financial institutions can also hedge interest-rate risk with other financial derivatives such as futures contracts and futures options. Interest-rate swaps have one big advantage over hedging with these other derivatives: They can be written for very long horizons, sometimes as long as 20 years, whereas financial futures and futures options typically have much shorter horizons, not much more than a year. If a financial institution needs to hedge interest-rate risk for a long horizon, financial futures and option markets may not do it much good. Instead it can turn to the swap market.

---

[8]For more details and examples of how interest-rate risk can be hedged with interest-rate swaps, see the appendix to this chapter which can be found on the book's website at **www.aw-bc.com/mishkin_eakins**.

Disadvantages of Interest-Rate Swaps

Although interest-rate swaps have important advantages that make them very popular with financial institutions, they also have disadvantages that limit their usefulness. Swap markets, like forward markets, can suffer from a lack of liquidity. Let's return to looking at the swap between the Midwest Savings Bank and the Friendly Finance Company. As with a forward contract, it might be difficult for the Midwest Savings Bank to link up with the Friendly Finance Company to arrange the swap. In addition, even if the Midwest Savings Bank could find a counterparty like the Friendly Finance Company, it might not be able to negotiate a good deal because it couldn't find any other institution to negotiate with.

Swap contracts also are subject to the same default risk that we encountered for forward contracts. If interest rates rise, the Friendly Finance Company would love to get out of the swap contract because the fixed-rate interest payments it receives are less than it could get in the open market. It might then default on the contract, exposing Midwest Savings to a loss. Alternatively, the Friendly Finance Company could go bust, meaning that the terms of the swap contract would not be fulfilled.

It is important to note that the default risk of swaps is not the same as the default risk on the full amount of the notional principal because the notional principal is never exchanged. If the Friendly Finance Company goes broke because $1 million of its one-year loans default and it cannot make its interest payment to Midwest Savings, Midwest Savings will stop sending its payment to Friendly Finance. If interest rates have declined, this will suit Midwest Savings just fine because it would rather keep the 7% fixed-rate interest payment, which is at a higher rate, than receive the rate-sensitive payment, which has declined. Thus a default on a swap contract does not necessarily mean that there is a loss to the other party. Midwest Savings will suffer losses from a default only if interest rates have risen when the default occurs. Even then, the loss will be far smaller than the amount of the notional principal because interest payments are far smaller than the amount of the notional principal.[9]

Financial Intermediaries in Interest-Rate Swaps

As we have just seen, financial institutions do have to be aware of the possibility of losses from a default on swaps. As with a forward contract, each party to a swap must have a lot of information about the other party to make sure that the contract is likely to be fulfilled. The need for information about counterparties and the liquidity problems in swap markets could limit the usefulness of these markets. However, as we saw in Chapter 15, when informational and liquidity problems crop up in a market, financial intermediaries come to the rescue. That is exactly what happens in swap markets. Intermediaries such as investment banks and especially large commercial banks have the ability to acquire information cheaply about the creditworthiness and reliability of parties to swap contracts and are also able to match up parties to a swap. Hence large commercial banks and investment banks have set up swap markets in which they act as intermediaries.

---

[9]The actual loss will equal the present value of the difference in the interest payments that the bank would have received if the swap were still in force as compared to interest payments it receives otherwise.

Case

ARE FINANCIAL DERIVATIVES A WORLDWIDE TIME BOMB?

With the bankruptcies of Orange County in 1994 (see the "Conflicts of Interest" box) and the Barings Bank in 1995 (discussed in Chapter 17)—both of which involved trades in financial derivatives—politicians, the media, and regulators have become very concerned about the dangers of derivatives. Indeed, Warron Buffet has called financial derivatives "financial weapons of mass destruction." This concern is international and has spawned a slew of reports issued by such organizations as the Bank for International Settlements (BIS), the Bank of England, the Group of Thirty, the Office of the U.S. Comptroller of the Currency (OCC), the Commodity Futures Trading Commission (CFTC), and the Government Accounting Office (GAO). Particularly scary are the notional amounts of derivatives contracts—over $100 trillion worldwide—and the fact that banks, which are subject to bank panics, are major players in the derivatives markets. As a result of these fears, some politicians have called for restrictions on banks' involvement in the derivatives markets. Are financial derivatives a time bomb that could bring down the world financial system?

There are three major concerns about financial derivatives. First is that financial derivatives allow financial institutions to increase their leverage; that is, they can in effect hold an amount of the underlying asset that is many times greater than the amount of money they have had to put up. Increasing their leverage enables them to take huge bets on currency and interest-rate movements, which if they are wrong can bring down the bank, as was the case for Barings in 1995. This concern is valid. As we saw earlier in the chapter, the amount of money placed in margin accounts is only a small fraction of the price of the futures contract, meaning that small movements in the price of a contract can produce losses that are many times the size of the initial amount put in the margin account. Thus although financial derivatives can be used to hedge risk, they can also be used by financial institutions to take on excessive risk.

The second concern is that financial derivatives are too sophisticated for managers of financial institutions because they are so complicated. Although it is true that some financial derivatives can be so complex that some financial managers are not sophisticated enough to use them—a possibility in the Orange County case—this seems unlikely to apply to the big international financial institutions that are the major players in the derivatives markets. Indeed, in the Barings case, the bank was brought down not by trades in complex derivatives but rather by trades in one of the simplest of derivatives, stock index futures. (Recall from Chapter 17 that Barings's problem was more a lack of internal controls at the bank than a problem with derivatives per se.)

A third concern is that banks have holdings of huge notional amounts of financial derivatives, particularly swaps, that greatly exceed the amount of bank capital, and so these derivatives expose the banks to serious risk of failure. Banks are indeed major players in the financial derivatives markets, particularly the swaps market, where our earlier analysis has shown that they are the natural market-makers because they can act as intermediaries between two counterparties who would not make the swap without

CONFLICTS OF INTEREST

The Orange County Bankruptcy

Orange County, California, one of the richest counties in the United States, was forced to declare bankruptcy on December 6, 1994, in the largest municipal bankruptcy filing ever. Orange County's downfall was the investment activities of its treasurer, Robert Citron, who was in charge of the $7.8 billion investment fund, which had not only $4.7 billion of funds from Orange County agencies but also $3.1 billion from 180 other municipalities and local government agencies. For years, the Orange County fund looked like a good investment, with the annual returns averaging 10% over the 15-year period to 1994. Unfortunately, these high returns were obtained with a highly leveraged strategy in which the fund purchased amounts of medium- to long-term bonds several times the value of the fund by borrowing with repurchase agreements. Everything was fine until interest rates began to rise in late 1993 and early 1994 and bond prices declined, leaving the fund with large losses.

We have already seen in our discussion of the Barings collapse how the principal-agent problem becomes especially severe once a trader or a manager of a fund starts to experience sizable losses. Once in the hole, the manager of the fund knows that his or her future depends on reversing these losses promptly. In this situation, the fund manager has a strong moral hazard incentive to take excessive risks. This is exactly what Citron did in late 1993 and early 1994 when he began buying large amounts of "inverse floaters," highly risky derivative securities that have high pay-

offs if long-term bond rates decline. Unfortunately for Citron, interest rates continued to rise, and the fund slipped deeper in the hole. When Peter Swan, the president of the Irvine Ranch Water District, became suspicious about the financial situation of the fund in November 1994 and asked to redeem $400 million, the jig was up for Citron because the fund did not have the cash to meet this redemption. Finally, on December 5, Citron was forced to resign, and the following day, Orange County declared bankruptcy. When bankruptcy was declared, the fund had estimated losses of $1.5 billion, and was found to have $20 billion of securities, $8.5 billion of which were derivatives, a risky portfolio indeed.

Although the role of derivatives in the Orange County debacle has often been emphasized, the problem here was really one of leverage and the principal-agent problem at work. Indeed, an important reason that Citron was able to get away with such a risky strategy, particularly after the fund sustained large losses, was that disclosure requirements were not as strong as they could be for municipal investment funds in the state of California. In contrast to other states, which require monthly or even daily disclosure of the market value of their municipal investment funds, California required this disclosure only once a year. If California had stricter disclosure requirements, investors in Citron's fund would have found out more quickly the risks he was taking, making it more likely that they would have pulled out their funds. This might have prevented Citron from taking on the risks that he did, and the Orange County bankruptcy would have been avoided.

their involvement. However, looking at the notional amount of swaps at banks gives a very misleading picture of their risk exposure. Because banks act as intermediaries in the swap markets, they are typically exposed only to credit risk—a default by one of their counterparties. Furthermore, swaps, unlike loans, do not involve payments of the notional amount but rather the much smaller interest payments based on the notional amounts. For example, in the case of a 7% interest rate, the payment is only $70,000 for the $1 million swap. Estimates of the credit exposure from swap contracts indicate that they are on the order of only 1% of the notional value of the contracts and that credit exposure at banks from derivatives is generally less than a quarter of their total credit exposure from loans. Banks' credit exposure from their derivatives activities are thus not out of line with other credit exposures they face. Furthermore, an analysis by the GAO indicates that actual credit losses incurred by banks in their derivatives contracts have been very small, on the order of 0.2% of their gross credit exposure.

The conclusion is that financial derivatives do have their dangers for financial institutions, but some of these dangers have been overplayed. The biggest danger occurs in trading activities of financial institutions, and as discussed in Chapter 20, regulators have been paying increased attention to this danger and have issued new disclosure requirements and regulatory guidelines for how derivatives trading should be done. The credit risk exposure posed by derivatives, by contrast, seems to be manageable with standard methods of dealing with credit risk, both by managers of financial institutions and their regulators.

Summary

1. Interest-rate forward contracts, which are agreements to sell a debt instrument at a future (forward) point in time, can be used to hedge interest-rate risk. The advantage of forward contracts is that they are flexible, but the disadvantages are that they are subject to default risk and their market is illiquid.

2. A financial futures contract is similar to an interest-rate forward contract in that it specifies that a debt instrument must be delivered by one party to another on a stated future date. However, it has advantages over a forward contract in that it is not subject to default risk and is more liquid. Forward and futures contracts can be used by financial institutions to hedge against (protect) interest-rate risk.

3. Stock index futures are financial futures whose underlying financial instrument is a stock market index like the Standard and Poor's 500 Index. Stock index futures can be used to hedge stock market risk by reducing systematic risk in portfolios or by locking in stock prices.

4. An option contract gives the purchaser the right to buy (call option) or sell (put option) a security at the exercise (strike) price within a specific period of time. The profit function for options is nonlinear—profits do not always grow by the same amount for a given change in the price of the underlying financial instrument. The nonlinear profit function for options explains why their value (as reflected by the premium paid for them) is negatively related to the exercise price for call options, positively related to the exercise price for put options, positively related to the term to expiration

for both call and put options, and positively related to the volatility of the prices of the underlying financial instrument for both call and put options. Financial institutions use futures options to hedge interest-rate risk in a similar fashion to the way they use financial futures and forward contracts. Futures options may be preferred for macro hedges because they suffer from fewer accounting problems than financial futures.

5. Interest-rate swaps involve the exchange of one set of interest payments for another set of interest payments and have default risk and liquidity problems similar to those of forward contracts. As a result, interest-rate swaps often involve intermediaries such as large commercial banks and investment banks that make a market in swaps. Financial institutions find that interest-rate swaps are useful ways to hedge interest-rate risk. Interest-rate swaps have one big advantage over financial futures and options: They can be written for very long horizons.

6. There are three concerns about the dangers of derivatives: They allow financial institutions to more easily increase their leverage and take big bets (by effectively enabling them to hold a larger amount of the underlying assets than the amount of money put down), they are too complex for managers of financial institutions to understand, and they expose financial institutions to large credit risks because the huge notional amounts of derivative contracts greatly exceed the capital of these institutions. The second two dangers seem to be overplayed, but the danger from increased lever-age using derivatives is real.

Key Terms

American option, *p. 656*
arbitrage, *p. 644*
call option, *p. 657*
currency swap, *p. 663*
European option, *p. 656*
exercise price (strike price),
    p. 655
financial derivatives, *p. 639*
financial futures contract,
    p. 642
financial futures option
    (futures option), *p. 656*

forward contract, *p. 640*
hedge, *p. 639*
interest-rate forward
    contract, *p. 640*
interest-rate swap, *p. 663*
long position, *p. 639*
macro hedge, *p. 645*
margin requirement, *p. 649*
marked to market, *p. 649*
micro hedge, *p. 645*

notional principal, *p. 664*
open interest, *p. 646*
option, *p. 655*
premium, *p. 656*
put option, *p. 657*
short position, *p. 639*
stock market risk, *p. 652*
stock option, *p. 656*
swap, *p. 663*

Questions

1. Why does a lower strike price imply that a call option will have a higher premium and a put option a lower premium?

2. If the finance company you manage has a gap of +$5 million (rate-sensitive assets greater than rate-sensitive liabilities by $5 million), describe an interest-rate swap that would eliminate the company's income gap.

Quantitative Problems

1. If the pension fund you manage expects to have an inflow of $120 million six months from now, what forward contract would you seek to enter into to lock in current interest rates?

2. If the portfolio you manage is holding $25 million of 6s of 2023 Treasury bonds with a price of 110, what forward contract would you enter into to hedge the interest-rate risk on these bonds over the coming year?

3. If at the expiration date, the deliverable Treasury bond is selling for 101 but the Treasury bond futures contract is selling for 102, what will happen to the futures price? Explain your answer.

4. If you buy a $100,000 June Treasury bond contract for 108 and the price of the deliverable Treasury bond at the expiration date is 102, what is your profit or loss on the contract?

5. Suppose that the pension you are managing is expecting an inflow of funds of $100 million next year and you want to make sure that you will earn the current interest rate of 8% when you invest the incoming funds in long-term bonds. How would you use the futures market to do this?

6. How would you use the options market to accomplish the same thing as in Problem 5? What are the advantages and disadvantages of using an options contract rather than a futures contract?

7. If you buy a put option on a $100,000 Treasury bond futures contract with an exercise price of 95 and the price of the Treasury bond is 120 at expiration, is the contract in the money, out of the money, or at the money? What is your profit or loss on the contract if the premium was $4000?

8. Suppose that you buy a call option on a $100,000 Treasury bond futures contract with an exercise price of 110 for a premium of $1500. If on expiration the futures contract has a price of 111, what is your profit or loss on the contract?

9. Explain why greater volatility or a longer term to maturity leads to a higher premium on both call and put options.

10. If the savings and loan you manage has a gap of −$42 million, describe an interest-rate swap that would eliminate the S&L's income risk from changes in interest rates.

11. If your company has a payment of 200 million euros due one year from now, how would you hedge the foreign exchange risk in this payment with 125,000 euros futures contracts?

12. If your company has to make a 10 million euros payment to a German company in June, three months from now, how would you hedge the foreign exchange risk in this payment with a 125,000 euros futures contract?

13. Suppose that your company will be receiving 30 million euros six months from now and the euro is currently selling for 1 euro per dollar. If you want to hedge the foreign exchange risk in this payment, what kind of forward contract would you want to enter into?

14. A hedger takes a short position in five T-bill futures contracts at the price of 98 5/32. Each contract is for $100,000 principal. When the position is closed, the price is 95 12/32. What is the gain or loss on this transaction?

15. A bank issues a $100,000 variable-rate 30-year mortgage with a nominal annual rate of 4.5%. If the required rate drops to 4.0% after the first six months, what is the impact on the interest income for the first 12 months? Assume the bank hedged this risk with a short position in a 181-day T-bill future. The original price was 97 26/32, and the final price was 98 1/32 on a $100,000 face value contract. Did this work?

16. Laura, a bond portfolio manager, administers a $10 million portfolio. The portfolio currently has a duration of 8.5 years. Laura wants to shorten the duration to 6 years using T-bill futures. T-bill futures have a duration of 0.25 years and are trading at $975 (face value = $1000). How is this accomplished?

17. Futures are available on three-month T-bills with a contract size of $1 million. If you take a long position at 96.22 and later sell the contracts at 96.87, how much would the total net gain or loss be on this transaction?

18. Chicago Bank and Trust has $100 million in assets and $83 million in liabilities. The duration of the assets is 5.9 years, and the duration of the liabilities is 1.8 years. How many futures contracts does this bank need to fully hedge itself against interest-rate risk? The available Treasury bond futures contracts have a duration of 10 years, a face value of $1,000,000, and are selling for $979,000.

19. A bank issues a $3 million commercial mortgage with a nominal APR of 8%. The loan is fully amortized over ten years, requiring monthly payments. The bank plans on selling the loan after two months. If the required nominal APR increases by 45 basis points when the loan is sold, what loss does the bank incur?

20. Assume the bank in the previous question partially hedges the mortgage by selling three 10-year T-note futures contracts at a price of 100 20/32. Each contract is for $1,000,000. After two months, the futures contract has fallen in price to 98 24/32. What was the gain or loss on the futures transaction?

21. Springer County Bank has assets totaling $180 million with a duration of five years, and liabilities totaling $160 million with a duration of two years. Bank management expects interest rates to fall from 9% to 8.25% shortly. A T-bond futures contract is available for hedging. Its duration is 6.5 years, and it is currently priced at 99 5/32. How many contracts does Springer need to hedge against the expected rate change? Assume each contract has a face value of $1,000,000.

22. From the previous question, rates do indeed fall as expected, and the T-bond contract is priced at 103 5/32. If Springer closes its futures position, what is the gain or loss? How well does this offset the approximate change in equity value?

23. A bank issues a $100,000 fixed-rate 30-year mortgage with a nominal annual rate of 4.5%. If the required rate drops to 4.0% immediately after the mortgage is issued, what is the impact on the value of the mortgage? Assume the bank hedged the position with a short position in two 10-year T-bond futures. The original price was 64 12/32 and expired at 67 16/32 on a $100,000 face value contract. What was the gain on the futures? What is the total impact on the bank?

24. A bank customer will be going to London in June to purchase £100,000 in new inventory. The current spot and futures exchange rates are as follows:

Exchange Rates (Dollars / Pound)

Period	Rate
Spot	1.5342
March	1.6212
June	1.6901
September	1.7549
December	1.8416

The customer enters into a position in June futures to fully hedge her position. When June arrives, the actual exchange rate is $1.725 per pound. How much did she save?

25. Consider a put contract on a T-bond with an exercise price of 101 12/32. The contract represents $100,000 of bond principal and had a premium of $750. The actual T-bond price falls to 98 16/32 at the expiration. What is the gain or loss on the position?

26. Consider a put contract on a T-bond with an exercise price of 101 12/32. The contract represents $100,000 of bond principal and has a premium of $750. The actual T-bond price is currently 100 1/32. How can you arbitrage this situation?

27. A banker commits to a two-year $5,000,000 commercial loan and expects to fulfill the agreement in 30 days. The interest rate will be determined at that time. Currently, rates are 7.5% for such loans. To hedge against rates falling, the banker buys a 30-day interest-rate floor with a floor rate of 7.5% on a notional amount of $10,000,000. After 30 days, actual rates fall to 7.2%. What is the expected interest income from the loan each year? How much did the option pay?

28. A trust manager for a $100,000,000 stock portfolio wants to minimize short-term downside risk using Dow put options. The options expire in 60 days, have a strike price of 9700, and a premium of $50. The Dow is currently at 10,100. How many options should she use? Long or short? How much will this cost? If the portfolio is perfectly correlated with the Dow, what is the portfolio value when the option expires, including the premium paid?

29. A swap agreement calls for Durbin Industries to pay interest annually based on a rate of 1.5% over the one-year T-bill rate, currently 6%. In return, Durbin receives interest at a rate of 6% on a fixed-rate basis. The notional principal for the swap is $50,000. What is Durbin's net interest for the year after the agreement?

30. North-Northwest Bank (NNWB) has a differential advantage in issuing variable-rate mortgages, but does not want the interest income risk associated with such loans. The bank currently has a portfolio of $25,000,000 in mortgages with an APR of prime + 150 basis points, reset monthly. Prime is currently 4%. An investment bank has arranged for NNWB to swap into a fixed interest payment of 6.5% on a notional amount of $25,000,000 in return for its variable interest income. If NNWB agrees to this, what interest is received and given in the first month? What if prime suddenly increased 200 basis points?

Web Exercises

Hedging with Financial Derivatives

1. We have discussed various stock markets in detail throughout this text. Another market that is less well known is the New York Mercantile Exchange. Here contracts on a wide variety of commodities are traded on a daily basis. Go to **http://www.nymex.com/jsp/index.jsp** and read the discussion explaining the origin and purpose of the mercantile exchange. Write a one-page summary discussing this material.

2. We leave the details of pricing option contracts to another course. However, the following site can be used to demonstrate how the features of an option affect the option's prices. Go to **http://www.intrepid.com/~robertl/** and click on one of the choices under "Option Pricer." Indicate what happens to the price of an option under each of the following situations:

   a. The strike price increases.

   b. Interest rates increase.

   c. Volatility increases.

   d. The time until the option matures increases.

Web Appendices

Please visit our website at **www.aw-bc.com/mishkin _eakins** to read the Web appendix to Chapter 25, *More on Hedging with Financial Derivatives*.

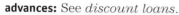

advances: See *discount loans*.

adverse selection: The problem created by asymmetric information before a transaction occurs: the people who are the most undesirable from the other party's point of view are the ones who are most likely to want to engage in the financial transaction. 26

agency theory: The analysis of how asymmetric information problems affect economic behavior. 377

American depository receipts (ADR): A receipt for foreign stocks held by a trustee. The receipts trade on U.S. stock exchanges instead of the actual stock. 290

American option: An option that can be exercised at any time up to the expiration date of the contract. 656

amortized: Paid off in stages over a period of time. Each payment on a loan consists of the accrued interest and an amount that is applied to repay the principal. When all of the payments have been made, the loan is paid off (fully amortized). 296

anchor currency: The currency to which a country fixes its exchange rate. 353

annuity: An insurance product that provides a fixed stream of payments. 567

appreciation: Increase in a currency's value. 319

arbitrage: Elimination of a riskless profit opportunity in a market. 644

asset: A financial claim or piece of property that is a store of value. 4, 71

asset management: The acquisition of assets that have a low rate of default and diversification of asset holdings to increase profits. 432

asset market approach: Determining asset prices using stocks of assets rather than flows. 81

asset transformation: The process by which financial intermediaries turn risky assets into safer assets for investors by creating and selling assets with risk characteristics that people are comfortable with and then use the funds they acquire by selling these assets to purchase other assets that may have far more risk. 26

asymmetric information: The inequality of knowledge that each party to a transaction has about the other party. 26

audits: certification by accounting firms that a business is adhering to standard accounting principles. 380

automated banking machine (ABM): An electronic machine that combines in one location an ATM, an Internet connection to the bank's website, and a telephone link to customer service. 457

automated teller machine (ATM): An electronic machine that allows customers to get cash, make deposits, transfer funds from one account to another, and check balances. 457

balance of payments: A bookkeeping system for recording all payments that have a direct bearing on the movement of funds between a country and all other countries. 352

balance-of-payments crisis: A foreign exchange crisis stemming from problems in a country's balance of payments. 359

balance sheet: A list of the assets and liabilities of a bank (or firm) that balances: total assets equal total liabilities plus capital. 425

balloon loan: A loan on which the payments do not fully pay off the principal balance, meaning that the final payment must be larger than the rest. 296, W-1

bank failure: A situation in which a bank cannot satisfy its obligations to pay its depositors and other creditors and thus goes out of business. 436, 514

bank holding companies: Companies that own one or more banks. 454

bank panic: The simultaneous failure of many banks, as during a financial crisis. 393

bank supervision: Overseeing who operates banks and how they are operated. 519

banker's acceptance: A short-term promissory note drawn by a company to pay for goods on which a bank guarantees payment at maturity. Usually used in international trade. 235

banks: Financial institutions that accept deposits and make loans (such as commercial banks, savings and loan associations, and credit unions). 8

Basel Accord: An agreement that requires that banks hold as capital at least 8% of their risk-weighted assets. 518

Basel Committee on Banking Supervision: A committee that meets under the auspices of the Bank for International Settlements in Basel, Switzerland, and that sets bank regulatory standards. 518

basis point: One one-hundredth of a percentage point. 264

bearer instrument: A security payable to the holder or "bearer" when presented. No proof of ownership is required. 231

behavioral finance: The field of study that applies concepts from other social sciences, such as anthropology, sociology, and particularly psychology, to understand the behavior of securities prices. 146

best-effort underwriting: An approach to underwriting in which the underwriter does not take ownership of the security issue and does not commit to sell the issue at a given price. Instead, the underwriter solicits, offers, and attempts to market the security for the best price possible. 596

beta: A measure of sensitivity of an asset's return to changes in the value of the market portfolio, which is also a measure of the asset's marginal contribution to the risk of the market portfolio.

Board of Governors of the Federal Reserve System: A board with seven governors (including the chairman) that plays an essential role in decision making within the Federal Reserve System. 153

bond: A debt security that promises to make payments periodically for a specified period of time. 4

bond indenture: Document accompanying a bond that spells out the details of the bond issue, such as covenants and sinking fund provisions. It states the lender's rights and privileges and the borrower's obligations. 252

book entry: A system of tracking securities ownership where no certificate is issued. Instead, the security issuer keeps records, usually electronically, of who holds outstanding securities. 228

branches: Additional offices of banks that conduct banking operations. 470

Bretton Woods system: The international monetary system in use from 1945 to 1971 in which exchange rates were fixed and the U.S. dollar was freely convertible into gold (by foreign governments and central banks only). 353

brokered deposits: Deposits that enable depositors to circumvent the $100,000 limit at each bank so that the total amount deposited is fully insured. 528

brokers: Agents for investors who match buyers with sellers. 21

bubble: A situation in which the price of an asset differs from its fundamental market value. 145

call option: An option contract that provides the right to buy a security at a specified price. 657

call provision: A right, usually included in the terms of a bond, that gives the issuer the ability to repurchase outstanding bonds before they mature. 254

capital account: An account that describes the flow of capital between the United States and other countries. 352

capital adequacy management: Managing the amount of capital the bank should maintain and then acquiring the needed capital. 432

capital call: A requirement of limited partners in a venture capital agreement to supply funds per their commitment with the partnership. 609

capital market: A financial market in which longer-term debt (maturity of greater than one year) and equity instruments are traded. 22

capital mobility: A situation in which foreigners can easily purchase a country's assets and the country's residents can easily purchase foreign assets. 328

captive finance company: A finance company that is owned by a retailer and makes loans to finance the purchase of goods from the retailer. W-8

cash flow: The difference between cash receipts and cash expenditures. 42, 393

casualty (liability) insurance: Protection against financial losses because of a claim of negligence. 573

central bank: The government agency that oversees the banking system and is responsible for the amount of money and credit supplied in the economy; in the United States, the Federal Reserve System. 8

Central Liquidity Facility (CLF): The lender of last resort for credit unions, created in 1978 by the Financial Institutions Reform Act. 504

certainty equivalent: An amount that will be received or spent with certainty. An insurance payment is a certainty equivalent since it removes the risk that unexpected amounts will need to be spent. 562

closed-end fund: A mutual fund that sells a fixed number of shares of stock and does not continue to accept investments. 542

coinsurance: An insurance policy under which the policyholder bears a percentage of the loss along with the insurance company. 578

collateral: Property that is pledged to the lender to guarantee payment in the event that the borrower should be unable to make debt payments. 374

collateralized mortgage obligation (CMO): Securities classified by when prepayment is likely to occur. Investors may buy a group of CMOs that are likely to mature at a time that meets the investors' needs. 312

common bond membership: A requirement that all members of credit unions share some common bond, such as working for the same employer. 502

common stock: A security that gives the holder an ownership interest in the issuing firm. This ownership interest includes the right to any residual cash flows and the right to vote on major corporate issues. 5, 274

compensating balance: A required minimum amount of funds that a firm receiving a loan must keep in a checking account at the bank. 620

competitive bidding: Competing in an auction against other potential buyers of Treasury securities. 227

confidential memorandum: A document that presents detailed financial information required by prospective buyers prior to making an offer to acquire a firm. 599

conflicts of interest: A manifestation of moral hazard in which one party in a financial contract has incentives to act in its own interest, rather than in the interests of the other party. 27, 403

conventional mortgages: Mortgage contracts originated by banks and other mortgage lenders that are not guaranteed by the FHA or the VA. They are often insured by private mortgage insurance. 303

costly state verification: Monitoring a firm's activities, an expensive process in both time and money. 385

coupon bond: A credit market instrument that pays the owner a fixed interest payment every year until the maturity date, when a specified final amount is paid. 44

coupon rate: The dollar amount of the yearly coupon payment expressed as a percentage of the face value of a coupon bond. 44

credit-rating agencies: Investment advisory firms that rate the quality of corporate and municipal bonds in terms of the probability of default. 104

credit rationing: A lender's refusing to make loans even though borrowers are willing to pay the stated interest rate or even a higher rate or restricting the size of loans to less than the amount being sought. 621

credit risk: The risk arising from the possibility that the borrower will default. 432

credit union: A financial institution that focuses on servicing the banking and lending needs of its members, who must be linked by a common bond. 501

Credit Union National Association (CUNA): A central credit union facility that encourages establishing credit unions and provides information to its members. 501

Credit Union National Extension Bureau (CUNEB): A central credit union facility established in 1921 that was later replaced by the Credit Union National Association. 501

creditor: A lender or holder of debt. 390, 501

currency swap: A swap that involves the exchange of a set of payments in another currency. 663

current account: An account that shows international transactions involving currently produced goods and services. W-45

current yield: An approximation of the yield to maturity that equals the yearly coupon payment divided by the price of a coupon bond. 51, 258

dealers: People who link buyers with sellers by buying and selling securities at stated prices. 21

debt deflation: A situation in which a substantial decline in the price level sets in, leading to a further deterioration in firms' net worth because of the increased burden of indebtedness. 395

deductible: An amount of any loss that must be paid by the insured before the insurance company will pay anything. 564

deep markets: Markets where there are many participants and a great deal of activity, thus ensuring that securities can be sold rapidly at fair prices. 227

default: A situation in which the party issuing a debt instrument is unable to make interest payments or pay off the amount owed when the instrument matures. 102

default-free bonds: Bonds with no default risk, such as U.S. government bonds. 102

default risk: The risk that a loan customer may fail to repay a loan as promised. W-3

deferred load: A fee on a mutual fund investment that is charged only if the investment is withdrawn. The amount of the deferred load usually falls the longer the investment is left in the fund. 549

defined-benefit plan: A pension plan in which the benefits are stated up front and are paid regardless of how the investments perform. 579

defined-contribution plan: A pension plan in which the contributions are stated up front but the benefits paid depend on the performance of the investments. 580

definitive agreement: A legally binding contract that details the terms and conditions for an acquisition of one firm by another. 599

demand curve: A curve depicting the relationship between quantity demanded and price when all other economic variables are held constant. 75

demand deposit: A deposit held by a bank that must be paid to the depositor on demand. Demand deposits are more commonly called *checking accounts*. 231

deposit outflows: Losses of deposits when depositors make withdrawals or demand payment. 431

deposit rate ceilings: Restrictions on the maximum interest rates payable on deposits. 462

depreciation: Decrease in a currency's value. 319

devaluation: Resetting of the par value of a currency at a lower level. 355

direct placement: An issuer's bypassing the dealer and selling the security directly to the investor. 234

dirty float: An exchange rate regime in which exchange rates fluctuate from day to day, but central banks attempt to influence their countries' exchange rate by buying and selling currencies. 353

discount bond: A credit market instrument that is bought at a price below its face value and whose face value is repaid at the maturity date; it does not make any interest payments. Also known as a *zero-coupon bond*. 44

discount loans: A bank's borrowings from the Federal Reserve System. Also known as *advances*. 427

discount points: Percentage of the total loan paid back immediately when a mortgage loan is obtained. Payment of discount points lowers the annual interest rate on the debt. 297

discount rate: The interest rate that the Federal Reserve charges banks on discount loans. 177, 433

discount window: The Federal Reserve facility at which discount loans are made to banks. 185

discount yield: See *yield on a discount basis*.

discounting: Reduction in the value of a security at purchase such that when it matures at full value, the investor receives a fair return. 226

disintermediation: A reduction in the flow of funds into the banking system that causes the amount of financial intermediation to decline. 462

diversification: Investing in a collection (portfolio) of assets whose returns do not always move together, with the result that overall risk is lower than for individual assets. 26, 538

dividends: Periodic payments made by equities to shareholders. 20

dollarization: A monetary strategy in which a country abandons its currency altogether and adopts that of another country, typically the U.S. dollar. 356

down payment: A portion of the original purchase price that is paid by the borrower so that the borrower will have equity (ownership interest) in the asset pledged as collateral. 306

dual banking system: The system in the United States in which banks supervised by the federal government and banks supervised by the states operate side by side. 453

due diligence period: A 20- to 40-day period used by the buyer of a firm to verify the accuracy of the information contained in the confidential memorandum. 599

duration: The average lifetime of a debt security's stream of payments. 61

duration gap analysis: A measurement of the sensitivity of the market value of a bank's assets and liabilities to changes in interest rates. 623

early-stage investing: Investment by a venture capital firm in a company that is in the very beginning stage of its development. 610

e-cash: A second form of electronic money used on the Internet to pay for goods and services. 459

econometric model: A model whose equations are estimated using statistical procedures. 94

economies of scale: Savings that can be achieved through increased size. 25

economies of scope: Increased business that can be achieved by offering many products in one easy-to-reach location. 404, 473

Edge Act corporation: A special subsidiary of a U.S. bank that is engaged primarily in international banking. 480

effective exchange rate index: An index reflecting the value of a basket of representative foreign currencies. 339

efficient market hypothesis: The hypothesis that prices of securities in financial markets fully reflect all available information. 132

e-finance: A new means of delivering financial services electronically. 9

electronic money (or e-money): Money that exists only in electronic form and substitutes for cash as well. 459

Employee Retirement Income Security Act (ERISA): A comprehensive law passed in 1974 that set standards that must be followed by all pension plans. 585

equities: Claims to share in the net income and assets of a corporation (such as common stock). 20

equity capital: See *net worth*.

equity multiplier: The amount of assets per dollar of equity capital. 437

Eurobonds: Bonds denominated in a currency other than that of the country in which they are sold. 23

Eurocurrencies: Foreign currencies deposited in banks outside the home country. 23

Eurodollars: U.S. dollars that are deposited in foreign banks outside of the United States or in foreign branches of U.S. banks. 23

European option: An option that can be exercised only at the expiration date of the contract. 656

excess demand: A situation in which quantity demanded is greater than quantity supplied. 79

excess reserves: Reserves in excess of required reserves. 176, 428

excess supply: A situation in which quantity supplied is greater than quantity demanded. 78

exchange rate: The price of one currency in terms of another. 6, 317

exchange rate overshooting: A phenomenon whereby the exchange rate changes by more in the short run than it does in the long run when the money supply changes. 338

exchanges: Secondary markets in which buyers and sellers of securities (or their agents or brokers) meet in one central location to conduct trades. 21

exercise price: The price at which the purchaser of an option has the right to buy or sell the underlying financial instrument. Also known as the *strike price*. 655

expected return: The return on an asset expected over the next period. 71

factoring: The sale of accounts receivable to another firm, which takes responsibility for collections. W-4

Federal Credit Union Act: Law passed in 1934 that allowed federal chartering of credit unions in all states. 501

federal funds: Short-term deposits bought or sold between banks. 229

federal funds rate: The interest rate on overnight loans of deposits at the Federal Reserve. 179

Federal Home Loan Bank Act of 1932: Law that created the Federal Home Loan Bank Board and a network of regional home loan banks. 487

Federal Home Loan Bank Board (FHLBB): Agency responsible for regulating and controlling savings and loan institutions, abolished by FIRREA in 1989. 487

Federal Open Market Committee (FOMC): The committee that makes decisions regarding the conduct of open market operations; composed of the seven members of the Board of Governors of the Federal Reserve System, the president of the Federal Reserve Bank of New York, and the presidents of four other Federal Reserve banks on a rotating basis. 153

Federal Reserve banks: The 12 district banks in the Federal Reserve system. 153

Federal Reserve System (the Fed): The central banking authority responsible for monetary policy in the United States. 8

Federal Savings and Loan Insurance Corporation (FSLIC): An agency that provided deposit insurance to savings and loans similar to the Federal Deposit Insurance Corporation which insured banks. FSLIC was eliminated in 1989. 487

financial crisis: A major disruption in financial markets, characterized by sharp declines in asset prices and the failures of many financial and nonfinancial firms. 391

financial derivatives: Instruments that have payoffs that are linked to previously issued securities and are extremely useful risk reduction tools. 456, 639

financial engineering: The process of researching and developing new financial products and services that would meet customer needs and prove profitable. 454

financial futures contract: A futures contract in which the standardized commodity is a particular type of financial instrument. 642

financial futures options: Options in which the underlying instrument is a futures contract. Also called *futures options*. 656

financial guarantee: A contract that guarantees that bond purchasers will be paid both principal and interest in the event the issuer defaults on the obligation. 258

Financial Institutions Reform Act: Law passed in 1978 that created the Central Liquidity Facility as the lender of last resort for credit unions. 504

Financial Institutions Reform, Recovery, and Enforcement Act: Law passed in 1989 to stop losses in the savings and loan industry. It reversed much of the deregulation included in the Garn–St Germain Act of 1982. 493

financial instrument: See *security*.

financial intermediaries: Institutions (such as banks, insurance companies, mutual funds, pension funds, and finance companies) that borrow funds from people who have saved and then make loans to others. 8

financial intermediation: The process of indirect finance whereby financial intermediaries link lender-savers and borrower-spenders. 24

financial markets: Markets in which funds are transferred from people who have a surplus of available funds to people who have a shortage of available funds. 3

financial panic: The widespread collapse of financial markets and intermediaries in an economy. 33

firm-commitment underwriting: Underwriting in which the underwriter agrees to buy the entire security issue at a prespecified price and then to resell it. This method ensures that the entire issue will be marketed. 593

Fisher effect: The outcome that when expected inflation occurs, interest rates will rise; named after economist Irving Fisher. 88

fixed exchange rate regime: Policy under which central banks buy and sell their own currencies to keep their exchange rates fixed at a certain level. 353

fixed-payment loan: A credit market instrument that provides a borrower with an amount of money that is repaid by making a fixed payment periodically (usually monthly) for a set number of years. 44

floating exchange rate regime: An exchange rate regime in which the value of currencies are allowed to fluctuate against one another. 353

floor plan: A type of loan for which inventory is pledged as security and a portion of the loan is repaid each time an item of inventory is sold. W-6

foreign bonds: Bonds sold in a foreign country and denominated in that country's currency. 22

foreign exchange intervention: An international financial transaction in which a central bank buys or sells currency to influence foreign exchange rates. 347

foreign exchange market: The market in which exchange rates are determined. 6, 317

foreign exchange rate: See *exchange rate*.

forward contract: An agreement by two parties to engage in a financial transaction at a future (forward) point in time. 640

forward exchange rate: The exchange rate for a forward (future) transaction. 319

forward rate: The interest rate predicted by pure expectations theory of the term structure of interest rates to prevail in the future. 124

forward transaction: An exchange rate transaction that involves the exchange of bank deposits denominated in different currencies at some specified future date. 319

free reserves: Excess reserves in the banking system minus the volume of discount loans. 197

free-rider problem: The problem that occurs when people who do not pay for information take advantage of the information that other people have paid for. 379

fully amortized loan: A fixed payment loan in which the lender provides the borrower with an amount of funds that must be repaid by making the same payment every period, consisting of part of the principal and interest for a set number of years. 44

fully funded: Describing a pension plan in which the contributions to the plan and their earnings over the years are sufficient to pay out the defined benefits when they come due. 580

fully subscribed: Describing a security issue for which all of the securities available have been spoken for before the issue date. 596

futures contract: A contract in which the seller agrees to provide a certain standardized commodity to the buyer on a specific future date at an agreed-on price. 456

futures options: See *financial futures options*.

gap analysis: A measurement of the sensitivity of bank profits to changes in interest rates, calculated by subtracting the amount of rate-sensitive liabilities minus rate-sensitive assets. Also called *income gap analysis*. 623

general obligation bonds: Bonds that are secured by the full faith and credit of the issuer, which includes the taxing authority of municipalities. 251

Glass-Steagall Act: Law that made it illegal for commercial banks to underwrite securities for sale to the public. 592

goal independence: The ability of the central bank to set the goals of monetary policy. 164

goodwill: An accounting entry to reflect value to the firm of its having special expertise or a particularly profitable business line. 489

hedge: To protect oneself against risk. 455, 639

hybrid funds: A mutual fund that is composed of both stocks and bonds. 546

incentive-compatible: Aligning the incentives of both parties to a contract. 387

income gap analysis: See *gap analysis*.

index fund: A mutual fund that is composed only of securities that are included in some popular stock index, such as the S&P 500. The fund is designed to mimic the returns generated by the underlying index. 548

indexed bonds: Bonds whose interest and principal payments are adjusted for changes in the price level and whose interest rate thus provides a direct measure of a real interest rate. 55

individual retirement account (IRA): Retirement account in which pretax dollars can be invested by individuals not covered by some other retirement plan. 587

initial public offering (IPO): A corporation's first sale of securities to the public. 246, 406, 594

insolvent: A situation in which the value of a firm's or bank's assets have fallen below its liabilities; bankrupt. 394

installment credit: A loan that requires the borrower to make a series of equal payments over some fixed length of time. W-1

instrument independence: The ability of the central bank to set monetary policy instruments. 164

insured mortgage: Mortgages guaranteed by either the Federal Housing Administration or the Veterans Administration. These agencies guarantee that the bank making the loan will not suffer any losses if the borrower defaults. 303

interest parity condition: The observation that the domestic interest rate equals the foreign interest rate plus the expected appreciation in the foreign currency. 328

interest rate: The cost of borrowing or the price paid for the rental of funds (usually expressed as a percentage per year). 4

interest-rate forward contracts: Forward contracts that are linked to debt instruments. 640

interest-rate risk: The possible reduction in returns that is associated with changes in interest rates. 59, 268, 432

interest-rate swap: A financial contract that allows one party to exchange (swap) a set of interest payments for another set of interest payments owned by another party. 663

intermediate target: Any number of variables, such as monetary aggregates or interest rates, that have a direct effect on employment and the price level and that the Fed seeks to influence. 194

intermediate-term: With reference to a debt instrument, having a maturity of between one and ten years. 20

international banking facilities (IBFs): Banking establishments in the United States that can accept time deposits from foreigners but are not subject to either reserve requirements or restrictions on interest payments. 481

International Monetary Fund (IMF): The international organization created by the Bretton Woods agreement whose objective is to promote the growth of world trade by making loans to countries experiencing balance-of-payments difficulties. 353

international policy coordination: Agreements among countries to enact policies cooperatively. 205

international reserves: Central bank holdings of assets denominated in foreign currencies. 347

inverted yield curve: A yield curve that is downward-sloping. 110

investment banker: A securities dealer who facilitates the transfer of securities from the original issuer to the public. 592

investment banks: Firms that assist in the initial sale of securities in the primary market. 21

January effect: An abnormal rise in stock prices from December to January. 140

junk bonds: Bonds rated lower than BBB by bond-rating agencies. Junk bonds are not investment grade and are considered speculative. They usually have a high yield to compensate investors for their high risk. 104, 256

large, complex banking organizations (LCBOs): Large companies that provide banking as well as many other financial services. 473

later-stage investing: Investment by a venture capital firm in a company to help the firm grow to a critical mass needed to attract public financing. 610

law of large numbers: The observation that when many people are insured, the probability distribution of the losses will assume a normal probability distribution. 568

law of one price: The principle that if two or more countries produce an identical good, the price of this good should be the same no matter which country produces it. 321

leasing: An arrangement whereby one party obtains the right to use an asset for a fee paid to another party for a predetermined length of time. W-5

letter of intent: A document issued by a prospective buyer that signals a desire to go forward with a purchase and that outlines the preliminary terms of the purchase. 599

leverage ratio: A bank's capital divided by its assets. 518

liabilities: IOUs or debts. 18

liability management: The acquisition of funds at low cost to increase profits. 432

lien: A legal claim against a piece of property that gives a lender the right to foreclose or seize the property if a loan on the property is not repaid as promised. 300

limit order: An order placed by a customer to buy stock that specifies a maximum price or an order to sell stock that places a minimum acceptable price. 601

liquid: Easily converted into cash. 21

liquidity: The relative ease and speed with which an asset can be converted into cash. 71

liquidity management: The decision made by a bank to maintain sufficient liquid assets to meet the bank's obligations to depositors. 431

liquidity preference framework: A model developed by John Maynard Keynes that predicts the equilibrium interest rate on the basis of the supply of and demand for money. W-27

liquidity premium theory: The theory that the interest rate on a long-term bond will equal an average of short-term interest rates expected to occur over the life of the long-term bond plus a positive term (liquidity) premium. 117

liquidity risk: The risk that a firm may run out of cash needed to pay bills and to keep the firm operating. W-3

liquidity services: Services that make it easier for customers to conduct transactions. 26

load fund: A mutual fund that charges a fee when money is added to or withdrawn from the fund. 549

loan commitment: A bank's commitment (for a specified future period of time) to provide a firm with loans up to a given amount at an interest rate that is tied to some market interest rate. 441, 620

loan sale: The sale under a contract (also called a *secondary loan participation*) of all or part of the cash stream from a specific loan, thereby removing the loan from the bank's balance sheet. 440

loanable funds: The quantity of loans. 80

loanable funds framework: Determining the equilibrium interest rate by analyzing the supply of and demand for bonds (loanable funds). 81

London interbank bid rate (LIBID): The rate of interest large international banks charge on overnight loans among themselves. 237

London interbank offer rate (LIBOR): The interest rate charged on short-term funds bought or sold between large international banks. 237

long position: A contractual obligation to take delivery of an underlying financial instrument. 639

long-term: With reference to a debt instrument, having a maturity of ten years or more. 20

macro hedge: A hedge of interest-rate risk for a financial institution's entire portfolio. 645

managed float regime: The current international financial environment in which exchange rates fluctuate from day to day, but central banks attempt to influence their countries' exchange rates by buying and selling currencies. Also known as a *dirty float*. 353

margin credit: Loans advanced by a brokerage house to help investors buy securities. 602

margin requirement: A sum of money that must be kept in an account (the margin account) at a brokerage firm. 649

marked to market: Repriced and settled in the margin account at the end of every trading day to reflect any change in the value of the futures contract. 649

market equilibrium: A situation occurring when the quantity that people are willing to buy (demand) equals the quantity that people are willing to sell (supply). 78

market fundamentals: Items that have a direct impact on future income streams of the security. 135

market maker: Dealers who buy or sell securities from their own inventories, thereby ensuring that there is always a market in which investors can buy or sell their securities. 604

market order: An order placed by a customer to buy stock at the current market price. 601

market segmentation theory: A theory of the term structure that sees markets for different-maturity bonds as completely separated and segmented such that the interest rate for bonds of a given maturity is determined solely by supply and demand for bonds of that maturity. 116

maturity: Time to the expiration date (maturity date) of a debt instrument. 20

mean reversion: The phenomenon that stocks with low returns today tend to have high returns in the future, and vice versa. 141

mergers and acquisitions market: An informal and unorganized market where firms are bought, sold, or merged with other firms. 599

micro hedge: A hedge for a specific asset. 645

monetary base: The sum of the Fed's monetary liabilities (currency in circulation and reserves) and the U.S. Treasury's monetary liabilities (Treasury currency in circulation, primarily coins). 176

monetary neutrality: A proposition that in the long run, a percentage rise in the money supply is matched by the same percentage rise in the price level, leaving unchanged the real money supply and all other economic variables such as interest rates. 337

monetary policy: The management of the money supply and interest rates. 8

money: Anything that is generally accepted in payment for goods or services or in the repayment of debts. Also called *money supply*. 8

money center banks: Large banks in key financial centers. 435

money market: A financial market in which only short-term debt instruments (maturity of less than one year) are traded. 22

money market mutual funds: Funds that accumulate investment dollars from a large group of people and then invest in short-term securities such as Treasury bills and commercial paper. 31, 546

money market securities: Securities that have an original maturity of less than one year, such as Treasury bills, commercial paper, banker's acceptances, and negotiable certificates of deposit. 225

money supply: See *money*.

moral hazard: The risk that one party to a transaction will engage in behavior that is undesirable from the other party's point of view. 27

mortgage: A long-term loan secured by real estate. 296

mortgage-backed security: A security that is collateralized by a pool of mortgage loans. Also called a *securitized mortgage*. 309

mortgage pass-through: A security that has the multiple borrowers' mortgage payments pass through a trustee before being disbursed to the investors. 310

mutual bank: A bank owned by the depositors. 486

mutual insurance company: An insurance company that is owned by the policyholders and has the objective of providing insurance for the lowest possible price. 565

named-peril policy: Insurance policy that protects against loss from perils that are specifically named in the policy. 573

National Association of Securities Dealers Automated Quotation System (NASDAQ): A computerized network that links dealers around the country together and provides price quotes on over-the-counter securities. 276

national banks: Federally chartered banks. 453

National Credit Union Act of 1970: Law that established the National Credit Union Administration (NCUA), an independent agency charged with the task of regulating and supervising federally chartered credit unions and state-chartered credit unions that receive federal deposit insurance. 503

National Credit Union Share Insurance Fund (NCUSIF): Agency established by the National Credit Union Act of 1970 that is controlled by the National Credit Union Administration and insures the deposits in credit unions for $100,000 per account. 503

natural rate of unemployment: The rate of unemployment consistent with full employment at which the demand for labor equals the supply of labor. 191

negotiable certificates of deposit: A bank-issued short-term security that is traded and documents a deposit and specifies the interest rate and the maturity date. 231

net asset value: The total value of a mutual fund's assets minus any liabilities, divided by the number of shares outstanding. 543

net interest margin (NIM): The difference between interest income and interest expense as a percentage of assets. 445

net worth: The difference between a firm's assets (what it owns or is owed) and its liabilities (what it owes). Also called *equity capital*. 382

no-load fund: A mutual fund that does not charge a fee when funds are added to or withdrawn from the fund. 549

nominal interest rate: An interest rate that is not adjusted for inflation. 52

nonbank banks: Limited-service banks that either do not make commercial loans or do not take in deposits. 629

noncompetitive bidding: Offering to buy Treasury securities without specifying a price; the securities are ultimately sold at the weighted average of the competitive bids accepted at the same auction. 227

notional principal: The amount on which interest is being paid in a swap arrangement. 664

off-balance-sheet activities: Bank activities that involve trading financial instruments and the generation of income from fees and loan sales, all of which affect bank profits but are not visible on bank balance sheets. 440, 518

official reserve transactions balance: The current account balance plus items in the capital account. W-47

open-end fund: A mutual fund that accepts investments and allows investors to redeem shares at any time. The value of the shares is tied to the value of investment assets of the fund. 542

open interest: The number of contracts outstanding. 646

operating expenses: The expenses incurred from a bank's ongoing operations. 443

operating income: The income earned on a bank's ongoing operations. 443

operating target: Any of a set of variables, such as reserve aggregates or interest rates, that the

Fed seeks to influence and that are responsive to its policy tools. 194

opportunity cost: The amount of interest (expected return) sacrificed by not holding an alternative asset. 221

options: Contracts that give the purchaser the option (right) to buy or sell the underlying financial instrument at a specified price, called the *exercise price* or *strike price*, within a specific period of time (the *term to expiration*). 655

overfunded: Describing a pension plan that has assets greater than needed to make the projected benefit payments owed by the plan. 580

oversubscribed: Having received more offers to buy than there are securities available for sale. 596

over-the-counter (OTC) market: A secondary market in which dealers at different locations who have an inventory of securities stand ready to buy and sell securities to anyone who comes to them and is willing to accept their prices. 21

passbook savings account: An interest-bearing savings account held at a commercial bank. 497

pecking order hypothesis: The hypothesis that the larger and more established is a corporation, the more likely it will be to issue securities to raise funds. 382

Pension Benefit Guarantee Corporation (Penny Benny): A government agency that performs a role similar to that of the FDIC, insuring pension benefits up to a limit if a company with an underfunded pension plan goes bankrupt. 585

pension plan: An asset pool that accumulates over an individual's working years and is paid out during the nonworking years. 579

perpetuity: A perpetual bond with no maturity date and no repayment of principal that makes periodic fixed payments forever. 49

political business cycle: A business cycle caused by expansionary policies before an election. 169

portfolio: A collection of assets. 26

preferred stock: Stock on which a fixed dividend must be paid before common dividends are distributed. It often does not mature and usually does not give the holder voting rights in the company. 274

premium: The amount paid for an option contract. 267, 656

present discounted value: See *present value*.

present value: Today's value of a payment to be received in the future when the interest rate is *i*. Also called *present discounted value*. 42

primary market: A financial market in which new issues of a security are sold to initial buyers. 20, 591

principal-agent problem: A moral hazard problem that occurs when the managers in control (the agents) act in their own interest rather than in the interest of the owners (the principals) due to differing sets of incentives. 383

private mortgage insurance (PMI): Insurance that protects the lender against losses from defaults on mortgage loans. 300

private pension plan: A pension plan sponsored by an employer, group, or individual. 581

property insurance: Insurance that protects against losses from fire, theft, storm, explosion, and neglect. 573

prospectus: A portion of a security registration statement that is filed with the Securities and Exchange Commission and made available to potential purchasers of the security. 594

prudent man rule: This rule states that those with the responsibility of investing money for others should act with prudence, discretion, intelligence, and regard for safety of capital as well as income. 608

public pension plan: A pension plan sponsored by a government body. 581

pure expectations theory: The theory that the interest rate on a long-term bond will equal the average of the short-term interest rates that people expect to occur over the life of the bond. 111

put option: An option contract that provides the right to sell a security at a specified price. 657

quotas: Restrictions on the quantity of foreign goods that can be imported. 324

random walk: The movements of a variable whose future changes cannot be predicted because, given today's value, the variable is just as likely to fall as to rise. 136

rate of capital gain: The change in a security's price relative to the initial purchase price. 57

rate of return: See *return*.

rational expectations: Expectations that reflect optimal forecasts (the best guess of the future) using all available information. 134

real bills doctrine: A guiding principle (now discredited) for the conduct of monetary policy that states that as long as loans are made to support the production of goods and services, providing reserves to the banking system to make these loans will not be inflationary. 199

real interest rate: The interest rate adjusted for expected changes in the price level (inflation) so that it more accurately reflects the true cost of borrowing. 52

real terms: Terms reflecting actual goods and services one can buy. 53

registered bonds: Bonds requiring that their owners register with the company to receive interest payments. Registered bonds have largely replaced bearer bonds, which did not require registration. 253

registration statement: Information about a firm's financial condition, management, competition, industry, and experience that must be filed with the Securities and Exchange Commission prior to the sale to the public of any security with a maturity of more than 270 days. 594

Regulation Q: The regulation under which the Federal Reserve System has the power to set maximum interest rates that banks can pay on savings and time deposits. 34

Regulation Z: The requirement that lenders disclose the full cost of a loan to the borrower; also known as the "truth in lending" regulation. W-8

regulatory arbitrage: An attempt to avoid regulatory capital requirements by keeping assets on banks' books that have the same risk-based capital requirement but are relatively risky, while taking off their books low-risk assets. 518

regulatory forbearance: Refraining from exercising a regulatory right to put insolvent savings and loans out of business. 489

reinsurance: Allocating a portion of the risk to another company in exchange for a portion of the premium. 574

reinvestment risk: The interest-rate risk associated with the fact that the proceeds of short-term investments must be reinvested at a future interest rate that is uncertain. 60

repossession: The taking of an asset that has been pledged as collateral for a loan when the borrower defaults. W-5

repurchase agreement: A form of loan in which the borrower simultaneously contracts to sell securities and contracts to repurchase them, either on demand or on a specified date. 185

required reserve ratio: The fraction of deposits that the Fed requires to be kept as reserves. 177, 428

required reserves: Reserves that are held to meet Fed requirements that a certain fraction of bank deposits be kept as reserves. 176, 428

reserve account: An account used to make insurance and tax payments due on property securing a mortgage loan. A portion of each monthly loan payment goes into the reserve account. 308

reserve currency: A currency such as the U.S. dollar that is used by other countries to denominate the assets they hold as international reserves. 353

reserve for loan losses: An account that offsets the loan accounts on a lender's books that reflects the lender's projected losses due to default. W-9

reserve requirements: Regulations making it obligatory for depository institutions to keep a certain fraction of their deposits in accounts with the Fed. 35, 179, 428

reserves: Banks' holding of deposits in accounts with the Fed, plus currency that is physically held by banks (vault cash). 176, 428

Resolution Trust Corporation (RTC): A temporary agency created by FIRREA that was responsible for liquidating the assets of failed savings and loans. 493

restrictive covenants: Provisions that specify certain activities that a borrower can and cannot engage in. 254, 375

return: The payments to the owner of a security plus the change in the security's value, expressed as a fraction of its purchase price; more precisely called the *rate of return*. 55

return on assets (ROA): Net profit after taxes per dollar of assets. 437

return on equity (ROE): Net profit after taxes per dollar of equity capital. 437

revaluation: Resetting of the par value of a currency at a higher level. 355

revenue bonds: Bonds for which the source of income that is used to pay the interest and to retire the bonds is from a specific source, such as a toll road or an electric plant. If this revenue source is unable to make the payments, the bonds can default, despite the issuing municipality's being otherwise healthy. 251

risk: The degree of uncertainty associated with the return on an asset. 26, 71

risk premium: The spread between the interest rate on bonds with default risk and the interest rate on default-free bonds. 102

risk sharing: The process by which financial intermediaries create and sell assets with risk characteristics that people are comfortable with and then use the funds they acquire by selling these assets to purchase other assets that may have far more risk. 26

risk structure of interest rates: The relationship among the various interest rates on bonds with the same term to maturity. 101

roll over: To renew a debt when it matures. W-3

seasoned issues: Securities that have been trading publicly long enough to have let the market clearly establish their value. 594

secondary market: A financial market in which securities that have previously been issued can be resold. 20, 591

secondary reserves: U.S. government and agency securities held by banks. 428

secured debt: Debt guaranteed by collateral. 374

secured loan: A loan guaranteed by collateral. 620

securitization: The process of transforming illiquid financial assets into marketable capital market instruments. 461

securitized mortgage: See *mortgage-backed security*. 312

security: A claim on the borrower's future income that is sold by the borrower to the lender. Also called a *financial instrument*. 4

seed investing: Investment by a venture capital firm in a company before it has a real product or is even clearly organized as a company. 610

Separate Trading of Registered Interest and Principal Securities (STRIPS): Securities that have their periodic interest payments separated from the final maturity payment and the two cash flows are sold to different investors. 250

share draft account: Accounts at credit unions that are similar to checking accounts at banks. 507

shelf registration: An arrangement with the Securities and Exchange Commission that allows a single registration document to be filed that permits multiple securities issues. 594

short position: A contractual obligation to deliver an underlying financial instrument. 639

short sale: An arrangement with a broker to borrow and sell securities. The borrowed securities are replaced with securities purchased later. Short sales let investors earn profits from falling securities prices. 146, 601

short-term: With reference to a debt instrument, having a maturity of one year or less. 20

simple loan: A credit market instrument providing the borrower with an amount of funds that must be repaid to the lender at the maturity date along with an additional payment (interest). 42

sinking fund: Fund created by a provision in many bond contracts that requires the issuer to set aside each year a portion of the final maturity payment so that investors can be certain that the funds will be available at maturity. 254

smart card: A more sophisticated stored-value card that contains its own computer chip so that it can be loaded with digital cash from the owner's bank account whenever needed. 459

special drawing rights (SDRs): A paper substitute for gold issued by the International Monetary Fund that functions as international reserves. 320

spot exchange rate: The exchange rate at a given moment. 124, 319

spot transaction: The immediate exchange of bank deposits denominated in different currencies. 319

state banks: Banks chartered by the states. 453

sterilized foreign exchange intervention: A foreign exchange intervention with an offsetting open market operation that leaves the monetary base unchanged. 349

stock: A security that is a claim on the earnings and assets of a corporation. 5

stock company: An insurance company that issues stock and has the objective of making a profit for its shareholders. 565

stock market risk: The risk associated with fluctuations in stock prices. 652

stock option: An option on an individual stock. 656

stop loss order: An order placed with a broker to buy or sell when a certain price is reached; designed to limit an investor's loss on a security position. 601

strike price: See *exercise price*.

superregional banks: Bank holding companies similar in size to money center banks whose headquarters are not based in one of the money center cities (New York, Chicago, San Francisco). 473

supply curve: A curve depicting the relationship between quantity supplied and price when all other economic variables are held constant. 78

swap: A financial contract that obligates one party to exchange (swap) a set of payments it owns for a set of payments owned by another party. 663

syndicate: A group of investment banks that come together for the purpose of issuing a security. The syndicate spreads the risk of the issue among the members. Each participant attempts to market the security and shares in losses. 595

systematic risk: The component of an asset's risk that cannot be eliminated by diversification.

T-account: A simplified balance sheet with lines in the form of a T that lists only the changes that occur in a balance sheet starting from some initial balance sheet position. 348, 429

tariffs: Taxes on imported goods. 324

term security: A security with a specified maturity date. 231

term structure of interest rates: The relationship among interest rates on bonds with different terms to maturity. 101

theory of efficient capital markets: The theory that prices of securities in financial markets fully reflect all available information. 132

theory of purchasing power parity (PPP): The theory that exchange rates between any two currencies will adjust to reflect changes in the price levels of the two countries. 322

thrift institutions (thrifts): Savings and loan associations, mutual savings banks, and credit unions. 29

tombstone: A large notice placed in financial newspapers announcing that a security will be offered for sale by an underwriter or group of underwriters. 595

trade association: A group of credit unions organized to provide a variety of services to a large number of credit unions. 506

trade balance: The difference between merchandise exports and imports. 352

transaction costs: The time and money spent trying to exchange financial assets, goods, or services. 25

Treasury bills (T-bills): Securities sold by the federal government with initial maturities of less than one year. They are often considered the lowest-risk security available. 225

underfunded: Describing a pension plan in which the contributions and their earnings are insufficient to pay out the defined benefits when they come due. 580

undersubscribed: Having received fewer offers to buy than there are securities available for sale. 596

underwriters: Investment banks that guarantee prices on securities to corporations and then sell the securities to the public. 565

underwriting: Guaranteeing prices on securities to corporations and then selling the securities to the public. 21

unexploited profit opportunity: A situation in which an investor can earn a higher-than-normal return. 134

unsecured debt: Debt not guaranteed by collateral. 374

unsterilized foreign exchange intervention: A foreign exchange intervention in which a central bank allows the purchase or sale of domestic currency to affect the monetary base. 349

U.S. Central Credit Union: A central bank for credit unions that was organized in 1974 and provides banking services to the state central credit unions. 504

usury: Charging an excessive or inordinate interest rate on a loan. W-9

vault cash: Currency that is physically held by banks and stored in vaults overnight. 428

venture capital firm: A financial intermediary that pools the resources of its partners and uses the funds to help entrepreneurs start up new businesses. 385

wealth: All resources owned by an individual, including all assets. 71

wholesale market: Market where extremely large transactions occur, as for money market funds or foreign currency. 220

World Bank: The International Bank for Reconstruction and Redevelopment, an international organization that provides long-term loans to assist developing countries in building dams, roads, and other physical capital that would contribute to their economic development. 353

World Trade Organization (WTO): The organization that monitors rules for the conduct of trade between countries (tariffs and quotas). 353

yield curve: A plot of the interest rates for particular types of bonds with different terms to maturity. 110

yield on a discount basis: The measure of interest rates by which dealers in bill markets quote the interest rate on U.S. Treasury bills. Also known as the *discount yield*. 260

yield to maturity: The interest rate that equates the present value of payments received from a credit market instrument with its value today. 45

zero-coupon bond: See *discount bond*.

INDEX

Note: Page numbers followed by letters f, n, and t refer to figures, notes, and tables, respectively.

Guide to Commonly Used Symbols

Symbol	Page Where Introduced	Term
Δ	66	change in a variable
π^e	53	expected inflation
σ	73	standard deviation
B^d	78	demand for bonds
B^s	78	supply of bonds
C	48	yearly coupon payment
D	103	demand curve
DUR	63	duration
DUR_{GAP}	628	duration gap
E	327	exchange (spot) rate
$(E^e_{t+1} - E_t)/E_t$	327	expected appreciation of domestic currency
EM	437	equity multiplier
GAP	623	income gap
i	42	interest rate (yield to maturity)